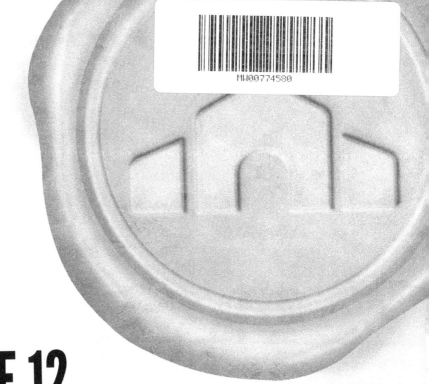

THE 12 NEW TESTAMENT MYSTERIES REVEALED

Rapture Wisdom For Christ's Bride

JESSE SMITH

CONTENTS

INTRODUCTION
God's Mysteries Are For You

"He answered and said unto them, Because it is given unto you to know the mysteries of the kingdom of heaven, but to them it is not given."

Matthew 13:11

I T IS AT SUCH a time as this—the time of the end, at the height of Satan's greatest deception in which he is trapping *"all nations"* in a modern Sodom and Gomorrah state, with the same *"days of Noah"* conditions of gluttony and drunkenness—that Jesus Christ, the True and Faithful Witness, has kept His promise to loose the mysterious seals on His Bible, and is revealing His secrets therein to you, His dearly beloved.[1]

God's eternal secrets are now at your fingertips. His revelations were not originally sent to me; I've only compiled them. The New Testament literally labels 12 individual doctrines as "mysteries", and if God is eternal, as He claims, then these doctrines are His eternal secrets. The premise of this book is to make you aware of God's mysteries He wants you to understand, share, and live by before His second coming.

---

1   *The Holy Bible*, Esther 4:14, Daniel 12:4, Luke 17:26-30, Philippians 1:4, Revelation 3:14, 6:1-17, 8:1, 10:1-11, 18:23

Perhaps the thought of God having secrets you *haven't* known up to this point in your life makes you nervous or uneasy. No one likes to be feel like they do not know enough. But don't fret. I want to encourage you that God has chosen this time of your life to reveal His mysteries to you. Solomon says our omniscient God has a time and season for every purpose under heaven.[2] Now is the season for you to allow God to reveal His mysteries to you as you read through this book. The Holy Spirit will *"break down"* any misunderstandings you may have about His plan of redemption that He may *"build up"* your faith in the truth.[3]

Much Biblical proof validates God's desire to reveal deeper, more intimate knowledge about Himself to you.

A HIDE-AND-SEEK ROMANCE DRAMA

The Bible contains the ultimate love story. You are probably aware of God's love, as Scripture says, *"For God so loved the world, that He gave His only begotten Son."*[4] But did you know that the Father's love was so great for mankind that He planned for His Son, the Lamb, to be slain for you *before* the foundation of the world?[5] Along with preplanning your salvation through the death of Christ, God also chose you *"in him before the foundation of the world."*[6] After choosing you, He predestined the events of your life so He would be close to you and that you could seek after and find Him.[7] God set up your life like a hide-and-seek romance drama.

A clear allegory of this divine romance is that of the husband and wife. Jesus is the heavenly bridegroom and Christians are His earthly bride.[8] Chapter 4 covers this *"great mystery"*[9] in full detail.

Jesus teaches that God's primary role is seeker in this romance, saying, *"Ye have not chosen Me, but I have chosen you."*[10] Paul says, *"There is*

2   Ecclesiastes 3:1
3   Ecclesiastes 3:3
4   John 3:16
5   Revelation 13:8
6   Ephesians 1:4
7   Romans 8:28-29, Acts 17:26-27
8   John 3:29, Ephesians 5:32
9   Ephesians 5:32
10   John 15:16

none that seeketh after God."[11] Ultimately, it is God Who seeks and gives every good and perfect gift, even our faith.[12] No man can boast for working to gain the salvation of the Lord.[13]

God loves to be on the seeker-side of the drama. Jesus says that God searches after souls who will worship Him in Spirit and truth.[14] In His own words, Christ said He came to *"seek and save that which was lost."*[15] Our Lord also stated His desire to hover over Jerusalem as a hen her brood—but they turned Him down.[16] God lovingly sought men's souls in the days of Noah, but found only one in the earth that walked with Him—Noah.[17]

In a minor way, God allows us to feel a need for Him, causing us to seek Him. Remember the marriage allegory? Solomon's relationship with his wife in Song of Solomon portrays this drama well. His wife is love-sick and seeking Solomon, but does not immediately find him.[18] But once reunited, marriage bliss ensues.

At times God hides Himself because He loves to be sought after and feel our love. Isaiah says, *"Verily thou art a God that hidest thyself, O God of Israel, the Saviour."*[19] After hiding, God will then honor those who diligently search for His love. Proverbs says, *"It is the glory of God to conceal a thing: but the honor of kings is to search out a matter."*[20]

Sometimes our Creator will withhold answers to our prayer requests until we cry out to Him in desperation. Solomon says, *"If thou criest after knowledge, and liftest up thy voice for understanding; if thou seekest her as silver, and searchest for her as for hid treasures; then shalt thou understand the fear of the LORD, and find the knowledge of God."*[21] God loves to hear our prayers and feel our need for Him.

11   Romans 3:11
12   Ephesians 2:8, James 1:17
13   Ephesians 2:9
14   John 4:23
15   Luke 19:10
16   Luke 13:34
17   Genesis 6:8-9
18   Song of Solomon 5:6-8
19   Isaiah 45:15
20   Proverbs 25:2
21   Proverbs 2:3-5

Its obvious God loves romantic suspense and fulfillment, so He placed this enjoyment in our lives, both naturally and spiritually. How wonderful it is to be loved and sought after by *"the King eternal, immortal, invisible, the only wise God"*![22] Perhaps this is why both children and adults enjoy fairy tales of heroic kings rescuing beautiful princesses. The tales remind us that our heroic God has defeated all enemies to save us— His spotless, glorious, beloved wife.[23]

Jesus' own words prove that your Creator wants to share His heart and mysteries with you.

JESUS' PREACHING ON THE MYSTERIES

Imagine you lived 2,000 years ago and were privileged to hear Jesus Christ preach the gospel. You, along with the multitudes of followers, would probably hang on His every word because of His reputation as a healer. Picture how you would feel if Jesus told the crowd He wanted to share God's secrets with them. Your heart would explode with excitement and anticipation, as God's deep intentions, feelings, and motives would be shared with you. But then to your surprise, He told simple parables about everyday work: planting seeds, fishing, and baking bread. How could God's intimate mysteries be revealed in such simple, everyday tasks? Yet, this is exactly what happened when Jesus preached and is recorded in three out of the four Gospels.[24]

In the Gospel of Matthew account, Jesus taught specifically on 7 mysteries related to the kingdom of heaven (see Chapter 8). There's five reasons Jesus preached about the mysteries of God based upon Matthew 13:3-51.

First, God's mysteries were special knowledge for believers only. Jesus Christ specifically stated this, saying that unbelievers would not receive God's mysteries. Both Jesus and Paul declared that unbelievers loved the world more than God, and thus would not desire the gospel.[25] Recall this

22   1 Timothy 1:17
23   Ephesians 5:27
24   Matthew 13:3-51, Mark 4:3-34, Luke 3:4-15, Luke 13
25   John 3:19, 2 Timothy 3:4

chapter's epigraph, wherein Jesus said it was *"given unto you to know the mysteries of the kingdom of heaven, but to them it is not given."*[26] Evidently, God gives the understanding of His mysteries only to those who believe in Him because only believers desire His knowledge. The mysteries are not given to rejectors of the Messiah. Scripture teaches that Jesus would preach to multitudes, but then would have private conversations with His disciples in order to confirm that they understood His messages.[27]

Second, Jesus taught the mysteries of God because He knew the knowledge would be valuable and precious to His followers. Everything about Christ is precious to the Christian, as Peter says *"unto you therefore which believe He is precious."*[28] Conversely, God's knowledge is not precious to unbelievers. In the discourse from the Gospel of Mark, Christ said His parables were just parables to unbelievers—meaningless stories. Messiah said, *"But unto them that are without, all these things are done in parables."*[29] To the unbeliever, Jesus' preaching was just mundane preaching. It was not inspirational, life-changing truth, like it was to true Christians.

Third, Jesus preached about the mysteries in order to fulfill prophecy about Himself.[30] 1,000 years before Christ, the psalmist foretold the coming mysteries of God. Generation after generation were longing for this knowledge. Over the centuries, millions of faithful Jews were prayerfully anticipating these amazing revelations from God's own heart. The Gospel of Matthew even recorded that Jesus would *"utter things which have been kept secret from the foundation of the world."*[31] So even before David and the Psalms, all the way back to Adam and Eve, God had secrets He was saving to reveal when His only begotten Son would roam the earth He created. Jesus said that many prophets and righteous men had desired to see and hear what the disciples had experienced but were not ordained for that earthly assignment.[32]

---

26   Matthew 13:11
27   Matthew 13:2, 36, 51
28   1 Peter 2:7
29   Mark 4:11
30   Matthew 13:34-35, Psalm 78:2-3
31   Matthew 13:35
32   Matthew 13:17

Fourth, Jesus preached the mysteries in parables to give everyone a fair chance at receiving eternal life. Scripture says God is not a respecter of persons and desires that all would be saved.[33] God freely offers salvation to all men in simplicity. In fact, Jesus' parables were so simple that they required hearers to humble themselves and become like a child in order to accept them.[34] Jesus rejoiced at the thought of God's parables being received by the humble but hidden from prideful, self-proclaimed wise men of the world.[35] The prophet Isaiah, nearly 800 years before Christ, prophesied that even a fool would not err in the way of salvation due to its simplicity.[36] God has made salvation such a simple subject to understand while revealing His creative power to all men so that all men will be without excuse on the Day of Judgment![37]

Lastly, and most importantly, God's mysteries contained the keys to receive eternal life. Jesus said that those who received His mysteries would gain the following spiritual abilities: *"see with their eyes...hear with their ears...understand with their heart"* while being *"converted"* and healed.[38] But sadly, in this same Scripture, Jesus taught that most hearers would purposely close their own eyes in order to continue in sin and not see His truth: *"their eyes they have closed."* Those who reject the mysteries will remain unconverted, sin-sick, with unforgiven sins. Your destiny hinges upon understanding and applying God's mysteries to your life.

JESUS' FRIENDS KNOW THE MYSTERIES

Jesus reveals His mysteries to only one group of people—His friends. Obedience is the only requirement for friendship with Jesus. Christ says, *"Ye are My friends, if ye do whatsoever I command you."*[39] Doers of the Word are God's righteous friends, as Paul says obedience leads to

---

33   Acts 10:34, 1 Timothy 2:4
34   Matthew 18:1-6
35   Luke 10:21
36   Isaiah 35:8
37   Romans 1:20
38   Matthew 13:15
39   John 15:14

righteousness: *"Know ye not, that to whom ye yield yourselves servants to obey, his servants ye are to whom ye obey; whether of sin unto death, or of obedience unto righteousness?"*[40] Proverbs declares God's *"secret is with the righteous."*[41]

God's requirement for friendship is obedience based upon love. In John chapter 14, Jesus repeatedly expresses that love motivates believers to obey God's commands, saying,

> *"If ye love Me, keep My commands...He that hath my commandments, and keepeth them, he it is that loveth me: and he that loveth me shall be loved of my Father, and I will love him, and will manifest myself to him...If a man love me, he will keep my words: and my Father will love him, and we will come unto him, and make our abode with him. He that loveth me not keepeth not my sayings: and the word which ye hear is not mine, but the Father's which sent me."*[42]

Undoubtedly, you can be God's friend if you love Him and keep His commands!

John called the believer's love for God, *"the love of the Father,"* teaching that *"if any man love the world, the love of the Father is not in him."*[43] Every human has the choice to either love the sinful things of the world or the holy things of God our Father. Jesus had the love of the Father to such a degree that He did only those things which pleased Him.[44]

As friends of Jesus, He gives us a status that is more personal than mere servants: *"Henceforth I call you not servants; for the servant knoweth not what his lord doeth: but I have called you friends; for all things that I have heard of My Father I have made known unto you."*[45] Jesus told His earthly disciples all that God showed Him, holding nothing back. We have the

40   Romans 6:16
41   Proverbs 3:32
42   John 14:15, 21, 23-24
43   1 John 2:15
44   John 8:29
45   John 15:15

same privilege today because Jesus said the Holy Spirit would guide us into all truth and tell us things to come that we might be prepared for His return.[46]

Abraham is privileged to be called the friend of God three times in Scripture because he believed God's promises.[47] Genesis says God knew Abraham would keep His commands and train his family to do so.[48] Based upon Abraham's faithfulness, God revealed His plans to destroy Sodom and Gomorrah. Abraham, the faithful friend of both God and man, responded by interceding in prayer to God for his nephew Lot, whom God saved from destruction.[49]

Friends of God in our time will make themselves ready for the second coming of Jesus Christ.[50] Paul says we will not live in sinful darkness, being overtaken as a thief in the night when judgment is poured out upon the earth.[51] Because we love the light of God's truth, He has *"not appointed us unto wrath, but to obtain salvation by our Lord Jesus Christ."*[52]

MYSTERIES ARE TREASURES

God's mysteries are invaluable, spiritual treasures that must be preached to God's people. Jesus says His Words are truth, spirit, and life.[53] Solomon says the value of God's wisdom is so great that nothing on earth can be compared to it![54] You'll soon learn His mysteries are also bread.

Jesus said God's mysteries were *"given"* to His apostles, who would then preach those truths to all who would listen: *"Go ye therefore, and teach all nations."*[55] God's mysteries are meant to be shared and this job so was important that Jesus prayed for His messengers and those

46   John 16:13
47   2 Chronicles 20:7, Isaiah 41:8, James 2:23
48   Genesis 18:19
49   Genesis 18:17-33
50   Revelation 19:7
51   1 Thessalonians 5:4
52   1 Thessalonians 5:9
53   John 6:63, 17:17
54   Proverbs 3:13-15
55   Matthew 13:11, 28:19

that would believe on Christ through their preaching: *"Neither pray I for these alone, but for them also which shall believe on Me through their word."*[56]

When His mysteries are preached, both *"new and old"* treasures of truth will be brought forth.[57] When we attend preaching services, we expect to be reminded of God's eternal truths but also hear new revelations to inspire our commitment to the gospel of Jesus Christ. Jesus promises that a spiritual hunger and thirst will be satisfied: *"Blessed are they which do hunger and thirst after righteousness: for they shall be filled."*[58]

To bring forth God's truth-treasures, ministers study and pray. Diligent studying and meditation upon the Word of God allows preachers to rightly divide the words of truth.[59] Jesus promises that praying in secret will produce an open, public reward for those who practice it.[60] The greatest reward a minister could receive is that both he and his hearers would be saved by the life-giving treasures of God's Word![61] Praying and meditating on the treasures of God was so critical that the early apostles created the deacon office to care for the physical needs of the people so that they could focus on the people's spiritual needs, which could be met only through the preaching of God's Word.[62]

STEWARDS OF THE MYSTERIES

God's mysteries are so valuable that Paul said all ministers of the gospel were *"stewards of the mysteries of God."* The Greek definition of "steward" is a "manager or superintendent."[63]

Since I am employed as a public school teacher, my mind cannot help but compare the job of a minister with a school district superintendent. In both occupations, the worker is a manager of someone else's resources

---

56 John 17:20
57 Matthew 13:52
58 Matthew 5:6
59 1 Timothy 4:15, 2 Timothy 2:15
60 Matthew 6:6
61 1 Timothy 4:16
62 Acts 6:1-4
63 "The Bible: Hebrew and Greek Lexicons." *Voice of God Recordings*, www.branham.org/en/messagesearch

and is accountable for his actions. The minister handles God's Word and people, while the superintendent handles the community's facilities, and its financial and human resources. My school district's budget is approximately 50 million dollars. Can you imagine being responsible for a sum that large? But in reality, the gospel minister is responsible for much more than the superintendent because earthly riches eventually perish but eternal life with Jesus Christ is never-ending. The fruits of a faithful ministry will be believers who live eternally with Jesus, walking on streets paved with pure, transparent gold![64]

Paul says ministers are required to be faithful managers of the mysteries of God, saying, *"It is required in stewards, that a man be found faithful."*[65] Ministers faithfully teach, uphold, and rightly divide the truth, for Jesus says the truth will set hearers free from sin.[66] The minister's spiritual labor makes him worthy of not honor, but *"double honor."*[67]

Preaching truth is such an honorable work that Paul says faithful ministers keep believers' souls from losing faith. He compares preaching false doctrine to being cankered, or having gangrene, a flesh-eating disease, saying, *"Their word will eat as doth a canker…and overthrow the faith of some."*[68] False doctrine is an evil sin that slowly consumes a worshipper's sincerity, causing him to give up his faith in Christ. The remedy is a God-sent preacher who will faithfully and uncompromisingly preach truth.

Jesus uses the illustration of a household manager to represent a minister in Luke chapter 12. He says a faithful and wise steward is blessed by God because he feeds his household *"their portion of meat in due season."*[69] God's truths are spiritual meals full of life-giving vitamins. David says about God's Word, *"O taste and see that the Lord is good"* and *"sweeter also than honey and the honeycomb."*[70] Jesus said His *"meat"* was

---

64   Revelation 21:21
65   1 Corinthians 4:2
66   John 8:32
67   1 Timothy 5:7
68   2 Timothy 17-18
69   Luke 12:42
70   Psalm 19:10, 34:8

"to do the will" of God, or the Word of God.[71] The church of Jesus Christ must be healthy, growing in grace and *"knowledge of our Lord and Savior Jesus Christ."*[72]

Being God's steward is a huge responsibility and includes tests. Sometimes stewards become discouraged or suffer persecution because Satan always attacks true stewards through false ones, as the children of the flesh will always persecute the children of the Spirit.[73] In Paul's stewardship, he experienced much persecution and often requested prayer that he would preach God's mysteries with boldness. He said, *"Praying...for me, that utterance may be given unto me, that I may open my mouth boldly, to make known the mystery of the gospel, for which I am an ambassador in bonds: that therein I may speak boldly, as I ought to speak."*[74] Stewards today, like Paul of old, need our prayers that they may declare the mystery of God boldly.

THE FINISHED MYSTERY OF GOD

The Bible foretold a time would come when all the mysteries of God are *"finished"*, or revealed. Revelation 10:7 says, *"But in the days of the voice of the seventh angel, when he shall begin to sound, the mystery of God should be finished, as he hath declared to his servants the prophets."* Now is the time in which God promised to reveal all His mysteries before the second coming of Jesus Christ to the earth.

First, Revelation 10 verses 1-6 show that Jesus is the *"mighty angel"* descending to earth to sound forth the contents of the heavenly Book that was previously sealed with seven seals.[75] Two descriptions of this *"mighty angel"* match previous descriptions of Christ from Revelation chapter 1: a *"face as it were the sun"*[76] and *"feet as pillars of fire."*[77] This visitation to earth is not the physical body of Jesus, for that body is not

---

71   John 4:34
72   2 Peter 3:18
73   Galatians 4:29
74   Ephesians 6:18-20
75   Revelation 5:1
76   Revelation 1:16, 10:1
77   Revelation 1:15, 10:1

an angel, being made a *"little lower than the angels"* that it might *"taste death for every man."*[78] The Revelation 10 visitation is that of Jesus' Spirit, or the Holy Spirit. God's Spirit is referred to as an angel, or messenger, many times in the Old Testament. The Angel of the Lord commissioned to Moses could forgive sins,[79] which only God can do. Hebrews calls Moses' angel *"Christ,"* saying, *"Esteeming the reproach of Christ greater riches than the treasures in Egypt."*[80]

Second, Revelation 10:3 describes the earthly voice of Christ as a roaring lion, which represents the Holy Spirit prophesying through a prophet. Amos 3:7-8 says, *"Surely the Lord GOD will do nothing, but he revealeth his secret unto his servants the prophets. The lion hath roared, who will not fear? the Lord GOD hath spoken, who can but prophesy?"* Notice that seven thunders uttered their voices after the lion roared. A thunder represents the voice of God.[81] The seven thunders must be God interpreting each of the Seven Seals that were loosed off the *"little book"* through a prophet prophesying on the earth. Every time a seal is loosed off the *"little book"*, a thunder sounds, as seen in Revelation 6:1: *"And I saw when the Lamb opened one of the seals, and I heard, as it were the noise of thunder, one of the four beasts saying, Come and see."*

Third, the *"seventh angel"* mentioned in Revelation 10:7 has to be a male human being because God's pattern is to save humans through the preaching of humans. Paul said, *"Ye are saved, if ye keep in memory what I preached unto you."*[82] God never used angels to preach salvation and bring conversions to men. The Bible fully supports this interpretation, as David, Paul, and a prophet in Revelation 22 are all referred to as *"angels."* David was *"as an angel of God"* to both Achish and Mephibosheth.[83] The Galatians received Paul *"as an angel of God, even as Christ Jesus."*[84] John was shown the Patmos vision by a prophet who was called an angel, identified

78   Hebrews 2:9
79   Exodus 23:20-21
80   Hebrews 11:26
81   Psalm 18:13, 29:3-11, John 12:28-29
82   1 Corinthians 15:2
83   1 Samuel 29:9, 2 Samuel 19:27
84   Galatians 4:14

as a fellow servant of John, of his *"brethren the prophets."*[85] Since the seventh angel's voice of Revelation 10:7 is finishing the mystery of God, he must be a human being. Chapters 7 and 13 prove this man was God's prophet William Branham (1909-1965). Appendix B lists his quotes supporting the Godhead mystery while the rest are available for free on my personal website: www.pastorjessesmith.com/12mysteriesbook.

Fourth, multiple prophets foretold of the opening of the seven-sealed book and the finished mystery, just as Revelation 10:7 says: *"as he hath declared to his servants the prophets."* Daniel declared the sealed book would be opened at *"the time of the end"* when *"many shall run to and fro, and knowledge shall be increased."*[86] Daniel predicted by the Spirit advances in transportation and the internet. Joel 2:23-26 speaks of a *"latter rain"* that will *"restore"* God's people back to spiritual prosperity. The prophet Malachi said the hearts of the children would be turned back to the hearts of their fathers, pointing to a time when Christians would experience God's presence like the early apostles in the Book of Acts.[87] Jesus, the God-Prophet, echoed Malachi's prediction that the Christian restoration would take place through a prophet anointed with the Spirit of Elijah, saying, *"Elias truly shall first come, and restore all things."*[88] The words of the prophets and Christ prove that God's mystery will be completed before the second coming of Jesus Christ.

Lastly, the Scriptures following Revelation 10:7, verses 8-11, describe how the spreading of the finished mystery actually completes Jesus' Great Commission because it must be preached world-wide. Revelation 10:11 says, *"prophesy again before nations, peoples, kings, and tongues."* John symbolizes the church who eats the open Book, and empowered by its revelations, takes the revealed mysteries around the world to prepare God's people for Jesus' second coming. Jesus says we are currently in the *"times of the Gentiles,"*[89] the time that God is offering salvation to

85   Revelation 22:8-9
86   Daniel 12:4
87   Malachi 4:5-6
88   Matthew 17:11
89   Luke 21:24

all nations while keeping the Jews blind to the gospel because of their rejection of Christ.[90]

THE 12 NEW TESTAMENT MYSTERIES

The New Testament mentions 12 mystery-doctrines that compose the complete *"mystery of God"* spoken of in Revelation 10:7. You may wonder why God chose 12 mysteries rather than another number. When searching Scripture, the meaning of 12 is government, rulership, or a kingdom. Examples include the 12 tribes of Israel,[91] 12 legions of angels,[92] 12 apostles of Christ,[93] and 12 pieces of shewbread in the holy place.[94] It is through the type of shewbread that we can understand why there are 12 New Testament mystery-doctrines.

In Hebrew, shewbread means "face" and has gained the title "bread of the face."[95] This indicates that through this bread God's face could be seen. Israel's high priest could only enter the Holy of Holies *"once a year"*,[96] representing seeing God's face. But every Sabbath, God had constant communion with Israel through the *"continual shewbread"*[97] that was laying *"before the LORD."*[98] The lesson is that through continual communion with God, you can come into His presence, His face.

For Israel, the 12 *"cakes"*, or pieces of shewbread, were placed before the Lord *"alway"* in the holy place.[99] God always wanted fresh bread before His face—the Holy of Holies—as His people daily approached Him in worship. There was never to be a time when God's people were lacking holy bread in their worship. After laying before the Lord for an entire week, the 12 loaves were eaten by the priests as a *"most holy"* offering when the 12 new loaves were set in place. Each tribe of Israel—the

---

90   Acts 18:6, Romans 11:7, 25
91   Genesis 49:28
92   Matthew 26:53
93   Matthew 10:2
94   Leviticus 24:5-9
95   "Shew-bread." *Bible Study Tools*, https://www.biblestudytools.com/dictionaries/smiths-bible-dictionary/shew-bread.html
96   Leviticus 16:34
97   2 Chronicles 2:4
98   1 Samuel 21:6
99   Exodus 25:30

entire kingdom—was symbolized as having communion with God through the weekly eating of 12 cakes. God sustained Israel's earthly kingdom through His holy bread. Today He sustains His earthly spiritual kingdom through His 12 mystery-doctrines.

For Christians, the shewbread foreshadowed that God is approached and known through the eating, or believing, of His fresh, sacred Word. Bread represents the Word of God, as Jesus, named *"the Word of God"*,[100] says *I am the bread of life."*[101] God's name, like the shewbread, is sacred, or hallowed.[102] Paul likens a true worship experience unto the *"unleavened bread of sincerity and truth."*[103] The apostle recorded that the Thessalonians received his preaching *"not as the word of men, but as it is in truth, the Word of God, which effectually worketh also in you that believe."*[104]

Christians, like Israel, have a spiritual government of 12 leaders. Jesus told His apostles they would *"sit upon twelve thrones, judging the twelve tribes of Israel."*[105] The spiritual lesson is that God has a Christian government representing the entire group of Jew and Gentile believers who are privileged with God's fellowship through His holy Word. We, as Jesus' spiritual kingdom on earth, have communion with Almighty God right now through His 12 mystery-doctrines that reveal His secrets.

Furthermore, just as Israel could see God only through continually eating the 12 cakes, we can see or understand God only when we have a true understanding of the 12 mystery-doctrines. Any other contradicting views or opinions would be unholy, spoiled, or stale bread. It is no coincidence that there are 12 doctrines labeled as "mysteries"—not 3, 5, or 10—in the New Testament. God is showing us, His New Testament *"kings and priests,"*[106] that we are to constantly feast on the preaching of His holy, fresh, and life-giving, mystery-truths!

100	Revelation 19:13
101	John 6:35
102	Matthew 6:9
103	1 Corinthians 5:8
104	1 Thessalonians 2:13
105	Matthew 19:28
106	Revelation 1:6

Each succeeding chapter in this book is dedicated to the following 12 New Testament mysteries:

- The mystery of the Godhead
- The mystery of Israel's spiritual blindness
- The mystery of the New Testament church composed of both Jew and Gentile
- The mystery of the New Testament church as the bride of Christ
- The mystery of godliness restored to man
- The mystery of Christ in you
- The mystery of the seven stars and seven golden candlesticks
- The mystery of the kingdom of heaven
- The mystery of Babylon
- The mystery of iniquity
- The mystery of God's will
- The mystery of the rapture

These 12 mysteries are your spiritual food for this season of your life. Just as the Jewish priests entered into the Holy Place to worship and commune with God, you can enter into a dedicated life with Christ as a spiritual priest and receive His nourishment, tasting His amazing grace and growing thereby.[107] Appendix A is a condensed Bible study reference list for teaching the first revelation, The Godhead. All other Bible study reference lists for the remaining 11 mysteries are available for free online at www.pastorjessesmith.com/12mysteriesbook.

SPEAKING THE MYSTERIES IN LOVE

God's gifted five-fold ministry of apostles, prophets, evangelists, pastors, and teachers preach the 12 New Testament mysteries.[108] Hearers of the five-fold ministry spiritually benefit by healthy growth, complete

---

107   1 Peter 2:2-3
108   Ephesians 4:11

maturity, edification, unity, and stability.[109] The end result is followers of Christ whose lives closely resemble the "*stature*" or character of Jesus Christ Himself.[110]

Another important benefit is "*speaking the truth in love*."[111] Jesus' true disciples are known by their love for both enemies and fellow Christians.[112] Love is the greatest gift God has given to His people.[113] Jesus sent out His first apostles as harmless doves.[114] Paul's tender love and gentleness for new converts characterized his missionary work in Thessalonica.[115]

One of the greatest dangers Christians face is receiving the revelations of God's mysteries intellectually instead of by faith. Genuine faith works through love.[116] Hebrews uses Israel as an example of hearing the Word but not mixing it with faith.[117] Paul witnessed the same type of people, who heard and understood God's mysteries but never received His love. He said, "*Though...I understand all mysteries...and have not charity, I am nothing.*"[118]

Let the Holy Spirit shed "*the love of God...abroad*" in your heart. Even if you can understand all the upcoming mystery-revelations, you will not be profited one benefit unless you plan to share God's truth with a loving spirit. God hates pride,[119] and He delights in an upright, innocent heart.[120]

CONCLUSION

This is God's season to reveal His mysteries to you that Jesus preached 2,000 years ago. He led you to this book. Your desire to love God and

109 Ephesians 4:12-14
110 Ephesians 4:13
111 Ephesians 4:15
112 Matthew 5:44, John 13:35
113 1 Corinthians 13:13
114 Matthew 10:16
115 1 Thessalonians 2:7-8
116 Galatians 5:6
117 Hebrews 4:2
118 1 Corinthians 13:2
119 Proverbs 8:13
120 Proverbs 11:20

obey His commands makes you His friend. The 12 New Testament mysteries are spiritual food you need to grow in this season of your life.

In order to be a faithful steward of the mysteries, I have organized each chapter to begin with the confusion surrounding the mystery, followed by the Biblical proof of its revelation. Last are the rewards for receiving the revelation and consequences for rejecting it.

Jesus says His mysteries were just for you—His friend, His beloved. Christ will help you correctly understand the Bible. By the grace of God, after reading this book you'll know where you came from, where you are now, and where you are going.

CHAPTER 1
The Mystery of The Godhead

"That their hearts might be comforted,
being knit together in love, and unto all riches
of the full assurance of understanding,
to the acknowledgement of the mystery of God,
and of the Father, and of Christ; In whom are hid
all the treasures of wisdom and knowledge."

Colossians 2:2-3

THE MOST NECESSARY PLACE to begin teaching on God's mysteries is with God Himself—the author of life, creator of the universe, giver of every good and perfect gift—*"the only wise God."*[121] Colossians 1:18 says Christ should have preeminence, or first place *"in all things,"* so He will be the first revealed mystery in this book.

In the epigraph, Colossians 2:2-3 speaks of the *"mystery of God, and of the Father, and of Christ."* From henceforth, I will refer to this mystery as the "Godhead" rather than the lengthier description.

Notice also from the epigraph that Paul wants Christians to acknowledge the mysterious aspect of the Godhead. This chapter acknowledges that Christians do not know everything about God, as it clearly states the one, final mystery that remains. While God is infinite and we are finite, we can know God's nature based upon His own Word while rejecting Satan's lies about God because we have the discerning power of God's sword, His Word.[122] Scripture must unveil Who God is, and Who God is not, for God has given us *"the spirit of wisdom and revelation in the knowledge of Him."*[123]

God manifests Himself to believers through revelation, or the spiritual unveiling of Himself. Jesus told Peter that the Heavenly Father could reveal Jesus' identity to Peter through revelation only, saying, *"Flesh and blood hath not revealed it unto thee, but my Father which is in heaven."*[124] Notice that Jesus' own flesh and blood, through His own human ability, could not reveal His identity to Peter. It took a revelation from the Heavenly Father for Peter to know that Jesus was the Christ! The same is true today: the Heavenly Father must reveal Jesus Christ to a person, or else he will not understand the Godhead.

THE CONFUSION ABOUT THE GODHEAD

The confusion about the Godhead centers on how many persons He is. Since nearly a third of the world's 7.3 billion people are professed Christians,[125] it can be estimated that nearly 2 billion Christians are trinitarians, believing God is three separate, distinct, co-equal persons. A small minority believe God is two persons and even fewer say He is one person.

122   Hebrews 4:12
123   Ephesians 1:17
124   Matthew 16:17
125   Hackett, Conrad and McClendon, David. "Christians Remain World's Largest Religion Group, But They are Declining in Europe." *Pew Research Center*, http://www.pewresearch. org/fact-tank/2017/04/05/christians-remain-worlds-religious-group-but-they-are-declining-in-europe/. Accessed 24 November 2018

The revelation of the mystery of the Godhead is God is one invisible person—three persons is essentially tritheism—Who created the body of His Son, Jesus, to be His one eternal image and tabernacle.

The trinitarian confusion is extremely vast and far-reaching because it started more than 1,800 years ago, and like the hidden leaven in Jesus' mystery-parable called The Leaven Hid in Three Measures of Meal (See Chapter 8), has had plenty of time to permeate into churches world-wide.

Around 180 A.D., Theophilus of Antioch first used the Greek form of the term Trinity, *trias*,[126] and shortly afterwards Tertullian coined the Latin form, *trinitas*.[127] The so-called "three persons" were declared as one God at the Council of Nicea in 325 A.D. and the Council of Constantinople in 381 A.D.[128] God's handpicked authors of the New Testament, Paul, Peter, James, and John, *never* used the term "Trinity," nor its definition of "God in three persons." Ultimately, the Trinity dogma pridefully and erroneously exalts man's false interpretation above God's revelation given to the New Testament authors.

There is absolutely no Biblical proof for a Trinity of three persons, so God should not be called such. Prayerfully consider that no doctor of divinity or seminary student can produce one Scripture in the Bible that literally says God is "three persons."

BIBLICAL PROOF FOR THE REVELATION ABOUT THE GODHEAD

The Bible defines God as one invisible Spirit who eternally exists as one person. Three verses say *"God is one"*[129] while seven Scriptures say God is *"one God."*[130] God alone is Savior, and there is no other god or person

---

126   "Trinity, The." *Encyclopedia Americana*. Grolier, 1996, pp. 116
127   "Trinity." *The Interpreter's Dictionary of the Bible*. Abingdon Press, 1962, pp. 711
128   "Trinity." *World Book*. 2003, pp. 447
129   Deuteronomy 6:4, Mark 12:29, Galatians 3:20
130   Malachi 2:10, Mark 12:32, Romans 3:30, 1 Corinthians 8:6, Ephesians 4:6, 1 Timothy 2:5, James 2:19

beside Him, for He says "*I, even I, am the LORD; and beside me there is no saviour.*"[131]

This one God manifests Himself in three ways to redeem mankind: Father, Son, and Holy Ghost. Three persons automatically equates to tritheism, or else language has lost its meaning completely. Trinitarianism, then, is a false doctrine.

The early church and Bible authors had the revelation that God is one person with three manifestations or offices. The apostles' collective revelation was one God with three titles: Father, Son, and Holy Ghost.

God chose His only begotten Son to be His one human image—"*the image of the invisible God*"[132]—placing "*the fulness of the Godhead*"[133] in the body of Jesus Christ. All of God was in Christ. Paul writes, "*To wit, that God was in Christ, reconciling the world unto himself.*"[134]

Thus, Jesus Christ is supreme deity. Jesus is God.

Just listen to deity speaking in Jesus Christ. In John 8:58 Jesus says, "*Verily, verily, I say unto you, Before Abraham was, I am.*" John 10:30 says, "*I and my Father are one*"—not two persons. When Philip asked to see the Father in John 14:8-10 Jesus said,

> "*Have I been so long time with you, and yet hast thou not known me, Philip? he that hath seen me hath seen the Father; and how sayest thou then, Shew us the Father? Believest thou not that I am in the Father, and the Father in me? the words that I speak unto you I speak not of myself: but the Father that dwelleth in me, he doeth the works.*"

The late reverend William Branham references Revelation 1:4-8 saying,

> "Just listen to these words again, 'I am Alpha and Omega, the Beginning and the Ending, saith the Lord, Which Is, and Which Was, and Which Is to Come, the Almighty.' This is

131   Isaiah 43:11
132   Colossians 1:15
133   Colossians 2:9
134   2 Corinthians 5:19

Deity. This is not simply a prophet, a man. This is God. And it is not a revelation of three Gods, but of one God, the Almighty."[135]

Additionally, Branham says, "But the Revelation through John by the Spirit to the churches was, 'I am the Lord Jesus Christ, and I am all of it. There isn't any other God.'"

Jesus was also fully human. Christ was a one-of-a-kind person unlike any man before or after—fully human and fully divine. Because Jesus' flesh was not divine, some interpret Him as being a separate person from God. But 1 Timothy 3:16 settles the question by saying, *"God was manifest in the flesh."* A second person did not come, but God came in another form, or manifestation. Hebrews 10:20 calls Jesus' body God's *"veil."* Jesus is the human form of God. He is God's human temple. Christ is the Father's image. Jesus is God's form, temple, image, and veil.

8 PROBLEMS WITH THE TRINITY DOGMA

There are eight glaring problems with the Trinity doctrine. **First, and most decimating to its validity, the Trinity dogma adds to the Bible.** The term "Trinity" and it's definition, "God in three persons," are nowhere found in Scripture. God's Word unleashes great curses and consequences upon anyone who adds to the Bible. Provers 30:5-6 commands us to not add to God's pure words, for those who do will be found as liars. Paul says those who pervert the gospel and change it are cursed.[136] The New Testament closes by warning those who add or take away from God's book will have plagues added to their punishment or their name taken off the book of life.[137] The term Trinity and its definition are blatantly absent from Scripture. The Trinity dogma is a house built upon sand, and great will be its fall on Judgment Day.[138]

The Trinity is not detailed in Scripture. The Catholic Encyclopedia states, "In Scripture there is as yet no single term by which the Three

135   Branham, William. *An Exposition of the Seven Church Ages.* 1965
136   Galatians 1:7-9
137   Revelation 22:18-19
138   Matthew 7:24-27

Divine Persons are denoted together."[139] The Encyclopedia of Religion says theologians agree that both the Hebrew Bible and New Testament do not contain an explicit doctrine of the Trinity, and "it is incontestable that the doctrine cannot be established on Scriptural evidence alone."[140] Millard Erikson declares the Trinity "is not overtly or explicitly stated in Scripture" and must be understood by inferences while exercising systematic theology.[141] Contrariwise, Jesus says He is known by revelation[142]—not theology! Just as the "masters in Israel" could not grasp the spiritual principles of Jesus' doctrine in His day,[143] trinitarian theologians miss the spiritual revelation of the Godhead today.

The specific words "triune" and "trinity" are not evil words of themselves. If used with correct biblical understanding, these words can be used to describe God's three manifestations. For example, God is triune, or three in one—three *manifestations* in one God. But God is *not* three *persons* in one, or else language has completely lost all meaning. God is also a trinity of manifestations if "trinity" is defined as "threefold" or "the state of being three." The impure words "three persons" cannot be used to understand God because they change God's testimony of Himself. My friend, Holden, summarized it well, saying, "God in three persons" is simply polytheism rebranded as the "Holy Trinity."

A brief study into ancient pagan religions shows numerous polytheistic religions worship a trinity-like group of deities, or gods. Nearly 5,000 years ago, Sumerians worshipped a triad of deities: Anu, Enlil, and Ea.[144] In the New Kingdom Egyptian age (1539-1075 B.C.) worship was given to a triad of gods: Osiris, Isis, and Horus.[145] Clearly "God in three persons" was polytheism rebranded, especially considering the word

---

139   "Trinity, The Blessed." *The Catholic Encyclopedia, Vol. 2.* New York: The Encyclopedia Press

140   "Trinity." *The Encyclopedia of Religion, Vol. 15.* New York: Macmillan Publishing Company, 1993, pp. 54

141   Erikson, Millard J. *Christian Theology.* Baker Publishing Group, 1986

142   Matthew 16:17

143   John 3:1-12

144   "Anu." *Encyclopedia Britannica.* www.britannica.com/topic/Anu. Accessed 31 January 2019

145   "The Gods." *Encyclopedia Britannica.* https://www.britannica.com/topic/ancient-Egyptian-religion/The-Gods. Accessed 31 January 2019

"trinity" and its definition were not coined until nearly 150 years after Christ. Although Islam is a false religion, I agree with Muslims on the Trinity, for they teach "the Christian dogma of a trinitarian god is a form of tritheism—of a three-god belief."[146]

Second, Jesus and His apostles taught and affirmed pure Hebrew monotheism rather than trinitarianism. Two texts show Jesus' affirmation of the Hebrew understanding of the Godhead: John 4:19-26 and Mark 12:28-34. In John 4:22, Jesus spoke with the Samaritan woman and told her, "*We know what we worship: for salvation is of the Jews.*" According to Christ, the Jews worship God in truth, and Judaism has always been the "purest monotheism" even from ancient times.[147] Mark 12 records Jesus' conversation with a scribe about the greatest commandment, and Christ confirms that God is one, not three. Jesus quoted Deuteronomy 6:4, the ancient Hebrew prayer known as the Shema, "*Hear, O Israel; The Lord our God is one Lord.*" Note that Jesus did not add to the Shema and say that God is "three persons." Our Lord always pointed people back to the Jewish faith of pure monotheism.

Jesus' apostles and early church leaders had no controversy about the subject of the Godhead in the first century. The New Testament, especially the Book of Acts, gives us a record of the councils and problems the apostles had, such as their command to Gentile Christians to abstain from eating blood and fornication in Acts chapter 15. But there's no record of the apostles having a disagreement about the Godhead because they all held the Hebrew, monotheistic understanding of God, like Jesus Himself. The early apostles had the true baptism of the Holy Ghost and all agreed on the Godhead, and today all those who have the same baptism of the Holy Ghost will agree with and teach the Godhead the same way as Christ and His apostles.

Third, the Athanasian Creed,[148] or sixth century trinitarian confessional, contains multiple contradictions to Biblical teaching on

---

146   "Monotheism." *Encyclopedia Britannica*, www.britannica.com/topic/monotheism. Accessed 31 January 2019
147   "Trinity, The." *Encyclopedia Americana*. Grolier, 1996, pp. 116
148   "Athanasian Creed." *Christ Reformed Church*, https://www.crcna.org/welcome/beliefs/creeds/athanasian-creed. Accessed 30 November 2018

the Godhead. Creeds always cause confusion because they are written by uninspired men who either add or take away from Scripture, immediately limiting the Holy One of Israel. Psalm 78:41 reads, *"Yea, they turned back and tempted God, and limited the Holy One of Israel."* Notice the Athanasian Creed's six contradictions:

- The creed says, "we worship one God in Trinity" but Jesus says we *"worship Him,"* God, the one person, not three persons, *"in spirit and in truth."*[149] Worship in the Spirit is walking in the Spirit by denying the sinful works of the flesh.[150] Worshipping in truth is believing only the Bible-testimony of the Godhead, which does not mention a three-person god. Jesus said *"Thy Word is truth"* in John 17:17, proving the Trinity cannot be truth since it is absent from the Word.

- The creed says, "the Son uncreated," but the Bible says the flesh of Jesus was created or *"made of a woman"*[151] in the womb of Mary by the Holy Ghost.[152] Also, Jesus calls Himself *"the beginning of the creation of God,"*[153] so how can the creed call him "uncreated"? Undoubtedly though, the Father that dwelt in Christ and spake through Christ was uncreated, which is why Jesus said in John 8:58: *"Before Abraham was, I am."* The great, uncreated I Am dwelt in the body of Jesus of Nazareth.

- The creed says, "the Son unlimited," but the Bible says Jesus' human knowledge was limited, for He did not know the identity of the woman with the blood issue who touched Him,[154] nor did He know the day and hour of His second coming to earth.[155]

149   John 4:24
150   Romans 8:1, Galatians 5:16-25
151   Galatians 4:4
152   Matthew 1:18, 20
153   Revelation 3:14
154   Mark 5:25-34
155   Mark 13:32

- The creed says, "the Son is of the Father alone," but the Bible says Jesus' body was conceived of the Holy Ghost, not specifically naming the Father, in the womb of Mary. The creed denies the Holy Ghost as the Father of Jesus, annulling Matthew 1:20. If the creed is true, then Jesus seems to have two fathers, since the one who conceives a child is the father. The truth is that the Bible reveals the Father and Holy Ghost as the self-same Person—not two separate persons.
- The creed says, "none is greater, or less than another," but the Bible says Jesus declared in John 14:28, "*The Father is greater than I.*" The truth is that the flesh of Jesus was mortal during His earthly ministry but God the Father is a Spirit and has been and always will be "*immortal.*"[156]
- The creed says God is "three persons," but the Bible never uses that language to describe God because He is one person. The Word teaches that the Father *is* the Holy Spirit, which decreases the Trinity's total down to only two persons: Father and Son. Then, the two will be decreased down to one because Hebrews 1:3 says the Son is the "*express image*" of the one "*person*" of God. As Colossians 1:15 says, Christ "*is the image of the invisible God.*" Christ is not a second person, but the visible image of the person of God.

Few trinitarians are aware that the first part of the Athanasian Creed was visually summarized as the Shield of the Trinity[157] (See Figure 1). This image creates unsound doctrine, contradicting itself. A contradiction is defined as a "statement of a position opposite to one already made."[158]

---

156 1 Timothy 1:17, 6:16
157 "Shield of the Trinity." *Wikipedia, The Free Encyclopedia,* https://en.wikipedia.org/w/index.php?%20title=Shield_of_the_Trinity&oldid=878878640. Accessed 26 January 2019
158 Apple. "Contradiction." *Dictionary,* Version 2.3.0. Accessed 26 January 2019

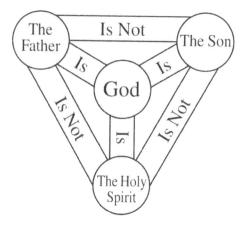

Figure 1

Claiming the "Holy Spirit is God" while also saying the "Holy Spirit is NOT the Father" is a contradiction of opposite statements. Ephesians 4:30 plainly states, *"And grieve not the holy Spirit of God."* Jesus prayed, *"Holy Father"* in John 17:11. The Father *is* the Holy Spirit, for there is only *"one Spirit."*[159]

The implications of "three persons" in the Godhead are doctrinally dangerous, proven by two examples. First, if the Holy Ghost is not the Father, then Jesus had two fathers. Jesus prayed to the heavenly Father but His physical body must have been conceived by another father, the Holy Ghost, because Matthew 1:20 says, *"That which is conceived in her is of the Holy Ghost."* Two fathers equals two persons, which equals two gods.

Second, if the Holy Ghost and Father are separate persons, then Jesus had two persons living inside Himself, the third person. Jesus said the Father dwelt in Him in John 14:10. Then, John 1:32 says the Holy Spirit *"abode"* or dwelt in Christ. Nowhere does the Bible tell us to believe that two eternal persons dwelt in a third eternal person. That would make three eternals, or three gods.

The truth is that the Father and Holy Ghost are the selfsame person. The Father came and lived in the temple, or body of His Son,

159   Ephesians 4:4

Jesus. The Father came and hid behind the veil of Jesus' flesh. Jesus was not a second person, but the image of God's one person. The Word made flesh.[160]

Thus, three personalities equal three separate person-gods, or else the English language has lost its meaning entirely. Three persons in the Godhead equals three gods, or tritheism. It's simply polytheism. This means trinitarianism is idolatry, which breaks first commandment!

Fourth, major Bible contradictions and inconsistencies exist among trinitarians. Most dangerous are those who lean more towards tritheism, the belief in three separate gods. For example, in his seminary thesis, one pastor wrote that God "exists in three equal beings" and is "three distinct beings." These phrases match the very definition of tritheism. Even though pastors who believe this often try to protect themselves by saying "yet God is one," they are nevertheless contradicting Scripture and propagating polytheism.

A great inconsistency among trinitarians is those who claim to worship "sola scriputra," Latin for "by Scripture alone," but then admit to understanding the Godhead using pagan ideology. For example, a prominent evangelical trinitarian scholar wrote that trinitarians tend to alternate between tritheism, a belief in three equal, closely related Gods, and modalism, a belief in one God who plays three different roles or reveals himself in three different fashions."[161] How incredibly deceptive and sad when Bible teachers admit to accepting pagan ideas into Christianity! Christians who claim to worship "by Scripture alone" should only worship by Scripture, never rotating between an error and Scripture. Can you imagine the evil of rotating between the sanctity of life (pro-life) and abortion, thinking that sometimes it is acceptable to kill a baby in the womb? It is foolish to rotate between good and evil. These trinitarians who rotate between tritheism and modalism are at best spiritual children in understanding, being *"tossed to and fro, and carried about with every wind of doctrine, by the sleight of men."*[162]

---

160 John 1:14
161 Erikson, Millard J. *Christian Theology.* Baker Publishing Group, 1986, pp. 340
162 Ephesians 4:14

Fifth, the early trinitarians did not affirm that the Holy Spirit was divine until the Council of Constantinople in 381 A.D.[163] This further proves that the Bible writers only—not the originators of the Trinity—had revelation on the Godhead because Luke, the author of Acts 5:3-4, used the words "Holy Spirt" and "God" interchangeably. Peter states that Ananias lied to the Holy Ghost in verse 3, and then in the next verse, Luke said Ananias lied to God. The early apostles and Bible authors instantly knew the Holy Spirit was God in 30 A.D., whereas the misguided trinitarians did not agree to this until about 350 years later!

Sixth, trinitarian images and artwork are often deceptive, creating false representations of the Godhead. Some images portray a heavenly scene containing two men sitting on two thrones—an old man representing the Father, and a young man as Christ. In the air between them is a white dove symbolizing the Holy Spirit. These images are not Scriptural, for no Bible text ever describes two thrones for two people in heaven, and there are no references to a dove flying around two men in heaven. These untrue images create a false security in trinitarians' minds, as some sort of visual evidence for their extra-biblical beliefs. As Christians, we must use discernment in the art we accept, for Paul says *"We ought not to think that the Godhead is like unto gold, or silver, or stone, graven by art and man's device."*[164]

When you get to heaven, and later when heaven comes down to earth, you will not see two persons and a dove, but you'll see one person, Jesus Christ, ruling from only one throne. This is because no one has seen, can see, nor ever will see the Father, for He is invisible.[165] The Book of Revelation says you will see Jesus' body only, for He is the image of the invisible God, Who suddenly appears among the eternal colors around the one throne.[166] Christ's human body with a countenance shining as the sun[167] is God's only image we will see—not a dove, nor a wrinkly old man.

---

163   "Trinity." *The Encyclopedia of Religion, Vol. 15*. New York: Macmillan Publishing Company, 1993, pp. 55
164   Acts 17:29
165   John 1:18, Colossians 1:15, 1 Timothy 6:16, 1 John 4:12
166   Revelation 4:3, 5:6
167   Revelation 1:16, 22:4-5

Seventh, some trinitarians use two fear tactics to persuade others to believe in the Trinity: heresy and hell. First, labeling non-trinitarians as heretics is a serious accusation, as the Greek meaning is "a body of men following their own tenants." Heretics, ultimately filled with the pride of life, will not inherit the kingdom of God.[168] Additionally, heresies show who God has rejected, and Christians are commanded to avoid heretics.[169]

A second fear tactic is repeating an anonymous saying: Try to explain it [Trinity], and you'll lose your mind; But try to deny it, and you'll lose your soul."[170] In other words, if you do not believe in the Trinity, you will go to hell. Nothing could be further from the truth! Your eternal destiny is not based upon your acceptance or rejection of the man-made Trinity dogma. Fear should never motivate blind faith in any doctrine. Instead, Christ's perfect love casts out all fear.[171] As you faithfully love God (Who is the Word[172]) over time, all your fears about your salvation will leave your mind because God promises to develop a divine, *"lively hope"*[173] in your heart.

Furthermore, Bible-believing Christians do not deny anything the Bible teaches about the Father, the Son, or the Holy Ghost. Rather, believers rejoice in the revelation of the Godhead and simply deny the false teaching. The false statements surrounding the Trinity doctrine essentially allow polytheism in the church, or the worship of more than one god, although it is not officially stated in that manner. God will *not* send anyone to hell because they rejected the Trinity doctrine and its additions to Holy Writ. Surely God will do the opposite—He'll save those who believe only the Bible's revelation and eternal truths of the Godhead.

Eighth, God sent a prophet named William Branham (See Chapters 7, 13) to warn Christians about the false Trinity doctrine.

168   Galatians 5:20-21
169   1 Corinthians 11:18-19, Titus 3:10
170   Erikson, Millard J. *Christian Theology*. Baker Publishing Group, 1986, pp. 342
171   1 John 4:18
172   John 1:1
173   1 Peter 1:3

In 1961, Branham declared, "Trinitarianism is of the devil. I say that, THUS SAITH THE LORD!"[174] While Branham believed trinitarians could still be genuine Christians, he said they were sincerely wrong about the Trinity. Recall some prophets God sent to warn His people: Noah to his generation, Jonah to Ninevah, and John the Baptist to the Pharisees. Likewise, God's faithful heart sent His prophet William Branham to this time period to warn His people of the trinitarian deception, in the name of the Lord, and its sinful addition to the faith. This prophet taught Christians to understand God using Bible terminology only.

GOD MANIFESTS HIMSELF IN THREE WAYS

In His redemption of man, the one God *manifests* Himself in three ways: Father, Son, and Holy Ghost. "Manifest" ("show" or "appear") is the key word to understanding the Godhead. The word "manifest" is specific Bible terminology used 11 times in connection to Jesus.[175]

A synonym for "manifest" is "form" in the King James Bible. Paul uses "form" to describe God's manifestation in Christ in Philippians 2:6, saying *"Who, being in the form of God, thought it not robbery to be equal with God."* The Greek Lexicon states *"form"* means "the form by which a person or thing strikes the vision; external appearance." As God the Father, He appeared in many forms to Israel. To redeem man by the cross, God took only one form, the Man Jesus Christ. To fill believers' souls on the Day of Pentecost, He took the form of the Holy Spirit. One God changing His form—not three persons.

God's one person (*"his person"*[176]) is made up of three manifestations: Father, Son, and Holy Ghost. Man is the same; he is one person made up of three aspects: body, spirit, and soul. Paul says, *"I pray God your whole spirit and soul and body be preserved blameless unto the coming of our Lord Jesus Christ."*[177] Since man is created in the image of God, after

---

174   "The Table." *Voice of God Recordings*, http://table.branham.org/#/en/main
175   John 1:31, 14:21, 17:6, 1 Corinthians 12:7, 1 Timothy 3:16, 2 Timothy 1:10, 1 Peter 1:20, 1 John 1:2, 3:5, 3:8, 4:9
176   Hebrews 1:3
177   1 Thessalonians 5:23

God's own image,[178] God cannot be three persons in one person because man is not three persons in one person. To make God into three persons is to break God's image He described in Genesis.

Three manifestations or forms do not equal three persons, especially when you consider God the Father's many manifestations, which include the human priest Melchisedec, a pillar of fire, a burning bush, a rock in the wilderness, and a voice in a whirlwind.[179] To understand God, you must use God's vocabulary words *"manifest"* or *"form,"* rather than adding man-made words like "three persons." The three manifestations or appearances of God—Father, Son, Holy Ghost—are the same person in a different form: God above us, God with us, God in us.

First, God manifested Himself as a father when He created male and female in Genesis chapter 1. Malachi 2:10 says, *"Have we not all one father? hath not one God created us?"* The Father is above us *"in heaven."*[180] God so powerfully, magnificently, and obviously manifests His creative work inside each and every human body that all men will be without excuse on the Day of Judgment, for they witnessed and experienced God's power in their own bodies.[181] In other words, no man will be able to deny God's fatherhood on the Day of Judgment!

Second, God was *"manifest in flesh"*[182] in the human body of Christ in order to redeem and reconcile His people back to Himself through the blood of Jesus' cross.[183] In His invisible Spirit-form, God could not redeem His sinful people because remission of sins came only by shed blood,[184] according to His own law. Invisible Spirit-God had to condescend into a flesh body that He Himself prepared for a *"once for all"*[185] sin sacrifice. God named that body Emmanuel, or *"God with us,"*[186] and then came and dwelt in Jesus' body, for Jesus said the Father dwelt in Him.[187]

178   Genesis 1:27
179   Genesis 14:18, Exodus 3:4, 13:21, Job 38:1, 1 Corinthians 10:4
180   Matthew 5:16
181   Romans 1:19-20
182   1 Timothy 3:16
183   Ephesians 2:13-16, Colossians 1:20, Revelation 5:9
184   Hebrews 9:22
185   Hebrews 10:10
186   Matthew 1:23
187   John 14:10

Jesus was not a second person of God, but was and is the visible image of the invisible God.[188]

Third, the Holy Ghost is the Father's Spirit manifest in the lives of humans on earth. Chapter 6 labors on this subject. In the Old Testament, the Holy Ghost was a strong, but temporary anointing on the believer's flesh and mind. A soul like Abraham's could have a small anointing on his soul, but the soul wasn't filled with God's Spirit. For Christians, the Holy Ghost is "God in us," abiding fully in our souls as a "*seal*,"[189] described by Jesus as the baptism of the Holy Ghost.[190] This baptism came after Jesus ascended to heaven when the eternal Spirit that was in Him divided itself and came to live in the Christians on the Day of Pentecost. This same Holy Spirit has been dwelling in the souls of true Christians ever since. The Holy Ghost is God manifest in believers. 1 Corinthians 12:7 declares, *"But the manifestation of the Spirit is given to every man to profit withal."*

It's essential to recognize that the Holy Ghost *is* the Father because *"God is holy"*[191] and *"God is a Spirit."*[192] The Holy Ghost is *literally* God the Father—not a third person in a trinity. The Bible never says that there are two different holy spirits, so *the* Holy Spirit is God the Father Himself.

Consider the multiple Scriptures that prove the Holy Ghost and Father are the same person. First, the body of Jesus was *"conceived...of the Holy Ghost,"*[193] proving the Holy Ghost is the Father of Jesus. Since Jesus can not have two fathers, the Bible-based conclusion is that the Father and Holy Ghost are the self-same person. Second, Jesus said the Father dwelt in Him[194] but the Bible also records that Holy Ghost abode upon Him and anointed Him.[195] Jesus did not have two separate persons anointing Him, but God's one Spirit. Third, God the Father promised to pour out His own Spirit—not a third person's spirit—on the Day of Pentecost according to Joel 2:27-29, saying *"I am the Lord your God...I will*

---

188   Colossians 1:15
189   Ephesians 1:13, 4:30
190   Acts 1:5
191   Psalm 99:9
192   John 4:24
193   Matthew 1:20
194   John 14:10
195   John 1:32, Acts 10:38

pour out My Spirit upon all flesh." God's own Spirit is not a separate person outside Himself. The sending of the Holy Ghost in Acts 2 was simply God the Father pouring out His Spirit into the souls of believers—not a third person coming, but the Spirit of the one and only living God being shared with humanity. Jesus named the Spirit's coming at Pentecost as *"the promise of My Father."*[196] Paul proved the Holy Ghost was the Father when he wrote, *"God hath said, I will dwell in them, and walk in them...and I will receive you, and will be a Father unto you."*[197]

MODALISM AND THE ONENESS MOVEMENT

Bible scholars label the true Godhead teaching—God in three manifestations—as modalism. Although modalism is closer to the truth than trinitarianism, Christians should not accept the modalist label because it contradicts Scripture at times.

Modalistic monarchianism, which emerged during the second century and eventually became labeled as heresy in the fourth century,[198] is defined as "the doctrine that the persons of the Trinity represent only three modes or aspects of the divine revelation, not distinct and coexisting persons in the divine nature."[199] This definition fully agrees with Scripture.

Digging deeper, though, Erickson says modalism teaches the Father, Son, and Holy Spirit are identical—they are successive revelations of the same person who has three different names, roles, or activities.[200] This is where modalism breaks down in two ways. First, while the Father and Holy Spirit are identical, the Father and Son are not fully identical. The Father and Son share the identical nature, as God is His Word and His Word became flesh in Christ, but their substance is different. Father's substance is an invisible, eternal Spirit but the Son had a human substance. Second, the Father, Son, and Holy Ghost have one name, not three. Matthew 28:19 says there is one *"name"*—not names—for the

196   Luke 24:49
197   2 Corinthians 6:16-18
198   "Monarchianism." *Encyclopedia Britannica*, www.britannica.com/topic/Monarchianism. Accessed 20 January 2019
199   Apple. "Modalism." *Dictionary*. Version 2.3.0. Accessed 19 January 2019
200   Erickson

Father, Son, and Holy Ghost. Scripture verifies this, as Jesus declared He came in His Father's name in John 5:43. So the name of the Father is "Jesus," since its Greek meaning is "Jehovah is salvation." The name of the Son is Jesus, for the Angel of the Lord told Joseph to name the son *"JESUS: for He shall save His people from their sins."*[201] Finally, Jesus said the Holy Ghost would come in His name, saying, *"But the Comforter, which is the Holy Ghost, whom the Father will send in my name, he shall teach you all things."*[202] Acts 4:12 says there is salvation in no other *"name."* Just as Zechariah 14:9 says there is *"one LORD and his name one,"* God has one name: the Lord Jesus Christ.

A third way modalism fails is its claim that "the Father suffered along with Christ, since He was actually present in and personally identical with the Son."[203] First, the Father cannot suffer physically since spirits do not have *"flesh and bones."*[204] Second, the Father forsook Jesus as Christ died on Calvary. Jesus cried, *"My God, my God, why hast thou forsaken me?"*[205] The Holy Spirit-anointing inside of Him, or the Father's Spirit, left Jesus somewhere between the Garden of Gethsemane and the cross. The Father had to leave Jesus' body because Christ was *"made a curse"*[206] for us and God *"hath made him to be sin for us."*[207] The Father could not curse Himself to redeem mankind, so He created a human form of Himself in order to pay sin's ransom.

Born again Christians do not need labels for their beliefs, especially regarding the Godhead. The Book of Acts is absent of believers debating about the number of persons God is. Early apostles were men *"full of faith"* and never called themselves trinitarians or modalists. Peter, James, John, and Paul didn't need creeds or fancy labels. Their only need was to know Christ, for once they knew Christ, Who is the Word, He would lead and guide them into *"all truth."*[208]

---

201   Matthew 1:20-21
202   John 14:26
203   Erickson
204   Luke 24:39
205   Matthew 27:46
206   Galatians 3:13
207   2 Corinthians 5:21
208   John 16:13

There is an increasingly popular religious label called "Oneness" which correctly rejects the Trinity and believes God is one person, but one does not need to attach labels to God's revelation. Additionally, some Oneness interpretations are false. The largest organization in the Oneness movement is the United Pentecostal Church International, which represents nearly 5 million believers world-wide.[209] While I rejoice that Oneness Pentecostals have received much truth, their major error is emphasizing speaking in tongues as the evidence for the baptism of the Holy Ghost. The erroneous and unbalanced evidence places excessive emphasis on a gift of the Holy Ghost rather than the Holy Ghost Himself. Jesus reveals the true evidence of the Holy Ghost in John 16:13—being guided *"into all truth."* The evidence of the Holy Ghost is taught in Chapter 6.

REDUCING PERSONS LEAVES THE MYSTERY OF PLURAL NOUNS

Based upon this overwhelming Biblical evidence, it is easiest to reduce the trinitarian false doctrine of three persons down to two persons by starting with God the Father and the Holy Ghost. If you can see that God the Father is the selfsame person as the Holy Ghost—since Jesus did not have two fathers—the three persons instantly reduces down to two. While two persons are closer to the truth than three, believers are faced with the fact that God never said, "I am two persons," so the only solution must be that God is one person. This brings us to the one and only mystery remaining about the Godhead.

Jesus' usage of first person plural pronouns like "we" and "us" when referring to the Father is the only remaining Godhead mystery. In John 14:23, Jesus says, *"If a man love me, he will keep my words: and my Father will love him, and we will come unto him, and make our abode with him."* Jesus uses "we," a plural pronoun, and "our," a possessive determiner, to speak of His and the Father's coming to dwell in the man who keeps His

---

209   "About The UPCI." *United Pentecostal Church International,* https://www.upci.org/about/about-the-upci

words. Then in John 17:21, Jesus uses "us" to refer to Himself and the Father, saying, *"That they all may be one; as thou, Father, art in me, and I in thee, that they also may be one in us."* If God is not two or three persons, why does Jesus use plural pronouns and possessive determiners?

The best Biblical answer is that Jesus was both fully human and fully divine, yet His human side was not divine. Therefore, Jesus had to use a separate pronoun for Himself, since He was mortal, unlike the immortal Father. Jesus experienced temptation in His human will, but the Father cannot be tempted. Jesus died but the Father can never die. Jesus is a human, but the Father is an eternal Spirit. Consequently, a separate pronoun was needed for Jesus, yet He was not a coequal, distinct person from the Father. He was the express image of the Father.

Consider that Jesus is a unique, one-of-a-kind *human* manifestation, completely unlike God's previous manifestations: Melchisedec, a pillar of fire, a burning bush, a rock in the wilderness, and a voice in the whirlwind. Jesus was born of a woman, Mary, unlike Melchisedec, who had no father or mother.[210]

The truth about God's need to use plural nouns lies somewhere between the two extremes of "Father and Son" beliefs: two coequal persons and total oneness. The truth is always in the middle of the road. Two coequal, eternal, separate, distinct persons is essentially polytheism and Jesus' own words reveal His Father is greater than He: *"For my Father is greater than I."* On the other end of the spectrum, total oneness isn't biblical because Jesus was not His own Father. In other words, the body of Jesus did not create itself. The Holy Ghost, Who is the eternal Spirit Father, created Jesus' body in Mary's womb. I've often heard the true statement, "God is not one like your finger." God and Christ are one, but only in a Scriptural way. The Father and Son are one by their sinless nature. The Father is an invisible Spirit, and the Son is the human temple of the Father.

Using plural nouns shows the difference between Jesus' flesh body and His immortal, invisible Spirit. God could not die as an eternal, immortal, invisible, omnipotent being so He created a Son that could

210 Hebrews 7:1-3

die. Jesus' flesh was *"made...to be sin for us,"*[211] or was *"made a curse for us,"*[212] as a substitutionary sacrifice for mankind, but God's eternal Spirit could not curse itself. Jesus was completely human, and His flesh had its own will it had to wrestle with in prayer against every temptation, but God's will can never be tempted by evil.[213]

While there were great differences between Jesus' flesh body and God's Spirit, there is one major similarity between the two—Jesus' nature, or character, was exactly the same as the Father's. Hebrews 1:3 says Christ is the *"express image,"* or "exact expression...precise reproduction" of God, according to the Greek Lexicon. When the Holy Ghost foreshadowed Mary's womb and created Jesus' body, all of God's character was in His Son. Throughout Jesus' earthly life, He never sinned. The tendency of His flesh was to always rely upon the Father's Word, always obeying God, always acting like God would act, for He was God's human image.

Furthermore, plural nouns were necessary because Jesus's body was a unique, one-of-a-kind manifestation and creation. Jesus of Nazareth was unlike any other human being in history. God will never make another human body to be His image, for Christ is His *"only begotten Son,"* as declared six times in Scripture. Also, God knew He'd be using His Son's physical body throughout all eternity, which is why Jesus said, *"We will come unto him, and make our abode with him."* By using *"we"* and *"our,"* God is revealing that Christians need both the Father and Son manifestations throughout eternity, as they are indispensable. The Son's physical body reveals the invisible Father, for the Father could not be seen without the Son.

This conclusion about plural nouns is both Scriptural and so much safer, reverent, and ultimately pleasing to God compared to the sin of adding uninspired words to God's eternal, inspired, inerrant Word. Proverbs 30:5-6 says adding to God's Word carries the accusation of being reproved as a liar by God Himself! Rest in the truth that God is not the author of confusion. He is not trying to confuse us by using plural

211   2 Corinthians 5:21
212   Galatians 3:13
213   Luke 22:42, Hebrews 4:15, James 1:13

nouns. Rather, He is helping us see the necessity of His manifestation in flesh—the body of Jesus Christ. Through His Son's body, God could be seen, held, and handled; for John says,

> *"That which was from the beginning, which we have heard, which we have seen with our eyes, which we have looked upon, and our hands have handled, of the Word of life; (For the life was manifested, and we have seen it, and bear witness, and shew unto you that eternal life, which was with the Father, and was manifested unto us.)"*[214]

If God is one person and not three, how should a Christian understand Scriptures like Genesis 1:26, Matthew 28:19, and 1 John 5:7 that reference the Father, Son, and Holy Ghost? By using God's provided words.

UNDERSTANDING GENESIS 1:26

Trinitarians often cite Genesis 1:26 as proof of multiple persons in the Godhead based upon the plural noun *"us,"* for God said, *"Let us make man in our image, after our likeness."* This does not prove multiple persons in the Godhead. Again, trinitarians are adding to the Word, since Genesis 1:26 does *not* say "Let three persons (us) make man in our image." Before guessing about the meaning of *"Let us,"* it's essential to examine *"make"* in this verse, for there is only one Maker—not two, and not three. Malachi 2:10 says we have *"one Father...one God created us."* There are not two creators—only one. Isaiah 44:24 plainly states, *"Thus saith the LORD, thy redeemer, and he that formed thee from the womb, I am the LORD that maketh all things; that stretcheth forth the heavens alone; that spreadeth abroad the earth by myself."* The LORD *alone* forms humans in the womb. He *alone* stretched out the heavens. The LORD did this all by Himself— not with two other persons.

There are two possible explanations for the usage of *"us"* in Genesis 1:26. First, God is referring to Himself and the angelic host because the Lord used *"us"* in this manner in two other passages: Genesis 11:7

214   1 John 1:1-2

and Isaiah 6:8. In Genesis 11:6-9, the LORD, or Jehovah, says *"Let us go down, and there confound their language"* and verses 8 and 9 record the LORD only scattering the men at Babel. It's likely God came with His angels to scatter and confound the men, just as God and two angels came down to earth to visit Abraham and Lot in Genesis chapters 18 and 19. Contrariwise, it's impossible that a three-person God visited Babel since the Bible never describes God as three people. Isaiah 8:1-8 describes Isaiah's heavenly vision in which he sees heavenly beings called seraphims. But then Isaiah sees only one person (not three) sitting on heaven's throne—the Lord, Yahweh. God was spiritually cleansing Isaiah in order to send him to His people, saying, *"Whom shall I send, and who will go for us?"* Notice God's use of "us" as it seems to refer to God and the seraphims. Isaiah's preaching ministry was a necessary warning from God and His angels to Israel before the backslidden nation was carried out of the promised land.

The second possibility is that *"Let us"* in Genesis 1:26 refers to the combined work of the Father and Son, and yet this would not equate to two individual persons. This would coincide with Jesus' usage of *"us"* in reference to the Father in John 17:21. In the beginning, *"Let us"* means the invisible Father used His Word—later acknowledged as Christ in John 1:1-3—to create man. Just as you use your spoken words to create your daily activities, the invisible God used His Words to create man and all things. Ephesians 3:9 supports this, saying, *"God...created all things by Jesus Christ."* God created *by* His Word. He created *by* speaking. Are your words separate persons from you? No, they are your thoughts expressed. In the same way, Jesus was God's thought expressed—not a second person. Later, God's Word became a man and it was necessary for mankind's redemption for Him to have attributes different from the Father, such as mortality and humanity, but that did not make Him a second person; it only made Christ the visible image of God's invisible person.

Additionally, the Father and Son shared one image—not two— in Genesis 1:26: *"And God said, Let us make man in our image, after our likeness."* This shows God's tendency to use a plural noun for His manifestations while having one image, since you already know God is invisible and Christ is God's one image.[215] In Genesis 1, God's two manifestations shared one image, which was a *"celestial"*[216] body. A celestial body is a spirit body, like an angelic body, and is invisible to the human eye under normal circumstances. The Father and Son shared a celestial body and each angel had their own separate celestial body. When God created man in Genesis 1, man was in a spirit body—not a flesh body— for that was God's image at that time. It wasn't until Genesis 2:7 when God put man's spirit (which had both masculine and feminine parts) in a body of flesh.

UNDERSTANDING MATTHEW 28:19 AND WATER BAPTISM

In Matthew 28:19, Jesus says, *"Go ye therefore, and teach all nations, baptizing them in the name of the Father, and of the Son, and of the Holy Ghost."* While this verse is probably the most commonly used proof of the Trinity, close examination of it actually reveals God's one name and three titles.

The first revelation in this Scripture is that there is one name—not three names—for the Father, Son, and Holy Ghost that is to be called upon at a believer's baptism. Jesus did *not* say to baptize "in the names"— He said "name," singular. Since God is one person, Jesus commanded God's followers to be baptized in one name, which the Book of Acts interprets as the "Lord Jesus Christ" (See Figure 2). Ten days after Jesus said to baptize in the one name of the *"Father, and of the Son, and of the Holy Ghost,"* Peter commanded thousands to be baptized in the name of "Jesus Christ." Since Peter was freshly filled with the Holy Ghost, he would not have contradicted Jesus' commandment about baptism; rather, Peter had the revelation that there is one name for the Father, Son, and Holy Ghost: the Lord Jesus Christ.

---

215   Colossians 1:15
216   1 Corinthians 15:40

	Father	Son	Holy Ghost
Matthew 28:19	Father	Son	Holy Ghost
Acts 2:38		Jesus	Christ
Acts 8:16	Lord	Jesus	
Acts 10:48	Lord		
Acts 19:5	Lord	Jesus	
Acts 22:16	Lord		
	Lord	**Jesus**	**Christ**

Figure 2

Later in Acts, you'll find that Philip and Paul also baptized believers the same way Peter did: in the name of *"the Lord Jesus,"* demonstrating unity among the Holy Ghost-filled preachers regarding the one name believers are to be baptized into. You can search the entire New Testament and you will never find one baptism recorded using the titles, "Father, Son, and Holy Ghost."

Biblical and historical records validate that Jesus' apostles used the "Lord Jesus Christ" baptism—which is referred to as the "apostolic baptism"—beginning on the Day of Pentecost around 30 A.D. to at least 100 A.D. when Christians were recorded as being baptized in the name of the "Lord Jesus" in Rome.[217] In other words, the only baptismal formula used by Jesus' apostles was the name of the "Lord Jesus Christ." Non-biblical records pinpoint 100 A.D. as the general time period the false trinitarian baptism—or "liturgical" baptism—was wrongly injected into Christian circles to replace the true water baptism in Jesus Christ's name:

- The Interpreter's Bible states that the early apostolic church had "no trace" of the "Father, Son, Holy Ghost" liturgical baptism and it "is not to be taken as part of Jesus' original commission, but comes from later liturgical use."[218]

217   *Time*, 5 December 1955, p. 5
218   *The Interpreter's Bible*. Abingdon-Cokesbury Press. 1954, p. 49

- The Encyclopedia Britannica states, "The trinitarian formula and triune immersion were not uniformly used from the beginning."[219]
- The New Standard Encyclopedia states, "At first only adults were baptized, generally by immersion, and in Christ's name only. By the second century, baptism in the name of the Holy Trinity, and soon the practice of infant baptism was introduced."[220]
- The Encyclopedia of Early Christianity records the "Father, Son, Holy Ghost" baptismal phrase "is frequently attested in the second century as a formula accompanying baptism."[221]
- The Interpreter's Dictionary of the Bible says the evidence from the Book of Acts "suggests that baptism in early Christianity was administered, not in the threefold name, but 'in the name of Jesus Christ' or 'in the name of the Lord Jesus."[222]

Be rebaptized if you were baptized incorrectly in the liturgical formula. According to the Book of Acts and history, correct baptism is the preacher pronouncing aloud your baptism in the "name of the Lord Jesus Christ" and not the titles "Father, Son, and Holy Ghost." You need not be ashamed if you need to be rebaptized, as rebaptism is Scriptural. In Acts 19:1-6, Ephesian believers learned from Paul that the water baptism required to be filled with the Holy Ghost was to be performed in the name of the Lord Jesus Christ. The Ephesians had previously been baptized through John the Baptist's method of water baptism, which purpose was only repentance, or justification. But upon hearing Paul's preaching, they were rebaptized in the name of the Lord Jesus and then filled with the Holy Ghost. When I learned this in 2002, I was rebaptized in the

---

219   *Encyclopedia Britannica: A Dictionary of Arts, Sciences, Literature and General Information.* University Press, 1910
220   "Baptism." *New Standard Encyclopedia.* Chicago, Standard Educational Corporation
221   "Baptism." *Encyclopedia of Early Christianity.* 1997, p. 161
222   "Baptism." *The Interpreter's Dictionary of the Bible.* Abingdon Press. 1962, p. 351

name of the Lord Jesus Christ because I wanted not only repentance, but the baptism of the Holy Ghost. I hope you'll have the literal name of the Lord Jesus Christ pronounced over you at your baptism or rebaptism.

Some trinitarians say that believers should use the "Father, Son, Holy Ghost" baptismal formula of Matthew 28:19 rather than the "Lord Jesus Christ" formula because Jesus' words have more weight than the apostles'. Although Jesus' words are infallible, their reasoning fails for three reasons. First, the apostles were filled with Jesus' Spirit, the baptism of the Holy Ghost, when they commanded new converts to be baptized in the name of the Lord Jesus Christ. Jesus said His Spirit would lead believers into all truth, and that is exactly what happened. The Holy Spirit taught the apostles that the name of the Lord Jesus Christ is the one name of the Father, Son, and Holy Ghost. Second, this illogical trinitarian argument pits Jesus against His apostles as if they were enemies. How sad to purposely create division among Jesus and His apostles just to scare people into accepting a creed-based baptism over the one, true water baptism! The truth is that Jesus and the apostles were in one accord because they all had the baptism of the Holy Ghost, bringing them into the *"unity of the Spirit."*[223] Third, denying and ignoring the five Book of Acts baptism examples would be taking away from the Word, which carries severe repercussions.[224]

God's one name is a revelation that was kept secret for 4,000 years until God unveiled it through His Son. As far back as Eden, God prophesied of the serpent-bruising Messiah;[225] and 3,000 years after Eden, King Agur inquired of Christ's name, asking, *"What is his name, and what is his son's name, if thou canst tell?"*[226] Messiah's name remained hidden because part of the prophecy related to Jesus' mission was to speak in parables (fulfilled in Matthew 13) and utter *"dark sayings"*[227] or enigmas, as the Hebrew Lexicon states. Christ's words about the "Father, Son, and Holy Ghost" in Matthew 28:19 were a fulfillment of the *"dark sayings"*

223 Ephesians 4:3
224 Revelation 22:19
225 Genesis 3:15
226 Proverbs 30:4
227 Psalm 78:2

prophecy. God had never spoken of "Father, Son, and Holy Ghost" in the Old Testament, making Jesus' words in Matthew 28:19 an enigma, or concept difficult to understand for the carnal mind. But Jesus opened His disciples' understanding regarding repentance and baptism before His ascension that they might know God's one name.[228] Matthew 28:19 is still an enigma to many millions of church goers. Thankfully, through the foretold restoration of the last days, God has revealed the enigma of His Son's name, that the Lord Jesus Christ is the name above all names.

MANY TITLES BUT ONE NAME

The three words "Father," "Son," and "Holy Ghost" are *titles*, not names. God has many, many titles, but just one name. Indeed, I hold at least eight titles—father, son, brother, husband, uncle, pastor, teacher, friend—but I am not eight separate persons. If you apply the false trinitarian logic of God being three persons because of the three titles in Matthew 28:19, then Satan would be four persons because he is called *"great dragon," "old serpent," "Devil,"* and *"Satan"* in Revelation 12:9. As Satan is not four persons, God is not three persons. God is one person who manifests Himself in three ways to redeem mankind.

Our Savior has numerous, beautiful, and meaningful titles, yet He is one person. In the Old Testament He is called Wonderful, Counselor, the Mighty God, the Everlasting Father, the Prince of Peace, the Righteous Branch, the Desire of All Nations, King, Messiah the Prince, Redeemer, the Head Stone of the Corner, and Sun of Righteousness to name a few.[229] Likewise in the New Testament He is called Rock, Root and Offspring of David, Bright and Morning Star, Resurrection and the Life, True Vine, True Light, the Word of God, Alpha and Omega, the Beginning and the End, and the First and Last.[230] As the four beasts repeatedly cry in heaven, Jesus is Lord God Almighty![231]

---

228   Luke 24:44-47
229   Isaiah 9:6, Jeremiah 23:5, Haggai 2:7, Zechariah 9:9, Daniel 9:25, Job 19:25, Psalm 118:22, Malachi 4:2
230   1 Corinthians 10:4, Revelation 22:16, John 11:25, John 15:1, John 1:9, Revelation 19:13, 22:13
231   Revelation 4:8

What a glorious list of Jesus' titles! Yet these titles are *not* His one "*name which is above every name*," which is Jesus Christ.[232] This is proven by the fact that demons were cast out only using the literal name of Jesus Christ,[233] not His titles. Believers were baptized only using the name of the Lord Jesus Christ,[234] not the titles Father, Son, and Holy Ghost. Miracles were done only using the name of Jesus Christ,[235] not the Righteous Branch, for instance. It is necessary to recognize that the literal name of God, the Lord Jesus Christ, is the name above all names. Once recognized, it can be used powerfully and reverently, as God desires.

POWER IN THE NAME OF JESUS

Once I recognized God's name, the Lord Jesus Christ, it became a source of power to accomplish His will in my life and ministry. First, when I became a Christian before my preaching ministry, I felt God's forgiveness when I was baptized in the name of the Lord Jesus Christ. I had been baptized twice before, once in the titles "Father, Son, and Holy Ghost" and once in "Jesus" name only, but never felt forgiven. Faith in God's true name allowed me to experience His saving grace when I was buried in the name of the Lord Jesus Christ. Second, I experienced freedom from numerous addictions through Jesus Christ's literal name as I would speak His name out loud against tobacco, pornography, idolatry, and more. Before recognizing God's name, the Lord Jesus Christ, I was a helpless slave to sin.

When my preaching ministry began, I spoke the name of Jesus Christ through His leading and watched His power cast out devils, heal the sick, bring deliverance to the addicted, bring forth babies for the barren, and more. While it may not be impossible, I have not yet witnessed any miracle or movement of God's Spirit by speaking aloud any of God's titles, such as Father, Son, Holy Ghost, Prince of Peace, or Righteous Branch. When I started speaking in God's literal name I began seeing the power and authority that accompanies it.

---

232   Philippians 2:9-11
233   Luke 10:17, Acts 16:18
234   Acts 2:38, 8:16, 19:5
235   Acts 3:6

The entire Bible teaches that God's name has power, and believers experience it when they have faith in His name according to Acts 3:16: *"And his name through faith in his name hath made this man strong."* When David defeated Goliath in 1 Samuel 17:45, he said he came against the giant *"in the name of the Lord of hosts."* Having faith in the Lord's name was the source of power and accuracy in David's stone and sling. John 1:12 teaches those that receive Christ receive His power because they believe in His name. Acts 4:7 emphatically declares a name is synonymous with power, for it says, *"By what power, or by what name, have ye done this?"* In this instance, Peter was being questioned how the previously lame man had received perfect soundness of health and the ability to walk. In verse 10, Peter's answer was *"by the name of Jesus Christ of Nazareth, whom ye crucified, whom God raised from the dead, even by him doth this man stand here before you whole."* The authority, or power in Jesus Christ's name made the lame man whole.

Humans can relate to the concept of a name representing power since human names carry reputations and have authority. Proverbs 22:1 says, *"A good name is rather to be chosen than great riches, and loving favour rather than silver and gold."* Your actions have a powerful influence on others, which create your "good name" or reputation.

Your name's authority is displayed when you purchase something with your credit card or with a check because the transaction isn't complete until you've applied your signature to the receipt or check. If I sign my checks with my titles, "father, son, and brother," my check will not be honored because they require the authority of my literal name. Another example is the name on a power of attorney document. Banks and businesses will honor only the one name that is certified and notarized as being a power of attorney. No other titles or names have power. In the same way, God's literal name, the Lord Jesus Christ, *"the name which is above every name,"* is the only name that carries authority or power when spoken in faith.

Paul declares that Christ's power, or name, would be denied in the *"last days"* by egotistical, self-absorbed imposters of Christianity who have a form of godliness, but not true godliness.[236] Are Christian churches teaching their members to cast out devils *in the name of Jesus Christ* as Paul did in Acts 16:18, or are they denying that power? Turn away from any church that denies this power! Very few churches teach the reality of the power in Jesus' name. This fulfills direct prophecy about the intent of the *"beast"* or antichrist spirit in Revelation 13:5-6, as Satan blasphemes God's name, tabernacle, and the saints in heaven. Blaspheme means to "slander" or "detract" in the Greek, meaning Satan reduces and takes away the value or worth of God's name. The popularity of the Trinity has valued and exalted the titles "Father, Son, and Holy Ghost" far above the name of Jesus Christ, thereby blaspheming God's true name, much to the enemy's delight. Few Christians are baptized in Jesus Christ's name. Even fewer perform miracles and cast out devils in Jesus Christ's name. Instead, they are taught to bless themselves using the sign of the cross in the titles "Father, Son, and Holy Ghost," and yet Scripture says blessing oneself is a sign that a heart is turned away[237] from serving God.

UNDERSTANDING 1 JOHN 5:7

1 John 5:7 reads, *"For there are three that bear record in heaven, the Father, the Word, and the Holy Ghost: and these three are one."* Does this prove God is three persons? No, for it never says God is three persons, but rather gives extra support that God is one person, for it says *"these three are one"*—not three.

What 1 John 5:7 does offer is more proof that God has three manifestations He uses to redeem mankind, just as Matthew 28:19 lists these three forms: Father, Son, and Holy Ghost. As evidence that "Son" is a title and not a name, this Scripture calls the Son *"the Word,"* which is a suitable alias for the same manifestation, for the Son is the Word made flesh. The gospel of John and Book of Revelation both teach this, saying *"In the beginning was the Word, and the Word was with God, and the Word was God. And the Word was made flesh, and dwelt among us,"*[238] and *"He*

---

236   2 Timothy 3:1-5
237   Deuteronomy 29:16-20
238   John 1:1, 14

was clothed with a vesture dipped in blood: and his name is called The Word of God."[239]

The little-known truth of God's three manifestations bearing record in heaven requires attention. God will use His three manifestations—Father, Son, and Holy Ghost—to serve as multiple witnesses in heaven either for or against all mankind. No matter which time period men lived in—before Christ's earthly ministry, during, or after—there will be a heavenly record of how they treated God's Word. The three bearing record in heaven cannot mean there are three persons sitting on judgment thrones in heaven, for Scripture never states there are three heavenly thrones, or even two for that matter. There is only one throne.

The Father is the heavenly witness either in favor of or against all men who lived before Jesus Christ walked the earth. The loving Father will witness that He sent men anointed of His Spirit to preach, warn, and lead the people. Enoch preached the Father's warning, for Jude says he

> *"prophesied of these, saying, Behold, the Lord cometh with ten thousands of his saints, To execute judgment upon all, and to convince all that are ungodly among them of all their ungodly deeds which they have ungodly committed, and of all their hard speeches which ungodly sinners have spoken against him."*[240]

Moses also served as the Father's witness when he reminded Israel of their covenant with Jehovah, saying, *"I call heaven and earth to record this day against you, that I have set before you life and death, blessing and cursing: therefore choose life, that both thou and thy seed may live."*[241] About 400 years before Christ, God the Father spoke through the prophet Malachi telling Israel how He was a witness that the men had *"dealt treacherously"* with their wives and He was no longer going to receive their offerings or tears.[242] This Scripture illuminates the fact that the Father's eyes plainly see into our homes and that nothing is hid from the Lord.

---

239   Revelation 19:13
240   Jude 1:14-15
241   Deuteronomy 30:19
242   Malachi 2:13-14

Jesus the Son is a heavenly witness because both His works and words will bear record of His ministry. Concerning His works Christ says, *"The works which the Father hath given me to finish, the same works that I do, bear witness of me, that the Father hath sent me. And the Father himself, which hath sent me, hath borne witness of me."*[243] Jesus' preaching will have an equally weighty heavenly witness on Judgment Day, for He says, *"The word that I have spoken, the same shall judge him in the last day."*[244] Jesus shockingly declared that the generation that rejected His earthly preaching would have two witnesses rise up against them in condemnation on the Day of Judgment: the men of Nineveh and the queen of the south.[245] The Ninevehites' repentance proves heaven is recording which people truly change their hearts and lives after hearing gospel preaching. Heaven also records the lengths people will go to hear God's preaching, as the queen of the south's testimony validates.

The Holy Ghost bares record on all mankind now because Jesus' body currently sits at the *"right hand of the majesty on high."*[246] Acts 5:31-32 teaches that the Holy Ghost currently gives witness to Jesus' death, resurrection, and exaltation. This witness is that the obedient Christian is born again, or given the Holy Ghost as a gift from God. The miracle-producing presence of the Holy Ghost in the ministries of genuine Christians is also God's witness to all generations, as taught in Hebrews 2:1-4. It's immensely important to recognize the witness of the Holy Ghost today, for Jesus said speaking against it will not be forgiven *"in this world, neither in the world to come!"*[247]

When 1 John 5:7 is closely examined, it's clear that John was not listing three persons, bur rather God's three manifestations that serve as heavenly witnesses for the actions of all humanity.

---

243   John 5:36-37
244   John 12:48
245   Matthew 12:41-42
246   Hebrews 1:3
247   Matthew 12:32

UNDERSTANDING JESUS' BAPTISM

Does Jesus' water baptism at the Jordan River prove God is three persons? No, for if it did, that would prove Christianity is tritheism—the belief in three distinct gods. To put it simply, Jesus' baptism shows God's power to manifest Himself simultaneously in multiple ways, an attribute He previously displayed in the Old Testament.

At the burning bush in Exodus 3:1-6, Moses witnessed God manifest Himself in two supernatural ways: by voice and fire. Some might see two persons here—Father as the voice and Holy Ghost as the fire. Recall that the Holy Ghost appeared as 120 licks of fire in Acts 2:3-4 but that does not mean He is 120 separate persons. Nothing in the Exodus text speaks of multiple personalities. The voice and fire were not showing God was two separate persons, but revealed His power to appear in different forms simultaneously. Paul says God's invisible Spirit hides inside the light of the fire in 1 Timothy 6:16: *"Who only hath immortality, dwelling in the light which no man can approach unto."*

When Jesus was baptized, many erroneously see three persons— Father as the voice, Son in the water, and Holy Ghost as the dove. The true understanding is that God spoke from heaven while His own Spirit (not a third person) descended like a dove upon the man Christ Jesus. God's three manifestations at Jesus' baptism do not prove three persons just as the 120 licks of fire on the Day of Pentecost do not prove the Holy Spirit is 120 separate persons!

When understood correctly, Jesus' baptism shows one invisible person anointing His visible human image. Since God the Father is the Holy Ghost, Jesus' baptism shows one invisible person coming to inhabit the body, or temple, He created. Imagine a hand filling a glove. Once inside the glove, the hand does not become a second, distinct hand. Rather, it's the same hand veiled behind an image. Like a glove, Jesus' body is the image God's person dwells within. Jesus is not a second person but the single, visual representation of God.

Consider the three errors of trinitarian logic regarding Jesus' baptism. First, it's an error to believe the coequal Son was anointed by the coequal

Holy Spirit. You're probably aware the Bible says Jesus was anointed of the Holy Ghost in Acts 10:38, so why does trinitarianism teach the Son needs a third person to anoint Him if He is already fully, eternal God? A fully-divine person should not need to be anointed by another fully-divine person. Here we see how trinitarianism leads to tritheism since one god needs anointed by another god. The truth is that Jesus' human body was powerless on its own, proven by Jesus' own words in John 5:19: *"Verily, verily, I say unto you, The Son can do nothing of himself, but what he seeth the Father do: for what things soever he doeth, these also doeth the Son likewise."* Jesus gave the Father credit for His miracles, as John 14:10 says, *"The Father that dwelleth in me, he doeth the works."* Christ needed to be filled with the Holy Ghost and received that filling at His River Jordan baptism. Prior to Jesus' resurrection, His human body was not immortal—it was mortal, didn't know all things, and died.

Second, trinitarianism has another problem related to the first. Supposedly, Jesus was filled with the third person of the Trinity at His baptism, but the doctrine doesn't explain when Jesus was filled with the first person—the Father. Jesus plainly said the Father dwelt in Him in John 14:10: *"But the Father that dwelleth in me, he doeth the works."* How could God the Father be pleased with His Son at His baptism, saying *"This is my beloved Son in whom I am well pleased,"* when He was not dwelling in Jesus? God the Father said He would put His own Spirit— not another person's spirit—in His Son in Isaiah 42:1, saying, *"Behold my servant, whom I uphold; mine elect, in whom my soul delighteth; I have put my spirit upon him."*

Third, trinitarianism implies Jesus had two separate, distinct persons living inside Him despite the Bible never saying two persons dwelt in Him. Scripture says both the Father (John 14:10) and Holy Ghost (Luke 4:1) dwelt in Jesus' body. If the Trinity is true, then two separate, distinct persons dwelt in one person. But the truth is that the Father and Holy Ghost are the selfsame person. Jesus did not suffer with DID, the multiple personalities disorder. Truly, Jesus' baptism shows the one person, the Father-Spirit, coming to fill and lead His human image, His Son.

Fourth, some believe the Holy Ghost that descended like a dove upon Jesus' body exists eternally as a visible dove. The Book of Revelation, along with the rest of the Bible, never mentions a third person as an eternal dove roosting in heaven next to two thrones although Trinitarian artwork displays this falsehood. The Holy Ghost is not a literal dove. He only appeared like a dove at Jesus' baptism as a sign for John the Baptist to identify the Lamb of God. The Holy Spirit changed its form from dove to 120 licks of fire in Acts chapter 2.

At His baptism in Matthew 3:15, Jesus said He must *"fulfill all righteousness,"* which has two meanings. First, He was setting the example of righteous obedience for New Testament believers to be baptized and filled with the Holy Ghost, which was later preached by Peter in Acts 2:38. Repentance is the prerequisite for water baptism, which is followed by the spiritual baptism of the the Holy Ghost. In Jesus' case, He didn't need repentance unto baptism like all believers need, but He did it as an example. However, Jesus *did* need to be filled with the Holy Spirit after His baptism, as Scripture says the Spirit descended from heaven and then abode (lived) and remained on Him when He came up out of the water.[248] Luke 4:1 says Jesus left Jordan *"full of the Holy Ghost"* and was immediately *"led by the Spirit into the wilderness."* Jesus was given the Spirit without measure[249] and personally verified He received the baptism of the Spirit, saying *"Are ye able to drink of the cup that I shall drink of, and to be baptized with the baptism that I am baptized with?"*[250] God's righteous design is that filling, or anointing comes *after* washing. Elijah's burnt sacrifice on Mount Carmel was first drenched with four barrels of water and then the fire of God fell from heaven.[251] Moses, Aaron, and his sons were commanded by God to wash in water before approaching God at the completion of the tabernacle in the wilderness and afterwards *"the glory of the LORD filled the*

---

248   John 1:32-33
249   John 3:34
250   Matthew 20:22
251   1 Kings 18:33-38

tabernacle."[252] Similarly, Jesus' *"temple of His body"*[253] had to be washed before the Holy Ghost filled Him.

Second, Christ was baptized in order to fulfill the righteous, Old Testament command for burnt offerings to be washed, according to Leviticus 1:1-9. Burnt offerings were *"a sweet savour unto the Lord,"* and Paul says Jesus *"hath given Himself for us an offering and a sacrifice to God for a sweet smelling savour."*[254] Jesus, being washed at His baptism, was later offered as God's perfect, complete, and acceptable burnt offering.

UNDERSTANDING JESUS' PRAYERS IN GETHSEMANE

Although Jesus prayed throughout His ministry, His Gethsemane prayers reveal His full humanity and help prove God's one personality. Jesus' prayers cannot prove God is three persons because the supposed coequal, coeternal Son would not need to pray to another coequal, coeternal person—the Father. Three eternal persons is always equivalent to polytheism.

Jesus' Gethsemane prayer shows Jesus was 100% human and 100% deity, yet this doesn't equal two coequal gods. The human part of the Son had a separate will than the eternal Father, as Christ says, *"Father, if thou be willing, remove this cup from me: nevertheless not my will, but thine, be done."*[255] Jesus' flesh, although sinless, did not want to die, but obediently surrendered to the will of the Father. Jesus' humanity *needed* God's deity, just as your humanity needs God's deity. The difference between Jesus and you is that Jesus' humanity had a Word-nature while your humanity has a sin-nature.

Does the mention of two wills—Jesus' fleshly will and the Father's will—equal two separate persons? No, but it does teach that Jesus' body was a one-of-a-kind human manifestation (*"God was manifest in the flesh"*) that had to have a separate will and pronoun in order to die for mankind since the immortal Spirit-God could never die. God didn't become a

---

252   Exodus 40:30-35
253   John 2:21
254   Ephesians 5:2
255   Luke 22:42

second person in the body of Jesus; He was the same person in another form. God in human form, manifest in the flesh. The Word became flesh. God became flesh. The Father and Son were one in nature—the Word—but with different characteristics.

OTHER THREEFOLD REFERENCES

Accompanying Matthew 28:19, 1 John 5:7, and Jesus' baptism are threefold references to the Godhead, such as both Paul and John's epistle greetings and benedictions. 2 Corinthians 13:14 is a widely known example, saying, *"The grace of the Lord Jesus Christ, and the love of God, and the communion of the Holy Ghost, be with you all."* Do threefold references to the Godhead like this prove God is three persons? No, for these references never call God "three persons" but they do prove how necessary it is for believers to recognize God's three manifestations.

Recall that 1 John 5:7 says the Father, Word, and Holy Ghost are heavenly witnesses for or against all mankind, proving the absolute necessity for believers to recognize God's three manifestations, including the one in which they live. For example, we are living in the age of the Holy Ghost manifestation, for the Son of Man is no longer on the earth and has ascended to the right hand of the Father. If we neglect or speak evil of the Holy Ghost today, there is no hope of forgiveness, for Christ says, *"But unto him that blasphemeth against the Holy Ghost it shall not be forgiven."*[256] In Jesus' earthly ministry, He harshly warned the Pharisees to not reject His "Son manifestation," saying, *"For if ye believe not that I am he, ye shall die in your sins."*[257] The Pharisees could apparently accept God in the Father manifestation, but not God's current manifestation in the Son, and so condemnation awaited their unbelieving hearts.

As you examine Paul and John's epistle greetings, you'll find their emphasis was on the Father and Son, and not upon worshipping three persons. Four examples of epistle greetings mention the Father and Son but nothing of the Holy Ghost: Romans 1:7, 1 Corinthians 1:3, 1 John

---

256   Luke 12:10
257   John 8:24

1:3, and 2 John 1:3. Does this mean Paul believed in only two persons, so he left out the third person of the Trinity? No, it means it was not necessary to mention the Holy Ghost because Paul knew the Father and Holy Ghost are the self same person.

Returning to Scriptures with threefold references, it seems God allows this to help believers better understand the enigma of the Father, Son, and Holy Ghost. In 2 Corinthians 13:14, Paul mentions *"The grace of the Lord Jesus Christ, and the love of God, and the communion of the Holy Ghost."* Although the three attributes all pertain to God—grace, love, communion—Paul uses each one separately to help believers appreciate each manifestation. For example, Paul said the grace of Christ would be with believers, which supports John's words that Christ was *"full of grace and truth"*[258] and by grace Jesus tasted death for every man.[259] Next, Paul emphasized the love of God. John 3:16 and Romans 8:38-39 explain God's great love that caused Him to send His Son to die for our salvation and speak of 10 things that cannot separate us from the love of God. Third, Paul ends the verse by wisely pointing out the believer's current *"communion of the Holy Ghost."* Christians today have communion with the Holy Ghost, Who is the selfsame person as the Father. God's plan was for the Son to have only about three and half years of earthly communion with Jesus' disciples. Peter, James, John, and the rest of the apostles were privileged to commune with the Son face to face. But our lot is communion with Christ through the Comforter, the Holy Ghost, just as Jesus taught in John 14:26, saying, *"But the Comforter, which is the Holy Ghost, whom the Father will send in my name, he shall teach you all things, and bring all things to your remembrance, whatsoever I have said unto you."*

IS JESUS THE "ETERNAL SON?"

Some trinitarians give Jesus the title "Eternal Son," which probably originates from the Athanasian Creed. The creed says, "The Father is eternal,

---

258   John 1:14
259   Hebrews 2:9

the Son is eternal, the Holy Spirit is eternal." But the "Eternal Son" title is both absent from the Bible and deceiving because it alludes to Jesus and the Father eternally existing as two separate persons in heaven. The truth is Jesus' human body did not exist until God's Spirit formed it in Mary's womb. Christ's body had a beginning but His Spirit or nature, the Word, did not. Jesus was and always will be the Word, God's nature, but Christ is not a separate person from God.

The "Eternal Son" title is self contradictory because the word "son" automatically suggests a beginning point. Branham says, "People talk about Jesus being the Eternal Son of God. Now isn't that a contradiction? Whoever heard of a 'Son' being eternal? Sons have beginnings, but that which is eternal never had a beginning. He is the Eternal God (Jehovah) manifested in the flesh."[260]

The implication of the "Eternal Son" dwelling with the "Eternal Father" and "Eternal Spirit" is the declaration of three gods, which is easily detected in today's influential pastors. With all due respect to Rick Warren, whose *Purpose Driven Life* book contains many truths, it also contains false trinitarian teachings. The first misunderstanding is Warren saying, "God invites us to enjoy friendship and fellowship with all three persons of the Trinity."[261] This falsehood is nowhere found in Scripture, but the opposite is true—the prophets Isaiah, Ezekiel, and John the revelator had fellowship with only one person in their heavenly visions.[262] No Bible passage ever teaches believers to have present or future fellowship with three separate persons. Thankfully, Christians do not have the pressure of giving equal fellowship with three separate persons.

Another error is Warren teaching "The Trinity is God's relationship to himself. It's the perfect pattern for relational harmony, and we should study its implications. God has always existed in loving relationship to himself, so he has never been lonely. He didn't need a family."[263] It's true that God has never been lonely, as Paul says God does not need anything

---

260   Branham, p. 21
261   Warren, Rick. *Purpose Driven Life.* Zondervan, 2012
262   Isaiah 6:1, Ezekiel 1:26-28, Revelation 4:2
263   Warren

in Acts 17:25. The Book of Isaiah states the Lord, who has no equal,[264] made all things alone, by Himself, proving creation was done by one person, not three.[265]

It's incorrect to say God has a relationship to Himself, which means He has relationships with two other Trinity members. The implication of a three person-god having a relationship to Himself is God managing a multiple personalities disorder. God is one person, with no coequal persons existing beside Him. God does not have to balance three personalities.

The truth is that God does have relationship with His manifested *thoughts*. God is the only one in the universe that has this power and privilege. As the omnipotent, eternal, ever-invisible, holy God, He dwelt alone with His thoughts inside His being well before He created angels and the universe. God wasn't having relationship with His thoughts because they needed to be expressed as individual persons before that could occur. Every Christian is a manifested thought of God. As 2 Corinthians 6:16 teaches, God expressed believers to be temples of His: *"As God hath said, I will dwell in them, and walk in them; and I will be their God, and they shall be my people."* You were previously an eternal thought of God and now that you're expressed in a flesh body, God can come and live and walk in you. God fellowships with you by living inside you.

Before God created humans, He did have a relationship with His Son, the Logos, but not as a separate person. Jesus confirms this twice in John 17, saying, *"O Father, glorify thou me with thine own self with the glory which I had with thee before the world was,"* and *"For thou lovedst me before the foundation of the world."*[266] This doesn't mean God is two persons, but it shows Jesus' spiritual body was God's first creation, since Jesus says He is *"the beginning of the creation of God."*[267]

Before earth and humans were created, a celestial body, or spirit body, came out of the invisible God. Scholars call this body the Logos,

---

264   Isaiah 40:25, 46:5
265   Isaiah 44:24
266   John 17:5, 24
267   Revelation 3:14

which is the Greek word for "Word" in John 1:1: *"In the beginning was the Word, and the Word was with God, and the Word was God."* In other words, in the beginning was the Logos, and the Logos was with God, and was God's visible image. The Logos is the Holy Spirit, only visible. This visible Logos was moved by the invisible Spirit hiding inside it, proving the Logos is not a second person, but the image of God's one person.

This Logos is personified as "wisdom" in Proverbs 8:12, 22-31. Listen to this loving description of the Father and Son, the Logos:

> *"I wisdom dwell with prudence, and find out knowledge of witty inventions.The Lord possessed me in the beginning of his way, before his works of old. I was set up from everlasting, from the beginning, or ever the earth was. When there were no depths, I was brought forth; when there were no fountains abounding with water. Before the mountains were settled, before the hills was I brought forth: While as yet he had not made the earth, nor the fields, nor the highest part of the dust of the world. When he prepared the heavens, I was there: when he set a compass upon the face of the depth: When he established the clouds above: when he strengthened the fountains of the deep: When he gave to the sea his decree, that the waters should not pass his commandment: when he appointed the foundations of the earth: Then I was by him, as one brought up with him: and I was daily his delight, rejoicing always before him; Rejoicing in the habitable part of his earth; and my delights were with the sons of men."*

This is the glory of Jesus' relationship with His Father before the world was in John 17:5.

It's undeniable that eternal life is *in* the Son, Jesus Christ. While Jesus is not the "Eternal Son," He does have eternal life. 1 John 5:11-12 mentions this fact twice, saying, *"God hath given to us eternal life, and this life is in his Son. He that hath the Son hath life; and he that hath not the Son of God hath not life."* The conclusion is that God's eternal life is in the Son because the invisible God created Jesus' body and forever dwells inside it.

THE REWARDS FOR RECEIVING THE REVELATION OF THE GODHEAD

There are at least three rewards for receiving the revelation of the Godhead. The first is that you will know God intimately, as He wants to be known, enjoying true fellowship with the Almighty. Monotheism is true, intimate worship. The ancient Hebrews were strict monotheists, so much so that Jesus told the Samaritan woman at the well that Jews *"know"* what they worship. Jews were not guessing God was one person—they knew God was one person!

It is only through monotheism that you can be a true, intimate worshipper. Jesus says the Father is currently seeking true worshippers.[268] Worshipping God as three persons is false worship, proven by the fact that many trinitarians sprinkle instead of fully immerse at baptism, call upon God's titles rather than His one name, and bless themselves with the sign of the cross and holy water. As you worship God's one personality, you are like Abel bringing the correct, acceptable sacrifice. False worshippers bring sacrifices of their own choosing, like Cain.

When you worship God as one person, the Lord grants you true communion with Himself. You don't have to worry about communing equally with each person of the Trinity. You don't have to wonder why you feel like you know the Father and Son so well but feel distant from the Holy Spirit. 1 John 1:3 says, *"Truly our fellowship is with the Father, and with his Son Jesus Christ."* When you believe on Jesus Christ, receiving the Son's work on Calvary, He reveals the Father, and the Father is the Holy Spirit. Matthew 11:27 declares, *"All things are delivered unto me of my Father: and no man knoweth the Son, but the Father; neither knoweth any man the Father, save the Son, and he to whomsoever the Son will reveal him."*

An example of this blessed communion is in daily prayer because God's three manifestations are active. The Holy Spirit anoints and leads Christians to have access in prayer to the Father (invisible Spirit) through the Son, as Ephesians 2:18 tells us, *"We both have access by*

---

268   John 4:24

one Spirit unto the Father." Christians come *"boldly"* to speak to the Father but it can only be done through the *"great high priest...Jesus the Son of God."*[269] Jesus' human body is the invisible Father's heavenly representation.

The second reward for receiving the true revelation of the Godhead is possessing God's overcoming power. Jesus promised this power to Peter, saying, *"the gates of hell shall not prevail against it"*—"it" being the revelation that Jesus was the Christ. Was Jesus' promise to Peter true? Yes. Did hell's counsel prevail against Peter? No, for even in Peter's greatest failure, publicly denying Christ three times before Jesus' crucifixion, Jesus personally showed Himself alive to Peter before the rest of the apostles after His resurrection.[270] Hell's counsels will not prevail against you even in the midst of your greatest failures because you have the same revelation about Jesus as Peter.

Paul lists 17 sins that you'll overcome (there could be more elsewhere in Scripture) by the Spirit of God in 1 Corinthians 6:9-10 and Galatians 5:19-21: idolatry, effeminate (child molestation), abusers of themselves with mankind (homosexuality), covetousness, drunkards, revilers, uncleanness, lasciviousness, witchcraft, hatred, variance, emulation, wrath, strife, seditions, heresies, and revelings. Knowing Jesus Christ in truth, with true revelation, gives you power to overcome every device of hell!

The third reward for receiving the Godhead revelation is the future reward of knowing Jesus' new name, which He will share with you. God is pleased that during your life you have confessed the name of the Lord Jesus Christ before family, friends, and associates. Like the church in Philadelphia, you have *"not denied"*[271] Jesus' holy name. Since you confessed Christ's name in life, Christ will confess your name before the Father[272] and then share His new name with you, the overcomer:

---

269   Hebrews 4:14-16
270   Luke 24:34, 1 Corinthians 15:5
271   Revelation 3:8
272   Matthew 10:32-33

"Him that overcometh will I make a pillar in the temple of my God, and he shall go no more out: and I will write upon him the name of my God, and the name of the city of my God, which is new Jerusalem, which cometh down out of heaven from my God: and I will write upon him my new name."[273]

Branham writes, "When all becomes new, then He will take upon Him a new Name and that Name will be the Name of the bride also. What that Name is, none dare conjecture. It would have to be a revelation of the Spirit given so conclusively that none would dare deny it. But no doubt He will leave that revelation to the day when He desires to give that Name forth. Suffice it to know that it will be more wonderful than we could ever imagine."[274]

THE CONSEQUENCES FOR REJECTING THE REVELATION OF THE GODHEAD

There are four possible consequences for rejecting the revelation of the Godhead. Let me state that these consequences do not refer to all trinitarians, but certainly most because Jesus said "few" would find the narrow road of truth.

First, many who reject God as one person and maintain He is three persons—without literal Bible evidence—will be guilty of idolatry (breaking the first commandment), lying by adding to God's pure words, and blaspheming God's name. The first commandment says, *"Thou shalt have no other gods before me,"*[275] but it's also apparent in this verse that God wants no other gods *with* Him. Isaiah records God saying six times there is no one else *"beside Me"*[276] and twice says He has no *"equal."*[277] Yet the Trinity fabricates two other *equal* persons *beside* God the Father, just as ancient religions concocted a triad of divine persons. The devil has succeeded in making idolators out of the masses through their complete ignorance and rejection of Scripture. Satan's Trinity deception has made

273   Revelation 3:12
274   Branham, p. 318
275   Exodus 20:3
276   Isaiah 43:11, 44:6-8, 45:5-6, 21,
277   Isaiah 40:25, 46:5

many trinitarians liars in God's sight, for anyone who willingly adds to Scripture will be called such, as previously referenced in Proverbs 30:5-6. The antichrist spirit is leading sinners to blaspheme God's name by substituting the titles "Father, Son, and Holy Ghost" in place of the all-powerful name, the Lord Jesus Christ. When Jesus Christ's name is denied when baptizing, casting out devils, and performing miracles, Satan has succeeded in blaspheming God's name.

A second, long term effect of rejecting the Godhead revelation is a slow, spiritual death as taught in James 1:15, for *"sin, when it is finished, bringeth forth death."* In fact, any false doctrine can have this effect, as Paul points out that the false doctrine that says the resurrection, or rapture, has already happened slowly overthrows *"the faith of some,"* spreading like a canker over their spiritual lives.[278] A canker in the Greek is gangrene, the slow, flesh-and-bone-eating disease. One false belief can cause a person to *"increase unto more ungodliness,"*[279] for accepting a second lie is easier than accepting the first. Jesus uses a similar illustration for false doctrine, calling it *"leaven,"*[280] which also slowly spreads until all the dough is leavened. If the false Trinity doctrine is accepted in a church, it's much easier for the rest of the church's teaching to become corrupted.

You can easily apply the gangrene or leaven effect to today's churches. Most church leaders allow their members to be lovers of pleasures more than lovers of God. The following sins are more widely accepted than ever, despite being plainly identified as evil in Scripture: adultery (being married to someone other than your first spouse while your first spouse is still alive), fornication (having sexual relations before marriage), homosexuality, drunkenness, cursing, watching sinful movies, listening to sinful music, cross dressing, immodest clothes, women cutting their hair, lying, stealing, and the like.

A third consequence is a greater likelihood of being given the status of a *"foolish"* Christian rather than wise, as taught by Christ in Matthew

278   2 Timothy 2:17-18
279   2 Timothy 2:16
280   Matthew 16:12

25:1-12. Chapters 6 and 8 contain a lengthy teaching on wise and foolish virgins. Our Lord says there are two kinds of Christians: wise and foolish. It's possible for a foolish Christian to be saved and go to heaven despite having made foolish decisions in his life in regards to the baptism of the Holy Ghost, and in this case, the Godhead. Trinitarians can still be saved, although it's foolish to add to the Bible, calling God "three persons" when He never reveals Himself thus. Jesus told His own followers they were *"fools"* for not believing *"all that the prophets"* had spoken regarding His coming.[281] The same is true today because scholars and doctors of divinity will not believe God's prophets (like Isaiah) who repeatedly declare that God is one and there is none beside Him. Because the foolish virgins failed to get the *"oil"* or baptism of the Holy Ghost, they could not be led by the Spirit into all truth, and thus continued to confess that God was "three persons."

A fourth and final consequence is not knowing and ignorantly worshipping God. On Mars Hill, Paul met Athenians who were ignorantly worshipping an unknown god.[282] A friend once shared her frustration with feeling well acquainted with the Father and Son, yet felt the Holy Spirit was a stranger. Sadly, my friend had attended church for over thirty years and in the current Holy Spirit-dispensation (the Old Testament Fatherhood and Sonship dispensations have already passed) admitted to not even knowing the Holy Spirit. If my friend was sincerely, yet ignorantly, trying to worship the "third person" of the Trinity after 30 years, how likely is it that many other life-long, trinitarian church members feel like they do not know God, or one of His persons? Furthermore, do trinitarians always know to which person of the Trinity they are praying? Like the Pharisees, many trinitarians today do not know Jesus because God's Word doesn't have a place in their hearts and minds.[283] Trinitarians often reject the plain, simple witness of Scripture in order to add "three persons" to the Bible.

281 Luke 24:25
282 Acts 17:16-34
283 John 8:19, 37

CONCLUSION

Although one mysterious element remains about the Godhead, God has revealed Himself as one person who manifests Himself in three ways to redeem mankind. All dark, shadowy confusion about God's number of persons scatters in the Light of Bible witnesses, revealing one, immortal, invisible, eternal person—the Lord Jesus Christ. Yes, Jesus Christ is supreme deity. Jesus Christ is God.

Theologians, scholars, historians, and preachers all admit that the doctrine of "three persons" is not implicitly taught in Scripture and there are at least eight, Bible-backed reasons why the Trinity doctrine is wrong. Indeed, God never called Himself "three persons." A "three person" god automatically injects tritheism into Christianity, expressly seen through Jesus supposedly having two fathers and being filled with two other coequal persons. What better way for Satan to blaspheme God's name than to change it to titles, "Father, Son, and Holy Ghost," and then convince billions of trinitarians to deny the power in the name of Jesus Christ? Ultimately, accepting the Trinity will likely lead to long term spiritual sickness in churches who embrace it because any doctrinal lie spreads like gangrene or leaven.

Accepting the revelation of the Godhead brings intimacy with Christ, overcoming power against the gates of hell, and a promise to share in Jesus' new name in the New Jerusalem. With this life-giving, prevailing Godhead revelation, you can now move on to the second mystery relating to God's blinding of His Old Testament people, Israel, and understand why most cannot see Jesus is the Messiah.

ACTION STEPS

1. If you're a former trinitarian, repent of purposely or ignorantly adding to God's known character. Rejoice in knowing God in truth, as one divine Person.

2. Although the revelation of the Godhead isn't required for salvation, be ready to share God's true revelation with others by citing Scripture alone, while explaining the danger of adding "three persons" to God's character.

3. Be aware to avoid lots of trinitarian references in songs (i.e. *Holy, Holy Holy*), statements of faith, and wedding or baptismal blessings.

4. Be careful when associating with trinitarians for the fact that one false doctrine often leads to many others.

FOLLOW UP

See Appendix A for a Bible Study Reference List with the Scriptures from this chapter.

See Appendix B for William Branham's quotes regarding this revealed mystery.

Free online videos and Bible studies related to this chapter: www.pastorjessesmith.com/12mysteriesbook

Email: jesse.smith11@sbcglobal.net

Text: 330-929-2037

CHAPTER 2

The Mystery of Israel's Spiritual Blindness

"For I would not, brethren, that ye should be ignorant of this mystery, lest ye should be wise in your own conceits; that blindness in part is happened to Israel, until the fulness of the Gentiles be come in."

Romans 11:25

BEFORE DISCUSSING ISRAEL'S BLINDNESS, it's important to understand her Biblical history. The Old Testament richly chronicles Israel's relationship with the one person God, Yahweh, the God of the Bible. This relationship begins in Eden, showing how God revealed Himself to Adam's faithful descendants, Israel, throughout the Old Testament, but later in the New Testament had to put spiritual blindness (that still exists today) upon the Jews that He might show mercy to the Gentiles.

Adam and Eve's godly seed proceeds through Seth's lineage to Noah. Between Noah's three sons—Ham, Shem, and Japeth—Shem emerges as the faithful servant to God, proven by the godly deeds of him and his descendants. The Lord promises to bless every nation through father Abraham—the ninth descendant from Shem—but specifically Isaac's seed is recognized as the true heirs of His everlasting covenant in Genesis 17:19-21:

> "And God said, Sarah thy wife shall bear thee a son indeed; and thou shalt call his name Isaac: and I will establish my covenant with him for an everlasting covenant, and with his seed after him. And as for Ishmael, I have heard thee: Behold, I have blessed him, and will make him fruitful, and will multiply him exceedingly; twelve princes shall he beget, and I will make him a great nation. But my covenant will I establish with Isaac, which Sarah shall bear unto thee at this set time in the next year."

Five generations from Isaac comes Moses, God's prophet sent to deliver the children of Israel out of Egyptian slavery. In Moses' time, God's compassionate description of His love for His people begins to manifest. Three months after the exodus in the desert of Sinai, God instructs Moses to tell Israel they are a special treasure to Him. Exodus 19:4-6 reads:

> "Ye have seen what I did unto the Egyptians, and how I bare you on eagles' wings, and brought you unto myself. Now therefore, if ye will obey my voice indeed, and keep my covenant, then ye shall be a peculiar treasure unto me above all people: for all the earth is mine: And ye shall be unto me a kingdom of priests, and an holy nation. These are the words which thou shalt speak unto the children of Israel."

Hardly more beautiful, comforting words could ever be received! Imagine the creator of the universe calling you His special treasure! Israel was indeed blessed and highly favored, being singled out from every nation under heaven as the holder of God's covenants and blessings. In fact, Paul says all other nations—Egypt, Persia, Greece, China, Japan, Russia, etc.—were *"aliens from the commonwealth of Israel, and strangers from the covenants of promise, having no hope, and without God in the world."*[284] Indeed, Israel was the chosen, special, privileged and peculiar people in the earth, thanks to God's gracious choosing.

But God had conditions to His covenant with Israel. He said *"if"* Israel obeyed His voice and kept His covenant, they would remain a kingdom of priests and holy nation unto Him.

Israel often wavered in devotion to God. Some 800 years before Christ, God anointed the prophet Isaiah to foretell Israel's spiritual blindness that would come upon them as a result of their rebellion to His holy covenant:

> *"And he said, Go, and tell this people, Hear ye indeed, but understand not; and see ye indeed, but perceive not. Make the heart of this people fat, and make their ears heavy, and shut their eyes; lest they see with their eyes, and hear with their ears, and understand with their heart, and convert, and be healed."*[285]

Then in Jeremiah's day, about 600 years before Christ, the LORD Himself called His people *"backsliding Israel."*[286] Israel had some godly leaders, such as Joshua, Samuel, David, Solomon, Hezekiah, and Josiah, but the majority were evil men who led God's people into evil, idolatrous lifestyles. Israel's disobedience, though, could not override God's grace to them. Nor could it hinder His amazing plan of redemption for all nations.

In His grace, 42 generations after Abraham[287] God sent His promised Son, Jesus Christ, to redeem Israel from their sins and fill their souls with the Holy Spirit. Jesus was the fulfillment of God's promises to Abraham to bless his seed and all nations. Messiah was God's antidote for their sin problem.

---

284   Ephesians 2:12
285   Isaiah 6:9-10
286   Jeremiah 3:6
287   Matthew 1:17

Note specifically Jesus' command for His disciples to preach to Israel, and not the other nations, which are all bundled together in one group called Gentiles. Matthew 10:5-7 says:

> "These twelve Jesus sent forth, and commanded them, saying, Go not into the way of the Gentiles, and into any city of the Samaritans enter ye not: But go rather to the lost sheep of the house of Israel. And as ye go, preach, saying, The kingdom of heaven is at hand."

Sadly, Israel rejected their Messiah, their antidote. Their literal words were, "Away with him, away with him, crucify him...We have no king but Caesar."[288] The once "kingdom of priests" rejected their King. John 1:11 reads, "He came unto his own, and his own received him not." Consequently, God gave Israel what they wanted—unbelief. Due to their disobedience, most Israelis were blinded to Jesus as Messiah. God then chose to temporarily put spiritual blindness upon backslidden Israel so He might save the Gentiles, giving them an opportunity for eternal salvation.

It's imperative to realize the Gentiles are not Israel, as some churches believe. Israel is forever her own independent nation before God and man due to the Abrahamic and Mosaic Covenants.

Numerous Scriptures clearly state Israel is spiritually blind. Jesus and Paul leave no confusion about this. All four gospels—Matthew 13:14-15, Mark 4:11-12, Luke 8:10, John 12:40—record Jesus quoting Isaiah 6:9-10, as you've already read.

While in Rome witnessing about Christ to Jews, some rejected Paul's teachings, causing him to quote Isaiah 6:9-10 in Acts 28:25-28:

> "And when they agreed not among themselves, they departed, after that Paul had spoken one word, Well spake the Holy Ghost by Esaias the prophet unto our fathers, Saying, Go unto this people, and say, Hearing ye shall hear, and shall not understand; and seeing ye shall see, and not perceive: For the heart of this people is waxed gross, and their ears are dull of hearing, and

*their eyes have they closed; lest they should see with their eyes,
and hear with their ears, and understand with their heart,
and should be converted, and I should heal them. Be it known
therefore unto you, that the salvation of God is sent unto the
Gentiles, and that they will hear it."*

The apostle Paul wrote four Scriptures in Romans 11:7-10, 25
explaining Israel's blindness. Paul says an elected, *"remnant"* group of
Israel received Christ and *"the rest were blinded"* to fulfill Isaiah 29:10 and
Psalm 69:22-23. The epigraph, Romans 11:25, denotes God's purpose in
blinding Israel—so He could save the Gentiles.

But the reason Israel was blinded was because they *"stumbled at the
stumblingstone"*—meaning they failed to believe in Christ. When Israel
rejected faith in Christ, God blinded them. Romans 9:31-33 declares
this truth:

*"But Israel, which followed after the law of righteousness, hath
not attained to the law of righteousness. Wherefore? Because
they sought it not by faith, but as it were by the works of the
law. For they stumbled at that stumblingstone; As it is written,
Behold, I lay in Sion a stumblingstone and rock of offence: and
whosoever believeth on him shall not be ashamed."*

It's apparent in Romans 11 that Israel's blindness is going to be taken
away in the future and she'll be *"graffed"*[289] back into God's blessings.
Romans 11:27 teaches the merciful God is going to remember His covenant and take away Israel's sins. But many remaining questions need
answered regarding the current 2,000 year period of blindness.

THE CONFUSION ABOUT ISRAEL'S BLINDNESS

The confusion surrounding Israel's blindness centers on whether or not
spiritually blinded Jews can be saved while awaiting a Messiah as they
currently reject Jesus Christ, the true Messiah. This question covers
the salvation of all blinded Jews who've lived for the past 2,000 years,

289   Romans 11:24

including those alive when Jesus walked the earth. Is it possible blinded Jews from Jesus' day can be saved? Can blinded Jews living now be saved?

The revelation of the mystery of Israel's blindness is that the covenant-keeping God still saves blinded Jews who faithfully follow Old Testament commands, promising them white robes of eternal life.

BIBLICAL EVIDENCE FOR THE REVELATION ABOUT ISRAEL'S BLINDNESS

Six Biblical evidences solidify the fact even blinded Jews can be saved: Jesus' prayer for forgiveness, Paul's Romans 11 teaching, foreshadowing in the life of Joseph, the Fifth Seal, God's righteous judgment based upon knowledge, and God's unconditional covenant with Israel through Abraham.

JESUS' PRAYER FOR FORGIVENESS

While hanging on His cross, Jesus Christ uttered forgiveness rather than condemnation in Luke 23:34: *"Then said Jesus, Father, forgive them; for they know not what they do. And they parted his raiment, and cast lots."* This is amazing grace! Although His own people, according to the flesh, called for His blood, He breathed mercy instead of judgment. Blinded Jews from Jesus' day could be saved.

Jesus' words reveal why some blind Jews from His time period could still be saved: they didn't know what they were doing. The principle is that spiritually blind Jews cannot fully understand the consequences of rejecting Christ. Just as a natural blind man innocently trips unawares over an object in his path, so some of the blinded Jews unintentionally stumbled over Jesus' life, actions, and words.

No doubt, some in the crowd calling for Jesus' crucifixion knew what they were doing, like Judas Iscariot knew he was selling out Messiah, a holy man. Psalm 69:20-28 says this group will have their names removed from the Book of Life, as will Judas.

But some in the multitude ignorantly got caught up in the moment and joined the mob unintentionally. For this group, Jesus prayed for mercy. Jesus wouldn't pray for their forgiveness in vain. Truly, Jesus knew God heard His every prayer![290] God definitely heard Jesus' prayer and will pardon the blinded Jews who didn't know what they were doing when they turned their backs on their own Savior. God's forgiveness is so great He pardons Jesus' own disciples who deserted Him in His greatest hour of trial, the crucifixion, except John, who was present at the cross.[291]

PAUL'S ROMANS 11 TEACHING

Paul's teaching in Romans 11 provides four foundational truths regarding Israel's blindness:

- The blinded Israelis are not forsaken for all time (verses 1 and 11)
- God is saving Gentiles while Israel is blinded (verses 11 and 15)
- Spiritual blindness is temporary—not permanent (verses 23 and 26)
- Spiritual blindness only set in on part of Israel—not the believing remnant (verse 25)

Only part of Israel was blinded to Christ's identity as Messiah. Paul calls the part that believes in Jesus as Christ the *"remnant"* in Romans 11:5: *"Even so then at this present time also there is a remnant according to the election of grace."* The apostle uses himself as an example of a Jew who believes in Christ in verse 1, calling himself *"an Israelite, of the seed of Abraham, of the tribe of Benjamin."* A small remnant of Jews in Paul's day believed in Christ as Messiah, and it's still possible for a Jewish remnant to "see" or believe in Christ today.

290   John 11:42
291   John 19:26

Despite the majority of Israelis being blinded, God has not completely forsaken Israel for all time. Twice Paul says "*God forbid*" that He would cast away His people and that they would stumble and fall completely away from God's grace. Paul says the Jews are provoked to jealousy[292] as they see the Gentiles receiving God's salvation that was first sent to them.

Israel experiences temporary spiritual blindness. Romans 11:23 says Israel will eventually overcome unbelief in Christ and "*shall be graffed in: for God is able to graff them in again.*" Observe Paul never condemns blinded Israel. Like a broken off branch, blinded Israel is detached from the God-tree, meaning they cannot possess God's eternal life, the baptism of the Holy Spirit, while living on earth (See Chapter 6). After the last Gentiles are saved, Israel's spiritual blindness will end and "*all Israel shall be saved,*"[293] which Revelation 7:4 tells us is 144,000 Jews.

Based upon Romans 11:11 and 15, God is focusing on saving, or "*reconciling*" the Gentiles while the majority of Israel is blinded. Shortly before His crucifixion in Luke 21:24, Jesus foretold God's desire to save Gentiles: "*And they shall fall by the edge of the sword, and shall be led away captive into all nations: and Jerusalem shall be trodden down of the Gentiles, until the times of the Gentiles be fulfilled.*" God is graciously giving the Gentiles an opportunity to be saved after Israel had nearly 1,500 years with salvation through Moses' law. Only God knows how much time the Gentiles have left to be saved. Foolish men constantly guess and miss the date of Jesus' return to earth. But once the last day is fulfilled, Jesus is returning to catch away His Gentile wife and then restore blindness-free salvation back to Israel.

FORESHADOWING IN THE LIFE OF JOSEPH

The life of Joseph, son of Jacob, foreshadows the life of Jesus Christ and shows how the blinded Jews can be saved at the White Throne Judgment despite rejecting Christ during their lifetimes. Joseph's life before slavery types Jesus' first coming to earth.

292   Romans 11:11
293   Romans 11:25-26

Jacob especially loved his son Joseph, as the heavenly Father loved Christ. Gifted in spiritual things, Joseph shared prophetic dreams with his brothers, who despised them. Christ's spiritual gifts of preaching and prophesying to Israel caused them to despise His words. Jacob sent Joseph to check on his brethren but they sold him to Egypt. God sent Christ to Israel but they sold him out to Rome. While in Egypt, they imprisoned Joseph on a false accusation. Rome arrested Jesus on a false accusation. While in prison, Joseph ministered to two prisoners. One lived, and one died. While on the cross, Jesus hung between two prisoners. One received a promise of eternal life in paradise, and the other lost. Joseph was resurrected out of prison and set as second in command to Pharaoh. Jesus was resurrected out of the tomb and ascended to the right hand of the majesty on high. While second in command, Joseph married an Egyptian, or Gentile wife. Jesus now offers salvation to the Gentiles, and the saved make up his spiritual wife, the New Testament church. During the famine, Joseph's brothers went to Egypt to get food but were blinded to their brother's identity, yet he's merciful to them. This example demonstrates that Jesus will be merciful to His blinded brethren, Israel. Joseph eventually revealed himself to his brothers and explained God allowed them to sell him into slavery in order to save lives during the famine. In type, Jesus's crucifixion saved all people—Gentiles and Jews—during the spiritual famine of the Seven Church Ages (See Chapter 7). As Joseph established his brothers in Goshen, Jesus will reveal Himself to the Jews during the Tribulation period and reestablish them in their promised land, Jerusalem.

The White Throne Judgment of "*all nations*" in Matthew 25:31-46 shows how Christ mercifully grants eternal life to surprised doers of good works who were seemingly blinded to His identity during their lives. Surely this group includes the nation of Israel, as all nations are gathered there. The "*blessed*" group of the saved were unaware of Christ's presence living inside His followers, the "*brethren*". In other words, they were blinded to Christ's body, His church, His bride. But Christians, like Paul, are not blinded to other Christians. Philippians 4:3 says that Paul knew Clement and a group of Christian women were saved and their *"names are in the book of life."* According to Jesus, this saved group in Matthew 25 helped Him by helping His followers. They gave food, drink, shelter, and clothing to Christians. They made sick visits and prison visits to Christians. They were blind to the fact they were actually helping Jesus. But Jesus, like Joseph, was not blinded to their identities and remembered their good works to His church, and so obtained mercy. Jesus' gracious judgment reminds you of Peter's words in Acts 10:34-35, how God accepts all persons, from all nations, who fear Him and work righteousness.

THE FIFTH SEAL, THE HEAVENLY ALTAR OF INCENSE, AND LOCATIONS AFTER DEATH

The Fifth Seal in Revelation 6:9-11 is irrefutable evidence that God saves blinded Jews, for the souls under the altar can be only Israelis. Four details prove this group is Israel.

First, they are martyrs *"slain for the word of God, and for the testimony which they held."* Notice, they are *not* slain for the testimony of Jesus. John, the author of Revelation, is described as having both the testimony of the Word of God and also of Jesus Christ in Revelation 1:2 and 9. John was a Christian and believed both the Word of God, Old Testament, and the testimony of Jesus Christ, the New Testament. But the Fifth Seal group faithfully believed the Word of God, or Old Testament, unto their deaths having no testimony of Jesus, showing they are Jews.

Second, they call for vengeance and judgment upon those who killed them. But Christians do not call for vengeance, as both Stephen (Acts 7:6) and Christ (Luke 23:34) pleaded for God's forgiveness upon their persecutors at their deaths.

Third, white robes were promised to them *after* their deaths. But Christians have white robes, representing eternal life, clothing their souls while they live on earth. Jesus says the Holy Ghost-filled Christian is *"endued,"*[294] or clothed with power upon receiving the Holy Spirit.

294   Luke 24:49

Paul tells believers, to *"Put ye on the Lord Jesus Christ"* in Romans 13:14. Christ offers a reminder of His imminent return in Revelation 16:15, telling saints to keep their garments: *"Behold, I come as a thief. Blessed is he that watcheth, and keepeth his garments, lest he walk naked, and they see his shame."* Note also how Jesus promises these Fifth Seal Israelis robes, just as Joseph gave his brethren new raiment in Genesis 45:22 after making himself known to them.

Fourth, Revelation 6:11 says there are more *"fellowservants,"* or *"brethren,"* of these Jews who must be martyred to fulfill a divine, appointed number. God alone knows this number because only He can calculate the punishment upon Israel for crucifying their own sinless, blameless Messiah. Matthew 27:25 says Israel called for Jesus' blood to be upon them and their children—and tragically it has been. More than 6 million Jews died in the Holocaust[295] and thousands, if not millions more have given their lives to fulfill this self-inflicted punishment. Yet, the merciful God of heaven will end this persecution at the conversion of the 144,000 Jews while granting eternal life to all Jewish martyrs who remain faithful to the Word of God.

Additionally, the Fifth Seal helps clarify the three different locations for souls after death: under the altar of incense, paradise, and prison. None need wonder where his soul will go upon death.

First, faithful, blinded Jews find shelter for their souls *"under the altar"* in heaven near the throne of Christ the Lord. What sweet confirmation for us to know how near Jewish martyrs are to Christ, the One who kept and fulfilled the Old Covenant, and that they can cry out loudly to Him and be heard!

Three Revelation Scriptures describe this golden altar of incense as having four horns while fiery incense is offered upon it with the prayers of the saints.[296] Recall Moses' earthly altar of incense was based upon this heavenly incense altar.[297] The altar of incense was the closest piece

---

295   "Introduction to the Holocaust." *United States Holocaust Memorial Museum*, https://encyclopedia.ushmm.org/content/en/article/introduction-to-the-holocaust

296   Revelation 8:3, 5, 9:13, 14:18

297   Exodus 25:40, 30:1

of furniture to the holiest of holies, yet it was separated by the veil. Likewise in heaven, the altar of incense is followed by a veil and a holiest of holies. Hebrews 6:19 reads, *"Which hope we have as an anchor of the soul, both sure and stedfast, and which entereth into that within the veil."* Saved, blinded Jews are close to Christ, but distance remains between them and the Lord.

Accompanying the altar of incense, there must be another heavenly altar where Jesus' blood lays as an atonement for sin. Two Revelation Scriptures show a portion of Jesus' blood is present in heaven. Revelation 5:6 pictures the heavenly Christ manifested as a slain Lamb and Revelation 19:13 says Jesus has a visible *"vesture dipped in blood"* when He returns on a white horse for the Battle of Armageddon. As Colossians 1:14 declares, we presently *"have redemption through his blood, even the forgiveness of sins."* Just as the earthly tabernacle of Moses required blood for atonement, so does the heavenly.

Paradise, a location even nearer to Christ's heavenly throne than the souls under the altar, is the second location souls go, but only born-again souls. Since the altar of incense is where Jews go—who were never born again by the baptism of the Holy Ghost—it must also be the location where Christians go who were never born again, for any believer not born again lacks a white garment. Jesus labels these Christians as foolish virgins in Matthew 25:1-13. The wise virgin Christians possessed the oil, representing the Holy Ghost baptism.

Paradise's location used to be *"in the heart of the earth,"* called *"Abraham's bosom"* by Jesus.[298] Luke 23:43 teaches Jesus took the repentant thief on the cross to *"paradise"* after their deaths on Good Friday. But upon Christ's resurrection, He led the previously-captive believers into His eternal captivity; and they resurrected in glorified bodies, appearing to many in Jerusalem. 40 days later, Jesus ascended to heaven with the resurrected saints, moving paradise close to His heavenly throne. In 2 Corinthians 12:1-4, Paul says he was caught up by vision to paradise, also known as the *"third heaven."* This is where Jesus lives with the heavenly

298   Matthew 12:40, Luke 16:22

host and believers. The first heaven must be the atmosphere around the earth, and outer space (all the remainder of our universe) is the second heaven.

Prison, also called "hell" in Luke 16:23, is located in the heart of the earth and is the third location. Only disobedient, unbelieving souls go there upon death. Jesus' story of the rich man and beggar Lazarus in Luke 16:19-31 vividly describes this prison of torment in which constant flames discomfort the unjust. In 1 Peter 3:18-20, Peter teaches Jesus preached to the disobedient souls in prison when He descended to hell following His crucifixion. Observe the loving, kind Jesus rebuking and preaching to the eternal lost souls in prison. These souls have no more chance to be saved and yet Jesus preaches to them, no doubt chiding them for rejecting Noah and all the other prophets Jesus sent to warn them of judgment for their unrepentant hearts. All disobedient souls in prison remain there until the White Throne Judgment when Jesus will command hell to deliver all these prisoners to their heavenly court trials to receive punishment "*according to their works.*"[299]

The Bible describes the conditions immediately after a person dies, or gives up the ghost. First, angels will usher the human spirit to either the third heaven (for the believer) or to hell's prison (for the unbeliever). Luke 16:22-23 say the righteous beggar, Lazarus, was "*carried by the angels into Abraham's bosom: the rich man also died, and was buried; And in hell he lift up his eyes, being in torments, and seeth Abraham afar off, and Lazarus in his bosom.*" Since Abraham's bosom, or paradise, moved its location to the third heaven, believers now ascend to heaven rather than descending to the heart of the earth. Faithful Jews and foolish virgin Christians go under the altar of incense while Holy Ghost-filled Christians go very near Jesus' throne in paradise.

A second condition is the human spirit retains its character, memories, convictions, and feelings—whether good or bad. In the Fifth Seal, faithful Jews cry out for vengeance. Death never took away their desire to be avenged. Death doesn't change a person's character, either. In Luke

299   Revelation 20:13

16, Jesus says the rich man in hell retained his unreasonable conviction that his brothers would repent and be saved if they saw miracles. But Abraham corrected him, saying his brothers would not believe a miracle if they would not hearken to Moses' law.[300] Witnessing a miracle doesn't save a person's soul. Faith and repentance lead to salvation.

Third, Holy Ghost-filled believers receive a new *"celestial,"*[301] or heavenly body, also called a theophany, after death. Paul in 2 Corinthians 5:1-8 says our celestial bodies await us and are *"eternal in the heavens."* A perfect, sinless theophany body awaits every Holy Ghost filled-Christian. Paul says, *"We groan, earnestly desiring to be clothed upon with our house which is from heaven."* Christians long to live in an eternally pure and holy body. The apostle likens this eternal body as clothing. Without the baptism of the Holy Ghost, a soul is naked before God, void of God's own life. 2 Corinthians 5:3 states, *"If so be that being clothed we shall not be found naked."* The saved under the altar of God—faithful Jews and Christians who were not born again—will be void of a celestial body but will be given it later at the White Throne Judgment.

Fourth, Holy Ghost-filled believers are present with the Lord after leaving their mortal bodies. Paul writes, *"We are confident, I say, and willing rather to be absent from the body, and to be present with the Lord."*[302] It is uncertain how much or how often you will see Jesus, as He is constantly making intercession for saints behind the veil.[303] But we will be present with him nonetheless according to Paul. Obviously, time moves differently in the heavenly dimensions, as God created time and works sovereignly within it, not being bound by it.

Fifth, you'll reunite with saved family members and recognize other believers you've never met before. Concerning family reunions, after the death of the newborn child produced through David and Bathsheba's adulterous act, David said, *"I shall go to him, but he shall not return to me."*[304] This is a great consolation to any parent who has lost a child through

---

300   Luke 16:27-31
301   1 Corinthians 15:40
302   2 Corinthians 5:8
303   Hebrews 6:19, 7:25
304   2 Samuel 12:23

tragedies like diseases, accidents, miscarriages, and more. As a believer, you'll instantly recognize saints who lived before you. During the Mount Transfiguration vision in Matthew 17, Peter, James, and John recognized Moses and Elijah—men who lived 1,500 and 900 years beforehand, respectively. Matthew 27:53 says after Jesus' resurrection many of the Old Testament saints raised with Him and *"went into the holy city, and appeared unto many."* For certain, God's Spirit within you will cause you to know another believer who possesses the Holy Spirit.

Lastly, believers will bask in and join in the angels' unceasing worship in glory. Revelation 4:8 says the four beasts *"rest not day and night, saying, Holy, holy, holy, Lord God Almighty, which was, and is, and is to come."* Christ is the focus and recipient of this devoted worship. He alone is worthy to receive all praise. Loud voices exclaim, *"Worthy is the Lamb that was slain to receive power, and riches, and wisdom, and strength, and honour, and glory, and blessing."*[305] In stark contrast, unbelievers and even a group of fallen angels suffer torment by flames in the darkness of hell awaiting judgment.[306]

GOD'S RIGHTEOUS JUDGMENT BASED UPON INHERENT KNOWLEDGE

Building upon the Fifth Seal, God's righteous judgment based upon each person's inherent knowledge supports the truth that blinded Jews can be given eternal life.

The Fifth Seal tells us blinded Jews are saved because God helped them have an overcoming testimony. Revelation 12:11 reiterates this, saying, *"They overcame him by the blood of the Lamb, and by the word of their testimony."* It's true all are saved by grace through faith,[307] but God honors a person's choice, for He cannot force anyone to accept grace and faith. Each person's free moral agency either accepts or rejects faith. After accepting, a believer has a testimony, report, or witness in both heaven and earth. In the case of blinded Jews, they could only understand the Old Testament and

305   Revelation 5:12
306   Luke 16:24, 2 Peter 2:4, Jude 1:6
307   Habakkuk 2:4, Ephesians 2:8

God will judge them accordingly. If they accepted faith in God's covenant, like Noah, Abraham, Moses, and others, they will be saved.

Rotating to a broader perspective, all humanity will be judged by what they knew about God and how they reacted to it. Men can also be judged by what they didn't know if they failed to seek God for it. Scripture calls this sin neglect, as both salvation and a person's individual gifts from God can be neglected.[308]

Christ's words in Matthew 25:20-21 and Luke 12:47-48 declare a person is rewarded or judged based upon their actions in response to their knowledge of God's will. Jesus said the following to the servant who doubled his five talents: *"Well done, thou good and faithful servant: thou hast been faithful over a few things, I will make thee ruler over many things."* This good servant knew what Christ wanted done and did it well, so he was rewarded with responsibility for many things.

Luke 12:47-48 say there are punishments for those who know God's will and refused to do it and those who *didn't* know God's will. It's easy to understand punishments for those who purposely refuse God's will. Jesus affirms this in Matthew 7:21 saying only those who do the will of God enter heaven.

Why would Christ punish someone who *didn't* know His will? The answer is the group had the opportunity but never asked God to know His progressive, or future will (See Chapter 11). They cared so little about spiritual things they never took time to pray and seek God. The reality is that all who want to know God on every continent, in every language, can know Him.[309] Every person has an awareness of God and a spiritual thirst for him. Christ promised all who asked would receive. Luke 11:10 reads, *"For every one that asketh receiveth; and he that seeketh findeth; and to him that knocketh it shall be opened."* It's Jesus' unfailing promise to reward everyone who seeks Him.

Romans 2:14-15 teaches a universal responsibility to God's law. Paul says God wrote His law upon every man's conscience. Therefore,

---

308   1 Timothy 4:14, Hebrews 2:3
309   2 Chronicles 16:9, Psalm 7:9, John 4:23, Acts 10:35, 17:27, Revelation 3:20

all men are *"without excuse"* on Judgment Day because of two things: God's inward law *"manifest in them"* and the witness of God's power in creation.[310] In each soul is the God-knowledge of good and evil. Each soul observes the undeniable power and beauty of God's creation and must choose whether to respond in love and appreciation or hatred and skepticism.

Blinded Jews from the days of Jesus' earthly ministry through today will be fairly judged by the law of Moses they heard—not Jesus' teaching if they were ignorant of it. Each person, being judged by their knowledge, will get a fair trial from the Righteous One.

GOD'S COVENANTS WITH ISRAEL THROUGH ABRAHAM

As seen in the Fifth Seal, God mercifully grants blinded Jews eternal life because of His covenants with Abraham and his offspring—Israel. Genesis 12:1-9 records God's unfailing promises to Abraham, his family's possession of Canaan's land, and the blessings for every nation. Abraham and his seed are God's chosen people perpetually, and through their family the entire world is blessed.

Undoubtedly, the amount of blessings within the covenant were based upon conditions, as Genesis 18:19 says Abraham's children *"after him"* must *"keep the way of the LORD...that the LORD may bring upon Abraham that which he hath spoken of him."* God foreknew the small remnant of Abraham's seed He could use to fulfill His promises.

Deuteronomy 11:26-28 records God's conditional promises—spoken with *"if"*—as Moses ministers to Abraham's seed:

> *"Behold, I set before you this day a blessing and a curse; A blessing, if ye obey the commandments of the LORD your God, which I command you this day: And a curse, if ye will not obey the commandments of the LORD your God, but turn aside out of the way which I command you this day, to go after other gods, which ye have not known."*

310   Romans 1:19-21

A thousand years after Abraham, his seed, Israel, possessed the promised land, yet they corrupted themselves through idolatry. Abraham's seed erroneously said God had forsaken them and forgotten about them. But the Israeli prophet Isaiah recorded Jehovah's comforting words for the rebellious people in Isaiah 49:13-16:

> *"Sing, O heavens; and be joyful, O earth; and break forth into singing, O mountains: for the LORD hath comforted his people, and will have mercy upon his afflicted. But Zion said, The LORD hath forsaken me, and my Lord hath forgotten me. Can a woman forget her sucking child, that she should not have compassion on the son of her womb? yea, they may forget, yet will I not forget thee. Behold, I have graven thee upon the palms of my hands; thy walls are continually before me."*

God promises Israel He can never forsake nor forget them by saying they are engraved upon His hands. Jesus' nail prints—which Thomas needed to see to believe in His resurrection[311]—would be God's proof of His unfailing covenant with Israel. The cross proves that His faithfulness and compassion is strong like a nursing mother's love for her baby, even in the midst of Israel's rebellion. A mother's love is deep, but there could be no deeper, devoted love than Jesus dying in our place.

Two hundred years after Isaiah, the prophet Jeremiah reiterated God's faithful love for Israel in beautiful terms. Jeremiah 31:31-34 records God's promise to give Israel a new covenant, which was preached by Jesus and His disciples. Afterwards, Jeremiah declared Israel would never cease from being God's nation and He'd never cast them off:

> *"Thus saith the LORD, which giveth the sun for a light by day, and the ordinances of the moon and of the stars for a light by night, which divideth the sea when the waves thereof roar; The LORD of hosts is his name: If those ordinances depart from before me, saith the LORD, then the seed of Israel also shall cease from being a nation before me for ever. Thus saith the*

---

311   John 20:25-27

LORD; If heaven above can be measured, and the foundations of the earth searched out beneath, I will also cast off all the seed of Israel for all that they have done, saith the LORD."

God attempts to convince backslidden Israel of His love by referencing the steadfastness of the sunlight, moon, stars, and oceans. Since these ordinances never cease, God's love for Israel will never cease. If anyone is able to measure the heavens, God will cast off Israel. But as the heavens are immeasurable, so is God's love for Abraham's seed, Israel. Indeed, God's unconditional love for Israel will be strong enough to grant salvation even to blinded Jews.

COVENANTS, TESTAMENTS, AND THE GENTILE TIME PERIOD

Examining God's covenants, testaments, and the Times of the Gentiles will help you understand His dealings with all mankind, in particularly the nation of Israel. It is the immutable power of God's covenants that allows even blinded Israelis to be saved.

Beginning with covenants and testaments, these two words are synonymous, meaning a compact or league. The Old Testament uses only "covenant" (never uses "testament") in the King James a total of 256 times. The New Testament uses both "covenant" and "testament" 24 and 13 times, respectively. The same Greek word, "diatheke," meaning "arrangement, a compact, a covenant, a testament," is interpreted as both "covenant" and "testament" repeatedly in the New Testament.

Christians sometimes use "dispensation" and "covenant" interchangeably, but their meanings are different. Dispensation's modern definition is a system of government at a particular time, but in the Greek Lexicon, a dispensation is a stewardship, or an overseeing job. The same Greek word for "dispensation" is also used for "stewardship" in Jesus' parable of The Unjust Steward in Luke 16:1-13. On the other hand, a covenant is a compact, or agreement.

Some say there are multiple dispensations throughout human history, and that is true if one is using the modern definition of dispensation, but not true if using the Scriptural one. The King James mentions the word "dispensation" four times, and Paul is the only Bible writer who uses it.[312] Three of these verses point to one dispensation that belonged to Paul—the Gentile dispensation of the gospel of Jesus Christ. The subject of Paul's dispensation is covered in Chapter 3. Since the Bible definition of dispensation is different than the modern one, I will not use "dispensation" to describe the 2,000 year period God is dealing with the Gentiles, which Jesus calls the Times of the Gentiles.

The fourth mention of "dispensation" in Ephesians 1:10 speaks of God gathering everything in Christ in the *"dispensation of the fulness of times."* Paul says God has one dispensation, or oversight, of all time periods and He'll gather everything together in Christ in the New Jerusalem, when all heaven and earth are subject to Him.

Returning to covenants, Paul points out God has given multiple covenants—not just one. Romans 9:4 says, *"Who are Israelites; to whom pertaineth the adoption, and the glory, and the covenants, and the giving of the law, and the service of God, and the promises."* Again in Ephesians 2:12 he writes, *"That at that time ye were without Christ, being aliens from the commonwealth of Israel, and strangers from the covenants of promise, having no hope, and without God in the world."* How many covenants has God made with man?

Scripture names eight covenants initiated by God and granted to man. Each covenant or compact established a new beginning for a group of people and is a further expression of God's love, grace, and faithfulness. In Biblical numerology, the number eight represents new creation or new beginning as seen in the following examples:

- God saved eight souls by water during the flood and gave humanity a new beginning (Genesis 8:18, 1 Peter 3:20).
- Every male Hebrew was circumcised on the eighth day representing their new beginning as part of Abraham's covenant (Genesis 17:12).
- God forgave Israel through sacrificial atonement, giving

312   1 Corinthians 9:17, Ephesians 1:10, 3:2, Colossians 1:25

them a new beginning, as the glory of God fell on the eighth day of sacrificing (Leviticus 9:1-24).

- A leper was declared clean at the door of the congregation on the eighth day of his or her recovery, a new beginning of cleanliness (Leviticus 14:10-11).
- Israel held a holy convocation, or sacred assembly, as an extra sabbath day on the eighth day of the Feast of Tabernacles to mark the beginning of the civil year (Leviticus 23:33-44).
- David, the youngest and eighth son, was chosen by God as a man after God's heart to give Israel a new beginning after King Saul's failure (1 Samuel 13:14, 16:10-11).
- Paralyzed Aeneas was healed by Peter in the eighth year of his infirmity as a new beginning of sound health (Acts 9:33).
- Paul lists eight things to meditate upon in order to renew your mind (Philippians 4:8).
- Charity is the eighth and final attribute in the Stature of a Perfect Man that makes you a new creation in Christ Jesus (2 Corinthians 5:17, 2 Peter 1:5-7).

The late Baptist minister Clarence Larkin (1850-1924) contributed much to the church's understanding of the eight covenants in his book, *Dispensational Truths*.[313] Some, but not all, of the following covenant details are referenced from Larkin's great work. For all eight covenants, you discover when they were initiated, their commands and conditions, and unique signs.

The Edenic Covenant is the first covenant found in Genesis 1:26-30 and 2:15-25. God initiated this covenant with Adam and Eve before sin entered humanity. The first two unclothed humans lived in complete innocence and obedience as God graciously commanded

---

313   "Clarence Larkin: Chapter 26 - The Covenants." *Blue Letter Bible*, https://www. blueletterbible.org/study/larkin/dt/26.cfm

them to reproduce and fill the earth with people, subdue the earth and keep the garden, and have dominion over the fish, birds, and all other living creatures. Man and animal were both limited to a vegetable diet.

The only condition for this holy covenant was Adam and Eve's abstinence from eating from the Tree of Knowledge of Good and Evil. Chapter 9 reveals the true identity of the forbidden fruit (it was not a physical fruit) and God's secret behind the real identity of the two trees: Tree of Life and Tree of Knowledge of Good and Evil. As long as the couple kept this condition, eternal life and peace was theirs, within their bodies.

After Eve was beguiled or deceived by the serpent into eating the forbidden fruit, Adam willingly sinned by partaking of the forbidden fruit,[314] plunging humanity into sin-slavery to the devil. 2 Peter 2:19 says, *"For of whom a man is overcome, of the same is he brought in bondage."* Paul calls Satan *"the god of this world"* in 2 Corinthians 4:4, and this was the moment he took that title.

After Adam broke God's covenant, the blessing of eternal life inside their bodies ended and death set in. God drove Adam and Eve out of the garden and set cherubims with flaming swords to keep mankind from accessing the Tree of Life. Still, the covenant's commands remained to reproduce, subdue the earth, and have dominion over all living things. These covenant-commands continue unending throughout all covenants, including the Eternal Covenant because the eighth mirrors the sinless condition of the first. The only difference is the Eternal has no conditions since Satan and sin are annihilated.

The Adamic Covenant is the second covenant found in Genesis 3:14-24. It was initiated by God's own animal sacrifice to make atonement for Adam and Eve's sin before sending them out of the garden. God made coats of skins to cover Adam and Eve's newly discovered nakedness. Here Adam and his offspring learned without shedding of blood there is no remission of sin.[315] *"By faith"* Adam, Abel, and their godly offspring understood how to offer offerings and gifts to God.[316]

---

314   Genesis 3:13, 2 Corinthians 11:3, 1 Timothy 2:13-14
315   Hebrews 9:22
316   Hebrews 11:4

In this covenant, God commanded curses and consequences for the serpent's beguiling and Adam and Eve's disobedience. The serpent is cursed above all cattle and beasts, forced to go upon his belly and eat dust. Note the serpent was an upright, standing creature before this curse.

While speaking to the serpent in Genesis 3:15, God places enmity or hatred between he and the woman and their separate offsprings. Most importantly, God declares the first prophecy of the cross of Jesus Christ 4,000 years in advance, promising a member of Eve's seed would bruise the serpent's head while the serpent would bruise his heel. Jesus indeed began to destroy the works of the devil, and His resurrection was a public triumph over every demon foe.[317] The Genesis 3:15 foretelling is expounded upon and fulfilled through four future covenants: Abrahamic, Mosaic, Davidic, and the New Covenant.

Eve's not cursed, but her consequences are multiplied sorrow in conception and bringing forth children. Additionally, her desire or longing is to be to her husband, which means her desire was previously for someone other than her husband—the serpent. Her last consequence is her husband will rule over her, meaning Adam is the leader in their marriage, and she is under submission to him, as taught in the New Testament as well.[318]

Like Eve, Adam's not cursed, but the ground is cursed for his sake. Adam would bring forth food through sorrowful, sweaty, hard work battling thorns and thistles.

All conditions and commands from this covenant remain to this day. God's promise to send Christ to bruise the serpent's head is His ultimate expression of love to us: *"But God commendeth his love toward us, in that, while we were yet sinners, Christ died for us."*[319]

The Adamic Covenant is fulfilled and ends when the Eternal Covenant begins because it seems the inhabitants of the earth during the Millennium will still be farming and working the land.[320] It also seems deaths still occur.[321]

---

317   Colossians 2:15, 1 John 3:8
318   1 Corinthians 11:3, Ephesians 5:22-24
319   Romans 5:8
320   Isaiah 65:21, Micah 4:3-4
321   Isaiah 65:20, Revelation 20:7-9

The Noahic Covenant is the third covenant found in Genesis 8:20-9:17. Nearly 1,700 years after the Adamic Covenant, the LORD initiated this covenant immediately following Noah's sweet smelling burnt offerings when he left the ark. The LORD's covenant is between Him and all living things—man and animals. He promises never to curse the ground again nor smite every living thing through a flood. But God will smite again all living things with fire in preparation for the eighth covenant according to 2 Peter 3:10: *"But the day of the Lord will come as a thief in the night; in the which the heavens shall pass away with a great noise, and the elements shall melt with fervent heat, the earth also and the works that are therein shall be burned up."*

God blesses Noah and his sons by reaffirming the *"be fruitful, and multiply, and replenish the earth"* command He previously gave in the Edenic Covenant. Animals will continue to fear and dread mankind, as man's dominion over all living things continues.

A new diet is allowed by God. Previously, mankind were vegetarians. Man can now eat the flesh of animals but must abstain from eating their blood.

God also commands capital punishment to be established in human government in Genesis 9:6, saying, *"Whoso sheddeth man's blood, by man shall his blood he shed: for in the image of God made he man."* This law is carried out using much discretion in the fear of the LORD, as both Moses and David killed men (David indirectly killed Uriah) and yet God let them live. Romans 13:4 shows capital punishment remaining in the New Testament.

To conclude this covenant, God provides the first token, or sign, for a covenant—the rainbow. The bow will be in the clouds and God will remember His covenant with man and all living things to never destroy the earth again through a flood. All commands and conditions of the Noahic Covenant remain to this day but it ends when the Eternal Covenant begins, for there is no more death.

The Abrahamic Covenant is the fourth covenant found in Genesis 12:1-3 and 17:9-14. About 400 years after Noah's covenant,

God initiated this covenant with Abraham and his offspring only. Previous covenants were promises to all mankind, but here God focused on one family. God confirmed His covenant with Abraham through a blood sacrifice in Genesis 15.

Even after Abraham's death, He visited Abraham's son, Isaac, and grandson, Jacob, in order to confirm this covenant with their family.[322] The LORD then focused in on one group of people to make a great nation through His holiness shortly after mankind's complete defiance at the Tower of Babel.

Through the Abrahamic Covenant, God created two groups of people—Jews and Gentiles. Jews are descendants of Abraham as the word "Jew" is short for Judah, the tribe named after the great grandson of Abraham. Gentiles encompass all other nations, peoples, and tongues.

The Lord promised Abraham to make a great nation of his seed, make his name great, bless him and all that bless him, curse those who curse him, and make him a blessing to all families on the earth. Like the Noahic Covenant, the Lord assigns a token for Abraham's covenant, but it is not in nature, like the rainbow. His everlasting token is in their flesh: male circumcision.

Abraham's Covenant has supernaturally shaped and transformed human history. During the seven years of famine in Genesis 41, Egypt was blessed and spared from destitution because they blessed Joseph, Abraham's great-great grandson. Under the faithful leadership of Moses, Joshua, David, and Solomon, many of Israel's enemies were cursed and defeated, helping to make the nation independent and powerful.

In modern history, the United States has become the world's super power because of its Judeo-Christian foundation and initial adherence to God's laws. The Constitution and Bill of Rights are heavily influenced by the Torah and Pauline epistles. America's prosperity has overflowed into nearly every other nation in part because of her continued support for Israel. Although other nations have their needs met, few experience the vast levels of freedom and prosperity as Americans.

322   Genesis 26:1-5, 28:10-25

The nation of Israel continues to experience prosperity and innovation because of God's faithfulness to Abraham's Covenant. Since becoming reestablished as a sovereign state in 1948, Israel has grown into a world leader in patents, research, entrepreneurship, and innovation. In recent years, all men witness "Israel's innovation story is extraordinary."[323]

Chapter 3 expounds on God mysteriously and graciously opening up this covenant to the Gentiles, as faith in Christ makes a believer Abraham's *spiritual* seed. Israel is Abraham's natural seed, or offspring. Faith in Jesus Christ makes a believing Jew or Gentile a member of Abraham's spiritual seed. Galatians 3:7 proclaims, *"Know ye therefore that they which are of faith, the same are the children of Abraham."* Since Abraham's true seed is spiritual, the circumcision token is now spiritual. Paul calls it the inward *"circumcision...of the heart"* in Romans 2:29.

All conditions and commands from this covenant remain to this day. However, as great as the Abrahamic Covenant was and is, it lacks a solution to man's sin problem. The answer is total forgiveness through Jesus' blood, the greatest of all blessings. Two covenants, though, preceded the New with important purposes.

The Abrahamic Covenant began some 1,900 years before Christ and ends when the Eternal Covenant begins because its purpose will be fulfilled. All alive then will already be eternally blessed with eternal life.

The Mosaic Covenant is the fifth covenant found in Exodus chapters 20-40 and Deuteronomy 30:1-10. About 400 years after Abraham, God initiated this covenant with Israel, generally referred to as the Law, through Moses on Mount Sinai. In Exodus 24, Moses sprinkles the people with blood enjoining[324] them to God's covenant.

Moses' Law can be divided into three groups: moral (Ten Commandments), civil (between Hebrews), and ceremonial (Levitical priesthood). The ceremonial law includes the creation of a priesthood

---

323 "Israel's Innovation Story is Extraordinary." *I Am Media*, https://www.iam-media.com/law-policy/israels-innovation-story-extraordinary-just-assuming-it-will-continue-would-be-big
324 Hebrews 9:19-20

to order worship in the Tabernacle. God called Israel to be a *"kingdom of priests."*[325]

The ark of the covenant symbolizes this covenant, representing the presence of God. Aaron's rod that budded, a pot of manna, and Moses' two tables of commandments were placed inside the ark. These three articles foretold the New Testament blessings of resurrection, believing the original truth, and the Holy Ghost seal, respectively.

Like the two previous covenants, this oath has a sign—Sabbath keeping.[326] Israelis worked for six days of the week but were forbidden to work on the seventh because the LORD made the earth in six days and rested on the seventh.

The entire chapter of Deuteronomy 30 expresses God's unfailing commitment to Israel despite His foreknowledge of her idolatry (causing her to be scattered all over the world) and rejecting the forthcoming Messiah. God promises to gather Israel from all nations, giving her a heart that completely loves Him, and causing her to forever posses the land of Israel.

This covenant's purpose is described by Paul in Galatians 3:24 as *"our schoolmaster to bring us to Christ."* The Law teaches how inherently evil we are to a holy God. Our sins demand a just penalty—death. Truly, the Law *"was added because of transgressions."*[327] The Law was *"holy, and just, and good"*[328] but also carried an insurmountable curse—breaking one command imputed to you the same guilt as breaking all the commands. James 2:10 explains, *"For whosoever shall keep the whole law, and yet offend in one point, he is guilty of all."*

All five offerings—sin, peace, meal, trespass, and burnt—and the vast amount required of each, point us to a desperately needed, once-and-for-all[329] sacrifice to put away all sin. The Law would continue *"til the seed should come,"*[330] the promised seed of the woman (Genesis 3:15) in

325   Exodus 19:6
326   Exodus 31:16-17
327   Galatians 3:19
328   Romans 7:12
329   Hebrews 10:10
330   Galatians 3:19

the Adamic Covenant. Our need is fully satisfied in the New Covenant through the death and resurrection of Jesus Christ.

Leviticus 26:41-42 highlights the principle that God's former covenant-blessings remain true even in the current covenant. God told Israel through Moses that they would possess the promised land but then fall away from His commands, causing Him to scatter Israel among heathen nations. But He promised to restore them to living in Palestine when they confessed their sins in humility. Israel's genuine repentance will cause God to say, "*Then will I remember my covenant with Jacob, and also my covenant with Isaac, and also my covenant with Abraham will I remember; and I will remember the land.*" God forever remembers His promises. Even during the period of Moses' Covenant, God still remembers and keeps the Abrahamic Covenant to give Abraham's seed the land of Palestine based upon the condition of their humble obedience. Israel's humble confession of sin and subsequent possession of all of Palestine is yet in the future to be fulfilled by the 144,000 Spirit-filled Jews spoken of in Revelation 7:1-8.

This Mosaic Covenant is the current covenant blinded Israel is under at this moment because they rejected the New Covenant preached by Jesus, Peter, Paul, and other "*remnant*" Jews who accepted Christ. Despite casting away the New Covenant in the 1st Century, blinded Israel retains God's blessings from all previous covenants: Mosaic, Abrahamic, Noahic, Adamic, and Edenic. Any blinded Jew will receive God's covenant blessings if he sincerely loves God and obeys Him. God cannot cast away all Israel because He promised to bless and never forget faithful Jews, and He will keep His Word.

The Mosaic Covenant began around 1,500 years before Christ and ended at Jesus' resurrection for Jesus-followers. Romans 8:4 explains Christians observe and obey the "*righteousness of the law,*" or moral commandments of the Law, through the Holy Spirit's power in the New Covenant. The Mosaic Covenant still continues, though, for the faithful, blinded Jews.

The Davidic Covenant is the sixth covenant found in 2 Samuel 7:4-17 and Luke 1:30-33. About 500 years after Moses' covenant, God initiates this oath to David through the prophet Nathan. Just like the Abrahamic Covenant, God again chooses to deal with one man and his offspring rather than making a world-wide covenant. Both covenants of Abraham and David start with one man but extend to bless and impact the entire world.

In the Davidic Covenant, God builds upon the Mosaic Covenant, which established the Law and priesthood. Through David, God promises a kingship, which points to the True King, Jesus Christ, Who will someday *"rule all nations with a rod of iron"*[331] in the Millennium and New Jerusalem.

Nathan tells David God will establish the throne, house, and kingdom of his son, Solomon, forever.[332] God says the same in Psalm 89:3-4: *"I have made a covenant with my chosen, I have sworn unto David my servant, Thy seed will I establish for ever, and build up thy throne to all generations."*

Of course, these promises were conditional and based upon Solomon and his sons' obedience, as recorded in 2 Chronicles 7:18-22. Verses 19-20 read:

> *"But if ye turn away, and forsake my statutes and my commandments, which I have set before you, and shall go and serve other gods, and worship them; Then will I pluck them up by the roots out of my land which I have given them; and this house, which I have sanctified for my name, will I cast out of my sight, and will make it to be a proverb and a byword among all nations."*

Solomon's sins and the many sins of his royal offspring eventually turned Israel away, and God plucked up the nation and scattered her abroad. The last king of Israel of David's seed was Zedekiah who was expelled from his throne around 587 B.C. Since that moment, there has not been a "son of David" ruling in Israel. God has postponed His promises until Jesus' second coming. Ezekiel 21:26-27 records this, showing

331   Revelation 12:5
332   2 Samuel 7:4-17

how the crown would be removed out of Israel *"until he come whose right it is"*—until Jesus returns:

> *"Thus saith the Lord GOD; Remove the diadem, and take off the crown: this shall not be the same: exalt him that is low, and abase him that is high. I will overturn, overturn, overturn, it: and it shall be no more, until he come whose right it is; and I will give it him."*

God will never do away with David's house. The gracious LORD promised to preserve the house of David because of His covenant promise in 2 Chronicles 21:7: *"Howbeit the LORD would not destroy the house of David, because of the covenant that he had made with David, and as he promised to give a light to him and to his sons for ever."*

Jeremiah 33:17-26 further witnesses God's promises to David are steadfast. God challenges Jeremiah's hearers to try to break the covenant of day and night to see if He will break His covenant with David. Certainly, man cannot alter the repetition of day and night, and so God will never alter His promises to David. Nor can man number the stars, heavenly hosts, and sands of the seas, and thus man cannot count how greatly God will multiply the seed of David. A few chapters previous to this, God tells Jeremiah He will not cast away Israel because His faithfulness to them is like the continual ordinances of day and night, moon, stars, and ocean waves.[333]

The prophet Isaiah and angel Gabriel give us further details about the deeper meaning of God's forever-covenant with David. The Davidic Covenant can be fulfilled only through Jesus Christ, who came through *"the seed of David according to the flesh."*[334] Isaiah 9:6-7 says the Messiah will have an unending throne and kingdom: *"Of the increase of his government and peace there shall be no end, upon the throne of David, and upon his kingdom, to order it, and to establish it with judgment and with justice from henceforth even for ever."* The angel Gabriel affirms this, telling Mary

---

333   Jeremiah 31:35-37
334   Romans 1:3

that her Son, Jesus, would be given *"the throne of his father David"* to reign over the house of Jacob forever with an unending kingdom.[335] The everlasting throne speaks of Jesus ruling in the Eternal Covenant in the New Jerusalem. Thus, the Davidic Covenant will be renewed once Jesus begins reigning on the earth during the Millennium and will continue without end throughout eternity.

It is noteworthy that the unending throne and kingdom of Israel was first offered to Saul but his disobedience and rebellion caused God to choose David and his seed as the kingly family. 1 Samuel 13:13 reads, *"And Samuel said to Saul, Thou hast done foolishly: thou hast not kept the commandment of the LORD thy God, which he commanded thee: for now would the LORD have established thy kingdom upon Israel for ever."* Only God knows the great blessings and rewards men lose due to their selfish disobedience.

The New Covenant is the seventh covenant found in Jeremiah 31:31-34 and Luke 22:20. Nearly 1,000 years after the Davidic Covenant, God institutes this covenant through Jesus' shed blood, instantly making Moses' covenant a thing of the past. The name, *"new covenant,"* contrasts with the *"old"* covenant given to Moses. Hebrews 8:13 reads, *"In that he saith, A new covenant, he hath made the first old. Now that which decayeth and waxeth old is ready to vanish away."* The Law was the Old Covenant but grace is the New Covenant.

In Luke 22:20, Messiah says the cup of the Lord's Supper *"is the new testament in my blood, which is shed for you."* Christ's death, through His blood sacrifice, and His resurrection caused this testament to take effect according to Hebrews 9:15-17. Verses 16 and 17 say this testament went into effect after Jesus' death: *"For where a testament is, there must also of necessity be the death of the testator. For a testament is of force after men are dead: otherwise it is of no strength at all while the testator liveth."*

On Calvary, Jesus' skin was opened up so much that His bare bones were exposed. God's sacrifice had to be torn open to institute the New Covenant because previous covenants were confirmed with torn-apart

335   Luke 1:32-33

sacrifices. Noah and Moses offered sacrifices from torn beasts. All five of Abraham's sacrifices were torn part before God's Spirit passed between the pieces.[336]

The pardoning power of Jesus' holy, sinless blood cannot be overemphasized. While other covenants were confirmed with shed blood—the coats of skins for Adam and Eve, Noah's burnt offering after exiting the ark, Abraham's sacrifice of five divided animals, and Moses' sprinkling the people with blood—only the New Covenant completely abolishes sin and a sinner's guilty conscience.[337] The sin question—"Am I truly forgiven in God's sight?"—is settled once and for all through Jesus' all-sufficient sacrifice. For those who truly love Christ and confess their sins, God forgives all their sins and trespasses. Colossians 2:13 says He's *"forgiven you all trespasses."* Not some. All!

Jesus' blood is the perfect remedy for sin, making the New Covenant the final covenant that requires blood. The Eternal Covenant and Edenic Covenant are bloodless. Hebrews 13:20-21 says Jesus' blood is the *"blood of the everlasting covenant"* and makes believers *"perfect in every good work to do his will, working in you that which is wellpleasing in his sight."*

The benefit and blessing of Jesus' precious blood makes the New Covenant a *"better covenant...established upon better promises."*[338] Each covenant God establishes gets progressively greater; and concerning forgiveness of sins, the New Covenant is God's triumphant masterpiece.

Accompanying the better promises comes greater responsibility for men to receive this covenant. The consequence for turning down such powerful, sin-cleansing blood is sore punishment. Hebrews 10:29 says, *"Of how much sorer punishment, suppose ye, shall he be thought worthy, who hath trodden under foot the Son of God, and hath counted the blood of the covenant, wherewith he was sanctified, an unholy thing, and hath done despite unto the Spirit of grace?"* God's Spirit of grace will cause the New Covenant good news to be preached and offered to every nation before

---

336   Genesis 15:10
337   Hebrews 10:1-39
338   Hebrews 8:6

the end of time.[339] The LORD has appointed a Day of Judgment to bring closure to this covenant and His Son's righteous blood will be the standard for judgment. Acts 17:31 promises, *"Because he hath appointed a day, in the which he will judge the world in righteousness by that man whom he hath ordained; whereof he hath given assurance unto all men, in that he hath raised him from the dead."*

The baptism of the Holy Ghost is the sign of the New Covenant, also called a *"seal"*[340] or mark in the believer's soul. Just like the rainbow and circumcision were tokens of previous covenants, the Holy Ghost-seal is the New Testament token. Unlike the previous covenants, the life of the sacrifice, Jesus' Spirit, now comes upon the believer.

The New Covenant was first sent to Israel through Jesus' earthly ministry but most Israelis rejected Messiah, becoming spiritually blind. God foreknew Israel's failure, allowing Him to have mercy upon the Gentiles for a season, saving their souls through the New Covenant (See Chapter 3). But the LORD promised to return to blinded Israel and give her another chance to receive the New Covenant, shortly after the rapture of the Gentile church.

It is certain 144,000 redeemed, guileless Jews will stand with Jesus Christ on Mount Zion according to Revelation 14:1-5. This mountaintop experience is preceded by Jesus revealing His identity to Israel, causing them to mourn in anguish upon realizing they crucified their Messiah 2,000 years ago. Zechariah 12:10-13:1 says Jews will go from house to house mourning after realizing their ancestors pierced Jesus, but then Christ opens a fountain of grace and forgiveness for them. Then Romans 11:26-27 is fulfilled: *"And so all Israel shall be saved: as it is written, There shall come out of Sion the Deliverer, and shall turn away ungodliness from Jacob: For this is my covenant unto them, when I shall take away their sins."*

The New Covenant began at Jesus' resurrection and ends after the White Throne Judgment because blood for forgiveness is no longer

---

339   Matthew 24:14
340   2 Corinthians 1:22, Ephesians 1:13, 4:30

needed. Death, hell, and Satan have all been cast into the lake of fire. Sin is forever defeated.

The Eternal Covenant is the eighth covenant found in Isaiah 65:17 and Revelation 21:1-5. God promises this unending covenant as a return to the sinless conditions of the Edenic Covenant. God and man will again enjoy close fellowship, but now it will be impossible for it to end because all God's enemies are destroyed.

Isaiah 65:17 offers the first glimpse of this covenant, saying, *"For, behold, I create new heavens and a new earth: and the former shall not be remembered, nor come into mind."* New heavens and a new earth simply means renovation and restoration. It doesn't mean God is going to blow up this earth and make a new one. No, God is going to redeem this earth and the heavens by holy fire. 2 Peter 3:10 reads, *"But the day of the Lord will come as a thief in the night; in the which the heavens shall pass away with a great noise, and the elements shall melt with fervent heat, the earth also and the works that are therein shall be burned up."*

Revelation chapters 21 and 22 build upon Isaiah's inspired promises in breathtaking detail. Notably, Revelation 21:1-5 says:

> *"And I saw a new heaven and a new earth: for the first heaven and the first earth were passed away; and there was no more sea. And I John saw the holy city, new Jerusalem, coming down from God out of heaven, prepared as a bride adorned for her husband. And I heard a great voice out of heaven saying, Behold, the tabernacle of God is with men, and he will dwell with them, and they shall be his people, and God himself shall be with them, and be their God. And God shall wipe away all tears from their eyes; and there shall be no more death, neither sorrow, nor crying, neither shall there be any more pain: for the former things are passed away. And he that sat upon the throne said, Behold, I make all things new. And he said unto me, Write: for these words are true and faithful."*

Indeed, the New Jerusalem is a significantly better Eden. Compare the two for a moment. God's two children, Adam and Eve, shared a garden. Now God's innumerable children share a massive city. Eden had a deadly adversary but New Jerusalem has only peaceful allies. Satan entered and brought a curse in Eden but he'll never step foot in the New Jerusalem and there will be no curses there. Eden had nightfall but our future home has "*no night there.*"[341] The Lamb, our Day Star, is the light in that city. The Tree of Life was just one of many trees in Eden but here it is elevated above all trees to the pinnacle of the city and so large until it encompasses *both* sides of the "*pure river of water of life.*"

This city is divine and unique. God is in everything. In this city, God is all and in all. 1 Corinthians 15:28 says, "*And when all things shall be subdued unto him, then shall the Son also himself be subject unto him that put all things under him, that God may be all in all.*" The city's precious stones; great, high wall; 12 gates; 12 foundations; and streets of pure, transparent gold all tell God's matchless redemption story. There'll be no need for men to build a temple "*for the Lord God Almighty and the Lamb are the temple of it.*"[342]

Peter says the New Jerusalem is the home of holiness. He writes, "*Nevertheless we, according to his promise, look for new heavens and a new earth, wherein dwelleth righteousness.*"[343] Finally, a kingdom of kindness, a reign of righteousness! Since you're drawn to this kingdom, Peter asks you to be diligent now to live without sin in true holiness. 2 Peter 3:14 says, "*Wherefore, beloved, seeing that ye look for such things, be diligent that ye may be found of him in peace, without spot, and blameless.*"

DANIEL'S 70 WEEKS PROPHECY

Many struggle to both understand the meaning and placement of the Daniel's 70 Weeks Prophecy, yet it directly connects to Israel's current blindness to the gospel. Where does this prophecy fit in the timeline of God's covenants?

Due to Israel's disobedience in the Mosaic Covenant, God expelled His people from their land into heathen lands, such as Babylon and

341   Revelation 21:25, 22:5
342   Revelation 21:22
343   2 Peter 3:13

Assyria.[344] Judah's last king, Zedekiah, was finally expelled from Jerusalem in 587 B.C. during the Babylonian Exile.

As a young man, the prophet Daniel was one of the prisoners led away into captivity to Babylon. Despite experiencing constant communion with God through prayer and seeing His miraculous power in being delivered from a den of lions, Daniel aged into an old man and yearned for the time his people would return to their promised land.

In Daniel chapter 9, you find Daniel reading Jeremiah's writings (see Jeremiah 25:8-14) and the Holy Spirit gives him understanding that Israel's 70 year period of expulsion from their land is coming to an end. Verses 4-19 record Daniel seeking God's face through fasting and intercessory prayer. He begins by worshipping God and thanking Him for His mercy and the keeping of His covenants. In humility, the prophet confesses his sins and the sins of Israel, specifically stating how they broke Moses' covenant and their just punishment.

The angel Gabriel appears to Daniel in verses 20-29, telling him how he is loved in heaven and his prayers were heard. Gabriel also says he is sent to give Daniel skill and understanding concerning the matter of Israel's return to Judea. The 70 Weeks Prophesy includes verses 24-27.

"Seventy weeks" equals 490 years because a week can mean seven years. Genesis 29:27 explains that Jacob fulfilled Rachel's *"week"* by working seven additional years for the right to marry her. So 70 Weeks means 70 times 7, equaling 490 years.

Daniel 9:24 introduces the prophesy *"upon thy people"* (Jews) and *"upon thy holy city"* (Jerusalem). It records Gabriel's list of six things that must happen at the end of a 490 year period so Daniel's prayers for national and spiritual restoration can be fulfilled:

- *"to finish the transgression"*—Israel's spiritual blindness causes transgressions or rebellion. The 2,000 year rebellion ends when the Jews with new sight accept Christ as their Messiah.

344   2 Kings 17:6, 24:15

- *"to make an end of sins"*—sin is ultimately unbelief and Israel's sin will end when they see the resurrected Jesus physically appear to them, just as Joseph revealed himself in-person to his 11 brothers in Egypt.
- *"to make reconciliation for iniquity"*—Israel's iniquity is pardoned in *"one day"*[345] when the 144,000 Jews are born again by the Holy Ghost, Who institutes the *"ministry of reconciliation."*[346]
- *"to bring in everlasting righteousness"*—the 1,000 year Millennium is the time of righteousness when the glory of the Lord fills the earth, and Satan is bound and unable to tempt anyone (Habakkuk 2:14, Revelation 20:1-7).
- *"to seal up the vision and prophecy"*—in Hebrew, *"seal"* means "to be stopped,"[347] showing Daniel's vision and this prophecy is complete at Jesus' second coming. Daniel 12:4 expresses the correct meaning of the 70 Weeks Prophesy would not be known until today, *"the time of the end."*
- *"to anoint the most Holy"*—at the beginning of the Millennium, Ezekiel 43:1-5 says the newly rebuilt Jewish Temple is anointed by the Holy Ghost as God's glory comes like a rushing mighty wind *"into the house by the way of the gate whose prospect is toward the east."* The Temple, not King Jesus, needs anointed, for Jesus is already eternally anointed by the Spirit. Christ never dies again, living with all of heaven's power (Matthew 28:18, Romans 6:9).

It's apparent none of these six events can happen until blinded Israel gains spiritual eyesight through repentance and acceptance of Jesus Christ. This monumental event takes place during the Tribulation, after

345 Isaiah 66:8
346 2 Corinthians 5:17-19
347 "The Bible: Hebrew and Greek Lexicons." *Voice of God Recordings,* www.branham.org/en/messagesearch

the New Testament church is raptured away to the Marriage Supper of the Lamb and the completed three and a half year ministry of Israel's two prophets—Moses and Elijah.[348]

   In verses 25-27 of Daniel chapter 9, the 490 year period is now divided up into three time periods: seven weeks (49 years), 62 weeks (434 years) and one week (7 years). This is the key to understanding the prophecy.

   The first two time periods (seven weeks plus 62 weeks) are combined to mark the point of Jesus' death. Then God cuts off Israel for rejecting Jesus, essentially causing a 2,000 year pause in this prophecy in order to save the Gentiles. The third period, or seven years that remain, occur during the seven year Tribulation period when God grafts Israel back into His grace.

   First time period of seven years: In verse 25, Gabriel tells Daniel there will be seven weeks, or 49 years, until the *"going forth of the commandment to restore and to build Jerusalem"* and *"the street shall be built again, and the wall, even in troublous times."* According to Larkin,[349] the starting date for this prophecy is 445 B.C when Artaxerxes Longimanus, king of Persia, ordered Israel's temple to be rebuilt.[350] The temple and its wall were finished 49 years later in 396 B.C. in troublous times. Nehemiah 4:17 confirms the troublesome conditions of rebuilding the wall, saying, *"They which builded on the wall, and they that bare burdens, with those that laded, every one with one of his hands wrought in the work, and with the other hand held a weapon."*

   Second time period of 434 years: This period of 62 weeks is also placed in verse 25 and must be added to the first-mentioned seven weeks, or 49 years, to know when the Messiah would appear as King to Israel. Daniel 9:25 says, *"Unto the Messiah the Prince shall be seven weeks, and threescore and two weeks."* John 12:13 captures the Jewish multitude acknowledging Jesus' royal, princely position as their King, only

---

348   Revelation 11:1-13

349   "Clarence Larkin: The Book of Daniel." *Earnestly Contending For The Faith,*
      https://www.earnestlycontendingforthefaith.com/Books/Clarence%20Larkin/
      Daniel ClarenceLarkinTheBookOfDaniel11.html

350   Nehemiah 2:1-8

to crucify Him within less than a week: "*Hosanna: Blessed is the King of Israel that cometh in the name of the Lord.*" Then in Daniel 9:26, the prophesy says Messiah would be "*cut off, but not for himself*" after the 62 weeks. This means we must add the previous seven weeks (49 years) to these 62 weeks, or 434 years. Jesus' crucifixion was His being "*cut off*" in order to bear all humanity's sins. Christ died for us, for our sins—not His. Hebrews 9:28 explains, "*So Christ was once offered to bear the sins of many; and unto them that look for him shall he appear the second time without sin unto salvation.*"

Adding the 62 weeks plus seven weeks yields 69 weeks, or 483 years (434 + 49 = 483). When you begin at Artaxerxes' order in 445 B.C. and add 69 weeks, or 483 years, you come to the year 38 A.D. as the date for Jesus' crucifixion. But there seems to be a problem—Jesus began preaching around 26 A.D. and was crucified after his 3.5 year preaching ministry in 30 A.D. There's an eight year difference between 30 A.D. and 38 A.D. There are 475 years from 445 B.C. to 30 A.D. but we need 483 years. How can God's prophecy be *short* 8 years? A simple resolution matches the dates correctly.

Two different calendars need examined to understand the prophecy—solar and prophetic. The solar calendar has 365 and 1/4 days per year while God's prophetic calendar has 360 days per year. A prophetic year is shorter than a solar year, as the solar calendar matches the amount of time it takes the earth to revolve once around the sun. More time passes on the prophetic calendar than the solar because its years are shorter.

Examining the prophetic year, we know God has 12 months in His year because Solomon had 12 officers over Israel, "*each man his month in a year.*"[351] Revelation 11:2-3 show 42 months equals 1,260 days. In God's prophetic calendar, each month has 30 days (1,260/42 = 30).

With these calculations verified by Scripture, you find the all-wise God hid the 483 prophetic years in man's 475 solar years! Isaiah 45:15 rightly declares, "*Verily thou art a God that hidest thyself, O God of Israel, the Saviour.*"

351   1 Kings 4:7

We must compare the number of days between the two calendars to see the time difference between them. The solar's 365 and 1/4 days times 483 years equals 176,415.75 days. God's prophetic calendar has 173,880 days (360 x 483), making the difference of 2,535.75 days. Now divide this number by 360 days and you arrive at 7.04 years. This means 7 extra prophetic years passed on the prophetic calendar (since it's a shorter year) during the 475 solar years.

Subtract the seven years from 38 A.D. and you land at 31 A.D. There seems to be one year remaining between Jesus' historical crucifixion date of 30 A.D. and 31 A.D. Keep in mind this extra year allows some "wiggle room" for the final six months or so of Jesus' ministry to be completed because we are not told Jesus' exact age at the start of His preaching ministry. Luke 3:21-23 gives Jesus' general age—*"about thirty years"*—when He was baptized, saying *"And Jesus himself began to be about thirty years of age."* This extra time also gave extra grace for the elected believers to recognize Jesus as Messiah, believing upon Him and following His ministry.

Finishing the latter details of Daniel 9:26, we read, *"And the people of the prince that shall come shall destroy the city and the sanctuary; and the end thereof shall be with a flood, and unto the end of the war desolations are determined."* The prince in this verse is not the Messiah, for Jerusalem (the city in which was the Temple, the sanctuary) was destroyed and made desolate by Titus' Roman army in A.D. 70. Observe the 40 year probation period from the time Israel crucified Christ—30 A.D.—to the time Titus came in 70 A.D., 40 years later. God did the same 40 year probation period with the generation who refused to possess the promised land after the exodus from Egypt. Hebrews 3:17 reads, *"But with whom was he grieved forty years? was it not with them that had sinned, whose carcases fell in the wilderness?"*

Like a school master putting a student in a time out or detention in discipline, God has put away or cast away[352] Israel from His New Covenant blessings based upon their disobedience. His focus has been

---

352 Romans 11:15

on the Gentile people from around 30 A.D. to the date of this publication, 2021. Through Israel's fall *"salvation is come unto the Gentiles."*[353]

God has put nearly a 2,000 year long pause on Daniel's 70 Week Prophesy to show His grace to the Gentiles. In other words, there's a near 2,000 year gap between the ending of the 69th week of Daniel's prophecy and the beginning of the 70th week. Hosea 3:4-5 beautifully foretell this long pause, calling it *"many days"*:

> *"For the children of Israel shall abide many days without a king, and without a prince, and without a sacrifice, and without an image, and without an ephod, and without teraphim: Afterward shall the children of Israel return, and seek the LORD their God, and David their king; and shall fear the LORD and his goodness in the latter days."*

Notice also Hosea 3:5 foretells Israel's return to the LORD. Paul agrees, saying, *"God is able to graff them in again"* and will do that when *"the fulness of the Gentiles be come in."*[354] Once every Gentile believer is saved, God will be done with the Gentiles and will return to Israel. Chapter 3 explains how God brought Gentiles into His family and Chapter 7 reveals God's historical dealings with them over the past 2,000 years, called the Gentile Church Ages.

Third time period of seven years: This final week, or seven year period, is the 70th week and is described in Daniel 9:27:

> *"And he shall confirm the covenant with many for one week: and in the midst of the week he shall cause the sacrifice and the oblation to cease, and for the overspreading of abominations he shall make it desolate, even until the consummation, and that determined shall be poured upon the desolate."*

The *"he"* in this verse cannot be Christ because our Lord would not purposely overspread abominations upon Jerusalem, as is the purpose

---

353   Romans 11:11
354   Romans 11:23, 25

of this man following his move to stop Jewish sacrifices. This "*he*" is connected to the last person mentioned in the previous verse—Titus the Roman general, the "*prince that shall come.*" The "*he*" in verse 27 is the person of the Antichrist, who will be the future Roman leader. Chapter 9 covers Scripture identifying the Antichrist, who will be a future Pope of the Roman Catholic Church.

The order of end-time events begins with the Holy Ghost-filled, New Testament church being raptured to meet Christ and the dead in Christ in the air. Jesus takes His faithful saints to heaven for the Marriage Supper of the Lamb. With the Gentile Church Ages being finished, God returns to His people, Israel. The Great Tribulation officially begins.

Shortly after the rapture, the Pope-Antichrist makes a "*one week*" or seven year covenant "*with many*" world leaders, including sinful Israel. The deceitful covenant is also called a peaceful "*league*" in Daniel 11:22-23. Paul says the world will be crying for "*peace and safety*"[355] and that is what the Pope-Antichrist will promise to deliver.

The 144,000 faithful Jewish remnant will refuse to bow to the Pope's flatteries, or not be a part of this covenant. It's likely all believing Israelis use this time to return to living in the Holy Land. Due to the Pope's world-wide peace agreement, which includes the oft-violent Palestinians, Israel will rebuild its Temple and reestablish animal sacrifices for the first time in almost 2,000 years. Christ foretold Israel's time of repossession of Jerusalem after the Gentile rapture in Luke 21:24: "*And Jerusalem shall be trodden down of the Gentiles, until the times of the Gentiles be fulfilled.*"

At the same time, Revelation 11:1-13 describes the supernatural ministry of Israel's two prophets in Judea. Verses 2 and 3 say these Spirit-empowered men prophesy for 3.5 years, or half of the last, or 70th week of Daniel. The next verses, 5 and 6, say their ministries match the Old Testament prophets Moses and Elijah, who had power to withhold rain, cause plagues, and turn water into blood. Great torments will begin, but the greatest judgments will happen after 3.5 years because the 144,000 Israelis must first accept Jesus as Messiah and be sealed by the Holy

---

355   1 Thessalonians 5:3

Ghost. Revelation 7:3 records the angel's command to hold off on the cataclysmic judgments until Israel is sealed: *"Saying, Hurt not the earth, neither the sea, nor the trees, till we have sealed the servants of our God in their foreheads."*

Half way through the seven year covenant, *"in the midst of the week,"* Daniel 9:27 teaches the Pope causes Israel's sacrifices and oblations to cease. This also marks the end of the 3.5 year ministries of the two Jewish prophets, who are slain by Satan, *"the beast,"* but are raised from the dead and raptured 3.5 days later in the sight of their enemies.[356] A great earthquake strikes Jerusalem, causing a tenth of the city to fall along with 7,000 deaths. The 144,000 remnant see God's power and give Him glory in the fear of the LORD.

Daniel 12:11 says one month, or 30 days after the broken covenant, Rome sets up an abomination[357] in Israel's Temple as the Pope sits in the Temple claiming he is god.[358] Then Rome and her allies send their armies to destroy Israel but God will fight for His covenant people.[359] Zechariah 12:9 foretells, *"And it shall come to pass in that day, that I will seek to destroy all the nations that come against Jerusalem."*

In the darkest hour, Israel's rejected King, Jesus Christ, returns to earth to destroy the armies. Next, Zechariah 12:9-13:6 says He physically reveals Himself to His 144,000 brethren and the spirit of grace and supplications pours upon them as a fountain, washing away their blindness. Crying and mournful Israelis weep from house to house, devastated their race crucified their own Messiah. Yet Jesus brings healing and following their heartfelt repentance, the 144,000 are sealed with the Holy Ghost.[360] Through Jesus' amazing grace, Israel's blindness is over. She was blind, but now she sees. The Messiah has done it—redeemed both Jew and Gentile.

Other events during the last 3.5 years include the wrath of God upon beast-worshippers who rejected Jesus Christ. This divine wrath

356 Revelation 11:7-13
357 Daniel 11:31
358 2 Thessalonians 2:3-4
359 Revelation 12:17, 17:12-14
360 Revelation 7:1-21, 14:1

is spoken of in the Sixth Seal of Revelation 6:12-17. The indescribable punishments in the Seven Trumpets that are mentioned in Revelation chapters 8, 9, and 11 fall upon mankind. The Seven Last Plagues or Vials are poured out according to Revelation chapters 15 and 16.

With the Sixth Seal nearly complete, Jesus returns from heaven as *"every eye"*[361] on earth sees Him as they wail, beholding His fiery eyes. The Battle of Armageddon ensues, based upon Revelation 16:16 and 19:11-21. Christ defeats the Pope-Antichrist and the evil spirit possessing him, and casts them both alive into lake of fire.

The remaining time of the last 3.5 period of Daniel's 70th Week comes to a close (See Figure 3 for a visual summary). Heavenly fire cleanses the earth in preparation for the 1,000 year honeymoon. Christ and His bride walk upon a new, sin-cleansed earth. Gabriel's sixfold purpose is complete. Everlasting righteousness will reign. The Millennial Temple will be anointed with Christ's glory. The earth is healed. Malachi 4:1-3 is realized:

> *"For, behold, the day cometh, that shall burn as an oven; and all the proud, yea, and all that do wickedly, shall be stubble: and the day that cometh shall burn them up, saith the LORD of hosts, that it shall leave them neither root nor branch. But unto you that fear my name shall the Sun of righteousness arise with healing in his wings; and ye shall go forth, and grow up as calves of the stall. And ye shall tread down the wicked; for they shall be ashes under the soles of your feet in the day that I shall do this, saith the LORD of hosts."*

361   Revelation 1:7

Daniel's 70 Weeks Prophecy - Daniel 9:24-27		
Time Period 1	Time Period 2	Time Period 3
7 weeks or 49 years	62 weeks or 434 years	1 week or 7 years
445 B.C. to 396 B.C.	396 B.C. to 30 A.D. The combined 483 years of the first two Time Periods must be converted to prophetic years rather than solar years. God hid 483 prophetic years in man's 475 solar years (445 B.C. to 30 A.D. is only 475 years) because prophetic years are shorter than solar years.	Future—begins after the rapture of the Gentile church. There is a currently a 2,000 year pause or gap between the ending of the 69th week and beginning of the 70th week of Daniel. This allows God to save Gentiles during the Church Ages, or Times of the Gentiles.

Figure 3

THE REWARDS FOR RECEIVING THE REVELATION OF ISRAEL'S BLINDNESS

Receiving the revelation of Israel's blindness gains a few rewards. First, believers inherit God's blessings upon their lives when they bless blinded, faithful Israel. This is because God's immutable covenant with Abraham and his seed remains in effect. As believers bless and pray for blinded Jews, the Lord blesses their health, finances, family, and more. God's divine law remains regarding the power of the tongue: "*Death and life are in the power of the tongue.*"[362] Genesis 12:3 holds true: "*And I will bless them that bless thee, and curse him that curseth thee: and in thee shall all families of the earth be blessed.*" Your family can be one of the many blessed through Abraham's obedience and now yours.

This doesn't mean believers bless the sinful acts of Jews who live in sin and reject the Mosaic Covenant. In fact, Paul dealt with these kind of

Jews, saying, "*As concerning the gospel, they are enemies for your sakes: but as touching the election, they are beloved for the fathers' sakes.*"[363] The apostle knew some Jews may be aggressively against Jesus but later turn to Him through God's election. We know the same is true now. Most Jews will sternly oppose Jesus' cross, but you know 144,000 will eventually experience the same grace you have through the resurrected Messiah.

The other reward is one you possess internally—hope for Israel. Without this revelation, your heart would feel devastation and despair for Israel, thinking she was cursed and bound for hell. But through Christ's Spirit in your soul, you realize Jesus *is* the hope of Israel. Paul writes it is the "*Lord Jesus Christ, which is our hope.*"[364] And with Jesus' everlasting grace, love, and wisdom, you know there is reason to hope for Israel's total restoration.

THE CONSEQUENCES FOR REJECTING THE REVELATION OF ISRAEL'S BLINDNESS

There are two possible consequences for rejecting the revelation of Israel's blindness. First, many believe Israel is forever-cursed because they crucified Jesus, their own Messiah. This faulty belief leads some to curse Jews in their angry hearts and with their words. In these cases, death is in their power of their tongues. Yet the Spirit of God cannot curse what God has blessed. Permanent curses must be differentiated from temporary ones. Sinful Jews (and sinful Gentiles, too) fall under temporary curses, also called spiritual captivity by Paul in 2 Timothy 2:26: "*And that they may recover themselves out of the snare of the devil, who are taken captive by him at his will.*" Another common word for a temporary curse is an addiction.

Before his miraculous conversion, Paul, then known as Saul, was persecuting Christians. Saul was hurting his own soul, taken captive to the lies he believed, such as Jesus not being Israel's Messiah. Acts 26:11 shows the belligerent Saul punished Christians and compelled them to blaspheme Jesus. When Christ met him on the road to Damascus, He

363   Romans 11:28
364   1 Timothy 1:1

told Saul he was kicking against the pricks.[365] This expression is taken from oxen who stubbornly kicked against the sharp goads used to prod them on. The ox only hurt itself and gained no relief. Saul was doing the same by dragging Christians to prisons—he was stubbornly destroying God's joy, peace, and love for his life. Many people destroy their own spiritual blessings by cursing others—including the Jews.

Anger towards Jews because they crucified Jesus should be abandoned because anyone in their position would have done the same. Do not let pride arise in your heart, thinking you would have stopped the angry mob from killing Jesus. Isaiah 53:3 and 6 washes all pride from our hearts by declaring, *"We hid as it were our face from him; he was despised, and we esteemed him not. . . All we like sheep have gone astray; we have turned every one to his own way; and the LORD hath laid on him the iniquity of us all."* If we had witnessed Jesus' arrest, flogging, and crucifixion, we would have hid, too. All of us would have forsaken Him. But this makes His grace so amazing in that He loved us first in our unlovable state.

A famous example of a Christian leader holding the wrong view of Jews is Martin Luther. The great Reformation leader of the 1500s repeatedly wrote with aggressive hostility towards Jews, calling them a serpent's brood.[366] Antisemitism is always wrong, even in Luther's case. Luther influenced some to expel Jews and burn their synagogues.[367] These are stains on his testimony, but Luther can plead ignorance for not having the revelation of Israel's blindness because all the mysteries of the Bible could not be revealed until the end time. Daniel 12:4 says God's book is sealed until *"the time of the end."* Had Luther lived in our day, he would have received the revelation of Israel's blindness, as evidenced by the truth that he received God's revelation about justification by faith in the time he lived.

Second, many Gentile religious groups are guilty of confusing their position with Israel's 144,000 future saints. These groups see blinded

365   Acts 9:5
366   "Luther's Jewish Problem." *The Gospel Coalition.org,* https://www.thegospelcoalition.org/article/luthers-jewish-problem/
367   "Martin Luther." *Britannica Online,* https://www.britannica.com/biography/Martin-Luther/Later-years

Israel as totally forsaken with no hope and consider themselves the spiritual Israel, or 144,000 remnant. They go as far as believing genuine Christians will suffer in the Tribulation period, which is unscriptural. Jehovah's Witnesses are best known for believing their followers make up the 144,000 believers. They misunderstand Romans 2:28-29 by thinking they replace the Jews, applying these verses to themselves. But Paul was writing only to Jewish born men who later became Christians, as Romans 2:17 suggests: *"Behold, thou art called a Jew, and restest in the law, and makest thy boast of God."* Without God's true revelation, most religious groups remain confused about their identity and position. 1 Corinthians 14:33 states, *"For God is not the author of confusion, but of peace, as in all churches of the saints."* If these groups would sincerely ask God for true revelation, He would give it to them. Jesus promises, *"Every one that asketh receiveth; and he that seeketh findeth; and to him that knocketh it shall be opened."*[368]

CONCLUSION

The six Biblical evidences reveal blinded Jews can be saved and have a heavenly home under the altar of incense. Jesus will grant them white robes of eternal life at right time.

In the meantime, God's covenants are immutable and steadfast.

Perhaps this generation will see the Joseph antitype, Jesus Christ, revealing His identity to His brethren, the 144,000 Jewish remnant. Like Joseph, Jesus will tell Israel God planned out everything in order to save lives. God uses all things for His glory—even His own covenant people's rejection of their Messiah. To God be all power, riches, wisdom, strength, honor, glory, and blessing!

368   Matthew 7:8

ACTION STEPS TO BLESS BLINDED ISRAEL

1. First repent if you have anger against Israel or if you have cursed them. God will forgive you and bless you in all your ways. Let your heart pity your blinded brethren, knowing Jesus' love and pity towards them.

2. Pray for blinded Israel to remain ever faithful to the Law of Moses. Pray for some of them to become Christians, as God's New Testament, Holy-Ghost filled church must be comprised of believers from all nations, including Israel (Revelation 7:9-17).

3. Prayerfully reach out to Jews you know and share the gospel, as they might be part of the Jewish remnant who are born again. If they turn down Jesus, bless them anyway and encourage them to serve God in the full capacity of their faith.

FOLLOW UP

Free online videos, Bible studies, and William Branham's quotes related to this chapter: www.pastorjessesmith.com/12mysteriesbook

Email: jesse.smith11@sbcglobal.net

Text: 330-929-2037

CHAPTER 3

The Mystery of The New Testament Church Composed of Both Jew and Gentile

"How that by revelation he made known unto me the mystery; (as I wrote afore in few words, Whereby, when ye read, ye may understand my knowledge in the mystery of Christ) Which in other ages was not made known unto the sons of men, as it is now revealed unto his holy apostles and prophets by the Spirit; That the Gentiles should be fellowheirs, and of the same body, and partakers of his promise in Christ by the gospel."

Ephesians 3:3-6

KNOWING ISRAEL'S POSITION THROUGH God's covenant promises is necessary so you can understand your own. For example, if you're born Jewish, either accept Christ as your Messiah or remain ever faithful to the Mosaic Covenant. If you're a Gentile, God has offered you a part of the New Covenant.

Whichever background you come from—Jew or Gentile—the next mystery shows how God planned and produced one New Testament church composed of both Jew and Gentile.

THE CONFUSION ABOUT JEWS AND GENTILES COMPOSING ONE CHURCH

The confusion about Jew and Gentiles composing one church centers on whether or not God would allow a previously unholy, sinful people—the Gentiles—into His holy, separated family. As you read the Old Testament, the LORD makes it clear only Israel is His people under the Mosaic Covenant. Deuteronomy 14:2 states, *"For thou art an holy people unto the LORD thy God, and the LORD hath chosen thee to be a peculiar people unto himself, above all the nations that are upon the earth."* Again, if Israel only obeyed God's commands, He would *"set thee on high above all nations of the earth: And all these blessings shall come on thee, and overtake thee, if thou shalt hearken unto the voice of the LORD thy God."*[369] Would Abraham's God raise up all other nations to the same honor and blessing as Israel? And if so, could Jews and Gentiles become one family in God, entitled to the same benefits and inheritances?

The revelation of the mystery of one church composed of Jew and Gentile is that every born again believer is a part of God's family and entitled to all its rights, benefits, and future inheritances.

While this may not seem like a confusing issue to you, it was a major issue during the first century. This subject might not seem mysterious because you're likely living in the Western civilization that's been established in Judeo-Christian culture for over 400 years.

The bulk of this chapter explores how God broke down the spiritual and physical walls that separated Jews and Gentiles through apostles

369   Deuteronomy 28:1-2

Paul and Peter. But a short section will address how Westerners, like myself and possibly you, may be surprised or even confused how Jews can be part of today's New Testament church. Since we've been accustomed to Gentiles-only in the New Covenant, it can be difficult to imagine how a Messianic Jew might worship Christ. Thankfully, our gracious God offers liberties within the New Covenant and values diversity within holiness.

BIBLICAL EVIDENCE FOR THE REVELATION ABOUT JEWS AND GENTILES COMPOSING ONE CHURCH

God hand-picked and separated Israel to be holy unto Himself, exclusive of other nations, thus forming the Abrahamic Covenant. Isaac was Abraham's true seed of promise, although Abraham had seven other sons. God furthered narrowed His choice on Isaac's son Jacob, out of whom came the 12 Tribes of Israel, although Esau was his firstborn.

Jacob's family went into Egypt with 75 people[370] but came out with possibly a few million because the first count of Israel's men was 600,000. According to Exodus 12:37-38, there were women, children, and a mixed multitude to add to this sum. As promised, God blessed the wombs of Israeli women through fruitfulness and multiplication. Yet God had made provision for Gentiles.

GOD'S PROVISION FOR GENTILE PROSELYTES IN THE OLD TESTAMENT

Although not specifically called to Judaism, Gentiles, called strangers or sojourners[371], were often accepted as proselytes.[372] Beginning with Abraham's covenant in Genesis 17:12 and 27, God prepared Abraham and his descendants to accept proselytes. The number of proselytes steadily increased until Solomon, 500 years after the Egypt exodus, gave a definite number of Gentiles sojourning with Israel to be 153,600.[373]

370 Acts 7:14
371 Leviticus 25:35
372 "Proselyte." *Bible Study Tools*, https://www.biblestudytools.com/dictionaries/eastons-bible-dictionary/proselyte.html
373 2 Chronicles 2:17

Male Gentile converts were required to be circumcised in accordance with Abraham's covenant.[374] Proselytes enjoyed many privileges within Mosaic Law, but males could never be priests, whose offices were designed only for sons of Levi.[375]

All Gentile proselytes kept Moses' Law, including commands such as:

- observing the Sabbath (Deuteronomy 5:14)
- keeping Passover laws (Exodus 12:19)
- rejoicing on feast days (Deuteronomy 16:11,14)
- ceremonial purifying from uncleanness through the red heifer's waters of separation (Numbers 19:10)

God chose to use numerous Gentiles in important and supernatural ways. Prominent Gentile converts within Judaism include:

- Rahab, the Gentile harlot of Jericho, the first recorded Gentile proselyte. Joshua chapters 2 and 6 show she was spared from her city's destruction when she received and protected Israel's two spies. Her red cord token signified her faith in Israel's God. Rahab later married Salmon, a prince of Judah and great-grandfather of David, putting her in the lineage of Jesus Christ.[376]
- Ruth the Moabitess, a childless widow who chose to sojourn back to Israel with her mother-in-law, Naomi, after hearing Israel had bread. Her godly virtue caught the attention of the wealthy Bethlehemite named Boaz, who redeemed both she and Naomi. Boaz was son of Salmon, Rahab's husband. Ruth and Boaz wed and she bore Obed, the grandfather of David, out of whose loins came Christ.
- Uriah the Hittite, husband of Bathsheba, whom David slew in order to take his wife.[377] Beforehand, he was one of

374   Genesis 17:12, Exodus 12:48
375   Leviticus 22:10
376   Matthew 1:5
377   2 Samuel chapters 11, 12

David's mighty men and chief officers (2 Samuel 23:39, 1 Chronicles 11:41). His loyalty to Israel, the Lord, and His battles demonstrate extraordinary devotion to Jehovah.

PROPHECY FORETELLING GENTILES RECEIVING GOD'S NEW COVENANT

Building upon those Gentile heroes, at least four Old Testament prophets foretold God's will to unite the Gentiles into His family through the New Covenant.

God Himself foretold His grace in Genesis 12:3, saying, "*In thee shall all families of the earth be blessed.*" Paul validates God's personal prophecy about the Gentiles in Galatians 3:8: "*And the scripture, foreseeing that God would justify the heathen through faith, preached before the gospel unto Abraham, saying, In thee shall all nations be blessed.*"

Four human prophets that foretell God's grace to the Gentiles are David, Isaiah, Hosea and Jeremiah. In the psalms, David twice mentions all nations worshipping the LORD. Psalm 22:27 reads, "*All the ends of the world shall remember and turn unto the LORD: and all the kindreds of the nations shall worship before thee.*" He adds, "*All nations whom thou hast made shall come and worship before thee, O Lord; and shall glorify thy name.*"[378]

Isaiah provides at least five references to the Gentiles. In chapter 9, verse 2 he writes, "*The people that walked in darkness have seen a great light: they that dwell in the land of the shadow of death, upon them hath the light shined.*" Matthew 4:13-16 explains this was prophecy fulfilled in Jesus' ministry to the Gentiles. Isaiah 11:10 says, "*And in that day there shall be a root of Jesse, which shall stand for an ensign of the people; to it shall the Gentiles seek: and his rest shall be glorious.*" Jesus is undoubtedly the "*root of Jesse*" as He brought the soul-rest of the baptism of the Holy Ghost, according to both Jesus and Paul.[379] A third reference is Isaiah

---

378   Psalm 86:9
379   Isaiah 28:12, Matthew 11:29, 1 Corinthians 14:21

42:1-9, and verse 1 reads, "*Behold my servant, whom I uphold; mine elect, in whom my soul delighteth; I have put my spirit upon him: he shall bring forth judgment to the Gentiles.*" Matthew 12:14-21 proves this was also fulfilled in Jesus' earthly ministry. Isaiah 49:6 prophesies that in addition to restoring the tribes of Israel, the Messiah would shine light for the Gentiles. Paul and Barnabas quote Isaiah, saying, "*For so hath the Lord commanded us, saying, I have set thee to be a light of the Gentiles, that thou shouldest be for salvation unto the ends of the earth.*"[380] Finally, Isaiah 60:3 tells us that "*the Gentiles shall come to thy light, and kings to the brightness of thy rising.*" Acts 26:23 reiterates that Christ's resurrection would "*shew light unto the people, and to the Gentiles.*"

Hosea 2:23 provides a well known Gentile prophecy: "*And I will say to them which were not my people, Thou art my people; and they shall say, Thou art my God.*" Paul is inspired by the Holy Spirit to cite Hosea in Romans 9:24-26 as proof of God offering His Spirit to the Gentiles:

> "*Even us, whom he hath called, not of the Jews only, but also of the Gentiles? As he saith also in Osee, I will call them my people, which were not my people; and her beloved, which was not beloved. And it shall come to pass, that in the place where it was said unto them, Ye are not my people; there shall they be called the children of the living God.*"

Jeremiah also prophesies of the Gentiles coming to know the true God in chapter 16, verses 19-21:

> "*O LORD, my strength, and my fortress, and my refuge in the day of affliction, the Gentiles shall come unto thee from the ends of the earth, and shall say, Surely our fathers have inherited lies, vanity, and things wherein there is no profit. Shall a man make gods unto himself, and they are no gods? Therefore, behold, I will this once cause them to know, I will cause them to know mine hand and my might; and they shall know that my name is The LORD.*"

---

380   Acts 13:47

JESUS FIRST OFFERS THE GOSPEL TO THE JEWS

As God's covenant people, Israel was obligated to have the first chance to receive the New Covenant. Jesus sent His disciples only to the Jews in Matthew 10:5-7:

> *"These twelve Jesus sent forth, and commanded them, saying, Go not into the way of the Gentiles, and into any city of the Samaritans enter ye not: But go rather to the lost sheep of the house of Israel. And as ye go, preach, saying, The kingdom of heaven is at hand."*

Jesus recognized the Gentiles' defiled condition in Matthew 15:22-24 calling them *"dogs"* while calling Israel *"children."* Later, though, after Israel steadfastly opposed His ministry, Jesus the *"one shepherd"* called the Gentiles His *"other sheep"* He must bring into His *"one fold"* in John 10:16.

Jesus' parable of The Wicked Husbandman in Matthew 21:33-46 tells the same story. God first offers His kingdom to Israel, the husband-man in the parable, but they kill the son of the husbandmen, representing Christ. Jesus interprets this parable for the Jews in their ears, saying, *"Therefore say I unto you, The kingdom of God shall be taken from you, and given to a nation bringing forth the fruits thereof."*[381]

Recall Isaiah 60:3, which says, *"the Gentiles shall come to thy light."* The Light of Jesus' gospel came to the Jews first. Acts 3:25-26 records Peter telling Jews God sent His Son Jesus *"unto you first"* to bless them with forgiveness of sins. Paul taught the power of God through Christ was preached first to the Jew in Romans 1:16. The gospel was meant to be their Light, as the prophets foretold. But once rejected and blasphemed,[382] the Light went to the Gentiles.

---

381   Matthew 21:43
382   Acts 13:45-46

THE BOOK OF ACTS AND PETER'S KEYS TO THE KINGDOM

Although most Jews rejected Jesus and supported His crucifixion, a small remnant of believers trusted in Him and knew He was alive and raised from the dead. A portion of this group waited in Jerusalem for 10 days, and on the Day of Pentecost received the New Covenant, the baptism of the Holy Ghost according to Acts chapters 1 and 2. Fittingly, Peter was Jesus' spokesman on that day, as 3,000 souls were added to the faith. Jesus previously gave Peter the keys to the kingdom in Matthew 16:18-19, and at Pentecost he used them first. Jesus says the kingdom of God is the baptism of the Holy Ghost within the believer in Luke 17:21: *"Behold, the kingdom of God is within you."* Both John the Baptist and Christ call the inward filling of the Holy Ghost a baptism in Matthew 3:11 and Acts 1:5, respectively.

Reading further in the Book of Acts, the gospel begins spreading to non-Jews, beginning with the Samaritans in Acts 8:1-40. Surprisingly, it was the persecution of Saul, later Paul, which brought about the spread of Christianity to the Gentiles. Before converting to Christianity, Saul indirectly helped spread it to the very people-group that Christ would later send him directly to! Paul helped the Gentiles receive Jesus' gospel both before he was converted and after his conversion.

Acts 8 shows Philip, the Jewish evangelist, preaching with miraculous signs and wonders to the Samaritans (half-Jews despised by full blooded Jews), causing many to repent of their sins and accept water baptism. Philip then calls for Peter and John to come pray and lay hands on them to receive the baptism of the Holy Ghost. Herein is the second time Peter uses the keys to the kingdom, for when he and John pray for the Samaritans, they are born again: *"(For as yet he was fallen upon none of them: only they were baptized in the name of the Lord Jesus.) Then laid they their hands on them, and they received the Holy Ghost."*[383]

Peter uses the keys to the kingdom a third time to open the door of salvation to Gentiles in Acts chapter 10. Following a supernatural vision

---

383   Acts 8:16-17

in which God shows Peter His soon intention to save the *"unclean"* Gentiles, the apostle goes with three men to the house of Cornelius, a Roman centurion. Cornelius was already a devoted follower of Christ, having a disciplined life of prayer, fasting, and alms giving, yet he hadn't been baptized yet. Peter's short sermon about God's divine plan to use Jesus' death and resurrection as a means to save and forgive *"whosoever believeth"* causes the Holy Ghost to fall *"on all them which heard the word."*[384] This is amazing news—the Gentiles are now receiving God's blessings equal to the Jews!

Upon hearing this news, the Jewish-Christians in Judea were upset and contended with Peter when he returned to their company. They accused Peter of defiling himself by eating with uncircumcised men. Peter recounts the events in Cornelius' house to the apostles and brethren, declaring that the Holy Ghost fell in Cornelius' house the same as it did on the Day of Pentecost, according to Jesus' promise to baptize believers with the Holy Ghost. Humbled by God's Spirit being poured out upon the Gentiles as a gift, Peter says, *"What was I, that I could withstand God?"* Peter's story satisfies the apostles, and Acts 11:18 reads, *"When they heard these things, they held their peace, and glorified God, saying, Then hath God also to the Gentiles granted repentance unto life."*

Cornelius' house, then, is a great turning point for the New Covenant because God now shares His Holy Spirit gift with Gentiles—even though the men had not kept the circumcision-token of Abraham's Covenant.

This turning point is a new spiritual time and season Jesus labels *"the times of the Gentiles"* in Luke 21:24, and Paul tells you it lasts for only a limited time. Romans 11:25 declares the Jews are blinded to Christ *"until the fulness of the Gentiles be come in."*

PAUL'S GENTILE DISPENSATION AND PETER'S APOSTLESHIP TO THE JEWS

You learned in Chapter 2 that the apostle Paul was given a dispensation, or stewardship, to preach Christ's gospel to the Gentiles according to 1

---

384   Acts 10:43-44

Corinthians 9:17, Ephesians 3:2, and Colossians 1:25. Herein we recognize Paul's divine assignment to the Gentiles.

1 Corinthians 9:17 says this dispensation was committed, or entrusted, to Paul:"*For if I do this thing willingly, I have a reward: but if against my will, a dispensation of the gospel is committed unto me.*"

Ephesians 3:1-2 tells you the Gentile dispensation was given to him by God: "*For this cause I Paul, the prisoner of Jesus Christ for you Gentiles, If ye have heard of the dispensation of the grace of God which is given me to you-ward.*" This verse proves Paul's dispensation was the time he would oversee the ministry of grace in a stewardship given solely to him by Jesus.

Colossians 1:25 explains his dispensation is a fulfillment of God's Word, or prophecy: "*Whereof I am made a minister, according to the dispensation of God which is given to me for you, to fulfil the word of God.*"

God specifically chose Paul to take the gospel to Gentiles while choosing Peter to take it to the Jews. These were not two gospels, but one, for this is "*one faith.*"[385] Scripture says both men had an apostleship to their respective group: Paul was God's apostle to the Gentiles, and Peter was the apostle to the Jews. Galatians 2:7-9 reads:

> "*But contrariwise, when they saw that the gospel of the uncircumcision was committed unto me, as the gospel of the circumcision was unto Peter; (For he that wrought effectually in Peter to the apostleship of the circumcision, the same was mighty in me toward the Gentiles:) And when James, Cephas, and John, who seemed to be pillars, perceived the grace that was given unto me, they gave to me and Barnabas the right hands of fellowship; that we should go unto the heathen, and they unto the circumcision.*"

Paul and Peter are significant choices as messengers of God's New Covenant, for both men had experienced Jesus' life-changing power. Paul had previously dragged Christians to jail, denying Christ and urging them to blaspheme Jesus. Peter had boasted of his devotion to Jesus

385   Ephesians 4:5

before denying Him with cursing three times on the night of Jesus' arrest. Paul and Peter's friends, families, and acquaintances witnessed their spiritual transformation from failures to bold followers of Jesus.

God's selection of Paul as the herald of this Gentile dispensation leaves no doubt to its authenticity because Paul was originally *"a Hebrew of Hebrews."*[386] In other words, Paul, or Saul, was a staunch, zealous Mosaic Covenant-Jew who likely despised Gentiles for their uncleanness. In our human minds, he would seem to be an unlikely choice to open the door of fellowship to Gentiles.

Previous to Christ humbling him through his conversion, Paul aggressively opposed any Gentile defiling his Hebrew synagogue and lifestyle. Saul kept Moses' Law along with the man-made traditions of the Pharisees. But once knowing Christ's love, Paul counted all his efforts in man-made, Pharisee-traditions as *"dung"* that he might *"win Christ."*[387] Paul knew what it meant to violently oppose God's plans but later receive grace from Jesus Christ. With this experience, he could freely preach grace to the Gentiles who also once opposed God's holiness.

THE MOMENT PAUL TURNED TO THE GENTILES

Acts 13:14-52 captures the moment Paul turned his ministry to the Gentiles. While on his first missionary journey with Barnabas in Antioch, Jewish leaders in a synagogue offer an opportunity for Paul and Barnabas to speak on the Sabbath. God's Word is so true—His gifts make room for themselves.[388] If God sends you to speak for Him, He will provide opportunities and listeners.

Paul stands and preaches Israel's history, beginning with the exodus from Egypt, then going through Joshua's conquest of Canaan, the judges, then kings, building to John the Baptist's words about the One coming after him—Jesus Christ. The apostle then shows forgiveness through Jesus' death and resurrection, followed by a warning to believe it. A week later, nearly the whole city comes to hear Paul preach. But certain Jews

386   Philippians 3:5
387   Philippians 3:6-8
388   Proverbs 18:16

were filled with envy after seeing other Jews and Gentiles believing in Christ. The angry Jews contradict and blaspheme Paul and Barnabas, causing the apostles to announce God's official turning from the Jews to the Gentiles:

> *"Then Paul and Barnabas waxed bold, and said, It was necessary that the word of God should first have been spoken to you: but seeing ye put it from you, and judge yourselves unworthy of everlasting life, lo, we turn to the Gentiles. For so hath the Lord commanded us, saying, I have set thee to be a light of the Gentiles, that thou shouldest be for salvation unto the ends of the earth. And when the Gentiles heard this, they were glad, and glorified the word of the Lord: and as many as were ordained to eternal life believed."*

This particular event gives evidence to blinded Jews being responsible for their blindness. Paul says Jews judged themselves unworthy of everlasting life. God did not forcefully blind Israel outside of their free moral agency. Rather, Israel wanted to disbelieve and blaspheme Christ. By foreknowledge God planned for this moment in advance, and prepared Paul and Barnabas to herald His loving grace to the spiritually-hungry Gentiles.

After many more missionary travels, Paul returned to Antioch and shared how God had opened the door of faith to the Gentiles in Acts 14:27: *"And when they were come, and had gathered the church together, they rehearsed all that God had done with them, and how he had opened the door of faith unto the Gentiles."* Since Israel would not return to Him in obedience, He would leave her and turn to the Gentiles.

PAUL'S GOSPEL IS CHRIST'S JUDGMENT STANDARD

To say Paul's teachings are important would be a gross understatement. Galatians 1:6-12 and Romans 2:16 boldly declare curses upon anyone who changes Paul's teachings because they will be Christ's judgment standard on Judgment Day.

Paul calls any variation to his teachings perversions in Galatians 1:6-7. Then in verses 8-9 he gives a double warning of a curse to those who change his original gospel message:

> *"But though we, or an angel from heaven, preach any other gospel unto you than that which we have preached unto you, let him be accursed. As we said before, so say I now again, If any man preach any other gospel unto you than that ye have received, let him be accursed."*

You might wonder, "Why such strong words?" Verses 10-13 state the reason—Paul received his initial gospel teachings, and thereby authority, directly from Jesus Christ Himself, and not from himself or other men. Anyone changing Paul's teachings were actually changing Christ's teachings, which would warrant a curse as Proverbs 30:5-6 and Revelation 22:18-19 support. Notice verse 8 again, how Paul says he and his fellow preachers—*"we"*— as well as angels cannot change one word Christ taught him.

It seems likely from Galatians 1:17 Paul received his revelations from Christ in the wilderness of Arabia. Jesus didn't send Paul to a seminary, although God used those in the past. Nor did Jesus send Paul to learn from Peter. No, Christ had a special ministry for Paul and needed to teach him personally, face to face. Imagine Paul communing with the same Light that caused his conversion on the road to Damascus, but now he's not persecuting Jesus, the Light, but letting the Light teach him the divine revelation of the mystery of God! Bible readers may be reminded of another prophet, Moses, communing with the eternal Light in the wilderness in order to receive the revelation of the Ten Commandments. A modern example of God meeting a prophet in the wilderness is detailed in Chapter 13.

Romans 2:16 says God will judge the secrets of men by Paul's gospel: *"In the day when God shall judge the secrets of men by Jesus Christ according to my gospel."* Of course, Paul is not claiming his teachings came from his own mind when he writes *"my gospel,"* but rather from his dispensation, or stewardship, from Jesus Christ, as Galatians 1:12 and Ephesians 3:2

state. Understand not every word Paul uttered from his lips, nor wrote with his pen was from Jesus as "Thus saith the LORD." Satan forever labors to deceive men into worshipping other men, as Paul experienced and recorded in 1 Corinthians 1:12-15. The apostle said he was thankful he baptized none of the Corinthians for they might have said they were baptized by Paul in Paul's name! Paul's own words admit he was not perfect, nor infallible. Only his teachings from Jesus Christ carried authority. The apostle writes in Romans 3:4, 13-14 that all men lie and let deceit and bitter words spew from their mouths. Paul also said he sinned and did things he hated in Romans 7:15-19. Although Paul was not infallible, his revealed gospel from Jesus Christ was.

Paul's revelation from Jesus was God's divine will for mankind, and all will be judged by Paul's epistles. This means Paul's inspired words about doctrine and Christian living need resounded today since much of Christendom rejects Jesus' revelation. The following divine gospel-truths will either witness for or against mankind on Judgment Day, and should not be added to nor deleted from pulpits:

- Water baptism is full immersion in water (not sprinkling) and should be administered in the literal name of Lord Jesus Christ.[389] No person in Scripture was baptized in the titles of Father, Son, and Holy Ghost. Paul baptized Ephesians in the literal name of the "*Lord Jesus*" in Acts 19:5.
- The Godhead, recognized as a genuine, divine mystery by Paul,[390] is never referred to as "three persons." Instead, Paul says Jesus is the image of the invisible God.[391] The Hebrews writer, likely Paul, says Jesus is the image of God's one person in Hebrews 1:3.
- Paul taught all churches appropriate hair length: men have short, cut hair while women have long, uncut hair according to 1 Corinthians 4:17 and 11:1-16.

389 Acts 2:38, 8:16, 10:48, 19:5, 22:16
390 Colossians 2:2
391 Colossians 1:15

- Modest clothing was commanded to Christian women by Paul in 1 Timothy 2:9. (I wrote my first book on this subject and I will provide you a free copy if you cannot afford one.)
- Women preachers were forbidden by Paul, who said men only can teach other men in 1 Timothy 2:12 and 1 Corinthians 14:34-35.
- Paul and the apostles never asked anyone to "invite" Jesus into their hearts for salvation, but rather preached repentance in anticipation for a later infilling of the Holy Ghost baptism.[392]

PAUL'S EXTENSIVE TEACHING ON THE REVELATION OF ONE CHURCH

Apostle Paul writes extensively on this revelation of Jews and Gentiles composing one church. He labels this subject as a mystery and fittingly provides sufficient evidence proving God accepts both Jew and Gentile into Christ's body, the church. The following Scriptures detail the one church: Romans 16:25-26, 1 Corinthians 12:13, Galatians 3:6-29, Ephesians 2:11-22, 3:1-21, and Colossians 1:27, 3:11, and 4:3.

It's essential to read the entire Book of Romans, as chapters 1-5 show the universal need for Jews and Gentiles to receive the righteousness of Jesus Christ He has graciously provided. Then, chapters 6-8 teach how the "new man" or Spirit-filled believer overcomes sin, understands the Mosaic Covenant, and walks in the Holy Spirit. Israel's downfall in unbelief, the mystery of her blindness, and her prophesied return to Christ are taught in chapters 9-11. The one faith, or guidelines for Christian living, are expressed in chapters 12-16.

In Romans 16:25-27, Paul ends his monumental teaching letter by telling believers God is going to establish and strengthen them according to the preaching of the *"revelation of the mystery"* of his gospel. Paul's revelation is that God wants all Gentiles to obey the one faith. This revelation

392   Acts 2:37-39, 3:19, 8:21-23, 9:17, 17:30, 19:1-7, 26:20

"was kept secret since the world began, But now is made manifest, and by the scriptures of the prophets, according to the commandment of the everlasting God, made known to all nations for the obedience of faith."

1 Corinthians 12:13 states Paul's revelation that both Jews and Gentiles become a part of Jesus' body through the baptism of the Holy Ghost: *"For by one Spirit are we all baptized into one body, whether we be Jews or Gentiles, whether we be bond or free; and have been all made to drink into one Spirit."* Any Jew or Gentile with the baptism of the Holy Ghost is part of the family of God, having the same benefits and inheritance.

ABRAHAM'S SPIRITUAL SEED

Galatians chapter 3 unpacks Paul's revelation from Jesus that anyone—whether Jew or Gentile—with faith in Christ is a spiritual seed of Abraham.

Paul's letter to the Galatians was probably one of his first epistles, and shows how directly and intensely he attacked legalism and heresies. In chapter 3, Paul pleads with the Galatians to avoid legalism, especially since they started serving Jesus by faith. The apostle refers his readers to Abraham and his justification by faith alone, and quotes Genesis 12:3 to prove Abraham's seed is now a spiritual seed with the same justification. It's amazing how much revelation God placed in this one short verse! God foretold the Times of the Gentiles 2,000 years in advance. Four verses teach that anyone with faith in Jesus is a spiritual seed of Abraham:

- Verse 7—*"Know ye therefore that they which are of faith, the same are the children of Abraham."*
- Verse 9—*"So then they which be of faith are blessed with faithful Abraham."*
- Verse 26—*"For ye are all children of God by faith in Christ Jesus."*
- Verse 29—*"And if ye be Christ's, then are ye Abraham's seed, and heirs according to the promise."*

The rest of chapter 3 highlights Jesus, the true seed of Abraham, taking the curse of the law upon Himself so that we might be justified by faith in Him. Paul then emphasizes *"the promise of the Spirit,"* or baptism of the Holy Ghost in their souls, calling it *"the blessing of Abraham."* The baptism of the Holy Ghost is a spiritual circumcision, the New Testament token for Abraham's seed. Romans 2:29 says it's the *"circumcision...of the heart."* The chapter ends by stating those *"baptized into Christ"* have put on Christ's righteousness and shall inherit all of Abraham's blessings. Genuine Christians are Abraham's spiritual seed by faith with the spiritual circumcision, given *"to the Jew first, and also to the Gentile."*[393]

To dissolve all doubts, Paul uses Galatians chapter 4 to further prove his point. Twice his emphasis is on the born again experience, the Holy Ghost-baptism of the soul. Verses 1-7 explain God's Spirit in your heart changes you from a slave to a son, which is called the *"adoption of sons."* A second mention is in verse 29 as Paul declares those *"born after the Spirit"* are children of the freewoman, meaning you are Abraham's true offspring, and therefore inherit the promised blessings.

CHRIST CREATES ONE BODY AND ONE TEMPLE

In Ephesians chapters 2 and 3, Paul both identifies and explains the mystery and revelation of God's new church.

Chapter 2 begins with 10 memorable verses magnifying God's work in saving us *"by grace...through faith."*[394] Beginning in verses 11 and 12, Paul tells the Ephesians to remember their hopeless Gentile condition prior to knowing Christ. They were *"without Christ, being aliens from the commonwealth of Israel, and strangers from the covenants of promise, having no hope, and without God in the world."* Verse 13 says they were *"far off"* from God but are now *"made nigh by the blood of Christ."*

In verse 14, Paul declares Jesus *is* our peace because He has made Jews and Gentiles one by breaking down *"the middle wall of partition"* between them. Paul is likely referring to the wall in Herod's Temple

393   Romans 2:10
394   Ephesians 2:8

separating Gentiles from Jews. Upon the wall hung an inscription, written in Latin and Greek, warning Gentiles of certain death if they entered the inner courts beyond their court, named the Court of the Gentiles. In other words, it was immediate war with Jewish temple guards if a Gentile attempted to get physically closer to worshipping Almighty God. Jews enjoyed worship closer to God, as the Court of Women and Court of Men surrounded the Court of Priests, where sacrifices were offered. Christ's blood tears down this wall, abolishing all the commandments against Gentiles, creating peace with God for both Jew and Gentile.

Paul paints two pictures of the new unity in Christ for Jews and Gentiles: one body and one temple. The cross makes them *"one new man...in one body"*[395] and Christ is the head[396] of this body. This new body has access to Father God through the *"one Spirit."* The one *"holy temple"* is Paul's second picture in verses 19-22. The apostle announces Gentiles are *"fellowcitizens"* alongside Jews in *"the household of God."* This new holy temple has Jesus Christ as the *"chief corner stone"* and the foundation of *"the apostles and prophets."* Christian Jews and Gentiles are built upon this magnificent foundation, making the temple grow together into God's dwelling place: *"an habitation of God through the Spirit."*

Paul's one temple imagery was divinely foreshadowed in the construction of Solomon's Temple 1,000 years before Christ. This awe-inspiring temple took seven years[397] to complete, which foreshadowed Jesus using Seven Church Ages to build His spiritual temple during the Times of the Gentiles. Fascinatingly, Solomon didn't rely solely upon Jewish help for its construction. 1 Kings 5 details Solomon's partnership with a Gentile king, Hiram of Tyre, in order to finish the temple. Both kings and their people—Jews and Gentiles—partnered together in making God's natural earthly habitation as a beautiful type of Christian Jews and Gentiles composing the one temple of God's spiritual habituation, the body of Christ. God's spiritual temple He dwells in today is currently under construction, being built with devoted Jewish and Gentile hearts.

---

395   Ephesians 2:15-16
396   Ephesians 1:22, 4:15, 5:23
397   1 Kings 6:38

In Ephesians chapter 3, Paul calls himself a prisoner of Jesus Christ *"for you Gentiles"* that he *"should preach among the Gentiles the unsearchable riches of Christ; And to make all men see what is the fellowship of the mystery."* Paul was a love-slave for Christ's will. His calling was to preach Jesus' amazing, multifaceted love to Gentiles, as verses 17-19 affirm.

The apostle wants all men to see the *"fellowship"* of the mystery, or "joint participation" in the Greek Lexicon. Verses 6 and 12 declare both Jews and Gentiles participate in partaking of God's promises by having full access to Jesus Christ.

Ephesians 3:5 emphatically declares this revelation was *"in other ages...not made known unto the sons of men, as it is now revealed unto his holy apostles and prophets by the Spirit."* You learn even God's prophets cannot know revelations until the Almighty ordains it. Additionally, there can be no hard feelings towards Jews for their previous separation from Gentiles because it was ordained by the Father. How exciting it must have been for Paul and those Ephesians to know God was *"now"*—presently—revealing a mystery and they were the first to hear it!

Another revelation of the mystery is that the one body of Christians, both alive on earth and those in heaven, have one family name—the Lord Jesus Christ—as verses 14 and 15 teach. The name above all names[398] is the Lord Jesus Christ, as the Book of Acts records believers being baptized in this name, devils being cast out in this name, and miracles being done in this all-sufficient name.[399] Acts 4:12 forever proclaims *"there is none other name under heaven given among men, whereby we must be saved."*

In Ephesians 3:14-21, Paul ends the chapter offering prayer that the Ephesians would experience *"the riches of his glory, to be strengthened with might by his Spirit in the inner man."* His emphasis is on Christ's Spirit dwelling inside each believer, also called the baptism of the Holy Ghost. Paul wants them to know the depths of Christ's love which allows believers to be *"filled with all the fulness of God."* Throughout all ages the church will glorify Christ for sharing His *"power that worketh in us."*

---

398   Philippians 2:9-10
399   Acts 2:38, 3:6, 8:12-16, 10:48, 16:18, 19:5

Although in prison, Paul beseeches the prayers of his Ephesian converts to pray for all men, including Paul. Ephesians 6:18-20 records Paul's main prayer request for boldness to share this beautiful revelation with anyone willing to listen: *"Praying always... And for me, that utterance may be given unto me, that I may open my mouth boldly, to make known the mystery of the gospel, For which I am an ambassador in bonds: that therein I may speak boldly, as I ought to speak."*

LETTER TO THE COLOSSIANS

Paul's letter to the Colossians, another prison epistle, supports the revelation of one church. A city in present-day Turkey about 100 miles east of Ephesus, Colosse had a Christian church through the missionary work of Paul's helper, Epaphras.[400]

This letter is perhaps best known for giving the most complete expression of Jesus Christ's supreme deity in chapter 1, verses 15-20. Immediately thereafter, Paul names another mystery God now manifest to the Gentiles—*"Christ in you, the hope of glory."* This is the doctrine of the baptism of the Holy Ghost (See Chapter 6). But later in chapter 3, verses 10-14, Paul has to remind the Colossians a Holy Spirit-filled believer is a *"new man"* and must treat everyone in Christ's one body with love. In Jesus' one Jew-Gentile church, He is all, and in all:

> *"And have put on the new man, which is renewed in knowledge after the image of him that created him: Where there is neither Greek nor Jew, circumcision nor uncircumcision, Barbarian, Scythian, bond nor free: but Christ is all, and in all. Put on therefore, as the elect of God, holy and beloved, bowels of mercies, kindness, humbleness of mind, meekness, longsuffering; Forbearing one another, and forgiving one another, if any man have a quarrel against any: even as Christ forgave you, so also do ye. And above all these things put on charity, which is the bond of perfectness."*

400   Colossians 1:7, 4:12

At the end of this letter in 4:2-4, Paul echoes the same prayer request he gave to the Ephesians, asking for open doors to share God's revelation: "*Continue in prayer, and watch in the same with thanksgiving; Withal praying also for us, that God would open unto us a door of utterance, to speak the mystery of Christ, for which I am also in bonds: That I may make it manifest, as I ought to speak.*"

BLESSINGS AND CHALLENGES WHEN TRANSITIONING TO ONE BODY

The revelation of the one church mystery brings intimacy, or partnership, between Jews and Gentiles as Paul wrote in Ephesians 3:9. Examining the Book of Acts and Paul's epistles reveals both the blessings of this partnership and the challenges that arose while transitioning to one body, or one church.

God's blessings were apparent in Paul's dealings with Gentile churches. Three heartfelt examples include the Philippians, Thessalonians, and Ephesians.

The church in Philippi was Paul's first European church, started during his second missionary journey. His letter to the Philippians has been called his warmest and most personal. In chapter 1, Paul thanked God every time he remembered this church, convinced God would finish the good work He began in them. These Christians had a place in Paul's heart, so much that he greatly longed to see them again. The Philippians' loyalty to following Paul's message was evident as they withstood heretics and legalists. In the final chapter, Paul thanks the Philippians for being the only church who contacted him about his physical needs, having sent provisions to Paul through Epaphroditus. Paul assures them God will supply their own physical needs, receive their giving as an offering to His glory, and record their generosity as a deposit in their heavenly rewards bank account.[401]

Paul's two letters to the Thessalonians demonstrate a deep, emotional bond between the Jewish apostle and these Gentiles despite his

---

401   Philippians 4:17-18

very short stay among them. This church was started during Paul's second missionary trip as Paul passed through Thessalonica, the capital city of Macedonia. Thanksgiving and prayers were always flowing from Paul's mouth for these believers because of their unceasing *"work of faith, and labour of love"* despite persecutions.[402] The apostle was like a gentle nurse and instructive father among them, taking nothing of theirs, but giving out love only.[403] His ministry was so effective they willingly forsook their dead idols to serve *"the living and true God."*[404] In 1 Thessalonians chapter 4, Paul provided much comfort to them regarding their deceased loves ones, promising them a future meeting in the air with their brethren and Jesus Christ at His return. But warnings about the antichrist spirit were communicated, and disorderly and lazy brothers were given correction in his second letter. In Paul's eyes, the Thessalonian converts were his heavenly crown and his *"glory and joy."*[405]

Paul's longest missionary stay was with the Ephesians during his third and final missionary trip, with whom he stayed three years according to Acts 20:31. It was through Paul's teachings that 12 Ephesians initially received eternal life, or the baptism of Holy Ghost.[406] In Paul's farewell with the Ephesians in Acts 20:17-38, one of the most touching and emotional scenes in Scripture unfolds. Paul reminds them to imitate his humble, selfless service and sincerity. He taught them the whole *"counsel of God,"* holding nothing good back from them. He knows he's facing imprisonment and likely martyrdom, but Paul urges the leaders to feed and protect the saints because Satan will send wolves into their flock. Finally, in sorrow the Jewish and Gentile group prays and weeps together before accompanying Paul to his departing ship, proving Christ's unsearchable love in His one body of believers:

402   1 Thessalonians 1:2-3, 2 Thessalonians 1:3-4
403   1 Thessalonians 2:7-11
404   1 Thessalonians 1:9
405   1 Thessalonians 2:19-20
406   Acts 19:1-7

"And when he had thus spoken, he kneeled down, and prayed with them all. And they all wept sore, and fell on Paul's neck, and kissed him, Sorrowing most of all for the words which he spake, that they should see his face no more. And they accompanied him unto the ship."

Many challenges sprang up as Jew and Gentile Christians transitioned into one body. The first challenge was likely Peter's mistreatment of Gentile Christians recorded in Galatians 2:11-21. It seems this struggle happened before the Jerusalem Council because Paul never cites the conclusions of the Council in the letter to the Galatians.

Galatians tells us Peter so feared legalistic Jews that he refused to eat with Gentiles. The very man who had the Keys to Kingdom from Jesus, received a vision straight from God about His cleansing of the Gentile people, and first saw the Holy Ghost baptize Gentiles into the body of Christ at Cornelius' house mistreated Christian Gentiles. Peter's influence was so great it caused Barnabas to join him in the sinful separation. But Paul would have none it, withstanding Peter to his face in front of all the apostles and elders blaming him for hypocrisy. It's believed Peter repented and again fellowshipped with Gentiles as he had before.

Circumcision was the second issue in Acts 15. Certain Jewish Christians from Judea were teaching Gentiles must be circumcised to be saved. Paul and Barnabas strongly resisted this teaching, causing the brethren to send Paul and Barnabas to Jerusalem to counsel with the apostles and elders about this doctrine. This is often called the Jerusalem Council.

Peter offers his conviction that Gentiles are in fact saved and no different from Christian Jews. Paul and Barnabas follow Peter by sharing testimonies about God's miracles and wonders done among Gentiles. James gives the final convincing words to settle the matter and bring peace to every heart, claiming Peter's words were correct because they aligned with Amos' prophecy that God would take the Gentiles for His name sake in Amos 9:11-12:

> *"In that day will I raise up the tabernacle of David that is fallen, and close up the breaches thereof; and I will raise up his ruins, and I will build it as in the days of old: That they may possess the remnant of Edom, and of all the heathen, which are called by my name, saith the LORD that doeth this."*

James' conclusion is not to trouble the Gentiles with forced circumcision but give them four guidelines for the time being in Acts 15:20:

- Abstain from pollutions of idols
- Abstain from fornication
- Abstain from things strangled
- Abstain from blood

Of course, in the years to come Jesus would reveal more truths for Gentiles to live by through Paul's epistles, who taught the Ephesians the whole counsel[407] of God within his three years with them. But here in Acts 15 the Jerusalem apostles and elders heartily receive James' sentence and send letters of this decision to all their churches, making the saints rejoice in their Christian freedoms.

A third example is again about circumcision but worthy of an individual mention, which is Paul's circumcision of Timothy. Some wander why Paul would refuse to let Titus be circumcised,[408] yet later Paul himself would perform Timothy's circumcision. The answer is each case had different conditions leading to different results.

Galatians 2:3-4 explains Titus, a pure Greek Gentile, was under pressure to come under the bondage of law-keeping from *"false brethren."* Paul vehemently opposed the false brothers, refusing to become a part of their heretical, legalistic movement.

Timothy's circumstances were much different because no one was pressuring him to be circumcised. He was half-Jew, half-Greek. His father didn't permit him to be circumcised as a baby, yet he was diligently trained in Judaism by his mother and grandmother. It appears Timothy

---

407   Acts 20:27
408   Galatians 2:3-5

voluntarily chose circumcision for three reasons: he wanted to honor his Judaic upbringing, he didn't want to offend the Jews he was associating with, and he believed his circumcision might cause non-believing Jews to listen to his gospel message. Acts 16:3 says, *"Him would Paul have to go forth with him; and took and circumcised him because of the Jews which were in those quarters: for they knew all that his father was a Greek."* As Paul's travel companion, Timothy was in constant contact with Jews and felt he could influence them if he had the token of Abraham's covenant in his flesh.

Timothy's selflessness in regards to his physical body in order to promote the spiritual body of Christians inspires believers to prayerfully seek any solution, within holiness, to overcome challenges to spreading the gospel of Jesus Christ. It seems Timothy followed Paul's example to go to any reasonable lengths to save souls:

> *"For though I be free from all men, yet have I made myself servant unto all, that I might gain the more. And unto the Jews I became as a Jew, that I might gain the Jews; to them that are under the law, as under the law, that I might gain them that are under the law; To the weak became I as weak, that I might gain the weak: I am made all things to all men, that I might by all means save some."*[409]

THE FEASTS AND HOLY DAYS OF ISRAEL

The Feasts of Israel are historical worship events mandated for Jews, but prophetically reveal God's redemptive plan for Jews and Gentiles. In particular, the fourth feast, the Feast of Weeks, reveals God's plan to unite Jews and Gentiles into one body, one church, and more time must be devoted to its essential details.

Kevin J. Connor's *The Feasts of Israel* provides an extensive teaching on the Feasts. Connor writes, "Ceremonies and all that pertains to the letter and ritual of the Law, are empty and vain apart from the reality in Christ."[410]

---

409   1 Corinthians 9:19-20,22
410   Connor, Kevin J. *The Feasts of Israel.* City Bible Publishing, 1980.

Under the Mosaic Covenant, God instituted three major feasts (two of which had two additional minor feast or holy days, for a total of seven feasting or holy days) in which Israeli males were to appear before Him with sacrifices:

> *"Three times in a year shall all thy males appear before the LORD thy God in the place which he shall choose; in the feast of unleavened bread, and in the feast of weeks, and in the feast of tabernacles: and they shall not appear before the LORD empty: Every man shall give as he is able, according to the blessing of the LORD thy God which he hath given thee."*

Leviticus 23 provides a chronological list of the feast and holy days along with imperative details Israel was to honor in both celebration and mourning, depending upon God's commands:

- Feast of Passover (23:4-5)
- Feast of Unleavened Bread (23:6-8)
- Feast of Sheaf of Firstfruits (23:9-14)
- Feast of Weeks (23:15-22)
- Feast of Trumpets (23:23-25)
- Holy Day of Atonement (23:26-32)
- Feast of Tabernacles (23:33-44)

God initiated these gatherings to meet with His people on His terms. The Holy One appointed the meeting place and sacrifices to be offered, giving His children annual meeting times to abstain from work in order to focus on their relationship with Him.

Each of the the seven feasts and holy days allows you to see God's historical and prophetic purposes for Israel and the Gentiles.

The Passover: Beginning on the fourteenth day of the first month of the new year at evening, each family in Israel sacrificed a one-year-old male lamb. They were to eat a meal—the lamb along with unleavened bread. Its historical purpose was to be a memorial of God delivering them from Egyptian slavery. Full details are found in Exodus 12:1-29, Leviticus 23:4-5, and Deuteronomy 16:1-8.

The Passover's prophetic purpose was fulfilled in Jesus' death on Calvary as He fulfilled every Old Testament detail to the letter. Truly, Messiah died for both Jews and Gentiles—the sins of the entire world. 1 John 2:2 says Jesus *"is the propitiation for our sins: and not for ours only, but also for the sins of the whole world."* Christ delivered all from the slavery of sin. Paul teaches in 1 Corinthians 5:7 believers experience a continual Passover and faithfully partake of the Lord's Supper[411] in remembrance of Him.

The Unleavened Bread: Beginning on the evening of Passover, this bread-feast lasted seven days, emphasizing a diet totally separate from leaven. It represented Israel partaking of no Egyptian influences, as leaven puffs up an entire lump of dough. Any Israeli with leaven found in his house was instantly cut off from the congregation. Once in the Promised Land, Jewish fathers were to explain this bread-feast to their children in memory of God's mighty hand to deliver Israel. All details are found in Exodus 12:8-39, 13:1-10, Leviticus 23:6-8, Numbers 28:17-25, and Deuteronomy 16:1-8.

Jesus Christ again fulfills the prophetic purpose of this Feast, for His death separated us from our sins, or leaven. His blood washed away all sins,[412] just as the Jewish houses were washed free from leaven. He is the true Bread of Life from heaven[413] all Christians feast on continually and exclusively. Christ manifested sinless perfection, being free from leaven, or sinful influences, unlike the Pharisees' leavened false doctrines in Matthew 16:11-12. Paul teaches we still keep this spiritual feast *"not with old leaven, neither with the leaven of malice and wickedness; but with the unleavened bread of sincerity and truth."*[414]

The Sheaf of Firstfruits: This was the final Feast of first month, observed on the day after the Sabbath (Sunday) following the Passover.

---

411   1 Corinthians 11:23-34
412   1 John 1:9, Revelation 1:15
413   John 6:48-50
414   1 Corinthians 5:8

A priest waved a sheaf of barley firstfruits before the Lord as a forerunner that the rest of the crop would later mature for harvest. Additionally, a lamb burnt offering was included along with a meal and drink offering. This Feast is taught in Exodus 23:19, Leviticus 23:9-14, and Numbers 28:26.

Prophetically, this Feast foreshadowed the greatest day in human history—the resurrection of Jesus Christ, which took place on a Sunday, the *"first day of the week."*[415] This Feast was fulfilled as God, not a priest, waved His resurrected Son before Israel as the *"firstborn from the dead"*[416] or *"first begotten from the dead."*[417] Jesus' resurrection demonstrates that all believers would also experience the resurrection at harvest time, or the end of the world. Romans 8:11 promises the same Holy Spirit that raised Christ from the dead shall also quicken our mortal bodies. Paul writes every man will be raised from the dead *"in his own order,"*[418] with Christ being the firstfruits. The wave sheaf and other offerings speak of Jesus' death and resurrection because they are inseparable. The burnt offering represents Jesus' sinless death through total obedience. The meal and drink offerings speak of believers' continual communion with Christ through the Lord's Supper.

THE FEAST OF WEEKS

Also known as Pentecost in the New Testament, the Feast of Weeks occurred in the third month, or fifty days after Firstfruits. The number 50 represents deliverance, liberty, or freedom for Israel, as every 50 years they celebrated the Jubilee year[419] in which slaves were released from bondage, and debts and all inheritances were restored to their original owners.

After Moses brought Israel out of Egypt following the Passover, they worshipped God and experienced the power and terror of His presence at Mount Sinai 50 days after the exodus while receiving the Ten

415   Matthew 28:1
416   Colossians 1:18
417   Revelation 1:5
418   1 Corinthians 15:20-23
419   Leviticus 25:8-17

Commandments. Once living in Canaan, Israel's Weeks Feast included numerous sacrifices. Two loaves of bread baked with leaven were waved before the Lord. Israel was commanded to bring the following freewill gifts: burnt, meat, drink, sin, and peace offerings. This Feast marked the beginning of the four-month-long harvest season in which Israel was to harvest most, but not all their crops, in order for the poor and stranger to have food. This Feast is detailed in Exodus 34:22-23, Leviticus 23:15-21, Numbers 28:26-31, and Deuteronomy 16:9-12.

Acts chapter 2 fulfilled the Feast of Weeks, also known as the Day of Pentecost. The 50th day after Firstfruits, Pentecost symbolized spiritual freedom and liberty for souls of men by the baptism of the Holy Ghost. Ten days prior to this pouring out of the Holy Ghost, Jesus promised His disciples He would send this spiritual baptism and commanded them to wait for it in Jerusalem:

> "And, being assembled together with them, commanded them that they should not depart from Jerusalem, but wait for the promise of the Father, which, saith he, ye have heard of me. For John truly baptized with water; but ye shall be baptized with the Holy Ghost not many days hence. But ye shall receive power, after that the Holy Ghost is come upon you: and ye shall be witnesses unto me both in Jerusalem, and in all Judaea, and in Samaria, and unto the uttermost part of the earth."[420]

Israel's reception of the Ten Commandments typed the pouring out of the Holy Ghost on the Day of Pentecost. In Figure 4, Connor beautifully compares and contrasts many, not all, of the aspects of the giving of Moses' Law to the giving of the Holy Ghost:

420   Acts 1:4-5,8

Old Testament Pentecost (Exodus 19, 20, 24)	New Testament Pentecost (Acts 2, 2 Corinthians 3)
Presence of God manifest in thunders, lightnings, thick clouds, fire, audible Voice	Presence of God manifest in rushing mighty wind, licks of fire, speaking in tongues
Occurred at Mount Sinai on 50th day	Occurred in Jerusalem, near Mount Zion on 50th day
Birthday of Judiasm through Old Covenant	Birthday of Christianity through New Covenant
Giving of the Law on tables of stone written by the finger of God	Giving of the Holy Ghost on fleshly tables of men's hearts written by the Spirit of God
3,000 souls died	3,000 souls added to the church
Ministration of death through the law of sin and death	Ministration of life through the law of the Holy Spirit
Glory on Moses' face	Glory of God in the face of Jesus Christ
Moses' face veiled so people could not see the glory	Believers have unveiled faces to be changed into the same glory
Glory to be done away with	Glory that remains

Figure 4

The most unique aspect of Weeks is the waving of two leaven-infused loaves of bread. Herein is the revelation of one church composed of both Jew and Gentile as these loaves are called "*a new meat offering unto the LORD.*"[421] Notice these two loaves are called one offering,

421   Leviticus 23:16

singular. The two loaves are one substance, just as the two peoples—Jew and Gentile—become one. Paul teaches this in 1 Corinthians 10:17: *"For we being many are one bread, and one body: for we are all partakers of that one bread."* Again, the apostle says, *"Having abolished in his flesh the enmity, even the law of commandments contained in ordinances; for to make in himself of twain one new man, so making peace."*[422]

When the priest waved two loaves in Israel, he foretold God waving both Spirit-filled Jews and Gentiles before the world. The first loaf waved was the 120 born again Jewish Christians on the Day of Pentecost. Soon afterwards, the Lord waved a second loaf, the Spirit-born Gentiles in Cornelius' house, before Peter and other witnesses.

The new aspect of this offering is the addition of leaven, which was forbidden in Passover and accompanied by the threat of excommunication. But in this third month of the year leaven is acceptable. Passover represented the sacrifice of the sinless Son of God, while Pentecost represents the ministry of the New Testament church and the sin-nature that remains inside their bodies. Holy Ghost-filled Jews and Gentiles still sin but do not let it have dominion[423] over their daily lives. Christians now present and give their lives as offerings unto God during this New Testament season.

Leaven is a common representation for evil and sin. Through the baptism of the Holy Ghost, Christians become *"new creatures"*[424] in Christ Jesus, just as the leavened wave loaves were new offerings. Spirit-filled Christians have both divinity (Christ's Spirit in their souls) and sin (in their flesh) dwelling inside them, as Paul explains in Colossians 1:27 and Romans 7:17 and 20, respectively. John goes as far as saying the believer's soul (the nature of the human spirit) anointed with the Holy Ghost, is the Christian's true identity and cannot sin: *"Whosoever is born of God doth not commit sin; for his seed remaineth in him: and he cannot sin, because he is born of God."*[425] Christ's new church would always have the

---

422 Ephesians 2:15
423 Romans 6:14
424 2 Corinthians 5:17, Galatians 615
425 1 John 3:9

element of sin to deal with, but she was given the Holy Spirit to bring unity to other Christians while overcoming sin's effects.

C.I. Scofield[426] describes the unique meaning of the two loaves contrasted to the one wave sheaf at Firstfruits: "Observe, it is now loaves; not a sheaf of separate growths loosely bound together, but a real union of particles making one homogenous body. The descent of the Holy Spirit at Pentecost united the separated disciples into one organism." At Pentecost, God united the souls of the Christians through the indwelling power of the Holy Ghost, causing them to have *"one heart and...one soul."*[427] This same unity spread to the Gentiles at Cornelius' house and then multiplied into many millions more Gentiles.

Leviticus 23:15-21 speaks of five additional sacrifices of this Feast that compliment the two wave loaves: burnt, meat, drink, sin, and peace offerings. Just as a burnt offering was totally consumed in devotion to God, Christians give themselves wholly[428] to God's work. Meat and drink offerings symbolize the bread and wine believers consume in the New Testament Lord's Supper. The sin offering represents our constant need for Jesus' forgiveness of our sins through His heavenly role as High Priest-Mediator.[429] The Hebrew definition for peace offerings teaches these oblations stood for voluntary expressions of thanksgiving[430] to God which Christians faithfully offer through vocal praises: *"By him therefore let us offer the sacrifice of praise to God continually, that is, the fruit of our lips giving thanks to his name."*[431]

Another aspect of the Weeks feast fulfilled in Acts 2 is the holy, euphoric worship by the 120 Holy Ghost-filled saints. Recall the 120 were so filled with God's Spirit they left the upper room around 9 A.M. and headed to Jerusalem's streets to boldly declare the *"wonderful works of God."* The onlookers from 17 nations were so amazed by the worship

426 "Leviticus 23." *Bible Study Tools*, https://www.biblestudytools.com/commentaries/scofield-reference-notes/leviticus/leviticus-23.html
427 Acts 4:32
428 1 Timothy 4:15
429 Hebrews 2:17-3:1, 1 John 1:7-2:1
430 "The Bible: Hebrew and Greek Lexicons." *Voice of God Recordings*, www.branham.org/en/messagesearch
431 Hebrews 13:15

they saw and heard[432] that they concluded they were drunk with wine. Acts 2 is clearly the fulfillment of Deuteronomy 16:10-12, which teaches Israel was to rejoice with many people before the LORD in remembrance of God granting them freedom from Egypt. Romans 14:17 validates this:

> "The kingdom of God is not meat and drink; but righteousness, and peace, and joy in the Holy Ghost."

Scripture says two different harvests took place in the first and third months: barley started in the first month at Firstfruits and continued through the second, while wheat harvest began in the third month at Weeks and lasted until the seventh month. Exodus 34:22 says Weeks was *"the firstfruits of wheat harvest"*, while Ruth 2:23 differentiates the two feasts: *"So she kept fast by the maidens of Boaz to glean unto the end of barley harvest and of wheat harvest; and dwelt with her mother in law."* Both Feasts had firstfruits waved in anticipation for the rest of the crop to mature, fulfilled by Jesus' resurrection and the 120 being filled with the Holy Ghost 50 days later.

The Feast of Pentecost initiated a four month long period of wheat harvest until the next Feast, Trumpets, began in the seventh month. The Week's four month period signifies the long, nearly-2,000-year period (30 A.D. to present) in which God would offer the New Covenant to both Jew and Gentile until the Times of the Gentiles were fulfilled. This left lots of time to labor and harvest before the next phase of life.

THE FORMER AND LATTER RAINS BEFORE THE FINAL HARVEST

Reaping the wheat harvest was the main task of the Feast of Pentecost, just as Jesus' Great Commission[433] emphasizes saving souls in the field of the world's nations. But no harvest is possible without both former and latter rains.

---

432   Acts 2:13, 33
433   Matthew 24:14, 28:19-20, Mark 16:15

Rain has a symbolism in both the Old and New Testaments. On the Day of Pentecost, Peter declares the falling of the Holy Spirit fulfilled Joel's prophecy of God pouring out His Spirit in Joel 2:28. Hosea 6:1-3 is another evidence that God symbolizes His Spirit coming upon the people as rain: "*His going forth is prepared as the morning; and he shall come unto us as the rain, as the latter and former rain unto the earth.*"

Now look at the truth of two rains necessary for harvest: former and latter. The purpose of the former rains were to water the seeds at the beginning of the autumnal growing season while the latter rains were the last rains necessary to bring the seed to maturity in the spring. Israel had a sacred year and civil year. The sacred year was from March/April to September/October. The civil year was from October/November to February/March.

The former rains fall around October or November and the latter rains fall in the first month of the sacred year, around March or April. Logically, the latter rain had to fall in or shortly before the first month just in time for Israel to harvest the barley firstfruits to be waved by the priest on the Feast of Firstfruits.

The former and latter rain truth must be applied prophetically to the Times of the Gentiles, or from 30 A.D. to the present. Christians today are in the spiritual Feast of Weeks, the long season of harvest before God returns to the Jews in the Feast of Trumpets.

Peter was clear that God was going to pour or rain His Spirit upon "*all flesh*"[434] which has been verified through the Gentiles receiving the Holy Ghost in the Book of Acts and all throughout 2,000 years of church history. Holy Ghost-rain showers have fallen upon every age and its leaders, from John the Divine to Irenaeus, from Columba to Luther, from Wesley to Wigglesworth.

But Jesus and other prophets foretold end-time conditions in the Times of the Gentiles before the final harvest would ultimately mirror a spiritual famine due to disobedience. Christ asked, "*Nevertheless when the Son of man cometh, shall he find faith on the earth?*" Paul calls it a "*falling*

434   Acts 2:17

away" or apostasy from truth caused by an influx of seducing teachers who grow increasingly more deceptive.[435] Then Amos 8:11-12 reads:

> *"Behold, the days come, saith the Lord GOD, that I will send a famine in the land, not a famine of bread, nor a thirst for water, but of hearing the words of the LORD: And they shall wander from sea to sea, and from the north even to the east, they shall run to and fro to seek the word of the LORD, and shall not find it."*

Jesus describes the final wheat harvest in Matthew 13:24-30 and 36-43. Christians are indeed labeled *"wheat"*—matching the wheat harvest of Israel's natural Feast of Weeks—and are gathered into Christ's barn. But the apostate tares are burned in fire.

Since Jesus' final harvest is required before the wrath and judgment of the Great Tribulation, former and latter rains are necessary to bring the wheat to maturity. James 5:7-8 support these prophesies, giving us a promise of one more former and latter rain before the last Gentile harvest:

> *"Be patient therefore, brethren, unto the coming of the Lord. Behold, the husbandman waiteth for the precious fruit of the earth, and hath long patience for it, until he receive the early and latter rain. Be ye also patient; stablish your hearts: for the coming of the Lord draweth nigh."*

The Holy Spirit's inspiration helps us find more details about the Gentile latter rain prophecy in Joel 2:23-26. It's a fitting location because the beginning of the New Covenant is also located in this chapter—Joel 2:28-32. Verses 23-26 describe what the former and latter rain Holy Ghost-anointings will produce in Christians' lives:

> *"Be glad then, ye children of Zion, and rejoice in the LORD your God: for he hath given you the former rain moderately, and he will cause to come down for you the rain, the former rain, and the latter rain in the first month. And the floors shall*

be full of wheat, and the fats shall overflow with wine and oil. And I will restore to you the years that the locust hath eaten, the cankerworm, and the caterpiller, and the palmerworm, my great army which I sent among you. And ye shall eat in plenty, and be satisfied, and praise the name of the LORD your God, that hath dealt wondrously with you: and my people shall never be ashamed."

The Hebrew word for *"former"* can mean "teacher," meaning Christians should expect a great teaching anointing to come in preparation for the rapture harvest. Chapter 13 explains this teaching ministry.

After the former rain, God plans to send a latter-rain anointing, or rapturing faith, as His church recognizes the conditions, times, and seasons of the rapture. She will begin seeking God for the latter rain through prayer as Zechariah 10:1 says: *"Ask ye of the LORD rain in the time of the latter rain; so the LORD shall make bright clouds, and give them showers of rain, to every one grass in the field."*

Jesus will then send His Spirit in the same measure as the Day of Pentecost, producing the same results. This divine, latter rain will restore back to the final church everything the early church possessed—wheat (Word), wine (joy) and oil (baptism of the Holy Ghost). Before the rapture harvest, Christ's church will have the same power, truth, miracles, and faith of the apostolic saints. Jesus promises to bring the last church right back to where she started at Pentecost in Acts 2. Joel 2:23 says the latter rain is sent in the *"first month"* and in Hebrew this phrase can mean "formerly, at first." Shortly before the rapture, the latter rain falls on the Gentile church as it did formerly, at first, on the Day of Pentecost.

THE FEASTS OF THE SEVENTH MONTH

Following the four month-long Feast of Weeks came two holy days and one feast in the seventh month, or September/October time period: Trumpets, Atonement, and Tabernacles. These final holy and feast days have nothing to do with the New Testament church, for she is already in heaven enjoying the Marriage Supper of the Lamb. Based upon 1 Thessalonians 4:17, the church was *"caught up"* or snatched off the earth by Jesus in the rapture-harvest before the Tribulation. Then God grafts Israel back into His blessings and immediate focus of ministry.

The Trumpets: On the first day of the seventh month Israel held a sabbath to blow trumpets and offer burnt, meat, and sin offerings made by fire unto the LORD. This day is called a *"holy convocation,"* or sacred gathering, or assembly. Trumpets were blown for many purposes but here they were to gather[436] Israel for the Day of Atonement, or national cleansing, nine days later. Trumpets was not a rejoicing time like Weeks, but rather a call to self examination. Israel knew Trumpets meant preparing them to appear for Atonement in mourning, for the tenth day was a day to afflict their souls, meaning humiliation and being downcast. Trumpets is taught in Leviticus 23:23-25 and Numbers 29:1-6.

Prophetically, the Feast of Trumpets represents the prophetic ministry of the two witnesses of Revelation 11:1-13 during the first 3.5 years of Daniel's 70th or final week. Prophets' voices are likened unto trumpets in Ezekiel 33:1-9, Isaiah 58:1, and Hosea 8:1. With the help of two prophets' supernatural ministry, the guileless 144,000 faithful Jews will be gathered in Jerusalem. Hearing the two prophets preach about Jesus Christ prepares them to receive Him at Atonement. As always, faith comes by hearing.

In the meantime, Israel is worshipping God in their newly rebuilt Temple. Three times Daniel foretells Israel offering animal sacrifices,[437] as they are currently forbidden to offer them due to their lack of a temple. Animal sacrifices will again be allowed as part of Israel's seven year covenant with the Pope-Antichrist, but he will cut them off in the midst of the week in order to enshrine his own abomination that works desolation.

The Day of Atonement: On the 10th day of the seventh month was Israel's national cleansing—the most holy day of the year. Jews came to the Temple fasting and mourning in complete humiliation of body and spirit before God Almighty in a day to *"afflict"*[438] their souls. Along with all routine sacrifices, two goats were offered to God for atonement—one

---

436   Numbers 10:4, Judges 6:34, Isaiah 27:13, Jeremiah 4:5
437   Daniel 9:27, 11:31, 12:11
438   Leviticus 16:29

died on the altar and the other carried Israel's sins far away into the wilderness. Connor describes more aspects of this Atonement Day, saying:

> "On this day only, which took place but once a year, the High Priest entered into the Holiest of All, within the veil, with the blood of the Lord's goat, the sin offering. Here he sprinkled the blood on the mercy seat. The blood of the sin offering on the great Day of Atonement brought about the cleansing of all sin, all iniquity, and all transgression. The priesthood, the sanctuary, and Israel as a nation experienced blood atonement, thus being reconciled to God."[439]

Atonement is taught in Leviticus 16:1-34, 23:26-32, and Numbers 29:7-11.

Prophetically, Atonement is fulfilled after the 3.5 year ministry of the two witnesses when Israel meets their Messiah, Jesus Christ, face to face. Israel will *acknowledge* their Atonement since she rejected the actual atonement 2,000 years prior—Jesus' death on the cross and heavenly acceptance.

Having seen their two prophets raptured to heaven, the 144,000 Jews glorify God as the realization of Jesus as their Messiah solidifies. Then the holy King of kings, and Lord of lords, Jesus Christ, physically appears to the faithful Jewish remnant. Seeing Jesus' scars, one brave Jew will ask, "*What are these wounds in thine hands?*"[440] Jesus sweetly answers, "*Those with which I was wounded in the house of my friends.*"

Instantly, the guilt and shame of their ancestors overtakes them. They're now aware how Israel willingly crucified God's Son, the "*root of Jesse,*" David's "*righteous Branch,*" the Seed of the Woman. This causes Israel to desperately mourn as never before. Despite their fatal move, the Crucified One now calls the Jews His "friends." Amazing grace overwhelms the remnant. Zechariah 12:10-14 captures their bitter humiliation:

439   Connor
440   Zechariah 13:6

156

"And I will pour upon the house of David, and upon the inhabitants of Jerusalem, the spirit of grace and of supplications: and they shall look upon me whom they have pierced, and they shall mourn for him, as one mourneth for his only son, and shall be in bitterness for him, as one that is in bitterness for his firstborn. In that day shall there be a great mourning in Jerusalem, as the mourning of Hadadrimmon in the valley of Megiddon. And the land shall mourn, every family apart; the family of the house of David apart, and their wives apart; the family of the house of Nathan apart, and their wives apart; The family of the house of Levi apart, and their wives apart; the family of Shimei apart, and their wives apart; All the families that remain, every family apart, and their wives apart."

Israel's souls are afflicted, and rightly so, but then God opens a fountain of forgiveness.

Zechariah 13:1 states, *"In that day there shall be a fountain opened to the house of David and to the inhabitants of Jerusalem for sin and for uncleanness."* Being forgiven and blameless, the 144,000 can be born again by the baptism of the Holy Ghost, also called the *"seal of God in their foreheads."*[441]

Isaiah 66:8 prophesied of Israel's incredible spiritual birthday, claiming it would happen in one day, saying, *"Who hath heard such a thing? who hath seen such things? Shall the earth be made to bring forth in one day? or shall a nation be born at once? for as soon as Zion travailed, she brought forth her children."*

With the 144,000 born again, three of Gabriel's six tasks listed in Daniel 9:24 are now complete: finish the transgression, make an end of sins, and make reconciliation for iniquity. Israel has finally been reconciled back to God. She's finally received the New Covenant!

Returning to the current New Testament believer, we experience our spiritual Day of Atonement when we're born again by the baptism of the Holy Ghost. One requirement of being born again is repentance according to Acts 2:38: *"Repent, and be baptized every one of you in the*

441   Revelation 7:3, 9:4

name of Jesus Christ for the remission of sins, and ye shall receive the gift of the Holy Ghost." In the Greek Lexicon, "repent" means an "abhorrence of one's past sins." This abhorrence matches the afflicted-soul requirement of the Old Testament Day of Atonement. After genuine repentance, the believer obeys God's Word and is soon born again by the Holy Ghost. Acts 5:32 reads, "And we are his witnesses of these things; and so is also the Holy Ghost, whom God hath given to them that obey him."

For this cause, the church did not need to go through the Tribulation Period as blinded Israel did. Her sins were already atoned for by the precious blood of Jesus Christ. Romans 5:11 declares, "And not only so, but we also joy in God through our Lord Jesus Christ, by whom we have now received the atonement."

The true, spiritual Day of Atonement took place on the morning of Christ's resurrection. Showing Himself to Mary Magdalene first, Jesus said, "Touch me not; for I am not yet ascended to my Father."[442] Christ forbid contact to fulfill other Scriptures. Through His death, He was not only the two goats, but also the spiritual red heifer of Numbers 19. Any priest or Jew who touched the sacrificed heifer or its ashes was instantly unclean. Jesus knew He should not be touched yet until He presented His blood to the Father. After talking with Mary, Jesus ascended to His Father in heaven to present His acceptable sacrifice and obtain our redemption according to Hebrews 9:11-12:

> "But Christ being come an high priest of good things to come,
> by a greater and more perfect tabernacle, not made with hands,
> that is to say, not of this building; Neither by the blood of goats
> and calves, but by his own blood he entered in once into the holy
> place, having obtained eternal redemption for us."

Once received in heaven and possessing our redemption, Christ descended back to earth on Resurrection Sunday and showed Himself alive to the disciples. No doubt He was embraced by His beloved disciples. One week later, He fulfilled Thomas' desire to touch His scars.

---

442   John 20:17

Jesus said, "*Reach hither thy finger, and behold my hands; and reach hither thy hand, and thrust it into my side: and be not faithless, but believing.*"[443] The sacrificial work is done. Jesus, with a new glorified body, can now be touched.

The Book of Hebrews unveils Jesus' complete redemptive work as God's one and only Atonement for sins. Christ's shed blood fulfilled every oblation and sacrifice, cleansed the heavenly sanctuary, and allowed Him to be both Mediator and High Priest between God and man.

Jesus can rapture His church off the earth before the Tribulation because she's already cleansed by the Atonement. She, having "*no condemnation*" through believing and receiving the baptism of the Holy Ghost, has already passed from death unto life.[444] Her soul is sealed unto the day of redemption.

The Tabernacles: Following the solemn Day of Atonement, came the celebratory Tabernacles, which occurred after the final harvest of the year—fruit. Tabernacles began on the 15th day of the seventh month and lasted eight days.

During the first seven days Israelis would rejoice while dwelling in temporary booths made from tree branches in remembrance of God making Israel dwell in booths after their exodus from Egypt. Each day involved its own burnt, meat, and drink offerings besides the routine, daily sacrifices unto God. The eighth day was a sabbath and included a final offering made by fire as a solemn assembly and holy convocation. This Feast is taught in Leviticus 23:33-44.

Prophetically, Israel's Tabernacles foretold Christ's 1,000 year Millennial reign, detailed in Isaiah 65:19-22 and Revelation 20:1-6. The Son's peaceful reign after the Tribulation and Battle of Armageddon fulfills the true meaning of this Feast.

This Feast follows the final fruit harvest which has its fulfillment in Revelation chapter 14. Verses 13-16 show the Son of Man reaping the harvest of the earth, which is the 144,000 being sealed by the Holy Ghost

---

443   John 20:27
444   John 5:24, Romans 8:1

in verses 1-5. They are called *"firstfruits unto God and to the Lamb"* in verse 4. Later in the chapter, verses 17-20 teach the gathering of the vine and its destruction through the wrath of God. All sinners who took the mark of the beast experience this awful judgment before the Millennium.

With all the harvests complete, you see the barley harvest of Firstfruits fulfilled by Christ's resurrection with the Old Testament saints. The wheat harvest of Weeks represented the one church composed of Jew and Gentile. Lastly, the fruit harvest before Tabernacles represented the Spirit-sealed 144,000 Jewish remnant.

Back to Tabernacles—the seven days of rejoicing represents God getting His seventh day with His creation. Recall from Genesis chapters 1 and 2 that God had six days, or 6,000 years of peace during His week of creation. 2 Peter 3:8 explains a day with God equals a thousand years of man's time: *"But, beloved, be not ignorant of this one thing, that one day is with the Lord as a thousand years, and a thousand years as one day."* But Satan interrupted God's seventh day of rest when he possessed the serpent and beguiled Eve into eating the fruit, who shared it with Adam, plunging mankind into sin bondage. Edenic conditions will be restored and God will have His sin-free rest day.

Living in temporary booths will be fulfilled as Christ's Spirit-filled followers build their own homes, harvest crops, and reign over cities and nations with Him. Isaiah 65:21-22 read:

> *"And they shall build houses, and inhabit them; and they shall plant vineyards, and eat the fruit of them. They shall not build, and another inhabit; they shall not plant, and another eat: for as the days of a tree are the days of my people, and mine elect shall long enjoy the work of their hands."*

Yes, the one Jew-Gentile church will rejoice for 1,000 years as Satan is bound and cast into the bottomless pit. With no tempter, the church experiences complete joy, fruitfulness, peace, and victory.

The eighth day holy convocation symbolized the beginning of the Eternal Covenant. Eight is God's number of a new beginning. Here the eighth day is the first day repeating, which speaks of the unending cycles of eternity. Time is over. The New Jerusalem, our eternal home, has come down to earth out of heaven. No more temporary booths, or homes. Christ's family has made it to her eternal home. Everything done on earth will be done as it were in heaven, since heaven has come down to earth.

THE MULTINATIONAL GREAT MULTITUDE

Revelation 7:9-17 gives you a glimpse of Christ's multinational New Testament church gathered before God's throne, calling her *"a great multitude, which no man could number, of all nations, and kindreds, and people, and tongues."* Christ's Word sent via the Great Commission did not return void. Every nation under heaven had the opportunity to repent and those who received it have eternal life and loudly worship their Savior with cries and palm-waving.

This great praise likely takes place in the New Jerusalem, as Jesus leads His people to living fountains of waters, the sun is not needed, and He wipes away all tears from their eyes, matching the future home description in Revelation 21:4 and 22:1-5.

Every skin and hair color imaginable is beautifully represented in this eternal gathering. This great, white-robed multitude is like a bride's expensive, radiant flower bouquet kept and preserved for decoration in the couple's first home. Jesus' one, Jew-Gentile church is a timeless, incorruptible bouquet-bride.

The multitude's journey to God's throne wasn't easy. The angel tells John they suffered through *"great tribulation,"* yet washed their robes white in the blood of the Lamb. Paul declares

> *"all that will live godly in Christ Jesus shall suffer persecution."*[445]
> All godly saints suffer some form of persecution but it's allowed
> so we'll know Christ in the fellowship of His sufferings.[446]

---

445   2 Timothy 3:12
446   Philippians 3:10

Since it's a church from all nations, Israel must be included. This shows not all Jews are blinded to Christ as their Messiah. Most are blinded, but not all. God's immutable purpose to have a church from every nation is accomplished. Believers from every nation are represented because *"God so loved the world."*

WESTERNERS UNDERSTANDING EASTERNERS CONVERTING TO CHRIST

The bulk of this chapter deals with Gentiles coming into relationship with the God of the Jews, a major issue in the first century. Today, though, Westerners must recognize and understand how the gospel is returning back to Easterners and God allows liberties and diversities of worship within our holy calling.

A brief look at the last 500 years of history allows you to trace God's revivals moving from east to west, and now back to the east. Germany experienced revival with Martin Luther in the 16th century. Two hundred years later, God moved mightily in England through John Wesley's ministry. The Azusa Street Revival manifested in California, USA, 100 years after Wesley. But the revival has left America because she left God's Word. America's laws no longer honor God, as she's legalized the killing of nearly 50 million babies along with the protection of homosexual marriage.

Indeed, God is currently stirring revival fires in the Middle East and China. Voice of the Martyrs Canada reports Middle Easterners are coming to Christ by "thousands upon thousands."[447] The Council on Foreign Relations says China's Christian revival is so great it may "have the world's largest population of Christians by 2030."[448] You've probably realized God's revival will end up back in the east where it started, in Jerusalem, when the 144,000 Israelis are sealed with the Holy Ghost during the Tribulation.

---

447   "Thousands of Muslims Reportedly Turning to Christ in Middle East." *Fox News*, https://www.foxnews.com/world/thousands-of-muslims-reportedly-turning-to-christ-in-middle-east

448   "Christianity in China." *Council on Foreign Relations*, https://www.cfr.org/backgrounder/christianity-china

These facts demonstrate your Scriptural knowledge of God's desire to have one Jew-Gentile church. No nation, tyrant, military, or leader can stop God's predestined plan to save souls in every nation. Chinese, Muslims, Hindus, and more are all coming into the open *"door of faith unto the Gentiles."*[449] Jesus assures us He is the Door and saves all who come through Him in John 10:9: *"I am the door: by me if any man enter in, he shall be saved, and shall go in and out, and find pasture."* It's necessary and natural for Western-born Christians to rejoice in God's mighty move in the east and pray for every lost soul to find salvation in Christ.

Concerning Christian liberties, God allows believers to express their faith in different ways within His holy plan. Four examples include foods, observance of holy days, wine, and jewelry.[450] A full teaching addresses these topics in my book, *Restoring Christian Modesty: God's Perfect Will For Your Outward Appearance.*

Eastern Christians may make different choices than Westerners in food, holy days, wine usage, and jewelry. Should we hear of Eastern Christians worshipping in ways different than our own, let us not be quick to judge. Instead, let us be quick to express patience with our Eastern brothers and sisters, and even reach out in love and seek to understand why they choose certain actions. Just as Paul wrote, we must respect others' convictions and be thankful they are trying their best to worship Jesus Christ. You can be confident that the God Who started the work of salvation in their lives will complete it.[451] If they are sensitive to the Holy Spirit, He will guide them into all truth.[452]

Specifically, Messianic Jews may worship in ways unfamiliar to us. They may keep the natural Feasts and Holy Days of Israel, Nazarite Vows, and other Old Testament commands while believing in Jesus Christ. Remember Paul took his liberties as a Jewish-Christian, keeping Jewish Feasts in Israel when possible and keeping vows to God.[453] These actions were no longer required under the New Covenant, but Paul knew he had

449   Acts 14:27
450   Romans 14:1-23, 1 Corinthians 8:1-13, 10:14-33
451   Philippines 1:6
452   John 16:13
453   Acts 18:18-21

liberty to express his faith through his personal convictions. Paul knew Jesus—the God Who gave him the bulk of the New Testament—was also the God of the Old Testament. As Jews, Chinese, Muslims, and Hindus all come to Christ by the thousands, let us rejoice in their salvation and respect their liberties.

Westerners need humility, including myself. Let's humbly acknowledge our extreme ignorance of Jewish and other Eastern traditions. Many gospel stories cannot be understood without valuable details from Jewish culture. May Westerners become meek and learn from the Meek One,[454] Christ Jesus, valuing God's vast, beautiful diversity.

THE REWARDS FOR RECEIVING THE REVELATION OF THE ONE CHURCH OF JEW AND GENTILE

Those who receive the revelation of one church composed of Jews and Gentiles gain the rewards of fellowship and promises.

Paul says all men can see the *"fellowship of the mystery,"* or partnership of the mystery. All Christians will benefit from godly partnership. No matter our race, culture, or skin color, Holy Ghost-filled Christians must partner together in strengthening each other. This may manifest in praying for one another and helping meet each other's physical needs as the Philippians met Paul's needs.[455]

Another form of partnership is having preachers cooperate in spreading the gospel. They must work together holding joint meetings in a city rather than competing against each other. The body of Jesus Christ edifies, or builds up itself in love[456]—not jealousy and competition. Leaders may agree to go separate directions in their ministries, yet fully support one another. Pastors and ministers must lead the way in this partnership, just as Paul and Peter modeled. Galatians 2:9-10 reads,

> *"And when James, Cephas, and John, who seemed to be pillars, perceived the grace that was given unto me, they gave to me and*

---

454 Matthew 11:29
455 Philippians 4:14-19
456 Ephesians 4:16

Barnabas the right hands of fellowship; that we should go unto the heathen, and they unto the circumcision. Only they would that we should remember the poor; the same which I also was forward to do."

A second reward is benefiting from God's promises, as Paul says all Spirit-filled Jews and Gentiles are *"fellowheirs, and of the same body, and partakers of his promise in Christ by the gospel."*[457] All Christians are privileged with the same promises of eternal rewards as well as the earthly benefits of salvation, divine healing, gifts and fruits of the Spirit, and more. God's promises give us *"boldness and access with confidence"*[458] to heaven's only High Priest, Jesus Christ. Certainly, the faithful prayers of both Jews and Gentiles can touch the heart of the invisible God through His Son, Who feels our pains and ever lives to make intercession for us.[459]

THE CONSEQUENCES FOR REJECTING THE REVELATION OF THE ONE CHURCH OF JEW AND GENTILE

There are three possible consequences for rejecting the revelation of the one church composed of Jew and Gentile. The sins can be labeled as prideful discrimination, cursing the blessed, and complacency.

Peter pridefully discriminated against Gentiles by refusing to eat with them due to peer pressure from other Jews who felt Gentiles were still unclean. Paul said Peter was *"to be blamed,"*[460] which in the Greek Lexicon means "find fault with, condemn." Peter's sin had brought temporary fault and condemnation upon him, and led by the Spirit, Paul called it out and corrected him. Christians today may fall under the same prideful, self righteous spirit, thinking they are more holy than other ethnic groups, thus separating themselves. Jude 1:19 warns that those who permanently separate themselves show they are carnal and sensual, likely

457 Ephesians 3:6
458 Ephesians 3:12
459 Hebrews 4:15, 7:25
460 Galatians 2:11

not having the baptism of the Holy Spirit. Let us physically gather more with saints as we see Christ's second coming swiftly approaching.

Cursing the blessed is a second consequence to rejecting the one church revelation. Just as taught in Chapter 2, some Gentiles may think Israel is forever-cursed and then condemn all Jews in their angry hearts for crucifying their own Messiah. When a person curses others in error, it reveals their own corrupt spiritual condition. According to 2 Timothy 2:26, these corrupted ones are caught in the *"snare of the devil"* and need deliverance through repentance.

Paul teaches complacency or lukewarmness is a major consequence of knowing God has opened the door of faith to the Gentiles but not taking advantage of the opportunity. Romans 11:18-22 explains how Gentiles are temped to *"boast...against the branches"* or Jews. But Gentiles must keep the fear of the Lord. Since God's goodness has extended to us, the Gentiles, we must continue in His goodness or else be cut off from God's blessings due to complacency. The apostle John in Revelation 3:14-19 identifies this same spirit of lukewarmness falling upon Gentile churches in the last days in his letter to the Laodiceans. Christians must constantly keep the spirit of revival in their lives, hungering and thirsting for more of Christ's righteousness. A Holy Ghost-filled Christian daily acknowledges his need to fully depend upon the Spirit's leading and strength. You desire to increase your obedience, *"perfecting holiness in the fear of God."*[461] You can't stay the same or grow complacent! You must and will overcome the inward sin nature violently battling against your mind. Jesus died and rose again to give you this victory.

461   2 Corinthians 7:1

CONCLUSION

God's loving heart desires unity, harmony, and partnership between Christians of all nations, kindreds, and tongues. He sent His Holy Spirit into believers' hearts to accomplish this divine oneness. The true, born-again church of Jesus Christ has always been and always will be one people by the Holy Ghost.

Jews and Gentiles are truly united in one body, as one bread, with a real merging of particles, united by the Fire of the Holy Spirt. The one church fulfills Jesus' prayer for perfect unity in John 17:23: *"I in them, and thou in me, that they may be made perfect in one; and that the world may know that thou hast sent me, and hast loved them, as thou hast loved me."*

ACTION STEPS TO JOINING AND BLESSING THE ONE CHURCH OF JEW AND GENTILE

1. Repent and seek the baptism of the Holy Ghost, for this is the Fire of God that will make your soul one with every born again Jew and Gentile on the earth. Being born again is the only way to join the one church.

2. Frequent prayer should be made for believers around the world, especially those facing persecution. Do not neglect your own spiritual body. Hebrews 13:3 tells you to *"Remember them that are in bonds, as bound with them; and them which suffer adversity, as being yourselves also in the body."*

3. Put your faith into action by financially supporting the body of Christ. Give to poor Christians in your area and be generous to missionaries who will take the gospel to future members of the one church worldwide.

FOLLOW UP

Free online videos, Bible studies, and William Branham's quotes related to this chapter: www.pastorjessesmith.com/12mysteriesbook

Email: jesse.smith11@sbcglobal.net

Text: 330-929-2037

CHAPTER 4

The Mystery of The New Testament Church as the Bride of Christ

"This is a great mystery:
but I speak concerning Christ and the church."

Ephesians 5:32

EQUIPPED WITH THE KNOWLEDGE that both Jew and Gentile compose the New Testament church, you will see the necessity for the next revelation of the one church as the bride of Jesus Christ. Here you grasp God's ordained position for His people as a "she," a feminine counterpart to His masculine role. With the knowledge of our position comes the revelation of our responsibilities, ministries, and destiny.

Recall the Introduction Chapter's section on "God's Hide and Seek Romance Drama". Your infinite, loving Lord has chosen you for His mate. He has preplanned your life's events so that you could come to love Him, accept His gift of salvation, and willingly seek His leadership all the days of your life. God loves romantic suspense and its fulfillment, graciously setting believers as the apple of His eternal eye.[462] Perhaps no simpler or significant words can be found to describe such unending love as Paul says in Ephesians 2:4: *"But God, who is rich in mercy, for his great love wherewith he loved us."* Jesus daily pursues you with great love.

THE CONFUSION ABOUT THE CHURCH AS THE BRIDE OF CHRIST

The confusion about the New Testament church as Jesus' bride centers on who she is. Which group of Christians is the true church? The evidence is not in what the groups say, but in the way they live. The group's size, name, or historical accomplishments are not the determining factor in identifying it as Christ's bride. The character of the people is the determining factor.

Rightly so, it has been said that the beauty of a church is the character of its people. A church's character is judged by how obedient the members are to Jesus' commands. Indeed, the groups that follow Paul's apostolic pattern and teachings make up the one true bride.

The revelation of the mystery of the church as the bride of Christ is the true church submits to all of Jesus' commands now with the promises of being raptured, and ruling and reigning with her Husband in the Millennium.

This chapter shows Christ as the Husband and the church as the wife, along with the attributes that define the true church. She is set apart as a bride to Christ, identified by her complete submission to the apostolic blue print given to Paul by Christ. The fruits of all major Christian groups will be examined by the Bible blue print, and identified as either the bride or not.

462   Psalm 17:8

You must test every group by its actions. Jesus says, *"Wherefore by their fruits ye shall know them,"*[463] and every *"tree is known by his fruit."*[464] Every tree, or church group, is known by its fruit. You do not have to wonder if you're in the true church. With Christ's applied eye salve, you can see plainly. With Jesus' Spirit of discernment, you can *"prove all things"* and *"hold fast that which is good."*[465] If you possess God's Spirit inside you, you won't believe every church. Instead you will *"try the spirits whether they are of God."*[466] Remember, Jesus promises His Spirit will guide you into all truth, as John 16:13 declares: *"Howbeit when he, the Spirit of truth, is come, he will guide you into all truth: for he shall not speak of himself; but whatsoever he shall hear, that shall he speak: and he will shew you things to come."*

BIBLICAL EVIDENCE FOR THE REVELATION ABOUT THE CHURCH AS THE BRIDE OF CHRIST

Scripture declares Jesus Christ to be the Husband or Bridegroom. In fact, Christ Himself says He is the Bridegroom in Mark 2:19-20:

> *"And Jesus said unto them, Can the children of the bridechamber fast, while the bridegroom is with them? as long as they have the bridegroom with them, they cannot fast. But the days will come, when the bridegroom shall be taken away from them, and then shall they fast in those days."*

Jesus also identifies Himself as the Bridegroom in three of His parables (See Chapter 8). The first is The King's Son from Matthew 22:1-14. Jesus places Himself as the espoused Son Who awaits believers who will accept the Father's invitation to His wedding and wear the appropriate wedding garments. In the second parable, The Ten Virgins, found in Matthew 25:1-13, Jesus is likened to the Bridegroom Whose imminent coming catches five wise virgins fully prepared with oil and five foolish

---

463   Matthew 7:20
464   Matthew 12:33
465   1 Thessalonians 5:21
466   1 John 4:1

virgins unprepared. The foolish miss His wedding due to their neglect. Thirdly, the parable of The Great Supper in Luke 14:15-24 portrays Christ as the host of a great supper, which speaks of the *"marriage supper of the Lamb"* from Revelation 19:9. Messiah again connects Himself with an upcoming marriage and His position as Bridegroom.

Jesus' forerunner, John the Baptist, labels Jesus as a Husband. John emphatically says Jesus has a bride, providing you with definitive proof that the one, Jew-Gentile church is to carry the "bride" title. Then John says Jesus is the Christ and His origin was in heaven in John 3:28-31:

> *"Ye yourselves bear me witness, that I said, I am not the Christ, but that I am sent before him. He that hath the bride is the bridegroom: but the friend of the bridegroom, which standeth and heareth him, rejoiceth greatly because of the bridegroom's voice: this my joy therefore is fulfilled. He must increase, but I must decrease. He that cometh from above is above all: he that is of the earth is earthly, and speaketh of the earth: he that cometh from heaven is above all."*

Yes, it is logical that Christ the Husband must have a wife, and the New Testament church is emphatically identified as his bride. The Book of Revelation mentions Jesus' bride twice. Most notable is Revelation 22:17, in which the bride is speaking with the Holy Spirit, inviting thirsty souls to come and drink of the Water of Life freely: *"And the Spirit and the bride say, Come. And let him that heareth say, Come. And let him that is athirst come. And whosoever will, let him take the water of life freely."* This is the same invitation I am echoing to you in this book.

The second mention is John being invited by the angel to witness the holy city, the New Jerusalem, descending from heaven upon the earth, describing it as a beautifully adorned bride. The city is not the bride; but the home of the bride and heavenly Bridegroom. Revelation 21:2-3 reads,

> *"And I John saw the holy city, new Jerusalem, coming down from God out of heaven, prepared as a bride adorned for her husband. And I heard a great voice out of heaven saying,*

*Behold, the tabernacle of God is with men, and he will dwell
with them, and they shall be his people, and God himself shall be
with them, and be their God."*

GOD'S SEARCH FOR A BRIDE IN ISRAEL, THEN THE WORLD

God's plan has always been to select a spiritual wife for Himself. The
nation of Israel was handpicked by God to be His peculiar treasure
because of His love for Abraham and his offspring. Deuteronomy 4:37
and 7:8 say God chose them *"because he loved"* their fathers, and the
nation of Israel, too.

Ezekiel 16 records God's depiction of His loving effort to rescue Israel
and marry her. The Lord describes Israel as a neglected baby in an open
field, laying in its own blood. He saves her life and nurtures her until she's
of marrying age. God enters into a marriage covenant with Israel. She
became His, clothed and decked in beauty, with worldwide renown. Sadly,
her pride caused her to become a harlot with every nation. She became
an idolater and aborted her own children to false gods. Israel forgot God's
grace in rescuing her from her bloody, polluted beginning. Israel would
suffer for her sins, but ultimately, God would forgive her. Verse 60 says,

*"Nevertheless I will remember my covenant with thee in
the days of thy youth, and I will establish unto thee an
everlasting covenant."*

Israel is now suffering the consequences of her sins in the Old
Testament, as well as her rejection of her Messiah, Jesus. Most Jews are
blinded to Christ by their own unbelief. When God cut or broke off the
Jewish branch,[467] He likened it unto a divorce from Israel, according to
Jeremiah 3:8: *"And I saw, when for all the causes whereby backsliding Israel
committed adultery I had put her away, and given her a bill of divorce; yet
her treacherous sister Judah feared not, but went and played the harlot also."*

467   Romans 11:19-20

Jeremiah chapter 3 contains the same story as Ezekiel 16. Verse 14 reads, "*Turn, O backsliding children, saith the Lord; for I am married unto you.*" Israel leaving her Husband is taught in verse 20: "*Surely as a wife treacherously departeth from her husband, so have ye dealt treacherously with me, O house of Israel, saith the Lord.*" Yet again, God's divine forgiveness is expressed in verse 22: "*Return, ye backsliding children, and I will heal your backslidings. Behold, we come unto thee; for thou art the Lord our God.*"

The prophet Hosea was used by God to portray Himself as a faithful Husband and Israel as an adulterous wife. God's prophet was told to marry the harlot, Gomer, to show Israel her marital unfaithfulness. In Hosea 3, the prophet buys back, or redeems his estranged wife after her period of whorish escapades. Hosea is confident Gomer will now be faithful to him alone, and God uses this relationship to affirm that Israel will be faithful to Him in the "*latter days.*"[468] This refers to the 144,000 Jewish remnant who will accept Jesus Christ as Savior during the Tribulation Period. This will lead to the fulfillment of Isaiah 54:5 during the Millennium, when Jesus will be Israel's Husband, and Lord of the whole earth: "*For thy Maker is thine husband; the Lord of hosts is his name; and thy Redeemer the Holy One of Israel; The God of the whole earth shall he be called.*" Isaiah calls Israel "Married Land" in Isaiah 62:4-5:

> "*Thou shalt no more be termed Forsaken; neither shall thy land any more be termed Desolate: but thou shalt be called Hephzibah, and thy land Beulah: for the Lord delighteth in thee, and thy land shall be married. For as a young man marrieth a virgin, so shall thy sons marry thee: and as the bridegroom rejoiceth over the bride, so shall thy God rejoice over thee.*"

God is finally going to have a bride, a beautiful Jew-Gentile one, and enjoy a joyful 1,000 year honeymoon with her.

Jesus was God's incarnation in His search for a faithful mate. Instead of Israel accepting Christ as their Messiah, they demanded His blood be shed and willingly accepted the guilt of His blood upon their race

468   Hosea 3:3-5

according to Matthew 27:25: *"Then answered all the people, and said, His blood be on us, and on our children."*

Israel's rejection of Jesus was a rejection of being called by His Name. God then turned to the Gentiles to find a bride who wanted to be called by His Name, just like a natural man marries a wife, and she takes his last name. James recognizes God's search for a wife among the Gentiles in Acts 15:14: *"Simeon hath declared how God at the first did visit the Gentiles, to take out of them a people for his name."* Spiritually speaking, God is now looking for a bride that will gladly accept His Name, and become Mrs. Lord Jesus Christ.

Just as a natural wife gets a new last name after the wedding, Christians get their new name after the rapture (spiritual wedding), Marriage Supper (reception) and Millennium (honeymoon). Jesus will write our new name upon us according to Revelation 3:12:

> *"Him that overcometh will I make a pillar in the temple of my God, and he shall go no more out: and I will write upon him the name of my God, and the name of the city of my God, which is new Jerusalem, which cometh down out of heaven from my God: and I will write upon him my new name."*

THE APOSTOLIC BLUEPRINT FOR BECOMING A BRIDE MEMBER

You become a bride member when you hear and receive a preacher's anointed message about Jesus Christ being your Lord and Savior. In 2 Corinthians 11:2, Paul tells the Corinthians he espoused them, or engaged them to Jesus Christ: *"For I am jealous over you with godly jealousy: for I have espoused you to one husband, that I may present you as a chaste virgin to Christ."* This espousal was affirmed through Paul's persuasive preaching ministry, recorded in Acts 18:1-11. Paul spent a year and half *"teaching the word of God among them."* The apostle was like Abraham's servant, Eliezer, who was sent to get a bride for Isaac. Eliezer shared the espousal terms with Rebekah, who eagerly accepted. Those who eagerly received Paul's espousal terms, which were given to him by Christ, immediately became Jesus' espoused, spiritually-virgin bride.

I must add an important truth at this point. Bride members are spiritually married when they become Christians but not physically married. The physical union takes place at the rapture, the meeting in the air as Paul taught in 1 Thessalonians 4:16-17. The engagement starts when you are saved, but the marriage ceremony is with Christ in the air at the rapture. There is also a presentation of Christ's bride after the rapture, sometime near the marriage supper of the Lamb. Recall Paul said he would present the Corinthians to Christ as a chaste virgin.

Some misunderstand Paul's teaching in Romans 7:4, which says, *"Wherefore, my brethren, ye also are become dead to the law by the body of Christ; that ye should be married to another, even to him who is raised from the dead, that we should bring forth fruit unto God."* Yes, you are spiritually married to Christ by the vow in your heart, but you are not physically with your Husband. His Spirit is inside you, like an engagement vow lives in your heart. But His nail-scarred body is not with you. Like Rebekah traveling upon her camel to meet Isaac, you are on your earthly journey to meet your Husband, but the wedding is yet in the future. The baptism of the Holy Ghost is your power, or camel, carrying to you meet your Bridegroom. Just water the camel and you'll make it. Water the Holy Spirit with praise and worship and you'll meet Jesus in the air.

Once Rebekah saw Isaac face to face, she never left him. When you finally see Jesus face to face, you'll ever be with the Lord. 1 Corinthians 13:12 reads, *"For now we see through a glass, darkly; but then face to face: now I know in part; but then shall I know even as also I am known."* You are officially married to Jesus when you have a body like His. Paul writes this in Philippians 3:20-21, *"For our conversation is in heaven; from whence also we look for the Saviour, the Lord Jesus Christ: Who shall change our vile body, that it may be fashioned like unto his glorious body, according to the working whereby he is able even to subdue all things unto himself."* 1 John 3:2 also promises, *"Beloved, now are we the sons of God, and it doth not yet appear what we shall be: but we know that, when he shall appear, we shall be like him; for we shall see him as he is."*

Apply Paul's Corinthian blueprint to the Day of Pentecost when 3,000 souls were espoused to Christ through Peter's sermon. Observe Acts 2:41-47 and see how faithfully the bride assembled, hungry for true teaching and worship, and enthusiastic to help each other with physical needs:

> *"Then they that gladly received his word were baptized: and the same day there were added unto them about three thousand souls. And they continued stedfastly in the apostles' doctrine and fellowship, and in breaking of bread, and in prayers. And fear came upon every soul: and many wonders and signs were done by the apostles. And all that believed were together, and had all things common; And sold their possessions and goods, and parted them to all men, as every man had need. And they, continuing daily with one accord in the temple, and breaking bread from house to house, did eat their meat with gladness and singleness of heart, Praising God, and having favour with all the people. And the Lord added to the church daily such as should be saved."*

Every new bride member became a new creature in Christ Jesus. Each left their previous, sinful way of life, whether it was the curse of trying to save oneself through Moses' Law, or a licentious, lustful lifestyle. Jesus charged Paul to direct sinners out of the darkness and into the light of being a forgiven bride member in Acts 26:18: *"To open their eyes, and to turn them from darkness to light, and from the power of Satan unto God, that they may receive forgiveness of sins, and inheritance among them which are sanctified by faith that is in me."* Paul knew this same dramatic joy of coming to Christ. He compared his previous life to dung while affirming the excellency of being a bride member in Philippians 3:8: *"Yea doubtless, and I count all things but loss for the excellency of the knowledge of Christ Jesus my Lord: for whom I have suffered the loss of all things, and do count them but dung, that I may win Christ."*

Paul, once a violent blasphemer, taught his miraculous salvation experience was a pattern to all future bride members in 1 Timothy 1:13-16:

> *"Who was before a blasphemer, and a persecutor, and injurious: but I obtained mercy, because I did it ignorantly in unbelief. And the grace of our Lord was exceeding abundant with faith and love which is in Christ Jesus. This is a faithful saying, and worthy of all acceptation, that Christ Jesus came into the world to save sinners; of whom I am chief. Howbeit for this cause I obtained mercy, that in me first Jesus Christ might shew forth all longsuffering, for a pattern to them which should hereafter believe on him to life everlasting."*

The apostle Paul embarked on three missionary trips to espouse more bride members to Christ, and repeatedly operated according to his blueprint. First, he would win new converts. Then he would spend significant time teaching them Christ's Word. Finally, before leaving he would ordain faithful men as elders and leaders to oversee the converts. The blueprint is most clearly seen on his first missionary journey in Acts 14:21-23:

> *"And when they had preached the gospel to that city, and had taught many, they returned again to Lystra, and to Iconium, and Antioch, Confirming the souls of the disciples, and exhorting them to continue in the faith, and that we must through much tribulation enter into the kingdom of God. And when they had ordained them elders in every church, and had prayed with fasting, they commended them to the Lord, on whom they believed."*

Paul's letters record his instructions to preachers, Titus and Timothy, to keep the same blueprint for all Christian churches. Both men learned Paul's requirements for pastors (also called elders or bishops), and deacons in Titus 1:6-9 and 1 Timothy 3:1-13.

The apostle told Titus to set the churches in order by ordaining elders in every city: *"For this cause left I thee in Crete, that thou shouldest set in order the things that are wanting, and ordain elders in every city, as I had appointed thee."*[469] Timothy was instructed to pass down God's revelations to faithful men in 2 Timothy 2:1-2: *"Thou therefore, my son, be strong in the grace that is in Christ Jesus. And the things that thou hast heard of me among many witnesses, the same commit thou to faithful men, who shall be able to teach others also."*

These Scriptures give you God's blueprint for how people become bride members through genuine missionary work, how their churches grow, and how to make more bride members.

THE UNCHANGING GOSPEL BLUEPRINT

It's imperative to show Paul's indictment upon anyone who would change even one word of the revelations Jesus taught him. Curses were to come upon anyone who changed Jesus' blueprint, or pattern for saving, teaching, and harvesting future bride members according to Galatians 1:6-12:

> *"I marvel that ye are so soon removed from him that called you into the grace of Christ unto another gospel: Which is not another; but there be some that trouble you, and would pervert the gospel of Christ. But though we, or an angel from heaven, preach any other gospel unto you than that which we have preached unto you, let him be accursed. As we said before, so say I now again, If any man preach any other gospel unto you than that ye have received, let him be accursed. For do I now persuade men, or God? or do I seek to please men? for if I yet pleased men, I should not be the servant of Christ. But I certify you, brethren, that the gospel which was preached of me is not after man. For I neither received it of man, neither was I taught it, but by the revelation of Jesus Christ."*

Every word Paul was given by Christ to write and share with the churches must be obeyed. Paul was faithful in teaching the whole counsel of God to every church he started or visited. 1 Corinthians 4:17 says, *"For this cause have I sent unto you Timotheus, who is my beloved son, and*

469   Titus 1:5

faithful in the Lord, who shall bring you into remembrance of my ways which be in Christ, as I teach every where in every church." Every bride-church heard the same, complete gospel from Paul. Paul told the Ephesians in Acts 20:27 that they heard the full counsel of God, and thereby were responsible for it: *"For I have not shunned to declare unto you all the counsel of God."* Bride members will not change one word of Jesus' revelation given to Paul. They know there is only *"one faith"* according to Ephesians 4:5, and Jude 3 says it is the one and only faith we must earnestly contend for.

Timothy received a direct charge from Paul to keep every Word of God in 1 Timothy 6:13-14: *"I give thee charge in the sight of God, who quickeneth all things, and before Christ Jesus, who before Pontius Pilate witnessed a good confession; That thou keep this commandment without spot, unrebukeable, until the appearing of our Lord Jesus Christ."*

Paul wept while writing the Philippians from prison due to the enemies of the cross who lived contrary to his example and teachings in Philippians 3:17-19:

> *"Brethren, be followers together of me, and mark them which walk so as ye have us for an ensample. (For many walk, of whom I have told you often, and now tell you even weeping, that they are the enemies of the cross of Christ: Whose end is destruction, whose God is their belly, and whose glory is in their shame, who mind earthly things.)"*

Paul rebuked false teachers by saying their false doctrines spread like gangrene, destroying the faith of potential bride members in 2 Timothy 2:16-18: *"But shun profane and vain babblings: for they will increase unto more ungodliness. And their word will eat as doth a canker: of whom is Hymenaeus and Philetus; Who concerning the truth have erred, saying that the resurrection is past already; and overthrow the faith of some."*

Jesus, Solomon, and John support Paul's insistence for believing all of God's Word without adding or taking anything away. Christ says God's Word will never pass away in Matthew 24:35: *"Heaven and earth shall pass away, but my words shall not pass away.*" Solomon teaches God will call men and women liars who add to or delete from His commands in Proverbs 30:5-6: "*Every word of God is pure: he is a shield unto them that put their trust in him. Add thou not unto his words, lest he reprove thee, and thou be found a liar.*" John warns those who would add or delete from the Bible, urging strict adherence to all God's Words in Revelation 22:18-19:

> "*For I testify unto every man that heareth the words of the prophecy of this book, If any man shall add unto these things, God shall add unto him the plagues that are written in this book: And if any man shall take away from the words of the book of this prophecy, God shall take away his part out of the book of life, and out of the holy city, and from the things which are written in this book.*"

Let God's Word be your Absolute—your final word, your unlimited source of strength. Let God be true and any word of man contrary to It a lie. Romans 3:4 declares, "*God forbid: yea, let God be true, but every man a liar; as it is written, That thou mightest be justified in thy sayings, and mightest overcome when thou art judged.*"

THE BRIDE'S SUBMISSIVE CHARACTER TO EVERY WORD OF CHRIST

In Ephesians 5:22-33, Paul uses the husband and wife imagery to express five attributes Christ desires in His bride. A woman is often used in Scripture to represent a church or even a nation. Ezekiel 16:7 shows God calling Israel a woman, and Acts 7:38 says Moses was part of the "*church in the wilderness.*" As proven earlier by numerous Scriptures, Jesus' church is also called a bride.

Paul's purpose for this Ephesians text is found in verse 32: "*This is a great mystery: but I speak concerning Christ and the church.*" Here you find the revelation of the true bride's Christian character.

The first attribute is Christ is the one and only head of the church. Ephesians 5:23 says, "*For the husband is the head of the wife, even as Christ is* the head of the church: and he is the saviour of the body." John 1:1 says Jesus is the Word, meaning the true revelation of the Bible. Bride members declare Jesus's Spirit—which wrote His Word, the Bible—is their only headship.

Sadly, most churches are headed up by man-made creeds, bylaws, and traditions that contradict the revelation Jesus gave to Paul. The Word doesn't rule them. The conditions today match those of Jesus' day, as the Pharisees had exalted their man-made interpretations above Moses' Law. One example is Jesus rebuking them harshly for mistreating their elderly parents, making the tradition of not supporting their parents their headship instead of Moses' teaching:

> "But he answered and said unto them, Why do ye also transgress the commandment of God by your tradition? This people draweth nigh unto me with their mouth, and honoureth me with their lips; but their heart is far from me. But in vain they do worship me, teaching for doctrines the commandments of men."[470]

Many examples can be given to show how churches reject Jesus' headship for both ministers and lay members, but here are just 10 of the most sinful teachings churches promote:

- Homosexual relationships, yet Paul's revelation condemns these as abominable (Romans 1:26-32, 1 Corinthians 6:9-11, 1 Timothy 1:10-11)
- Adulterous relationships (couples married more than once), yet Paul's revelation demands marriage last until death, and warns that adulterers will not inherit God's kingdom (Romans 7:1-3, 1 Corinthians 6:9-10)
- Fornication (sexual intercourse before marriage), yet Paul's revelation says fornicators will not inherit God's kingdom (1 Corinthians 6:9-10)
- Murdering babies through abortion and birth control pills, yet Paul's revelation says murderers will not inherit God's kingdom (Galatians 5:21)

470   Matthew 15:3,8-9

- Women preachers, yet Paul's revelation forbids any woman from teaching a man (1 Corinthians 14:34-36, 1 Timothy 2:11-15)
- Substance abuse (smoking cigarettes, drunkenness, etc.), yet Paul's revelation says these acts defile the body, the temple of the Holy Ghost, and should not be done as long as the world stands (Romans 14:21, 1 Corinthians 3:17, 6:19-20, 8:13)
- Viewing sinful movies and television shows, yet Paul's revelation was to avoid all appearance of evil (1 Thessalonians 5:22)
- Shameful hair lengths (women cutting their hair and men growing long hair), yet Paul says women should never cut their hair and men should keep theirs short (1 Corinthians 11:1-16)
- False conversations (saying converts are filled with the Spirit at initial confession or working miracles is proof of salvation), yet Paul's revelation is that you must continue believing, and you will receive the Holy Ghost sometime after you initially believe (Matthew 7:21-23, Acts 19:1-7, Galatians 4:19, Ephesians 1:13)
- Immodest clothing (sexy, revealing outfits), yet Paul commands modest clothing (1 Timothy 2:9)

Surely you can see Jesus Christ and His Word are not the head of most churches. Concerning these 10 teachings, they are completely one-sided, and have no examples of God allowing them. You'll never find homosexual relationships celebrated in God's Eternal Word, nor will you find a godly woman preaching or cutting her hair. May you follow the Spirit's leading to assemble with bride members who give Jesus His rightful place as head of the church. Who do you know that loves Jesus so much they obey God's Word in all 10 of these areas?

A second bride-attribute is complete submission in everything. Verse 24 says the *"church is subject to Christ...in everything."* Bride members are happy to read the Bible with a desire to know more of God's will so that they might obey it. Their goal is to live like Jesus, Who knew man does *"not live by bread alone, but by every word that proceedeth out of the mouth of God."*[471] Obeying her Husband is not a grievous task for the bride because she is born again, as 1 John 5:3-4 teach: *"For this is the love of God, that we keep his commandments: and his commandments are not grievous. For whatsoever is born of God overcometh the world: and this is the victory that overcometh the world, even our faith."* The bride's goal is total submission to her Husband in all things. She wants to be holy because Jesus is holy, as Peter declares: *"As obedient children, not fashioning yourselves according to the former lusts in your ignorance: But as he which hath called you is holy, so be ye holy in all manner of conversation; Because it is written, Be ye holy; for I am holy."*[472]

A third bride-attribute is submission to Christ's washing process. Ephesians 5:26 reads, *"That he might sanctify and cleanse it with the washing of water by the word."* Jesus cleanses your life as you hear His Word and obey it. 1 Peter 1:22 says you are purified *"in obeying the truth through the Spirit."* Acts 22:16 says Paul's sins were washed away at his repentance and water baptism. We know water itself cannot forgive sins, but rather Paul's obedience caused God to forgive him.

Overcoming sin in the midst of persecution and temptation is the washing process the bride goes through according to Revelation 1:5 and 7:14. Jesus washes His bride by anointing preachers to share His Word which cleanses the hearers. 1 Corinthians 1:18 declares preaching is the power of God unto salvation. Jesus' five preaching gifts—apostle, prophet, pastor, teacher, and evangelist—perfect, edify, and unify His bride.[473]

The reason most churches do not get washed is because they do not preach and obey all of Paul's revelation, as shown by the 10 bulleted examples above. Upon obeying Jesus' commands, your mind is renewed, or washed. Paul validates this in Ephesians 4:22-32 and Titus 3:3-8. Verse 5 in Titus 3 says Christians are saved *"by the washing of regeneration, and*

---

471   Matthew 4:4
472   1 Peter 1:14-16
473   Ephesians 4:8-13

renewing of the Holy Ghost." As Christ's bride, you must be constantly washed and prepared for your wedding day, your great day of presentation to your Husband, the Word.

Being joined (or glued to in the Greek Lexicon) to Christ is the bride's fourth attribute. Ephesians 5:31 says, "*For this cause shall a man leave his father and mother, and shall be joined unto his wife, and they two shall be one flesh.*" Jesus' true bride is glued to His fellowship and that of His people. Christians are to constantly meditate upon the Lord, speaking to Him in unceasing prayer.[474]

The bride will also gather with other believers, and their physical gathering will increase as Jesus' second coming nears. Hebrews 10:24-25 explains, "*And let us consider one another to provoke unto love and to good works: Not forsaking the assembling of ourselves together, as the manner of some is; but exhorting one another: and so much the more, as ye see the day approaching.*" You cannot separate the bride from her Husband, nor from her spiritual family. Many church members are glued to their sinful television shows, movies, and sports, too busy to fellowship with Christ and His church.

The fifth bride-attribute is the attitude of reverence. Ephesians 5:33 commands: "*Nevertheless let every one of you in particular so love his wife even as himself; and the wife see that she reverence her husband.*" Reverence means "to be in awe of" in the Greek. Just speaking her Husband's name is a sacred, hallowed thing to the bride. Her Husband is great in her eyes, causing her to be meek and humble. She is careful which words come out of her mouth, possessing quiet strength. Bride members own the treasure of a meek and quiet spirit just as natural wives should: "*But let it be the hidden man of the heart, in that which is not corruptible, even the ornament of a meek and quiet spirit, which is in the sight of God of great price.*"[475]

Paul closes Ephesians 5 by reminding men to love their wives, so I will close this section by reminding you of Jesus' love for you. Paul says

474   1 Thessalonians 5:17
475   1 Peter 3:4

God has *"great love"*[476] for you, and he also lists 17 things that cannot separate us from Christ's love in Romans 8:35-39. Jesus' commands for His bride are for her good—her safety, protection, provision, and growth. Romans 8:28 says all things—not some—work together for good to them that love the Lord. This is forever Christ's purpose for His commands—our good. God told the same to Moses in Deuteronomy 6:24-25: *"And the Lord commanded us to do all these statutes, to fear the Lord our God, for our good always, that he might preserve us alive, as it is at this day. And it shall be our righteousness, if we observe to do all these commandments before the Lord our God, as he hath commanded us."* Your Husband's commands will always work for your benefit. Your obedience to Jesus is the greatest expression of your love for Him, for He delights in obedience more than sacrifice. Jesus pleads, *"If ye love me, keep my commandments."*[477]

Keep the true bride's attributes in mind because Chapter 9 unveils the sinful attributes of the false bride, the Mother Harlot.

JUDGING CHRISTIAN GROUPS AND DENOMINATIONS BY THEIR FRUITS

Based upon Paul's bride-attributes, the Holy Spirit helps us judge Christian groups by their fruits. You can know a person's purity by their actions. You might use the word "discern" instead of judge, but they mean the same thing. It is necessary for you to *"prove all things"* and test every spirit. Jesus specifically warns us of men—false prophets. Matthew 24:4 states, *"And Jesus answered and said unto them, Take heed that no man deceive you."*

Please understand the following judgments upon church groups are not eternal judgments, as only God judges eternal destinations. I am only judging each church's adherence to Paul's revelation from Jesus Christ, as well as the rest of the Holy Bible. With the internet, it's easier than ever to judge churches through their online statements of faith.

476 Ephesians 2:4
477 John 14:15

Jesus instructs us to judge individuals and situations with righteous judgment in John 7:24: *"Judge not according to the appearance, but judge righteous judgment."* Paul's prayer for the Philippians is for them to approve holy things as they grow in judgment in Philippians 1:9-10: *"And this I pray, that your love may abound yet more and more in knowledge and in all judgment; That ye may approve things that are excellent; that ye may be sincere and without offence till the day of Christ."* The Hebrews writer states mature Christians skillfully discern or judge between good and evil. Baby Christians refuse to judge right and wrong:

> *"For when for the time ye ought to be teachers, ye have need that one teach you again which be the first principles of the oracles of God; and are become such as have need of milk, and not of strong meat. For every one that useth milk is unskilful in the word of righteousness: for he is a babe. But strong meat belongeth to them that are of full age, even those who by reason of use have their senses exercised to discern both good and evil."*[478]

In 2010, the Pew Research Center estimated the following sizes for Christian groups that combine for about 2.5 billion members worldwide.[479] As you read through this list consider which group keeps all 10 doctrines listed earlier, along with the rest of God's commands.

- Roman Catholic: 1.3 billion
- Protestant: 900 million
- Eastern Orthodox: 270 million
- Anglican: 110 million
- Oriental Orthodox: 62 million
- All Others: 37 million

---

478 Hebrews 5:12-14
479 "Global Christianity-A Report on the Size and Distribution of the World's Christian Population." *Pew Research Center*, https://www.pewforum.org/2011/12/19/global-christianity-exec/

If you are thinking, "None of these named groups keep all 10 doctrines," you are right. They are guilty of either adding to God's Word or taking away from it. It is with love and compassion that I claim all these churches are guilty of transgressing Jesus' commands. Jesus says we must do His commands if He truly is our Lord in Luke 6:46: "*And why call ye me, Lord, Lord, and do not the things which I say?*"

Friend, this is a serious subject. Before we examine these denominational groups, remember the bride church will not have creeds, bylaws, or traditions that contradict Paul's revelation, for they are cursed if they do.

In addition to the 10 doctrines already listed, the following further illustrate how the bride church keeps all of God's commands as a woman separate from all church systems:

- Water baptisms are performed as full immersions in water, calling upon the name of the Lord Jesus Christ—not by sprinkling, and not by speaking the titles Father, Son, and Holy Spirit (Acts 2:38, 8:16, 10:48, 19:5, 22:16).

- Believers are taught to receive the baptism of the Holy Ghost in their souls—the third work of grace—after justification and sanctification (Matthew 11:29, Mark 4:26-28, John 17:17, 20:22, Acts 1:5, 19:1-7).

- God is known as one Person—not three persons (Job 13:8). Thus, the Trinity dogma is wrong. God says He is the only God, and there was no one beside Him (Isaiah 43:11, 44:6-8). Jesus is the image of the invisible God, the express image of His Person (Colossians 1:15, Hebrews 1:3).

- Men and women wear separate garments because cross dressing (transgender movement) is an abomination to God (Deuteronomy 22:5). This means men only will wear pants. Women will abstain from wearing men's garments (pants, even if they are women's pants), and wear modest skirts and dresses.

- Supernatural power currently operates all nine gifts of the Holy Ghost (Mark 16:16-18, 1 Corinthians 12:1-11).

Beginning with Roman Catholics, Chapter 9 explores the depths of their wicked doctrines. Additionally, they confess God is three separate, co-equal persons, which is polytheism. They consider their communion wafer to be the literal body of the crucified Jesus, which is an idolatrous fantasy. Mary is exalted higher than Christ for she is called the "Mother of God." Women cut their hair and wear men's clothing. With just these few examples, Roman Catholics cannot be the bride.

Most Protestants confess a three-person God, and permit adulterous marriages, cross dressing (women wearing pants), and women cutting their hair, excluding them from being bride. Going further, most Baptists claim you are filled with the Holy Ghost at repentance (denying the baptism of the Holy Ghost), and allow women preachers. Their loud cheering at sporting events is louder than their praises in church, manifesting their idolatry. They are not the bride. Lutherans often allow members to drink alcohol heavily, and have no modesty standards. They cannot be the bride. Seventh Day Adventist's make Sabbath keeping the evidence for being born again, which is just as erroneous as Pentecostals teaching speaking in tongues is the evidence. You cannot emphasize the gift, tongues, more than the Giver, the Holy Spirit. Those groups cannot be the bride. Jehovah's Witnesses deny supernatural healings. They cannot be bride. Mormons teach you're born again after baptism only (Acts 10:44-48 shows believers can be born again before baptism), and add an entire Testament to the Bible—The Book of Mormon—which carries severe punishments on Judgment Day. Mormons are not Christ's bride. Similar discernments for each Protestant group could be made in order to prove who is bride and who isn't.

Eastern Orthodoxy erroneously exalts tradition to be equal with Scripture, celebrates the Eucharist, intercedes for the dead, and venerates icons. Despite being orthodox by name, this group is not Jesus' bride, nor are Anglicans and Oriental Orthodox. Anglicans recite three powerless creeds (the Apostles' Creed, Nicene Creed, and Athanasian Creed), and declare Christ's real presence is in the Eucharist. Oriental Orthodox deny Jesus' dual nature (human and divine), and require sacraments for salvation.

These few examples prove we are living in the time of the great *"falling away,"*[480] or the apostasy. Most churches have fallen away from Paul's teachings. But remember, Jesus will have a bride-church, and she will allow Him to wash her with the waters of His Word, week-in and week-out, preaching service after preaching service.

Not for a moment do I say there are no saved believers in the groups listed above, as God has children in every organization. God doesn't accept organizations, only sincere individuals within them. But the saved in these organizations cannot be born again, Holy Ghost-filled bride members if they are part of any church that rejects even a portion of God's Word. This is true because God searches the world for genuine worshippers, who fear Him through worshipping in the Spirit and truth.[481] Bride members may start their Christian journey in the false churches, but then the Lord calls them out of false church systems, saying, *"Come out of her, my people, that ye be not partakers of her sins, and that ye receive not of her plagues."*[482] One major purpose of being born again is for Jesus to lead you into all truth,[483] so staying in a church that allows sin is against Jesus' nature. He sends His Spirit with the intent to separate His bride from those who love pleasures more than God.

Jesus says there are three kinds of Christians: workers of iniquity (imposters), foolish, and wise.[484] Chapters 8, 10, and 12 focus on this subject, but for now you must know that workers of iniquity have gifts to perform miracles under the true anointing of the Spirit, but their souls are void of God's anointing. These imposters enjoy working in God's Spirit for financial and selfish gain. Therefore, they are lost. Foolish virgins will be saved at the White Throne Judgment, but will miss the rapture, Marriage

480   2 Thessalonians 2:3
481   2 Chronicles 16:9, John 4:23-24, Acts 10:35
482   Revelation 18:4
483   John 16:13
484   Matthew 7:20-23, 25:1-13

Supper of the Lamb, and Millennium because they failed to prepare oil for the tarrying bridegroom. This means foolish Christians today fail to receive the baptism of the Holy Ghost by foolishly choosing to invest their time and energy into worldly cares. They are "virgin" in that they had no obvious interaction with idolatry, lusts, addictions, and the like. But like Israel stopping at Kadesh-Barnea for fear of the giants, they failed to possess all of God's promises for fear of losing out on worldly opportunities. They could have had all the truth, but failed to ask for it. Jesus promised to give the Holy Ghost to them that asked in Luke 11:13.

WHO IS THE BRIDE AND WHERE IS SHE LOCATED?

Sincere hearts want to know who the true bride is and where she is located. Truly, the climatic book of the Bible, Revelation, holds this subject at its very core. John's work is a dramatic unveiling of Jesus, His true bride, and the false bride.

Revelation chapter 1 reveals Jesus Christ the Bridegroom in His seven-fold glory of Supreme Deity. Revelation chapters 2 and 3 reveal the bride's overcoming character, and Chapter 7 of this book is devoted to explaining this subject. The false bride, the Mother Harlot-church, is exposed in Revelation chapter 17 and 18 as the imposter church who loves abominations and self-indulgent living more than God's Word. Chapter 9 of this book covers the Mother's attributes, but also the daughter-churches who hold their Mother's beliefs. The true bride's eternal home then descends to earth in Revelation chapters 21 and 22. With the Holy Spirit's discernment, you are able to distinguish the imposter-church from the true bride-church. Begin by using the 15 doctrinal examples listed above. The Word is your standard, forever settled in heaven, never to pass away, and will judge the secrets of every heart at Jesus' White Throne.

Yes, Jesus' true bride believes God is one Person, just like the apostles believed. She has the supernatural power of the Holy Ghost working in her midst through the Spirit's nine gifts. New converts are baptized in the name of the Lord Jesus Christ, and continue on into sanctification to receive the baptism of the Holy Ghost sometime afterwards. The bride is Pentecostal by experience, but not by organization. Her members believe in holiness and dress modestly with separate garments for both genders. Her women have uncut hair and men short hair as Paul commanded. Bride members marry between men and women only, and their marriages last until death. They live holy lives, abstaining from cigarettes, social drinking, and all other substance abuse.

I believe I'm part of this Bible-based bride, which is the reason I've written this book. I believe every Word in the Bible, just as it is written. Paul's teachings are the unchanging, eternal truth of God for us to believe and live by.

So, where is the bride? Her members are gathered in small churches worldwide, as Jesus' rapture description says some will be sleeping when the rapture happens while others will be working in the field or grinding at the mill.[485] She is part of Pew Research Center's "All Others" group, but separate from most of those due to her love for truth. She could take the names "Holy Ghost Filled Church," "Wise Virgin Church," or "Bible Believing Church," but she has no official name. Her heavenly name is the Lord Jesus Christ, along with the family of God.[486] This is the reason she baptizes her converts in the literal name of the Lord Jesus Christ. Her members are both Jew and Gentile.

This bride group will be Spirit-organized through her heavenly headquarters, following Paul's apostolic pattern. She has no earthly headquarters to enact man-made control over her members. Instead, she is organized and unified exactly as Paul organized the early church—through the power of the Holy Spirit.

JESUS' BRIDE FORESHADOWED IN EIGHT OLD TESTAMENT WOMEN

Not only did God foretell His taking a Gentile wife through an Old Testament prophet,[487] He also used the following women's lives to type

---

485   Matthew 24:40-41, Luke 17:34-36
486   Ephesians 3:14-15
487   Amos 9:11-12, Acts 15:14

or foreshadow the bride-church and her past and future events: Sarah, Rebekah, Asenath, Rahab, Samson's bride from Timnath, Ruth, Esther, and Solomon's wife, the Shulamite. A type foretells someone or some event to come in the future.

Sarah, the wife of Abraham, bearing Isaac at 90 years old types the rapture of the Jew-Gentile church. Galatians 3:7 says anyone with faith in Christ is a child of Abraham. Isaac's birth foretells Jesus' second coming to earth because both are promised sons, and Isaac's birth happened about the same time as Sodom's destruction. Jesus promised His second coming would occur at a time when the world was again in Sodomite conditions according to Luke 17:28-30.

Since Sarah's womb was dead[488] and it was impossible for her to conceive before Isaac's birth, God had to transform her body with new life. Her body change foreshadowed the body change Christians will experience at the rapture: *"Behold, I shew you a mystery; We shall not all sleep, but we shall all be changed, In a moment, in the twinkling of an eye, at the last trump: for the trumpet shall sound, and the dead shall be raised incorruptible, and we shall be changed."*[489]

Without God, it is impossible for our bodies to change and meet Christ in the air. But with God, all things are possible. Sarah even doubted God's promise to bring seed through her womb, but God fulfilled His promise to Abraham about his promised seed. So will God keep His promise to Christians despite their occasional doubts, and fulfill 1 Thessalonians 4:15-18.

Rebekah's espousal and marriage to Isaac in Genesis 24 types the bride's spiritual espousal and heavenly marriage to Christ the Bridegroom. Eliezar, Abraham's chief servant, is guided by God to find a suitable wife for Isaac. Chapter 13 shows God's current choice for a human servant to espouse a bride-church for His Son, Jesus.

Once Rebekah is found and accepts the marriage proposal, Eliezar bestows upon her gifts of valuable jewelry. These gifts type the nine gifts

488   Romans 4:19
489   1 Corinthians 15:51-52

of the Holy Ghost given to Jesus' bride as love tokens, which the true bride will possess and operate for His glory. Eliezar endeavors to quickly return her to Isaac, and Rebekah agrees. The servant, Rebekah, and her maidens make the long journey by camel to Abraham's country. The power of the camels symbolizes the power of the Holy Ghost that makes the church's long, earthly journey possible. Just as the camels needed watered and fed, our souls need a constant feeding of God's Word during our lives.

When Isaac comes into view, he is outside his tent, meditating in the field. Rebekah then meets him in the field, typing our meeting *"the Lord in the air"*[490] at the rapture. We won't meet Jesus in His tent, or heavenly house, but in between, in the air.

Asenath, the Egyptian wife of Joseph, types the New Testament church, composed of both Jew and Gentile. Her status as a Gentile marrying a Jew, Joseph, types Paul espousing Gentile believers in a spiritual marriage with Christ. If you're a Gentile, you are the antitype of Asenath.

Joseph's life before marrying Asenath clearly types Jesus' earthly ministry. Joseph and Jesus were both rejected by their brethren, and sold for 20 and 30 pieces of silver, respectively. Joseph's time in prison, in which one inmate was killed and the other spared, typed Jesus on the cross. The unrepentant thief's soul was lost, but the other thief was saved, as Jesus promised him paradise. Joseph's exaltation to second in command to Pharaoh typed Jesus' resurrection and placement at the right hand of the majesty on high. Once in his ruling position, Joseph married Asenath. Likewise, after Jesus sat down on His heavenly throne, He began to call and espouse a Gentile wife to Himself.

Joseph revealing his identity to his brethren types the event of Jesus revealing Himself to the faithful, 144,000 Jewish remnant after the rapture. Joseph's 11 brothers were blinded to his true identity, just as Israel is currently blinded[491] to recognizing Jesus as Messiah. This revelation

---

490   1 Thessalonians 4:17
491   Romans 11:7

came after Joseph put out everyone from His presence, meaning Asenath was in her royal quarters, not present as he revealed himself. This type means Jesus' true bride will be in her heavenly, royal quarters as Jesus descends to Mount Zion[492] to reveal Himself to the Jews.

The rescue of Rahab, the Gentile harlot, from Jericho's destruction types the rapture event from 1 Thessalonians 4:15-18. Her Gentile lineage speaks of God rescuing the Gentile people in the Times of the Gentiles. Just as Rahab was saved by Israel's trumpet and shout in Joshua 6:5, the Jew-Gentile bride is raptured by Christ's "*shout...voice...and trump of God.*"[493]

The Book of Joshua shows Rahab being spared from her city's destruction, because in faith, she received and protected Israel's two spies.[494] Her red cord signified her faith in Israel's God, typing the token or seal of the Holy Ghost baptism believers must have on display in order to go in the rapture. Chapters 6, 8, and 12 in this book detail Jesus' two symbols for the Holy Ghost baptism: oil and a wedding garment. Only Rahab and those within her house were spared from death when Jericho's walls fell, foreshadowing the certain death for all who miss the rapture in the awful time that follows, the Tribulation.

After being rescued, this once ill-famed, sexually immoral woman became a faithful, godly wife and mother, insomuch God placed her in David's lineage, which produced the Christ child.[495] Rahab's rags-to-riches testimony speaks of Gentile Christians being dead in sins and trespasses before Christ's Spirit quickens and raises them to sit in the honorable state of heavenly places in Christ Jesus.[496]

Samson's Philistine wife from Timnath types Jesus' Gentile bride. Samson's parents were at first shocked that Samson didn't take a Jewish wife, but Judges 14:4 says it was God's plan for Samson to take a wife from among the Philistines that he might destroy them and deliver Israel. The Holy Spirit revealed this revelation to my brother, Cameron, who

492   Revelation 14:1
493   1 Thessalonians 4:16
494   Hebrews 11:31
495   Matthew 1:5
496   Ephesians 2:1-6

is also a pastor, and then shared it with me. God's purpose is to take a Gentile bride in mercy, not judgment, but God must pour out His wrath upon most Gentiles during the Tribulation because they have rejected His Spirit.

Judges 14:3 says Samson chose his wife because she pleased him. Jesus' bride-church pleases Him as well as she walks in the Spirit and not the flesh. This dedicated walk proves she has the Spirit of Christ and belongs to Him.[497] Paul taught believers how to please God through His commandments and sacrificing for others.[498]

Before marrying her, the Spirit of LORD comes upon Samson, and he slays a young lion who roared against him. After a short meeting with his espoused bride, Samson finds bees and honey in the lion's carcass, which he eats and shares with his parents without telling them where he got it. The slain lion represents God delivering Jesus, the Lion of the Tribe of Judah, to be slain before the Gentile marriage. Acts 2:23 says Jesus was *"delivered by the determinate counsel and foreknowledge of God"* to be crucified and slain. Unsearchable riches, spiritual treasures, and delicious revelations are gained from Jesus' death. Peter says God's Word has a gracious taste.[499] John was commanded to eat the Open Book, formerly sealed with seven seals, and testified it tasted like honey in Revelation 10:10.

Finally, Samson hosted a seven day wedding feast to celebrate his new bride. Proudly, he put forth a riddle to challenge 30 Philistine men, promising them new clothing if they could solve it. In Judges 14:14 you find the riddle: *"Out of the eater came forth meat, and out of the strong came forth sweetness."* The men were confounded for six days so on the seventh day they secretly threatened to burn the bride's father's house if she didn't get the answer from Samson for them. In tears, the bride gains the answer from Samson and shares it with the men. Samson realizes what has happened, but still pays them the garments he promised. Soon after, Samson goes to Ashkelon and slays the men, taking back his garments.

---

497   Romans 8:8-9
498   1 Thessalonians 4:1-2, Hebrews 13:15-16
499   1 Peter 2:2-3

This strange, amazing story is fulfilled in the Times of the Gentiles, from 53 A.D. to the present day. The seven day feast symbolizes the Seven Church Ages (See Chapter 7). Samson's riddle represents *"the mystery of God"* spoken of in Revelation 10:7 that can only be revealed on the seventh and final day, or seventh and last church age, the Laodicean Church Age. John was told to take the Open Book, or revealed Bible-truths that denominations had lost for centuries, eat and prophecy them again around the world.[500] It's my humble opinion that the book you are reading contains the answer to Samson's riddle, or the revelation of God's Holy Bible, and it could only be revealed in the last day.

Just as Samson's wife was the only one who had the answer to his riddle, only Christ's bride has the revelation of the previously seven-sealed Book, or Bible. The Timnath bride had to lay before Samson and seek his love in order to get the revelation. Today's bride church stays in God's presence, like Mary, the sister of Lazarus, and receives the sweet tasting Bible revelations. You can only find these rich, sweet, Bible revelations being preached by Jesus' bride, for out of the Eater, Jesus, came forth meat and sweetness. Jesus' *"strong meat"* is spiritual discernment to judge between good and evil.[501] Jesus' honey-like sweetness is His revealed, unveiled, open Bible.[502] You are tasting it now, and I hope you can agree with its sweetness like David did in Psalm 119:103: *"How sweet are thy words unto my taste! yea, sweeter than honey to my mouth!"*

Samson destroying the 30 men for threatening his bride is fulfilled during the Tribulation when heaven's wrath is poured out upon all those who persecuted Christ's bride. Revelation 18:20 and 24 captures Jesus' revenge upon the false church, her daughter churches, and sinners: *"Rejoice over her, thou heaven, and ye holy apostles and prophets; for God hath avenged you on her. And in her was found the blood of prophets, and of saints, and of all that were slain upon the earth."*

Ruth, the Gentile Moabitess, types the Gentile church's marriage to Jesus. Ruth's childless state as a widow represents the church's fruitless

---

500   Revelation 10:9-11
501   Hebrews 5:12-14
502   Revelation 10:9-11

life before coming to Christ and her first hopeless marriage to the law. Her marriage to Boaz symbolizes the bride-church's marriage to Jesus according to Romans 7:4: "*Wherefore, my brethren, ye also are become dead to the law by the body of Christ; that ye should be married to another, even to him who is raised from the dead, that we should bring forth fruit unto God.*" Thus, the death of Ruth's husband represents her being loosed from the curse of the law.

Before marrying Boaz, Ruth's choosing to travel back to Israel with her elderly mother-in-law, Naomi, types Gentile Christians leaving their sinful lives and following the "*old paths*"[503] of serving God in love. Naomi types the old, strict, teaching of Judaism, for it was "*our schoolmaster to bring us unto Christ.*"[504] Naomi led Ruth back to Israel and ultimately to Boaz, a type of Christ.

The timing of Naomi and Ruth's return to Israel is perfect because it also types Gentile salvation through the cross of Jesus Christ. The women arrived in time for the barley harvest.[505] Chapter 3 shows how the barley harvest occurred in the third month, at the time of the Feasts of Passover, Unleavened Bread, and Firstfruits. Ruth's arrival at barley harvest represents Gentile Christians coming to faith in Christ by experiencing the spiritual blessings of His death (Passover), burial (Unleavened Bread), and resurrection (Firstfruits). Recall Paul said Christians continually benefit from the spiritual feasts of the Passover, Unleavened Bread, Firstfruits, and even Pentecost because of the filling of the Holy Ghost.[506] The bride-church, like Ruth, came to Christ in a timely manner. She'll enjoy all the blessings of Passover and the final harvest of Pentecost, the rapture.

In Ruth's remaining story, Boaz redeems Naomi in order to purchase and marry Ruth in Ruth 4:9-10. This types Jesus shedding His blood on the cross in order to purchase both Jew (Naomi) and Gentile (Ruth). Acts 20:28 says Jesus "*purchased*" us "*with his own blood.*" After their marriage,

---

503   Jeremiah 6:16
504   Galatians 3:24
505   Ruth 1:22
506   1 Corinthians 5:7-8, Ephesians 5:18

Ruth bears a son named Obed, and lets Naomi nurse her son, her seed. This types the Seed-Life of the Gentile church, the Holy Spirit, returning to the once-blinded Jews after the rapture, or wedding of the bride church. All the Israeli women rejoice for Naomi who now has a kinsman, nourishment, and a restored life through Boaz and Ruth. The 144,000 Jewish remnant enjoy the same—a Kinsman Redeemer in Christ, spiritual nourishment through the New Testament truths, and restored spiritual life through the seal of the Holy Ghost in their foreheads.

Esther, the Jewish queen of the Persian king Xerxes during 6th Century B.C., types the New Testament bride-church. Xerxes' previous queen, Vashti, whom he put away, types Israel being put away, or blinded, as God put Israel away via a *"bill of divorcement"* in Isaiah 50:1 and Jeremiah 3:8. Having put Israel away, Christ could find a people for His Name's sake to be His new bride. Mordecai, Esther's cousin, urges her to enter the contest to become Xerxes' new wife. Mordecai, the elder, staunch Jew, again types the holy Law of Moses as a schoolmaster to point us to Jesus Christ.

Required to be a virgin to marry the king, Esther's virginity types complete devotion to Christ with no worldly intercourse. Amazingly, not one evil word is recorded about Esther's character. 2 Corinthians 11:2 says, *"For I am jealous over you with godly jealousy: for I have espoused you to one husband, that I may present you as a chaste virgin to Christ."* Esther wins Xerxes' beauty contest by adorning herself according to Hegai's requirements and nothing more.[507] Hegai, the king's chamberlain and keeper of the women, types the Holy Spirit's sanctification work, or second work of grace, which needs nothing extraneous added to it. Esther lived by every word that proceeded from Hegai as the bride-church lives by every Word of God in preparation for her marriage to Jesus. Esther' wedding night types the Christian's born again experience, as the new birth is likened unto receiving seed in 1 Peter 1:23.

Although Esther was Jewish, her Israeli identity was at first unknown to the king and all Shushan. In other words, everyone considered her a

507   Esther 2:15

virgin Gentile. Esther never even lived a day in Jerusalem. These facts about Esther type today's spiritually virgin, bride-church composed of Jew and Gentile, but inwardly she's a spiritual Jew, meaning her heart has been circumcised by the Holy Ghost; she is born again. Romans 2:29 reads, *"But he is a Jew, which is one inwardly; and circumcision is that of the heart, in the spirit, and not in the letter; whose praise is not of men, but of God."*

Haman's plot to kill all Jews, including Mordecai and Esther, types the very end of the Times of the Gentiles. This is when the *"beast...out of the earth"* in Revelation 13:11-18 plots to kill all—*"both small and great, rich and poor, free and bond"*—who do not take his antichrist mark. His deceitful theme will be a promise of *"peace and safety"*[508] while outlawing true Christianity and instituting unionized religion. Just as Haman's plot was foiled by Esther's prayerful, humble intercession, so will the beast's plot be foiled by the bride-church's prayers.

Esther and the Jews fasted for three days before the queen put on *"her royal apparel"*[509] and stood before the king. Though it could have cost her her life, Esther was willing to die to save her people, and knew she was ordained queen *"for such a time as this."*[510] Esther's approach to Xerxes types the bride prayerfully approaching Christ, clothed in the Holy Spirit's anointing, in her spiritual roles as king and priest unto God.[511] Esther had access to the highest authority, as Christians have *"access by faith into this grace wherein we stand."*[512]

Just as Esther felt political pressure, there is coming a time of political pressure, or a squeezing time, upon the bride-church. At some point in the future, false churches will unite with political leaders to change laws requiring all churches to join an evil ecumenical union. Bride-churches will feel the pressure of the movement, but will be kept from actually having to decide upon the mark of the beast, as Jesus promised in Revelation 3:10: *"Because thou hast kept the word of my patience, I also*

508 1 Thessalonians 5:3
509 Esther 5:1
510 Esther 4:14-17
511 Romans 13:14, Revelation 1:6, 5:10
512 Romans 5:2

will keep thee from the hour of temptation, which shall come upon all the world, to try them that dwell upon the earth."

In the political squeeze, the true church will do what Esther did—hold two wine banquets for the king. Wine represents the joy and boldness God's Spirit brings to the believer, as taught in Psalm 16:11, Acts 2:4-21, and 4:31. Instead of choosing fear in her time of trouble, the bride will honor her King with praise, joy, and bold rejoicing to magnify His name. Dual wine banquets also speak of the former and latter rains from Joel 2:23 (See Chapter 3). Note also how Isaiah likens the rapture—validated by Paul in 1 Corinthians 15:51-54—unto a wine feast in Isaiah 25:6-8:

> *"And in this mountain shall the Lord of hosts make unto all people a feast of fat things, a feast of wines on the lees, of fat things full of marrow, of wines on the lees well refined. And he will destroy in this mountain the face of the covering cast over all people, and the vail that is spread over all nations. He will swallow up death in victory; and the Lord God will wipe away tears from off all faces; and the rebuke of his people shall he take away from off all the earth: for the Lord hath spoken it."*

Observe Esther sitting at a table with her husband and her greatest enemy, Haman. Like David wrote in Psalm 23:5, Esther was at a table in the presence of her enemies, but God's anointing upon her led her to victory and deliverance: *"Thou preparest a table before me in the presence of mine enemies: thou anointest my head with oil; my cup runneth over."* Though political pressure may come to the bride's table, or churches, even shutting her doors, the latter rain anointing will ensure her deliverance. David knew his victory came not by his own power but by God's anointing. Today's bride-church knows the same.

It was on the day of the second wine banquet when Esther finally revealed her petition to her husband, the king, who saved her from her accuser, Haman. Esther never had to suffer through the hour of death

Haman planned because Xerxes did away with him. So will the bride-church be saved from living in the Tribulation when the mark of the beast will be laid down. Christ will remove His church from the earth before the Tribulation.

Esther's story ends with Mordecai's ascension to increased power and authority in the king's house. The Jews, Esther's people, were given permission to defend themselves against Haman's death sentence, and they fought and defeated all their foes, causing the creation of the celebratory Feast of Purim. Complete Jewish victory in Shushan types the complete victory of the 144,000 Jewish believers during the Tribulation. Though the Antichrist and every nation will come against her, Jesus will physically come to protect and save His covenant people whose names are on the Book of Life.[513]

The "*Shulamite,*"[514] Solomon's love interest in the Book of Song of Solomon, types the bride of Christ because she is his only love throughout the entire book, and she is never divorced or put away as Israel was. She is his one and only, his "*lily among thorns,* the "*fairest among women.*"[515] The Shulamite was likely a Jew, as Easton's Bible Dictionary says Shulamite means "from Shunem," which is a little village in the tribe of Issachar.[516] Song of Solomon 3:9-11 names Solomon, proving he is indeed both the Shulamite's lover and king.

Chapters 1-3 trace their romance from its beginning to the end of their engagement. The Shulamite asks to be drawn into fellowship by her lover despite her black, sunburnt skin. She is a Jewish vineyard laborer and not of royal ascent, as royalty do not work in the hot sun. Right away she connects her skin color with the Gentile clan of Kedar[517] (Ishmaelites) giving evidence she is a type of the New Testament church composed of Jew and Gentile.

---

513   Daniel 12:1
514   Song of Solomon 6:13
515   Song of Solomon 1:8, 2:2, 6:9
516   "Shulamite, The." *Bible Study Tools*, https://www.biblestudytools.com/dictionaries/smiths-bible-dictionary/shulamite-the.html
517   Song of Solomon 1:5

The Shulamite loves him in her soul,[518] the center of her existence. God's Holy Spirit reaches to the depths of the bride's soul, purifying it as the seal upon her soul.[519] The couple dream of their wedding night and enjoy short vacations together in the spring until Solomon's arrival for their wedding in chapter 3:6-11.

Chapter 4 details their wedding night, as the couple compliments each other's head-to-toe beauty. The marriage is consummated as Solomon enters his spouse, his garden, and tastes of his honey. Here, physical intercourse types the baptism the Holy Ghost in the believer's soul because Peter likens the new birth to receiving God's incorruptible seed,[520] as a woman receives her husband's seed on the wedding night.

Chapters 5-7 detail the Shulamite's struggles to respond quickly to her husband and her diligent seeking of his presence. The couple again compliments each other's beauty in every body part as the wife longs to get away on vacation in order to give him her love. Any Christian can relate to the Shulamite's desires to appropriately respond to Christ's Spirit and constantly live in His presence. The body of Christ is completely lovely in Christ's eyes, for He has washed it Himself with His Word.

In the eighth and final chapter, the couple's love is best described as a seal upon their hearts, stronger even than death. Adam proved love is stronger than death, for he, like Christ after him, purposely chose to die in order to be with Eve. He knew she was part of him and he could not deny himself. Jesus' love for His people was stronger than death, for He raised from the dead to justify her. Jesus' church loves Him so much she willingly gives her life for Him, either through martyrdom or life long service.

In Bible days, nothing was more permanent than a king's seal, as Esther 8:8 says the king's proclamation sealed with his ring is irreversible. The couples' love is irreversible, unending, and eternal. Jesus' love is the seal of the Holy Ghost upon a Christian's soul. It's an unending, spiritual love. Ephesians 4:30 promises the believer is *sealed unto the day of*

---

518   Song of Solomon 1:7, 3:1-4
519   Ephesians 4:30, 1 Thessalonians 5:23, 1 Peter 1:22
520   1 Peter 1:23

redemption." Romans 5:5 says *"the love of God is shed abroad in our hearts by the Holy Ghost which is given unto us."*

Song of Solomon ends identically to the New Testament, as both books have brides eager for their bridegroom's return. Song of Solomon 8:14 records the wife urging Solomon to return quickly like a speedy gazelle running down a mountain, saying, *"Make haste, my beloved, and be thou like to a roe or to a young hart upon the mountains of spices."* After Jesus promises to come quickly, John agrees, saying *"Amen. Even so, come, Lord Jesus."*[521] Christ's bride is greatly anticipating His return at the rapture.

LESSONS LEARNED THROUGH BIBLE BRIDES, WIVES, AND WOMEN

Today's New Testament bride can learn valuable lessons she can instantly apply to her life from the women's lives recorded in the Holy Bible.

Eve, the first female, came from Adam as she was formed from his rib. She is a representation of Christ's bride originating from God's mind, as we were *"chosen…in him before the foundation of the world."*[522] You came from the mind of God; you are one of His eternal thoughts. This means your soul is eternal. You came from God, and you will go back to God. You are a part of His Word, which inspires you to daily live out His Word.

The first female was deceived into sinning by the Satan-filled serpent. Chapter 10 details Satan injecting his nature into the human race. Christians don't put excessive guilt and blame upon Eve, for any of us in her position would have done the same. But the lesson is to never add or take away from God's Word, as repeatedly taught in Scripture. Eve's desire should have been to Adam. The bride-church's desire must only be to Christ. The bride-church observes Eve accepting the serpent's addition to God's command and learns not to repeat her error. The serpent added one word—not—saying, *"Ye shall not surely die."*[523] True churches will not add one thing to God's commands.

---

521   Revelation 22:20
522   Ephesians 1:4
523   Genesis 3:4

Redemption's story is seen in Eve's life, first in Adam willingly sinning. Adam knew he would die if he partook of the forbidden fruit, but he loved Eve too much to live without her. She was part of him, so he took her sin upon himself, trusting God's mercy to redeem them. Eve was deceived but Adam wasn't. This is allegorical of Christ willingly taking all sin upon Himself and dying on the cross for our redemption.

You also see God providing an animal sacrifice to forgive and redeem them both. Like God providing a ram to take Isaac's place, God prepared a body for Christ to take your place on the cross. Adam and Eve were clothed in their sacrifice, wearing coats of skins in Genesis 3:21. Jesus' forgiven bride-church is spiritually clothed in His righteousness. Isaiah 61:10 reads, *"I will greatly rejoice in the Lord, my soul shall be joyful in my God; for he hath clothed me with the garments of salvation, he hath covered me with the robe of righteousness, as a bridegroom decketh himself with ornaments, and as a bride adorneth herself with her jewels."*

Eve is forever connected with Adam, just as the bride-church is connected with Christ. Jesus is called the *"last Adam"* in 1 Corinthians 15:45 because he is the true, faithful Adam. Where Adam failed, Jesus conquered. Paul writes further, *"For since by man came death, by man came also the resurrection of the dead. For as in Adam all die, even so in Christ shall all be made alive."*[524] So if Jesus is the Last Adam, the bride-church must be the Last Eve—the obedient one, desiring only her Husband, and she cannot be deceived.

Jochebed, the mother of Moses, along with her husband, are examples of trusting in God in the face of governmental oppression. Egypt was killing all Hebrew baby boys, but Jochebed's faith caused her to reject fear[525] and cast Moses upon the waters in an ark rather than let him die by Egyptian hands. God honored her faith, ordaining Pharoah's daughter to find him. Jochebed was eventually paid by the government to raise her own son!

---

524   1 Corinthians 15:21-22
525   Hebrews 11:23

Christ's bride learns to honor God's Word despite persecution. As Peter says, *"We ought to obey God rather than men."*[526] Trust God with your children's destiny and God will reward you in ways you cannot imagine. Go to all lengths to love, protect, and train the children God gives you with confidence that God has a divine commission for their lives. Just as Moses began following God at 80 years old, have faith your children will someday repent and serve God. Proverbs 22:6 declares, *"Train up a child in the way he should go: and when he is old, he will not depart from it."*

Deborah, a prophetess and wife of Lapidoth, became a judge in Israel during a period of spiritual decline when Israel was without male prophetic leadership. God used her accurate prophesies to inspire Barak in his victorious attacks against the Canaanites, like He used Sarah to move Abraham in sending away Hagar and Ishmael.[527]

Jesus' bride learns the power of prophecy from Deborah's example. The *"testimony of Jesus is the spirit of prophecy,"*[528] and Ezra 6:14 says believers always prosper through prophecy. You should expect prophetic words, as Jesus in John 16:13 says the Holy Ghost will tell us things to come. Although Paul says women can not preach to men due to Eve's deception,[529] the New Testament does give both men and women the right to prophecy and manifest all nine gifts of the Holy Ghost.[530] The bride-church will have all nine gifts of Spirit operating in her midst.

Michal, the daughter of king Saul and wife of David, once saved David's life by helping him escape Saul's wrath. But after being given in marriage to another man and then reclaimed by David, she despises and mocks David's Spirit-led dancing and worship as he brings the ark into Jerusalem. She's condemned to a life of barrenness, having no children.[531]

Bride members glean the importance of Spirit-inspired worship expressed in singing, dancing, shouting, and more. Paul writes in 1 Thessalonians 5:19, *"Quench not the Spirit."* David knew music led by the

---

526   Acts 5:29
527   Genesis 21:12
528   Revelation 19:10
529   1 Timothy 2:11-15
530   Acts 21:9, 1 Corinthians 12:1-3
531   2 Samuel 6:16-23, 1 Chronicles 15:28-29

Holy Ghost would cast out devils,[532] and Jesus' bride knows the same. Churches who reject the emotional blessings of the Holy Ghost will go childless, meaning their members will never be born again by the Spirit. Just as natural babies are often born with noisy crying, spiritual babies are baptized with the Holy Ghost through a bold, emotional experience (See Chapter 6).

Michal is best resembled by Judas Iscariot, the betrayer of Jesus, when he degraded Lazarus' sister Mary. Judas was upset Mary used very costly spikenard to anoint Jesus' feet and wipe them with her long, uncut hair in John 12:1-8. Unlike Judas, bride-churches follow the apostolic example of Acts 4:24-31 by getting in the Spirit and fully, loudly worshipping God with their bodies and emotions, despite reproach from Judas Iscariot-type mockers.

Hannah, the wife of Elkanah and mother of the prophet Samuel, is known for desperately and emotionally seeking God for a child that she be not barren. While pouring out her soul before the LORD, Eli the priest mistakes her emotion for drunkenness, but Hannah explains her sincere desire. Eli announces God's approval of and answer to her request and vow. After weaning Samuel, Hannah keeps her promise and leaves Samuel to minister in the priesthood.[533]

Lessons about the value of natural and spiritual children are learned here. While most professing Christian churches condone the killing of millions of babies, both by abortions and birth control pills,[534] true churches abhor death and value all life. Yes, birth control pills cause millions of abortions by preventing new children, embryos, from attaching to the uterine wall. Bride-churches are desperate to see new life come forth in the natural womb of mothers and in spiritual womb of the church.

During my ministry, I have desperately prayed for two barren couples to have children, and God heard the prayers for both. Now we rejoice

---

532   1 Samuel 16:23
533   1 Samuel 1:1-28
534   "Can Birth Control Pills Kill Unborn Babies?" *ChristianAnswers.Net*, https://christiananswers.net/q-eden/edn-bcpill.html

like Hannah in 1 Samuel 1:27: *"For this child I prayed; and the Lord hath given me my petition which I asked of* him."

Bride churches must also pray earnestly for new converts to be born again by the Holy Ghost baptism. Acts chapters 1 and 2 show the early apostles praying for 10 days before receiving the new birth. Paul says in Galatians 4:19 he was willing to again *"travail in birth"* until the Galatians were truly born from above. Their reverting to legalistic teachings proved they were not born again at first and Paul was willing to help bring them to the born again experience they previously fell short of.

Many more lessons abound for bride members in the lives of Biblical women:

- Abigail, beautiful and wise, was exalted to wife of king David following her reverent approach to him and the death of her first husband, evil Nabal (1 Samuel 25). The bride-church's first husband, the law, also dies and she offers pleasing sacrifices to her royal Husband, King Jesus (Romans 7:4, Hebrews 13:15, 1 Peter 2:5, Revelation 19:16).

- Bathsheba, disgraced by adultery before legally becoming David's wife, was forgiven by God, blessed with four sons, and helped to secure Solomon's succession to the throne (1 Chronicles 3:5, 1 Kings 1). Bride members rest in God's complete washing away of sexual immortality, and use all their power and influence to ensure Christ rules with preeminence both in the church and their hearts (1 Corinthians 6:9-11, Colossians 1:18, 3:15).

- Mary, the wife of Joseph and mother of Jesus, is the epitome of child-like faith, humbly receiving the angel Gabriel's promise she would conceive the Christ child in her virginity, and decades later, received the Spirit of Christ in the upper room (Luke 1:26-38, Acts 1:14, 2:4). Her testimony inspires bride members to live as chaste virgins to Jesus, quickly accept God's promises, and obey every Word until the new birth comes (Acts 5:32, 2 Corinthians 11:2, 1 Thessalonians 2:13).

- Anna, an elderly widowed prophetess, *"served God with fastings and prayers night and day,"* and gave witness of baby Jesus being the promised Messiah-Redeemer at the same instant Simeon prophesied of Jesus' mission (Luke 2:22-38). Bride members understand life-long, faithful decades of service to God and His house yield untold spiritual rewards and experiences. God *"is a rewarder of them that diligently seek him"* (Hebrews 11:6).

- Mary Magdalene was healed from seven demons by Christ and then faithfully followed and supported His ministry, being present at the cross (Matthew 27:56, Luke 8:2). Jesus rewarded her faith by making her the first to see Him after His resurrection (Mark 16:9). The bride church enjoys the same freedom from devils as Mary, and seeks to imitate her unwavering devotion despite trials, with the same promise to one day see the Resurrected One face to face.

- The Samaritan woman Jesus meets at Jacob's well instantly recognizes Jesus' prophetic gift when He reveals her secrets, causing her to boldly testify to her city, making many more converts to Christ (John 4:1-42). Believers experience the same discernment ability of the living Word today (Hebrews 4:12) and women in particular learn the power of testifying to others about Jesus without preaching. Christian women testify, but do not preach (1 Timothy 2:11-15).

- Mary of Bethany, a sister of Jesus' close friend Lazarus, serves as a powerful example of hearing the Word and acting upon it. Despite her sister's objection, Mary chose to sit and listen to Jesus rather than complete house work, and Christ approved of Mary's decision, saying all she heard would never be taken away (Luke 10:39-42). Christians today realize the revelations received during the preaching are eternal and the gates of hell will never prevail against them (Matthew 16:17-18).

- Priscilla, the wife of Aquila, shows diligence in the faith by working alongside her husband to help Paul, host church services in her house, and testify to Apollos about God's further revelations (Acts 18:2-26, Romans 16:3, 1 Corinthians 16:19). Bride members glean the importance of staying in your position, supporting preachers, opening your home to the gospel, and the power of testimonies.

THE PROVERBS 31 WOMAN TYPES JESUS' BRIDE

I would be remiss if I left out the Proverbs 31 Woman. Few portions of Scripture place such a high value upon a godly, holy woman. Proverbs 31:10 declares, *"Who can find a virtuous woman? for her price is far above rubies."* A simple online search about the value of rubies shows a single carat can be worth 2 million dollars.[535] A real Christian woman's value, equivalent to numerous rubies, far exceeds millions and billions of dollars. In the spiritual sense, Jesus' bride was so valuable He gave His innocent life for her guilty life, shedding His precious blood to save her soul.

Surely this distinguished woman points to Christ's New Testament bride. Like the Shulamite, the Proverbs 31 Woman is singled out and exalted above all women: *"Many daughters have done virtuously, but thou excellest them all."*[536] Ephesians 5:27 describes Christ's bride-church as being free from spot, wrinkle, or blemish. She is heaven's one, blood-washed, great multitude from every nation who serves Him and never leaves His side.[537]

The Proverbs 31 Woman is the culmination of the Book of Proverbs. The first chapter begins with symbolic Lady Wisdom seeking to pour

---

535   International Gem Society, *https://www.gemsociety.org*
536   Proverbs 31:29
537   1 Thessalonians 4:17, Revelation 7:9-17

out her Spirit upon any and all listeners.[538] In the final chapter you see a woman who embodies wisdom. The wisdom has become flesh. Just as Jesus was the Word made flesh,[539] the bride-church will become the manifestation of Christ's Word-image.[540]

It may surprise you to learn that Proverbs 31:10-31 is an acrostic poem,[541] meaning each verse begins with a different Hebrew letter, beginning with the first letter, aleph, and ending with the last, tav. Thus, the Proverbs 31 Woman is all of it—she is completely wise, like the wise virgin of Matthew 25:2. By grace, Jesus' wife is just like Jesus, Who is the *"Alpha and Omega,"*[542] alpha being the first and omega being the last letter of the Greek alphabet. Additionally, the Shulamite was all-beautiful, head to toe, according to Solomon. The bride of Jesus will live all the Word prophesied about her—from the first prophecy to the last—through obedience to the Holy Spirit. Her entire being—body, spirit, soul—is foretold to be preserved blameless unto the day of the Lord Jesus Christ.[543] Proverbs 31:1 says this all-wise woman is a prophecy: *"The words of king Lemuel, the prophecy that his mother taught him."* How exciting to know Proverbs 31 is a prophecy about Jesus' desire for your total obedience to His Word!

Proverbs 31 traces the God-designed path wisdom travels: mother to child, then child to community. Verses 1-9 state wisdom begins with a godly mother who urges her son, the future king, to be wise in every way, but especially in his choice of a wife, which is the purpose of verses 10-31. She knows her son and his wife will influence the entire kingdom, so the gravity of her duty to teach him is apparent. As a son receives teaching from his mother, a believer receives instruction from the church. Remember that you, too, are a spiritual king and priest based upon Revelation 1:6 and 5:10, and you must *"reign in life by one, Jesus Christ."*[544]

538　Proverbs 1:20-23
539　John 1:14
540　Romans 8:29
541　"Proverbs 31 As An Acrostic Poem." *Bible Odyssey,* https://www.bibleodyssey.org/en/passages/related-articles/proverbs-31-as-an-acrostic-poem
542　Revelation 1:8, 11, 21:6, 22:13
543　1 Corinthians 1:8, 1 Thessalonians 5:23
544　Romans 5:17

The Proverbs 31 Woman is highly valued and praised because of two attributes that drive her life: she fears the LORD and does good to her husband all the days of her life.[545] Our closest relationships reveal our true spiritual conditions. Everyone knew this woman feared God, her heavenly Head, because of the attitude and actions towards her earthly head, her husband. Christians who have spiritual treasure in their hearts, or knowledge of Jesus Christ,[546] will also have the treasure of loving relationships in their homes. Proverbs 15:6 says, *"In the house of the righteous is much treasure."* Jesus wants us to treasure our relationships, not our financial gains.

A Holy Ghost-filled bride member will manifest her love for Christ through her everyday actions, blessing those in her home, church, and community. Proverbs 31:10-31 focuses on her life long impact throughout the seasons of life. A natural wife goes from a newly wed, to a mother, to an empty nest. God ordained these seasons, and each has its unique responsibilities. Ecclesiastes 3:1 says, *"To every thing there is a season, and a time to every purpose under heaven."*

A Proverbs 31 Woman's highest priority is her home life, for her daily interactions with her family proves her status as a chaste virgin to Christ, and also shapes the spiritual condition of the next generation. Proverbs 31 explains how Christian women practically apply God's Word to their everyday lives. In her home, her nest, she is:

- Completely trustworthy with her husband and family resources (31:11-12)
- Taking initiative to work with her hands (31:13, 18-19, 22, 24)
- Ready to serve her family at all hours (31:15)
- Shrewd in business transactions and investments (31:16, 24)
- Healthy, physically fit, and adorned in her best clothes (31:17, 22)

---

545   Proverbs 31:12, 30
546   2 Corinthians 4:6-7

- Ready to respond to help the poor (31:20)
- Prepared, a shrewd planner, and alert (31:18, 21, 27)
- Anointed with God' strength and humbly saving celebrations for the future (31:25)
- Speaking kind, wise words (31:26)

Each Christian mother should strive to have these attributes, and Christian husbands should love their wives in a way that helps her achieve these actions in the appropriate seasons of life. Husbands are called to love like Jesus loved, giving up their own selfish desires for their family's benefit. The Proverbs 31 Woman, after many days of both happiness and struggles, witnesses her children and husband blessing and praising her holy efforts. Proverbs 31:28 reads, *"Her children arise up, and call her blessed; her husband also, and he praiseth her."* Likewise, Jesus' bride will be called *"blessed and holy"* for overcoming life's struggles and obtaining the rapture, or first resurrection.[547]

THE REWARDS FOR RECEIVING THE REVELATION OF THE CHURCH AS JESUS' BRIDE

Those who receive the revelation of the church as Jesus' bride experience great rewards now and in the heavenly home.

In this earthly life, bride members have eternal assurance through the seal of the Holy Ghost-baptism. The Holy Spirit is Jesus' nature ruling their human nature. They are marked in their souls as Christ's bride because they were in His mind before the world was. Through anointed preaching, she will be faithfully washed from all iniquities and transgressions, confident of Jesus' return for her, His bride.

The bride is rewarded with seeing the fruits of her decisions. Her wise decisions, as the wise virgin group, are undeniable to those around her. Her separated, holy life is acknowledged as Jesus teaches in Matthew 5:16: *"Let your light so shine before men, that they may see your good works, and glorify your Father which is in heaven."* She has left both the "foolish

547   Revelation 20:6

virgin" churches and the Mother Harlot church, and enjoys *"a quiet and peaceable life in all godliness and honesty."*[548] She is not totally free from trials, but her physical and spiritual separation from worldly influences yields a special oneness with her Lord, her Husband.

If you and your spouse receive this revelation, you'll experience all the home-life blessings spoken of in Proverbs 31. God's presence in your home will be your treasure, as parents and children love one another in godly harmony. Home will resemble heaven on earth.

Heavenly rewards include experiencing the rapture, the meeting in the air. Chapter 12 details this climatic event of human history. During the Tribulation, you will sit with bride members from all ages at the Marriage Supper of the Lamb, enjoying communion with your Bridegroom, Jesus.

Following the supper, you'll reign with Christ on the earth for 1,000 years. Revelation 20:4-6 promises this, as only bride members live and reign during this time period. The *"rest of the dead"*—foolish virgins, make believers, and unbelievers—do not live until after the 1,000 year honeymoon is completed:

> *"And I saw thrones, and they sat upon them, and judgment was given unto them: and I saw the souls of them that were beheaded for the witness of Jesus, and for the word of God, and which had not worshipped the beast, neither his image, neither had received his mark upon their foreheads, or in their hands; and they lived and reigned with Christ a thousand years. But the rest of the dead lived not again until the thousand years were finished. This is the first resurrection. Blessed and holy is he that hath part in the first resurrection: on such the second death hath no power, but they shall be priests of God and of Christ, and shall reign with him a thousand years."*

As Christ's beautiful wife, the bride-church sits next to Him on thrones, judging nations for a millennium. This magnifies the importance of judging truth and error now, for you cannot be a judge there

548   1 Timothy 2:2

unless you judge righteously here. You will suffer rejection, mockery, and perhaps even physical persecution for judging earthly matters correctly. Endure these sufferings and temptations so you can reign later. 2 Timothy 2:11-12 promises, "*It is a faithful saying: For if we be dead with him, we shall also live with him: If we suffer, we shall also reign with him: if we deny him, he also will deny us.*"

Two more heavenly rewards await Jesus' bride: she will sit with Him in judgment at His White Throne, and live with Him in the New Jerusalem. Just as Jesus promised to raise up the Queen of the South and the men of Nineveh on Judgment Day,[549] so will He use His bride's testimonies against unbelievers. Revelation 3:21 says you'll sit with Him on that day: "*To him that overcometh will I grant to sit with me in my throne, even as I also overcame, and am set down with my Father in his throne.*" Paul says your testimony will judge unbelievers and fallen angels in 1 Corinthians 6:2-3.

In the New Jerusalem, Jesus' bride is ever with Him, being fed by Him and serving His desires. Her eternal privilege is seeing His loving face forever. Revelation 22:3-4 declares, "*And there shall be no more curse: but the throne of God and of the Lamb shall be in it; and his servants shall serve him: And they shall see his face; and his name shall be in their foreheads.*"

THE CONSEQUENCES FOR REJECTING THE REVELATION OF THE CHURCH AS JESUS' BRIDE

Rejecting the fact that God has a special people designated as His bride leads to the deception of universalism. Many live under the lie that "We are all God's children, God loves us the same, and we are all going to heaven." While it is true that God's love is impartial, God's love must be received. When churches willingly disobey any part of God's Word, they forfeit either part or all of God's blessings. Disobedience also signifies hatred for God since Jesus taught obedience signifies your love for God in John 14:15, 21, and 23-24.

---

549   Luke 11:31-32

Doubters of this revelation will have chaos in their homes as another consequence. When God's Word is either discredited or not preached, the listeners go home unwashed, without spiritual correction and power. Family chaos ensues, as 2 Timothy 3:1-2 foretells: *"This know also, that in the last days perilous times shall come. For men shall be lovers of their own selves, covetous, boasters, proud, blasphemers, disobedient to parents, unthankful, unholy."* Husbands will love themselves more than their wives and children. Teenagers and children alike will violently rebel against the ones who nurtured them and gave them life. Instead of treasure in their homes, corruption will abide.

For those who will eventually be saved but reject this revelation, their highest spiritual attainment is the "foolish virgin" category as taught by Jesus and Paul. They will squander their precious time wandering from activity to activity. Ephesians 5:15-17 says, *"See then that ye walk circumspectly, not as fools, but as wise, Redeeming the time, because the days are evil. Wherefore be ye not unwise, but understanding what the will of the Lord is."* Foolish virgins are not quite sure what God's will is for their lives. Rather than being conformed to Jesus' Word-image[550] like the bride was, they conformed to the world's standards. Paul pleads with us to conform our minds to Jesus' Words in Romans 12:1-2:

> *"I beseech you therefore, brethren, by the mercies of God, that ye present your bodies a living sacrifice, holy, acceptable unto God, which is your reasonable service. And be not conformed to this world: but be ye transformed by the renewing of your mind, that ye may prove what is that good, and acceptable, and perfect, will of God."*

Future consequences are most awful for those who reject and blaspheme this revelation. They may even become part of a church, whether the Mother Harlot or one of her daughters. As a result, their lives will be filled with demonic influences in their bodies and minds, through movies, television shows, and more. Mother Harlot churches are the homes

---

550   Romans 8:29

of every kind of devil according to Revelation 18:2. Choosing to be part of the false bride brings plagues. Revelation 18:4 warns, *"And I heard another voice from heaven, saying, Come out of her, my people, that ye be not partakers of her sins, and that ye receive not of her plagues."* The last, miserable consequence for these lost souls is eternal separation from God in the lake of fire.

CONCLUSION

Jesus is looking for a bride that will submit to His every Word, and accept her responsibilities and ministries. Will you let Jesus wash away your every sin-stain through the Water of His Word? Jesus offers this cleansing and thirst-quenching Water to every individual: *"If any thirst, let him come unto me, and drink."*[551]

You need not have to wonder if you are part of Jesus' bride. The Bible doctrines and commands that any person can read straight out of the Bible must be followed. Those who obey are the true bride, separated from the foolish and evil women. Christ came to seek and save His bride, and you will know His voice as you hear His Word preached in its fullness and truth.

In becoming Jesus' bride, you find your eternal destiny and position by His side. Your only word will be His Word. His thoughts will be your thoughts. Just as Adam said of Eve, *"This is now bone of my bones, and flesh of my flesh,"*[552] Jesus says you are a Word of His Word, Life of His Life, and Spirit of His Spirit.

ACTION STEPS

1. Repent for disobeying any Bible command and seek the baptism of the Holy Ghost. Express your desire to fully submit to every Word of God. If you surrender fully, He'll come in fully.

551   John 7:37-39
552   Genesis 2:23

2. In kindness and respect, separate yourself from both foolish and false churches. If you are in need of a bride-church, please contact me. Revelation 22:17 says the Spirit and the bride are inviting you to come and drink of the Waters of Life freely. If you desire a true church, there has to be a church God has prepared for you. Psalm 42:7 says, *"Deep calleth unto deep."* If you have a deep call and desire for truth, God has a response waiting for you, even if you have to start a bride-church yourself.

3. Continue to grow in grace and knowledge of the Lord through continual sanctification. The bride not only begins holiness, but perfects and completes it. 2 Corinthians 7:1 reads, *"Having therefore these promises, dearly beloved, let us cleanse ourselves from all filthiness of the flesh and spirit, perfecting holiness in the fear of God."*

FOLLOW UP

Free online videos, Bible studies, and William Branham's quotes related to this chapter: www.pastorjessesmith.com/12mysteriesbook

Email: jesse.smith11@sbcglobal.net

Text: 330-929-2037

CHAPTER 5
The Mystery of Godliness Restored to Man

"And without controversy great is the mystery of godliness: God was manifest in the flesh, justified in the Spirit, seen of angels, preached unto the Gentiles, believed on in the world, received up into glory."

1 Timothy 3:16

GODLINESS IS A PRECIOUS, mysterious, yet obtainable level of Christian character that few worshippers reach. Like Paul, you are one of the true worshippers seeking to *"press toward the mark for the prize of the high calling of God in Christ Jesus."*[553]

In the Greek Lexicon, *"godliness"* means "reverence, respect, piety towards God." Other words that help explain its meaning are loyal, faithful, devoted, and dutiful.

You can also say godliness is "being like God." What a glorious invitation—God is offering you a chance to be like Him! You might be thinking, "I can't be like God." But be encouraged, for Jesus says you can. Our Lord says, *"Be ye therefore perfect, even as your Father which is in heaven is perfect."*[554] Godliness is a state of loyalty all true Christians desire based upon Jesus' invitation.

If Jesus asks us to be perfect, or complete, He has to make a way for us to achieve that condition. He has, and this chapter reveals Christ's process to our godliness.

In the epigraph above, Paul declares the mystery of godliness in context of Jesus' life: *"God was manifest in the flesh, justified in the Spirit, seen of angels, preached unto the Gentiles, believed on in the world, and received up into glory."* In other words, Jesus' earthly life manifested true godliness as the epitome of godliness. In stark contrast is Satan, the epitome of iniquity (See Chapter 10).

You see the true expression of godliness as you read about Jesus Christ in the four gospels because He lived by every Word of God. Jesus is God's manifestation of His own character in a flesh body. To understand godliness, you need only look to Jesus Christ's behavior.

Jesus manifested godly character by constantly increasing His wisdom. Godliness is attained through a slow, steady growth. Even at 12 years old, Jesus' heart was burdened with doing His *"Father's business."*[555] Scripture records that *"Jesus increased in wisdom and stature, and in favor with God and man."*[556] Godliness was mysteriously manifested in the life of Christ as He daily increased His devotion and loyalty to God the Father. As always, His life is the guidance for understanding our lives.

THE CONFUSION ABOUT THE MYSTERY OF GODLINESS

The confusion about godliness centers around human effort and its attainability. Is human effort required to reach godliness? If so, how

554 Matthew 5:48
555 Luke 2:49
556 Luke 2:52

much effort is needed? Can godliness even be attained? If churches teach human effort is required, some will instantly accuse them of legalism and works-based salvation. The age-old "Works or Faith" debate is revived as you study godliness, but God's Word settles this debate once and for all as God's revelation on godliness unfolds in this chapter.

The revelation of the mystery of godliness is that God uses Works of Grace to incrementally anoint Christians with measures of Christ's own godly character as they lovingly yield all their human strength.

BIBLICAL EVIDENCE FOR THE REVELATION OF GODLINESS

Jesus eliminates all confusion about obtaining godliness through His teaching about the two greatest commandments in Matthew 22:37-39: *"Jesus said unto him, Thou shalt love the Lord thy God with all thy heart, and with all thy soul, and with all thy mind. This is the first and great commandment. And the second is like unto it, Thou shalt love thy neighbour as thyself."* Human effort is required to reach godliness and its motivation is love. In fact, Jesus says you must use *"all"* your human effort or strength in a parallel passage in the gospel of Mark: *"And thou shalt love the Lord thy God with all thy heart, and with all thy soul, and with all thy mind, and with all thy strength: this is the first commandment."*[557] All your human effort and strength is required to manifest godliness.

If absolutely no human effort or action is required for salvation, then all sinners will be saved. It's ridiculous to think Judas Iscariot, whom Jesus said was lost in John 17:12, and the rich man literally in hell in Luke 16:23 will be saved. The reason they are lost is because they refused God's love into their souls, a choice necessary for salvation. Humans must do something for salvation, and it is believe.

557   Mark 12:30

Surprising to some, all human actions are based upon love, whether the person is a sinner or saint. Sinners are lost and go to hell because they love the pleasures of the world. Love for unbelief motivates their human effort. Jesus says in John 3:19, *"And this is the condemnation, that light is come into the world, and men loved darkness rather than light, because their deeds were evil."* Paul echoes this truth by teaching sinners are *"traitors, heady, highminded, lovers of pleasures more than lovers of God."*[558] Paul never said these sinners didn't love God. Their fatal problem was that they loved the world *more* than they loved God.

Jesus silences the legalism accusation. Legalism is defined as "excessive adherence to law or formula,"[559] meaning legalism is an addition to the Word of God. Scripture condemns anyone who adds to God's Word in Proverbs 30:5-6 and Revelation 22:18-19. An obvious Bible example of legalism is Paul encountering legalistic Jewish teachers who were requiring circumcision for salvation, which he condemned as a fall from grace.[560] Jesus never asks us to do anything outside the Bible's commands. Rather, He empowers our human effort to do all His commands by His love, which is shed in our hearts: *"And hope maketh not ashamed; because the love of God is shed abroad in our hearts by the Holy Ghost which is given unto us."*[561]

Obeying God with all your love and human strength is attainable through a self-crucifixion of your sinful human will. Jesus declares in Luke 14:27: *"And whosoever doth not bear his cross, and come after me, cannot be my disciple."* Jesus' true disciples follow His commands through a daily death to selfishness. This is the only way to live in the Holy Spirit, as Romans 8:13 says, *"For if ye live after the flesh, ye shall die: but if ye through the Spirit do mortify the deeds of the body, ye shall live."* Paul again writes, *"Mortify therefore your members which are upon the earth; fornication, uncleanness, inordinate affection, evil concupiscence, and covetousness, which is idolatry: For which things' sake the wrath of God cometh on the*

558   2 Timothy 3:4
559   "Legalism." *Oxford English Dictionary*, https://en.oxforddictionaries.com/definition/legalism
560   Acts 15:24-29, Galatians 5:1-6, 6:12-15
561   Romans 5:5

children of disobedience."[562] Paul experienced this daily, self-crucifixion personally, saying, *"I protest by your rejoicing which I have in Christ Jesus our Lord, I die daily."*[563]

Scripture teaches you yield your will and human strength to one of two masters. Jesus says you cannot serve both God and mammon, meaning riches, in Luke 16:13: *"No servant can serve two masters: for either he will hate the one, and love the other; or else he will hold to the one, and despise the other. Ye cannot serve God and mammon."* Which master do you love more—God or riches? Paul says you'll either yield to sin or God in Romans 6:13: *"Neither yield ye your members as instruments of unrighteousness unto sin: but yield yourselves unto God, as those that are alive from the dead, and your members as instruments of righteousness unto God."* If you yield to God with all your strength, you'll achieve godliness.

TWO TYPES OF GODLINESS

Scripture differentiates two types of godliness. One is an initial level of devotion you receive as you approach your spiritual birth, or before you are born again through the baptism of the Holy Ghost. This measure or portion of godliness is the sixth character trait God adds to your being after He's saved your soul through the substance of faith.

The second type of godliness is a mature, rare, spiritual state of devotion a believer manifests *after* he is born again. Chapter 6 gives a full teaching on the born-again experience, the baptism of the Holy Ghost. This mature godliness is the *"mystery of godliness"* seen in Jesus' life as He fully and constantly obeyed the Father.

The fact that there are two types of godliness gives this subject its mysterious nature. It is no different from the mystery of two kinds of fillings of God's Spirit—one in your mind and another in your soul (see Chapter 6). Often when something seems confusing in Scripture, God is hiding in mystery behind it urging you to dig deeper in search of revelation.

---

562   Colossians 3:5-6
563   1 Corinthians 15:31

Paul and Peter repeatedly mention the mature state of godliness. Paul's instructions to Timothy, a preacher,[564] are to exercise himself *"unto godliness"* as he follows after godliness.[565] In Paul's mind, Christians are actively seeking to display *"all godliness."*[566] Peter echoes the same, saying Christians ought to be dedicated persons *"in all holy conversation and godliness, looking for and hasting unto the coming of the day of God, wherein the heavens being on fire shall be dissolved, and the elements shall melt with fervent heat."*[567] Both apostles are pointing us to mature godliness like Christ's, Who says He does *"nothing of himself, but what he seeth the Father do."*[568] Jesus did only what His Father told Him to do. You are approaching mature godliness when your daily actions are only those that God leads you to do. Christ spoke only the words His Father gave Him, as evidenced by John 8:38: *"I speak that which I have seen with my Father."*

MORE OF PAUL'S TEACHING ABOUT MATURE GODLINESS

The apostle Paul provides five texts—the most of any New Testament author—about the mature state of godliness that help us understand its meaning and application to our lives.

Beginning in Titus 1:1-2, Paul says he is *"a servant of God, and an apostle of Jesus Christ, according to the faith of God's elect, and the acknowledging of the truth which is after godliness."* Christians acknowledge the truth is *"after"* or *"according to"* godliness. Recognizing the one and only true religion—Christianity—promotes godliness. Paul, a former *"Hebrew of the Hebrews,"*[569] a zealous Pharisee and law keeper, assures all Christians that their faith follows godliness.

In the second text of 1 Timothy 2:1-3, Paul says it's good and acceptable in the sight of God when Christians *"lead a quiet and peaceable life in*

---

564 2 Timothy 4:2
565 1 Timothy 4:7, 6:11
566 1 Timothy 2:2
567 2 Peter 3:11-12
568 John 5:19
569 Philippians 3:5-6

all godliness and honesty." In context, Paul encourages Christians to pray for all men, including our government officials. Notice that *"all godliness"* is attainable and pleases our Lord. Christians do not settle for partial godliness; they set their sights on accomplishing complete godliness.

The third text, 1 Timothy 4:7-8, follows Paul's identification of Jesus' life as the mysterious *"godliness"* (1 Timothy 3:16) and then says Christians obtain godliness through the imagery of spiritual exercise. Just as physical exercise helps you reach healthiness, Paul says vigorous spiritual exercise helps you reach godliness. Paul rebukes heavily exercising our minds in fiction, or listening to *"profane and old wives' fables."* The apostle says *"exercise thyself rather unto godliness. For bodily exercise profiteth little: but godliness is profitable unto all things, having promise of the life that now is, and of that which is to come."* In the Greek Lexicon, *"exercise"* means "to exercise vigorously, in any way, either the body or the mind." Your mind exercises by repeatedly meditating on things that are true, honest, just, pure, lovely, virtuous, and praiseworthy.[570] Paul says you must *"set your affection on things above"*[571] and the final result will be your spiritual transformation.[572]

1 Timothy 6:3-12, Paul's fourth and most thorough teaching on godliness, mentions "godliness" four times. He begins by affirming that the doctrine of Jesus Christ *"is according to godliness"* and warns of false teachers who suppose financial gain is a sign of godliness. Paul urges you to withdraw from the prosperity gospel and its preachers. God does not promise riches to the godly. True Christians seek spiritual prosperity, not financial prosperity. Rivers of truth flow from Paul's pen as he describes our fight to be both godly and content:

> *"But godliness with contentment is great gain. For we brought nothing into this world, and it is certain we can carry nothing out. And having food and raiment let us be therewith content. But they that will be rich fall into temptation and a snare, and into many foolish and hurtful lusts, which drown men in*

570 Philippians 4:8
571 Colossians 3:2
572 Romans 12:2

destruction and perdition. For the love of money is the root of
all evil: which while some coveted after, they have erred from
the faith, and pierced themselves through with many sorrows.
But thou, O man of God, flee these things; and follow after
righteousness, godliness, faith, love, patience, meekness. Fight
the good fight of faith, lay hold on eternal life, whereunto thou
art also called, and hast professed a good profession before
many witnesses."

Always remember that you are fighting to obtain mature godliness while simultaneously remaining content with worldly possessions.

In his final letter before his martyrdom, Paul teaches again on godliness in 2 Timothy 3:1-17. While prophesying, he warns believers about the *"perilous"* or dangerous spiritual conditions *"in the last days."* Paul lists 18 sinful attributes—including covetousness, pride, unthankfulness, and being boastful—men will exhibit while maintaining a *"form of godliness"*. In the Greek Lexicon, *"form"* means "shaping, the mere form, semblance." How deceptive Satan is, for he enslaves the masses into a hollow or false godliness by training them to love sin more than God. No doubt men and women faithfully attend and give some money to churches. Some spend time in Bible devotions and yet do not attain true godliness. This happened in Jesus' day, as the Holy Spirit instantly brings to mind the Pharisees' form of godliness. Jesus said they were beautiful in outward appearance yet full of extortion, excess, hypocrisy, and iniquity.[573] Pharisees were devoid of true godliness yet faithfully attended and prayed publicly in the Temple and were devout donors.[574] You glean that genuine godliness comes from a pure heart that loves God far more than worldly pleasures. In your lifetime, these *"last days,"* you're warned false, hollow godliness will *"wax worse and worse, deceiving, and being deceived."* You can obtain true godliness by living selflessly and continuing in the *"holy scriptures, which are able to make thee wise unto salvation through faith which is in Christ Jesus."*

---

573   Matthew 23:25-28
574   Matthew 6:5, 23:6,23

PETER'S STEPS TO INITIAL GODLINESS

Here is where you focus on the other type of godliness—the initial anointing of godliness before you are born again.

Christ anoints Peter to reveal the exact steps God uses to help believers obtain an initial measure of godliness in 2 Peter 1:1-15. God gives eight spiritual portions of character to believers as they mature in Christianity with godliness being the sixth measure (See Figure 5). It is striking to discover that Jesus gave Peter both *the keys to the kingdom of heaven*[575] and the steps for godliness. The Book of Acts records how Peter took the *"keys"* or power and authority to unlock the door to *"the promise of the Father,"*[576] the born-again experience (See Chapter 6).

#1 Character quality	Faith
#2 Character quality	Virtue
#3 Character quality	Knowledge
#4 Character quality	Temperance
#5 Character quality	Patience
#6 Character quality	Godliness
#7 Character quality	Brotherly Kindness
#8 Character quality	Charity

Figure 5

575　Matthew 16:19
576　Luke 24:49, Acts 1:4, 2:33

Each of the eight steps involves God adding a portion or measure of His *"divine nature"* to a Christian's spiritual character. Notice the word "measure." The idea of God giving us eight spiritual measures of His nature comes from Romans 12:3: *"For I say, through the grace given unto me, to every man that is among you, not to think of himself more highly than he ought to think; but to think soberly, according as God hath dealt to every man the measure of faith."* Paul teaches God gives every man a measure or portion of faith. Recall in Figure 5 that *"faith"* is the first character quality given to believers, *"for by grace are ye saved through faith."*[577] As you will learn, faith is the beginning point of your relationship with Almighty God.

Peter uses the exact word *"add,"* which means "to supply, furnish, present", to describe how man receives the eight Christ-like character qualities. How marvelous is the truth that you can have Christ's own mentality or disposition! The faithful God supplies you with the necessary spiritual portion during each step of your Christian journey. God the Father did the same for Jesus as Luke 2:52 records, *"And Jesus increased in wisdom and stature, and in favour with God and man."* God increased, or added to Jesus' character as He grew.

Combining Peter's text with a similar text about becoming a complete, mature Christian in Ephesians 4:8-24, this eight-step spiritual building process can be called "The Stature of a Perfect Man." In the Greek, *"stature"* means "maturity." These steps show how you become a mature, living dwelling place of the living God, for your body is the temple of the Holy Ghost. 1 Corinthians 6:19-20 declares, *"What? know ye not that your body is the temple of the Holy Ghost which is in you, which ye have of God, and ye are not your own? For ye are bought with a price: therefore glorify God in your body, and in your spirit, which are God's."*

Ephesians 4:8-24 emphasizes five preaching gifts God uses to impart the eight character qualities in the Stature of a Perfect Man: apostle, prophet, evangelist, pastor, and teacher. Once Jesus ascended to heaven to sit at the right hand of His Father, these five gifts are what He *"gave...*

577   Ephesians 2:8

unto men...for the perfecting of the saints...Till we all come in the unity of the faith, and of the knowledge of the Son of God, unto a perfect man, unto the measure of the stature of the fulness of Christ." It shouldn't surprise you that preaching brings complete maturity to Christians because it is preaching that initially brings you to salvation. The Bible says, "*it pleased God by the foolishness of preaching to save them that believe.*"[578] How comforting to know that the same method Christians are saved by will also be used to impart further Christ-like character! In our earthly journey, God will always use preaching to increase our maturity: "*So then faith cometh by hearing, and hearing by the word of God.*"[579] Faithful preachers are used by God to impart the following benefits:

- Perfecting of the saints (Ephesians 4:12)
- Work of the ministry (Ephesians 4:12)
- Edifying of the body of Christ (Ephesians 4:12)
- Unity of faith and knowledge of the Son of God unto a perfect man (Ephesians 4:13)
- Maturity and doctrinal stability (Ephesians 4:14)

Each character quality is a spiritual crossroad on a believer's journey. Just as Israel made an exodus out of Egypt following every move of the Pillar of Fire, Christians leave a sinful life while following every leading of the Holy Ghost. Believers must decide whether to continue growing in God's Word by walking in obedience to His commands or reject His leadership. Figure 6 shows why believers must accept the character qualities from God at each crossroad, or stage, of their Christian journey, and why they must reject Satan's bait. Just as God told Moses, life and death is set before every believer. Good and evil were set before Adam and Eve. You must either accept or reject God's gifts in every season of life.

578 1 Corinthians 1:21
579 Romans 10:17

	Accept	Reject
#1 Character quality	Faith is the substance needed to choose God's way.	Unbelief
#2 Character quality	Virtue is the strength needed to daily walk God's way.	Hypocrisy
#3 Character quality	Knowledge is the understanding needed to know why you walk in all God's ways.	Human reasoning
#4 Character quality	Temperance is the self control needed to remain on God's way.	Sensuality
#5 Character quality	Patience is the steadfastness needed to be content on God's way.	Haste
#6 Character quality	Godliness is the devotion needed to be just like God on God's way.	Irreverence
#7 Character quality	Brotherly Kindness is the selflessness needed to live for your Christian family on God's way.	Selfishness
#8 Character quality	Charity is God's abiding, loving presence needed to completely manifest the will of God for your life.	Resistance

Figure 6

CHARACTER QUALITY #1: FAITH

Faith is the foundational character quality. Hebrews 11:1 defines faith as *"the substance of things hoped for, the evidence of things not seen."* Additionally, Hebrews 11:6 says, *"Without faith it is impossible to please him: for he that cometh to God must believe that he is, and that he is a rewarder of them that diligently seek him."* Faith is the first and most necessary character quality needed to please God.

Faith is a gift from God. Salvation is indeed a gift to all who will receive it, as Ephesians 2:8 says, *"For by grace are ye saved through faith;*

and that not of yourselves: it is the gift of God: Not of works, lest any man should boast." Faith is not earned by human effort; rather, it is freely given. Paul writes in Romans 8:32, *"He that spared not his own Son, but delivered him up for us all, how shall he not with him also freely give us all things?"* 2 Peter 1:3 says, *"According as his divine power hath given unto us all things that pertain unto life and godliness, through the knowledge of him that hath called us to glory and virtue."* Jesus says *"few"*[580] will accept saving faith, so choose to be one of the few who accept this eternal gift.

A Christian's spiritual journey begins with faith. Before faith comes, a person is lost in unbelief, or spiritually dead. Ephesians 2:1 says unbelievers are *"dead in trespasses and sin."* Believing in Jesus Christ as Savior brings spiritual life, as Jesus says believers pass *"from death unto life."*[581]

Faith comes when a believer rejects unbelief, repents from his sins, and trusts in Christ for forgiveness. In the Greek, repent means "to change one's mind for better, heartily to amend with abhorrence of one's past sins." Scripture calls this change of mind a "turning of the heart." John the Baptist's preaching was to *"turn the hearts of the fathers to the children, and the disobedient to the wisdom of the just; to make ready a people prepared for the Lord."*[582] Similarly, Paul's preaching would *"open their eyes, and to turn them from darkness to light, and from the power of Satan unto God, that they may receive forgiveness of sins, and inheritance among them which are sanctified by faith that is in me."*[583]

Both John the Baptist and Jesus Christ preached repentance and remission of sins as the starting place for serving God. Mark 1:4 says, *"John did baptize in the wilderness, and preach the baptism of repentance for the remission of sins."* Then Mark 1:14-15 says, *"Now after that John was put in prison, Jesus came into Galilee, preaching the gospel of the kingdom of God, And saying, The time is fulfilled, and the kingdom of God is at hand: repent ye, and believe the gospel."* Jesus instructs us to believe the gospel, or good news, that we can be forgiven all our sins and become part of

580 Matthew 7:14
581 John 5:24
582 Luke 1:17
583 Acts 26:18

God's kingdom. Christ says, "*I came not to call the righteous, but sinners to repentance.*"[584]

At the moment a person is saved through repentance, he receives life, the spiritual substance of faith in his soul. 1 Thessalonians 5:23 teaches every man has three parts to his being: body, human spirit, and soul. This faith-substance is a small, but powerful anointing of the Holy Ghost in the soul. Faith in the soul is likened unto a seed in a seed packet. The seed is not yet growing, but life is inside it, and it has so much potential!

The new believer feels new life upon receiving faith. Prior to faith coming he "*walked according to the course of this world, according to the prince of the power of the air, the spirit that now worketh in the children of disobedience.*"[585] In other words, he used to be anointed by and obedient to demonic spirits, or death, but now he's anointed with a measure of life, God's Spirit—the substance of faith.

Zacchaeus and the woman at Simon's house are examples of Scripture capturing the very moment believers pass from death to life. Once faith entered his soul, Zacchaeus vowed to restore all he'd stolen. Jesus identified that day as his day of salvation, saying, "*This day is salvation come to this house, forsomuch as he also is a son of Abraham. For the Son of man is come to seek and save that which was lost.*"[586] You can know the very day salvation comes to your heart! Galatians 3:7 supports Jesus' declaration of Zacchaeus as a son of Abraham, saying, "*Know ye therefore that they which are of faith, the same are the children of Abraham.*" At Simon the Pharisee's house, a sincere, repentant woman called a "*sinner*" found salvation through Christ as she washed Jesus' feet with her tears.[587] Her faith moved her to wash and anoint Jesus' feet, and through her faith she was saved. Our Lord first pronounced her forgiveness and then said, "*Thy faith hath saved thee; go in peace.*"

New Testament believers are immediately baptized, or fully immersed in water as a public testimony of their new life, or faith in

584 Mark 2:17
585 Ephesians 2:2
586 Luke 19:9-10
587 Luke 7:36-50

Christ Jesus. In Acts 8:26-40, the Ethiopian eunuch stopped his chariot in the middle of his travels home so Philip could immediately baptize him in water moments after his heart turned, believing in Christ as Messiah. At Paul's miraculous turn to faith the scales fell from his eyes, and he was immediately baptized.[588] Jesus' purpose for Paul was to help others experience the same turn to faith that he had experienced. Paul's life is a striking example of turning from death to life. The man who once jailed Christians and consented to Stephen's death because he was a Christian is now sent to preach freedom, liberty, and *"the newness of life"*[589] through Jesus Christ. Furthermore, the beginning of the Book of Acts illustrates in-depth how beautifully faith comes to new Christians.

Acts chapter 2 demonstrates how 3,000 new Christians were baptized after receiving God's gift of faith.[590] The Day of Pentecost begins with 120 believers being filled with the Holy Spirit early in the morning in a private, upper room setting. Their joyful, loud, and exuberant worship could not be contained in the upper room and flowed into the streets of Jerusalem, becoming a 9:00 AM worship service—*"seeing it is but the third hour of the day."*[591] Their Holy Ghost baptism-experience gets *"noised abroad"* Jerusalem, causing a *"multitude"*[592] to gather around them. Some mock their worship, calling them drunk. Peter, freshly anointed with the Holy Spirit, stands up and preaches the gospel with a loud voice, beginning his sermon by identifying the Scripture the Christians are fulfilling, Joel 2:28-32. Peter says his group has not received *"new wine,"* but the Spirit of the living God. His next point is to indict the multitude's wicked act of delivering Christ, the God-approved miracle worker, to be crucified. Peter continues by quoting Psalm 16:8-11, proving that Jesus is the foreknown Holy One, or Messiah, God would raise from the dead, and David was not speaking of himself. The apostle declares himself to be a witness of Jesus' resurrection and the events of the morning to be the the fulfillment of the

588   Acts 9:18
589   Romans 6:4
590   Acts 2:41
591   Acts 2:15
592   Acts 2:6

Heavenly Father's *"promise of the Holy Ghost."*[593] The sermon is concluded by Peter's declaration to the house of Israel that *"God hath made that same Jesus, whom ye have crucified, both Lord and Christ."*

Stop and recognize that Peter had to preach both "bad news" and "good news." The bad news was the followers of Judaism were guilty of letting their innocent Messiah be crucified by wicked men. Peter indicted Israel for rejecting their own Savior! The good news was Jesus defeated death, resurrected to heaven at the right hand of God, and was now pouring out His promised Spirit upon believers. The bad news convicted the 17-nation multitude, for they were *"pricked in their heart,"*[594] or sorrowful, agitated, and pained in the mind according to the Greek Lexicon. Bad news really hurts, but can cause hearts to seek deliverance. The multitude's humble response to Peter's sermon was, *"Men and brethren, what shall we do?"* The walking-on-water apostle delivers what may be called the true church's "first and only creed" recorded in Acts 2:38-39, preaching, *"Repent, and be baptized every one of you in the name of Jesus Christ for the remission of sins, and ye shall receive the gift of the Holy Ghost. For the promise is unto you, and to your children, and to all that are afar off, even as many as the Lord our God shall call."* Observe that faith comes after God's Word convicts guilty sinners who admit and turn from their hopeless wickedness (repentance), desiring to trust in Jesus Christ for complete forgiveness. This pattern for receiving faith worked 2,000 years ago and still works today.

If you haven't repented and been baptized in the name of Jesus Christ for your remission of sins with the accompanying gift of the baptism of the Holy Ghost, won't you seek this eternal blessing today?

LOVE PRODUCES FAITH, THEN FAITH PRODUCES WORKS

Another of Jesus' comments to the "sinner" woman at Simon's house unveils the origin and order of all works: love, faith, works. Notice Jesus'

---

593   Acts 2:33
594   Acts 2:37

words to forgiven woman in Luke 7:47: "*Her sins, which are many, are forgiven; for she loved much: but to whom little is forgiven, the same loveth little.*" Clearly, this woman's love for Jesus moved her to do the work of washing and anointing His feet. Love is the only motivation God accepts for all Christian acts or works. Paul says love comes before faith and works, because "*faith…worketh by love.*"[595] The forgiven woman first loved Jesus Christ, which helped her receive faith in Christ. Her faith then went to work, causing her to wash and anoint Jesus' feet. Figure 7 shows the order of all Christian works through this woman's example.

	Love	Faith	Works
Forgiven Woman in Luke 7:36-50	In her sinful state, the woman somehow learned of Jesus and deeply fell in love with Him and His godly character. Perhaps she saw Him preach and perform miracles. Maybe she saw Jesus' disciples baptizing new believers after Jesus forgave them. One thing is certain—Jesus said, "*For she loved much.*"	She had faith she could be forgiven of her many sins. She saw herself as a sin-debtor, which is how Jesus described her condition. Her faith in Christ moved her to prepare to do the work of washing and anointing Jesus. She brought an alabaster box of ointment to Simon's house and waited for the right moment to begin washing His feet. Paul said, "*Faith...worketh by love.*"	The woman worked by letting her tears wash Jesus' feet, using her hair as a towel to clean His dirty feet. She then kissed His feet and anointed them with ointment. After Jesus saw her love empower her faith, and her faith manifest a good work upon Him, He said "*Thy faith hath saved thee.*" Jesus always sees works as faith-in-action, like the men who let down the palsy-stricken man through the roof tiles in Luke 5:17-26. Luke says, "*And when he [Jesus] saw their faith, he said unto him, Man, thy sins are forgiven thee.*"

Figure 7

595   Galatians 5:6

Christians are not saved by works according to Ephesians 2:8, but once saved, Christians recognize God created them to do good works according to Paul in Ephesians 2:10: *"For we are his workmanship, created in Christ Jesus unto good works, which God hath before ordained that we should walk in them."* The forgiven woman was created to wash Jesus' feet at Simon's house and therefore walked in God's plans for her life! Before she could do that, she had to fall in love with Jesus. Once full of love for Him, her faith went to work.

The age-old "Faith Versus Works Debate" is now made plain. You are saved by God's amazing grace. Your experience begins when your heart begins to love God. This love produces faith in His eternal Word. Faith, motivated by love, works out God's plan for your life. Genuine works of obedience always originate with a loving heart that brings faith into the soul.

JUSTIFICATION BY FAITH

At the moment a believer is saved by grace through faith, he is justified in the sight of God. Paul devotes significant time to solidifying God's promise to justify believers in Romans chapters 3-5, and Galatians chapters 2 and 3.

In the Greek Lexicon, justification means "to show one to be righteous" and "to declare one to be just." When you stand before the judgment seat of Christ—Paul says *"we shall all stand before the judgment seat of Christ"*[596]—you desperately want Him to declare you righteous, not unrighteous. Just as you'd want an earthly judge to declare you righteous in court, you want heaven's Judge to justify you before the throne of God.

Romans 3 explains how sinful men and women can be righteous and just in God's sight. But Paul begins Romans 3:10-12 by explaining mankind's hopeless situation apart from Christ, saying, *"There is none righteous, no, not one: There is none that understandeth, there is none that seeketh after God. They are all gone out of the way, they are together become*

596 Romans 14:10

unprofitable; there is none that doeth good, no, not one." In Romans 3:19-31, Paul says "all the world" is guilty before God—"for all have sinned, and come short of the glory of God"—and unable to be justified by human efforts to keep God's law. Through Christ's blood, there is a "righteousness of God without the law" God is offering to all. The "righteousness of God" is "unto all and upon all them that believe." By God's own design, genuine belief or trust in Christ's sacrifice is all that is required for salvation:

> "Being justified freely by his grace through the redemption that is in Christ Jesus: Whom God hath set forth to be a propitiation through faith in his blood, to declare his righteousness for the remission of sins that are past, through the forbearance of God; To declare, I say, at this time his righteousness: that he might be just, and the justifier of him which believeth in Jesus. Where is boasting then? It is excluded. By what law? of works? Nay: but by the law of faith. Therefore we conclude that a man is justified by faith without the deeds of the law."

The Just One, Christ, justifies all who believe in Him. Jesus declares His righteousness for the remission of our sins. No man can brag about his own righteousness because he has none.

Romans 4:3 explains that Christians are justified in the same way Abraham was—he simply "believed God, and it was counted unto him for righteousness." God counts your simple, humble faith as righteousness. Romans 4:5 says, "But to him that worketh not, but believeth on him that justifieth the ungodly, his faith is counted for righteousness." God's Spirit anointed David to describe this amazing promise 1,000 years before Christ: "Even as David also describeth the blessedness of the man, unto whom God imputeth righteousness without works, Saying, Blessed are they whose iniquities are forgiven, and whose sins are covered. Blessed is the man to whom the Lord will not impute sin." And all these indescribable blessings flow from the cross and resurrection, for Christ "was delivered for our offences, and was raised again for our justification."[597]

---

597   Romans 4:25

In Romans 5:1-2, Paul states, "*Therefore being justified by faith, we have peace with God through our Lord Jesus Christ: By whom also we have access by faith into this grace wherein we stand, and rejoice in hope of the glory of God.*" Again, observe how God's grace brings you to the state of justification. By believing in Christ's blood, you have peace with God. One Greek meaning of "*peace*" is "exemption from the rage and havoc of war." God is not angry with believers. He's not enraged at their sins, nor warring against their every decision. The Heavenly Father patiently chastens believers like a father pities his children.[598] Indeed, every justified Christian has no charges nor accusations against them before God's throne, for Paul declares "*Who shall lay any thing to the charge of God's elect? It is God that justifieth.*"[599] Jesus Christ has entered "*into heaven itself, now to appear in the presence of God for us*"[600] and "*he is able also to save them to the uttermost that come unto God by him, seeing he ever liveth to make intercession for them.*"[601]

Galatians chapters 2 and 3 address justification by faith, saying no flesh can be justified by the law in the sight of God. Justification is by faith for both Jew and Gentile, being foretold for Gentiles in Genesis 12:3 and Habakkuk 2:4. God promised to bless all nations through Abraham, saying, "*And I will bless them that bless thee, and curse him that curseth thee: and in thee shall all families of the earth be blessed.*" Over 600 years before Christ, the prophet Habakkuk wrote God's vision that "*the just shall live by his faith.*" The law of Moses served as a "*schoolmaster,*" or tutor, "*to bring us unto Christ, that we might be justified by faith.*"[602]

Some say James 2:24 causes confusion in the "Faith Versus Works Debate," but those accusations are wrong. This verse states, "*Ye see then how that by works a man is justified, and not by faith only.*" Some argue that "faith alone" is not enough to save a sinner because James writes a man is justified by works and "*not by faith only.*" Reading James chapter 2 in context reveals that James is rebuking "*dead*" faith, meaning a faith-confession

---

598   Pslam 103:13, Hebrews 12:6
599   Romans 8:33
600   Hebrews 9:24
601   Hebrews 7:25
602   Galatians 3:24

that honors God with words only. Empty words without action reveal an absence of faith. James is correct to denounce false professors of faith who spurt out empty, vain words. His example is a person who gives verbal well-wishes to a cold, hungry Christian but does not give him clothes and food. A real, faith-filled Christian will give a cold, hungry Christian *"those things which are needful to the body."*[603] When understood correctly, James' words agree with Paul's, for genuine faith works by love, doing the *"good works, which God hath before ordained that we should walk in them."*

INTELLECTUAL HUMAN FAITH

Every human being possesses an intellectual human faith that is different from God's gift of divine, saving faith. God's saving faith is part of the *"divine nature,"*[604] the same faith Jesus Christ possesses. Christ's faith is added to a Christian as a gift, just as Peter said each character quality must be added to the believer—*"add to your faith virtue."*[605] Paul said he lived by Christ's supernatural faith, not his own faith. Galatians 2:20 says *"I am crucified with Christ: nevertheless I live; yet not I, but Christ liveth in me: and the life which I now live in the flesh I live by the faith of the Son of God, who loved me, and gave himself for me."* Paul had received God's gift of supernatural saving faith, a measure of Jesus' own faith, the faith of the Son of God.

Human faith that simply acknowledges truth is not saving faith, as proven in Hebrews 10:26-27: *"For if we sin willfully after that we have received the knowledge of the truth, there remaineth no more sacrifice for sins, But a certain fearful looking for of judgment and fiery indignation, which shall devour the adversaries."*

Many Jews acknowledged Jesus as a special messenger from God in Jesus' lifetime. Nicodemus admitted that the Sanhedrin Council's members knew Jesus was from God, telling Jesus in John 3:2, *"Rabbi, we know that thou art a teacher come from God: for no man can do these miracles that thou doest, except God be with him."* Just as Muslims believe Jesus Christ is a prophet with human faith, the Israeli Sanhedrin Council knew and

---

603   James 2:16
604   2 Peter 1:4
605   2 Peter 1:5

believed with human faith that Jesus was from God. But human faith is not sufficient for salvation. Repentance from sin, while trusting in the blood of Jesus Christ for forgiveness, is God's requirement for salvation. Muslims and other world religions can possess the knowledge of the truth that Jesus is the Christ and still not be saved.

Fallen angels, like humans, can genuinely believe in God and still exist in complete rebellion to Him. James 2:19 states that all fallen angels, or devils, believe in and tremble at the one God: *"Thou believest that there is one God; thou doest well: the devils also believe, and tremble."* Angels have the intellectual capacity to believe in Christ while trying to work against Him, but must obey His every command. Luke 4:34 records an unclean devil crying out to Jesus, saying, *"I know thee who thou art; the Holy One of God."* The destiny of all fallen angels is judgment unto annihilation, for Jude 1:6 says, *"And the angels which kept not their first estate, but left their own habitation, he hath reserved in everlasting chains under darkness unto the judgment of the great day."*

THE GIFT OF FAITH

There are two other kinds of faith that must be differentiated from saving faith: the gift of faith and the fruit of faith.

The gift of faith is one of the nine spiritual gifts Paul describes in 1 Corinthians 12:1-11 (see Figure 8). In the Greek, a gift, or charisma, is "a favor with which one receives without any merit of his own" and "grace or gifts denoting extraordinary powers, distinguishing certain Christians and enabling them to serve the church of Christ."

The Nine Spiritual Gifts of the Holy Ghost		
Wisdom	Knowledge	Faith
Healing	Miracles	Prophecy
Discerning of spirits	Divers kinds of tongues	Interpretation of tongues

Figure 8

The Bible describes the gift of faith as power to move obstacles, figuratively described as mountains, by speaking God's Word according to Mark 11:23 and 1 Corinthians 13:2. Two clear Bible examples of mountain-moving faith include the Roman Centurion and Paul.

In Matthew 8:1-13, a Roman Centurion came to Christ for the healing of his sick servant who suffered from paralysis. Jesus agreed to come to his house and heal the servant, but the centurion said He needed to *"speak the word only"* for the servant to be healed. Jesus marveled at the centurion's *"great faith"* and said, *"As thou hast believed, so be it done unto thee."* The centurion's great faith in Christ, spoken from his anointed heart to Christ, caused the Savior to speak the Word, moving the mountain of paralysis *"in the selfsame hour."*

While in Lystra (modern day Turkey), Paul's gift of faith operated on a crippled man who had never walked. Acts 14:8 says the crippled man was *"impotent in his feet"* but heard Paul speaking. The Holy Spirit anointed Paul to perceive the cripple *"had faith to be healed,"* so he *"said with a loud voice, Stand upright on thy feet. And he leaped and walked."* How could Paul loudly command a man to walk who had never walked? Through the mountain-moving gift of faith. In this case, the mountain of impotent feet was moved by speaking God's Word in faith.

The gift of faith is different from saving faith because the gift is always present in a person's human spirit from birth. Figure 9 shows the location of both kinds of faith in relation to man's three parts. On the other hand, saving faith only comes upon a believer *after* genuine repentance from sins.

God graces every Christian—and surprisingly—even every unbeliever with at least one of the nine spiritual gifts, for Paul says, *"the manifestation of the Spirit is given to every man to profit withal,"*[606] and *"all these worketh that one and the selfsame Spirit, dividing to every man severally as he will."*[607] Some saints have multiple gifts like Paul, who prophesied, had gifts of healing, and spoke in tongues.[608]

---

606   1 Corinthians 12:7
607   1 Corinthians 12:11
608   Acts 27:21-26, Acts 28:1-10, 1 Corinthians 14:18,

Man's Three-Part Being (1 Thessalonians 5:23)	
Body	Sinful nature (Romans 7:18-23)
Human Spirit or Mind	Faith (Saving Faith) Virtue Knowledge Temperance Patience Godliness Brotherly Kindness Nine Gifts of the Spirit
Soul	Charity or filling of the Holy Ghost

Figure 9

Gifts are given to every person, as Romans 11:29 teaches, *"the gifts and calling of God are without repentance."* Even before a believer repents, God has already given him a spiritual gift. Conversely, even if an unbeliever will not repent, God has already given him a spiritual gift. Every spiritual gift is a built-in component and special ability in each person's human spirit. Gifts can be likened unto the *"talents"* that Jesus graciously distributes, detailed in Matthew 25:14-30. Christians are accountable for investing in their valuable, divine abilities—like faith—given them by Jesus.

Although shocking to some, six Bible texts validate unbelievers possessing gifts of the Spirit despite lacking saving faith. First, 2 Peter 2:15-17 teaches Balaam's destiny was hell—the *"mist of darkness…for ever"*—yet he had a gift of prophecy that correctly predicted *"a Star out of Jacob"*[609] would lead the wise men to Christ. Second, Matthew 10:1-15 explains how Judas Iscariot, eventually lost to hell as the son of perdition, and the eleven other apostles were given gifts of healing: *"When he had called unto him his twelve disciples, he gave them power against unclean spirits, to cast them out, and to heal all manner of sickness and all manner of disease."*

609   Numbers 24:17

Next, Luke 10:1-20 describes Jesus' seventy disciples He sent out to cities with power to cast out devils—the gift of miracles according to Mark 9:38-39. John 6:66 suggests these seventy left Christ because His preaching was offensive to them, saying, "*From that time many of his disciples went back, and walked no more with him.*" The reality of Jesus' gifts of healing and miracles was not enough to keep these disciples following Christ. They walked away from eternal life, Christ, because they were offended by His preaching.

Matthew 7:21-23 provides a fourth example. Jesus sends workers of iniquity to hell because He never knew them and they failed to do the will of God. The large, lost group of "*many*" people also did "*many wonderful works*" in Jesus' name, such as prophesying and casting out devils. Jesus warned us of these "*false Christs and false prophets*" in Matthew 24:24 who temporarily have the anointing of God upon them, but live sinfully after operating God's gifts. It's crucial Christians do not make the ability to repeatedly and correctly operate gifts as the evidence of a person's salvation—whether the gift is speaking in tongues or performing miracles.

Fifth, Hebrews 6:1-12 describes a group who taste of heavenly gifts and powers but are still lost. After initially enjoying God's gifts, they become spiritually slothful and fall away, unwilling to repent. This group treats Christ to an "*open shame,*" or public disgrace by their sinful lives, crucifying Jesus "*afresh.*" God's Word again uses botany life—Jesus used wheat and tares in Matthew 13—to help readers understand the lost, comparing their lives to thorn-producing plants. The lost produce thorns and briers rather than the holy, righteous fruits of the Holy Spirit.

Finally, a sixth example is found in 1 Corinthians 13:1-3, which specifically mentions the gift of faith, saying, "*and though I have all faith, so that I could remove mountains, and have not charity, I am nothing.*" You learn that faith is a powerful gift that removes mountains, or imposing obstacles, but you also understand that exercising the gift of faith without God's love equals spiritual bankruptcy. Love is the only true and acceptable motivation for trying to do God a service because love empowers faith, and living faith produces works.

THE FRUIT OF FAITH

There are nine fruits of the Holy Spirit, taught by Paul in Galatians 5:16-26 and seen in Figure 10. The apostle lists 17 sinful works of the flesh to contrast the nine, divine fruits. Faith is the seventh fruit on the list.

The Nine Fruits of the Holy Spirit		
Love	Joy	Peace
Longsuffering	Gentleness	Goodness
Faith	Meekness	Temperance

Figure 10

The fruit of faith is the rarest form of faith because it's only man-ifested in mature, seasoned Christians. Anyone—sinner or saint—can manifest a gift of faith. Saving faith is more rare than the gift of faith, being only present in the *"few"* believers Jesus said would find the narrow path to eternal life.

Understanding the fruit of the Holy Spirit comes from examining natural fruit from the earth. A ripe apple, a natural fruit, is the product of an apple seed. It takes from six to eight years for the apple seed to grow and mature before it produces substantial fruit.[610] Spiritual fruit then is a product of the seed-Word of God according to 1 Peter 1:23: *"Being born again, not of corruptible seed, but of incorruptible, by the word of God, which liveth and abideth for ever."* Peter symbolizes being born again, or the new birth, as receiving an incorruptible seed, producing fruits of the Spirit years later, in due time.

Jesus teaches a parable about being patient for fruit to be produced. In Luke 13:6-9, Christ's parable tells of a *"certain man"* who plants a fig tree in his vineyard but the tree produces no fruit after three years. The vine-dresser suggests the certain man cut down the fig tree, but the merciful,

---

610 "Apple Fruit and Tree." *Encyclopedia Britannica,* https://www.britannica.com/plant/apple-fruit-and-tree

patient man decides to leave it alone for another year and fertilize the tree in hopes of fruit in the fourth year. Christ seems to be symbolizing Israel as the fig tree and Himself as the "*certain man*" because Christ's earthly ministry lasted about three and a half years. But Christians can glean Jesus' patience to wait for believers to manifest fruit of the Spirit, as Paul stresses patience with all men in 1 Thessalonians 5:14-15: "*Now we exhort you, brethren, warn them that are unruly, comfort the feebleminded, support the weak, be patient toward all men. See that none render evil for evil unto any man; but ever follow that which is good, both among yourselves, and to all men.*" There is no set amount of time Christians must wait to see maturity in each other, but fruits of Spirit must and will manifest in all born again Christians.

The spiritual fruit of faith is a mature level of faith. Fully-developed fruit is the goal of Christianity, as proven by John 15:1-16 and Matthew 13:3-8 and 18-23. In John 15, Christ paints a picture of God the Father as a "*husbandman*," or farmer, Himself as the "*true vine*," and believers as branches. Jesus promises that branches who abide in Him, being kept clean through His Word, will glorify the Father through much fruit bearing. Pruning is required for all branches, as the faithful Savior will take away parts of our character that do not produce the fruit of the Spirit. Jesus assures Christians are chosen and ordained to bear fruit that lasts. Matthew 13 records Jesus' teaching that every human heart will culminate in one of four conditions and the only honorable condition is a fruitful heart (See Chapter 8). Luke 8:15, a parallel passage, describes the fruitful heart as "*the good ground...which in an honest and good heart, having heard the word, keep it, and bring forth fruit with patience.*"

Paul and John are key examples of mature, experienced believers, whose faith-fruit had fully developed. Converted to Christianity around 34 A.D., Paul faithfully served God's purpose until his martyrdom in Rome in 66 A.D. Throughout his ministry, Paul's faith was tested severely by being stoned, shipwrecked three times, whipped five times, beaten with rods, suffering frequent imprisonments, and countless perils.[611] Even so, Paul's faith knew death had lost its sting because of Christ's victorious resurrection[612] and a crown of righteousness—from the Righteous Judge— was *"laid up"*[613] for him after death. After 32 years of ministry, the apostle was ready to die as a martyr, writing, *"For I am now ready to be offered, and the time of my departure is at hand. I have fought a good fight, I have finished my course, I have kept the faith."*[614]

The apostle John—the *"disciple whom Jesus loved"*—followed Christ during His three and a half-year earthly ministry and was born again on the Day of Pentecost in 30 A.D. John's ministry lasted over 60 years, writing three epistles (I, II, and III John) and his Gospel around 80 A.D. before recording the Book of Revelation in 95 A.D. John's epistles strengthen the saints' faith by making their joy full, encouraging abstinence from sin, stressing avoidance of seducing teachers, and assuring their possession of eternal life through belief in Christ.[615] The Gospel of Saint John emphasizes the deity, divine power, and preexistence of Jesus Christ as foundational in the Christian faith. John's mature, fully-developed faith is powerfully displayed in the circumstances surrounding the writing of his final letter, the Book of Revelation. Even at the ripe age of around 80 years old, John's faith so was evident that Emperor Domitian imprisoned him to the Isle of Patmos in the Aegean Sea for a year and a half. While banished on the island, John's faith chose to walk *"in the Spirit"*[616] rather than self pity, and then he received the *"revelation of Jesus Christ."*[617] As a result of John's faith, the Book of Revelation has been called a "complete overview of theology" due to its teachings on sin, redemption, angels, demons, Israel, Gentiles, and Christ's divinity. The beauty of Revelation is that it shows your daily choices and actions determine which end time events you'll experience. John's mature faith has provided us an intimate, glorious glimpse

---

611   2 Corinthians 11:23-27
612   1 Corinthians 15:55-57
613   2 Timothy 4:8
614   2 Timothy 4:6-7
615   1 John 1:4, 2:1, 2:26, 5:13
616   Revelation 1:10
617   Revelation 1:1

of Christ's plans for the end of human history and beginning of the eternal day.

THE FAITH FOUNDATION

Much more could be said about faith, as this crucial subject fills New Testament Scripture, being mentioned over 220 times. As you move on to the second character quality, rejoice in the rock-solid foundation of faith God has given you by His grace. Your foundation will hold in your greatest temptations, just as Peter's faith held him in his hardest trial—his denial of Christ before the crucifixion. Our Lord said, *"Simon, Simon, behold, Satan hath desired to have you, that he may sift you as wheat: But I have prayed for thee, that thy faith fail not: and when thou art converted, strengthen thy brethren."*[618] Jesus' prayer kept Peter's faith-foundation from failing even after denying Christ three times! Peter didn't commit suicide like Judas, or leave Judea as a vagabond like Cain left God's presence. Rather, he hung around until he could experience Christ's forgiveness because he knew there was no other place to go for eternal life. Peter said in John 6:68, *"Lord, to whom shall we go? thou hast the words of eternal life."*

Be encouraged that Jesus prayed the same for you in John 17:20-21, for you have believed on Him through the words of His original disciples: *"Neither pray I for these alone, but for them also which shall believe on me through their word; That they all may be one; as thou, Father, art in me, and I in thee, that they also may be one in us: that the world may believe that thou hast sent me."* Since your faith is motivated by love, your faith foundation will be the rock upon which God can build your spiritual house—the Stature of a Perfect Man. Jesus says, *"Therefore whosoever heareth these sayings of mine, and doeth them, I will liken him unto a wise man, which built his house upon a rock: And the rain descended, and the floods came, and the winds blew, and beat upon that house; and it fell not: for it was founded upon a rock."*[619]

618   Luke 22:31-32
619   Matthew 7:24-25

As an overcomer, you have rejected Satan's bait of unbelief and have let God add faith to your being. What a wonderful decision! You've chosen God's way to heaven by repentance and water baptism in the name of the Lord Jesus Christ. The great and wise Master-builder, Jesus Christ, is now ready to add His next character quality to you: virtue.

CHARACTER QUALITY #2: VIRTUE

2 Peter 1:5 reads, *"And beside this, giving all diligence, add to your faith virtue."* The second step on your way to godliness is virtue, which is a second measure or portion of Holy Ghost-anointing God wants to add to your being.

In the Greek Lexicon, virtue is defined as "a virtuous course of thought, feeling and action; virtue, moral goodness" and "moral excellence." A Hebrew definition is "strength, might, efficiency." Combining these definitions, the Bible places virtue as the strength to daily walk in God's way. Logically, God must first give you faith to choose the right way to walk and secondly empower you with the virtue to daily walk in His narrow path.

Christians who ask for and receive God's virtue must first reject the sin of hypocrisy. The Greek definition of hypocrisy is "the acting of a stage player." A modern definition is "the practice of claiming to have moral standards or beliefs to which one's own behavior does not conform."[620] Jesus witnessed much hypocrisy during His earthly ministry, calling out the scribes and Pharisees in Matthew 23:25 and 28 for presenting a false moral strength to the public. Christ says, *"Woe unto you, scribes and Pharisees, hypocrites! for ye make clean the outside of the cup and of the platter, but within they are full of extortion and excess…Even so ye also outwardly appear righteous unto men, but within ye are full of hypocrisy and iniquity."*

Virtue is power to consistently live out your faith for Christ publicly and privately, before family, coworkers, friends, and strangers. In Matthew 10:32-42, Jesus requires that all believers confess Him before men and their families, saying,

620   Apple. "Hypocrisy." *Dictionary*. Version 2.3.0. Accessed 22 May 2019

"For I am come to set a man at variance against his father, and the daughter against her mother, and the daughter in law against her mother in law. And a man's foes shall be they of his own household. He that loveth father or mother more than me is not worthy of me: and he that loveth son or daughter more than me is not worthy of me."

Since Jesus' requirement is public and private confession of His great name, He provides the anointing of virtue to all believers.

EXAMPLES OF VIRTUOUS BIBLE CHARACTERS

Ruth from the Old Testament is a shining example of virtue. Boaz, the wealthy Bethlehemite *"lord of the harvest,"* was kinsman to Mahlon, Ruth's first husband, who died without any children to carry on his name. Ruth laid at Boaz's feet, initiating him to claim his right to be her kinsman redeemer and fulfill Deuteronomy 25:5-10, and Boaz quickly promised to marry her. Ruth 3:11 expresses Boaz's confidence in Ruth's virtue known to the entire city: *"And now, my daughter, fear not; I will do to thee all that thou requirest: for all the city of my people doth know that thou art a virtuous woman."* When a believer has divine virtue, he can live out his faith at all times and in all public settings. Boaz further pointed out that Ruth could have followed a younger man, rich or poor, to attempt having children but she instead choose to honor God's kinsman requirement. Temptations ran rampant in Ruth's life, just as in your life, but her virtue empowered her to overcome every test. Righteous Ruth's testimony proclaims the power, or virtue, to obey God's Word publicly despite financial and sensual temptations.

Solomon offers further examples of virtue in Proverbs 31:10-31, focusing on virtuous women. Above all, Solomon says a virtuous woman possesses the fear of the Lord, promising *"she shall be praised."* Wisdom is the result of godly fear, according to Proverbs 9:10: *"The fear of the Lord is the beginning of wisdom."* Therefore, virtuous women make wise decisions in motherhood, personal finances, and business deals. A virtuous woman is trustworthy: *"The heart of her husband doth safely trust in her.*[621] A virtuous woman is busy meeting everyone's needs and *"eateth not the bread of idleness."*[622] She is spiritually clothed with strength and honor as she serves her family both inside and outside the home. As seen in Ruth's example, Solomon agrees that a virtuous woman's value is great: *"her price is far above rubies."*[623]

The prophet Daniel is an example of a virtuous man. He was so dedicated to God that his coworkers could not find one thing wrong with his work, which made them concoct a devious plan to entrap him into breaking a new law they wrote themselves forbidding prayer to his God, Jehovah, in Daniel 6. Daniel's inner virtue, or strength, led him to continue his three daily prayers without hesitation although he knew the law and its consequences. Daniel's virtue amidst his arrest and sentence to be thrown into a den of hungry lions caused God to send an angel to shut the lions' mouths, securing Daniel's deliverance. This is the power of divine virtue—public strength to do what is right in God's sight even when you know you will suffer.

JESUS' EXAMPLES OF VIRTUE

Jesus' teachings in Matthew chapters 5 and 6 contain simple, concrete examples of how Christians can manifest virtue in both public and private settings. In these settings, divine virtue is needed for spur-of-the-moment public requests as well as planned out, private giving.

In Matthew 5:38-42, Christ teaches four virtuous responses to public trouble and surprising or unplanned requests. First, if you're smitten on the right cheek, let your enemy smite your left cheek. Second, if you're sued in court for your coat, or undergarment, give your adversary your cloak, or outer garment as well. Third, if you're compelled to carry someone's message for a mile, be willing to go two miles. Fourth, give to those who ask for your possessions and be willing to let others' borrow them.

In Matthew 6:1-4, Jesus teaches about alms giving in private. Our Lord encourages believers to *"take heed"* or pay special attention to giving

621   Proverbs 31:11
622   Proverbs 31:27
623   Proverbs 31:10

alms or charity in secret, and not before men. Jesus knows it takes His virtue to give in secret. Christ says, "*Therefore when thou doest thine alms, do not sound a trumpet before thee, as the hypocrites do in the synagogues and in the streets, that they may have glory of men. Verily I say unto you, They have their reward.*" Recall hypocrisy is the sin that must be rejected in order to receive God's virtue. True almsgiving can only be done with the virtue-anointing. With Jesus' virtue, you will not seek glory of men, but glory of your Heavenly Father.

JESUS' HEALING VIRTUE

Jesus' healing virtue must be differentiated from divine virtue. Healing virtue is synonymous with a gift of healing and is different from the second character quality Peter describes in the Stature of a Perfect Man.

Mark 5:25-30 and Luke 6:18-19 detail Jesus' healing virtue. In both cases, sick people were healed after touching Jesus. Scriptures says, "*And the whole multitude sought to touch him: for there went virtue out of him, and healed them all.*" One woman with an issue of blood for 12 years touched Jesus' garment and instantly "*felt in her body that she was healed of that plague.*" The Heavenly Father had not previously told His Son about this encounter, so Christ was surprised to feel His healing power flow out of His spirit into the sick woman. He turned around and said, "*Who touched my clothes?*" When she heard His request, she humbly came before the Savior, and He honored her faith saying, "*Daughter, thy faith hath made thee whole; go in peace, and be whole of thy plague.*"

Healing virtue is not given to every Christian, just as the other eight gifts are given at God's choosing—not ours. Paul plainly states that not everyone has every spiritual gift in 1 Corinthians 12:29-30: "*Are all apostles? are all prophets? are all teachers? are all workers of miracles? Have all the gifts of healing? do all speak with tongues? do all interpret?*" It would be erroneous to say every Christian is an apostle, or missionary. If that was true, there would be no need of local pastors because each missionary would be traveling to spread the faith. Similarly, if everyone spoke in unknown tongues, there would be no interpreters to make known the meaning of the unknown tongues. Rejoice in Jesus' healing virtue and those who have that gift today, but do not confuse the spiritual gift of healing with the second character quality of virtue. You do not need to have healing virtue—the gift of healing—in order to be virtuous. You'll have healing virtue only if God has ordained a healing ministry for your life.

PETER'S LOSS AND RESTORATION OF VIRTUE

Peter, God's chosen author of the Stature of a Perfect Man, is a prime example of gaining virtue, losing it, then gaining it again with no worry of losing it.

Examining Peter's life, Mark 1:14-18 shows that Peter received faith, the first character quality of Christ, when he repented and began following Jesus, as Christ's first sermons dealt with repentance. John 4:1-2 records that Peter and Jesus' disciples baptized new believers, but Jesus did no baptizing. Peter must have been baptized after his repentance, as Peter would not be permitted to baptize others unless he himself had been baptized.

Shortly afterwards, Peter received the character quality of virtue because he publicly preached Christ in his hometown and other cities. Matthew 11:1 says, *"And it came to pass, when Jesus had made an end of commanding his twelve disciples, he departed thence to teach and to preach in their cities."* Luke 9:1-6 says Jesus gave Peter and the apostles *"power and authority over all devils, and to cure diseases"* and they *"went through the towns, preaching the gospel, and healing everywhere."* Peter's virtue strengthened him to unashamedly declare Jesus' gospel publicly in his hometown.

Sadly, a few years later Peter lost his virtue when he denied Christ three times on the night before the crucifixion. Due to the threat of arrest or imprisonment, Peter let fear come over him and the adversary spoiled his virtue. When confronted by a maid and a crowd who associated him with Jesus, Scripture says Peter *"began…to curse and to swear, saying, I know not the man. And immediately the cock crew. And Peter remembered the word of Jesus, which said unto him, Before the cock crow, thou shalt deny me thrice. And he went out, and wept bitterly.*"[624] How could a man that walked on water, had the keys to the kingdom, had preached and healed in cities for Christ's sake, and known Jesus for over three years deny Him? The evil spirit of fear that robs believers of their power had overcome Peter in this temptation. 2 Timothy 1:7 says, *"For God hath not given us the spirit of fear; but of power, and of love, and of a sound mind."*

Despite losing his virtue, Peter never lost his faith-foundation because Jesus interceded in prayer for him prior to Peter's three denials. Luke 22:31-32 reads, *"And the Lord said, Simon, Simon, behold, Satan hath desired to have you, that he may sift you as wheat: But I have prayed for thee, that thy faith fail not: and when thou art converted, strengthen thy brethren."* How marvelous and strong are the prayers of Jesus! Despite Jesus' warning, Peter pridefully declared, *"Lord, I am ready to go with thee, both into prison, and to death."* This boast was proven untrue within a matter of hours, but Jesus' prayer kept Peter from permanently falling away from his faith, unlike Judas Iscariot.

God's rich mercy restored Peter's virtue during the 50 day period from the Passover, Christ's crucifixion, to the Day of Pentecost. Jesus showed himself alive to Peter on multiple occasions,[625] giving both Peter and the apostles *"many infallible proofs"*[626] of the resurrection. Then on the Day of Pentecost, Peter was one of the 120 who received the baptism of the Holy Ghost, the promise of the Father, empowering him never to deny Christ again. The Book of Acts records multiple examples of Peter being threatened and imprisoned for Christ, and each time he displayed unwavering virtue to publicly witness Jesus' resurrection without recanting.[627] The difference in Peter's life was that virtue, knowledge, temperance, patience, godliness, and brotherly kindness had all been added to his faith and sealed into him by baptism of the Holy Ghost. After being born again, Peter never lost his virtue again because it was sealed into him.

---

624   Matthew 26:69-75
625   John 20:19, 20:30, 21:1-14, 1 Corinthians 15:5
626   Acts 1:3
627   Acts 4:1-22, 5:17-42, Acts 12:5-19

GAINING AND LOSING THE CHARACTER QUALITIES: FAILING GRACE

Peter's virtue example reveals people can gain and lose God's character qualities, known as failing or despising grace. Peter was saved, of course, regaining his virtue and being a Holy Ghost-filled Christian after Pentecost. But Judas Iscariot was lost, for he never regained the virtue he once had after selling out Christ.

The spiritual life of Judas Iscariot requires an in-depth study. Judas temporarily received Christ's character qualities, walking in the anointing of God's Spirit for nearly three years before deciding to betray Jesus and be filled with Satan's spirit. Luke 22:3 says, *"Then entered Satan into Judas"* and John 13:27 says, *"And after the sop Satan entered into him."* Judas's life had an eternally sad ending.

Judas's ministry started correctly. After all night prayer in Luke 6:12-16, Jesus called Judas Iscariot and the 11 other disciples to be His apostles. John 4:1-2 tells us Jesus' apostles baptized new believers, which proves Judas must have first confessed his faith in Jesus as Messiah and been baptized before he would be ordained to baptize others. Judas received faith in Christ, believing just as strongly as the other 11 apostles as he witnessed Jesus' miracles, for John 2:11 says, *"This beginning of miracles did Jesus in Cana of Galilee, and manifested forth his glory; and his disciples believed on him."*

As one of Jesus' 12 apostles, Judas was sent out with the same supernatural commission from the lips of Christ Himself with *"power against unclean spirits, to cast them out, and to heal all manner of sickness and all manner of disease."*[628] Judas no doubt experienced God's power and anointing to do miracles and was faithful to his calling for nearly three years. After Judas' death, the apostles even bore witness of Judas' ministry, apostleship, and bishoprick in Acts 1:15-26. Peter said Judas *"obtained part of this ministry"* but fell *"by transgression"* from it. Judas possessed some of the divine character qualities but departed from or abandoned them for monetary gain. Jesus did not cast away Judas—Judas cast away

628   Matthew 10:1-8

Jesus and His divine nature. John 6:37 declares Jesus' promise to not cast away anyone who comes to Him: *"All that the Father giveth me shall come to me; and him that cometh to me I will in no wise cast out."*

Apparently, Judas lived a relatively clean, obedient life to Christ's commands throughout Jesus' three year ministry, as evidenced on the night Judas betrayed Jesus. During the Passover supper, Jesus shared that one of His disciples would betray Him. Notice none of the apostles instantly pointed at Judas and said, "Judas has been a devil all along. We always knew he'd betray Jesus." In fact, each disciple became *"exceeding sorrowful"*[629] and asked Jesus one by one if he would be the betrayer.[630] When it came to Judas' turn, Matthew 26:25 records, *"Then Judas, which betrayed him, answered and said, Master, is it I? He said unto him, Thou hast said."*

There was a moment Judas' spiritual weakness was seen before his final betrayal of Christ for thirty pieces of silver. Six days before he betrayed Christ, Judas disdained Lazarus' sister, Mary, for anointing Jesus' feet with very costly spikenard in preparation for His burial. John 12:5-8 records Judas' complaint about and Jesus' protection of Mary:

> *"Why was not this ointment sold for three hundred pence, and given to the poor? This he said, not that he cared for the poor; but because he was a thief, and had the bag, and bare what was put therein. Then said Jesus, Let her alone: against the day of my burying hath she kept this. For the poor always ye have with you; but me ye have not always."*

It's implied from John 12:6 that Judas was stealing money from Jesus' ministry throughout his time as Jesus' treasurer but he kept his secret sin from being discovered by the other apostles. Only God knows how much and how often he stole from our Lord's money.

According to Jesus, many—not few—follow Judas's pattern of selling out the gospel for worldly lusts. Matthew 7:21-23 contains Jesus' exact

---

629   Matthew 26:22
630   Mark 14:19

description of the many Judas-like churchgoers who temporarily receive God's anointing but then reject it for a life of iniquity, or wicked living:

> *"Not every one that saith unto me, Lord, Lord, shall enter into the kingdom of heaven; but he that doeth the will of my Father which is in heaven. Many will say to me in that day, Lord, Lord, have we not prophesied in thy name? and in thy name have cast out devils? and in thy name done many wonderful works? And then will I profess unto them, I never knew you: depart from me, ye that work iniquity."*

Choose to be one of the few saved Christians who walks the narrow road of holiness, leading to eternal life.[631]

Six texts support the truth that many will be like Judas, temporarily receiving the character qualities of Christ, but will ultimately reject them and be damned on Judgment Day: Matthew 12:29-30, 43-45, Luke 8:1-18, Hebrews 3:7-4:16, Hebrews 6:1-12, Hebrews 10:19-39, and 2 Peter 2:19-22.

Matthew 12:29-30 and 43-45 illustrate a man as a house that is filled with good things, or God's spiritual character qualities such as faith and virtue. The only way this person can be demon possessed is if he lets a demon *"bind"* him, allowing the demons to *"spoil his house."* This means the man stops obeying God's Word and submits to the will of demons. The "goods" the man once had, perhaps faith and virtue, are taken away, meaning the man no longer has those divine attributes of God. Jesus gives more detail about this spiritual robbery in verses 43-45, saying demons that are cast out of a man will get help from seven other demons and return to the man to *"enter in and dwell there,"* making *"the last state of that man...worse than the first."* This is what happened to Judas. He began as a clean house but eventually he was deceived into betraying Christ and Satan himself—not eight demons—entered into him on Passover night. Friend, your three-part being—body, spirit, soul[632]—is a

---

631   Matthew 7:14
632   1 Thessalonians 5:23

battlefield that you must daily fight for and conquer through obedience to the Holy Ghost.

Luke 8:1-18 records Jesus' parable of the sower and the seed sown represents the Word of God. The four grounds represent four kinds of hearts that hear the Word. The second, rocky ground receives the Word and *"for a while"* believes but eventually falls away in a *"time of temptation."* In the parallel passage in Matthew 13:21, Christ says this person *"dureth for a while,"* which in the Greek means he believes "for a season, enduring only for a while, temporarily." People can genuinely possess the seed-Word of divine faith for a while and then forsake it, deserting and withdrawing into death, destruction, and hell.

Hebrews 3:7-4:16 is an extensive passage that provides a powerful and crucial illustration of gaining and losing spiritual character qualities. The Hebrews author, most likely Paul, uses Israel's exodus out of Egypt and journey to possess the Promised Land as an allegory of the New Testament Christian's journey from faith to charity. Figure 11 shows the three stages of Israel's journey as allegorical to the Christian's three stage journey to the baptism of the Holy Ghost. The text teaches the Israeli hearts were soft in the first stage but became *"hardened through the deceitfulness of sin"* during the wilderness testing, or second stage. Jeremiah 2:2 adds to this, saying that Israel loved God when they went after Him in the wilderness. Hebrews 3:14 states there are conditions to every promise of God, saying, *"For we are made partakers of Christ, if we hold the beginning of our confidence stedfast unto the end."* If believers keep believing God's Word and faithfully serve Jesus, they will enter *"into his rest"*—the third stage, the soul-rest, or the baptism of the Holy Ghost Jesus spoke of in Matthew 11:29 and John 7:37-39. Deuteronomy 3:20 says possessing the Promised Land is Israel's rest. The Israeli souls who died in the wilderness had gained many miles in their journey but lost many benefits when unbelief ruled their hearts, doubting they could possess Canaan due to the evil report of the 10 spies in Numbers 13:31-14:3.

Stage	Israel	New Testament Christian
1: Justification By Faith	Exiting Egypt and Crossing Red Sea Waters	Repentance and Water Baptism
2: Sanctification	Wilderness Testing	Sanctification
3: Rest, or Baptism of the Holy Ghost	Possessing Canaan	Baptism of the Holy Ghost

Figure 11

In Hebrews 6:1-12, the author again illustrates the Christian life as a journey, saying believers leave or are sent forth from the introductory *"principles of the doctrine of Christ"* and *"go on unto perfection"* by God's permission. The text affirms that it's *"impossible"* for one who falls away from faith to be renewed *"again unto repentance."* Notice the one who fell away did indeed repent at one time, meaning he had faith. Mark 1:15 teaches faith (or belief) comes at repentance. What did the person fall away from? The text says the person was *"enlightened"* by the Holy Spirit, *"tasted of the heavenly gift,"* and was made a partaker *"of the Holy Ghost."* Judas Iscariot is again our prime example of one who fell away despite being enlightened by the Messiah, tasting the heavenly gifts of healing and miracles, and partaking of the Holy Ghost-anointed ministry given to him by Christ. Judas put Christ to *"an open shame,"* publicly betraying Him with a kiss[633] that led to His arrest and crucifixion. Judas partook of heavenly gifts, even tasting *"the good word of God, and the powers of the world to come"* but fell away from them. Believers are urged to show *"the same diligence to the full assurance of hope unto the end: That ye be not slothful, but followers of them who through faith and patience inherit the promises."* Just like Peter twice emphasized diligence in 2 Peter 1:5 and 10, the Hebrews author says diligence is required to finish the Christian journey and inherit God's promises.

633   Luke 22:48

Two more Scriptures show many people will fall away from faith in the last days. In 2 Timothy 3:1-7, Paul declares the *"last days"* will be *"perilous times"* in which men will be lovers of pleasures more than lovers of God. The apostle further writes in 2 Thessalonians 2:3 the *"man of sin,"* or person of the Antichrist, can be revealed only after a great *"falling away"* or apostasy from the Christian faith. Sinners who never know the way of righteousness cannot fall away from faith, as taught in 2 Peter 2:21. Only believers with faith can fall away from Christianity, and Bible prophecy says your day is a perilous, dangerous time to live in when many will forsake truth. We must be fortified with the full armor of God, *"Praying always with all prayer and supplication in the Spirit, and watching thereunto with all perseverance and supplication for all saints,"*[634] if we expect to withstand this evil day.

Another Hebrews text, chapter 10:19-39, shows how people can *"draw back unto perdition,"* or lose their confession of eternal life, not believing *"to the saving of the soul."* In the Greek, *"draw back"* means retreating or shrinking back. On the narrow road to eternal life, you choose one of three options: finishing the journey in strength, becoming idle by staying in one place, or retreating from the narrow road to the broad road. This Hebrews text begins with the reality of our prayerful approach to God's heavenly throne through a *"true heart in full assurance of faith."* After a command to assemble more with Christians as Christ's return approaches, verses 26 and 29 detail how sinning willfully, on purpose, after knowing truth, is grounds for sore punishment from God. Verse 29 emphatically declares, *"Of how much sorer punishment, suppose ye, shall he be thought worthy, who hath trodden under foot the Son of God, and hath counted the blood of the covenant, wherewith he was sanctified, an unholy thing, and hath done despite unto the Spirit of grace?"* The main phrase to notice is *"wherewith he was sanctified,"* proving a person can be genuinely sanctified—meaning separated from profane things and dedicated to God in the Greek—and yet retreat from this spiritual condition and be lost. Reference Figure 11 and recall sanctification is the second

---

634 Ephesians 6:18

stage of a Christian's journey to the baptism of the Holy Ghost. Just as all Israel came to Kadesh-Barnea,[635] the border of the Promised Land, or third stage of their journey, and provoked God by rejecting His leadership to possess Canaan, people journey through the first two stages of the Christian journey (justification and sanctification) and provoke God, drawing back into a sinful lifestyle without being born again by the Holy Ghost. Verses 38 and 39 are a beautiful, encouraging conclusion to this text, saying, *"Now the just shall live by faith: but if any man draw back, my soul shall have no pleasure in him. But we are not of them who draw back unto perdition; but of them that believe to the saving of the soul."*

Figure 12 shows how the three-stage journey matches the Stature of a Perfect Man. Faith is the character quality you receive when you are justified. During sanctification, God gives you the character qualities of virtue, knowledge, temperance, patience, godliness, and brotherly kindness. The third stage is when charity, the love of God, or God's Holy Spirit, baptizes your soul into the kingdom of God as a seal unto the day of your redemption.

Three Stages and the Stature of a Perfect Man	
First Stage: Justification	Faith
Second Stage: Sanctification	Virtue Knowledge Temperance Patience Godliness Brotherly Kindness
Third Stage: Baptism of the Holy Ghost	Charity

Figure 12

635   Numbers 13:26

The sixth and final text is 2 Peter 2:19-22, in which Peter teaches people can escape *"the pollutions of the world through the knowledge of the Lord and Savior Jesus Christ"* but become *"again entangled therein, and overcome"* back into their corrupt lifestyle. Peter compares this backslider to a pig, or *"sow"* that can be washed and made clean, but then return to wallow *"in the mire."* Jesus says the only way to be clean is through His Word in John 15:3: *"Now ye are clean through the word which I have spoken unto you."* A sow-like person can indeed receive God's Word and be washed with His divine character traits temporarily only to forsake them later, returning to a sin-addicted lifestyle.

The example of the saved thief on the cross shows how swiftly you can gain the character qualities of God. Most know the thief on Jesus' right hand was saved because Christ told him, *"Verily I say unto thee, To day shalt thou be with me in paradise."*[636] But few people know that the saved thief was initially mocking and reviling Jesus along with passersby, chief priests, scribes, and elders. Matthew 27:44 reads, *"The thieves also, which were crucified with him, cast the same in his teeth."* At some point during their hours on the cross together, the saved thief received faith and enough virtue to publicly stand for Christ's innocence and plead for eternal life. He also rebuked the lost thief saying, *"Dost not thou fear God, seeing thou art in the same condemnation? And we indeed justly; for we receive the due reward of our deeds: but this man hath done nothing amiss. And he said unto Jesus, Lord, remember me when thou comest into thy kingdom."*[637] The lesson is Jesus will quickly and faithfully pardon all those who glory in His sinlessness and humbly plead for eternal life.

RECOGNIZING OR WEIGHING A LACK OF CHARACTER

Jesus Christ recognizes a lack of divine character in the "rich young ruler," recorded in three gospels: Matthew 19:16-30, Mark 10:17-31, and Luke 18:18-30.

---

636   Luke 23:43
637   Luke 23:40-42

Mark 10:21 says Jesus loved this young man, for he had kept *"all"* six of the commandments Christ listed from his childhood (Ten Commandments five through nine plus Leviticus 19:18). What a rare specimen of obedience! His sincerity was apparent because he came running—not walking—and kneeling before Christ.[638] Yet despite all this, the man knew he lacked eternal life, saying, *"What lack I yet?"* God puts a conscience in every heart, including yours and mine, so we know how far we have come with God and if we yet lack His character qualities. Jesus agreed, saying, *"One thing thou lackest: go thy way, sell whatsoever thou hast, and give to the poor, and thou shalt have treasure in heaven: and come, take up the cross, and follow me."* The ruler left Jesus, grieved and sorrowful, *"for he had great possessions."*

Your story doesn't have to end like this ruler's. By grace, you can *"add"* to your character, as this story implies God's Spirit gives a true, honest spiritual assessment for every person through preaching, Bible reading, and witnessing. Not only does God love you like He loved this ruler, but He offers explicit directions on what you must do to continue growing in grace and knowledge of the Lord Jesus Christ. Right now you can know where you are in God's plan for your life. You can look at Figure 12 and ask the Holy Spirit to reveal which stage you are in. Have you recently been baptized in the name of the Lord Jesus Christ with divine faith? Then you are in stage one and ready to move into stage two, seeking virtue. Have you received divine virtue, living boldly for Christ in public settings and ready to go further into divine knowledge, or beyond into temperance or patience? Or are you ready to be baptized by the Holy Ghost in stage three, seeing godliness, brotherly kindness, and the other stage two qualities manifesting in your life?

Jesus' body is in heaven, but His Holy Spirit is present and near to every heart attempting to show his current character and offer a greater experience serving Christ. Acts 17:26-28 says,

---

638   Mark 10:17

"And hath made of one blood all nations of men for to dwell on all the face of the earth, and hath determined the times before appointed, and the bounds of their habitation; That they should seek the Lord, if haply they might feel after him, and find him, though he be not far from every one of us: For in him we live, and move, and have our being; as certain also of your own poets have said, For we are also his offspring."

Scripture declares God weighs each person's character in Proverbs 16:2: *"All the ways of a man are clean in his own eyes; but the LORD weigheth the spirits."* God's Word is the measuring stick or balance that measures or weighs your character. Paul says in Philippians 3:16 Christians should walk by the *"same rule,"* which means "a measuring rod, rule; a carpenter's line or measuring tape" in the Greek. The reason God gave us His Word is so we can measure our lives by its truths. Someday all will be judged by the Word, for Paul declares, *"God shall judge the secrets of men by Jesus Christ according to my gospel."*

Joining the rich ruler, Belshazzar and Job are two more Bible examples of men aware that their lives were being weighed by God. Belshazzar, king of Babylon at the time of its fall, profaned Israel's holy temple vessels by feasting with them while praising idols. Supernatural fingers interrupted the evil feast by writing the king's doom on the palace wall, which Daniel interpreted as *"Thou (Belshazzar) art weighed in the balances, and art found wanting."*[639] The king was guilty of refusing to learn humility from Nebuchadnezzar's life and offer glory to the one true God. In God's sight, Belshazzar's character was *"wanting,"* or deficient of humility. Job had his patience tested to its limit, yet passed the test. After suffering the loss of his livestock, servants, and children by Satan's desire, Job kept his integrity by worshipping God and not charging *"God foolishly."*[640] Job endured months[641] of tests and pleaded with God, saying, *"Let me be weighed in an even balance, that God may know mine integrity."*[642] God had

639   Daniel 5:27
640   Job 1:13-22
641   Job 7:3, 29:2
642   Job 31:6

weighed Job's life and deemed it acceptable, telling his three friends that Job had spoken right and they had spoken wrong.[643]

Paul explains in 2 Corinthians 4:16-18 that trials and tests of faith produce an *"eternal weight of glory."* What is this eternal weight? It must be heavenly awards that await Christians, such as the *"crown of life"*[644] and memorials God keeps as witnesses of His children's righteous acts of faith. Acts 10:4 says an angel let Cornelius know that a memorial of his prayers and alms giving were *"before God"* in heaven. May you set your affection on things above and live for eternal rewards in the midst of your tests. Peter says our tests of faith are *"much more precious than of gold that perisheth."*[645] Jesus wants to help you recognize your current character and what is lacking so that you may accept His portion of divine character, which will help you store up an eternal weight of glory in heaven.

CHARACTER QUALITY #3: KNOWLEDGE

2 Peter 1:5 reads, *"And beside this, giving all diligence, add to your faith virtue; and to virtue knowledge."* Knowledge is the third step on your way to godliness. It's a third measure or portion of Holy Ghost-anointing God wants to add to your spirit.

In the Greek, knowledge is defined as "general intelligence, understanding; the deeper more perfect and enlarged knowledge of this religion, such as belongs to the more advanced, especially of things lawful and unlawful for Christians." Based upon this definition, the Bible places knowledge as a deep understanding of Christianity you need to advance on God's way. Logically, God must give you knowledge, a deep understanding of God, after you have faith and virtue. Faith helped you choose the right way to walk, and virtue was moral power to daily walk in His narrow path. But knowledge helps you understand deeper truths about what pleases God and why He requires certain behaviors since His judgments are *"unsearchable...and his ways past finding out."*[646]

---

643   Job 42:7-9
644   James 1:12
645   1 Peter 1:7
646   Romans 11:33

Christians who ask for and receive God's knowledge must first reject the sin of reasoning, or human understanding. You must differentiate honest, spiritual reasoning from sinful reasoning. God gave you the gift to use spiritual reasoning in your daily life. In Isaiah, God lovingly invited Israel to reason with Him, promising to wash their sins white as snow if they were willing, obedient, and did well.[647] This glorious, spiritual reasoning leads to eternal life! But sinful reasoning is different. It's a thought process exalting Satan's, or man's will, above God's.

Genesis 3 provides the first example of humans choosing sinful reasoning over God's knowledge. The subtle serpent beguiled Eve into eating the forbidden fruit through false reasoning. God had previously told Adam he'd *"surely die"* if he partook of the fruit in Genesis 2:17, and Eve had this same knowledge according to Genesis 3:2-3. But the serpent exalted his will above God's, claiming Eve would *"not surely die"* because she would be wise like a god, *"knowing good and evil."* Even after Eve's beguilement, Adam willingly chose to join in his wife's disobedience, plunging humanity into utter chaos. Both of their reasoning was completely contrary to God's knowledge and produced incalculable effects upon human history. Every emergency siren screams out because of sinful reasoning. Each natural disaster ravages the land because of human reasoning. Every skin wrinkle and gray hair is the result of Eve's false reasoning. Every funeral is the result of the serpent's sinful reasoning. Thankfully, Jesus' spiritual reasoning to *"do always those things that please"*[648] the Father has resulted in redemption for all believers. Romans 5:18-19 declares,

> *"Therefore as by the offence of one judgment came upon all men to condemnation; even so by the righteousness of one the free gift came upon all men unto justification of life. For as by one man's disobedience many were made sinners, so by the obedience of one shall many be made righteous."*

647   Isaiah 1:16-20
648   John 8:29

In Capernaum, the Lord Jesus confronted scribes about their sinful reasoning when He forgave the palsy-stricken man's sins in Mark 2:1-12. The scribes, along with *"all the region around about Galilee"*[649] had heard of Jesus' famous authority over demons and His miracles, and should have understood that He, the Christ, had power to forgive sins. After all, scribes knew Isaiah's prophecies that the Messiah was *"The mighty God, The everlasting Father."*[650] The merciful Messiah gave the scribes another chance to reject their sinful reasoning by healing the man of palsy, saying, *"But that ye may know that the Son of man hath power on earth to forgive sins, (he saith to the sick of the palsy,) I say unto thee, Arise, and take up thy bed, and go thy way into thine house."*[651]

Paul models a faithful example of godly reasoning *"out of the scriptures"* in Acts 17:1-12. For three straight Sabbath days Paul uses Old Testament Scripture to reason with Thessalonians about prophecies of Jesus' death and resurrection, causing some to believe. When the apostle moves on to Berea and reasons again in the synagogue, the new believers react in the best manner—supporting their godly reasoning by searching the Scriptures themselves. Acts 17:11 says, *"These were more noble than those in Thessalonica, in that they received the word with all readiness of mind, and searched the scriptures daily, whether those things were so."* You manifest honest spiritual reasoning when you hungrily seek God's Word for yourself.

KNOWLEDGE AS A KEY, LIGHT, AND FRAGRANCE

Three Bible metaphors describe knowledge as a key, light, and fragrance, providing Christians three perspectives on the life-changing power of divine knowledge.

Jesus calls knowledge a key in Luke 11:52: *"Woe unto you, lawyers! for ye have taken away the key of knowledge: ye entered not in yourselves, and them that were entering in ye hindered."* Our Lord makes a similar statement to the Pharisees in Matthew 23:13: *"But woe unto you, scribes and*

---

649   Mark 1:28
650   Isaiah 9:6
651   Mark 2:10-11

Pharisees, hypocrites! for ye shut up the kingdom of heaven against men: for ye neither go in yourselves, neither suffer ye them that are entering to go in." In both statements, Jesus rebukes religious men for disallowing people from entering into the kingdom of heaven. These evil men took away the *"key of knowledge"* so people could not enter the kingdom of heaven through Jesus' ministry. The Jewish rulers had the true knowledge about Jesus. Nicodemus expressed that he and the Sanhedrin Council knew Jesus was a teacher sent from God,[652] yet Jewish leaders threatened to excommunicate anyone from the synagogue who believed in Jesus as Messiah.[653] How was this done? Satan anointed false teachers with *"doctrines of devils"* and *"commandments of men"* to point followers away from entering into Christ the Door: *"I am the door: by me if any man enter in, he shall be saved, and shall go in and out, and find pasture."*[654]

To ensure His followers entered into eternal blessings, Jesus gave Peter the *"keys of the kingdom of heaven"* in Matthew 16:19. After he received the Holy Ghost on the Day of Pentecost, the Book of Acts records that Peter used the keys to unlock salvation and the Holy Ghost baptism to three different groups: Jews, Samaritans, and Gentiles.

The Jews received salvation from Peter's preaching in Acts 2:14-47. The keys, or promises of God, Peter used to help 3,000 souls enter the kingdom of heaven are found in Acts 2:38: *"Repent, and be baptized every one of you in the name of Jesus Christ for the remission of sins, and ye shall receive the gift of the Holy Ghost."* The Samaritans needed Peter's keys to be born again in Acts 8:1-17, having been previously saved and baptized through Philip's ministry. Once Peter and John arrived they prayed for and laid hands upon the new believers and the Holy Ghost fell upon them, birthing spiritual children into God's kingdom. The Gentiles also received the Holy Ghost through Peter's keys in Acts 10:34-48. While Peter preached at Cornelius' house, *"the Holy Ghost fell on all them which heard the word."* Peter later rehearsed these events to Jews in Acts 11:1-18, declaring that God was granting to the Gentiles *"repentance unto life."*

652 John 3:1-2
653 John 9:22
654 John 10:9

Peter faithfully and powerfully used the keys Jesus gave him to allow three different groups to access eternal life.

Acts 16 details Paul's first European convert from Thyatira (in modern day Turkey) named Lydia. Sent by vision to Macedonia, Paul went to pray at a river side and spoke to a group of women about Jesus Christ. Lydia received Paul's knowledge of Christ and she and her household were baptized. The key of knowledge opened Lydia's heart: *"And a certain woman named Lydia, a seller of purple, of the city of Thyatira, which worshipped God, heard us: whose heart the Lord opened, that she attended unto the things which were spoken of Paul."*[655]

Every promise of God is obtained by knowledge or understanding God's will. 2 Peter 1:3-4 reads,

> *"According as his divine power hath given unto us all things that pertain unto life and godliness, through the knowledge of him that hath called us to glory and virtue: Whereby are given unto us exceeding great and precious promises: that by these ye might be partakers of the divine nature, having escaped the corruption that is in the world through lust."*

All spiritual blessings come through the knowledge of Him—God—whether you need salvation, cleansing, bodily healing, or deliverance.

Light is a second metaphor Paul uses to describe knowledge in 2 Corinthians 4:6-7, located in our hearts, or spirits: *"For God, who commanded the light to shine out of darkness, hath shined in our hearts, to give the light of the knowledge of the glory of God in the face of Jesus Christ. But we have this treasure in earthen vessels, that the excellency of the power may be of God, and not of us."* David writes the same in Psalm 119:130, saying, *"The entrance of thy words giveth light; it giveth understanding unto the simple."* The knowledge of God's Word *"is a lamp unto my feet, and a light unto my path,"*[656] giving understanding to the humble.

---

655   Acts 16:14
656   Psalm 119:105

Anywhere salvation through the gospel of Jesus Christ is preached in truth, the light of knowledge is shining. Paul and Barnabas first preached the light of God's knowledge to Jews in Antioch who blasphemed it, causing the apostles to focus on preaching to Gentiles:

> *"Then Paul and Barnabas waxed bold, and said, It was necessary that the word of God should first have been spoken to you: but seeing ye put it from you, and judge yourselves unworthy of everlasting life, lo, we turn to the Gentiles. For so hath the Lord commanded us, saying, I have set thee to be a light of the Gentiles, that thou shouldest be for salvation unto the ends of the earth."*[657]

Jesus says the gospel's knowledge-light will shine upon every nation, then the end of the world will come.[658]

Fragrance is the third metaphor Scripture uses to explain knowledge. Paul writes in 2 Corinthians 2:14-16:

> *"Now thanks be unto God, which always causeth us to triumph in Christ, and maketh manifest the savour of his knowledge by us in every place. For we are unto God a sweet savour of Christ, in them that are saved, and in them that perish: To the one we are the savour of death unto death; and to the other the savour of life unto life. And who is sufficient for these things?"*

The savor, or fragrance, of divine knowledge is spread by Christians in every place they preach. To believers, their knowledge is fragrance unto life but to sinners, its fragrance unto death.

PRINCIPLES OF KNOWLEDGE

Divine knowledge is founded on the principles that God cannot lie, the Bible is free from contradictions, and God still works through supernatural gifts of the Holy Ghost. These principles ensure your advancement in deeper Christian truths because you know God is trustworthy.

---

657   Acts 13:46-47
658   Matthew 24:14

God cannot lie. Many scoffers say God changes His mind, deceives mankind, and doesn't keep His promises. Nothing could be further from the truth. Scripture shouts every man is a liar, or has told a lie at some point during his lifetime, and God is the only truth-teller: "*God forbid: yea, let God be true, but every man a liar; as it is written, That thou mightest be justified in thy sayings, and mightest overcome when thou art judged.*"[659]

God told Noah to build an ark because He would flood the earth in judgment upon wicked-hearted men. Noah faithfully prepared the ark for around 55-75 years[660] before one drop of rain fell. God's Word stood true despite over a half century of waiting upon it.

25 years after God promised Abram He'd make a "*great nation*"[661] out of him, Isaac was born to his wife Sarah. Despite both of their occasional, doubtful laughter at God's promise over a two-decade wait, the Word came to pass. God repeatedly strengthened Abraham's faith until he was "*fully persuaded that, what he [God] has promised, he was able also to perform.*"[662]

Over 800 years before Jesus' birth, the prophet Isaiah foretold it, saying, "*Behold, a virgin shall conceive, and bear a son, and shall call his name Immanuel.*"[663] Eight centuries of theological skepticism could not stop God from keeping His promise by visiting a highly favored virgin named Mary, causing her to conceive Jesus, the Son of God.

It's crucial to understand God makes both conditional and unconditional promises. His promise that a virgin would conceive the Messiah was unconditional, but His warning to destroy Ninevah was conditional: "*And Jonah began to enter into the city a day's journey, and he cried, and said, Yet forty days, and Nineveh shall be overthrown.*"[664] God's Word doesn't record the conditional aspect of His warning; it only states its overthrowing. The lesson is to seek understanding if a promise of God is conditional or unconditional.

---

659 Romans 3:4
660 "How Long Did It Take Noah To Build The Ark?" *Answers In Genesis*, https://answersingenesis.org/bible-timeline/how-long-did-it-take-for-noah-to-build-the-ark/
661 Genesis 12:2
662 Romans 4:20-21
663 Isaiah 7:14
664 Jonah 3:4

Any unconditional promise God speaks today, just as in the past, will come to pass. Conditional promises require mature spiritual discernment, since failed prophecies, spoken in God's name, were not spoken by God, but rather by an evil, lying spirit impersonating the Holy One.[665]

The Bible is free from contradictions. Since God sent Jesus as *"the way"*[666] to save sinners because He *"so loved the world,"*[667] He is obligated to give us an infallible, written record of instructions for how to walk this way. The just and fair God must provide a clear path to heaven if He is warning mankind with everlasting judgment for willful disobedience to His eternal life offer. Humanity will be judged by God's Word. Romans 2:16 says, *"In the day when God shall judge the secrets of men by Jesus Christ according to my gospel."* Jesus is the Word of God,[668] and the true Word of God is found in the King James Version of the Holy Bible.

Floyd Nolen Jones' book *Which Version is The Bible?* details the validity and reliability of the King James Version in contrast to modern Bible versions. Jones "proclaims from the outset that the King James or Authorized Version is the Word of God translated into the English language to the extent that it is the final authority in all matters of conduct and faith."[669] The KJV is set apart from modern versions because its New Testament is translated from the most accurate Greek manuscripts, the Textus Receptus, whereas modern versions use the corrupted Greek texts called the Codex Vaticanus B. Two men—B.F. Westcott (1825-1901) and F. J. A. Hort (1828-1892)—produced this polluted "radical Greek text" in 1881. Examples abound of modern versions—through Westcott and Hort's efforts—omitting God's pure words, proving just how dangerously deceptive these versions are. Estimated by Jones, Westcott and Hort changed, added, or subtracted 7% of the 140,521 Greek words in the Textus Receptus. Revelations 22:18-19 warns of the awful, eternal repercussions for adding to God's Words or taking away

---

665 1 Kings 22:22, Jeremiah 29:23
666 John 14:6
667 John 3:16
668 John 1:1-14, Revelation 19:13
669 Jones, Floyd Nolen. *Which Version is the Bible?* KingsWord Press, 2006

from them because *"every word of God is pure,"*[670] and taking away from the Word is exactly what modern versions do.

Colossians 1:14 says *"we have redemption through his blood, even the forgiveness of sins"* in the KJV. But the NIV, ESV, and NASV omit *"through his blood."* Certainly the enemy, Satan, wants Jesus' blood omitted as much as possible because he knows the *"blood of the everlasting covenant"* makes believers *"perfect in every good work to do"* God's will.[671] Christians daily access the cleansing power of Jesus' blood, for we wash our robes *"white in the blood of the lamb."*[672]

The KJV of Isaiah 14:12 identifies Satan as *"Lucifer, son of the morning,"* but modern versions omit *"Lucifer"* and give Satan titles that belong only to Christ. The NIV of Isaiah 14:12 calls Satan *"morning star,"* which is a title only given to Christ in Revelation 22:16. God is not the author of confusion. He does not share His name or titles with anyone else, but Satan wants to be like Christ and seeks to steal His worship according to Isaiah 14:13-14. The ESV and RSV make a similar error in Isaiah 14:12, calling Satan the "Day Star." But Jesus Christ is the single *"day star"* that has risen in our hearts according to 2 Peter 1:19. The KJV is the only version that preserves God's original, full revelation of Himself and His will.

Some say the King James Version contains contradictions, but that is false. One example of a supposed contradiction concerns how many died in the plague after the feast of Baal-peor. Numbers 25:9 says 24,000 died while 1 Corinthians 10:8 says 23,000. Which is it? The key is understanding the wording. Notice the words *"fell in one day,"* found in 1 Corinthians 10:8. There is no contradiction between the two Scriptures because 23,000 died in one day and 1,000 more died either the next day or in the following days thereafter to bring the total fallen to 24,000. Careful, prayerful Bible study allows Christians to maintain full assurance that God's Word is contradiction-free.

God still works through the supernatural gifts of the Holy Ghost. Many follow the cessation doctrine, believing the gifts of the Holy Ghost

---

670   Proverbs 30:5
671   Hebrews 13:20-21
672   Revelation 7:14

have ceased. Without going into great depth on this subject, know that the cessation doctrine is wrong for a number of reasons.

First, Jesus put the gifts into the church as part of the Great Commission and never took them out. Mark 16:15-18 records Jesus' promise that gifts like speaking in tongues, casting out devils, and healing the sick would follow *"them that believe"* as the gospel was preached in all the world, to every creature. In a parallel passage on the Great Commission, our Lord said, *"Lo, I am with you alway, even unto the end of the world. Amen."*[673] Genuine manifestation of spiritual gifts are evidence of Christ's Spirit being present and working with all believers, in all generations, until the end of the world. Christ never limited these gifts to just the apostles, but said the gifts were for *"them that believe"*—any true believer.

Some think 1 Corinthians 13:8-13 teaches the gifts ended with the completion of the written New Testament. Careful examination of this text proves otherwise, for Paul states perfection will come when we are *"face to face"* with Christ. Since living Christians are not yet face to face with Christ, we still need prophecies, tongues, and knowledge to operate *"in part,"* meaning through and despite the veil of our sinful bodies. Once we have new, eternal bodies, or *"that which is perfect,"* then *"that which is in part shall be done away with."* Our human bodies will be changed into glorified, or perfect bodies when we see Jesus. That is the moment we will not need spiritual gifts. 1 John 3:2 teaches, *"When he [Jesus] shall appear, we shall be like him; for we shall see him as he is."* Paul writes, *"Who shall change our vile body, that it may be fashioned like unto his glorious body, according to the working whereby he is able even to subdue all things unto himself."*[674]

Second, Paul ordained the nine gifts of the Spirit to the Corinthians,[675] and all Christians, over 20 years after Jesus ascended to heaven. Paul received his revelation from Jesus Christ Himself and warned that

---

673   Matthew 28:18-20
674   Philippians 3:21
675   1 Corinthians 12:1-31

if anyone changed it, they were cursed.[676] In this same letter to the Galatians, the apostle defends the gifted members among them who were working miracles by the *"hearing of faith"* rather than the works of the law.[677] Paul never condemned gifted workers of miracles, nor did he tell them to cease operating in spiritual gifts.

Third, many supporters of the cessation doctrine say only the apostles of Christ were to use the gifts, and then the gifts would cease. This argument is extremely shallow and proven false by a casual reading of the New Testament. Philip the evangelist had four virgin daughters—obviously not among the 12 apostles—who prophesied according to Acts 21:8-9. Agabus was a prophet who correctly predicted the *"great dearth throughout all the world"* in Acts 11:28. Paul told the Thessalonians not to despise prophesies by quenching the Holy Spirit, but rather to prove them to be sure they were from God.[678] This was the same principle Paul taught the Corinthians: gifts are welcome to operate as long as they are tested and proven to be truly from the Lord.[679]

To conclude this subject, Christians *"covet earnestly the best gifts"* but their operation must be motivated by love, as love is *"a more excellent way."*[680] Those who operate gifts of God are not always among the saved, so greater emphasis should be placed upon loving obedience to every Word of God rather than seeking the operation of gifts. God is the only one who determines when gifts operate. In Paul's life, God led him to do many great miracles, but he couldn't heal himself from the thorn in his own flesh.[681] He left Trophimus sick at Miletum in 2 Timothy 4:20, and told Timothy to use a little wine for his sick stomach and *"often infirmities."*[682] Paul couldn't heal others at his own will. God will lead His people to do miracles and all other gift operations at His sovereign will, and not at the will of man.

---

676   Galatians 1:6-12
677   Galatians 3:5
678   1 Thessalonians 5:19-21
679   1 Corinthians 14:26-33
680   1 Corinthians 12:31
681   2 Corinthians 12:8-9
682   1 Timothy 5:23

THE GIFT OF THE WORD OF KNOWLEDGE

The gift of the word of knowledge is one of the nine gifts of the Spirit listed in 1 Corinthians 12:8-10. Like the separate gift of faith (1 Corinthians 12:9) and the character quality of faith (2 Peter 1:5), the gift of the *"word of knowledge"* is different than the character quality of knowledge. Gifts are placed in a person's human spirit by God from his birth and can operate regardless of whether a person is saved or not.

The Greek definition for the character quality of knowledge (2 Peter 1:5) and the gift of the word of knowledge (1 Corinthians 12:8) is the same: "a deep understanding of things lawful and unlawful for advanced, mature Christians." But the gift of the word of knowledge must be the ability to minister a deep understanding of God's Word to others. It's a gift or key of knowledge that allows someone to enter into the promises of God. Three examples from the Book of Acts demonstrate this gift of knowledge in the lives of Peter, Philip, and Paul.

In Acts 2, the baptism of the Holy Ghost falls upon 120 of Jesus' followers and a multitude of Jews witness their exuberant praise and adoration. The multitude thinks these 120 believers are drunk, but Peter's gift of knowledge helps them understand the Scriptural promise God is fulfilling—Joel 2:28-32. He concludes his sermon by giving the multitude the key of knowledge they need to become Christians: repent and be baptized in the name of Jesus Christ. That day, 3,000 people entered into salvation through Peter's word of knowledge.

Philip uses God's gift of knowledge in Acts 8:26-40 by sharing the understanding of Jesus' fulfilling of Isaiah 53:7-8 to an Ethiopian eunuch. Philip helps the eunuch understand Jesus was the Lamb of God brought to slaughter on Calvary to save mankind. Philip continues to preach to the eunuch, who sees water and asks to be baptized. The chariot is made to stand still while Philip baptizes him, helping him enter into salvation and eternal life through the knowledge of God.

Acts 19:1-6 records Paul's gift of knowledge opening the door for 12 Ephesians to receive the baptism of the Holy Ghost. Previous to Paul's coming, the Ephesians believed in Jesus Christ, and had been saved through Apollos' Scriptural teachings, for Apollos *"mightily convinced the Jews, and that publicly, shewing by the scriptures that Jesus was Christ."*[683] It's clear the Ephesians already had the character quality of knowledge, but lacked the knowledge of God the Father's promise to baptize believers with the Holy Ghost according to Luke 24:49 and Acts 1:4. God graciously sends Paul to Ephesus to help them enter into the third step of the Christian journey, who asks *"Have ye received the Holy Ghost since ye believed?"*[684] Once the 12 receive this knowledge, Paul lays his hands on them; and the Holy Ghost comes on them, manifesting through tongues and prophesy.

Whether knowledge is added to an individual's character or the gift of knowledge helps one Christian minister understanding to another, it's a life-changing, enlightening anointing of the Holy Spirit.

CHARACTER QUALITY #4: TEMPERANCE

2 Peter 1:6 reads, *"And to knowledge temperance."* Temperance is the fourth step on your way to godliness, a fourth measure or portion of Holy Ghost-anointing God wants to add to your spirit.

The Greek definition of temperance is "self control; the virtue of one who masters his desires and passions, especially his sensual appetites." Temperance is the self control you need to remain on God's way. After choosing God's way through faith, having virtue to publicly and daily walk the way, and knowledge to more deeply understand the way, God desires you crucify any remaining lusts of the flesh and mind so you can remain on the way.

Temperance empowers you to be more spiritual than carnal. You have five carnal, fleshly senses you must bring into subjection to the Holy Ghost: sight, taste, touch, smell, and hearing. Once you've added temperance to your character, by God's grace, you will be able to trust in your "sixth sense," faith, rather than your five senses. Faith is a spiritual sense because it is an inward, spiritual evidence you have of things not

---

683   Acts 18:28
684   Acts 19:2

seen. Hebrews 11:1 says, *"Now faith is the substance of things hoped for, the evidence of things not seen."*

Galatians 5:24-25 sums up this "spiritual versus natural" battle well: *"And they that are Christ's have crucified the flesh with the affections and lusts. If we live in the Spirit, let us also walk in the Spirit."* Your victory to be spiritually-minded is accomplished through crucifying your fleshly lusts. Crucifixion is a slow, cruel death, as seen in Jesus' self-sacrificial death on the cross. Jesus calls you to *"take up"* your *"cross daily and follow me."*[685] Christians, like Paul, *"die daily"*[686] to the temptations endured through their five senses.

Christians who ask for and receive God's temperance must first reject the sin of sensuality. Scripture repeatedly warns to flee from sensual lusts. The experienced preacher, Paul, told the young preacher, Timothy, to *"Flee also youthful lusts: but follow righteousness, faith, charity, peace, with them that call on the Lord out of a pure heart."*[687] Christians recognize sensual lusts and run from them, just as Joseph fled from the daily, lustful advances of Potiphar's wife in Genesis 39:7-12. More on Joseph later in this chapter.

Over time, you can identify true, temperate Christians just by their physical location because Scripture says sensual ones will ultimately separate from Spirit-filled believers and gather with other lust-seekers. Jude 1:18-19 affirms the sensual ones separate and cannot have the Holy Spirit: *"How that they told you there should be mockers in the last time, who should walk after their own ungodly lusts. These be they who separate themselves, sensual, having not the Spirit."*

In 1 Corinthians 3:1-7, Paul describes the damage sensual, carnal sins had upon the Corinthian church. He compared the Corinthians to babies that could only handle *"milk"* or elementary preaching rather than *"meat"* or deep preaching because of their carnality. Their sensuality manifested itself among the church members with *"envying, and strife, and divisions"* while they exalted their favorite preachers above others.

---

685   Luke 9:23
686   1 Corinthians 15:31
687   2 Timothy 2:22

The apostle affirms that all preachers are equal in importance and mission, planting and watering God's seed-Words. But God is the only great One in the church. 1 Corinthians 3:7 says, "*So then neither is he that planteth any thing, neither he that watereth; but God that giveth the increase.*" Preachers cannot create spiritual life in new converts at their bidding. God reserves this power to save converts to Himself.

LUSTS OF THE FLESH AND EYES, AND THE PRIDE OF LIFE

Sensual temptations come through one of three categories: lust of the flesh, lust of the eyes, and pride of life. 1 John 2:15-16 says: "*Love not the world, neither the things that are in the world. If any man love the world, the love of the Father is not in him. For all that is in the world, the lust of the flesh, and the lust of the eyes, and the pride of life, is not of the Father, but is of the world.*" All earthly sins fit into one of these three categories. You have and will be tempted through individual categories but also by multiple categories simultaneously.

The lust of the flesh is the first category and consists of sinful acts that bring your flesh pleasure or satisfaction. Bible examples include but are not limited to the following:

- Drunkenness: Being drunk perverts moral judgment (Proverbs 31:4-5) and drunkards will not inherit the kingdom of God (1 Corinthians 6:10).
- Overeating: Gluttony leads to poverty (Proverbs 23:20-21). Paul says enemies of Jesus' cross are those who make their bellies their god (Philippians 3:18-19).
- Sexual sins: Amnon, son of David, was so vexed with fleshly lust that he raped his half-sister, Tamar, and he was later murdered by her full-brother, Absalom (2 Samuel 13:1-39). Paul told the Corinthians to "*purge out*" and "*put away*" from their church a wicked brother who was fornicating with his step mother (1 Corinthians 5:1-13).

- Drugs: Linked to and labeled as *"witchcraft"* by Paul, using drugs to experience a high is condemned and those guilty will not inherit the kingdom of God (Galatians 5:20-21).

The lust of the eyes consists of looking at and desiring things in a covetous manner. Covetousness is closely connected to the lust of the eyes because humans often covet things they see. The following four examples are good things to behold with righteous intentions, but Satan often tries to pervert good intentions. Bible examples of lusting with the eyes include but are not limited to the following:

- Sexual attraction: Between a lawful husband and wife, sexual attraction is a blessing. Any attraction outside marriage must be overcome. Neglecting his war duties, King David sees beautiful Bathsheba bathing and immediately takes her to commit adultery. After she conceives, David has Joab assign Uriah, Bathsheba's husband, to a battle position where Uriah is killed (2 Samuel 11:1-27). Jesus says to look and lust upon a woman in your heart is the same as committing the literal act of adultery (Matthew 5:27-29).
- Property: Possessing and defending property is a blessing, and God-given right.[688] Desire to possess property must not supersede the kingdom of God. Jesus' *"great supper"* parable describes a man who turns down a great supper—symbolizing the post-rapture marriage supper of the Lamb—because he first *"must needs go and see"* his recently purchased land (Luke 14:18).
- Material possessions: God blesses believers with material possessions they need to enjoy life, but He requires contentment. Achan saw, coveted after, and took a Babylonian garment, silver, and gold, leading to the death

688 Exodus 3:8, 2 Samuel 23:11-12

of 36 Israeli soldiers (Joshua 7:1-26). Judas Iscariot, infamous traitor of our Lord Jesus, sold out Christ's location for 30 pieces of silver (Matthew 27:3-10).

- Financial prospects: God makes some believers rich, and others poor.[689] Again, contentment with God's will is the goal. When given the choice of a dwelling place, Lot, nephew of Abraham, chose the plain of Jordan which eventually drew he and his family into the vexing, wicked Sodomite culture (Genesis 13:10-11, 2 Peter 2:7-8). Balaam, the unfaithful prophet from Moses' time, greedily rejected God's perfect will in order to seek King Balak's lucrative offer and cause Israel to stumble (Numbers 22:17, Jude 1:11, Revelation 2:14).

The pride of life consists of seeking self-promotion, self-will, and praise. Bible examples include but are not limited to:

- Reputation: A good name is better than riches,[690] but believers must let God spread their reputations. The men who partially built the Tower of Babel desired to reach heaven and make a name for themselves (Genesis 11:1-9). Herod was smitten by the angel of the Lord and worm-eaten because he accepted praise as God rather than giving God the glory (Acts 12:22-23).
- Greatness: Before receiving the Holy Ghost, Jesus' disciples battled self-promotion because they argued about who was greater (Luke 22:24-26). God let King Nebuchadnezzar wander with the beasts of the field for seven years with a beast's mind because he believed it was his own power that established the Babylonian kingdom (Daniel 4:30).
- Strife: Korah electioneered for his group to take Aaron's position as priest but God opened the earth to swallow

689 Proverbs 22:2
690 Proverbs 22:1

them up alive (Numbers 16:1-50). King Uzziah did likewise, encroaching upon a spiritual office not belonging to him, attempting to offer incense to God as a priest, but the Lord smote him with leprosy until the day he died (2 Chronicles 26:1-23).

- Murder: After God rejected Cain's bloodless, self-will offering and accepted Abel's offering, the enraged, wrathful Cain murdered his brother (Genesis 4:1-8).

To conclude this section, consider the contrast between Eve and Jesus's three-fold temptations in Genesis 3 and Matthew 4, respectively. Both Eve and Christ were tempted in all three categories—lust of the flesh, lust of the eyes, pride of life—but only Christ overcame the enemy three times.

In Genesis 3:6, Eve is tempted with the lust of the flesh because *"the tree was good for food."* She was tempted with the lust of the eyes because the tree *"was pleasant to the eyes."* Eve fell to the pride of life because the tree would make her wise. After her submission to all three temptations, Eve partook of the fruit, beguiled or wholly seduced and deceived by the serpent's subtilty.[691] God now forbids women to preach His Word and lead His people because Eve let down her spiritual armor.[692]

Matthew 4:1-11 details Satan's greatest temptation ever upon a man, but his temptation failed because he was tempting the righteous God-man, Christ Jesus. Truly, no man has ever been, nor ever could be, tempted more fiercely than Jesus was tempted. The Savior was tempted by Satan Himself—not just a lower ranking, less powerful demon. Additionally, Christ was hungry after fasting for 40 days and His flesh was desperately weak. This was his test regarding the lust of the flesh, which was followed by the pride of life and lust of the eyes. Yet our Lord proved the weakest Christian overcomes Satan's greatest attacks by quoting the rightly divided Word of God.

---

691   2 Corinthians 11:3
692   1 Timothy 2:11-15

Note Satan's second temptation challenged Christ to cast Himself down from a pinnacle in hopes the angels would bear Him up. Basically, Satan urged Christ to produce a miracle at His own will by misquoting Scripture: Psalm 91:10-12. Satan deceives many Christians by misapplying Scripture and urging them to act upon their own thinking rather than God's. Thankfully, our Lord Jesus Christ rightly divided God's Word, and quoted Deuteronomy 6:16, saying, "*It is written again, Thou shalt not tempt the Lord thy God.*"[693] God asks us to prove Him in tithes and offerings,[694] but not in hazarding our lives by jumping off colossal buildings to show off our power, since we have none. Christ's lesson is this: you quoting *and* obeying God's Word will defeat Satan himself anytime, anywhere, anyplace.

1 Samuel 4:1-22 shows the importance of both quoting and obeying God's Word. Backslidden Israel was quoting God's promise given to Moses in Numbers 10:35 to save them from their enemies through the Ark of the Covenant. Of course, it was obedience to God's Presence in the Ark—not just possessing the Ark itself—that gave the victories. Even though the earth rang with Israel's hopeful shouts for victory, the Philistines easily defeated Israel because they were living in disobedience to God. Quoting part of God's Word without obeying the whole gets you nowhere.

Speak God's Word, obey it, stand upon it, and watch Satan leave you for a season,[695] just as he temporarily left Christ. Never forget that God will not give you a temptation too difficult for you to conquer. 1 Corinthians 10:13 says, "*There hath no temptation taken you but such as is common to man: but God is faithful, who will not suffer you to be tempted above that ye are able; but will with the temptation also make a way to escape, that ye may be able to bear it.*"

THE FRUIT OF TEMPERANCE

Just as faith is both a character quality and fruit of the Spirit, temperance is both as well. Figure 10 lists temperance as a fruit of the Holy Spirit

693   Matthew 4:7
694   Malachi 3:10
695   Luke 4:13

in a mature Christian's life and is the rarest form of temperance found under heaven.

Joseph, son of Jacob, displays mature temperance by fleeing the sexual advances of Potiphar's wife in Genesis 39:7-12. Joseph was around 28 years old at the time of this sexual temptation. He was sold into slavery at 17 years old, faithfully served Potiphar for 11 years before being falsely accused, and spent two years in prison (after interpreting the butler and baker's dreams) before being exalted to Pharaoh's right hand at 30 years old.[696] At the time of the *"day by day"* sexual temptations, Joseph wasn't married and was in the prime of his life when his fleshly lusts were at their peak. Given the power and authority Joseph had, he would have known Potiphar's schedule and had access to privacy in order to fulfill the lusts of his flesh. But Joseph overcame the temptation. How did Joseph display such mature temperance, day after day, at such a young age? Genesis 39:9 reveals that he feared God more than fulfilling the lust of the flesh. He boldly defied the seductress saying, *"How then can I do this great wickedness, and sin against God?"* How many church-going men today—regardless of age—would be able to turn down a woman constantly begging them for sexual pleasure? Joseph's temperance over the lust of the flesh strengthens and inspires believers of all ages to honor God with their bodies, for their bodies belong to God.[697]

The apostle Paul's writings reveal his divine measure of temperance, for he says Christians are *"temperate in all things"* in 1 Corinthians 9:24-27. Paul uses imagery of athletic games, similar to the Olympics, to compare Christians to professional runners. Just as runners train their bodies through self-denial with strenuous workouts and strict diets, Christians deny their fleshly lusts and strictly control their bodies that they might win the incorruptible crown of eternal life. A Christian is self-controlled or temperate in his speech, diet, spending, exercise, work, and every other area of his life.

696 Genesis 37:2, 41:1, 41:50
697 1 Corinthians 6:19

Paul's letter to the Philippians shows his advanced temperance just two years before his martyrdom. At the time of this letter in 64 A.D., Paul had served Jesus for 30 years. Instead of increasing financial prosperity, Paul experienced frequent imprisonments and poverty. Christ was stripping him of the pride of life and helping him crucify the lusts of the flesh. He rejoiced in the care the Philippians had shown to his physical needs, not because he desired gifts, but because he knew God was going to add rewards to their accounts in heaven.[698] Paul admits he was learning contentment whether his stomach was full or empty. It is in this context of hunger pains that Paul is quoted as saying, *"I can do all things through Christ which strengtheneth me."* Rest assured that Christ's strength is readily available for you in times and seasons of suffering and want. You can crucify the lust of the flesh, lust of the eyes, and the pride of life through Christ Who strengthens you with a measure of His own temperance.

CHARACTER QUALITY #5: PATIENCE

2 Peter 1:6 reads, *"And to knowledge temperance; and to temperance patience."* Patience is the fifth step on your way to godliness, a measure or portion of Holy Ghost-anointing God wants to add to your spirit.

The Greek definition of patience is "steadfastness, constancy, endurance, perseverance" even in the "greatest trials and sufferings." Patience is the steadfastness needed to be content on God's way. No matter what tests, trials, persecutions, or sufferings you encounter, God's anointing of divine patience empowers you to endure the spiritual battles and come forth as a better Christian. Right in the middle of your storm or test, God's patience will hold you unwavering in your convictions. As my friend Kidri preaches: you are tested in order to gain a testimony! You are confident God allows your tests to make you more obedient to Him. Job knew this fact and proclaimed, *"When he [God] hath tried me, I shall come forth as gold."*[699]

698 Philippians 4:10-17
699 Job 23:10

To receive God's divine patience you must reject the sin of haste. In our instant society with instant messenger, instant pots, instant money transfers, quick fixes, and 5G internet speeds, we have grown accustomed to instant gratification. Almost unconsciously, our culture teaches us impatience. Contrariwise, God still teaches His children through the same, time-tested method: patience. Delays. Waiting. Obstructions. In fact, if God answered every prayer of yours instantly, you'd be only more impatient. Our flesh hates waiting, but God knows it is the only way we learn contentment.

Additionally, the Bible states exactly when patience is gained: in the middle of your tribulation. Romans 5:3-4 says, "*And not only so, but we glory in tribulations also: knowing that tribulation worketh patience; And patience, experience; and experience, hope.*" Tribulation, distress, or life's pressures accomplish patience when you purposely choose to think about God's goodness rather than your disappointments. Isaiah 26:3 says, "*Thou wilt keep him in perfect peace, whose mind is stayed on thee: because he trusteth in thee.*" Patience is the outcome of faithfulness. Offering thanksgiving to God while praying about your tribulation is being faithful. This accomplishes patience according to Philippians 4:6-7: "*Be careful for nothing; but in every thing by prayer and supplication with thanksgiving let your requests be made known unto God. And the peace of God, which passeth all understanding, shall keep your hearts and minds through Christ Jesus.*"

A major temptation is making speedy decisions without proper prayer, counsel, and contemplation. Decision-making in haste and sinful urgency is repeatedly condemned in God's Word, particularly in Proverbs. Sinners "*make haste to shed blood*"[700] and a hasty spirit "*exalteth folly.*"[701] Too often people quickly praise foolish things, like famous singers, athletes, politicians, and even technological advances, but Jesus says "*that which is highly esteemed among men is abomination in the sight of God.*"[702] Be careful who or what you praise. Proverbs 29:20 says, "*Seest*

---

700   Proverbs 1:16
701   Proverbs 14:29
702   Luke 16:15

thou a man that is hasty in his words? there is more hope of a fool than of him." Concerning money, never be impatient for riches. Proverbs 28:22 says, *"He that hasteth to be rich hath an evil eye, and considereth not that poverty shall come upon him."*

Israel's first king, Saul, lost unimaginable rewards because of impatience. Although we know Saul was saved (Samuel told Saul he would be with him in paradise[703]), he lost out on God's establishing his kingdom *"forever"*[704] because he couldn't wait a *few extra hours* for Samuel to arrive and sacrifice a burnt offering. God wasn't asking Saul to wait extra weeks, months, or even years. Saul had to wait only a few extra hours to the end of the seventh day but he failed by forcing himself to offer his own burnt offering. David, on the other hand, is an example of exercising divine patience. As Saul's royal replacement and the man God recognized as chasing after His heart, David received God's promise and anointing to be king from Samuel when he was around 15 years old, but waited around 15 more years in order to inherit the promise because he was crowned king of Hebron at 30 years old.[705] David's divine patience kept him from hastening his ascent to Israel's throne, as he could have killed Saul on two occasions but would not harm the Lord's anointed.[706]

During those years of waiting, David endured death threats from Saul, his own father-in-law, enduring a fugitive's life. David wrote many of the psalms during these years of waiting, even psalms about avoiding Saul, like Psalm 18, 52, 54, 57, and 59. David's lesson is to sing to and about God in order to increase your patience. While running for his life, divine patience anointed David to sing, *"I trust in the mercy of God for ever and ever. I will praise thee for ever, because thou hast done it: and I will wait on thy name; for it is good before thy saints."*[707] Surely if David could joyfully sing to God with patience for deliverance, waiting upon God's name with a bounty on his head, you can worship and praise Jesus' name in the midst of your trial.

703   1 Samuel 28:19
704   1 Samuel 13:13-14
705   2 Samuel 5:4-5
706   1 Samuel 24:1-7, 26:5-10
707   Psalm 52:8-9

JOB: THE PATIENCE POSTER CHILD

The Bible teaches Job is the prime example of patience. You could call him the poster child for unwavering steadfastness. James 5:11 says, *"Behold, we count them happy which endure. Ye have heard of the patience of Job, and have seen the end of the Lord; that the Lord is very pitiful, and of tender mercy."*

Most know Job was both the richest and wisest man in the east, as men sat at his feet awaiting his counsel as they would wait upon a chief and king.[708] Job manifests patience with God and the tragic events of his life after suffering the excruciating loss of his livestock, children, and personal health. His intense physical suffering with open skin sores from his head to his feet lasted for months and caused sleepless nights.[709]

Patient Job endures the false accusations of his three friends before God Himself descends in a whirlwind to humble Job by asking him over 60 questions without directly answering Job's questions. God's first question is as unanswerable as the rest, asking, *"Where wast thou when I laid the foundations of the earth? declare, if thou hast understanding."*[710] Most importantly, God's visit brings Job to repentance and a greater appreciation and respect for the Almighty God.[711] Soon after, the Lord restored Job's family and possessions, blessing *"the latter end of Job more than his beginning."*[712]

Scripture records that Job's great victory was his integrity because he did not speak evil things against God, even resisting his wife's urge for him to curse God.[713] Job's patient words in the midst of suffering revealed his patient heart. Jesus says evil words defile a person because the words originate from the heart.[714] Matthew 12:34 says, *"For out of the abundance of the heart the mouth speaketh."* Let God add divine patience to your heart and you will speak patient words amidst your sufferings like Job did amidst his.

708 Job 1:1-3, 29:21-25
709 Job 2:7, 7:3-4, 29:2
710 Job 38:4
711 Job 42:1-6
712 Job 42:12
713 Job 1:22, 2:9-10
714 Matthew 15:18

THE PATIENCE OF THE PROPHETS

James 5:10 speaks about prophets being our examples for patience, say-ing *"Take, my brethren, the prophets, who have spoken in the name of the Lord, for an example of suffering affliction, and of patience."*

Examples abound of patient prophets that will strengthen your faith. You've probably heard that Abraham waited 25 years[715] between the time God promised him a son and the time when Isaac was born. The ark-building prophet Noah spent at least 55 years[716] building the ark, although he may have worked for up to 120 years. Either way, God's warning to Noah kept him patiently working for multiple decades on the ark *"to the saving of his house."*[717] At 80 years old[718] Moses delivered Israel out of Egyptian bondage but he first waited 40 years in Midian after smit-ing an Egyptian[719] before God visited him at the burning bush.

Have you considered the prophet Hosea's patience after God com-manded him to marry a harlot? Hosea's first thought may have been, "How can God ask me, a distinguished, holy prophet to marry a defiled, filthy whore?" Yet Hosea faithfully obeyed, endured the public shame, trusting God's plan as he took Gomer as his wife. The Lord said Hosea's wife had to be *"a wife of whoredoms and children of whoredoms."*[720] Not only was Gomer a whore, but her family members were known for their whoredoms.

Despite having three children together—Jezreel, Loruhamah, and Loammi—Hosea's patience was again tested when Gomer left him and committed adultery,[721] living with another man. But Hosea was patient because he knew God ordained his marriage to represent unfaithful Israel's constant rebellion and God's merciful forgiveness. Hosea fol-lowed the Word of the Lord and redeemed Gomer out of slavery for 15 pieces of silver and barley to signify God's redeeming love through

715 Genesis 12:4-7, 21:5
716 "How Long Did It Take Noah To Build The Ark?" *Answers In Genesis*, https://answersingenesis.org/bible-timeline/how-long-did-it-take-for-noah-to-build-the-ark/
717 Hebrews 11:7
718 Exodus 7:7
719 Acts 7:23-24
720 Hosea 1:2
721 Hosea 3:1

Jesus Christ laying His life down for both *"the lost sheep"* of Israel and the *"other sheep,"* the Gentiles.[722]

One final patience example is the prophet Joseph, son of Jacob and Rachel. After being sold into slavery by his brothers at 17 years of age, Joseph faithfully served Potiphar for 11 years before being falsely accused and imprisoned for trying to commit adultery with Potiphar's wife. While in prison, the Word of God came to Joseph about the destinies of the butler and baker, but the restored butler forgot to mention Joseph to Pharaoh. Finally, after waiting 2 years, Joseph was released from prison when another interpretation came to him about Pharoah's dream regarding seven years of plenty and seven years of famine. Psalm 105:19 says Joseph was in prison *"Until the time that his word came: the word of the Lord tried him."*

Like Joseph's life, God's promised Word always tries or tests believers. Scripture lists patience as the second step in the order to receive a promise from God. First, you must do the will of God, obeying His command. Second, you must be patient. Lastly, you will receive the promise. Hebrews 10:36 validates this order, saying, *"For ye have need of patience, that, after ye have done the will of God, ye might receive the promise."* You and I must follow Joseph's example, along with all those faithful saints who have inherited God's promises. Hebrews 6:12 states, *"That ye be not slothful, but followers of them who through faith and patience inherit the promises."*

CHARACTER QUALITY #6: GODLINESS

2 Peter 1:6 says, *"And to knowledge temperance; and to temperance patience; and to patience godliness."* Godliness is the sixth character trait the Lord adds to your being during the second stage of sanctification. This is the general measure or portion of godliness all Christians receive before being born again by charity, or the Holy Ghost.

The measure or character quality of godliness is distinct from the state of mature godliness—the *"mystery of godliness"* Paul writes about—that

---

722   Matthew 10:6, Luke 1:68, John 10:15-16

Jesus Christ modeled for us by being completely loyal and obedient to every command of God. Figure 13 details this understanding in the Third Stage. You will be most like God after being born again and experiencing years of learning and conforming to God's Word. You will most please and obey God after seasons of suffering, for it is through suffering you will learn to obey God according to Hebrews 5:8: *"Though he were a Son, yet learned he obedience by the things which he suffered."* Christ suffered great temptations but learned to obey His Father during those seasons. The sufferings of God's Son helped Him declare the singular statement His holy lips alone could utter: *"For I do always those things that please him."*[723]

Three Stages and the Stature of a Perfect Man	
First Stage: Justification	Faith
Second Stage: Sanctification	Virtue Knowledge Temperance Patience Godliness Brotherly Kindness
Third Stage: Baptism of the Holy Ghost	Charity ...which produces: Fruits of the Holy Spirit Also known as: Adoption Mature Godliness Keeping the Faith Fighting a Good Fight

Figure 13

723   John 8:29

The fact that godliness is the sixth character quality is significant because it relates to man being created by God on the sixth day of creation, according to Genesis 1:24-31. Both 6s represent godliness. Upon God creating Adam, he immediately possessed godliness. He was sinless, with dominion over all creatures and *"over all the earth."* Adam was so much like God as an amateur god by God's own design. Recognizing God's desire for Adam to be godly, you can understand God's desire for you to take dominion over your life. Paul says you have this Scriptural right in Romans 5:17 because you *"reign in life by one, Jesus Christ."*

What do you specifically reign over? Demonic powers and temptations. Paul says you wrestle *"against principalities, against powers, against the rulers of the darkness of this world, against spiritual wickedness in high places."*[724] Your enemies are unseen demonic influences and you constantly defeat them through *"the whole armor of God"*[725] as you cast down *"imaginations, and every high thing that exalteth itself against the knowledge of God, and bringing into captivity every thought to the obedience of Christ."*[726] Satan and his demons must flee from you as you quote God's Word through your lips and refuse their temptations.[727] As you exalt God's Word in your mind and obey His commands, you subdue demonic powers and reign over sin, the flesh, the world, and Satan.

GODLY BEHAVIOR TOWARD SINNERS AND ENEMIES

In His Sermon on the Mount, the Lord Jesus Christ teaches exactly what He requires for us to obtain godliness, and it centers around how we treat sinners and unbelievers. Believers must reject the sin of irreverence towards sinners and unbelievers. God is good to sinners, and so must we do likewise. To be *"perfect, even as your Father which is in heaven is perfect,"* Jesus asks us to love, bless, do good to, and pray for our enemies. Muse on Matthew 5:43-48:

724 Ephesians 6:12
725 Ephesians 6:13
726 2 Corinthians 10:5
727 Luke 4:12-13, James 4:7-8

"Ye have heard that it hath been said, Thou shalt love thy neighbour, and hate thine enemy. But I say unto you, Love your enemies, bless them that curse you, do good to them that hate you, and pray for them which despitefully use you, and persecute you; That ye may be the children of your Father which is in heaven: for he maketh his sun to rise on the evil and on the good, and sendeth rain on the just and on the unjust. For if ye love them which love you, what reward have ye? do not even the publicans the same? And if ye salute your brethren only, what do ye more than others? do not even the publicans so? Be ye therefore perfect, even as your Father which is in heaven is perfect."

Being a Christian, anointed with divine godliness, makes you compassionate towards the lost and unbelievers. If you are like God, you will hope for all men to be saved, although you know few will be saved. Peter says God is *"not willing that any should perish"*[728] while Paul says God wishes *"all men to be saved."*[729] Ezekiel 33:11 states clearly God does not delight in the death of sinners: *"As I live, saith the Lord GOD, I have no pleasure in the death of the wicked; but that the wicked turn from his way and live: turn ye, turn ye from your evil ways; for why will ye die, O house of Israel?"*

Examples abound of the righteous hoping and desiring for sinners to be saved, which is a true expression of godliness. Paul says he had *"great heaviness and continual sorrow"* in his heart wishing he could be cursed instead of his Israeli brethren who had rejected Christ as Messiah.[730] Stephen, the first Christian martyr, loudly asks Jesus to *"lay not this sin to their charge"*[731] as Jews stone him to death. Our Lord Jesus, during His crucifixion, uttered forgiveness to His mockers as some of his final words before His death, saying, *"Father, forgive them; for they know not what they do."*[732]

Ezekiel 9:1-11 records a remarkable instance of God sparing a small remnant of Israeli believers from His wrath against Jerusalem. This

---

728   2 Peter 3:9
729   1 Timothy 2:4
730   Romans 9:1-4
731   Acts 7:60
732   Luke 23:34

faithful remnant was spared because they sighed and cried *"for all the abominations"* done in Jerusalem. Not only does true godliness separate you from fellowshipping with sinners and despising their choices, but it also makes you weep and sigh in your private prayers to God. Godliness makes you so burdened and concerned about others' destinies that you cry and plead with God to show mercy on the disobedient and unholy. David experiences this burden in Psalm 119:136, saying, *"Rivers of waters run down mine eyes, because they keep not thy law."* Historically, Ezekiel's vision is fulfilled in 2 Chronicles 36:17-20 as Nebuchadnezzar's Babylonian forces slay many, carry others away into slavery, burn the house of God, and break down the wall of the city.

The anointing of godliness is given so it can lead you to show mercy or pronounce judgment according to God's leadership. But prepare to rule your heart by being *"slow to anger"*[733] just as God is slow to anger.[734] In Matthew 5:7 Jesus says, *"Blessed are the merciful: for they shall obtain mercy."* Wisdom teaches you to begin with merciful, gracious words for sinners and enemies.

There were times Jesus was very harsh and judgmental towards sinners, such as with the scribes and Pharisees in Matthew chapter 23. But Christ's mercy and forgiveness is what we admire and worship Him for. Paul, God's *"minister to the Gentiles,"*[735] issues harsh judgment but shifts to gracious mercy within a matter of a few sentences in 2 Timothy 4:14-18. The apostle says the Lord will reward Alexander the coppersmith for all the evil works he committed against him, but two verses later prays for God to not lay a charge to those men who forsook him. A godly person is so near to God's heart, through constant prayer, that God leads him to speak God's will in every situation. Godliness tells your heart to trust in and wait upon God before making a judgment, for He has *"mercy on whom he will have mercy"*[736] and *"he delighted in mercy."*[737]

733 Proverbs 16:32
734 Nehemiah 9:17, Psalm 103:8, 145:8
735 Romans 15:16
736 Romans 9:18
737 Micah 7:18

CHARACTER QUALITY #7: BROTHERLY KINDNESS

2 Peter 1:7 says, "*And to godliness brotherly kindness; and to brotherly kindness charity.*" Brotherly kindness is the seventh character trait the Lord adds to your being during the second stage of sanctification. This is the final character quality or portion of anointing Christians receive before being born again by charity, or the Holy Ghost.

The Greek word for brotherly kindness is "philadelphia," meaning "love of brothers or sisters; the love which Christians cherish for each other as brethren." Christianity puts a great emphasis on serving its members, as Paul says, "*As we have therefore opportunity, let us do good unto all men, especially unto them who are of the household of faith.*"[738] Our Lord Jesus says love among Christians is the primary way sinners will recognize Christians are Jesus' true disciples.[739] You are a true disciple of Jesus when you fervently love other Christians.

Brotherly kindness is the last character quality before a Christian is born again and makes him focus on his Christian brothers and sisters more than himself. It is as if God is saying, "I've graciously built you up into a godly, spiritual being but before I officially adopt you into my family by the seal of the Holy Ghost, I'm giving you brotherly kindness so you will serve and love My other children I've adopted." God is not going to birth a child into His kingdom without first adding brotherly kindness, for that person would not be kind to the rest of the body of Christ. It's easy to see why Christians must reject the sin of selfishness in order to receive the anointing of brotherly kindness.

Jesus prophesies love among mankind is going to continually decrease as His second coming approaches. Matthew 24:12 says, "*And because iniquity shall abound, the love of many shall wax cold.*" You will see less and less brotherly kindness in the world. Iniquity and unconfessed sins are causing love to decrease. Paul prophesies where love is being directed in the "*last days*," saying men will be "*lovers of their own selves*" and "*lovers of pleasures more than lovers of God.*"[740] But Paul also

---

738   Galatians 6:10
739   John 13:35
740   2 Timothy 3:1-4

prays for an increase in love among Christians that you can fulfill in 1 Thessalonians 3:12: *"And the Lord make you to increase and abound in love one toward another, and toward all men, even as we do toward you."* Let the world decrease its love while you choose to increase your brotherly love.

LOCATING AND LIVING FOR YOUR CHRISTIAN FAMILY

The character trait of brotherly kindness inspires a believer to locate and live for his Christian family. Locating and joining a Christian church family is an important part of serving God. Jesus modeled faithful church attendance for Christians to imitate. According to Luke 4:14-17, Christ's *"custom"* or habit was to be in the synagogue on the Sabbath day. Make it your custom to be gathered in public worship with other Christians every Sunday, as modeled by Paul and the Ephesians in Acts 20:7: *"And upon the first day of the week, when the disciples came together to break bread, Paul preached unto them, ready to depart on the morrow; and continued his speech until midnight."*

Just as every sheep needs a flock and a shepherd, every Christian needs a church family and pastor. Jesus was moved with compassion when He saw multitudes of people without pastors and urged His disciples to pray for the Lord to send laborers *"into his harvest."*[741] Shortly after His resurrection and ascension to heaven Jesus sent five preaching gifts to His church,[742] one of which is the pastor. Along with the preaching gifts of the apostle, prophet, teacher, and evangelist, the pastor gift benefits the church by equipping its members for their individual ministries, teaching precise truth, and promoting unity. The five-fold preaching ministry also protects believers from immaturity, doubt, hesitation, and deception.[743]

You can live for your Christian church family in at least five ways. First, brotherly kindness moves believers to meet the physical needs of other Christians. The early Christians provided daily food for poor

741 Matthew 9:36-38
742 Ephesians 4:8-11
743 Ephesians 4:11-14

widows[744] and James says genuine faith moves a true Christian to provide clothes and food for needy Christians.[745] Meeting physical needs is such a heartfelt act in Jesus' sight that He will grant eternal life as a reward for individuals who demonstrate six different acts of compassion upon His *"brethren,"* or other Christians, according to Matthew 25:31-46. In Philippians 2:3-4, Paul teaches Christians to have a *"lowliness of mind"* so they can esteem others *"better than themselves."* This humility causes us to *"look not every man on his own things, but every man also on the things of others."* Brotherly kindness causes you to consider others' needs more important than your own as you train your eyes to focus on others more than yourself.

Second, brotherly kindness promotes radical forgiveness towards fellow Christians. Matthew 18:21-35 details Jesus' attitude towards forgiveness. Peter asks Jesus if he should forgive his brother seven times but Christ says to multiply that estimate by 70! After this astounding news, Peter and the rest of the apostles say, *"Lord, Increase our faith"*[746] in Luke's parallel passage. In Matthew 18, the parable of the unmerciful servant follows, and Jesus teaches us God's forgiveness of our sin-debts are so great that we should freely forgive those who sin against us because their sin-debts are tiny in comparison. The divine lesson is to continually forgive your brother and sister just as Christ continually forgives you all your trespasses. Paul's letter to Philemon expresses Paul's request for Philemon to offer generous forgiveness to Onesimus, Philemon's former slave. Onesimus had been an unprofitable servant to Philemon and owed him money while wronging him.[747] Paul writes that he led Onesimus to salvation in Christ and the new convert is now profitable for both men. The apostle implores Philemon to receive Onesimus as a brother, laying any debt on Paul's account which he promises to repay to Philemon. When you offer a brother or sister a second chance, you are expressing brotherly kindness.

744   Acts 6:1
745   James 2:14-17
746   Luke 17:5
747   Philemon 1:10-19

Thirdly, increasing the number of gatherings with Christians is an attribute of brotherly kindness. In Hebrews 10:24-25, Paul teaches us to assemble ourselves together *"so much the more, as ye see that day approaching."* During our increasing number of visits, Christians will provoke or stimulate each other to do good deeds and provide exhortation or encouragement.

Additionally, seek to spend time with the least esteemed, or less popular Christians. Paul pens Romans 12:16, saying, *"Be of the same mind one toward another. Mind not high things, but condescend to men of low estate. Be not wise in your own conceits."* When you're at a church fellowship, find the ones who have no one to talk to and begin pleasant conversation with them. You can also host your own fellowship and Jesus promises to bless you when you invite *"the poor, the maimed, the lame, the blind"* because they cannot repay you.[748]

Fourth, Christians offer brotherly kindness with impartiality regardless of socioeconomic status. Carnal Christians exalt rich church members above the poor members. But James tells Christians it's a sin to be partial to rich Christians who have expensive jewelry and clothing by offering them comfort and rest with the best seats while making others stand in a church assembly.[749]

Fifth, brotherly kindness leads Christians to pray for one another. Ephesians 6:18 says a fully armored Christian is *"Praying always with all prayer and supplication in the Spirit, and watching thereunto with all perseverance and supplication for all saints."* Pray for all Christians, near and far. When you hear of Christians suffering persecution, you feel their pain and care enough to pray for them. 1 Corinthians 12:25-26 reads, *"That there should be no schism in the body; but that the members should have the same care one for another. And whether one member suffer, all the members suffer with it; or one member be honoured, all the members rejoice with it."*

To conclude brotherly kindness, notice it is the seventh and last trait before charity caps off your being. Seven is a Scriptural number

---

748   Luke 14:12-14
749   James 2:1-9

representing completion and in this case brotherly kindness signifies a Christian's complete sanctification or cleansing. Psalm 12:6 teaches complete purification comes through seven steps: *"The words of the LORD are pure words: as silver tried in a furnace of earth, purified seven times."* Brotherly kindness completes your purification as you graduate to charity, the baptism of the Holy Ghost.

CHARACTER QUALITY #8: CHARITY

2 Peter 1:7 says, *"And to godliness brotherly kindness; and to brotherly kindness charity."* Charity is the eighth and final character trait the Lord adds to your being as you enter the third and final stage of your Christian walk. Resistance is the sin you must reject to receive charity, as Stephen said in Acts 7:51: *"Ye do always resist the Holy Ghost."*

This section is purposely shortened because the proceeding chapter is fully devoted to the third stage or baptism of the Holy Ghost (See Figure 13). Although this is the last stage, it's the greatest stage because you experience sealing, adoption, fruit-bearing, and a state of mature godliness. The first two stages—justification and sanctification—prepare you *for* service. The third stage puts you *into* service.

The Greek word for charity is "agape" meaning "brotherly love, affection, good will, love, benevolence." Agape love is a greater love than brotherly kindness. It is a permanent portion of God's divine love living in you. In fact, it is a larger measure of God's own Spirit coming to live inside your soul because 1 John 4:8 says, *"God is love."*

Follow these next thoughts to understand how God, love, the baptism of the Holy Ghost, and charity are all synonymous. God is the Holy Ghost because Jesus says *"God is a spirit,"*[750] or ghost, and there is only *"one Spirit."*[751] The Holy Ghost is Jesus' promise to His disciples in Acts 1:5: *"For John truly baptized with water; but ye shall be baptized with the Holy Ghost not many days hence."* Jesus originates the baptism of the Holy Ghost doctrine. Furthermore, the baptism of the Holy Ghost

---

750   John 4:24
751   1 Corinthians 12:13

is love because Paul says *"the love of God is shed abroad in our hearts by the Holy Ghost."*[752] Peter supports Paul's claim, saying this *"promise of the Father,"* or baptism of the Holy Ghost promised by Jesus,[753] was *"shed forth"* on the Day of Pentecost in Acts 2:33. Both love and the Holy Ghost were shed forth on the Day of Pentecost because they are one and the same. The entire chapter of 1 Corinthians 13 describes the effect of charity, or love, or the baptism of the Holy Ghost, upon your soul.

Since charity is the last character quality—the eighth out of eight— charity is the marking or sealing of Christ's character inside your being, called a *"seal"* in three Scriptures: 2 Corinthians 1:22, Ephesians 1:13 and 4:30. The eighth character quality seals God's Spirit of love into your being; specifically into your soul. The Person of Love, Jesus Christ, now abides in your soul because you've been conformed into Christ's image and learned to love and serve both enemies and God's family.

Having the baptism of the Holy Ghost seals the previous seven character qualities into your soul: faith, virtue, knowledge, temperance, patience, godliness, and brotherly kindness. You are *finally* ready to start living! The longer you live in obedience, the more mature godliness you will manifest in your flesh.

THREE STAGES OR WORKS OF GRACE

Figures 11 and 12 show how the three stages of Israel's journey from Egypt to the Promised Land is allegorical to the Christian's journey from faith to the baptism of the Holy Ghost, or charity. The three stages have also been called the Three Works of Grace in some Christian circles. While "Works of Grace" may sound like a contradiction, the Bible teaches that God's grace causes Christians to work for God. The three works are God's works in a surrendered believer. The believer simply surrenders, or yields, to God's works. As Paul says in Philippians 2:13, *"It is God which worketh in you."* A repentant Christian recognizes God's

752   Romans 5:5
753   Luke 24:49, Acts 1:4-5

goodness,[754] making him love God. This love motivates faith in God, and faith produces works.[755]

2 Corinthians 6:1 says, *"We then, as workers together with him, beseech you also that ye receive not the grace of God in vain."* Paul urges you to work *with* God—not alone. In fact, God cannot work through a human without him allowing it through submitted free moral agency. If God alone is working, then humans are mere choice-less robots, but you know that's not the case. It's also implied Christians work because they have received the gift of grace. An individual claiming to be a Christian without works has not truly received God's grace.

Paul again says he did not receive God's grace in vain in 1 Corinthians 15:10. As humbly as possible, Paul says he worked more than all the apostles, including Peter and James.[756] He attributes his vast works to grace being with him, saying, *"But by the grace of God I am what I am: and his grace which was bestowed upon me was not in vain; but I laboured more abundantly than they all: yet not I, but the grace of God which was with me."* Grace—God's unmerited favor to you—has always been and always will be your pure source of motivation.

Figure 14 shows eight examples of the Three Works of Grace throughout Scripture, including man's natural birth and spiritual birth, Israel's exodus from Egypt, Israel's three-court tabernacle, the earth's cleansing, Ezekiel's new heart prophecy, stages of the wheat plant (See Chapter 8), and Jesus as the way to heaven. Three is God's number of divine perfection in design, and these examples showcase God's perfect design in processes.

---

754   Romans 2:4
755   Galatians 5:6
756   1 Corinthians 15:1-10

Process	First Work	Second Work	Third Work
Man's Natural Birth	Water breaks	Blood	Breath of life
Man's Spiritual Birth	Justification	Sanctification	Baptism of the Holy Ghost
Israel's Exodus	Leaving Egypt	Wilderness	Promised Land
Tabernacle's Cleansing	Outer court	Holy place	Holiest of holies
Earth's Cleansing	Noah's flood	Jesus' blood	Fervent heat
Ezekiel's Prophecy Ezekiel 36:26-27	New heart	New spirit	"*My Spirit*" or God's Spirit
Growing Wheat Plant Mark 4:28	Blade	Ear	Full corn
Jesus as the Way to Heaven John 14:3-6, 17:17	Way	Truth "*Sanctify them through thy truth*"	Life

Figure 14

GROWING IN THE STATURE OF A PERFECT MAN

The seventh example in Figure 14 identifies the three stages of growth in the wheat plant taught by Jesus in His parable of the seed cast into the ground in Mark 4:26-29. Notice how the three stages in the wheat's maturity match the three stages to Christian maturity: justification, sanctification, and the baptism of the Holy Ghost.

The Lord Jesus emphasizes the seed grows up without man knowing how in Mark 4:27. It is man's duty to plant and water the seed but it is God Who gives the increase. The same is true with the gospel: "*I have planted, Apollos watered; but God gave the increase. So then neither is he that planteth any thing, neither he that watereth; but God that giveth the increase.*"[757] No man causes his own spiritual increase. In other words, you cannot add any character quality to yourself, such as temperance, at your own will. You must confidently trust in God's growing process, just as a farmer does.

Your job is accept each of God's promises by planting each promise in your heart. Believe God will add faith, then virtue, and the rest of the character qualities. Then water every seed-promise with prayer, praise, Bible reading, and thanksgiving. In the right season, you will see the faith-blade, then the ear of virtue, knowledge, temperance, patience, godliness, and brotherly kindness. Lastly, you'll experience the baptism of the Holy Ghost, or full corn, at the right time. Ecclesiastes 3:11 declares, "*He hath made every thing beautiful in his time.*"

KNOWING YOUR SPIRITUAL LOCATION

God has given you the Three Works of Grace and Peter's eight steps to the Stature of a Perfect Man so you can assess your current spiritual location. By prayerfully examining your life, you can know whether you are in the first, second, or third Work of Grace. Paul commands, "*Examine yourselves, whether ye be in the faith; prove your own selves.*"[758] The apostle admonishes you to "*work out your own salvation with fear and trembling.*"[759]

757   1 Corinthians 3:6-7
758   2 Corinthians 13:5
759   Philippians 2:12

God did the same thing with Israel. In reference to Israel's three stage exodus, God told both Moses and the people He was going to take them out of Egypt and into the Promised Land of Canaan.[760] The Sinai Peninsula lay between Egypt and Canaan. God was going to use *"the wilderness of Shur,"*[761] *"the wilderness of Sinai,"* and the *"wilderness of Paran"*[762] to test Israel's trust in Him. The Lord declared He led Israel through the wilderness to humble and prove them whether they would obey Him or not, and so they would know to live by every Word of God.[763] The Promised Land journey was a three stage process. At all times, Moses and the people could easily assess their physical location and how close they were to their destination.

So can you know at all times your spiritual location in Christianity. Are you in the first stage, seeking to be saved out of the world, like Israel was saved out of Egypt? Then you can *"repent, and be baptized...in the name of Jesus Christ for the remission of sins."*[764] God will bring you through the Red Sea as you joyfully dance at the sight of all your dead taskmasters, or sinful addictions. Are you in the second stage, having already been saved and baptized, but going through the wilderness of sanctification, being daily tested and tried as you learn to obey? Then you can examine the six character qualities of sanctification—virtue, knowledge, temperance, patience, godliness, and brotherly kindness—to assess which ones you need added to your life. Ask Jesus for His character traits, for He offers, *"And all things, whatsoever ye shall ask in prayer, believing, ye shall receive."*[765] Are you in the third stage, born again of God's Spirit and already *"endued with power from on high?"*[766] Then obey Hebrews 12:1, laying aside every weight of sin that easily besets you and run the race set before you with patience. Serve God wholeheartedly. Die to your human desires daily. Abide in Christ the Word and bring forth *"much fruit"* of the Holy Ghost.[767]

---

760   Exodus 3:17, 13:5
761   Exodus 15:22
762   Numbers 10:12
763   Deuteronomy 8:2-3
764   Acts 2:38
765   Matthew 21:22
766   Luke 24:49
767   John 15:4-5

Based upon Jesus' teaching that few will find the narrow road to eternal life in Matthew 7:14, most people will start the Christian journey but not finish. Like Israel leaving Egypt, many will be baptized but will wander in the wilderness, never possessing the Promised Land, or baptism of the Holy Ghost. There is no need for Christians to wander aimlessly in religion. The Stature of a Perfect Man divinely outlines our journey from sinner to Holy Ghost-filled saint. Out of the original group of Israelis who left Egypt, only two made it to Canaan—Joshua and Caleb. Scripture says the majority of them died in the wilderness for their rebellion after God saved them out of Egypt. Jude 1:5 says, *"I will therefore put you in remembrance, though ye once knew this, how that the Lord, having saved the people out of the land of Egypt, afterward destroyed them that believed not."*

If you feel stranded, in a rut, or you're wandering from church to church, get down to business with God. Examine the Stature of a Perfect Man, assessing your true character by the Word. You will find your next step as you honestly examine your life through meditation. As David thought upon his ways, he turned his feet to God's path. Psalm 119:58-60 reads, *"I intreated thy favour with my whole heart: be merciful unto me according to thy word. I thought on my ways, and turned my feet unto thy testimonies. I made haste, and delayed not to keep thy commandments."* You can do the same. It only requires an honest and good heart. Jesus teaches, *"But that on the good ground are they, which in an honest and good heart, having heard the word, keep it, and bring forth fruit with patience."*[768]

JESUS' 12 APOSTLES AND THE STATURE OF A PERFECT MAN

Jesus' 12 apostles are prime examples of believers working their way up the Stature of a Perfect Man by grace and serve as measuring sticks for our lives. The four gospels reveal the apostles' journey from faith to brotherly kindness, in unflattering ways at times, so we might relate to and learn from them. The Book of Acts details the moment they received

768   Luke 8:15

charity (Acts 2:4), the baptism of the Holy Ghost, and its effects upon their lives.

Here are examples proving that Jesus' disciples were saved but not born again until the Holy Ghost fell in Acts chapter 2:

- **Faith**: The disciples believed Jesus was the Messiah[769] and their faith led them to forsake family and careers to follow Christ.[770]
- **Virtue**: The disciples possessed virtue allowing them to go into cities two by two publicly preaching and healing before Jesus visited the cities,[771] but they all lost their virtue on the night of Jesus' arrest, being scattered like sheep[772] through fear of arrest. Excluding Judas Iscariot, the 11 disciples, and Peter in particular, never lost their faith because Jesus prayed that their faith would *"fail not."*[773]
- **Knowledge**: While most Jews misunderstood Jesus' parables and teachings, the disciples assured Jesus they understood them.[774] But the disciples lacked understanding about how men are defiled, the leaven of the doctrine of the Pharisees and Sadducees, and Jesus' resurrection.[775]
- **Temperance**: The disciples exercised exemplary self control over their sensual desires, but 10 disciples did become indignant against James and John when their mother asked Jesus if her two sons could sit on His right and left hand.[776]
- **Patience**: The 12 apostles patiently stayed with Jesus after many of His disciples forsook Him, knowing Christ

769   John 6:69
770   Mark 10:28
771   Luke 10:1
772   Mark 14:27
773   Luke 22:32
774   Matthew 13:51
775   Matthew 16:5-12, Mark 7:14-23, Luke 18:31-34
776   Matthew 20:24

had eternal life.[777] But the disciples hastily asked Jesus to send away the woman of Canaan who repeatedly cried for Jesus to heal her vexed daughter, which request Jesus miraculously fulfilled.[778]

- **Godliness**: Jesus extinguished James and John's ungodly desire to call fire down from heaven upon the Christ-rejecting Samaritans.[779] Peter violently cut off Malchus' ear trying to defend Jesus, proving he had not received love for his enemies.[780]

- **Brotherly Kindness**: Multiple times the disciples lacked brotherly kindness, such as when they argued about which of them was greatest, forbade a brother from casting out devils because he didn't follow the 12,[781] and forbade their Christian sisters from bringing their infants and toddlers to Jesus. Peter struggled with Jesus' requirement to forgive his brother 70 times more than he had first estimated.[782]

- **Charity**: After His resurrection, Jesus breathed on His disciples, urging them to receive the baptism of the Holy Ghost.[783] Christ used the 50 days from His resurrection to Pentecost to rebuild the disciples' character, giving them many infallible proofs of His resurrection for the first 40 days[784] and then letting them pray for the final 10 days in the upper room until they were in *"one accord."*[785] Love, or charity, fell into the disciples' souls on the Day of Pentecost. Paul says *"the love of God is shed abroad in our hearts by the Holy Ghost which is given unto us."*[786]

---

777   John 6:66-68
778   Matthew 15:21-28
779   Luke 9:51-56
780   John 18:10
781   Mark 9:33-40
782   Matthew 18:21-22, Luke 17:3-5
783   John 20:22
784   Acts 1:3
785   Acts 1:13-14, 2:1
786   Romans 5:5

JOSEPH'S LIFE AND THE STATURE OF A PERFECT MAN

Joseph, son of Jacob and Rachel, displayed and foreshadowed the Stature of a Perfect Man in the Old Testament because he was a type of Christ, and Christ's life expressed the complete *"mystery of godliness."*

Joseph's life both displayed (the first seven steps) and foreshadowed (the eighth step) the Stature of a Perfect Man. John 7:37-39 teaches Old Testament saints like Joseph could not receive the baptism of the Holy Ghost (eighth step) because Jesus had not yet raised from the dead. Joseph's character qualities are seen in the following examples:

- **Faith**: Joseph's faith trusted God's way for his life as he unashamedly shared his dreams with his family (Genesis 37:5-11).
- **Virtue**: Joseph's virtue, or moral strength in slavery, caused his daily work to prosper in Potiphar's house (Genesis 39:1-3).
- **Knowledge**: Joseph's knowledge, or understanding, helped promote him to overseer of all Potiphar's possessions in his house and field (Genesis 39:4-6).
- **Temperance**: Joseph's temperance kept him from committing adultery with Potiphar's wife despite her daily seductions (Genesis 39:7-20).
- **Patience**: Joseph's patience, or contentment, allowed him to prosper while waiting in prison for two years until the butler remembered him and informed Pharaoh of Joseph's spiritual gift of interpretation (Genesis 41:1-13).
- **Godliness**: Joseph's godliness made him so much like God that Pharaoh knew God's Spirit was in Joseph after God gave him the interpretation of Pharaoh's dreams (Genesis 41:14-57).
- **Brotherly Kindness**: Joseph's brotherly kindness led him to freely forgive his brothers for selling him into slavery

because he recognized God used their actions to save the world from famine (Genesis 45:1-15).

- **Charity**: Joseph lovingly embraced his father, Jacob, when he came to abide with him in Egypt (Genesis 46:29). This father-and-son embrace foreshadowed Christians uniting with their loving Father, or charity, for Father-God *is* love.

Recall from Chapter 2 that the number eight has a significant meaning in Scripture, speaking of a new beginning. This chapter highlights the eight steps in the Stature of a Perfect Man that lead to a new beginning, as Paul says any man who is *"in Christ"* is *"a new creature: old things are passed away; behold, all things are become new."*[787] A born again, Holy Ghost-filled Christian is a new creature, living a new life of divine power.

THE REWARDS FOR RECEIVING THE REVELATION OF GODLINESS

Those who receive the revelation of godliness will be rewarded with spiritual fruitfulness in this life and an entrance into the heavenly kingdom.

2 Peter 1:8 says if these eight character traits are abounding in your life, you will be fruitful *"in the knowledge of our Lord Jesus Christ."* You will produce the precious Christian fruit God desires as you daily express faith, virtue, knowledge, temperance, patience, godliness, brotherly kindness, and charity with the world around you. The longer you express these eight character qualities, the more spiritual fruit you will see God produce in your life: love, joy, peace, longsuffering, gentleness, goodness, faith, meekness, and temperance. Chapter 8 details the fact that spiritual fruitfulness is your goal because it is the only kind of heart that bears and brings forth fruit unto God.

Peter further states if you *"do these things"*—the eight character traits—you *"shall never fall: For so an entrance shall be ministered unto*

787   2 Corinthians 5:17

you abundantly into the everlasting kingdom of our Lord and Saviour Jesus Christ."[788] Heaven's door will open for you like it did for John in Revelation 4:1: "*After this I looked, and, behold, a door was opened in heaven: and the first voice which I heard was as it were of a trumpet talking with me; which said, Come up hither, and I will shew thee things which must be hereafter.*" Do these things Peter wrote: Do faith. Do virtue. Do knowledge. Do temperance. Do patience. Do godliness. Do brotherly kindness. Do charity. Take action upon God's Word to assure you'll never fall.

Having done these eight things, you'll possess Christ-like character in your human spirit and soul, which is the only thing you are taking with you to the next life. 1 Timothy 6:7 says, "*For we brought nothing into this world, and it is certain we can carry nothing out.*" Your hands won't carry anything out of this world but you will be adorned in white raiment as you leave this world. In Revelation 3:18 Jesus says this white raiment, or eternal life, is available now. Your character, or life, must come from Jesus Christ, and it comes through these eight character traits. Paul says the souls of sinners will be "*found naked*"[789] when they die for they possess not eternal life, or Christ-like character.

Your character-produced good works (inspired by love and grace) will meet you at the judgment. Paul writes this in 1 Timothy 5:24-25: "*Some men's sins are open beforehand, going before to judgment; and some men they follow after. Likewise also the good works of some are manifest beforehand; and they that are otherwise cannot be hid.*" Either now or later, your good works will be known. The opposite is true for sinners. But God records all good works in the Book of Life[790] and there is a Book of Remembrance listing the names of those who feared Him, meditated on His Word, and constantly talked about Him on earth. Malachi 3:16 reads, "*Then they that feared the LORD spake often one to another: and the LORD hearkened, and heard it, and a book of remembrance was written before him for them that feared the LORD, and that thought upon his name.*" Perhaps the angel who visited Cornelius gazed upon these heavenly books, for

---

788   2 Peter 1:10-11
789   2 Corinthians 5:3
790   Revelation 20:12

he told him, "*Thy prayers and thine alms are come up for a memorial before God.*"[791] Choose godliness, and heaven will rejoice in your good works.

THE CONSEQUENCES FOR REJECTING THE REVELATION OF GODLINESS

The most serious consequence for rejecting godliness is living a life of ungodliness, resulting in suffering the wrath of God after Judgment Day in the lake of fire. An entrance into the everlasting kingdom of Christ will not be granted to the ungodly.

Individuals can still be saved even if they reject the revelation of godliness. Faith alone is required for salvation, as seen in both the Old and New Testaments. While under the final moments of the Old Testament, the saved thief on the cross received salvation by grace through faith from Christ Himself. In the New Testament, Paul declares a believer can be saved even after being excommunicated from a Christian assembly for pridefully committing sexual immorality. Of course, the excommunicated would be driven to saving repentance before his death through the God-permitted "*destruction of the flesh*" at the hands of Satan.[792]

2 Peter 1:8 teaches barrenness and unfruitfulness are consequences to rejecting godliness. A barren Christian is one who is inactive in the work of God. In the Greek, barrenness also means idleness. Jesus compares barren or idle persons as those standing in a marketplace who have not begun to toil in a vineyard. Without the Stature of a Perfect man, you are wasting your life instead of investing it in laboring for the Lord of the Harvest, Jesus Christ. Regarding unfruitfulness, Matthew 13:3-9 and 18-23 shows there are four heart-reactions to the gospel of Christ (See Chapter 8). Three reactions bring forth no fruit: letting Satan quickly snatch the Word from your heart, believing the Word for only a while before abandoning it, and allowing cares and pleasures of the world to stop God's Word from yielding fruit. Only the heart that hears the Word and understands it is fruitful.

---

791   Acts 10:4
792   1 Corinthians 5:1-5

Peter goes on to say a man without godliness *"is blind, and cannot see afar off, and hath forgotten that he was purged from his old sins."*[793] Spiritual blindness occurs when a heart is hardened to truth[794] and refuses repentance and the healing benefits of the Holy Spirit. Blinded eyes see only this earth because they are set on worldly pleasures rather than heaven above. Paul admonishes you to *"set your affection on things above, not on things on the earth."*[795] You are racing to heaven, *"looking unto Jesus the author and finisher of our faith."*[796] As you gaze upon Jesus, He tells you to continue adding His eight character qualities. Placing your eyes upon sin and selling out Jesus' words can cause you to lose some or all of your character qualities just as Judas sold out Christ and fell from his bishoprick.[797]

Those without godliness even forget they were purged from old sins. Peter again explains this phenomenon, saying, *"Dearly beloved, I beseech you as strangers and pilgrims, abstain from fleshly lusts, which war against the soul."*[798] Frequent submission to fleshly lusts rather than the Holy Ghost creates a war against your soul. Your confused mind doesn't know if your soul is saved because your constant indulgence in fleshly lusts makes you feel like the flesh is winning the war. Additionally, the longer a person wanders in the wilderness of sanctification without moving forward to the baptism of the Holy Ghost, like Israel's self-imposed 40 year wilderness wandering, the more distant their forgiveness seems. This magnifies the necessity of the eight character traits, especially the power of temperance to mortify sensual cravings. However, the obedient are not forgetful of Christ's forgiveness. What a precious memory you have recalling the day you experienced Christ's purging power that separated you from your sins *"as far as the east is from the west"*![799] Just like Israel rehearing the memory of supernaturally crossing the Red Sea, you can rehearse crossing over from sinner to saint at the foot of Jesus' cross.

793   2 Peter 1:9
794   John 12:40
795   Colossians 3:2
796   Hebrews 12:1-2
797   Acts 1:20, 25
798   1 Peter 2:11
799   Psalm 103:12

CONCLUSION

The immensity of this chapter signifies God's immense desire for you to experience godliness. Just as God drew Israel to Himself *"in lovingkindness,"*[800] God is patiently and lovingly drawing you to receive His divine character qualities.

Take heed to Paul's suggestion about your salvation: *"Work out your own salvation with fear and trembling."*[801] Nothing could be more important than being assured of your salvation, or your spiritual condition. Search the Scriptures daily and pray earnestly to your Heavenly Father for His help to yield your will to Him as you serve God rather than sin.

God wants you to be like Him. He says, *"Be ye holy; for I am holy."*[802] He has made the way for you to manifest true godliness in your flesh, just as Jesus Christ manifested God in the flesh: *"And without controversy great is the mystery of godliness: God was manifest in the flesh."* Follow the Stature of a Perfect Man and grow in grace and knowledge of our Lord Jesus Christ.

ACTION STEPS TO GODLINESS

1. Be sure you have the rock-solid foundation of genuine faith in the shed blood of Jesus, expressed by being baptized (fully immersed) in water in the name of the Lord Jesus Christ. Contact me if you need to be baptized or rebaptized in Christ's literal name.

2. Prayerfully examine your actions and habits to see which character qualities you have and which you are lacking, and ask the Lord to add those attributes to your being as you reject the corresponding temptation at each step on the Stature of a Perfect Man. Jesus says, *"If ye then, being evil, know*

800 Hosea 2:19
801 Philippians 2:12
802 1 Peter 1:16

how to give good gifts unto your children: how much more shall your heavenly Father give the Holy Spirit to them that ask him?"[803]

3. Once you're born again, live boldly and faithfully for Christ Jesus and you'll see the fruits of the Spirit begin manifesting in your life. Chapter 11 details the Bible's instructions on how you can be certain you are doing God's perfect will for your life.

FOLLOW UP

Free online videos, Bible studies, and William Branham's quotes related to this chapter: www.pastorjessesmith.com/12mysteriesbook

Email: jesse.smith11@sbcglobal.net

Text: 330-929-2037

803   Luke 11:13

CHAPTER 6

The Mystery of Christ In You: The Baptism of the Holy Ghost

"To whom God would make known what is the riches of the glory of this mystery among the Gentiles; which is Christ in you, the hope of glory."

Colossians 1:27

URING YOUR EARTHLY JOURNEY, you could have no greater privilege than for Jesus Christ's Spirit to permanently live inside you all the days of your life. The epigraph shows how Paul calls this abiding presence *"Christ in you."* Similarly, Jesus calls it the baptism of the Holy Ghost.[804] This permanency-privilege was unavailable in the Old Testament and is one of the major purposes and benefits of the New Testament.

The baptism of the Holy Ghost is one of the *"better promises"* contained in the *"better covenant,"*[805] or New Testament. God walked *with* Adam in Eden, but He wanted something better. Now He wants to walk *in* you. God says, *"I will dwell in them, and walk in them; and I will be their God, and they shall be my people."*[806]

The verse preceding the epigraph—Colossians 1:26—calls the Holy Ghost baptism *"the mystery which hath been hid from ages and from generations, but now is made manifest to his saints."* The baptism of the Holy Ghost is a hidden mystery God purposely kept from ancient ages, generations, and saints. As you'll soon see, Job, David, and other saints knew they lacked something—or rather, Someone. Namely, they lacked the Comforter in their souls. The Spirit of Truth. The Holy Ghost!

Beginning with Moses and extending the next 1,500 years, the Lord first had to show the weakness of the law through human flesh. The failure of the law would magnify the need for the Holy Ghost baptism. God then sent His Son, Jesus, as the first to be filled with and walk according to the Holy Spirit. In the fulness of time, the Holy Ghost came rushing into the believers' souls on the Day of Pentecost so man for the first time could *"walk not after the flesh, but after the Spirit."*[807]

THE FORETELLING AND ANNOUNCING OF THE BAPTISM OF THE HOLY GHOST

The prophets Joel, Jeremiah, and Ezekiel foretold the permanent anointing of the baptism of the Holy Ghost some 800 and 600 years before Christ. This long awaited promise of God's indwelling, permanent power was first experienced on the Day of Pentecost in Acts chapter 2.

Joel described this experience as God freely pouring out His Spirit upon believers of all ages[808] and Peter validated Joel by quoting him in Acts 2:16-21. Jeremiah fashioned this baptism as God writing His commands upon the hearts of His believing children[809] and the writer of

805   Hebrews 8:6
806   2 Corinthians 6:16
807   Romans 8:4
808   Joel 2:28-32
809   Jeremiah 31:33

Hebrews confirmed this in Hebrews 8:10. Ezekiel 36:27 says the Holy Ghost baptism, or God's *"Spirit within you"*, would *"cause"* or empower God's saints to walk in His statutes, keep, and do His judgments.

The New Testament opens with John the Baptist baptizing repentant ones. John is aware his baptism unto repentance is solely an immersion in water. He knows he is *"sent…to baptize with water."*[810] His close relationship with God gave him knowledge to announce that the coming Messiah would baptize His followers with something greater than water—the Holy Ghost. Mark 1:8 records John saying, *"I indeed have baptized you with water: but he shall baptize you with the Holy Ghost."* Although baptism unto repentance is a necessary experience, John knew there was a greater experience than just being baptized in water.

Mark 1:9-12 records Jesus' water baptism administered by John. This was no ordinary baptism, for the heavens opened and God's Spirit descended in the form of a dove. A parallel passage in John 1:33 says the Spirit descended and remained upon Christ. Indeed, the Spirit *"abode upon him."*[811] Luke 4:1 describes Jesus as being *"full of the Holy Ghost"* after John baptized him. You conclude that Jesus Christ is the first to be baptized with the Holy Ghost and is commissioned to baptize others into this blessed fellowship after His resurrection. This explains why Jesus foretells His disciples they would experience the same Holy Ghost baptism He had, saying, *"Ye shall drink indeed of my cup, and be baptized with the baptism that I am baptized with."*[812] Jesus Himself says He was *"sealed"*[813] by the Father and the word "seal" is repeatedly used by Paul to describe the baptism of the Holy Ghost in 2 Corinthians 1:22, Ephesians 1:13 and 4:30.

The four gospels contain Jesus' announcements of the baptism of the Holy Ghost during His earthly ministry after He Himself was filled with God's Spirit. In the first year of Jesus' public ministry you read His first extensive teaching on the baptism of the Holy Ghost, found in

810   John 1:33
811   John 1:32
812   Matthew 20:23
813   John 6:27

John 3:1-12, during his conversation with a Pharisee named Nicodemus. Four times Jesus says believers must be *"born again"*, or *"born of the Spirit."* Christ foretold the sudden, powerful appearing of the soul-baptism by comparing it to the wind: *"The wind bloweth where it listeth, and thou hearest the sound thereof, but canst not tell whence it cometh, and whither it goeth: so is every one that is born of the Spirit."* When Nicodemus couldn't understand the born again requirement, Jesus challenged him by saying, *"Art thou a master of Israel, and knowest not these things?"* It seems Jesus expected a master-scholar like Nicodemus to recall the aforementioned Old Testament prophesies of the Holy Ghost from Joel, Jeremiah, and Ezekiel.

In Jesus' second year of ministry He preaches the Sermon on the Mount. Christ's fourth beatitude hints of the baptism of the Holy Ghost. Matthew 5:6 says, *"Blessed are they which do hunger and thirst after righteousness: for they shall be filled."* Later, while teaching His disciples to pray, Messiah explains the simplicity in which we ask for the Holy Ghost and the Heavenly Father gives it. Luke 11:13 reads, *"If ye then, being evil, know how to give good gifts unto your children: how much more shall your heavenly Father give the Holy Spirit to them that ask him?"*

During Christ's third year of ministry He gave, arguably, the boldest, most public invitation for the soon-to-be-available baptism of the Holy Ghost in John chapter 7. Verse 2 informs us Jesus is with thousands of Jews celebrating the Feast of Tabernacles in Jerusalem. 18th century theologian John Gill provides contextual insight on the astounding meaning of this passage.[814] Gill describes a Jewish traditional ceremony of drawing and pouring water that occurred during the solemn assembly on the last day of the feast, the eighth day, in which no servile work was done.[815] Since Moses ordained this last feast to be a time of rejoicing in Leviticus 23:40, Jews would shout and dance as the priests drew water from the pool of Siloam and poured it into a basin at the altar to fulfill Isaiah 12:3: *"Therefore with joy shall ye draw water out of the wells of*

---

814   "John 7:37." *Bible Study Tools*, https://www.biblestudytools.com/commentaries/gills-exposition-of-the-bible/john-7-37.html. Accessed 7 December 2019.
815   Leviticus 23:33-44

salvation." This ceremony had dual purposes; the first was to rejoice in God's annual pouring out of the water of His Spirit to wash and forgive Israel through the Day of Atonement. Second, prayer was offered beseeching God for sufficient natural rains for the ensuing agricultural year. Israel was approaching God in thanksgiving for the waters of forgiveness and seeking God for natural water for their crops.

At some point *"on the last day"* of *"that great day of the feast, Jesus stood and cried, saying, If any man thirst, let him come unto me, and drink. He that believeth on me, as the scripture hath said, out of his belly shall flow rivers of living water."* John 7:39 says Christ was referring to the Living Waters of the Holy Spirit that would be given *after* Jesus received His glorified body, following His resurrection. More about Jesus' glorified body will be explained later in this chapter. But imagine the thousands of Jews silent and stunned viewing the young, controversial rabbi loudly declaring He was offering eternal Water greater than the upcoming rains Israelis were trusting in to sustain their natural life. Jesus was the very God they were praying to, standing among them, offering them eternal water for their souls.

Shortly before His arrest and crucifixion in His third and final year of ministry, Christ taught His apostles about the Holy Ghost baptism during their final, intimate hours after the Passover on their way to the Garden of Gethsemane in John chapters 14 through 17. Indeed, Christ promised to send *"another Comforter...even the Spirit of truth"*, later naming the Comforter as the Holy Ghost,[816] Who *"shall be in you."*[817] Christ continually emphasized His future dwelling inside His disciples—meaning inside their souls—saying, *"I in you"* in John 14:20. Jesus later says twice, *"I in them"* in John 17:23 and 17:26.

On at least two occasions following His resurrection, Christ instructed His apostles to wait or tarry for the Holy Ghost, which He refers to as the *"promise of the Father."*[818] Despite following Jesus and performing miracles for over three years, the apostles were not born again.

---

816   John 14:26
817   John 14:16-17
818   Luke 24:49, Acts 1:4-5

Following Jesus' death and resurrection, He urged His disciples to receive this soul baptism. John 20:22 reads, "*And when he had said this, he breathed on them, and saith unto them, Receive ye the Holy Ghost.*" Some of His final words before leaving His disciples assured them He would send the baptism of the Holy Ghost, recorded in Acts 1:5-8. Christ uttered, "*For John truly baptized with water; but ye shall be baptized with the Holy Ghost not many days hence. But ye shall receive power, after that the Holy Ghost is come upon you.*"

Finally, fifty days after Jesus' resurrection, on the Day of Pentecost, 120 disciples received the baptism of the Holy Ghost while tarrying in an upper room. Acts 2:4 records, "*And they were all filled with the Holy Ghost, and began to speak with other tongues, as the Spirit gave them utterance.*" This Holy Spirit baptism caused the once timid and fearful disciples to flow into the streets of Jerusalem and saturate the city with loud, noisy praise at 9:00 in the morning! Thankfully, the same Holy Spirit is available to us today, but many are confused about how and when He comes.

THE CONFUSION ABOUT THE MYSTERY OF THE HOLY GHOST BAPTISM

The confusion around the baptism of the Holy Ghost doctrine, or born again experience, is widespread and carries massive repercussions. When and how is a believer baptized with the Holy Ghost?

The revelation of the Holy Ghost baptism is Christ's Spirit permanently indwelling and sealing (marking) the believer's soul as the Third Work of Grace.

I'll first show the two false extremes most churches gravitate towards before using Biblical proof to identify precisely when and how a believer is born again.

There are two extremes most churches erroneously gravitate towards: unemotional confession or emotional speaking in unknown tongues.

Evangelicals foster the unemotional confession while charismatics and Pentecostal denominations demand emotional speaking in unknown tongues. From this point forward, charismatics and Pentecostal denominations will be referred to in one group as "charismatics."

Many evangelicals say you're already born again as soon as you invite Jesus into your heart or recite the "Sinner's Prayer." Sadly, no Scripture teaches new believers to recite a scripted, generic, unemotional prayer to invite Jesus into their hearts. Instead, the Book of Acts models zealous repentance from sin, followed by water baptism in the name of the Lord Jesus Christ, and then a sealing with the baptism of the Holy Ghost.[819] In most cases, the born again experience follows water baptism at a future date. True repentance is turning from and hating your previous sin, which is often left out of the stoic, evangelical salvation prayer.

The charismatics swing to the other extreme, urging and requiring new believers to emotionally utter unknown words as evidence of being born again. While having an emotional experience with God is impactful, speaking in unknown tongues as the evidence of being born again is unscriptural. On the Day of Pentecost, all 17 nationalities heard and understood Peter and the Christians declaring the *"wonderful works of God"* in their own native languages.[820] The 120 believers spoke in other languages unknown to them, such as Iranian, Greek, Persian, Latin, Coptic, and more, but the tongues were all understood. Modern charismatics showcase their erroneous teachings when they speak in unknown languages and no one understands their words. In Acts chapter 2, all inspired tongues were understood by the hearers. Today in charismatic churches, most tongues confuse the hearers. God is not the author of confusion in the assembly of the saints. Tongues-as-the-evidence churches are majoring on a minor, emphasizing the gift of tongues rather than the Giver of the gifts. Figure 15 shows the correct, middle-of-the-road approach to the baptism of the Holy Ghost, and the two, erroneous approaches that are on the fringes of the road to heaven.

---

819   Acts 2:38-39
820   Acts 2:4-11

Extreme Emphasis on Confession	True Baptism of the Holy Ghost	Extreme Emphasis on Tongues
"Dangerous Fringe"	"Middle of the Road"	"Dangerous Fringe"
On one fringe, the new believer publicly confesses faith in Jesus Christ as Savior but neither seeks nor shows emotion. His clergy completely avoid using the "baptism of the Holy Ghost" terminology despite the fact Jesus used it in Acts 1:5.	In the middle of the road lays the truth. The believer publicly confesses faith in Jesus Christ and seeks to receive God's Spirit with a bold, liberating, emotional experience based upon God's choosing. The believer may prophecy, speak in an unknown tongue, shout, weep, dance, scream, or show other emotions. Sinners who witnessed this experience would call the believer drunk.	On the other fringe, after publicly confessing faith in Jesus Christ as Savior, the believer seeks to boldly speak with unknown tongues as evidence of the new birth based upon man's choosing. In Acts 2, all the tongues were understood, but today few or none understand what is spoken when people speak in tongues. Sadly, this believer seeks the unknown tongues gift rather than the Giver of the gifts, the Holy Ghost.

Figure 15

The negative repercussions of both fringe teachings hurt millions of church goers because they lack the permanent, indwelling presence of Christ. The baptism of the Holy Ghost is a seal *"unto the day of redemption"*,[821] meaning it's a permanent mark of God's anointing and influence upon a believer's soul. This anointing never leaves the believer. Without this permanent seal, the evangelicals and charismatics are like Jesus' description of home owners who build their houses upon sand rather than rock in Matthew 7:24-27. When the storms of life come in various forms of temptations, those without the permanent seal of God often see their testimony fall apart as they indulge in adultery, greed, idolatry, drugs, and other sins. Temporary testimonies abound in their churches rather than permanent, life-long memorials of obedience and dedication to the glory of Jesus Christ.

821   Ephesians 4:30

For evangelicals, many are deprived of personally experiencing God's power in any form. In Luke 24:49, Jesus says believers are endued, or clothed, with power upon receiving the Holy Ghost. But unemotional confessions usually lead to compromising, sin-loving church members because they never receive God's power to overcome temptations. Without supernatural power, church members submit to temptations and learn to live in idolatrous sins under the guise of liberty or freedom in Christ. As 2 Timothy 3:5 says, they have a *"form of godliness"* but deny the power thereof.

Charismatics exalt personal experience above Bible truth. While they may experience God's power in the form of emotional tongue-speaking, they often stop short of experiencing God's power in their souls. Hebrews 4:10 speaks of this power, calling it a *"rest"* from selfish, individual works. The repercussion, then, of exalting tongues-speaking above the true, Holy Ghost baptism in the soul is coming short of the new birth and God's full inheritance. Just as Israel tasted the massive grapes of Canaan[822] before rejecting God's leading to possess the land, charismatics taste of the glorious gifts of the Holy Ghost (like tongue-speaking) but reject God's desire to possess their every decision. The obvious result for charismatics is wandering for decades in the same false doctrine of unknown tongues as the evidence of the Holy Ghost, just as Israel wandered in the wilderness for 40 years.[823]

BIBLICAL EVIDENCE FOR THE REVELATION OF THE HOLY GHOST BAPTISM

Now that the two extremes have been described and debunked, here is Biblical proof for *when* and *how* a believer is baptized with the Holy Ghost.

When is a believer baptized with the Holy Ghost? A Christian is born again sometime *after* he is justified (saved) and completely sanctified (rid of sinful habits). In short, you're born again after the first two

---

822   Numbers 13:24, Hebrews 6:4-6
823   Numbers 14:33

Works of Grace are complete. Chapter 5 fully details the Three Works of Grace needed for God's Spirit to completely possess a Christian: justification, sanctification, and the baptism of the Holy Ghost. God gives the Holy Ghost, the Third Work of Grace, *"to them that obey him"*[824] by being justified and sanctified. Four examples from the Book of Acts validate this truth.

The first text, Acts 1:12-15, records *"about an hundred and twenty"*[825] Christians, which included Jesus' 11 remaining apostles and godly women, gathering in an upper room in Jerusalem to receive the Holy Ghost. When did they receive the Holy Ghost? 10 days later on the Day of Pentecost, after God finished sanctifying them. Acts 2:1-4 describes their Holy Ghost baptisms. The Holy Ghost fell in a group setting after they *"all continued with one accord in prayer and supplication"*[826] in the upper room for 10 days. Although they were saved at different times before gathering in the upper room, their complete sanctification came at the same time through group prayer and supplication.

Consider the Three Works of Grace in the life of Mary the mother of Jesus. She was saved at some point prior to her meeting with Elizabeth, for she declared God as her Savior in Luke 1:46-47: *"And Mary said, My soul doth magnify the Lord, And my spirit hath rejoiced in God my Saviour."* Mary's sanctification must have lasted well over 30 years. She first had to give birth to Jesus, and then His ministry began at the age of 30 and lasted over three years. But the faithful God finished her sanctification by giving her the gift of the Holy Ghost at Pentecost. Mary is recorded as being in the upper room in Acts 1:14.

Acts 8:5-25 is a second text about Philip's evangelistic ministry in the city of Samaria. When did the Samaritans receive the baptism of the Holy Ghost? After Peter and John laid hands on them and prayed for them to receive the Holy Ghost. It's crucial to recognize that the Samaritans were already believers before Peter and John laid hands on them, for they

824   Acts 5:32
825   Acts 1:15
826   Acts 1:14

had seen miracles[827] and were baptized in water.[828] This text wonderfully proves the difference between water baptism and the Holy Ghost baptism, as you can believe in Jesus Christ, have been baptized in His name, and yet still *not* be baptized with the Holy Ghost in your soul. Reading Acts 8:15-17 unveils this revelation, for Peter and John had to pray for the Samaritans to receive the Holy Ghost because "*he was fallen upon none of them: only they were baptized in the name of the Lord Jesus. Then laid they their hands on them, and they received the Holy Ghost.*" What you and every believer needs today is for the Holy Ghost to fall upon your soul, baptizing your nature with God's "*divine nature.*"[829] Although salvation is a magnificent step, God wants complete preeminence in Christians' lives. He wants believers daily empowered by the Holy Ghost.

The Samaritans, then, quickly experienced the Three Works of Grace. In Acts 8:5-13, Samaritans witnessed miracles and were justified, being saved and "*baptized in the name of the Lord Jesus*"[830]—not the titles "Father, Son, and Holy Ghost" (See Chapter 1). Sanctification took place in their lives from the time they were baptized until Peter and John arrived after news spread to Jerusalem of their conversions. The Holy Ghost fell upon them as Peter and John laid their hands on them and prayed.

The third text of Acts 10:1-48 shows a scene in Caesarea in which Gentiles in the house of Cornelius the centurion receive the baptism of the Holy Ghost. When did Cornelius and the "*many*"[831] in his house receive this soul-baptism? They received the Holy Ghost baptism while Peter preached to them. Acts 10:44 states, "*While Peter yet spake these words, the Holy Ghost fell on all them which heard the word.*"

Concerning the Three Works of Grace, Cornelius and his household were already saved and sanctified before meeting Peter. Acts 10:36-37 proves Cornelius had heard about Christ and believed, although he had not yet been water baptized. Peter said, "*That word, I say, ye know,*"

827   Acts 8:5-8
828   Acts 8:12
829   2 Peter 1:4
830   Acts 8:12, 16
831   Acts 10:27

which was the truth that God preached *"peace by Jesus Christ"* to Israel. Consider how sanctified Cornelius was before he met Peter and compare your life to his for a moment. Scripture calls Cornelius *"a devout man"* who constantly prayed, fasted, and gave alms to people insomuch that the visiting angel told him heaven had a memorial of all his prayers and alms.[832] Being in this sanctified condition, it's easy to see how Peter could preach a short, 10-verse-long sermon and the Holy Ghost could fall upon Cornelius and his household, forever baptizing their souls into the kingdom of God.

Amazingly, this text gives one more astounding fact many don't recognize: God can fill believers with the Holy Ghost *before* they are baptized in water. Yes, God can send the spiritual soul baptism before a man knows about the natural water baptism. Acts 10:47-48 records Peter's command for Cornelius and his house to be baptized in water after they had been baptized with the Holy Ghost, saying, *"Can any man forbid water, that these should not be baptized, which have received the Holy Ghost as well as we? And he commanded them to be baptized in the name of the Lord. Then prayed they him to tarry certain days."* You learn the physical act of being baptized in water doesn't save and forgive sins. Water alone has no virtue to save. Calling upon the Lord in obedience to His command for repentance has virtue to save. Romans 10:12-13 reads, *"For there is no difference between the Jew and the Greek: for the same Lord over all is rich unto all that call upon him. For whosoever shall call upon the name of the Lord shall be saved."* Water baptism is simply an outward expression of the inward work of grace that has taken place. You also learn through the example of Cornelius' household that anyone who is spiritually baptized with the Holy Ghost will immediately be baptized in water when commanded to do so.

Before Peter preached in his house, Cornelius was already saved by believing in Christ for the forgiveness of sins and was sanctified, living a selfless life of prayer, fasting and almsgiving. No one knows why he hadn't yet been baptized in water, but one possibility is there was a separation

---

832   Acts 10:2, 4, 30-31

of Jews and Gentiles in those days. Cornelius, a Gentile, would not have been allowed to be in the company of Jews, and therefore could not hear preaching about being baptized in water. Before Peter's great sheet vision, the Jewish-Christians had not yet received the revelation of God's grace extending to the Gentiles. Peter acknowledged the end of this Jew-Gentile segregation, saying, *"Of a truth I perceive that God is no respecter of persons."* In fact, the whole point of Peter's *"great sheet"* vision in Acts 10:9-16 was to prepare him to see God pour out the Holy Ghost upon the Gentiles whom he had previously considered too unclean to be God's people.

Acts 19:1-7 is a fourth text in which Paul meets 12 disciples of John the Baptist in Ephesus, a city in modern day Turkey. When did these 12 Ephesians receive the baptism of the Holy Ghost? After Paul opened their understanding to the existence of the baptism of the Holy Ghost! This shows believers can be justified and sanctified without having knowledge of the Third Work of Grace: the baptism of the Holy Ghost.

As taught in Acts 18:24-28, the Ephesian church was led by its bold and eloquent teacher, Apollos. He was *"mighty in the scriptures"* and *"instructed in the way of the Lord."* Apollos' fervency caused him to diligently and publicly proclaim the repentance doctrine of John the Baptist. Undoubtably, his teaching caused believers to be justified and sanctified before God. Later, Aquila and Priscilla helped increase Apollos' understanding of *"the way of God"* and Apollos *"mightily convinced the Jews... shewing by the scriptures that Jesus was Christ."* Apollos and his group were justified and sanctified, but unaware of the Holy Ghost-baptism until God sent His hand-picked apostle, Paul, on his third and final missionary journey.

Upon his arrival, we are only told Paul's one question for these saved and sanctified Ephesians: *"Have ye received the Holy Ghost since ye believed?"* Paul didn't doubt their belief in Christ; he wondered whether Christ was inside their souls. Their response was that they had not heard of the Holy Ghost baptism. Paul knew what most preachers today do not—the Holy Ghost fills you sometime *after* you believe; not *when* you believe. God doesn't fill a vessel until it is justified, or declared His, and also sanctified, or cleaned out. You wouldn't immediately use a cup you found laying on the grass at the park, no matter how pretty or what the name brand was. You'd first take it home and wash it before filling and using it. God showed Paul the Three Works of Grace and he wrote the same in Ephesians 1:13 saying, *"In whom also after that ye believed, ye were sealed with that holy Spirit of promise."* The Holy Ghost-filling comes some time *after* you believe as a seal for your soul. Truly, Acts chapters 2, 8, and 10 agree with chapter 19 and validate Christians receive the Holy Ghost after believing, or after their moment of salvation, and after being sanctified from sinful habits.

Two more points can be made from Paul's Ephesus visit. First, in Paul's day there were two different water baptisms: John the Baptist's and the Lord Jesus Christ baptism. John the Baptist's water baptism represented repentance unto salvation, but the Lord Jesus Christ water baptism represented the desire to obtain the spiritual soul-baptism of the Holy Ghost. This situation was prevalent in Paul's day because believers were leaving the Old Testament for the New, and John's baptism was a preliminary act to *"prepare...the way of the Lord"*[833], meaning it prepared New Testament believers for the spiritual baptism of the Holy Ghost. The Lord Jesus Christ water baptism with the promise to receive the baptism of the Holy Ghost is your golden opportunity to enter God's kingdom. The Ephesians could not be born again without knowledge of and obedience to the Lord Jesus Christ water baptism because they were ignorant of its existence. Nor can believers today be born again without the knowledge of the full soul-baptism of the Holy Ghost. This two-baptism situation still exists today in a different form because most churches don't teach the necessary doctrine that the water baptism is different from the soul baptism. Most clergy tell new converts they are already born again when they are water baptized, but this is a major error.

A second point is that God allows re-baptism in water. Acts 19:3-5 says the Ephesians were already water baptized unto John's water baptism,

833   Mark 1:3

but Paul informed them they needed to be water baptized in the literal name of the "*Lord Jesus*." The Ephesians knew of and believed in Christ, but were ignorant of the Lord Jesus Christ water baptism. Upon their obedience and water baptisms, Paul "*laid his hands upon them*" and "*the Holy Ghost came on them.*"

In your case, you may need rebaptized and this is acceptable unto God according to Acts 19:1-7. If you were sprinkled or if the titles "Father, Son, and Holy Ghost" were invoked at your previous baptism, you need rebaptized, fully immersed in water while calling upon the literal name of the Lord Jesus Christ. A few of my brothers were sprinkled as babies, but upon seeing God's revelation of the Lord Jesus Christ baptism, they were gladly rebaptized and filled with the Holy Ghost afterwards. In my life, I was wrongly baptized in the titles, "Father, Son, and Holy Ghost," and also in the "Jesus only" format, but God graciously allowed me to be correctly baptized on my third attempt in the name of the Lord Jesus Christ. God's peace will fill your soul when you've been correctly baptized in water and spiritually baptized with the Holy Ghost.

How is a believer baptized with the Holy Ghost? He's born again by the Spirit of God falling[834] into His soul from heaven causing a bold, liberating, emotional worship experience. I call it the See and Hear Principle, because that is what Peter called it. Every time a believer was filled with the Holy Ghost in the Book of Acts, observers could "*see and hear*"[835] the outward effects of their inward soul baptism. Just as you "see and hear" a natural baby's birth, you "see and hear" a Christian's spiritual birth. Five texts from the Book of Acts illustrate this revelation and Acts 11:15 proves the Holy Ghost will fall into the souls of men in a similar, worshipful manner every time: "*And as I began to speak, the Holy Ghost fell on them, as on us at the beginning.*" Yes, the spiritual birth experience will be a bold, liberating, worship experience for every Christian.

Every Christian must have an experience of being baptized with the Holy Ghost, but not every experience is the exactly the same. There is not

---

834   Acts 8:16, 11:15
835   Acts 2:33

one specific, outward evidence of the soul baptism, as I'll soon explain. There can be varieties of expressions at the literal moment of receiving the baptism of the Holy Ghost, such as speaking in tongues so others can understand the gospel, declaring God's wonderful works, prophesying, or magnifying God, but each experience is unashamedly life changing. A believer's experience must also be Word-based, meaning the Christian can identify how his experience matches one of those in the Book of Acts when the Holy Ghost fell upon souls. It's as if *you* were there in the upper room in Acts chapter 2 because you've had a similar experience. Lyrics to Isaiah Martin's 1906 hymn "I'm Glad I'm One of Them" joyfully ring in the hearts of all born again believers:

> They were gathered in the upper room,
> All praying in His name.
> They were baptized with the Holy Ghost,
> And power for service came.
> Now, what He did for them that day,
> He'll do for you the same.
> I'm so glad that I can say I'm one of them.
> One of them, one of them.
> I'm so glad that I can say I'm one of them.
> One of them, one of them.
> I'm so glad that I can say I'm one of them.

While emotion comes with the See and Hear experience, it's not the focus of it. Lots of worshippers get emotional, but never fully repent of their sins to experience a changed life. The focus at the beginning of the See and Hear experience is lovingly praising God while asking Him to fill your soul. Our Father loves to hear His children pray and ask Him to fulfill His Word, just as earthly fathers enjoy meeting their children's requests. Jesus says in Luke 11:13, "*If ye then, being evil, know how to give good gifts unto your children: how much more shall your heavenly Father give the Holy Spirit to them that ask him?*"

In Acts 2:1-33, Peter originates the See and Hear Principle by telling the multitude, "*Therefore being by the right hand of God exalted, and having received of the Father the promise of the Holy Ghost, he hath shed forth this, which ye now see and hear."* Earlier in the chapter, the 120 believers got so full of the Holy Ghost, that they left the upper room and went into the streets of Jerusalem about 9:00 a.m. declaring the *"wonderful works of God"* in such a way that they were accused of being drunk on wine.[836] The Holy Ghost in the souls of these freshly filled Christians caused the praises of God to flow out of their souls, into their minds, and then further out into their bodies and mouths, as they moved around the streets and boldly spake of God's works. It's been said a natural birth is a mess and so is a spiritual birth. All the joy, loud worship, emotion, and victory comes flowing out at once. It looks messy to the world—like natural drunkenness—but it's a spiritual birth. It's an emergence. It's eternal life!

Acts 2 was not an unemotional, scripted "Sinner's Prayer" experience. This was the promised *"living water"* Jesus spoke about,[837] flowing out of satisfied souls, freshly filled with eternal life. Note how Acts 2:6-11 teaches the multitude understood everything these Holy Ghost-filled Galileans were saying.

The See and Hear Principle is seen a second time in Acts 4:31 as recently born again Christians prayed for boldness to speak God's Word, and Scripture says the Holy Ghost filled all saints who were praying for this petition. This powerful prayer meeting followed the miraculous healing of a lame man at the gate Beautiful. After performing the miracle through God's power, Peter and John were arrested and threatened to not speak Jesus' name anymore. Once released and among the brethren again, Acts 4:24 says *"they lifted up their voice to God with one accord."* Their prayers asked for signs, wonders, and miracles to *"be done by the name of thy holy child Jesus."* God was so pleased that He shook the building and those who had not been born again were immediately filled, for *"the place was shaken where they were assembled together; and they were all filled with the Holy Ghost, and they spake the word of God with boldness."*

---

836   Acts 2:11-13
837   John 7:38

Observe all you can *"see and hear"* in this event: a shaking building and many loud, bold voices. The Heavenly Father smiled as His spiritual babies were born.

Acts 8:14-25 depicts the Samaritans receiving the baptism of the Holy Ghost, and The See and Hear Principle is evident. The same worship experience from Acts 2 in Jerusalem is now happening nearly 100 miles away in Samaria. After Peter and John lay hands upon the Samaritans and the Holy Ghost falls upon them, a former sorcerer and recent Christian convert named Simon is so amazed by how the Samaritans act upon receiving the Holy Ghost that he offers Peter money if he will give him the power to lay hands on people to impart the Holy Ghost. Simon was well acquainted with seeing Satan manipulate, molest, and bewitch people though his own evil sorceries,[838] but he had never witnessed such genuine, pure, holy, and righteous empowerment as saints receiving the baptism of the Holy Ghost. Ultimately, Simon pleads with Peter for prayer that God will forgive him of thinking he could purchase the power to impart the Holy Ghost to believers' souls. Simon had to learn what John the Baptist taught—it is Jesus Christ alone Who baptizes with the Holy Ghost—not any other person.

A third text about how the Holy Ghost falls is Acts 10:44-48. Though small, this text and its description in the following chapter provides great support for the See and Hear Principle. During Peter's sermon inside Cornelius' house *"the gift of the Holy Ghost"* is *"poured out"* upon many Gentiles. The Jews with Peter *"heard them speak with tongues, and magnify God."* Praise and worship directed to God always flows out the mouths of spiritual babes. These tongues were no doubt understood by the Jews and anyone else in hearing distance because Peter later returned to Jerusalem and told his Jewish brethren that God gave the Gentiles the gift of the Holy Ghost *"like...as he did unto us."*[839] Acts 11:15 proves the Holy Ghost fell on Gentiles in the same way it fell upon Jews in Acts chapter 2.

---

838   Acts 8:9
839   Acts 11:1-18

Additionally, Peter's Jerusalem testimony in Acts 11 teaches the presence of the Holy Ghost inside a Holy Ghost-filled believer's soul can recognize when someone else has received the baptism of the Holy Ghost. Watching the Samaritans receive the Holy Ghost brought Jesus' words to Peter's remembrance in Acts 11:15-18:

> *"And as I began to speak, the Holy Ghost fell on them, as on us at the beginning. Then remembered I the word of the Lord, how that he said, John indeed baptized with water; but ye shall be baptized with the Holy Ghost. Forasmuch then as God gave them the like gift as he did unto us, who believed on the Lord Jesus Christ; what was I, that I could withstand God? When they heard these things, they held their peace, and glorified God, saying, Then hath God also to the Gentiles granted repentance unto life."*

A believer with God's own eternal life can often recognize when a fellow believer is born again. Paul confirms this truth in Romans 8:16, saying, "*The Spirit itself beareth witness with our spirit, that we are the children of God.*" 1 John 5:6 and 8 say, "*It is the Spirit that beareth witness, because the Spirit is truth*", and "*There are three that bear witness in earth, the Spirit, and the water, and the blood: and these three agree in one.*"

The final time recorded in Acts in which believers received the Holy Ghost is chapter 19:1-7, and the See and Hear Principle is displayed by two expressions: speaking with tongues and prophesying. Acts 19:6 says, "*And when Paul had laid his hands upon them, the Holy Ghost came on them; and they spake with tongues, and prophesied.*" God sent tongues to share His works with the Ephesians. It's implied that these disciples were not alone. There must have been unbelievers amongst the group of 12 because tongues are a sign for unbelievers—not believers. 1 Corinthians 14:22 reads, "*Wherefore tongues are for a sign, not to them that believe, but to them that believe not.*" Prophecy, a dramatic gift to assure believers of God's foreknowledge and omniscience, accompanied the tongues, foretelling things to come they would soon witness the fulfillment of.

Revelation 19:10 promises prophecy for those with Jesus' Spirit, saying, *"The testimony of Jesus is the spirit of prophecy."* Supernatural prophecy will be present among Christians, but know not all Christians prophesy according to 1 Corinthians 12:29-31.

UNKNOWN TONGUES ARE NOT THE EVIDENCE OF THE HOLY GHOST BAPTISM

Millions of charismatic churches worldwide erroneously teach speaking in unknown tongues is the initial evidence of the baptism of the Holy Ghost. While the See and Hear Principle agrees believers must have an emotional, bold, and liberating worship experience at the initial moment of receiving the baptism of the Holy Ghost, the Bible allows for different expressions in the worship experience. Unknown tongues-speaking is not the evidence of being born again. Six proofs validate this claim:

First, all instances of speaking in tongues in the Book of Acts were understood by the hearers, but today they are mostly unknown. Genuine tongues from the Holy Ghost, in the Book of Acts, were always understood by the hearers when sent by God. All hearers always understood what was said in Acts 2:4-12, 10:44-46, and 19:1-6 when the Holy Ghost fell and tongues were manifested. The proof of this is found in Acts 11:15, when Peter said the Holy Ghost fell at the house of Cornelius the same way it did on the Day of Pentecost. Since all the tongues that manifested on the Day of Pentecost were understood by the 17 nations of hearers, then any other tongues given when the Holy Ghost fell in the Book of Acts had to be understood as well, based upon the testimony of Peter and the fact that God and His ways are unchanging. In modern services, there are usually unknown tongues and no one understands what is being spoken, which is completely opposite of what took place in Acts chapters 2, 10, and 19.

Second, the Bible does not record tongues being manifested every time believers were born again. Speaking in tongues is mentioned three out of five times in the Book of Acts when the Holy Ghost fell and filled believers—but not five out of five. This proves speaking in tongues is not present every time the Holy Ghost comes. God must have a need to manifest the power of tongues or He will not send that manifestation. Tongues were present in Acts 2:1-5, 10:44-46, and 19:5-6, but not in Acts 4:31 and 8:17. The two instances without tongues—Acts 4:31 and 8:17—show God must not have needed tongues because all the believers present spoke the same language.

Third, Paul taught not all Christians speak in tongues. 1 Corinthians 12:29-31 says, "*Are all apostles? are all prophets? are all teachers? are all workers of miracles? Have all the gifts of healing? do all speak with tongues? do all interpret? But covet earnestly the best gifts: and yet shew I unto you a more excellent way.*" Paul's repeated questioning proves there is diversity in gifts of the Holy Ghost. Not all speak with tongues. Therefore, it's wrong to try and convince every believer that they must speak in unknown tongues. This ungodly teaching is like pressuring every Christian to perform a miracle, like Satan twice pressured Jesus to tempt His Father to perform miracles.[840] Note, though, Paul wrote in 1 Corinthians 14:4-5 he wished all believers would speak in tongues because of the powerful edification that the gift brings to the individual, and the potential edification it can bring to an entire congregation if the unknown tongue would be interpreted so everyone understood what the tongue said.

Fourth, tongues are signs for unbelievers—not believers. Tongues are *not* signs for believers according to 1 Corinthians 14:22: "*Wherefore tongues are for a sign, not to them that believe, but to them that believe not: but prophesying serveth not for them that believe not, but for them which believe.*" This means tongues cannot be a sign to believers who are seeking the baptism of the Holy Ghost, yet many charismatic churches teach the opposite.

A man seeking the baptism of the Holy Ghost is already a believer and doesn't need the sign of speaking in unknown tongues to believe he is born again. The seeker does need a See and Hear experience, but it's wrong to require him to speak in an unknown tongue. Gifts are

---

840   Matthew 4:3-7

determined by God, not man. 1 Corinthians 12:11 and 18 say God divides gifts to each man based upon His will, as it pleases Him.

In Acts chapter 2, the first tongues were spoken by the 120 saints in order to get the unbelievers to believe. This matches what Paul says in 1 Corinthians 14:22. Tongues are a sign to unbelievers. The 120 spoke in unknown tongues so the foreigners from 17 different locations could hear the wonderful works of God and then repent, be baptized, and filled with the Holy Ghost.[841]

Fifth, no one knows the source of an unknown tongue without an interpretation. The problem with unknown tongues being the absolute evidence a person is born again is that no one knows the source of the tongue unless it is interpreted and judged. This is why Paul says in 1 Corinthians 14:28-29 all tongues and interpretations need judged, and if there are no interpreters for those who speak in unknown tongues, the tongues should be kept silent in the church. The fact is most initial-evidence churches don't judge unknown tongues.

Unknown tongues cannot be the evidence of the Holy Ghost baptism because if it is, then you would have to accept every kind of unknown tongue, from any person, as an evidence of being born again. But speaking in tongues can be easily impersonated by the devil and his servants, as reports from missionaries verify this. Religious encyclopedias describe one of the evidences of demon possession as speaking in an unknown tongue, commonly called glossolalia. Witches and other workers of witchcraft are not born again by the Spirit of God just because they speak in unknown tongues.

God desires tongues of men and angels to be manifested among His people, as Paul taught that the gift of tongues should be in the church, but it must be used properly and kept in order.[842] Paul placed great emphasis on understanding the meaning of tongues in 1 Corinthians 14:6, 11 and 19, saying unknown tongues only profit if they are interpreted. The apostle said he'd rather speak five words with understanding than 10,000 in

841   Acts 2:37-39
842   1 Corinthians 12:10, 14:40

unknown tongues. Speakers in unknown tongues seem like barbarians to the listeners without interpretations.[843] The 3,000 souls saved on the Day of Pentecost didn't think the 120 Holy Ghost-filled saints were barbarians; they understood the wonderful works of God they were declaring and received Christ for themselves.

The Holy Ghost does *not* come with one, mandated observation—unknown tongues—as Jesus taught in Luke 17:20: *"The kingdom of God cometh not with observation."* It comes with a powerful, dynamic worship experience others can *"see and hear."* A pure, godly, and overcoming life follows the See and Hear experience, which leads to the next proof unknown tongues are not an evidence of the new birth.

Sixth, Jesus taught what the real evidence of receiving the Holy Ghost is—and it isn't unknown tongues. In John 14:26 and 16:13, Jesus says the evidence of being born again is being led by the Spirit into all truth. John 14:26 reads, *"But the Comforter, which is the Holy Ghost, whom the Father will send in my name, he shall teach you all things, and bring all things to your remembrance, whatsoever I have said unto you."* John 16:13 declares, *"Howbeit when he, the Spirit of truth, is come, he will guide you into all truth: for he shall not speak of himself; but whatsoever he shall hear, that shall he speak: and he will shew you things to come."*

The evidence you are a child of God is that you can be taught to continually live a more holy, obedient, and righteous lifestyle. John 6:45 says, *"It is written in the prophets, And they shall be all taught of God. Every man therefore that hath heard, and hath learned of the Father, cometh unto me."* This evidence manifested in Christ's own earthly life. Luke 2:52 says, *"Jesus increased in wisdom and stature, and in favour with God and man."* Christ's holy character will manifest in every believer's life. Meekness and humility are prerequisites for the high calling of living a Christ-like life, for Jesus says, *"Take my yoke upon you, and learn of me; for I am meek and lowly in heart."*[844] Both sinners and Christians are growing in their endeavors. Sinners will *"increase unto more ungodliness"*[845] and *"evil men*

---

843   1 Corinthians 14:11
844   Matthew 11:29
845   2 Corinthians 2:16

and seducers shall wax worse and worse, deceiving, and being deceived"[846], but Christians *"grow up into him in all things… even Christ."*[847] Proverbs 4:18 supports progressive holiness, saying, *"But the path of the just is as the shining light, that shineth more and more unto the perfect day."*

Before concluding this subject, I've personally witnessed numerous examples of people who spoke in tongues but later rejected righteousness and turned to unrighteousness. These broken lives prove speaking in tongues is only a temporary anointing of a gift and not the seal, or permanent abiding presence of Christ. Two examples from my college days bear retelling.

First, a friend I'll call Graham confessed in tears that he pretended to speak in tongues during a revival service at his church. He said he didn't want to pretend, but felt intense pressure to perform an unknown tongue when the preacher stuck the microphone under his mouth and spoke to the entire congregation, saying, "Did you receive the Holy Ghost, Graham?" Feeling singled out in front of the entire church and afraid the group would ridicule him if he didn't say yes, he loudly answered, "Yes!" Unexpectedly, the preacher stuck the microphone back into his face and shouted, "Then speak in tongues for everyone to hear!" Graham didn't have the courage to tell the truth, so he blabbered an unknown tongue into the mic to the delight of the preacher and congregation. My prayer is that Graham has found forgiveness and redemption through the Spirit of truth.

A second college friend I'll call Billy got saved during his freshman year through a revival sponsored by an initial evidence church. Being tall, handsome, and charismatic, the initial evidence church quickly groomed him to the pulpit as a preacher. Visiting their church, I watched he and his fiancé repeatedly speak in unknown tongues. Afterwards, I shared my differing opinion about the initial evidence, but we agreed to disagree. Billy eventually married his fiancé, but less than three years into their marriage, his wife committed adultery with another man, divorcing him

---

846 2 Timothy 3:13
847 Ephesians 4:13

and leaving him alone. Her adulterous act proved she never had the baptism of the Holy Ghost, despite frequently speaking in unknown tongues, because 1 Corinthians 6:9-10 says, *"Neither... adulterers... shall inherit the kingdom of God."* The seal of the Holy Ghost seals out Satan's power to persuade believers to commit adultery, among other sins. Billy's ex-wife may have had a genuine gift to speak in tongues, but it was wrong for her church to teach her to seek after the gift of tongues rather than the Giver of the gifts, Jesus Christ. Had she received Jesus Christ, our Lord would have washed away her desire to commit adultery, and she would be married to Billy to this day.

Speaking in unknown tongues can be easily impersonated as a carnal, fleshly evidence. But the real evidence is faith that produces the life of Christ in a believer's daily life.

Hebrews 11:1 is the only New Testament Scripture that uses the word *"evidence"*, and it never mentions unknown tongues: *"Now faith is the substance of things hoped for, the evidence of things not seen."* Invisible faith that produces progressively-holy, Christ-like works is the evidence a Christian has been truly born again.

MORE ABOUT THE GENUINE EVIDENCE OF THE HOLY GHOST BAPTISM

More can be said regarding the sixth reason why tongues isn't the evidence of the Holy Ghost baptism. Yes, Jesus taught the real evidence for receiving the baptism of the Holy Ghost is being guided by the Holy Spirit into all Bible-truth, but He also provided concrete examples to help clarify the nature of the Spirit's guidance. A Christian life guided into all truth includes:

- Love for other Christians—John 13:35 says, *"By this shall all men know that ye are my disciples, if ye have love one to another."*
- Supernatural signs and wonders done by the Holy Ghost—Mark 16:17-18 says, *"And these signs shall follow them that believe; in my name shall they cast out*

devils...speak with new tongues...lay hands on the sick, and they shall recover."

- Remembering Jesus' words—John 14:26 says, *"The Holy Ghost...shall...bring all things to your remembrance, whatsoever I have said unto you."*
- Testifying about and glorifying Jesus—John 15:26 and 16:14 say, *"The Spirit of truth...he shall testify of me"*, and *"He shall glorify me."*
- Being convicted of and overcoming sin—John 16:8 and 1 John 5:4 say, *"He will reprove the world of sin"*, and *"For whatsoever is born of God overcometh the world."*
- Knowing future events—John 16:13 says, *"The Spirit of truth...will shew you things to come."*
- Listening to and believing the human messengers sent to preach during their lifetimes—John 17:20-21 says, *"Neither pray I for these alone, but for them also which shall believe on me through their word; That they all may be one."*

The above seven examples demonstrate the nature of the Spirit's guidance for New Testament believers, but what about Old Testament saints? Generally speaking, it can be said the Spirit guided Old Testament into all of God's revelation available to them during their lifetimes. They had to be in the Word all the way for their day. While saints like Noah, Joshua, Caleb, and John the Baptist couldn't receive the baptism of the Spirit in their souls, they could be led by it.

Noah was one of eight believers who were led by the Spirit into all the truth for his day, which meant living all of God's righteous commands and physically separating themselves into Noah's ark before the flood. The evidence Noah's group were genuine believers was their full obedience to God's Word in their lifetimes. Joshua and Caleb were the only two out of the multitude that left Egypt to inherit the Promised Land. Numbers 14:24 says Caleb had *"another spirit"* and it was that

Spirit that led he and Joshua to receive the messenger of their day, Moses, and to obey all the truth of Moses' message. John the Baptist was the messenger for his day and all true believers heard him, confessed their sins in repentance, and were baptized. In Luke 7:30, the Pharisees and lawyers rejected God's counsel given to John and refused to be baptized. Consequently, John called those who rejected his message a *"generation of vipers."*[848] Later in this chapter, more will be taught on the Holy Ghost and the Old Testament saints.

UNIFYING AND DIFFERENTIATING TERMINOLOGY

Terminology about the baptism of the Holy Ghost needs both unified and differentiated from the other two Works of Grace. Chapter 5 covers the Three Works of Grace: justification, sanctification, and the baptism of the Holy Ghost.

It's absolutely essential for believers to have this understanding to rightly divide the word of truth about the three stages in a Christian's experience. Without this understanding, churches will falsely assure new believers, who have only recently been baptized in water, they are already born again. But in reality, the new believers are only justified; not sanctified and certainly not *"endued with power from on high."*[849] Sadly, I've witnessed a Bible teacher try to convince children as young as five years old that they already had Jesus' full power and could do greater works than Him (misinterpreting John 14:12), yet most of these children did not show any fruits of repentance (justification), nor the signs of a sanctified, transformed human spirit. Along with spreading confusion when teachers reject or are ignorant of the Three Works of Grace, the power of God is reduced to a stale, emotionless moment of "inviting Jesus in your heart." Thankfully, the Bible offers us so much more hope than this.

Figure 16 shows the Three Works of Grace and unifies terminology for each stage. The first stage, justification, is often referred to as being *"saved"* and Ezekiel calls it the *"new heart."* Justification corresponds to

848   Matthew 3:7
849   Luke 24:49

Israel's exodus out of Egypt, wherein they were saved from bondage and cleansed through the Red Sea, representing the New Testament water baptism.

Justification	Sanctification	Baptism of the Holy Ghost
Salvation, Justified, or Saved (Luke 19:9, 1 Corinthians 1:18-21, 6:11, Titus 3:5,7)	Sanctified (John 17:17, 1 Corinthians 6:11)	Baptism or Filling of the Holy Ghost (Matthew 3:11, Acts 1:5, 2:4)
New heart (Ezekiel 36:26)	New spirit (Ezekiel 36:26)	My Spirit (Ezekiel 36:27)
Blade (Mark 4:28)	Ear (Mark 4:28)	Full corn (Mark 4:28)

Figure 16

Sanctification, the second stage, is called the "*new spirit*" by Ezekiel because God is renewing the believer's mind, or human spirit. Another word for sanctification is purification. God cleans out the believer's mind in this stage. In the purest sense, it is a brain washing, or human spirit-washing by the "*washing of water by the Word.*"[850] Formerly, the Christian was under the spirit of disobedience[851], but sanctification teaches him to obey the Word. This stage corresponds to Israel's wilderness journey in which they were tested by God that He might "*know what was in thine heart,*" whether Israel would "*keep the commandments, or no.*"[852]

The baptism of the Holy Ghost is the third stage specifically reserved for New Testament Christians. Old Testament saints could never attain to this stage because Jesus' blood had not yet atoned for mankind's sins and

850   Ephesians 5:26
851   Ephesians 2:2
852   Deuteronomy 8:2

He was not yet glorified.[853] Note this following list of terms and descriptors for the Holy Ghost baptism. It far exceeds the previous two stages:

- Converted (Luke 22:32)
- Endued with power from on high (Luke 24:49)
- Born again or new birth (John 3:7)
- Receiving eternal life (John 10:28, 1 John 5:11-13)
- Love, or charity (Romans 5:5, 1 Corinthians 13:1-13, 2 Peter 1:7)
- The Holy Spirit dwelling in you (Romans 8:11)
- The Spirit of adoption (Romans 8:15)
- God the Father dwelling and walking in you (2 Corinthians 6:16,18)
- Seal, or spiritual mark (Ephesians 1:13, 4:30)
- Christ in you (Colossians 1:27)
- Washing of regeneration and renewing of the Holy Ghost (Titus 3:5)
- Washed robes made white in the blood of the Lamb (Revelation 7:14)

Most of these terms and phrases are not found in the Old Testament, proving they were reserved by God for the New Covenant when He would live in believers' souls. Old Testament believers could not be labeled as "born again," "baptized with the Holy Ghost," "sealed," or "regenerated." Only New Testament believers are able to presently possess love, "eternal life," the "Spirit of adoption," and have God daily "walking in them."

Let it be clearly and emphatically stated that the following terms and phrases are speaking of the one and same experience of the baptism of the Holy Ghost: new birth, born again, filled with the Holy Ghost, sealed, Christ in you, possessing eternal life, converted, adopted, regenerated, charity, love, and endued with power from on high.

For your benefit, it bears revisiting that "love" and "charity" are identical terms and are synonymous for the baptism of the Holy Ghost. The

---

853   John 7:37-39, Hebrews 9:12-15, 13:20

Bible twice says, "*God is love.*"[854] Chapter 1's section called "God Manifests Himself In Three Ways" introduces the truth that God the Father and the Holy Ghost are the selfsame person. God is the Holy Spirit—the Person of Love Who comes to abide in your soul. If this seems confusing, go back and read Chapter 5's section called "Character Quality #8: Charity." Eight Scriptures reveal this truth and help bring harmony to Bible terminology about the Holy Ghost baptism.

THE HOLY GHOST BAPTISM COMES UPON ONE OF MAN'S THREE PARTS

As explored in Chapter 5, every human has three parts to his or her being: body, human spirit, and soul. 1 Thessalonians 5:23 provides this fact, saying, "*And the very God of peace sanctify you wholly; and I pray God your whole spirit and soul and body be preserved blameless unto the coming of our Lord Jesus Christ.*" Figure 17 provides a visual of man's threefold division. Some may suggest man has fewer or more parts to his being, but the Bible limits it to only three parts.

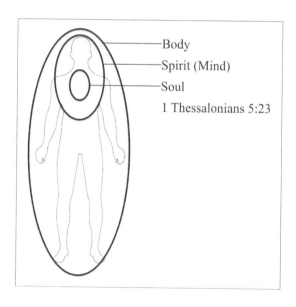

Figure 17

854   1 John 4:8,16

If each man has three parts, which part receives the seal of God, or baptism of the Holy Ghost that Jesus promised? The body, spirit, or soul? Recall Jesus' words in John 7:37-39 about the Holy Ghost not being given until *after* He was resurrected and glorified. Which part of man was awaiting a spiritual baptism? The soul.

Equipped with the knowledge that man only has three parts to his being, you can use the process of elimination to rule out the two parts that do not experience the baptism of the Holy Ghost—body and human spirit—and find that part that does—the soul.

THE BODY DOES NOT RECEIVE THE BAPTISM OF THE HOLY GHOST

Starting from the outside and working inward, the body or flesh does not receive the baptism of the Holy Ghost. Paul says *"For I know that in me (that is, in my flesh,) dwelleth no good thing."*[855] The apostle knew his flesh had a totally depraved sin-nature, twice more saying sin dwelt inside his flesh.[856] Galatians 5:17 says, *"For the flesh lusteth against the Spirit, and the Spirit against the flesh: and these are contrary the one to the other: so that ye cannot do the things that ye would."* The flesh is completely defiant against the Holy Spirit and always lusting after sin.

At times the flesh—equipped with its five senses—can certainly feel the anointing of the Holy Ghost, but it is always temporary. At Paul's conversion on the Damascus road in Acts 9:1-6, Christ's heavenly light shined so brightly that he fell to the ground and physically trembled under Jesus' holiness. But Paul wasn't baptized with the Holy Ghost until a later date, after he received his eye sight and was baptized in water.[857]

THE HUMAN SPIRIT DOES NOT RECEIVE THE BAPTISM OF THE HOLY GHOST

Moving inward beyond the flesh is the human spirit, or mind. Thinking takes place here in the human spirit. This second part of man is the part

855 Romans 7:18
856 Romans 7:17, 20
857 Acts 9:17-18

many erroneously say receives the seal of God, but these professors are mistaken because the human mind needs daily renewed and refreshed by the Holy Ghost. Romans 12:1 says a Christian conforms or fashions his mind through spiritual transformation. Then, 2 Corinthians 4:16 teaches this renewing happens daily: *"For which cause we faint not; but though our outward man perish, yet the inward man is renewed day by day."*

Contrariwise, the baptism of the Holy Ghost, or seal of God upon man's soul, is a permanent anointing that lasts *"unto the day of redemption."*[858] When God seals a man's soul, the work is "one and done." But the human mind must be daily made new and forced to serve the law of God by man's free moral agency. Romans 7:25 reads, *"I thank God through Jesus Christ our Lord. So then with the mind I myself serve the law of God; but with the flesh the law of sin."*

THE FIVE ASPECTS TO THE HUMAN SPIRIT

Scripture teaches there are five aspects to the human spirit: conscience, memory, reason, affection, and imagination. Each aspect is temporarily anointed by the Holy Ghost when the believer brings his mind into obedience to God's Word. It's noteworthy that the human spirit, or mind, is like a battlefield between Satan and the believer. The enemy has free access to your mind and can inject evil thoughts without your permission. Ephesians 6:16 likens this unto Satan shooting fiery darts into your mind. You can't stop him from attacking, but you can stop the fiery darts from hitting you. With the mighty weapons of your Christian warfare, such as the shield of faith, you can cast down all *"imaginations and every high thing"* that exalts itself against God's Word.[859] Definitions and Bible examples of these five aspects include:

- Conscience is the moral compass that guides man to recognizing right and wrong. The scribes and Pharisees were *"convicted by their own conscience"*[860] and decided not to stone the woman caught in adultery after Jesus directed

858   Ephesians 4:30
859   2 Corinthians 10:4-5
860   John 8:9

them to examine their own guilt first before judging the woman.

- Memory is the ability to store and recall information. Peter's memory of Jesus' promise to baptize with the Holy Ghost helped calm and convince Jews that God had granted the Gentiles *"repentance unto life"* in Acts 11:1-18. One benefit of the baptism of the Holy Ghost is that He will *"bring all things to your remembrance"*[861] when needed.

- Reason is the ability to explain the cause or justification of an action or event. Jesus perceived the scribes' evil reasoning in Mark 2:1-8. After Messiah declared a paralyzed man forgiven, the scribes silently reasoned Jesus blasphemed because only God can forgive sins. But Christ proceeded to prove He was God by miraculously causing the man to walk. Godly reasoning is a powerful tool used to explain the Scriptures, as Paul caused many Thessalonians to believe the gospel by reasoning Old Testament Scriptures about Jesus' death and resurrection in Acts 17:1-4.

- Affection is the emotional component of the human spirit. Paul says Titus, one of his fellow workers in the gospel, had an abundant *"inward affection"* towards the believers in Corinth.[862] All believers must set their affections *"on things above, not on things on the earth."*[863]

- Imagination is the ability to mentally form new ideas, concepts, or images not present. God flooded the earth in Noah's day because every imagination of the thoughts of men's hearts were only evil continually. Christians use their imaginations to receive revelation from God as they consider the future joys of heaven, which God has prepared for those He loves. Note how 1 Corinthians

861   John 14:26
862   2 Corinthians 7:14-15
863   Colossians 3:2

2:9-10 says God has *already* revealed unimaginable, deep things to His children: *"But as it is written, Eye hath not seen, nor ear heard, neither have entered into the heart of man, the things which God hath prepared for them that love him. But God hath revealed them unto us by his Spirit: for the Spirit searcheth all things, yea, the deep things of God."*

THE SUPERNATURAL HUMAN SPIRIT

Man's human spirit is the supernatural part of him God designed to live for thousands or more years. For example, Cain's human spirit is one of the millions that lived 6,000 years ago in the days of man's origin. The human spirit of Cain and all the lost of his day are still alive in hell awaiting judgment at the White Throne. 1 Peter 3:18-20 teaches that Jesus *"preached unto the spirits in prison"* who disobeyed Noah's message and lived over 2,000 years before Christ's earthly ministry.

Three Biblical examples teach human spirits keep both their strengths and weaknesses, or character, even after death. First, the prophet Samuel remained a prophet four years after his death when his spirit was called up to earth by the witch of Endor. His righteous character remained in tact, for he foretold, or prophesied, the death of Saul and his sons the day before it happened,[864] proving he still had the prophetic gift in his human spirit. Once a prophet, always a prophet. Interestingly, this story also shows how a diviner, or necromancer, was able to bring up Samuel's spirit from Abraham's bosom. Thankfully, this is no longer possible because Jesus' death and descent into hell allowed Him to take the keys of death and hell[865] before resurrecting in power and leading the saints to heaven. More on the keys of death and hell later in this chapter.

Found in Luke 16:19-31, Jesus' story of the rich man and beggar named Lazarus is a second example of human spirits keeping their character after death. Following death, the rich man finds himself tormented in the flames of hell while Lazarus rests comfortably with Abraham. The

864   1 Samuel 28:19
865   Revelation 1:18

rich man's human spirit remained prideful even after death, as seen in his discourse with Abraham. Having five brothers, the rich man wanted Abraham to send Lazarus back from the dead to testify to his brothers so they would believe God's Word and escape hell. Abraham refused, saying his brothers only needed to hear Moses and the prophets to be saved. Arrogantly, the rich man tried to correct father Abraham by saying the miracle of Lazarus raising from the dead would convince his brothers to be saved. Death never changed the rich man's selfish, prideful character. Wisely, Abraham uttered, *"If they hear not Moses and the prophets, neither will they be persuaded, though one rose from the dead."* Witnessing miracles does not bring salvation. Repentance from sin brings salvation.

A third example of human spirits keeping their character after death is the souls under the altar in Revelation 6:9-11. In this Fifth Seal, souls in the heavenly dimension are crying out for revenge. You learned in Chapter 2 of this book that these souls are Jews who have been martyred for their faith in *"the word of God,"* or Old Testament, from the days of Jesus to the present. This includes all the slain Jews during the New Testament, from the first century, up to the 6 million Jews murdered during the Holocaust, to the persecuted Jews of today. Note they did not have the *"testimony of Jesus Christ"* like the apostle John had in Revelation 1:2 and 1:9. Yes, these Jews were faithful to Moses' Law but their human spirits still seek vengeance for their blood. The human spirits of Holy Ghost-filled Christians seek not vengeance, but ask forgiveness for their persecutors. Stephen, the first recorded Christian martyr by stoning, kneeled down at his death *"and cried with a loud voice, Lord, lay not this sin to their charge."*[866] The ultimate example of a human spirit offering forgiveness is Jesus Christ at His crucifixion. Messiah breathed, *"Father, forgive them; for they know not what they do."*[867]

866   Acts 7:60
867   Luke 23:34

THE HUMAN SPIRIT RECEIVES A TEMPORARY ANOINTING

The fact that the human spirit only receives a temporary anointing is a prominent revelation in this chapter. Every church that makes speaking in tongues the evidence of receiving the Holy Ghost fails this revelation because they only receive a temporary anointing on their human spirits rather than a permanent one. The Holy Spirit anoints their minds, causing them to operate the gift of tongues, but the anointing eventually leaves. Afterwards, worldliness usually creeps into their lives, and genuine fruits of the Holy Spirit cannot be produced.

Jesus promised believers power when baptized with the Holy Ghost, but many tongues-speakers only have power to speak in unknown tongues and lack the power to overcome the lusts of the eyes, lusts of the flesh, and pride of life. It does no good to utter unknown languages at church but utter gossip, cursing, lies, and praise for worldliness outside the church.

Even born again Christians battle the lusts and pride of life. Some mornings when you wake up, your human spirit has backslid into total defiance to God's Word, and your flesh doesn't feel like seeking God through morning prayer and Bible reading. But as a spiritual king, you must exercise dominion over both the flesh and human spirit, bringing them into subjection to the Holy Ghost. Ruling over the flesh and spirit is walking in obedience to God's Spirit. Living spiritually minded is your daily victory of life and peace. Romans 8:4-7 says,

> "That the righteousness of the law might be fulfilled in us, who walk not after the flesh, but after the Spirit. For they that are after the flesh do mind the things of the flesh; but they that are after the Spirit the things of the Spirit. For to be carnally minded is death; but to be spiritually minded is life and peace. Because the carnal mind is enmity against God: for it is not subject to the law of God, neither indeed can be."

THE DIVIDING LINE BETWEEN THE TEMPORARY AND PERMANENT ANOINTING

You can understand the difference between the Holy Ghost's temporary anointing on the human spirit versus the permanent anointing upon the soul by using three Scriptures: John 7:39, Acts 1:5, and Acts 2:4. These Scriptures create a dividing line at the Day of Pentecost. With full Bible authority, Acts 2:4 is the first time believers (all but Jesus) received the permanent anointing of the Holy Ghost in their souls. Every other time the Bible speaks of the anointing, or filling of the Holy Ghost, previous to the Day of Pentecost, it is referring to the temporary anointing on the human spirit, not the soul. This means every Old Testament Scripture that refers to the Holy Ghost anointing men and women was a temporary anointing upon their human spirits and not their souls. Additionally, it means anyone anointed by the Holy Ghost in the four Gospels (excluding Jesus Christ at His water baptism) only received a temporary anointing.

Examining John 7:39, the baptism of the Holy Ghost in the soul could only be given *after* Jesus was glorified: *"(But this spake he of the Spirit, which they that believe on him should receive: for the Holy Ghost was not yet given; because that Jesus was not yet glorified.)"* When was Jesus glorified? Christ was glorified, or received a new, glorified body, at the moment of His resurrection. John 12:23-24 records Jesus saying His death meant the hour of His glorification was near, saying, *"The hour is come, that the Son of man should be glorified. Verily, verily, I say unto you, Except a corn of wheat fall into the ground and die, it abideth alone: but if it die, it bringeth forth much fruit."*

Two more Scriptures—John 2:22 and 12:16—place Jesus' glorification after His resurrection because Christ's disciples only gained understanding of His prophesies after Jesus rose from the dead. John 12:16 reads, *"These things understood not his disciples at the first: but when Jesus was glorified, then remembered they that these things were written of him, and that they had done these things unto him."* Shortly after the Day of Pentecost, Peter performed a miracle in Christ's name and said God had already glorified His Son Jesus: *"The God of Abraham, and of Isaac, and of Jacob, the God of our fathers, hath glorified his Son Jesus."*[868]

Acts 1:5 records Jesus' red letter words of promise to baptize His disciples with the Holy Ghost 10 days before it happened: *"For John truly baptized with water; but ye shall be baptized with the Holy Ghost not many days hence."* This was the soul-baptism both Christ and John the Baptist foretold. Luke 3:16 records John differentiating his water baptism from the soul-baptism that Christ would unleash at Pentecost: *"John answered, saying unto them all, I indeed baptize you with water; but one mightier than I cometh, the latchet of whose shoes I am not worthy to unloose: he shall baptize you with the Holy Ghost and with fire."*

OLD TESTAMENT EXAMPLES OF THE TEMPORARY ANOINTING

Now that you've learned the human spirit, the second part of your being, is only anointed temporarily by the Holy Ghost, you can understand Old Testament Bible examples referring to believers being *"filled"* with the Holy Ghost. You know these temporary fillings only anointed their minds, not their souls, because Jesus was not yet glorified.

Pharaoh recognized God's Spirit in Joseph in Genesis 41:38, saying, *"Can we find such a one as this is, a man in whom the Spirit of God is?"* In Exodus 28:3, wise-hearted Jews were *"filled with the spirit of wisdom"* in order to make Aaron's priestly garments. Bezaleel was *"filled...with the spirit of God...in all manner of workmanship"*[869] to help build the tabernacle of Moses. But it was his human spirit that was filled with God's Spirit, not yet his soul, because Hebrews 10:4 says it was impossible for the blood of bulls and goats, which sacrifices he was living under, to take away his sins. Numbers 14:24 says Caleb *"had another spirit with him"* which caused him to follow God fully in the days of Joshua. In Numbers 27:18, Joshua had God's Spirit, for the Lord told Moses, *"Take thee Joshua the son of Nun, a man in whom is the spirit, and lay thine hand upon him."*

---

868   Acts 3:13
869   Exodus 31:2-5

Micah knew his mind was filled with God's Spirit, saying, *"But truly I am full of power by the spirit of the LORD, and of judgment, and of might, to declare unto Jacob his transgression, and to Israel his sin."*[870] All prophets had God's Spirit temporarily anointing them. Numbers 11:25-29 shows how God put a portion of His Spirit that was already upon Moses on 70 elders, causing them to prophesy without ceasing.

Closely examining three Old Testament individuals helps further prove the Spirit's anointing was temporary: Samson, Saul, and David. Samson is known both for his supernatural strength via the Holy Ghost, but also for his immorality. Judges 13:25 and 14:6 record the Spirit mightily moving upon him, but later his disobedience and sensuality caused the Lord to depart from him.[871] Surely God's Spirit was anointing Samson to fulfill his life's purpose of delivering Israel from the Philistines. But it wasn't the Lord's anointing causing him to commit fornication with a prostitute.[872] The New Testament believer is empowered by the baptism of the Holy Ghost in his soul to abstain from fornication, since fornicators will not inherit the kingdom of God,[873] but this soul-anointing wasn't available in Samson's lifetime.

At the beginning of his reign, Saul was anointed king of Israel and the Spirit of God came upon him in 1 Samuel 10:1-10. Through his rebellion against God, an evil spirit came upon Saul, but departed as David played his harp.[874] After David slew Goliath in 1 Samuel 18:6-12, the evil spirit returned to Saul because he was jealous when dancing Israeli women proclaimed David the better warrior. The evil spirit would come and go. Saul even unsuccessfully attempted to murder David twice in 1 Samuel 19:8-18. Next, Saul and his servants went to Ramah to dispose of David, but instead all prophesied as the *"Spirit of God"*[875] came upon them. Saul spent many of his remaining years on earth harboring a murderous spirit as he hunted down David. God grew weary of Saul's disobedience, ultimately

---

870   Micah 3:8
871   Judges 16:20
872   Judges 16:1
873   1 Thessalonians 4:3, Galatians 5:19-21
874   1 Samuel 16:14-23
875   1 Samuel 19:18-24

taking away both His mercy from Saul and the kingdom of Israel.[876] Saul experienced only the temporary anointing of God's Spirit upon his human spirit. New Testament believers with the permanent seal of God's Spirit in their souls will not harbor murderous spirits because Jesus says, *"Behold, the kingdom of God is within"* their souls. Murderers will not inherit the kingdom of God.[877] 1 John 3:15 teaches no murderer has eternal life. Every born again Christian, though, already possesses eternal life.[878]

David's life may serve as the most profound example of the Holy Spirit's temporary anointing upon the human spirit because his victories and failures were so great. Even before his epic victory against the giant Goliath, God's anointing came upon David as Samuel poured a horn of natural oil on his head and pronounced him the next king.[879] Along with being the universal symbol for a giant-killer, David is also well known for having a heart that chased after God's heart.[880] David loved God's anointing and you read of his love for God and His law in scores of worship songs in the Book of Psalm. Many of his psalms prophesied of Jesus Christ, including Psalm 16, 22, and 110. Indeed, over 1,000 years before Jesus' crucifixion, the Holy Spirit took David so deep into revelation that he foretold Messiah's suffering and some of His very words from the cross by writing, *"My God, my God, why hast thou forsaken me?...all my bones: they look and stare upon me. They part my garments among them, and cast lots upon my vesture."*[881] David humbly and accurately said in 2 Samuel 23:2, *"The Spirit of the Lord spake by me, and his word was in my tongue."* 2 Peter 1:21 rightly describes David's experiences, saying, *"Holy men of God spake as they were moved by the Holy Ghost."*

On the other side of the spectrum, David experienced the pain, agony, and shame of rejecting the anointing in his human spirit when he harbored and acted upon lustful thoughts about another man's wife: Bathsheba. 1 Kings 15:5 says this situation was David's one time he

---

876   1 Samuel 15:28, 1 Chronicles 17:13
877   Galatians 5:21
878   1 John 5:13, 20
879   1 Samuel 16:12-13
880   1 Samuel 13:14
881   Psalm 22:1, 17-18, Matthew 27:35, 46

purposely turned aside from God's command: *"Because David did that which was right in the eyes of the Lord, and turned not aside from any thing that he commanded him all the days of his life, save only in the matter of Uriah the Hittite."* Without the permanent seal of the Holy Ghost in his soul, David radically turned aside from the anointing of God's Spirit and committed horrendous evils.

Told in 2 Samuel chapters 11 and 12, David's first mistake was neglecting his kingly war duties. At the time of his downfall, he was in Jerusalem, but should have been out with Israel's army battling the Ammonites. You must learn to never neglect your responsibilities, as all Old Testament Scripture is written for your benefit.[882]

Next, David stood on his rooftop at night and saw Bathsheba bathing. Consumed by her beauty, he enquired of her identity and then sent messengers to bring her to him. Consider the time that passed between the moment David first saw Bathsheba and the time he lay with her, in which he could have repented of his lust and chose obedience to God's commands. He had at least two ways out. First, with God's anointing, he could have cast out this lustful temptation from his mind. Second, the king, who had at least 8 wives and 10 concubines,[883] could have easily satisfied his sensual passions with one of his legal wives, but instead took another man's *only* wife. David willingly ignored the conviction of the Holy Spirit and Scripture says he *"despised the commandment of the Lord"*[884] that forbid adultery. David chose to commit adultery with Bathsheba and after he received word from her that she was pregnant, he repeatedly tried to cover up his sin. This moved David to place Bathsheba's husband, loyal solider Uriah, in the middle of a violent battle that led to his death. The prophet Nathan put the blame of murder upon David, saying, *"Thou hast killed Uriah the Hittite with the sword, and hast taken his wife to be thy wife, and hast slain him with the sword of the children of Ammon."*[885] In all of this, Scripture gives no clues about Bathsheba's

---

882   1 Corinthians 10:11, 2 Timothy 3:16-17
883   2 Samuel 5:13, 11:27, 20:3, 1 Chronicles 3:1-3
884   2 Samuel 12:9
885   2 Samuel 12:9

motives, but David admits his blame saying, "*I have sinned against the LORD.*"[886]

Like all children of God, David suffered grave consequences for his evil actions, foretold by the prophet Nathan, as the sword never departed from his house. He and Bathsheba's first child died shortly after birth. David's daughter, Tamar, was raped by her half-brother, Amnon, who was then murdered by Absalom, David's son. Soon after that, Absalom stole the hearts of the people and the kingdom from David, forcing his father into exile. Absalom then slept with his father's concubines publicly as divine retribution for his secret adultery with Bathsheba. Adonijah, another son of David, was executed after David's death as a traitor.[887] Friend, God is not mocked. Whatsoever a man sows, that shall he reap.

Psalm 51 is universally acknowledged as a divine song of repentance after David committed adultery with Bathsheba. In verses 10-12, David requests God recreating a clean heart within him and a renewal of the right spirit. He pleads for God not to cast him away from His holy presence, saying, "*Take not thy holy spirit from me.*" This statement shows David knew God's anointing upon him was temporary. The king then asks for a restoration of joy and God's upholding power for his human spirit.

Herein lays the truth that under the Old Testament, David could kill a giant (Goliath) outside his body, but not the giant of lust within his body because he lacked the inward power of the baptism of the Holy Ghost. New Testament teaching states adulterers cannot inherit the kingdom of God.[888] This is because power is now available to overcome adultery and every other sin. In short, a New Testament believer who is truly baptized with the Holy Ghost will not commit adultery. He may commit adultery before being born again, but not after. Spirit-filled Christians are sealed, or marked, as God's eternal property and are guarded by the power of God from committing adultery and other grave sins. 1 Peter 1:5 says we are kept, or guarded, "*by the power of God through faith.*"

886   2 Samuel 12:13
887   1 Kings 2:24-25
888   1 Corinthians 6:9-10

Preachers and lay members alike may erroneously use David's failures to justify their own lusts, claiming they, too, can be men or women after God's heart despite adulteries, fornications, and multiple marriages. But the revelation of the Holy Ghost-baptism unveils their folly by showing a higher holiness standard for New Testament saints based upon access to greater power. Wolves in sheep's clothing live by the motto, "If God forgave David for his sexual sin, then God will forgive me." Sadly, these wolves plan out their sins, like adulteries, despite Romans 13:14 admonishing us to *"put ye on the Lord Jesus Christ, and make not provision for the flesh, to fulfil the lusts thereof."* False preachers devise, plan, and execute their sexual escapades, but godly preachers depart from all iniquity. 2 Timothy 2:19 reads, *"Nevertheless the foundation of God standeth sure, having this seal, The Lord knoweth them that are his. And, Let every one that nameth the name of Christ depart from iniquity."*

While David was guilty of his failures, his life proves Old Testament believers lacked the permanent dwelling of God's presence because God was hiding it until Pentecost. If David had been born again, the Holy Ghost seal inside him would have caused him to overcome adultery with Bathsheba and refrain from Uriah's murder rather than despising God's commands. God's soul-seal offers Christians power to *"cause"* them to obey God according to Ezekiel 36:27.

NEW TESTAMENT EXAMPLES OF THE TEMPORARY ANOINTING

John the Baptist and his parents, Zacharias and Elisabeth, are three New Testament examples of the temporary anointing of God's Spirit. Technically, the New Testament did not begin until after Jesus' death and resurrection. Hebrews 9:16-17 validates this, saying, *"For where a testament is, there must also of necessity be the death of the testator. For a testament is of force after men are dead: otherwise it is of no strength at all while the testator liveth."* These three individuals are classified as New Testament examples because their temporary anointing is recorded in Luke's gospel, which is considered part of the traditional New Testament canon.

Luke chapter 1 records John and his parents being filled with the Holy Ghost. Luke 1:15 says, *"For he* [John] *shall be great in the sight of the Lord, and shall drink neither wine nor strong drink; and he shall be filled with the Holy Ghost, even from his mother's womb."* Speaking of Elisabeth, Luke 1:41 says, *"And it came to pass, that, when Elisabeth heard the salutation of Mary, the babe leaped in her womb; and Elisabeth was filled with the Holy Ghost."* Luke 1:67 mentions Zacharias, saying, *"And his father Zacharias was filled with the Holy Ghost, and prophesied."*

Weigh these three experiences with Jesus' words in John 7:39: *"(But this spake he of the Spirit, which they that believe on him should receive: for the Holy Ghost was not yet given; because that Jesus was not yet glorified.)"* Based upon the Messiah's declaration, John and his parents were temporarily filled with the Holy Ghost in their human spirits and not their souls. Additional proof is found in John's doubt of Christ as Messiah. Matthew 11:2-3 reads, *"Now when John had heard in the prison the works of Christ, he sent two of his disciples, And said unto him, Art thou he that should come, or do we look for another?"* The pressure, stress, and agony of prison life had caused John to doubt his earlier experience of seeing the Holy Ghost descend and remain upon Christ at His baptism that he performed.[889] John could doubt his supernatural experience because his soul was not sealed. Indeed, John lacked the greater power in his soul to be an unwavering witness that only the Holy Ghost-baptism could provide. Acts 1:8 identifies this power, saying, *"But ye shall receive power, after that the Holy Ghost is come upon you: and ye shall be witnesses unto me both in Jerusalem, and in all Judaea, and in Samaria, and unto the uttermost part of the earth."*

Three other New Testament passages teach of the temporary anointing of God's Spirit upon the human spirit. Matthew 7:21-23 shows that many persons who had God's anointing temporary will be lost and sent to hell because they chose to work iniquity rather than righteousness. See Chapter 8's parables called "The Wheat and the Tares" and "The Net Cast Into the Sea" for a full study on this passage. Hebrews 6:4-8 describes

889   John 1:32-34

wicked people who temporarily enjoy the blessings of the Holy Spirit. The Hebrews author clearly states these reprobates can be enlightened of the Spirit, taste of heavenly gifts, partake of the Holy Ghost, but still fall away from living a true Christian life. Lastly, Hebrews 10:26-29 speaks of those who sin willfully after receiving the knowledge of the truth. God's *"judgment and fiery indignation"* is against those who serve God with His anointing long enough to be sanctified, but then *"trodden under foot the Son of God"* and live *"despite...the Spirit of grace."*

THE SOUL RECEIVES THE PERMANENT ANOINTING OF THE HOLY GHOST

Using the process of elimination among the three parts of man's being—body, human spirit, and soul—the soul is the only realm of man left that can logically receive the baptism of the Holy Ghost. The body and human spirit have already been ruled out as God's permanent abode. But does Scripture give enough support for the soul as God's permanent dwelling place within man? The answer is a resounding yes.

Contrast David's Old Testament description of God's temporary anointing with New Testament descriptions of the permanent anointing. Psalm 51:11 says, *"Take not thy holy spirit from me,"* implying David knew the feeling of God's anointing leaving him. But Paul's words in Ephesians 4:30 say the seal of the Holy Ghost cannot be taken away and lasts *"unto the day of redemption"*—or, until you die, or your body is changed at the pre-tribulation rapture.

Now insert Jesus' promises for His Spirit to indwell and never leave believers. John 14:16 records Messiah saying, *"And I will pray the Father, and he shall give you another Comforter, that he may abide with you for ever."* Jesus promised believers would know He was living *in* them and that He had made His *"abode"* with them in John 14:20 and 23. Christ's parting words to His disciples in Matthew 28:20 were, *"Lo, I am with you alway, even unto the end of the world."* He would be with them by dwelling inside their souls. Twice in John 17, Jesus says He'll achieve oneness with His disciples by His Spirit living inside them. John 17:23 says, *"I in them, and thou in me, that they may be made perfect in one.*" John 17:26 reads, "*And I have declared unto them thy name, and will declare it: that the love wherewith thou hast loved me may be in them, and I in them.*"

God permanently dwelling in believers' souls is a major part of God's better covenant, as He declares, "*I will dwell in them, and walk in them; and I will be their God, and they shall be my people.*"[890] New Testament saints, permanently born again in their souls, have the benefit of greater obedience, constancy, and stability compared to Old Testament saints because the human will is fully surrendered to God's will. Remember David's fall into the shameful, public adultery with Bathsheba? He lacked the power and stability of baptism of the Holy Ghost in his hour of temptation. Likewise, before Pentecost, Peter fell in a shameful, public denial of Christ while speaking with a lowly maid. The difference for Peter was Pentecost, which was unavailable to David. Before the upper room, Peter even cowardly ran for his life at the threat of arrest, but afterwards he was boldly crucified upside down as a martyr for Christ in 64 A.D..[891] Once filled with the Holy Ghost in his soul, Peter could not deny his Lord and Savior.

WHAT IS THE SOUL?

The soul is defined as the nature, will, or desire of the human spirit. The soul is closely connected to the human spirit, but is separate from it. The soul is the inside core of the human spirit.

From birth to the age of accountability, every human soul has a holy thirst for God. Psalm 42:2 says, "*My soul thirsteth for God, the living God.*" This was by God's perfect design because He wants fellowship with His creation. Just as the body has an innate, natural thirst for water, so the soul has an innate, spiritual thirst for God's acceptance and fellowship. If the body is denied water, it dies. The soul dies, or is eternally separated from God, if it denies itself fellowship with God's Spirit. Isaiah 26:7-9 beautifully describes the soul's thirst, or desire for God:

---

890   2 Corinthians 6:16
891   "St. Peter the Apostle." *Encyclopedia Britannica*, https://www.britannica.com/biography/Saint-Peter-the-Apostle

"The way of the just is uprightness: thou, most upright, dost weigh the path of the just. Yea, in the way of thy judgments, O LORD, have we waited for thee; the desire of our soul is to thy name, and to the remembrance of thee. With my soul have I desired thee in the night; yea, with my spirit within me will I seek thee early: for when thy judgments are in the earth, the inhabitants of the world will learn righteousness."

The Lord built this holy thirst into each person's soul so all *"are without excuse"* on the Day of Judgment. Romans 1:18-21 teaches God manifests Himself to all men through the amazing design of their human bodies and the indescribable majesty of the heavens, earth, and universe. These three elements—holy thirst, design of the human body, and majestic universe—form an undeniable group of witnesses to God's unfathomable love for His creation. Paul speaks truth when he says, *"But God, who is rich in mercy, for his great love wherewith he loved us."* No man will be able to say God did not love him because Christ has provided witnesses both within—holy thirst, design of the human body—and without man—creation.

The holy thirst in every soul produces a longing to worship. Every person in every culture longs to worship a higher being. No matter how advanced or primitive, wealthy or poor, urban or rural, mankind longs to worship and does worship someone or something. Most often, men try to satisfy this thirst with false religion because it pleases their selfish, fleshly, and sinful desires. But God searches the earth until He identifies small groups of honest worshippers who will not stop searching until they find His true spiritual Water that alone quenches the spiritual thirst inside them. Peter preached this truth in Acts 10:34-35, saying, *"Of a truth I perceive that God is no respecter of persons: But in every nation he that feareth him, and worketh righteousness, is accepted with him."* Jesus says the Father is seeking true worshippers.[892] Zechariah 4:10 agrees, saying God's eyes *"run to and fro through the whole earth."* 2 Chronicles 16:9 also describes that God's eyes searching the whole earth in order *"to shew himself strong in the behalf of them whose heart is perfect toward him."* Rest assured, the loving Heavenly Father will search out and find every soul longing for fellowship with Him.

Free moral agency, or the power of autonomous choice, originates within man's soul as a gift from God. Life on earth is a gift, but salvation unto eternal life is an even greater gift and is yours to gain or lose. To accept salvation is to keep your soul; to reject it is to lose your soul as Jesus teaches in Mark 8:36: *"For what shall it profit a man, if he shall gain the whole world, and lose his own soul?"* The Lord does not force any soul to follow Him or repent from his sins, but graciously offers mercy and warnings to all persons.

The soul-nature ultimately directs a person's destiny to heaven or hell. Your soul directs your way, whether it's the correct or erroneous way. James 5:20 reads, *"Let him know, that he which converteth the sinner from the error of his way shall save a soul from death, and shall hide a multitude of sins."* God mercifully gives each person the way, or desire, of their heart. Psalm 37:4 says God gives the righteous the desires of their hearts. Romans 1:28 implies He gives sinners their evil desires, saying, *"And even as they did not like to retain God in their knowledge, God gave them over to a reprobate mind, to do those things which are not convenient."* Those who want to be saved will be, and those who desire a life and eternity without God will receive the same.

Through the soul's free moral agency, every person either chooses faith or unbelief. If faith is chosen, God directs the believer to heaven. If faith is rejected, unbelief is the default state of the unbeliever and Satan directs him to hell. Unbelief is the absence, or rejection of faith in God. Continual sin leads to complete unbelief. To reject faith is the ultimate, final sin because it determines a person's eternal destiny. Ezekiel 18:4 says, *"the soul that sinneth, it shall die."* Sinning means missing the mark, or wandering from the way in Hebrew. Therefore, it is man's soul, via free moral agency, that chooses every action. The soul either does good (faith) or evil (unbelief). Romans 2:9-10 confirm this, saying, *"Tribulation and anguish, upon every soul of man that doeth evil, of the Jew first, and also of the*

Gentile; But glory, honour, and peace, to every man that worketh good, to the Jew first, and also to the Gentile."

Every soul worships someone or something. The souls of faith-rejectors chose to disbelieve God, but their soul still worships Satan according to their own wills. Appropriately, Paul calls all false worship "will worship" in Colossians 2:23 after condemning the worship of angels and legalistic teachings in verses 16-22. Will worship, or worshipping in self will, is the default mode of soul worship for all who reject God's requirements for true worship. Jesus teaches true worshippers *must*—not should—worship in Spirit and in truth in John 4:24: "God is a Spirit: and they that worship him must worship him in spirit and in truth." Cain is the first human will worship example in Genesis 4:1-7. Instead of being happy that God had accepted his brother Abel's offering and following his example to please God, Cain became "very wroth" against God. The merciful God offered Cain another chance at true worship through obedience and the opportunity to be spiritual head of his brother, but he flatly refused God's counsel. Cain then murdered Abel and lied about it to God. Worshipping like Cain in self will, according to your own requirements, is a soul-damning decision. This is why Cain is called the son of Satan in 1 John 3:11-12: "For this is the message that ye heard from the beginning, that we should love one another. Not as Cain, who was of that wicked one, and slew his brother. And wherefore slew he him? Because his own works were evil, and his brother's righteous."

Cain foolishly rejected the simple way to salvation. John 14:6 says Jesus is God's one way to salvation—"I am the way, the truth, and the life"—and Isaiah 35:8 says this way is so simple a fool will not error therein: "And an highway shall be there, and a way, and it shall be called The way of holiness; the unclean shall not pass over it; but it shall be for those: the wayfaring men, though fools, shall not err therein."

IMAGERY AND FORESHADOWING OF THE SOUL RECEIVING THE BAPTISM OF THE HOLY GHOST

Scripture uses at least eight images with corresponding Old Testament foreshadowing to help us understand how the soul, or human nature, is born again. All eight representations are fulfilled simultaneously at the moment a Christian is born again.

The soul needs filled with God's nature. More than 10 times the New Testament mentions believers being filled with the Holy Ghost, which suggests man's soul, or will, begins *empty* of the divine nature. Without the full anointing of God's Spirit, the human soul only has a finite, human nature, which ultimately leads itself to destruction. Ephesians 2:3 says we *"were by nature the children of wrath"* before our conversions to Christianity. But beginning in Acts 2:4, believers were *filled* with the divine nature, or divine will of God, and were appropriately described as having *"one soul."*[893] The fourth verse of 2 Peter 1 states this truth plainly, saying Christians are now *"partakers of the divine nature."* Paul likens believers unto vessels that must be *"filled with the Spirit,"* having previously been sanctified, ready for the Master's use.[894] Similarly, Jesus likens believers unto houses that must be cleaned out of devils in Matthew 12:29, 43-45. The obvious implication is that our houses, or bodies, must be filled with the Holy Ghost.

Elisha's miracle of filling the widow woman's borrowed pots with oil in 2 Kings 4:1-7 foreshadows the filling of the Holy Ghost. In the New Testament, God will fill every "empty vessel," or soul, who comes to Him to be filled and He'll only stop when no more Gentiles seek His Spirit.

The soul needs sealed or marked as God's eternal property. Seven New Testament Scriptures call the baptism of the Holy Ghost a seal, and in the Greek it means both a "mark" and a "sealing up." Both definitions accurately depict what happens at the new birth. God's abiding Spirit becomes a permanent property-mark or stamp on the

---

893   Acts 4:32
894   Ephesians 5:18, 2 Timothy 2:21

believer's soul, keeping it from being marked or claimed by Satan. God puts His spiritual mark upon His children as a token they've received His New Testament Covenant.

It's also a seal to close up the soul like an envelope until it reaches its heavenly home after death. God's will is sealed in to the soul while Satan's will is sealed out. Beginning with Cain, sinners have been taking Satan's mark on their souls. Romans 1:18-32 and 2 Thessalonians 2:9-14 detail how Satan' mark comes as the "point of no return" when sinners reject God's truth for the last time. In return, God gives them over to their reprobate minds, letting them believe lies unto their own destruction because they loved not the truth.

Ephesians 4:30 says God seals His divine nature into the Christian *"unto the day of redemption."* This eternal seal lasts longer than the time from one annual church revival event to the next. It lasts forever, without end because God's seal is His Holy Spirit, which is the one and only eternal Spirit. As you'll soon see in 1 John 3:9, unbelief is sealed out of the soul and faith is sealed in.

Ezekiel 9:1-7 foreshadows the marking of the Holy Spirit, comparing it to a scribe marking faithful believers who sighed and cried against abominations. Kings sealed off their gardens and fountains in Bible times. Solomon likens his wife to a sealed garden and fountain in Song of Solomon 4:12: *"A garden inclosed is my sister, my spouse; a spring shut up, a fountain sealed."* This foreshadows Jesus sealing off His spouse, the bride, the New Testament church, with the soul-seal of the Holy Ghost.

The soul needs clothed in divine power. In Luke 24:49, Jesus says the Holy Ghost baptism is a garment of power, for the Spirit is power. Luke 4:14 says, *"And Jesus returned in the power of the Spirit into Galilee."* Man's sinful soul is naked, or lacking divine power. In Colossians 3:7-10, Paul calls this sinful, powerless soul the *"old man"* and says his works are *"anger, wrath, malice, blasphemy"*, among other sins. The *"old man"* must be *"put off"*, or taken off like a garment, and the *"new man"* must be *"put on."* The Holy Ghost baptism is power to do God's will. The apostle admonishes believers to *"put ye on the Lord Jesus Christ, and make not provision for the flesh, to fulfil the lusts thereof."*[895]

Additionally, sinful souls are spiritually naked after death, meaning they lack a celestial, eternal body, also called a theophany. Paul teaches this in 2 Corinthians 5:1-5, saying believers groan to be clothed with their celestial or heavenly bodies. Souls of sinners are *"found naked"*, void of the clothing of the Spirit's power.

Elisha receiving Elijah's mantle, or anointing, in 2 Kings 2:14 foreshadows the soul-clothing of the baptism of the Holy Ghost.

The soul needs its unbelief removed or circumcised. In Romans 2:28-29, Paul claims the Holy Ghost-filled Christian is a spiritual Jew, having the *"circumcision...of the heart, in the spirit."* He again teaches this truth in Philippians 3:3 and Colossians 2:11, saying, *"We are the circumcision, which worship God in the spirit"* and have *"the circumcision of Christ."* Indeed, it is Christ Who uses His Sword, the Word, to permanently cut off the evil desires of the human will, severing it from the soul, never to return again.

Abraham's circumcision in Genesis 17:1-14 was a sign of the covenant between he and God, foreshadowing the soul-circumcision of the New Testament Christian.

The soul needs born or brought forth from above. A birth is a bringing forth, a start of new life. Your first birth, from your mother's womb, is your natural birth. But Christ promised and required heavenly birth for your soul, saying, *"Ye must be born again"* in John 3:7. In the Greek Lexicon *"again"* means *"from above."*[896] Your body birthed on earth was your first birth, through your father's corruptible seed. But your soul's birth from heaven is another birth experience, through your Heavenly Father's seed. 1 Peter 1:23 plainly states, *"Being born again, not of corruptible seed, but of incorruptible, by the word of God, which liveth and abideth for ever."* Your body will die and perish, but your soul will live eternally because it has God's own life, or seed. 1 John 3:9 boldly claims your soul *cannot* sin because its seed-life is

895   Romans 13:14
896   "The Bible: Hebrew and Greek Lexicons." *Voice of God Recordings*, www.branham.org/en/messagesearch

from God: "*Whosoever is born of God doth not commit sin; for his seed remaineth in him: and he cannot sin, because he is born of God.*" The apostle Paul taught his flesh and mind sinned, but not himself—his soul. Romans 7:17 states, "*Now then it is no more I that do it, but sin that dwelleth in me.*"

The born again soul is a new spiritual creature like a natural baby is a new creature. It's a start of a new life—eternal life. 2 Corinthians 5:17 says, "*Therefore if any man be in Christ, he is a new creature: old things are passed away; behold, all things are become new.*" Indeed, God's foreknowledge knew you'd desire the new birth, so He foreordained it in His will. Like first time parents plan for and eagerly anticipate their first child's arrival, your Heavenly Father planned your spiritual birth in His will at the perfect time and season. John 1:12-13 says sons of God are born again "*not of blood, nor of the will of the flesh, nor of the will of man, but of God.*"

Seth, son of Adam and Eve, foreshadows the New Testament new birth. Eve said Seth was "*another seed*", or second seed from God, to replace "*Abel, whom Cain slew.*"[897] Eve needed a new creature, a new son. Christians need another seed, a second seed, an Incorruptible Seed from above, in order to be a new creature. Seth was actually the second seed of Adam, as Cain was the seed of the serpent according to Genesis 3:15 and 1 John 3:12. Chapter 10 details the serpent's seed and Cain's true father.

The soul needs quickened or made alive through God's eternal life. Your human soul has a supernatural life, but doesn't have the fullness of eternal life until it's born again. Your soul receives a faith-seed for salvation through preaching, but the seed needs "*quickened*"[898], or "made alive", according to the Greek. In order for a natural seed to grow, it needs three conditions met: light, water, and fertile soil. The seed cannot be quickened until all three conditions are present. Likewise, the spiritual seed in your soul is quickened when the three following conditions are met.

897 Genesis 4:25
898 Ephesians 2:5

The Word-seed in a believer's soul needs spiritual light, soil, and water to be quickened, and these conditions were met on the Day of Pentecost. Spiritual light is the knowledge of Jesus' work on the cross that Paul says shined in our hearts. 2 Corinthians 4:6 reads, *"For God, who commanded the light to shine out of darkness, hath shined in our hearts, to give the light of the knowledge of the glory of God in the face of Jesus Christ."* This spiritual light shined brightly upon dark hearts as Peter preached to the 17 nationalities in Acts 2:14-36. The second condition is fertile soil, which Jesus says is *"an honest and good heart"* in Luke 8:15. This condition was met at Pentecost when the new believer's hearts were *"pricked"* in Acts 2:37, leading to their repentance and water baptism in the name of Jesus Christ. Spiritual water is the third and final condition which represents the Holy Spirit that fell on the Day of Pentecost. Peter said this divine Water was poured out upon he and the other 119 believers in the upper room in Acts 2:17. After Peter's Pentecost sermon, the spiritual water fell upon the new believers shortly after their water baptisms because Scripture says 3,000 souls were added to the church that very day.

Aaron's dead rod that budded overnight in the Holiest of Holies in Numbers 17:8 foreshadows the baptism of the Holy Ghost. The lifeless rod received resurrection power in the third realm of Moses' Tabernacle, typing the Third Work of Grace. The Outer Court and Holy Place type justification and sanctification, respectively.

The soul needs immersed or baptized in God's nature. The Son of God Himself depicted the born again experience as a spiritual *"baptism"* for the soul in Acts 1:5: *"But ye shall be baptized with the Holy Ghost not many days hence."* The human soul is fully immersed in God's nature, or will, when it's born again. As Ezekiel says, this divine nature will *"cause"* you to keep God's commands just like water causes a seed to carry out its genetic code.

Reverting to the seed imagery, water is one of the three elements a seed needs to germinate, but the right amount of water is essential. Too much water and the seed dies waterlogged lacking oxygen. Too little water and the seed coat remains hard and doesn't germinate. But when evenly moist soil surrounds the seed, this baptism causes life to spring forth.

Naaman's bodily cleansing after his seventh dip, or baptism, in the Jordan River in 2 Kings 5:14 foreshadows our spiritual cleansing through the Holy Ghost baptism.

The soul needs rest for doing its own will. The Lord Jesus Christ specifically preached His promise to give rest for our souls in Matthew 11:28-29: *"Come unto me, all ye that labour and are heavy laden, and I will give you rest. Take my yoke upon you, and learn of me; for I am meek and lowly in heart: and ye shall find rest unto your souls."* Without Christ's rest, all souls are restless, working to feel justified with God. The human will labors in vain to try to do good deeds, but ultimately fails. All religions outside of Christianity, including all nonreligious self help programs are self-serving, self-motivated, and selfish. They all do man's will rather than God's.

Judaism is called the *"deeds of the law"* in Romans 3:20 because all human deeds and efforts of sinful, fallible flesh cannot be justified in God's sight. It's true the law is holy, just, and spiritual but we are carnal, *"sold under sin."*[899] What the human will needs is a rest from its carnal will and a full submission and obedience to the will of God. This privilege is provided by the baptism of the Holy Ghost.

Another way to express being *"sold under sin"* is slavery, or the *"spirit of bondage."* The soul is under slavery, labor, and bondage until it's set free by the Holy Ghost baptism, appropriately called *"the Spirit of adoption"* in Romans 8:15. You're officially adopted into God's family as His child through the new birth. Paul says in Galatians 4:5 we receive the *"adoption of sons."* You can rest knowing you're a child of God with a family kinship to Him, and not a slave. Romans 8:23 tells you the adoption process is completed when you receive your new, glorified body: *"And not only they, but ourselves also, which have the firstfruits of the Spirit, even we ourselves groan within ourselves, waiting for the adoption, to wit, the redemption of our body."*

899 Romans 7:12-14

Hebrews 4:1-12 beautifully explains the New Testament rest for the soul. The author gives two examples of resting—God resting from His creative work on the seventh day, and most of Israel failing to enter into their rest in the Promised Land—before urging Christians to labor to enter into the new rest for *"the people of God."* This rest must be both the same rest Christ promised in Matthew 11:29 and a new rest different from the Sabbath day Moses instituted in Exodus 20. The New Testament rest is ceasing from your own works and doing God's works. Hebrews 4:10 validates this: *"For he that is entered into his rest, he also hath ceased from his own works, as God did from his."* In Colossians 1:29, Paul states his labors are God's Spirit laboring through him: *"Whereunto I also labour, striving according to his working, which worketh in me mightily."*

You must know the New Testament Sabbath is not resting every Saturday, as Seventh Day Adventists teach. While you should rest your body while worshipping with other believers every Sunday like Acts 20:7 and Hebrews 10:25 show, the baptism of the Holy Ghost is the soul-rest Jesus promised—not a body rest. Old Testament saints already had the body rest under the 4th Commandment. Colossians 2:16-17 state Saturday Sabbath days were a *"shadow of things to come."* Isaiah boldly prophesied the shadow, or Saturday Sabbath, would vanish on the Day of Pentecost by saying, *"This is the rest"* in Isaiah 28:11-12. The prophet foretold the real, soul-rest would be stammering lips spoken to God's people. Paul says Isaiah's prophecy was fulfilled on the Day of Pentecost in 1 Corinthians 14:21. In the born again experience, a Christian rests or walks according to the Spirit and does not fulfill the lusts of the flesh. For the remainder of his Christian walk, the believers rests or ceases from sinful habits and establishes holy habits. Now that's a true rest!

The New Testament soul-rest gives believers the *potential* (but it remains impossible due to our bodily sin-nature) to always obey God's Word if we only wait and listen for God's Spirit to speak to us in every situation. This is true because our souls cannot sin or disbelieve once baptized with the Holy Ghost. Recall 1 John 3:9: *"Whosoever is born of God doth not commit sin; for his seed remaineth in him: and he cannot sin, because he is born of God.*" But of course, we don't wait and pray enough on a daily basis. We often choose to make decisions based upon the feelings of the flesh or human spirit, rather than the soul. The greatest lessons in life are learning to listen to and rest upon the revelations from God's Spirit in our souls. Listen to God first, then act. Wait upon His leading. Calm yourself to hear the still, small Voice in your soul. You'll never regret resting from your works and doing God's.

Truly, the rest Jesus offers you today is a glorious soul-rest, one in which Isaiah promised 800 years before Emanuel came. Isaiah 11:10 reads, "*And in that day there shall be a root of Jesse, which shall stand for an ensign of the people; to it shall the Gentiles seek: and his rest shall be glorious.*" By the Holy Ghost baptism, we partake in the divine, glorious rest of God.

Ruth's rest while waiting for Boaz to finish the kinsman redeemer work foreshadows the baptism of the Holy Ghost. Her life fits the Three Works of Grace framework. She was first justified, or saved, after deciding to believe and follow Naomi's God, Jehovah. Secondly, her sanctification came as she served and labored in Boaz's field, gleaning every ear of corn to ensure Naomi's and her own survival. Ruth 3:18 records Naomi's wisdom for Ruth to rest in Boaz's redemption work: "*Then said she, Sit still, my daughter, until thou know how the matter will fall: for the man will not be in rest, until he have finished the thing this day.*" Christians do the same, resting from their own works and trusting in the finished work of Jesus' cross and resurrection.

To conclude this imagery section, Scripture offers numerous symbols for the Holy Ghost, including, but not limited to:

- Oil (1 Samuel 16:13, Zechariah 4:1-6, 11-14, Matthew 25:1-13)
- Dove (Matthew 3:16)
- Water (John 4:14, 7:37-39, Revelation 22:17)
- Rain (Acts 14:17)
- Fire (Acts 2:3-4)
- Wind (John 3:8)

- Standard (Isaiah 59:19)
- Clothes (Luke 24:49)
- Quickened seed (1 Peter 1:23)

REFILLINGS OF THE HOLY GHOST HAPPEN IN THE HUMAN SPIRIT

You may hear preachers or believers say they were "refilled" with the Holy Ghost. Based upon Scripture, a refilling of the Holy Ghost can only happen in the human spirit and not the soul. 2 Corinthians 4:16 and Ephesians 4:23 teach your human spirit can have a fresh refilling, or renewing. These Scriptures say you're renewed daily *"in the spirit of your mind."*

No Scripture teaches souls are refilled or reborn after the initial fill-ing or birth. Ephesians 4:30 says the seal of God lasts until your day of redemption—not for a year or until the next church revival meeting. God's seal marks and protects you until you die and cross over into the heavenly dimension, or until your physical body gets *"swallowed up"*[900] in a glorified body at the pre-tribulation rapture.

Some may read the context of Acts 4:31 and think souls can be refilled with the Holy Ghost, but careful examination and Scriptural comparison leads us to believe differently. Peter and John had returned to their *"company"*, or fellow Christians, after being threatened to stop speaking in Jesus' name. After loud group prayer, the Holy Ghost shook the building *"and they were all filled with the Holy Ghost."* Some in the company may have received the Holy Ghost baptism for the first time, but not all, and certainly not Peter and John. Acts 1:13 says Peter and John were among the group that was already filled with the Holy Ghost when the Spirit fell in Acts 2:4. This means Peter and John got a Spirit-refilling in their human spirits to refresh their minds, but not another soul-sealing because their soul baptism in Acts 2:4 lasted *"unto the day of redemption."*

900   1 Corinthians 15:51-54

THE SOUL OF THE OLD TESTAMENT BELIEVER

Since only New Testament believers can have their souls filled, sealed, clothed, circumcised, born, quickened, baptized, and at rest, what did Old Testament saints have in their souls? The answer is faith. Hebrews 11:1 describes faith as a spiritual *"substance"*, or a small portion of God's Spirit.

Abraham, *"the father of us all"*[901], can be used as an example to illustrate an Old Testament believer's soul-change from unbelief to faith. Yet, according to Jesus, the Holy Ghost could not be given in full measure to Abraham.

Like all persons, Abraham was born a sinner, or unbeliever, with an inherent sin-nature. David wrote, *"Behold, I was shapen in iniquity; and in sin did my mother conceive me."*[902] Romans 3:23 reads, *"For all have sinned, and come short of the glory of God."* Abraham was raised in *"Ur of the Chaldees"*[903], a southern Babylonian city. Even as a sinner, Abraham's soul was thirsting for God, but barren of faith. Therefore, his soul was in the state of unbelief, yet thirsting for truth.

One wonderful day in Mesopotamia *"the God of glory appeared"*[904] to Abraham (although he was still known as Abram until Genesis 17:5) and in his free moral agency received God's Word, becoming a believer. Abraham freely chose to believe God and now had faith in God, which set his way, or course, to acceptance with God in heaven. Indeed, Abraham had been converted *"from the error of his way"* according to James 5:20. Hebrews 11:8-10 details how *"by faith"* his faith-infused soul directed his earthly course:

> *"By faith Abraham, when he was called to go out into a place which he should after receive for an inheritance, obeyed; and he went out, not knowing whither he went. By faith he sojourned in the land of promise, as in a strange country, dwelling in tabernacles with Isaac and Jacob, the heirs with him of the same*

901   Romans 4:16
902   Psalm 51:5
903   Genesis 11:28
904   Acts 7:2

promise: For he looked for a city which hath foundations, whose builder and maker is God."

Lot, Abraham's nephew, undoubtedly experienced this same salvation in his soul. 2 Peter 2:7-9 says Lot was a *"righteous man"* with a *"righteous soul."* Faith in his soul directed his earthly course to resist and rightfully accuse the Sodomites of their wickedness.[905] God then mercifully[906] delivered him from the judgment of Sodom and Gomorrah.

Figuratively, the Seed of God's Word had fallen upon Abraham's soul, but not yet quickened. The Seed contained powerful potential to produce great fruits of the Spirit, but could not due to the spiritual conditions of Abraham's lifetime.

A natural seed lays dormant until three conditions are met: sufficient water, light, and fertile soil. The spiritual Seed of God's Word also needs three conditions met. In Abraham's lifetime, two of the three spiritual conditions needed to quicken the Seed in his soul were unavailable. The Water of the Spirit was available to believers, as you've already read of numerous Old Testament saints being powerfully anointed of the Holy Spirit in their human spirits. God graciously anointed believers' minds and bodies who longed for His presence. But spiritual Light and fertile soul were unavailable.

Spiritual Light is knowledge of Jesus Christ and forgiveness of sins through His cross.[907] Jesus' cross and pardoning blood were nearly 2,000 years in the future ahead of Abraham, and thus, unavailable. Spiritually fertile soil was unavailable, too, because of the weakness of animal sacrifices. Jesus says a fertile heart is *"an honest and good heart"* in Luke 8:15. According to Hebrews 9:9-14, Abraham's flesh could be purified after animal sacrifice, but his human spirit, or heart, didn't completely feel *"good."* Specifically, Abraham's conscience could not be fully purged *"from dead works to serve the living God."* Imagine Abraham sacrificing and worshipping in sincerity trusting he was *"forgiven"* and righteous in

---

905   Genesis 19:7
906   Genesis 19:16
907   Acts 26:18, 2 Corinthians 4:6

God's sight by meeting His requirements,[908] but leaving his altar with an unclean, guilty conscience remembering his past sins.

After each of Abraham's animal sacrifices, Hebrews 10:3-4 says there was a "*remembrance again...of sins every year*" because it was "*not possible that the blood of bulls and of goats should take away sins.*" Animal blood purged the flesh, but not the human spirit. With an unclean human spirit, God could not baptize Abraham's human spirit with His Spirit, let alone his soul. It's clear the conditions for the soul-baptism weren't right.

The remembrance of sins is observable in the lives of Old Testament saints, especially in Job and David. Job 9:2 and 33 show Job's desire to feel "*just with God*" through a mediator that would bring peace between he and God. That Mediator would later come as Jesus Christ, the "*one mediator between God and men.*"[909] Job's many previous animal sacrifices were accepted by God[910], but it wasn't possible for the blood of those animals to make Job feel truly justified. Job knew he lacked a Person—his Mediator, Jesus Christ. David knew he lacked the same, echoing similar thoughts in Psalm 130:3 and 143:2. Israel's king asked, "*If thou, LORD, shouldest mark iniquities, O Lord, who shall stand?*" David said, "*In thy sight shall no man living be justified.*" Paul said the law couldn't justify believers like Job and David when he said, "*Therefore by the deeds of the law there shall no flesh be justified in his sight.*"[911] Job and David's words explain their lack of rest, or lack of the Holy Ghost baptism. But to their credit, God was hiding it from every Old Testament age and generation.

In accordance with the forth coming "Paradise and the Keys of Death and Hell" section, Abraham and the Old Testament saints lived a life subject to bondage and the fear of death due to the weakness of animal sacrifices. But this fit into the plan of God to magnify the power of Jesus' blood. The law was a teacher, a "*schoolmaster to bring us unto Christ.*"[912] Weak animal sacrifices emphasize the need for the powerful, sinless, holy sacrifice of Christ.

908   Romans 4:3-8
909   1 Timothy 2:5
910   Job 1:5,8
911   Romans 3:20
912   Galatians 3:24

Before the cross, Satan stood before God like a cruel lawyer accusing all believers of sins based upon God's own law. Lucifer is rightly named *"the accuser of our brethren."*[913] Colossians 2:14 makes it seem Satan had compiled a written record of the sins of the Old Testament saints as *"handwriting of ordinances that was against"* them. Thankfully, Jesus' death blotted out the handwriting, taking it *"out of the way, nailing it to his cross."* Indeed, all the evidence of our sins was nailed to His cross and taken *"out of the way."* Isaiah 53:6 rightly declares, *"The LORD hath laid on him the iniquity of us all."* Our ransom, or sin-debt, was paid-in-full by the substitutionary sacrifice of Jesus Christ. Three Scriptures say Jesus gave His life as a ransom payment for all sinners.[914]

Returning to Abraham and Lot, both men had righteous souls by obeying God's animal sacrifice-requirements, but their degree of dedication to God's Word and separation from sin differed. Abraham lived in total surrender to God while Lot pitched his tent toward Sodom before eventually becoming a resident in the sin-saturated city. Lot's testimony only produced the saving of two souls out of Sodom (his virgin daughters) before its destruction. Previous to losing his wife to the pillar-of-salt-condemnation and his other daughters and son-in-laws in the fire and brimstone, Lot experienced daily vexation from everything he saw and heard in Sodom.[915] Abraham's life was peaceful; not of torment, as Lot's was. Genesis 18:19 and 26:5 portray the father-of-faith patriarch as an obedient, diligent teacher and keeper of God's commands among his family and household servants.

Recalling the Stature of a Perfect Man from Chapter 5, Abraham and Lot both advanced in character, adding traits to their faith. With souls anointed with faith, both men yielded their humans spirits to God's service. It seems Abraham obtained the seventh trait, brotherly kindness, because he rescued Lot from the kings, gave Lot the first choice on land to inhabit, and then dramatically interceded with God for Lot and the believers' souls in Sodom. Abraham's soul, though, couldn't be

---

913 Revelation 12:10
914 Matthew 20:28, Mark 10:45, 1 Timothy 2:6
915 Genesis 19:14-26, 2 Peter 2:7-8

born again due to weakness of the law and animal blood. It's likely Lot only reached the fourth trait, temperance, because he was not content living away from Sodom's riches (impatient), purposely lived amongst the ungodly Sodomites (ungodly), and took the first choice of land to inhabit rather than allowing his elder uncle the first choice (lacked brotherly kindness). Like Jesus' disciples, Old Testament saints could gain and lose the divine character qualities in their human spirits.

SOUL REDEMPTION THROUGH CHRIST'S BLOOD

Peter writes of both the soul's redemption through Christ's blood and its purification by the Spirit in his first epistle. He declares Christians *"were not redeemed with corruptible things, as silver and gold...But with the precious blood of Christ, as of a lamb without blemish and without spot."*[916] In the Greek, "redeemed" means "to release on receipt of ransom" and "liberate by payment of ransom; to cause to be released to one's self by payment of a ransom, to deliver." New Testament saints experience liberated souls, meaning the souls of Old Testament saints were not yet released from Satan's authority. Hence, all believing souls in the Old Testament were kept in Abraham's bosom in the heart of earth, separated only by a great chasm from the unbelievers in hell. The devil had brought all men's souls into bondage to sin by overcoming Adam in Eden. Jesus' self-sacrificial blood literally purchased the believers' souls back to God. Acts 20:28 says Christ purchased the church *"with his own blood."* Since the wages of sin was death,[917] death of an innocent substitute was lawful payment, or ransom, for the redemption of believing souls. Matthew 20:28 says *"the Son of man came not to be ministered unto, but to minister, and to give his life a ransom for many."* Friend, Jesus' blood bought your soul. You *"are bought with a price: therefore glorify God in your body, and in your spirit, which are God's."*[918]

Now that Christ's blood has paid-in-full the ransom for every believing soul, there's *"now no condemnation to them which are in Christ*

916　1 Peter 1:18-19
917　Romans 6:23
918　1 Corinthians 6:20

Jesus, who walk not after the flesh, but after the Spirit."[919] New Testament believers can serve God with great freedom and liberty through a clean, holy conscience. Hebrews 9:14 reads, "*How much more shall the blood of Christ, who through the eternal Spirit offered himself without spot to God, purge your conscience from dead works to serve the living God?*" If Abraham could faithfully command and teach others God's will with a defiled conscience, "*how much more*" should we serve our living God through the conscience-purging blood of Jesus Christ? Let us serve Him in complete liberation from condemnation. Romans 5:1 rings true: "*Therefore being justified by faith, we have peace with God through our Lord Jesus Christ.*"

PARADISE AND THE KEYS OF DEATH AND HELL

Before Calvary, Satan held the keys of death and hell. Hebrews 2:14 labels Satan's keys as the "*power of death*" since they are not literal keys, but spiritual authority. Satan earned the keys by beguiling Eve into sinning which was followed by Adam's willful sin.[920] Through the fall, Satan conquered Adam, God's chosen ruler of the earth,[921] and all mankind came into bondage to Satan and sin according to God's law. 2 Peter 2:19 says, "*For of whom a man is overcome, of the same is he brought in bondage.*"

For the next 4,000 years after Adam during the Old Testament, mankind lived under this bondage and "*fear of death*"[922] as slaves to sin.

Thankfully, another portion of God's law, written in heaven before written on earth,[923] provided forgiveness of sins through the shedding of innocent blood. This was certainly one of the "*better promises*"![924] Hebrews 9:22 declares, "*Without shedding of blood is no remission.*" Substituting innocent blood in payment for someone else's sin is called a ransom, or price for redeeming. God ordained animal sacrifices to provide a temporary covering for sin in the Old Testament, but not a total abolishment of sin. Truly, the blood of bulls and goats could never

---

919   Romans 8:1
920   1 Timothy 2:14
921   Genesis 1:26-28
922   Hebrews 2:15
923   Psalm 119:89
924   Hebrews 8:6

take away sins,[925] which allowed Satan to use the keys of death to keep all believers captive in the heart of the earth after their deaths.

Animal sacrifices were limited in power, only purifying the flesh and not the human spirit, or conscious of man. Since a human (Adam) caused the fall, a human life—not an animal life—had to pay the ransom for sin. 1 Corinthians 15:21-22 verify this, saying, *"For since by man came death, by man came also the resurrection of the dead. For as in Adam all die, even so in Christ shall all be made alive."* A holy, human sacrifice was needed to obtain eternal redemption for us and pay the full ransom for sin. Where could God get a holy, sinless human being to become a willing offering for all humanity's sins?

God in His Spirit form could not die and shed blood, so He prepared Himself a body, His Son, and Jesus willingly died on the cross *"to give his life a ransom for many."*[926] Just as God provided Himself a sacrifice to save Abraham's natural seed, Isaac, God again provided His own sacrifice for Abraham's spiritual seed, the New Testament church. Hebrews 9:12-14 validates this, saying,

"Neither by the blood of goats and calves, but by his own blood he entered in once into the holy place, having obtained eternal redemption for us. For if the blood of bulls and of goats, and the ashes of an heifer sprinkling the unclean, sanctifieth to the purifying of the flesh: How much more shall the blood of Christ, who through the eternal Spirit offered himself without spot to God, purge your conscience from dead works to serve the living God?"

In the next chapter, Hebrews 10:1-18, these truths are expounded upon. God prepared a body for Himself, since Jesus is called *"Emmanuel,"* meaning "God with us" in the Greek. By Jesus' crucifixion, *"we are sanctified through the offering of the body of Jesus Christ once and for all."*[927] Jesus' pure, sinless life made Him the one and only acceptable sacrifice

925   Hebrews 10:4
926   Matthew 20:28
927   Hebrews 10:10

unto God, allowing our sins and iniquities to be completely abolished. Hebrews 10:14, 17-18 reads, *"For by one offering he hath perfected for ever them that are sanctified…And their sins and iniquities will I remember no more. Now where remission of these is, there is no more offering for sin."*

Hebrews 2:14-18 brings a great climax to this section, pronouncing Jesus' death destroyed Satan's hold on the Old Testament saints and delivered them from bondage. Hebrews 2:14-16 reads,

> *"Forasmuch then as the children are partakers of flesh and blood, he also himself likewise took part of the same; that through death he might destroy him that had the power of death, that is, the devil; And deliver them who through fear of death were all their lifetime subject to bondage. For verily he took not on him the nature of angels; but he took on him the seed of Abraham."*

By Jesus paying the sin ransom with His holy blood, He destroyed Satan's influence over mankind.

As Jesus' dead body lay in Joseph of Arimathaea's tomb, Christ went by the Spirit to hell,[928] located in the *"heart of the earth,"*[929] and took the keys of death and hell from Satan. Christ now possessed the power of death. This was a total surprise attack and raid upon hell! Neither Satan nor the kings of the earth had predicted Jesus' redemption of the keys of death and hell that Adam forfeited. 1 Corinthians 2:7-8 says *"none of the princes of this world knew: for had they known it, they would not have crucified the Lord of glory."* If Herod, Pilate, and especially Satan had known what Jesus would accomplish after His death, they would not have helped crucify Him. But God brilliantly hid Jesus' raid on hell and subsequent resurrection in one of the 23,000 Old Testament verses. Psalm 16:10 contains one of God's better promises—Jesus seizing the keys of death and hell. David, speaking of Christ, wrote, *"For thou wilt not leave my soul in hell; neither wilt thou suffer thine Holy One to see corruption."*

928 1 Peter 3:18-19
929 Matthew 12:40

Satan and the princes of the world didn't understand the ramifications of the Psalm 16:10 prophecy, allowing Jesus to resurrect from the dead. Through Jesus' innocent death, he paid our ransom, conquering death. Acts 2:24 reads Christ *"loosed the pains of death: because it was not possible that he should be holden of it."* Jesus paid our penalty and took death's keys from Satan.

With the keys of death in His hand, Jesus the Lion of the Tribe of Judah, led many of the Old Testament saints, previously dwelling in Abraham's bosom, up to the earth's surface on Easter morning. Christ first opened His grave and then many other graves of the saints who *"came out of the graves after his resurrection, and went into the holy city, and appeared unto many."*[930] Job's prophecy had finally come true! A resurrected Job was standing in a new, glorified body on the earth with his Redeemer, just as his vision predicted nearly 1,600 years before Christ:

> *"For I know that my redeemer liveth, and that he shall stand at the latter day upon the earth: And though after my skin worms destroy this body, yet in my flesh shall I see God: Whom I shall see for myself, and mine eyes shall behold, and not another; though my reins be consumed within me."*[931]

Jesus was seen for 40 days after His resurrection[932] and it seems likely the Old Testament saints were also seen for this time period. Imagine the thrill for believers living in Jerusalem to know they could see a resurrected Christ, as well as a resurrected Abraham, Sarah, Job, Joseph, or David around any corner! But imagine the shame and mental torment for men like Caiphas and Pilate, who might have seen the resurrected ones and heard report after report of Jesus and the saints being alive.

At the conclusion of the 40 day period, Jesus ascended to heaven in a cloud in sight of His apostles[933] to sit at the right hand of the majesty on high. As He went out of their sight, ascending towards His heavenly

---

930   Matthew 27:52-53
931   Job 19:25-27
932   Acts 1:3
933   Acts 1:1-9

throne, He was joined by the resurrected, Old Testament saints. The saints followed their leader, the Son of God, towards glory, as Ephesians 4:8 says, "*When he ascended up on high, he led captivity captive.*" Jesus led captivity captive, meaning He led the Old Testament saints out of captivity from the heart of the earth and into God's possession, or divine captivity.

By God's power, they rose higher and higher until they reached heaven's gates. Psalm 24:7-10 records the dialogue between Christ, the resurrected saints, and the angel-doorkeepers as the resurrected ones arrive at heaven's doors. Jesus' voice shouts, "Lift up your heads, O ye gates; and be ye lift up, ye everlasting doors; and the King of glory shall come in!" The doorkeepers dutifully ask for identification upon entrance into heaven, saying, "Who is this King of glory?" Abraham, Sarah, Job, and the resurrected saints proclaim their King's credentials, saying, "The LORD strong and mighty, the LORD mighty in battle!" How strong, mighty, and glorious was Christ when He was slapped, buffeted, spit on, beaten, scourged, stripped, crucified, and stabbed in obedience to the Father's will. Christ endured the unfathomable brutality and shame of the cross for this moment, the moment of joyfully entering His kingdom with His redeemed, forgiven subjects. Hebrews 12:2 says, "*Looking unto Jesus the author and finisher of our faith; who for the joy that was set before him endured the cross, despising the shame, and is set down at the right hand of the throne of God.*"

The dialogue repeats in Psalm 24:9-10, as Jesus again commands for heaven's gates to be lifted up so the King of glory can enter. The doorkeepers again ask, "Who is this King of glory?" and the resurrected saints declare their Savior, Jesus Christ, as "The LORD of hosts, he is the King of glory!" Jesus is the Lord of hosts, proving His supremacy over all creatures, including the heavenly armies. Did not Jesus say He had the option of asking His Father for 12 legions of angels[934] to appear at His side? The Greek meaning of "legions" is 6,826 men,[935] exacting 12 legions or nearly

934 Matthew 26:53
935 "The Bible: Hebrew and Greek Lexicons." *Voice of God Recordings,* www.branham.org/en/messagesearch

82,000 angels. According to Colossians 1:15-17, Christ is the image of the invisible God, firstborn of every creature, creator of all things, before all things, and by Him all things consist. The Lord Jesus Christ is the King of glory.

Since Jesus' ascension to heaven with the resurrected, Old Testament saints, He has been fulfilling His *"high priest"* office, seated on His heavenly throne making intercession for the saints living on earth.[936] In the New Testament, Satan can no longer empower necromancers, like the witch of Endor, to access believer's souls because they are protected in heaven by the blood of Jesus Christ. God's Son bruised the serpent's head on the cross, crushing his venomous power of death. Life conquered death and now all who believe are freely forgiven all their trespasses. Saints ascend to heaven upon death, rather than descending to the lower parts of the earth.

Paul knew upon his death he would ascend to heaven and put on his eternal body that awaited him there. 2 Corinthians 5:1-2 says, *"For we know that if our earthly house of this tabernacle were dissolved, we have a building of God, an house not made with hands, eternal in the heavens. For in this we groan, earnestly desiring to be clothed upon with our house which is from heaven."* Paradise is no longer in the heart of the earth; it's located in heaven. In 2 Corinthians 12:4, the apostle said he *"was caught up into paradise."* Upon death, Christians' souls ascend up to paradise; not down. Christians are assured to be present with the Lord after leaving their earthly bodies: *"We are confident, I say, and willing rather to be absent from the body, and to be present with the Lord."*[937]

SOULS AND THE BOOK OF LIFE

As illustrated in Jesus' Sower and the Found Grounds parable in Matthew 13:3-9 (See Chapter 8), each soul, or ground, has the opportunity to receive God's Word, or seed. The mysterious truth of the second ground, called the *"stony ground,"* teaches souls (like Judas Iscariot) can

936   Hebrews 7:25-26
937   2 Corinthians 5:8

temporarily receive the Word (faith) and grow thereby for a period of time before ultimately rejecting it, leaving their souls lost and bound for the lake of fire. The stony ground's loss of seed-life explains the oft misunderstood subject of names being blotted out from the Book of Life.

When a name is blotted out of the Book of Life the person loses the gift of salvation. It's true a person can believe in Christ for salvation but later reject Christ, just like a person can receive a Christmas gift but later discard it. Both gifts—salvation and a Christmas present—are given by unmerited grace, but the receiver must accept and keep the gift. Salvation is a promise based upon conditions *"if"* you believe[938] and *"endure unto the end."*[939] Hebrews 10:39 says you must *"believe to the saving of the soul."* Chapter 8 will deal more with this subject in light of Judas Iscariot's falling away from salvation, as John 17:12 says *"none of"* the disciples were *"lost, but the son of perdition."* Jesus said He kept the other 11 disciples, but Judas was lost. Judas was saved, but later forfeited salvation for money. He even obtained part of a Holy Ghost ministry. God took away *"his part out of the book of life"*[940] when he betrayed Christ. You can read Hebrews 6:4-8 and 10:26-29, and 38-39 in the meantime for more of this truth.

Some often repeat the phrase, "Once saved, always saved", but Judas proves this phrase incorrect. The true phrase is, "Once sealed, always sealed", based upon Ephesians 4:30. Once a believer's soul is sealed by the Holy Ghost baptism, he is destined for heaven.

Is there eternal security for Christians? Yes, every Christian who meets God's salvation requirements is eternally secure. Your faith is the evidence of your eternal security. John 10:27-29 says Jesus' sheep hear His voice and He gives them eternal life. Messiah promises, *"No man is able to pluck them out of my Father's hand."* But transgressors, workers of iniquity, the slothful, and wicked have no eternal security because they forfeit eternal life for temporal pleasures of this life.

Four astounding truths exist regarding the Book of Life. First, it's located in heaven and those whose names are on it should rejoice

---

938   Acts 8:37
939   Matthew 24:13
940   Revelation 22:19

according to Luke 10:20. Second, it is the Faithful Witness, the Lord Jesus, Who wrote the Book of Life, but also He alone blots names out according to Exodus 32:32-33, Deuteronomy 29:20, and Revelation 3:5. These Scriptures also teach Christ blots out the names on the grounds of willfully sinning against Him, or failing to overcome the world.

Third, two Scriptures—Revelation 13:8 and 17:8—say all the names within the Book of Life were written *before* the foundation of the world through God's foreknowledge, meaning there is no present compiling of names. Your name wasn't written on the Book of Life the day you were saved, like many believe. Rather, God foreknew you'd be saved and wrote it before the foundation of the world. Revelation 13:8 and 17:8 also reveal the fourth truth that unbelievers' names, or the *"way side"* souls, have never been nor ever will be written on the Book of Life. Figure 18 rightly divides the location of names in heaven's books based upon Jesus' classification of souls into four categories. Obviously, the names of unbelievers are recorded in some heavenly books referred to in Revelation 20:12, but the only Book with eternally-saved names is *"another book, which is the book of life."*

"Good" Souls Matthew 13:23	"Thorny" Souls Matthew 13:22	"Stony" Souls Matthew 13:20-21	"Way" Side Souls Matthew 13:19
Names written in the Lamb's section of the Book of Life before the foundation of the world. Also known as Wise Virgins in Matthew 25:1-13.	Names written in the Book of Life before the foundation of the world and left remaining therein. Also known as Foolish Virgins in Matthew 25:1-13.	Names were written in the Book of Life section before the foundation of the world, but blotted out due to their sins.	Names were never written in the Book of Life, but were recorded in other books.

Figure 18

Both the Old and New Testaments offer examples of names being blotted out of the Book of Life. The Old has three examples and the New alludes to one.

Beginning in the Old, Israel's worship of the golden calf in Exodus 32 serves as the first witness of God blotting out names from the Book of Life. Moses unselfishly stood in the gap for idolatrous Israel, offering for his name to be blotted out instead of Israel's. But *the Lord said unto Moses, whosoever hath sinned against me, him will I blot out of my book."* Hebrews 3:16-19 and Jude 1:5 affirm that many Israelis who fell in the wilderness were lost, their names being blotted out of the Book of Life.

Two of the 12 Tribes of Israel—Dan and Ephraim—had their names blotted out from *"under heaven"*—not *"in heaven"*—for committing idolatry. Dan and Ephraim were listed as part of the 12 sons of Jacob that went into Egypt in Genesis 35:22-26. Both names remained in their tribal order after leaving Egypt in Numbers 10:11-28. But Deuteronomy 29:16-20 had pronounced the blotting-out warning to any Israeli *"who would go and serve the gods of these nations"* saying, *"The Lord shall blot out his name from under heaven."* The tribe of Dan's idolatry is recorded in 1 Kings 12:25-30 and Ephraim's joining to idols is found in Hosea 4:17. The consequences for their idolatry is nearly 3,000 years without tribal recognition, proven in Revelation 7:4-8 as Dan and Ephraim's tribal names are missing from the 144,000 Jews who are marked in their foreheads before the great destructions of the Tribulation. Surprisingly, though, God's amazing grace restores their tribal names in the Millennium according to Ezekiel 48:1-8 and 22-29 because Dan and Ephraim, as literal sons of Jacob, will be resurrected as overcomers to inherit their tribe's portion of land.

The third blotting out took place at the very conclusion of the Old Testament—at Jesus' crucifixion. After Pilate's attempt to wash his hands of guilt and claim his innocence in Jesus' death, *"all the people"* answered him, *"His blood be on us, and on our children."* The Israeli multitude willingly rejected (some ignorantly though, as Jesus prayed for their forgiveness) their own Messiah and Paul says they were *"broken off,"* or cut off, from the life of God, or Holy Spirit, in Romans 11:19. Psalm 69:20-28 prophesied of Christ's Calvary-humiliation, and also the blotting out of the workers of iniquity who consented to Jesus' death. Verse 21 says, *"They gave me also gall for my meat; and in my thirst they gave me vinegar to drink"*, and then verse 28 reads, *"Let them be blotted out of the book of the living, and not be written with the righteous."* Many Jews who rejected Jesus had their names blotted out of the Book of Life. But the apostle reassures us not all Israel is lost, though, saying, *"Even so then at this present time also there is a remnant according to the election of grace."*[941] Even though the majority rejected their Messiah, God still saved the small remnant who worshipped in Spirit and truth.

Judas Iscariot is the New Testament example for an individual's name being blotted out of the Book of Life. Chapter 5 details his reception and eventual rejection of salvation. But now you must know he was *"chosen"*[942] by Christ, believed in Christ,[943] was baptized unto repentance, and baptized others.[944] Judas was commissioned by Christ with the same Holy Ghost-anointed ministry as the other 11 apostles in Luke 9:1-2. Then in Luke 10:17-24, Judas was among the group that Jesus said had their names written in heaven. Sadly, Judas fell from his salvation by the wicked transgression[945] of betrayal, going to *"his own place"*, or hell. Jesus says Judas is lost. He lost his soul, his name's part on the Book of Life. Judas was overcome by the love of money. He didn't overcome sin, and consequently Jesus was required to blot his name off the Book of Life.[946] Had Judas fully repented of his transgression and went to Pentecost to receive the baptism of the Holy Ghost, he would have been eternally sealed. His name could have remained on the Book, but he departed from the faith. Like the stony ground, Judas *"for a while"* believed"[947], but then rejected the truth since he had no *"root in himself"*[948]—no deep, genuine love for Christ—since Paul

941 Romans 11:5
942 John 6:70
943 John 2:11
944 John 4:1-2
945 Acts 1:25
946 Revelation 3:5
947 Luke 8:13
948 Matthew 13:21

says Christians are *"rooted and grounded in love."* Judas let the Word-seed grow a little, making some progress, but later let it die.

While the Book of Life was written *before* the foundation of the world and doesn't have names added to it during human history, there is another heavenly book called the Book of Remembrance that is written in real time before the Lord, in His presence. Its purpose is to record the thoughts, words, and deeds of them that fear the Lord. Malachi 3:15 says, *"Then they that feared the LORD spake often one to another: and the LORD hearkened, and heard it, and a book of remembrance was written before him for them that feared the LORD, and that thought upon his name."* In Hebrew, *"remembrance"* means *"memorial."* Notice godly words and deeds are written therein. Acts 10:3-4 seems to refer to this Book, as *"an angel of God"* tells Cornelius his *"prayers...and alms are come up for a memorial before God."* The Book of Remembrance will be useful in the future assigning of heavenly rewards.

Finishing the Book of Life teaching, there will be a future writing and compilation of names in a book in the New Jerusalem, also called *"mount Sion...the city of the living God"* in Hebrews 12:22. God foreknows all future inhabitants of this holy city. Psalm 87:6 shows God will make a revised roll of names who remained in the Book of Life after the second resurrection: *"The LORD shall count, when he writeth up the people, that this man was born there. Selah."* Herein is the final roll call in heaven. How we want our names to be in that number!

SOUL SEARCHING

You may have heard Christians say they searched their soul for answers in the midst of life's trials. Most likely, we can all relate to a time of soul-searching—a time to make major life decisions like salvation, marriage, family, ending relationships, or moving locations. The Bible calls this "communing with your own heart," as explained by David, Asaph, and Solomon. This truth helps you understand how you can know your soul condition—whether faith is present (the soul is saved) or absent (the soul is lost).

You might also call soul-searching a testing time, or trial of your faith. Peter admits there are seasons in which your faith will undergo fiery tests in 1 Peter 1:6-8. Despite unspeakable loss, suffering, and disappointment, the prophet Job eventually recognized his faith was on trial. He put his confidence in God and knew the outcome would produce godly character. Job 23:10 reads, *"But he knoweth the way that I take: when he hath tried me, I shall come forth as gold."*

In Psalm 4:4 David writes, *"Stand in awe, and sin not: commune with your own heart upon your bed, and be still."* Soul-searching is best accomplished during distraction-free quiet time. Asaph's words in Psalm 77:6 provide the great revelation that the human spirit, or mind, stills itself before searching the soul: *"I call to remembrance my song in the night: I commune with mine own heart: and my spirit made diligent search."*

It is during the still moments and hours of soul-searching that God leads and accompanies every heart on its soul-search. The gentle Spirit of God anoints each human mind to search its motives and objectives that originated in the soul. Recall the soul is home of free moral agency: the human will. As each soul comes in God's view, He weighs the actions, thoughts, and decisions, and gives each person the fruit of their doings. 1 Chronicles 28:9 says, *"The LORD searcheth all hearts, and understandeth all the imaginations of the thoughts: if thou seek him, he will be found of thee; but if thou forsake him, he will cast thee off for ever."* Jeremiah 17:10 adds, *"I the LORD search the heart, I try the reins, even to give every man according to his ways, and according to the fruit of his doings."* Jesus is this LORD, for Revelation 2:23 is Jesus proclaiming, *"I am he which searchest the reins and hearts: and I will give unto every one of you according to your works."*

At the conclusion of the search, every soul decides to continue in their own will or abandon it for God's. A worthy soul abandons their selfish will and seeks God's will, as He promises to be found. Jeremiah 29:13 states, *"And ye shall seek me, and find me, when ye shall search for me with all your heart."* God satisfies the holy thirst inside worthy souls.

An unworthy soul is like the rich man in Jesus' parable in Luke 12:16-21. The context is Jesus encouraging a man to not covet his father's inheritance in verses 13-15. Jesus portrays a rich man communing with his own soul. The rich man's human spirit tells his soul to take its ease. In other words, the man tells his own soul to take peace and comfort in his riches and to cease from trusting in God. In Luke 12:19, Jesus makes it seem the human spirit, or consciousness, actually talks to the soul because it says, "*And I will say to my soul, Soul, thou hast much goods laid up for many years; take thine ease, eat, drink, and be merry.*" Truly, your consciousness either satisfies the holy thirst to know God in your soul or silences it.

Jesus' parable about the rich man building greater barns is a classic example of a soul drawing back from living by faith. The rich man told his soul to cease trusting in God and to trust in his great barns. Similarly, Judas Iscariot's drawing back moment was his decision to leave Jesus and His apostles at the Last Supper, betraying his Lord. John 13:2 reads, "*And supper being ended, the devil having now put into the heart of Judas Iscariot, Simon's son, to betray him.*" Judas leaving the communion table symbolized him leaving faith. Judas left grace; grace never left him. He embodied Hebrews 12:15 which says men can fail, or fall back from, the grace of God. Judas did "*despite unto the Spirit of grace*"[949], meaning he insulted the Holy Ghost. He cast aside his faith and its absence allowed Satan to enter Judas' heart. Luke 22:3 explains, "*Then entered Satan into Judas surnamed Iscariot, being of the number of the twelve.*"

I'm persuaded you can choose a better destiny than Judas. Hebrews 6:9-12 declares:

> "*But, beloved, we are persuaded better things of you, and things that accompany salvation, though we thus speak. For God is not unrighteous to forget your work and labour of love, which ye have shewed toward his name, in that ye have ministered to the saints, and do minister. And we desire that every one of you do shew the same diligence to the full assurance of hope unto the end: That ye be not slothful, but followers of them who through faith and patience inherit the promises.*"

949   Hebrews 10:29

DIVIDING ASUNDER SOUL AND SPIRIT

While the soul and human spirit are closely connected, Scripture says they can be differentiated in order to allow individual ministry and care.

Your soul is like the core of the human spirit and they are interdependent. Adam became a living soul when both his human spirit and soul entered his body. Genesis 2:7 says Adam became a *"living soul"* as God *"breathed into his nostrils the breath of life."* Once Adam's human spirit and soul were placed inside his body, he was alive. Contrariwise, at Adam's passing away his human spirit and soul left his body and he was dead, or separated from this earth.

A seed serves as a suitable illustration for man's three parts. The seed coat is like the body, the stored food like the human spirit, and the embryo represents the soul. A complete seed always has all three parts just as a human being is complete with a body, human spirit, and soul.

As a seed can be divided into its three parts, man's three parts can be divided, or differentiated, by God's Word. Hebrews 4:12 declares, *"For the word of God is quick, and powerful, and sharper than any twoedged sword, piercing even to the dividing asunder of soul and spirit, and of the joints and marrow, and is a discerner of the thoughts and intents of the heart."* The Word reveals the location of the spiritual battle—whether in the soul or human spirit. It also discerns, or judges, the thoughts and intents of the human spirit and soul.

When you hear it said, "I'm having a mind battle," you know the person's human spirit is under attack. This is when your mind feels foggy and confused. Paul says the Word of God is our mighty weapon amidst mind battles in 2 Corinthians 10:5: *"Casting down imaginations, and every high thing that exalteth itself against the knowledge of God, and bringing into captivity every thought to the obedience of Christ."* Battle-ready Christians cast down, or reject evil thoughts, choosing to dwell on God's Word in order to win mind battles. Paul says God's peace comes to those who purposely think on things that are true, honest, just, pure, lovely, of good report, virtuous, and praise worthy.[950]

950   Philippians 4:7-9

If someone says, "I'm going through a soul-searching time," it usually means their soul is at war, with possibly both the flesh and human spirit attacking it. You already learned soul searching is when major choices are made and when faith is tested and tried. Peter confirms how the flesh wars against the soul saying, *"Dearly beloved, I beseech you as strangers and pilgrims, abstain from fleshly lusts, which war against the soul."*[951] A young Christian man in the Corinth church was so overtaken by the fleshly lust of sexual immorality that Paul excommunicated him from the church in hopes his soul would be saved.[952] Paul recognized the battle for the deputy's soul in Acts 13:6-12 when Elymas the sorcerer tried to stop the deputy from hearing Paul's preaching. The deputy's soul *"desired the hear the word of God"* being preached. The Spirit led Paul to pronounce temporary blindness upon Elymas so the deputy's hungry soul could receive the Word. Upon seeing this mighty sign, the deputy believed the gospel.

All Christians benefit from God's Sword-Word separating the soul from the human spirit in order to faithfully minister to their individual needs. Most often this happens as Christians listen to preaching. Romans 10:17 reads, *"So then faith cometh by hearing, and hearing by the word of God."* Through my own church attendance and preaching, I've seen the Holy Spirit minister to believers' minds by presenting new Scriptures they had never seen before, thereby helping them understand God's will and truth. Other times, the Word preached brings peace to unsettled minds. I've also seen the Word minister to the needs of the soul as God seeks His children's obedience, submission, and praise. Indeed, *"the preaching of the cross is to them that perish foolishness; but unto us which are saved it is the power of God."*[953]

Ephesians 4:11-16 teaches the Holy Spirit anoints the five-fold preaching ministry to equip and edify believers while bringing a unity of faith and knowledge about Jesus Christ. The Word conforms us to be Christ-like, transforming our thinking to renew our minds. Then the

---

951   1 Peter 2:11
952   1 Corinthians 5:1-5
953   1 Corinthians 1:18

renewed human spirit can *"prove what is that good, and acceptable, and perfect, will of God."* A renewed mind clearly understands God's perfect will for its soul (See Chapter 11).

JESUS' UNIVERSAL INVITE TO RECEIVE THE SOUL BAPTISM

Jesus, Paul, and His New Testament church sound a universal invitation to receive both salvation and the baptism of the Holy Ghost. Christ doesn't discriminate age, race, or gender. All who want to be saved and filled with the Holy Ghost can be.

Jesus in John 7:37-39 offered the living water of the Holy Spirit to any man, saying, *"If any man thirst, let him come unto me and drink."* In Matthew 11:28-30, Jesus invites *"all"* to come unto Him for soul-rest: *"Come unto me, all ye that labour and are heavy laden, and I will give you rest."* Paul says more of the same in Romans 10:12-13: *"For there is no difference between the Jew and the Greek: for the same Lord over all is rich unto all that call upon him. For whosoever shall call upon the name of the Lord shall be saved."* The Holy Spirt in the bride, or New Testament church, freely offers the water of life to everyone in Revelation 22:17: *"And the Spirit and the bride say, Come. And let him that heareth say, Come. And let him that is athirst come. And whosoever will, let him take the water of life freely."* If you're thirsty for eternal water, God is ready to quench your thirst.

This gracious, universal invitation will be referenced on Judgment Day, as everyone will admit to having an opportunity to repent and accept Jesus Christ as their Savior. Recall Romans 1:20 teaches there'll be no excuses on Judgment Day. Yes, Romans 2:16 says that day is coming—*"the day when God shall judge the secrets of men by Jesus Christ according to my gospel."*

No secret will be kept from Jesus Christ at that day. The gospel He commissioned and revealed to Paul will be His judgment standard. Respond to His loving, universal invitation by receiving Christ as Savior and as your soul's rest.

PREDESTINED TO RECEIVE THE SOUL BAPTISM

Although the invitation is universal, its reception is not. Jesus said *"few"* will find the narrow road that leads to life.[954] But Scripture gives us an assurance that all of God's predestined, elected, and foreknown sons and daughters will receive the baptism of the Holy Ghost.

Paul is the main teacher about God's foreknowledge and predestination. Ephesians 1:4-5 say God chose us *"in him before the foundation of the world"* and then *"predestinated us unto the adoption of children by Jesus Christ to Himself."* Imagine that—before the world was founded, God knew human history and chose you in His mind to be adopted into His family by Jesus Christ's Spirit! God didn't force you to choose Him. He knew you would choose Him and with that foreknowledge, He predestined how and when you'd be born again by His Spirit. God knows all who will receive and those who will not. Romans 8:29-30 provide the divine order of His own counsel:

> *"For whom he did foreknow, he also did predestinate to be conformed to the image of his Son, that he might be the firstborn among many brethren. Moreover whom he did predestinate, them he also called: and whom he called, them he also justified: and whom he justified, them he also glorified."*

God's three steps in His eternal order for salvation is foreknowledge, predestination, and calling. The Almighty begins by knowing your ultimate choice about salvation, then predestinates the events of your life so you can receive His calling to the new birth. He already knows you'll receive Him and be baptized with His Holy Spirit. After explaining this, it seems Paul is supercharged with faith because his next words are, *"What shall we then say to these things? If God be for us, who can be against us?"*[955]

Peter's first epistle also identifies foreknowledge as God's determining factor for salvation. Through eternal, infinite foreknowledge, the Lord knows who will accept the gospel. Then He elects, or chooses,

---

954   Matthew 7:14
955   Romans 8:31

believers for His purposes. 1 Peter 1:2 proclaims, *"Elect according to the foreknowledge of God the Father, through sanctification of the Spirit, unto obedience and sprinkling of the blood of Jesus Christ."*

Paul's letter to the Galatians provides the capstone on the baptism of the Holy Ghost revelation. Galatians 4:1-7 likens us to servants to sin until God adopted us into His family through Christ's redemptive work on the cross. Why did we receive the baptism of the Holy Ghost? Because we already were sons in God's mind! Galatians 4:6 declares, *"And because ye are sons, God hath sent forth the Spirit of his Son into your hearts, crying, Abba, Father."* God's foreknowledge, before the world was founded, told Him you'd choose Him, so you've always been a son or daughter in His thinking. Even before you knew you loved God, you already were His child.

The prodigal son parable in Luke 15:11-32 perfectly expresses this thought. Just like the prodigal left his father's house, we willingly leave righteousness and run from truth. Some of us run for longer than others, but eventually we come to ourselves as the prodigal did amongst the swine. Was the prodigal any less of a son while eating the swine's husks? No, he was fully a son, just out of position until he repented. I remember the moment I came to myself and knew I could return to my Heavenly Father—do you? And I remember the feeling of the Father running to receive me back into His family. After the prodigal's repentance, the father gave him shoes, a ring, and change of clothes, which typed the baptism of the Holy Ghost. The prodigal was freshly clothed, or *"endued"*, with power—authority from his father—just as Jesus says His born again child receives power from on high.[956] Because the prodigal was a son, the father could give him the clothes. And because you're a child of God, He can give you the baptism of the Holy Ghost despite your disgraceful past. This is amazing grace!

Knowing God's foreknowledge helps you understand Scriptures that may have been perplexing beforehand. No one rebuked the unbelieving Jews as much as Christ when he proclaimed the devil was their

956   Luke 24:49

father[957] and said their converts were twofold more children of hell than they were.[958] Was Jesus being unfair or partial? Of course not. He was speaking by the foreknowledge God had made known to Him about their eternal destinies, for Jesus said He only spoke what God showed Him.[959] In John 14:17, Christ goes as far as saying worldly persons *cannot* receive the Holy Spirit: "*Even the Spirit of truth; whom the world cannot receive, because it seeth him not, neither knoweth him: but ye know him; for he dwelleth with you, and shall be in you.*" Jesus' sheep, His predestinated children, will hear and obey His voice. God's sheep have eternal security because God knows they will faithfully believe. The goats will not believe. John 10:26-28 reads:

> "*But ye believe not, because ye are not of my sheep, as I said unto you. My sheep hear my voice, and I know them, and they follow me: And I give unto them eternal life; and they shall never perish, neither shall any man pluck them out of my hand.*"

Our human perspective can only hope and wish for people to be saved and baptized with the Holy Ghost, but God's eternal perspective allows Him to foreknow all who will receive Him. God created time, space, and matter, so He's outside of time limits. He knows the beginning from the end, having no "*beginning of days, nor end of life.*"[960] In the midst of any obstacle to win souls, believers must continue to finish the Great Commission while sharing Jesus' confidence that every predestined believer will come home to the Heavenly Father. Messiah says, "*All that the Father giveth me shall come to me; and him that cometh to me I will in no wise cast out.*"[961]

---

957   John 8:44
958   Matthew 23:15
959   John 5:20; 8:28, 38; 12:49-50
960   Hebrews 7:3
961   John 6:37

THE REWARDS FOR RECEIVING THE REVELATION OF THE BAPTISM OF THE HOLY GHOST

Outstanding rewards await those who receive the revelation of the baptism of the Holy Ghost—both in this life and the life to come.

The great rewards in this life are possessing eternal life, experiencing God's fellowship, possessing spiritual sight, manifesting the fruits of the Spirit, and a small remnant will escape death altogether in the rapture.

Eternal life as a personal possession during this life serves as an anchor for your soul. Anchors usually ground boats to rocks below, but the soul-anchor lifts you upward. Do you know where your soul-anchor catches? Within the Holiest of Holies in heaven! Hebrews 6:19-20 says, *"Which hope we have as an anchor of the soul, both sure and stedfast, and which entereth into that within the veil; Whither the forerunner is for us entered, even Jesus, made an high priest for ever after the order of Melchisedec."* Paul agrees, saying we are seated *"together in heavenly places in Christ Jesus."*[962] The eternal soul-anchor again gives you assurance of eternal life. Since the Holy Ghost is eternal life—called the *"eternal Spirit"* in Hebrews 9:14—every born again Christian possesses a small portion of God's own life. Death is passed out of your soul. In John 5:24, Jesus says, *"Verily, verily, I say unto you, He that heareth my word, and believeth on him that sent me, hath everlasting life, and shall not come into condemnation; but is passed from death unto life."* This eternal, internal assurance is available to you now, but wasn't obtainable for Adam, Noah, Abraham, Moses, and the rest of the Old Testament saints.

Second, Spirit-filled believers experience a divine partaking of Christ's fellowship while living in this corrupt world. Through meditation, prayer, and worship, you can know Christ intimately. Paul was born again[963] and said he *knew* Christ in two ways: in His resurrection power, and in the fellowship of His sufferings.[964] You were dead in sins but now your soul is alive through resurrection power! None but Jesus walks with you during your sufferings, whether you're physically or mentally persecuted. These

962   Ephesians 2:6
963   Acts 9:17, 13:9
964   Philippians 3:10

dreadful seasons may actually best manifest Christ's fellowship with you as you learn to lean upon Him rather than men. As your fellowship increases with Christ, your fellowship with the world, family, friends, and associates decreases. The longer Paul preached, the more he was rejected by men, such as the so-called believers in Asia, and also Demas.[965] But Paul had consolation Christ's grace was with him throughout his sufferings and he'd receive a crown of life upon entering heaven.

Third, Holy Ghost-filled saints, or wise virgin Christians, are the only group on earth that possess spiritual eyesight, or understanding. Starting with Jews and Gentiles, Paul says most Jews are blinded to the gospel in Romans 11:25. Their eyes will be opened to Christ after the Times of the Gentiles is over. Moving on the Gentiles, there are three types: sinners, foolish virgin Christians, and wise virgin Christians. 2 Corinthians 4:4 says Satan has *"blinded the minds of them which believe not."* Sinners' minds denounce the spiritual light, or knowledge, of Jesus' glorious gospel. Some might think foolish virgins have spiritual eyesight, but three texts—Matthew 25:8, John 3:3, and Revelation 3:17—prove otherwise. In Matthew 25:8, the lamps of foolish virgins are gone out—no fire, no light. This means the fulness of the Holy Ghost has not shined in their souls. Foolish virgins are saved, being spiritual virgins, but did not fully prepare to possess the oil of the Holy Ghost baptism. Therefore, they do not fully know Christ in His resurrection power and the fellowship of His sufferings. God's Light has *"shined in our hearts"*—our souls—and *"we have this treasure in earthen vessels."*[966] True spiritual eyesight lets us see the world through God's eyes. Our worldview matches God's because we hate all sin, choosing to love holiness, obedience, and righteousness. Jesus says you can only see, or understanding, the kingdom of God when you're born again in John 3:3. Foolish virgins then, cannot understand, and thus cannot obey kingdom truths. Foolish virgins are part of the blind, lukewarm group in Revelation 3:14-22, fluctuating between occasional love for God and love for worldly pleasures.

---

965   2 Timothy 1:15, 4:10
966   2 Corinthians 4:6-7

A common example of American lukewarmness in my region is church members loving both football games and their Sunday worship service. These foolish Christians spend their entire Saturday and Sunday evening (each weekend from September to February) worshipping for 6 or more hours at the throne of the Ohio State Buckeyes and Cleveland Browns football teams. Some will even go to Friday night high school football games, wasting another 3 hours. Yet, they will enjoy their 1-2 hours at their Sunday morning church services. Their weekends are grossly lukewarm; not "hot", or fully focused, on serving Jesus Christ.

Fourthly, born again Christians are the only group on earth who manifest the fruits of the Holy Ghost. Jesus' The Sower and the Four Grounds parable, found in Matthew 13:3-9 and 18-23, reveals there are four reactions to hearing Christ's gospel. Only one reaction, from the *"honest and good heart"*, brings forth fruit. Galatians 5:22-23 lists the nine precious and rare fruits of the Spirit: *"love, joy, peace, longsuffering, gentleness, goodness, faith, Meekness, temperance."* All other religions produce imitation fruit. They promote good works, but without the Seed of God's Word and the truths of Jesus Christ's gospel, there is no real fruit production. 1 Corinthians 13:1-3 says good works done without Christ's love—even giving away all your money and dying at the stake as a martyr—profit the worker nothing.

Fifth, a small remnant of Holy Ghost-filled Christians who live until the end of the Gentile Church Ages (See Chapter 7) will experience the earthly reward of escaping death. Their bodies will be changed, swallowed up in life at the *"last trump"*[967] and they will need no funeral. Christ will snatch them away in the rapture before the awful Tribulation Period. Chapter 12 fully details this earthly reward for the soul-baptized saints who are privileged to live until Christ's literal coming.

Heavenly rewards are numerous as well for those receiving the privilege of obtaining the first resurrection, or rapture. Chapter 12 details the heavenly rewards, which include meeting Jesus and the resurrected saints at the meeting in the air, the wedding supper of the Lamb, and the

967   1 Corinthians 15:51-54

1,000 year earthly millennial reign. Paul said he would press towards the mark and go to *"any means"* to *"attain unto the resurrection of the dead"*[968] and so should we be willing to lose our lives in order to gain heaven's future rewards. Revelation 20:6 gives two descriptions for Christians who attain the first resurrection: *"blessed and holy."*

Immediately following the millennium is the climatic White Throne Judgment, in which every soul that ever lived will be judged by their works and either granted eternal life or cast into the lake of fire. There is a one special reward for the Holy Ghost-baptized saint at this judgment: sitting with Christ in His throne. This is the final reward spoken to the overcomer in the Laodicean Church Age in Revelation 3:21: *"To him that overcometh will I grant to sit with me in my throne, even as I also overcame, and am set down with my Father in his throne."* Obviously, every overcomer from every age will inherit this reward, based upon Revelation 21:7: *"He that overcometh shall inherit all things; and I will be his God, and he shall be my son."*

Muse about this reward and consider how all men and women, throughout earth's history will be gathered at this second resurrection. Matthew 25:32-33 describes it as all nations being gathered in one place in order to be separated into two groups: the saved and lost. Cain, Abel, and Nimrod will be there, along with Jacob and Esau. Moses and Pharaoh will be present. In attendance will be famous men like Goliath, Buddha, Cyrus, Confucius, Darius, Cicero, and Julius Caesar. Men that other men esteemed great, like Alexander the Great, will all stand face to face with the true Great One: the Lord Jesus Christ.

What excuse will these men be able to make for not obeying the portion of God's truth that was available during their lifetimes? If they refused God's Word, there will be no excuses. Jesus tells us He will raise up witnesses who endured identical temptations, but were overcomers. 1 Corinthians 10:13 teaches our temptations are *"common to man"*, or all the same; therefore we are all judged by the same standard. Unrepentant ones who possessed great earthly power, perhaps like Alexander the

968   Philippians 3:11

Great, will not be able to plead that their temptation was too great to overcome because God will raise up Moses as a witness, since he overcame the temptation of riches and power in Egypt. Hebrews 11:24-27 says Moses refused royal Egyptian status, pleasures, and riches in order to be a part of God's people. You can do the same!

Matthew 12:41-42 shows how Jesus will use the men of Nineveh and the queen of the south as witnesses against the unbelievers (Pharisees, Sadducees, etc.) of His earthly ministry—which lived 800 and 1,000 years beforehand, respectively. The men of Nineveh are witnesses because they repented at the preaching of a lesser preacher than Jesus—Jonah. The queen of the south is a witness because she traveled a great distance to hear a less-gifted man than Jesus—Solomon. You learn God only requires respect for His preaching servants in every generation. Respect to a lesser gift of God will witness against those who disrespected a greater gift.

And where will Moses, the men of Nineveh, and the queen of the south be sitting at this judgment? They'll be sitting with Jesus, on His throne, as He promised in Revelation 3:21. Paul promises the same, that "*the saints will judge the world*" and even angels in 1 Corinthians 6:2-3. Yes, if you're an overcomer you will sit by Jesus and judge the very demons that tempted and attacked you. 2 Peter 2:4 and Jude 1:6 teach some fallen angels are already awaiting judgment. Paul describes human history as a theatre, or "*spectacle unto...angels*", in 1 Corinthians 4:9. Fallen angels watch our lives like spectators sitting in a theatre, and then plan and carry out evil against us. But through the grace of Jesus Christ, every overcomer testifies against the demons at the great white throne judgment and becomes a spectator as the wicked angels are cast into the lake of fire.

THE CONSEQUENCES FOR REJECTING THE REVELATION OF THE BAPTISM OF THE HOLY GHOST

Returning to Jesus' Sower and Four Grounds parable from Matthew 13, there are serious consequences to the three other heart-reactions that reject the revelation of the Holy Ghost baptism. Recall the four reactions to hearing Christ's gospel: (1) honest and good, (2) thorny, (3) stony, and (4) way side. This section details the consequences for the thorny, stony, and way side.

The thorny reaction is the foolish virgin Christian who is indeed eternally saved, but misses being part of the rapture and millennium because he failed to prepare oil for the bridegroom's coming. In short, he foolishly stopped short of his soul being sealed by the Holy Ghost. Like Israel's exodus from Egypt, he came all the way to the Jordan River, or Holy Ghost baptism, only to shrink back in unbelief.

The honest and good heart had fruit, representing the nine fruits of the Spirit. But the thorny hearted believers brought forth no fruit. Any farmer or common homesteader knows the disappointment at harvest time when there's a lack of fruitfulness. They understand the painful feelings of knowing an opportunity was lost and potential wasn't reached. You can begin to see God's disappointment at the lack of spiritual fruit in the foolish virgins, as He is the Lord of the soul-harvest. Yet He's patient, as the divine husbandman, to wait for the precious fruit of the earth according to James 5:7.

You might wonder why such harsh consequences exist to the saved, thorny-hearted believer. Isaiah 35:8 holds the answer: "*And an highway shall be there, and a way, and it shall be called The way of holiness; the unclean shall not pass over it; but it shall be for those: the wayfaring men, though fools, shall not err therein.*" God's command for believers to walk in holiness is so simple and He's provided such great, mighty weapons of warfare[969] that only a fool would squander the once-in-a-lifetime opportunity to be a part of the Holy Ghost-kingdom of God. So God calls them fools who fall short of the seal of God. Combine with this the fact that everyone is freely and repeatedly invited to receive the Holy Ghost baptism, and it causes the foolish virgin to miss out on indescribably honorable events like the rapture, the wedding supper, and the millennium.

Putting three other Scriptures together you see more obvious, foolish attributes of this thorny-hearted group. First, Luke 11:13 records

969   2 Corinthians 10:4

Jesus' pledge to give the Holy Spirit to anyone who asks. The context is God the Father portrayed as a generous father who delights in giving his children gifts. This shows thorny hearts do not pray enough, failing to ask God for the soul-baptism. Next, Matthew 5:6 says foolish virgins neglect their spiritual hunger and thirst. This is true because in Christ's beatitude He promised to fill those who hungered and thirsted for righteousness. The fact the foolish virgins were not born again shows they neglected their soul's thirst for God. Third, Ephesians 5:15-17 identifies faulty time management as an attribute of the foolish virgins because Paul says the wise Christians redeem their time. Foolish Christians waste their time on frivolous cares of the world: movies, sports, entertainments, comedy, riches, social media, and more. Time-wasting was an attribute of the foolish virgins in Matthew 25:3. They didn't plan ahead for the fact the bridegroom might tarry, which he did. In the spiritual sense, they didn't pray, seek God, repent, or worship enough. They were invited to the rapture but didn't prepare in time. Jesus Christ didn't have preeminence in their lives.

A stony heart—one who temporarily believes in Christ but then rejects Him—inherits awful consequences for devaluing the baptism of the Holy Ghost. There are different degrees of punishment for those who once believed the gospel but left it. Luke 12:47-48 records Jesus' own words you must heed: "*And that servant, which knew his lord's will, and prepared not himself, neither did according to his will, shall be beaten with many stripes. But he that knew not, and did commit things worthy of stripes, shall be beaten with few stripes.*" Here you learn punishment is based upon how much truth a person knew.

Judas Iscariot is the infamous example of someone who knew very much about the gospel, but forfeited it. He believed and served Jesus for a season (at least three years) before betraying our Messiah. It would have been better for Judas to have never been born compared to the woes that await him in torment. No doubt he, like others who serve Christ but later betray Him, will be beaten with many stripes. Matthew 26:24 records Jesus' words about Judas' awaiting judgment: "*The Son of man goeth as it is written of him: but woe unto that man by whom the Son of man is betrayed!* *it had been good for that man if he had not been born."* Your heart sinks for Judas because he had the highest calling in Scripture—apostle—and had the greatest, completely blameless leader—Jesus Christ—and still forsook truth. Furthermore, he was less than two months away from receiving the baptism of the Holy Ghost in the upper room in Acts 2. He turned his back on Christ despite being so incredibly close to the spiritual Promised Land of the new birth.

Finally, the way side heart—one who briefly entertains believing Christ before letting Satan snatch God's Word from his soul—also receives disgraceful, dejected, and sorrowful consequences. Many way side hearts spitefully work against the Lord Jesus and purposely deceive, distract, tempt, or destroy others. They'll have degrees of damnation based upon the level of evil their souls created.

Religious unbelievers, like the scribes and Pharisees of Jesus' day will *"receive the greater damnation"*[970] because they blasphemed Christ, but also kept others from entering into God's promises. Any city that rejected the preaching of Jesus' disciples will have more intense punishment than the Sodomites according to Christ in Luke 10:1-12. Jesus specifically names the cities of Chorazin, Bethsaida, and Capernaum as having worse torment than Tyre and Sidon because they saw more *"mighty works"*[971] and failed to repent.

CONCLUSION

Jesus Christ's own words in John 7:37-39 combine with Paul's declaration in Colossians 1:26 that the baptism of the Holy Ghost was hidden from ages and generations. Old Testament saints could only experience a limited, temporary anointing of the Holy Ghost upon their flesh and minds, but New Testament saints are privileged to possess the permanent, eternal seal of the Holy Ghost in our souls.

---

970   Matthew 23:13-14
971   Luke 10:13-16

The baptism of the Holy Ghost revelation can hardly be overemphasized because without God's soul-seal a person profits nothing. 1 Corinthians 13:1-3 says you can understand all the mysteries—all 12 taught in this book—and yet not have charity, the baptism of the Holy Ghost. God's presence in your soul is the relationship element of your walk with God Almighty. Revelation without relationship profits little to nothing. Peter is the prime example, for he possessed revelation that Jesus was the Christ in Matthew 16:16-17, but you know he later denied Christ to a young maid three times. Peter received the relationship with Christ, the Holy Ghost baptism, in Acts 2:4 and was a new man afterwards, being crucified upside down at the end of his life as a martyr to honor Jesus. Relationship, or oneness with Christ, profits your soul eternally. My prayer for you is that you'll soon have a See and Hear experience like Peter's, if you haven't yet already.

Now that you've received this revelation, the Bible makes sense and you understand the unified terminology for the baptism of the Holy Ghost. Most importantly, you understand the need for all believers to understand and experience a deeper, fuller experience with the Holy Ghost. Christ's blood purchased not only our forgiveness, but the right for His Spirit to baptize our souls into His kingdom. Because of His great sacrifice on the cross, we are motivated to share His desire to constantly walk, talk, and dwell in His children's souls. Jesus wants more than a Sinner's Prayer and a speaking in unknown tongues experience. Christ longs for intimate oneness with your soul.

ACTION STEPS TO THE BAPTISM OF THE HOLY GHOST

1. If you haven't been baptized in the name of the Lord Jesus Christ, obey this command. If you have, repent thoroughly of every known sin. Commune with Christ upon your bed, or in your prayer closet, and let Him walk you through your mind and soul that you can see the current state of each.

2. Look at the seven character traits of the Stature of a Perfect Man and ask God to add His character to your being. While waiting for the new birth, devote yourself to a season of prayer and worship as you wait upon the Lord's timing.

3. Recall Cornelius' life and imitate it in love—fast, pray, and give alms. Empty yourself of selfishness and live for others. Then God will come and fill you.

FOLLOW UP

Free online videos, Bible studies, and William Branham's quotes related to this chapter: www.pastorjessesmith.com/12mysteriesbook

Email: jesse.smith11@sbcglobal.net

Text: 330-929-2037

CHAPTER 7

The Mystery of The Seven Stars and Seven Golden Candlesticks

"The mystery of the seven stars which thou sawest in my right hand, and the seven golden candlesticks. The seven stars are the angels of the seven churches: and the seven candlesticks which thou sawest are the seven churches."

Revelation 1:20

THE BOOK OF THE Revelation of Jesus Christ, the climatic finale of the New Testament, contains the seventh mystery of the seven stars and seven golden candlesticks. The number seven is referenced 36 times in Revelation, as its spiritual meaning is completion. Genesis 1 shows God creating for six days, but completing His work and resting on the seventh.

The Greek meaning of "Revelation" is "laying bear, disclosure of truth, appearance."[972] In Revelation, Jesus lays bear or unveils His plan to bring redemption, restoration, and completion to humanity through seven churches, seven Spirits, seven golden candlesticks, seven stars, seven lamps of fire, seven seals, seven horns, seven eyes, seven trumpets, seven angels, seven thunders, a seventh angel, seven thousand men, seven heads, seven crowns, seven last plagues, seven golden vials, seven mountains, seven kings, and a seventh stone.

While some shy away from Revelation, Jesus promises blessings upon those who read, hear, and keep it in its third verse: *"Blessed is he that readeth, and they that hear the words of this prophecy, and keep those things which are written therein: for the time is at hand."* If you are born again, you have no fear of misinterpreting Revelation because Jesus promised His Spirit would *"guide you into all truth."*[973] Through divine inspiration, John's writing from the Isle of Patmos pulls back the curtain to dramatically unveil Jesus and His true bride, along with Lucifer and the false bride, the Mother Harlot.

At the onset of this chapter I strongly advise you to read William Branham's *An Exposition of the Seven Church Ages* for a thorough explanation of Revelation chapters 1-3. I have always considered this book the second most important text I've read outside *The Holy Bible*. I will share more about this monumental book at the end of the chapter.

THE CONFUSION ABOUT THE MYSTERY OF THE SEVEN STARS AND SEVEN GOLDEN CANDLESTICKS

Jesus leaves no confusion about the meaning of the seven stars and seven golden candlesticks because Revelation 1:20 declares the stars are angels and the candlesticks are seven churches: Ephesus, Smyrna, Pergamos, Thyatira, Sardis, Philadelphia, and Laodicea.

The confusion about the stars and candlesticks centers around two questions: what are the identities of the seven star-angels and were the

---

972   "The Bible: Hebrew and Greek Lexicons." *Voice of God Recordings*, www.branham.org/en/messagesearch
973   John 16:13

messages to the seven churches only for those local churches around 95 A.D. or were they prophetic to future ages and generations?

The revelation of the mystery of the seven stars and seven candlesticks is Jesus ordained seven men to declare truth and model holy living during the Times of the Gentiles, or Seven Church Ages.

Scripture and history validate the seven stars, or angels, are men Jesus anointed to let their lights *"so shine before men"*[974] in their generations. These seven preachers most closely adhered to Paul's gospel blueprint. The letters to the seven churches apply both to seven local churches, but are also prophetic warnings and blessings about the conditions Christians would experience in future time periods.

BIBLICAL EVIDENCE FOR THE REVELATION OF THE SEVEN STARS AND SEVEN GOLDEN CANDLESTICKS

Beginning with the seven stars, Jesus calls them *"seven angels,"* but they were seven literal men, not heavenly angels. The first proof of this is found in Revelation 2:1: *"Unto the angel of the church of Ephesus write."* Why would Jesus tell John to author a handwritten letter to a heavenly angel at Ephesus? God speaks directly to heavenly angels, sending them from His throne to minister to believers *"who shall be heirs of salvation."*[975] The Lord does not need to write letters to angels. The truth is Jesus was assigning John to write to an earthly man at Ephesus who would preserve the letter for upcoming generations to whom it would also apply to.

Secondly, the seven angels are symbolic of human preachers because men are sometimes referred to as angels in Scripture. The Hebrew definition of "angel" is "messenger", and Jesus appropriately calls John the Baptist God's *"messenger"* in Matthew 11:10. The prophet David is twice

974 Matthew 5:16
975 Hebrews 1:7, 14, Revelation 7:11

called "*an angel of God*" in 1 Samuel 29:9 and 2 Samuel 19:27. Paul says the Galatians received him "*an an angel of God, even as Christ Jesus*" in Galatians 4:14. A final witness is Revelation 22:8-9, as "*the angel*" sent to John to show him the prophesies was actually a fellow servant of his, a prophet who kept the sayings of Revelation.

A third fact is God uses men to help save men. Angels assist men, but men are God's primary tool for sharing His way to salvation. Romans 10:14 says, "*How shall they hear without a preacher?*" Mark 16:20 explains Jesus' disciples "*preached every where, the Lord working with them, and confirming the word with signs following.*"

Fourthly, notice the location of the stars—they are in Jesus' right hand. Both Moses and Jesus define God's right hand as His power and authority,[976] strictly reserved for Christ and not angels according to Hebrews 1:13. But Jesus promised men would inherit God's power to witness His resurrection.[977]

Lastly, Abraham's seed—faith-filled humans—are referred to as stars in Genesis 15:5. Daniel 12:3 likens the saved and soul winners to stars, saying, "*And they that be wise shall shine as the brightness of the firmament; and they that turn many to righteousness as the stars for ever and ever.*" John the Baptist, God's messenger, is likened unto a star, a burning light in John 5:35: "*He was a burning and a shining light: and ye were willing for a season to rejoice in his light.*"

Jesus interprets the seven golden candlesticks as the seven churches of seven Gentile cities located in Turkey. No Jewish churches are mentioned because John wrote this around 95 A.D. and God had already blinded Israel because of their unbelief and turned to the Gentiles nearly 50 years prior.[978] Jesus Christ calls God's focus on saving the Gentiles "*the times of the Gentiles*" in Luke 21:24.

In Matthew 21:33-46, Jesus plainly teaches He is going to take the kingdom from Israel and give it to the Gentiles. Verse 41 says, "*He will miserably destroy those wicked men, and will let out his vineyard unto other*

---

976 Exodus 15:6, Matthew 26:64
977 Acts 1:8, 4:33
978 Acts 13:44-48, Romans 11:1-8, 25-29

husbandmen, which shall render him the fruits in their seasons." The *"wicked men"* are the Jews and the *"other husbandmen"* are the Gentiles, and they rendered their fruits to Jesus in their individual season, or Church Age.

Jesus (in Luke 21:24) and Paul teach the Times of the Gentiles have an ending point. Paul says God will return to offering the Jews the Holy Ghost kingdom when the *"fulness of the Gentiles be come in."*[979] After the last elected, foreknown Gentile saint is sealed by the Holy Ghost into the kingdom, God raptures the bride-church and returns to Israel.

Another term for the Times of the Gentiles is the Seven Church Ages because Jesus lists seven churches (not less or more) and His many-membered Gentile bride is called His *"church"* on many occasions, but most notably in Romans 16:16, Ephesians 3:21, and 5:23-32.

Is the term "Church Ages" Biblically acceptable? Yes, Paul twice says the Old Testament had ages in Ephesians 3:5 and Colossians 1:26, and it's apparent the 2,000 year New Testament time period does also. The apostle speaks of future ages beyond his in Ephesians 3:21: *"Unto him be glory in the church by Christ Jesus throughout all ages, world without end."* If there are past and future ages, there must always be ages.

Scripture foretells the 2,000 year Gentile Church Ages in Hosea 6:1-3:

> *"Come, and let us return unto the LORD: for he hath torn, and he will heal us; he hath smitten, and he will bind us up. After two days will he revive us: in the third day he will raise us up, and we shall live in his sight. Then shall we know, if we follow on to know the LORD: his going forth is prepared as the morning; and he shall come unto us as the rain, as the latter and former rain unto the earth."*

The prophet says God will revive Israel on the third day, or after 2 days, or 2,000 years of dealing with the Gentiles. One day represents 1,000 years in God's sight. 2 Peter 3:8 says, *"One day is with the Lord as a thousand years, and a thousand years as one day."* God will revive the 144,000 Israeli remnant with the seal of the Holy Ghost after He

---

979   Romans 11:25

is done with the raptured Gentiles. In Acts 2:17, Peter says the Spirit will be poured out in the *"last days,"* or last 2,000 years, before the Great Tribulation and Millennium. Paul says, *"In the last days, perilous times shall come,"*[980] and the last 2,000 years have been extremely dangerous for Christians. God has blinded Israel for the past 2,000 years, or two days, to graft in the Gentiles to take a bride for His name's sake.[981]

Our Lord likens the seven Gentile Church Ages unto the seven branches of the golden candlestick Moses constructed for the Tabernacle in the wilderness in Exodus 25. Six candlesticks proceeded out of the main, central candlestick, and all seven had lit, fiery wicks drenched in the same oil. This foretold every Church Age would burn with the same Holy Ghost anointing that fell at Pentecost, as oil represents the Holy Ghost in Zechariah 4:1-6. Peter guaranteed the oil, or *"gift of the Holy Ghost"*, was for all Seven Church Ages in Acts 2:38-39. Verse 39 reads, *"For the promise is unto you, and to your children, and to all that are afar off, even as many as the Lord our God shall call."* Each successive Church Age burns brightly with the light of the Holy Ghost.

In Revelation 1:13-16, Jesus' location standing *" in the midst of the seven candlesticks"* with the seven stars in His hand proves His constant presence with the one, Jew-Gentile church during the Seven Church Ages. Observe Jesus, the stars, and candlesticks are associated together in unity. The same Jesus, in His same Holy Ghost power, would be with every church in every age until the end. Before Christ left His disciples He said, *"Lo, I am with you alway, even unto the end of the world."*[982] As God's Spirit was with the apostles, so is it with believers today. Christ promised *"the Spirit of truth"* would dwell with us and in us in John 14:17.

THREE APPLICATIONS FOR THE SEVEN LETTERS

John's seven letters from Jesus to the seven Gentile churches have at least three applications—applying literally, prophetically to the future Gentile ages, and also to individual Christians.

---

980   2 Timothy 3:1
981   Acts 15:14
982   Matthew 28:20

THE SEVEN LETTERS APPLIED LITERALLY TO CHRISTIANS AROUND 95 A.D.

John's seven letters applied directly to Christians living in the seven Gentile cities around 95 A.D. For example, Scripture confirms both Ephesus and Laodicea had established churches in Ephesians 1:1 and Colossians 2:1 and 4:13-16, respectively. All seven cities have historical roots to Christianity. One notable example is the Council of Laodicea held in the 4th Century.[983] Jesus knew the exact spiritual conditions of those churches, admonishing some while rebuking others.

John's letters to the seven Asian churches seem to be Jesus' final call for them to repent because all Asian churches had rejected Paul by the end of his ministry, which was around 67 A.D.: *"This thou knowest, that all they which are in Asia be turned away from me; of whom are Phygellus and Hermogenes."*[984] Here in 95 A.D., the gracious Savior gives them one final offer to repent.

THE SEVEN LETTERS WERE PROPHETIC TO FUTURE AGES

Second, the seven letters were prophetic to the future spiritual conditions of the Seven Church Ages. Revelation 1:3 declares its prophetic nature: *"Blessed is he that readeth, and they that hear the words of this prophecy."* Verse 19 of the same chapter repeats this prophetic aspect: *"Write the things which thou hast seen, and the things which are, and the things which shall be hereafter."* Here you see how John wrote about the current spiritual conditions of those churches in his lifetime yet they foretold future conditions. Much of the remainder of this chapter shows the divine parallels between seven cities to the seven future ages Christians would live through.

Three clear-cut examples prove the seven letters prophesied of future events and conditions. First, Jesus warned the church in Symrna would *"have tribulation ten days"* but must be *"faithful unto death"* in Revelation

---

983   "Synod of Laodicea (4th Century)." *New Advent*, https://www.newadvent.org/fathers/3806.htm

984   2 Timothy 1:15

2:10. The ten days are historically accurate in one or two ways: either as the 10 persecutions on the Ante-Nicene Church or Diocletian's 10 year persecution. Beginning with Nero and ending with Diocletian, there were 10 major Christian persecutions from 64 A.D. to 303 A.D.[985] Since one day can be symbolic of a year,[986] the 10 days Jesus warned Christians about can also be the dreadful, decade-long Christian persecution initiated by the Roman Emperor Diocletian[987] from 303-313 A.D. Emperor Constantine I is credited with bringing an end to this madness.[988] Many holy martyrs died, but thanks to Jesus' warning through John's letter 200 years beforehand, their faith-unto-death attitude inspired Christianity to abound even more.

Second, Jesus foretold there were be an *"open door"* missionary age to the church of Philadelphia,[989] or time period from 1750-1906 A.D. During this age, the world saw the greatest missionary efforts through men like William Carey in India and David Livingstone in Africa. The final example is the lukewarm condition of the final church of Laodicea, which represents today's churches falling away from the faith, putting Jesus' Spirit outside of their churches.[990] This prompted Jesus to ask if He would find faith on the earth at His return in Luke 18:8: *"Nevertheless when the Son of man cometh, shall he find faith on the earth?"*

THE SEVEN LETTERS SPEAK PROPHETICALLY TO INDIVIDUALS IN ALL AGES

The third application of the seven letters is they prophetically speak to both individuals and individual churches in every age. Every honest Christian knows what it's like to desire to return to his *"first love"* as taught in the Ephesian letter.[991] Thanks to Jesus, you know how to

---

985   Coxe, A. Cleveland. *Ante-Nicene Fathers: Volume 4.* 1885, p. 125
986   Numbers 14:34, Ezekiel 4:5-6
987   "Diocletian." *Encyclopedia Britannica*, https://www.britannica.com/biography/Diocletian/Domestic-reforms#ref1832
988   "Edict of Milan." *Encyclopedia Britannica*, https://www.britannica.com/topic/Edict-of-Milan
989   Revelation 3:8
990   2 Thessalonians 2:3, 2 Timothy 3:1, Revelation 3:14-22
991   Revelation 2:4

return: do your first works! Smyrna's letter inspires today's persecuted Christians, as Jesus says *"I know thy works, and tribulation... Fear none of those things which thou shalt suffer."*[992] Holy Ghost-filled saints from all ages have benefited from Laodicea's warning against lukewarmness and constantly strive to be on fire for Jesus' sake. Of course, 1 John 3:9 teaches that a born again believer's soul cannot sin or become lukewarm. But we become weary and lukewarm in our minds. Paul and Peter admonish us to *"stir up"* our minds,[993] which means "to kindle up, inflame one's mind" in the Greek.

Individual churches today and throughout history have gone through the Ephesus-to-Laodicea cycle, with Ephesus representing the best condition and Laodicea the worst. You'll soon see how revivals start with great potential, but once organized, denominated, and limited by man, God's Spirit departs to the next group and the organized group dies. True holiness-loving churches have and will remain in the Ephesus condition, breaking the lukewarm cycle, keeping Jesus as their first love.

HOW THE STAR-MESSENGERS ARE IDENTIFIED AND THEIR NAMES

Identifying the seven stars, or men anointed by the Holy Ghost, to influence each Church Age over the past 2,000 years is done by this principle: God and His ways are unchanging. Hebrews 13:7-8 best expresses this principle: *"Remember them which have the rule over you, who have spoken unto you the word of God: whose faith follow, considering the end of their conversation. Jesus Christ the same yesterday, and to day, and for ever."* Ecclesiastes 3:14-15 agrees, saying, *"I know that, whatsoever God doeth, it shall be for ever: nothing can be put to it, nor any thing taken from it: and God doeth it, that men should fear before him. That which hath been is now; and that which is to be hath already been; and God requireth that which is past."* And of course, Malachi 3:6 reads, *"For I am the LORD, I change not."*

992   Revelation 2:8-10
993   2 Timothy 1:6, 2 Peter 1:13, 3:1

Our unchanging God has and always will choose and equip one man to lead and influence the rest of his Church Age with God's revealed Word. He is the one, major leader who teaches other local leaders, who then lead their people. Paul taught this pattern to Timothy in 2 Timothy 2:1-2: "*Thou therefore, my son, be strong in the grace that is in Christ Jesus. And the things that thou hast heard of me among many witnesses, the same commit thou to faithful men, who shall be able to teach others also.*" Indeed, he is the star in Jesus' nail-scarred hand.

Observing Old Testament history, you find Seth leading the way for the godly seed to praise and seek God.[994] That lasted until God chose Noah to influence his age via warning of oncoming destruction, followed by Abraham, Moses, and Joshua, among others. Even in the days of the judges, God followed this pattern when the Spirit of the Lord came upon Othniel to lead Israel, delivering them from their enemies.[995] Sadly, after the death of each judge, Israel would backslide into sin and bondage until the people would cry out to God for deliverance. Graciously, the Lord would send them another deliverer. A similar pattern exists in the New Testament Church Ages, as each messenger came on the scene at the beginning of the Church Age with the purpose of bringing revival to the people and, in the later Church Ages, restoration.

Each star-messenger meets three requirements exemplified by Paul's ministry: true teaching of God's Word, powerful manifestations of the written and spoken Word, and soul winning.

Using Paul's life, he was true to the Word Christ revealed to him, even correcting Peter when he erroneously disassociated himself from fellowship with Gentiles.[996] Paul said anyone who altered the gospel was accursed and charged Timothy to invest all his time in rightly dividing the Word of truth.[997] Any spiritual person, according to Paul, would recognize God's Word came to him and thus should be obeyed: "*What? came the word of God out from you? or came it unto you only? If any man*

---

994   Genesis 4:26
995   Judges 3:9-12
996   Galatians 2:11-14
997   Galatians 1:8-9, 1 Timothy 4:12-16, 2 Timothy 2:15

think himself to be a prophet, or spiritual, let him acknowledge that the things that I write unto you are the commandments of the Lord."[998]

Holy Ghost-power in the form of the written and spoken Word constantly flowed from Paul's life, as seen in him casting out devils, loudly instructing an impotent man to walk for the first time, and raising Eutychus from the dead.[999] Paul's written Word was just as powerful, authoring most of the New Testament, and causing the Corinthians to repent in godly sorrow from his written rebukes in 2 Corinthians 7:8-12.

No one can calculate how many souls Paul led to Christ, but there is undoubtedly much fruit to his ministry. In this area, Paul knew he was *"nothing...behind the very chiefest apostles,"* having labored more than any other apostle through three grueling missionary trips.[1000] The apostle told his Corinthian converts they were the *"seal of"* his *"apostleship...in the Lord"*, and informed both the Philippians and Thessalonians they were his joy and crown.[1001] Paul said he had godly jealously over his converts, desiring their chaste virginity to Christ while making mention of them in every prayer.[1002] Soul winning mattered more to Paul than money and every worldly temptation.

As church history demonstrates, Jesus' seven star-messengers to each Church Age who meet the three messenger-requirements are:

- Ephesus: Paul (5-67 A.D.)
- Smyrna: Irenaeus (130-202 A.D.)
- Pergamos: Martin (315-399 A.D.)
- Thyatira: Columba (521-597 A.D.)
- Sardis: Martin Luther (1483-1546 A.D.)
- Philadelphia: John Wesley (1703-1791 A.D.)
- Laodicea: William Branham (1909-1965 A.D.)

---

998   1 Corinthians 14:36-37
999   Acts 14:8-10, 16:18, 20:9-12
1000 1 Corinthians 15:10, 2 Corinthians 12:11
1001 1 Corinthians 9:2, Philippians 4:1, 1 Thessalonians 2:19
1002 2 Corinthians 11:2, Philippians 1:4

HOW THE DATES AND LENGTHS OF THE CHURCH AGES ARE DETERMINED

The following dates and lengths of the Seven Church Ages are approximate, determined by matching Jesus' seven city descriptions with major events in church history. Figure 19 shows Clarence Larkin[1003] and William Branham[1004] agree on most dates and lengths, with slight differences between Ephesus, Philadelphia, and Laodicea. Note also the star-messengers ministered during the beginning of their respective Church Ages as proof of God's longsuffering, allowing time for their revivals and revelations to fully spread.

Church Age	Star Messenger	Larkin	Branham
Ephesus	Paul, 5-67	70-170	53-170
Smyrna	Irenaeus, 130-202	170-312	170-312
Pergamos	Martin, 316-397	312-606	312-606
Thyatira	Columba, 521-596	606-1520	606-1520
Sardi	Luther, 1483-1546	1520-1750	1520-1750
Philadelphia	Wesley, 1703-1791	1750-1900	1750-1906
Laodicea	Branham, 1909-1965	1900-?	1906-?

Figure 19

The Ephesian Church Age lasted from about 53 A.D. to 170 A.D. Its starting point was Paul's three year ministry in Ephesus in which many received the baptism of the Holy Ghost.[1005] The Ephesian church was founded on Paul's third missionary journey, along with churches in Philippi, Thessalonica, Berea, and Corinth, among others, detailed in Acts chapters 16-20.

Ephesus means "permitted" in the Greek, and Larkin adds the synonymous phrase "to relax" to its definition, which matches Jesus's main concern for this age. This age started in great zeal, but decades later many left their *"first love"*.

1003   Larkin, Clarence. *Dispensational Truths or God's Plan and Purpose in the Ages.* 1918
1004   Branham, William. *An Exposition of the Seven Church Ages.* 1965
1005   Acts 19:6, 20:31

The Smyrnaean Church Age began around 170 A.D. and ended about 312 A.D. Smyrna means "myrrh" in the Greek which speaks to myrrh's use as a costly perfume and embalming antiseptic. Myrrh's connection with death aligns perfectly with Jesus' prophesy that this time period would be an age of martyrs: *"Be thou faithful unto death, and I will give thee a crown of life."*[1006] This age fittingly began with the martyrdom of Justin Martyr and his six disciples, and ended with the gruesome 10 year Christian persecution under Diocletian beginning in 303 A.D.

The Pergamean Age lasted from around 312 A.D. to about 606 A.D. It began with Emperor Constantine I's reign over the Western Empire, which later expanded to the entire Roman Empire in 324 A.D.[1007] As Jesus foretold in Revelation 2:14, many in this age would succumb to an unholy religious union similar to the one of Balaam and Balak, the union of church and state. False Christianity in Rome united with Constantine, who stopped Christian persecution, donated property to Christians, and had many churches constructed. However, he remained a murderer, as he had his eldest son and wife killed after his supposed conversion.[1008] Constantine's conversion to Christianity, then, was likely false and incomplete.

The Thyatirean Age was the longest age, beginning around 606 A.D. and finishing about 1520 A.D. Thyatira means "odor of affliction" in the Greek, and Christian persecution long lingered during the Dark or Middle Ages. Pope Boniface III's acceptance of the title "Universal Bishop" in 606 A.D.[1009] signaled the beginning of the darkest time period in church history, as the Jezebel spirit took the Roman church to the *"depths of Satan"* through fornication, idolatry, and many more doctrines of devils.

It is my humble opinion that the Thyatirean Age may have began earlier, though, around 560 A.D. in order to allow for its star-messenger,

---

1006   Revelation 2:10
1007   "Constantine I." *Encyclopedia Britannica*, https://www.britannica.com/biography/Constantine-I-Roman-emperor
1008   Ibid.
1009   Coxe, A. Cleveland. *Ante-Nicene Fathers. Volume 8: The Twelve Patriarchs, Excerpts and Epistles, The Clementina, Apocrypha, Decretals, Memoirs of Edessa and Syriac Documents, Remains of the First Ages,* 1886

Columba, to have labored during its time period. Additionally, a Holy Ghost-and-power movement in Phrygia from 560-565 resembled the Day of Pentecost, as all nine gifts of the Spirit were honored and operated.[1010] It seems likely Thyatira began with a revival, just as Laodicea began with the 1906 Azusa Street Revival.

The Sardis Church Age began around 1520 A.D. and stopped about 1750 A.D. On October 31, 1517, Martin Luther nailed his 95 Theses to the church door in Wittenberg, Germany, beginning the Protestant Reformation period. But it was three years later in 1520 when he published "three great documents which laid down the fundamental principles"[1011] of the reformers. As Jesus said only "*a few names…in Sardis*" had "*not defiled their garments*," this was a difficult age wherein many fell away from the faith after the deaths of reformers like Luther, Zwingli, and Calvin.

The time period of brotherly love, the Philadelphian Age, started around 1750 A.D. and lasted until 1906 A.D. This age, labeled as the "*open door*" age by Christ, saw men like George Whitefield, John Wesley, William Carey, and David Livingstone evangelize the world, teaching saints to keep Jesus' Word, Name, and patience. Just as seasons slowly transition from one to the next, the Philadelphian Age had a "first sign of spring" in 1739, when Whitefield's first American preaching tour providentially and supernaturally began in Philadelphia, Pennsylvania.[1012]

The final and current age, Laodicea, began around 1906 and continues today with the rapture as its unknown ending point. The 1906 Azusa Street Revival indicated a new age as the gifts of the Spirit were restored as God promised in Joel 2:25: "*And I will restore to you the years that the locust hath eaten, the cankerworm, and the caterpiller, and the palmerworm, my great army which I sent among you.*" Sadly, Pentecostals and all denominations and independents have grown lukewarm upon Jesus' Word and Spirit, wanting no more Bible revelation and kicking Jesus out of their

---

1010   Hazeltine, Rachel. *How Did It Happen?* 1958, p. 338

1011   "Modern History Sourcebook: Martin Luther (1483:1546): Address to the Nobility of the German Nation, 1520." *Fordham University*, https://sourcebooks.fordham.edu/mod/luther-nobility.asp

1012   "George Whitefield." *Christianity Today*, https://www.christianitytoday.com/history/people/evangelistsandapologists/george-whitefield.html

churches. Yet our merciful Messiah still stands at their doors, knocking, trying to enter with loving rebukes, chastening, and fellowship.

THE GAINING, LOSING, AND RESTORING OF TRUTH DURING THE CHURCH AGES

Before digging into specific church history by each age, it's imperative to see God's design for giving and restoring truth to the Seven Church Ages. Although God is unchanging, He never said the church was. No, the church would change because it would be persecuted, afflicted, and tested, but this was done to strengthen the faithful *"few"*,[1013] allowing them to truly know Christ in the power of His resurrection and the fellowship of His sufferings. Since the church loved Christ and wanted to reign with Him, it was necessary for her to suffer like Him.

The seven stars or messengers are called thus because of the profound spiritual darkness upon the earth. Jesus specifically called Paul, the star-messenger to the Ephesian Age, a light to the Gentiles, to *"turn them from darkness to light."*[1014] Spiritual darkness, or life under Satan's power, has covered earth since the fall, as he is the *"god of this world."*[1015] But due to increased iniquity and deception,[1016] darkness grows increasingly black during the spiritual nighttime of the past 2,000 years of Gentile Church Ages. Remember, the end time is a spiritual blackout, as Revelation 18:3 and 23 say *"all nations"* will be deceived by the beast and false prophet's religious system. In every age, though, Jesus promised His followers light in John 8:12: *"I am the light of the world: he that followeth me shall not walk in darkness, but shall have the light of life."*

Scripture proves the early church began with the full written Word and power of the Holy Ghost, and the final true church in the Laodicean Age, albeit a very small minority, will have it all restored before the rapture. Logically, in between the beginning and end would be a time where the church lacked the fulness of Word and power.

1013   Matthew 7:14, Luke 13:23-24, Revelation 3:4
1014   Acts 13:47, 26:18, 23
1015   2 Corinthians 4:4
1016   Matthew 24:12, 2 Timothy 3:13

Holy Ghost power was at its fullness at Pentecost, for not long after-wards the Spirit led Peter to pronounce a lame man healed. Peter said, *"Silver and gold have I none; but such as I have give I thee: In the name of Jesus Christ of Nazareth rise up and walk."*[1017] Peter had divine power given to him by Jesus! Joyfully, the healed man leaped, walked, and praised God, and these types of miracles followed all the apostles, for they were given *"great power"* as witnesses *"of the resurrection of the Lord Jesus."*[1018] Peter later wrote that God had given believers not some, but *"all things that pertain unto life and godliness."*[1019] Before leaving Ephesus after a three year apostleship there, Paul said he had declared to them *"all the counsel of God"* in Acts 20:27. While not all churches had all of Paul's epistles, the four gospels, and the rest of the New Testament canon at first, the born again believers had the Holy Ghost baptism, which Jesus said guided them into all truth in John 16:13.

Before Jesus returns to rapture His bride, He must restore all things the church had at Pentecost. Christ was the first to prophesy this end-time restoration in Matthew 17:11: *"And Jesus answered and said unto them, Elias truly shall first come, and restore all things."* Note that Jesus says a man anointed with the spirit of Elijah would restore all things. This man could not be Elijah the Tishbite back from the dead to restore Moses' Law because Hebrews 8:13 says the law has decayed, waxed old, and vanished away for good. The Elijah Jesus is speaking of, then, has to restore the New Testament truths. Chapter 13 details this revelation.

Peter also prophesied of restitution, or restoration, in Acts 3:20-21: *"And he shall send Jesus Christ, which before was preached unto you: Whom the heaven must receive until the times of restitution of all things, which God hath spoken by the mouth of all his holy prophets since the world began."* Heaven will keep Jesus until all things are restored, then Christ will phys-ically return to earth for His bride.

Joel 2:23-26 promises that the power of the Holy Ghost will be restored through the spiritual wine and oil of the former and latter rains:

1017   Acts 3:6
1018   Acts 4:33
1019   2 Peter 1:3

"Be glad then, ye children of Zion, and rejoice in the Lord your God: for he hath given you the former rain moderately, and he will cause to come down for you the rain, the former rain, and the latter rain in the first month. And the floors shall be full of wheat, and the vats shall overflow with wine and oil. And I will restore to you the years that the locust hath eaten, the cankerworm, and the caterpiller, and the palmerworm, my great army which I sent among you. And ye shall eat in plenty, and be satisfied, and praise the name of the Lord your God, that hath dealt wondrously with you: and my people shall never be ashamed."

Furthermore, combining Daniel 12:4 and 12:9 with Revelation 10:7-11 and Matthew 24:14, you find full support for this same conclusion: the end of human history cannot come until the mystery of God is finished and preached in all the world for a witness unto all nations! This can only happen in the technology age, for Daniel said the Book would be sealed until *"the time of the end"* when *"knowledge shall be increased."*

In between the beginning and end of the Seven Church Ages would be a time of loss. Ecclesiastes 3:6 teaches there *"is a time to get, and a time to lose."* Many truths and the glory from Pentecost would fade in the first four ages, but restoration would begin in the fifth and sixth. Jesus says believers in the fourth age, Thyatira, would have to overcome the depths of Satan, proving this age was a low point of truth and power. Just as John 12:24 likens Jesus unto a corn of wheat that had to fall into the ground and die in order to bring forth more fruit, the true church would experience the same. It would slowly die and lose truth and power through the first four ages, but in the fifth age, the Sardisean Age of the Reformation, the seed would spring forth in strength as God began incrementally restoring truth. Then in the final age, the Laodicean Age, all things would be restored.

Reading Revelation chapters 2 and 3, you see Jesus addressing two vines, or two groups, in every age: workers of righteous and workers of iniquity. Both are religious, but only the righteous true vine overcomes Satan's temptations throughout the ages.

Starting with the Ephesian Age, most worshippers left their first love and needed to repent. But the true vine hated the deeds of the Nicolaitans that the religious false vine had adopted. In the second age, Jesus instructed the true vine in Smyrna to not fear the persecution coming from the false vine. The false church progressed from hateful deeds into a full synagogue for Satan. The third age, Pergamos, shows Jesus having a few things, not just one thing, against the true vine, showing their decline in faith. Meanwhile, the false vine had fully erected a seat for Satan.

In the Thyatirean Age, the fourth age containing the Dark Ages, the true vine increased their works but Christ still had a few things against them, such as allowing the Jezebel spirit to teach and seduce His servants. Jesus simply said, *"hold fast"* what they already had. They had lost much of what Pentecost had had and it was not the hour for restoration. The false vine's Jezebel-like doctrines took it into the depths of Satan, making this the darkest age of all. It is undeniable that Rome took away the privilege of simply knowing and reading Scripture from millions. Alexander Hislop writes, "In the hands of Roman priests, that ushered in the dark ages, when, through many a dreary century, the Gospel was unknown, and the Bible a sealed book to millions who bore the name of Christ."[1020] Thyatira was an age of great loss.

The fifth age, Sardis, begins a hopeful restoration for the believing remnant known as the Reformation. The Reformation was possible because the Gutenberg Press produced millions of Bibles, translated by godly men, and placed truth in many believers' hands for the first time.[1021] Jesus admonishes a few worthy, undefiled saints to be watchful, strengthen the things which remain, hold fast, and to repent. Notice Jesus saying there are only a *"few"*[1022] worthy believers in the entire age, proving the massive decrease of true believers. The false vine adopted religious names, but were spiritually dead.

1020 Hislop, Alexander. *The Two Babylons.* 1853.
1021 "The Gutenberg Press" *The Museum of the Bible,* https://museumofthebible.org/book/minutes/440
1022 Revelation 3:4

There was more growth, or truth, in the sixth age, the Philadelphian Age, for the true vine had a *"little strength"* to walk through Jesus' open door and work for His name. Believers kept Jesus' Word and name, and Christ made the false vine in Satan's synagogue bow at the feet of their Open Door Ministry.

The last age, Laodicea, sees a huge spiritual decline into materialism and lukewarmness, and the false vine removes Jesus from their churches altogether. Christ urges the true vine to zealously repent. These overcomers, inspired by the message of restoration, buy spiritual gold and white raiment from Jesus, and anoint their eyes with eye salve to become *"hot"*,[1023] or on fire for Christ, right before the rapture.

HISTORICAL EVIDENCE AND REVELATIONS FOR THE SEVEN STARS AND SEVEN GOLDEN CANDLESTICKS

The church history of the past 2,000 years validates and parallels Jesus' prophetic promises regarding the Seven Church Ages. In Jesus' seven addresses, He reveals aspects of His divinity, His messages to both vines, and rewards for the overcomers.

THE EPHESIAN CHURCH AGE (53-170) IN REVELATION 2:1-7

Star: Paul is the angel-star to the first age. He identified 9 out of 12 mysteries and authored 14 of the 27 New Testament books—far more than any other man. 1 Corinthians 15:10 says God's grace enabled Paul to labor more than any other apostle. Jesus was going to use Paul's gospel to judge the secrets of men, and curses come upon anyone who changes the gospel Christ gave to him.[1024] Not only did Peter submit to Paul's face-to-face rebuke about his discrimination against Gentiles,[1025] but Peter acknowledged Paul's letters were Scripture in 2 Peter 3:15-16.

Some may argue that Paul cannot be the angel to this age because he wasn't alive at the time Jesus gave this revelation to John around 95 A.D.

1023 Revelation 3:15
1024 Romans 2:16, Galatians 1:7-9
1025 Galatians 2:11-14

While it is true that Paul died around 67 A.D., his legacy is immeasurable, far exceeding any other man due to his mission work and doctrinal revelations. Also, God often sends messengers who are not recognized until after they die, as in the case of John the Baptist. Jesus told His disciples that "*Elias*", or John the Baptist, had come already and they had not recognized him in Matthew 17:12-13. It would fit Jesus' pattern to send Paul as an angel-messenger, but not make it known to others until after Paul went to heaven.

As evidence Paul is the star-messenger to this age, his epistles teach exactly the same message Jesus gives to the true vine in this age: work and labor for Christ, flee all appearances of evil, hate evil, test self-labeled apostles to prove them, be patient, repent, and renew yourself daily.[1026]

Christ's Divinity: Jesus begins His address to His churches by showing His omnipotence, omnipresence, and sovereignty. He holds the seven star-angels in His right hand, symbolizing the authority and power He has given them. God's Son walks in the midst of the seven golden candlesticks, showing His unchanging presence in every age. As He says in Hebrews 13:5, "*I will never leave thee, nor forsake thee.*" He is with you just as He was with Paul, Peter, and all other saints.

Message to the True Vine: Our Lord tells this age He knows their works, tireless labor, and patience for His name's sake. The true vine could not bear evil ones and tried self-exalted liars, and found them to be false apostles. In love, Christ rebukes His church for leaving their first love, but provides the simple way back: repentance through doing the first works.

Just as Paul's ministry matches Jesus' message to the Ephesian Age, the life of Polycarp (60-160), the Greek bishop, does the same. Learning at the feet of the apostle John, Polycarp deeply loved our Lord Jesus and became head of the church at Smyrna at a young age.[1027]

Polycarp could not bear false teachers and tried them, as "he would not even talk with Marcion and Valentinian who were the great Roman

---

1026   Romans 5:3-4, 12:9, 2 Corinthians 4:16, 7:9-10, 1 Thessalonians 5:21-22, Titus 2:14
1027   Hazeltine, p. 112

leaders of false doctrines at that time."[1028] Even at 90 years of age, Polycarp determined to travel more than 1,500 miles to plead with Anicetus, the bishop of the first church in Rome, to repent of his participation in pagan Easter celebrations. In every city he visited while approaching Rome, he preached Christ and saw miracles and healings.

Once in Rome, Polycarp visited the first church and witnessed their worship of images, Peter, and the Eucharist. After Anicetus refused correction, Polycarp visited the second and third churches of Rome and saw God pour out Rome's last recorded revival. The sick were healed, demons cast out, and dead were raised to life. Before leaving, Polycarp also brought many of "the straying Valentinians and the Marcionites" out of false doctrine and into truth, their first love.[1029]

Polycarp returned to Smyrna and eventually turned himself into the pagans demanding his life in order to spare other Christians' lives. He was burned to death, and as a testimony of how Christ-like Polycarp was

> "...the pagans would not allow his disciples to have his corpse because they said the disciples would claim he had revived and raised from the dead like the Master (Christ) at Jerusalem. So they flayed the flesh from the bones, then ground the bones to powder and cast the ashes over a running stream."[1030]

Yet the true vine had to diligently examine itself to be sure it was keeping its first love. Edmund Broadbent writes, "As the churches increased, the first zeal flagged and conformity to the world and its ways increased also."[1031] Every age must battle and overcome spiritual complacency. In 156 A.D., Montanus, who might have been saved under Polycarp's ministry, protested against "the prevailing laxity in the relations of the church to the world."[1032] The true vine repented and did the first works to return to their first love.

1028 Ibid.
1029 Hazeltine, p. 114
1030 Hazeltine, p. 116
1031 Broadbent, E.H. *The Pilgrim Church.* 1935, p. 11
1032 Broadbent, p. 12

Iniquity of the False Vine: By Satan's design, vast numbers of lying false apostles rose up in the first age, as John recognized there were *"many antichrists"* in 1 John 2:18. Though Jesus called for their repentance, the false vine grew in sinful, hateful deeds.

After first receiving the gospel around 36 A.D. from the apostles Andronicus and Junia,[1033] the first church in Rome fell away during a 13 year period, 41-54 A.D., in which faithful apostles were banned from the city. With the faithful expelled, worship of Baal and Ashtoreh flourished in the midst of the lukewarm church members. When the apostles returned, the pagan-infused church repulsed them.[1034] Consequently, Jesus removed His candlestick, or Spirit-filled preaching ministry, from the first church in Rome as He had warned.

In this Ephesian Age, Jesus says He and the true vine hate the deeds of the Nicolaitans. Observe these are *"deeds"*, which are defined as "acts, undertakings" in the Greek Lexicon. These common, undetected deeds would later advance to become official, universal doctrines in the Pergamean Age (Revelation 2:15), but in the first age Satan deceived immature believers with seemingly harmless deeds.

The word "Nicolaitanes" might refer to a heretical group who followed a man named Nicolas, who were given over to prostitution, but I found only one reference for this theory.[1035] One certain meaning is found in the Greek meaning of Nicolas, which is "victor of the people."[1036] Satan would get victory over the people through religious leaders legalizing sinful deeds in churches. Jesus warned this age that the majority of religious people would be conquered by allowing sinful deeds into their worship. James 1:14-15 lists sin's progression: *"But every man is tempted, when he is drawn away of his own lust, and enticed. Then when lust hath conceived, it bringeth forth sin: and sin, when it is finished, bringeth forth death."*

Beginning in 41 A.D. the first church of Rome slowly and consistently added pagan deeds into their worship until they rejected

---

1033 Romans 16:7
1034 Hazeltine, pp. 108-109
1035 Hazeltine, p. 91
1036 Ibid.

the traditional, holy Passover observance, fully embracing the pagan Easter feast of Ishtar when Polycarp arrived around 150 A.D. The faithful bishop also detested their wicked deeds of idolizing statues and Eucharist worship.

The evil deed of changing water baptism—since there is only "*one baptism*"[1037]—also took place in the Ephesian Age, as the first century document, *The Didache,*[1038] records. The document's seventh chapter removes the name of the Lord Jesus Christ at baptism, substituting the titles "in the name of the Father, and of the Son, and of the Holy Spirit." Five examples from the Book of Acts show baptism should be performed in the literal name of the Lord Jesus Christ.[1039] *The Didache* also adds the false deed of pouring water, or sprinkling, at baptism, but Scripture shows only full immersion in water is God's acceptable baptismal deed.[1040] Truly, changing one word about water baptism would eventually lead to many more doctrinal changes, causing spiritual death in the false vine.

The devil also conquered the people by the deed of exalting the clergy above the laity. Clergymen were given more power than allotted by God. Ignatius, who died early in the second century, erred by giving "to the bishop a prominence and authority, not only unknown in the New Testament, but also beyond what was claimed by Clement."[1041] Hebrews 13:7-8 and 13:17 teach God-called men rule in the church, but only by the revealed Word of God, the Bible. However, men in the Ephesian Age had already begun leading by their own tenants rather than the Word, and Jesus hated it.

The Reward: Jesus promises overcomers in the Ephesian Age the blessing of eating from the Tree of Life in the midst of the paradise of God. In the New Jerusalem, Christ, the Tree of Life, will give His Words for food as a spiritual partaking of the one and only life, eternal life.[1042]

1037 Ephesians 4:5
1038 "Didache." *Encyclopedia Britannica,* www.britannica.com/topic/Didache
1039 Acts 2:38, 8:16, 10:48, 19:5, 22:16
1040 John 3:23, Acts 8:38, Romans 6:4, Colossians 2:12
1041 Broadbent, p. 8
1042 John 5:40, 14:6, 1 John 5:11-20

Justin Martyr will enjoy the reward of eating from the Tree of Life. Like spring blends into summer, the Church Ages gradually overlap as seen through Justin's martyrdom around 165 A.D. As the Ephesian Age transitioned into the Smyrnaean, the foretold persecution increased. Justin and his six disciples boldly defied the emperor and were beheaded for refusing to sacrifice to the gods. Being threatened with death, Justin overcame with these words: "Through prayer we can be saved on account of our Lord Jesus Christ, even when we have been punished, because this shall become to us salvation and confidence at the more fearful and universal judgment-seat of our Lord and Saviour."[1043]

THE SMYRNAEAN CHURCH AGE (170-312) IN REVELATION 2:8-11

Star: Irenaeus is the star-messenger to this second age. He was born in Greece[1044] and became the bishop of Lyons, having learned the gospel from Polycarp.[1045] Hazeltine writes the churches in France had all the gifts of the Holy Spirt operating through Irenaeus' teaching, including speaking in tongues, healings, and miracles, such as the dead being raised.

It is important to note Irenaeus had the true understanding of the Godhead, which would soon be lost even to genuine believers until its restoration in the end time. Irenaeus said God was not "beings" but one Being with numerous titles:

> "All the other expressions likewise bring out the title of one and the same Being; as, for example, The Lord of Powers, The Father of all, God Almighty, The Most High, The Creator, The Maker, and such like. These are not the names and titles of a succession of different beings, but of one and the same, by means of which the one God and Father is revealed, He who contains all things, and grants to all the boon of existence."[1046]

1043   Coxe, A. Cleveland. *Ante-Nicene Fathers: Volume 1: The Apostolic Fathers, Justin Martyr, Irenaeus.* 1885

1044   Foxe, John. *Foxe's Book of Martyrs.* 1563, p. 40.

1045   Hazeltine, p. 104

1046   Coxe, A. Cleveland. *Ante-Nicene Fathers: Volume 1*, p. 413

The Smyrnaean star is known for perpetually resisting the bishops of Rome, like Victor and Zephyrinus,[1047] because of their idolatrous practices. Irenaeus combated many heresies and authored one celebrated and extremely influential tract called *Against Heresies*.[1048] John Foxe, on page 717 of his classic text *Foxe's Book of Martyrs*, said Irenaeus' writings pointed to "no transubstantiation" concerning the Lord's Supper. Irenaeus' battle against Victor, bishop of the first church in Rome, to keep Easter a pure worship feast led to his martyrdom. Victor influenced Septimius Serverus to behead Irenaeus in 202 A.D.[1049]

Irenaeus' teachings on authentic Christianity, salvation, the gifts of the Spirit, and Godhead, along with his staunch stand against the first Roman church make him an obvious choice for star of the Smyrnaean Age.

Christ's Divinity: Our Lord builds upon His divine description by saying He is "*the first and the last, which was dead, and is alive.*" Jesus reveals His deity to Smyrna, showing He was "*before all things*" as the "*beginning of the creation of God.*"[1050] Jesus is the one true God, and there is none beside Him. Trust Jesus because He existed before you; He preserves your life now, and He promises you grace for the Day of Judgment, and a home in the New Jerusalem for the last, eternal day.

The Messiah says He was dead, but is now alive. He resurrected, conquering the grave in order to give us both a natural and a spiritual resurrection. If we die before the rapture, our bodies will rise in resurrection power at the meeting in the air, but Jesus offers a spiritual resurrection now. Paul says Christ resurrects our lives which were dead in sins and trespasses, making us "*sit together in heavenly places in Christ Jesus.*" Jesus describes it best in His parable of the prodigal son returning to the father's house: "*Thy brother was dead, and is alive again; and was lost, and is found.*"[1051] You can be alive now, spiritually, with a promise for your body to live again in the first resurrection.

1047   Hazeltine, p. 150
1048   Foxe, p. 40
1049   Hazeltine, p. 350
1050   Colossians 1:17, Revelation 3:14
1051   Luke 15:32

Message to the True Vine: Christ knows the works, tribulation, and poverty of this age and tells the saints to be faithful unto death. The Lord says, *"fear not those things which thou shalt suffer,"* which includes a 10 day period of tribulation.

Jesus' timely warning of persecution fits Smyrna since it means "myrrh" in the Greek. Myrrh is a gum associated with death, being used for embalming dead bodies, and mingled with wine and offered to the dying.[1052] This was the age of increased martyrdom. Jesus says be faithful *"unto death"*—not *until* death—emphasizing many believers would have to seal their testimony as martyrs.

Although the first church of Rome was growing in corruption and evil power, God's anointing strengthened many to resist unto death and overcome torture. Men like Irenaeus, Tertullian, Origen, and Novatianus are credited with defying Rome's iniquity, and they often paid the price with their blood, being faithful unto death.

Tertullian (155-230) was a lawyer in Rome before being converted through the evangelistic efforts of the second church of Rome.[1053] He saw the evangelist Montanus and his disciples perform miracles in a Holy Ghost revival. This experience led Tertullian to receive the Holy Ghost baptism during that time. After his new birth, Tertullian influenced believers through teaching and writing, and in 197 he condemned baptizing the dead and baptizing infants.[1054] Tertullian took the bishopric in Carthage around 207, separating from Rome and its challenges, and became a great leader in the African churches.

While visiting one of Tertullian's prayer meetings, Novatianus received the Pentecostal gift of the Holy Ghost, which changed the whole course his life. Another visitor, Origen, met with Tertullian before going to Rome in hopes of restoring them to the apostolic ministry. On Origen's trip home from Rome, he informed Tertullian an even worse spiritual condition existed in Rome than he had previous thought, due to their adoption of many pagan customs.

1052   Mark 15:23, John 19:39
1053   Hazeltine, pp. 146-151
1054   Broadbent, p. 9

Tertullian believed the church should be holy and clean, zealous of good works. He even traveled to France to plead for Iraenaus' life, though unsuccessfully. The first church of Rome called Tertullian a heretic for frequently exposing their devilish doctrines in his writings, which were burned by Rome not long after his death.

Not all of Tertullian's doctrines are accepted by Christians, such as the three person Trinity. Around 180, Tertullian was first recorded using the Latin form of Trinity, and Theophilus was first to use the Greek form. Calling God "three persons" does not eternally condemn a person's soul, but it does show a huge step out of God's Word and the original revelation given to Paul and all other New Testament authors. However, it is undeniable that Tertullian defied Rome's pagan corruption, inspired many believers to live holy, and pleaded for the life of this age's star, Irenaeus. Tertullian's stumble into the unscriptural belief in a three person God is evidence that each age lost some of the original apostolic revelation, like a withering wheat plant. But in this current Laodicean Age, God has restored the revelation of His divine oneness.

Origen (185-254) is called "one of the greatest teachers, as well as one of the most spiritually-minded of the fathers."[1055] At 17 years old, he witnessed his father's arrest and martyrdom for Christ, and would have joined him had it not been for his mother, who hid his clothes to keep him from leaving his house.[1056]

On a trip to Rome, he witnessed filthy deeds firsthand, like bishops and priests taking bribes to forgive sins, blackmail, adulteries, and more. Origen wrote, "Rome did not wish to retain the Scriptures in their hearts, so God gave them a strong delusion that they might believe a lie." A great gift Origen left to the churches was his list of martyrs in Rome. Peter's name is not on the list, giving many confidence that Peter was not the first pope.[1057]

1055 Broadbent, pp. 9-10
1056 Coxe, A. Cleveland. *Ante-Nicene Fathers: Volume 4: Tertullian, Part Fourth; Minucius Felix; Commodian; Origen, Part First and Second.* 1885
1057 Hazeltine, pp. 136-143

Like Tertullian, some of Origen's beliefs are denounced by Christians today, but he sealed his testimony as a martyr at Tyre and upon his death, his writing on Rome's martyrs became very precious to the saints, second in their hearts behind the Word of God.

Novatianus (189-253) "was an evangelical Christian who opposed the pagan forms of the bishop of the first Roman church."[1058] He became bishop of the second church of Rome, ordained by another martyr, Fabian. God blessed their church with tongues, prophecy, and the dead raised to life. Cyprian was one of his adversaries, accusing Novatianus of forsaking the Mother Church, or first church of Rome.[1059]

The power of the Holy Ghost was changing lives in Rome's second church, and the first church of Rome despised it. They called on the emperors to rid the city of Novatianus and God's move, which was accomplished in 251. Novatianus and his church fled, but God used it to spread His gospel to the far corners of the empire. With Novatianus' apostle-heart, he helped start evangelical churches all over the Roman Empire. In 253, Novatianus gave his life for Jesus Christ, earning the martyr's crown of eternal life.

Iniquity of the False Vine: Jesus summarizes the false vine's iniquity by rebuking their blasphemy, synagogue of Satan, imprisonments, trials, and 10 day persecution of the saints.

Like the Nicolaitanes of the first age and Antipas of the third age, there is little historical information about the lying group of false Jews of this second age. However, Jesus says they, the false vine, were claiming to be Jews in order to gain preeminence as the original church. At Pentecost, the Holy Ghost first filled Jews like Peter and Mary, and so the false vine pretended to be Jews. They blasphemed God and the true vine through their lies, and were Jews by name only. No, they were not Jews by natural birth, nor were they spiritual Jews by spiritual birth.

A fascinating fact is that Jesus called them the literal synagogue of Satan, meaning this group no longer hid their murderous ways. Like

1058   Hazeltine, pp. 202-204
1059   Broadbent, pp. 110-115

Cain, this false vine was full of Satanic hatred for the true vine, for the false vine will always hate and kill the true vine. The seemingly harmless deeds of the first age had now advanced into a completely sin-saturated, Satan-seduced synagogue of sinister souls in the second.

Chief of Satan's synagogues was the first church of Rome. Polycarp's trip to Rome to correct their errors allowed him to witness their worship service first hand. The laity came in, lighting candles and placing them before a stature of St. Peter while prostrating themselves.[1060]

Adding to this idolatry, they participated in pagan Easter celebrations, accepted bribes, legalized adulteries, and committed blackmail. The clergy were exalted above the laity by their power to manifest transubstantiation, the changing of common bread and wine into the literal body and blood of Christ. With idolatry and lies like these, Satan succeeded in creating his own synagogue, a man-made organization fully devoid of Bible truth.

On page 151 in Hazeltine's writing about Tertullian's time period, the first church of Rome grew through the aide of the emperors. Rome's evil bishops would report names of genuine Christians who opposed them to the emperors, who would have them exiled or killed: "The emperors were murderous and the bishops of the first Roman church loved it so." Carnal, pretend Christians of the false vine always kill the saints of the true. Galatians 4:29 reads, *"But as then he that was born after the flesh persecuted him that was born after the Spirit, even so it is now."*

Yes, the saints of the Smyrnaean Age were hunted down, imprisoned, put on trial, and martyred for Jesus' sake. The false vine continually increased their brutality, so much so that Tertullian was said to have used his astute skills as a lawyer to plead many times for the lives of Christians on trial.[1061]

10 Roman Emperors—Nero, Trajan, Hadrian, Aurelius, Severus, Maximin, Decius, Valerian, Aurelian, Diocletian—initiated ten awful persecutions upon Christians, with Diocletian's being the worst and

---

1060 Hazeltine, p. 114
1061 Hazeltine, p. 132

lasting 10 years. The 10 years of extreme violence occurred through Diocletian's four edicts:

- "An issue to tear down the churches to the foundations and to destroy the Sacred Scriptures by fire; and commanding also that those who were in honourable stations should be degraded if they persevered in their adherence to Christianity"
- "The order that the bishops, presbyters, and deacons should be imprisoned"
- The order that the bishops and other clergymen "should be tortured and compelled by every means to sacrifice"
- The order that the laity should be tortured. "The atrocious cruelty with which these edicts were enforced, and the vast numbers of those who suffered for the Faith are attested by Eusebius and the Acts of the Martyrs. We read even of the massacre of the whole population of a town because they declared themselves Christians."[1062]

The Rewards: Our Savior offers two rewards for overcomers: the crown of life and escape from the second death. While every reward uniquely matches its respective age, every overcomer from every age inherits all the rewards. Revelation 21:7 promises, *"He that overcometh shall inherit all things; and I will be his God, and he shall be my son."*

Every overcomer gets an incorruptible crown of life because they overcame death's corruptible rewards during their earthly journey. Millions upon millions earned the crown of life as a martyr in this Smyrnaean Age, but Paul says there is a crown for all who love Jesus' appearing in 2 Timothy 4:8: *"Henceforth there is laid up for me a crown of righteousness, which the Lord, the righteous judge, shall give me at that day: and not to me only, but unto all them also that love his appearing."*

1062 "Diocletian." *New Advent: The Catholic Encyclopedia,* https://www.newadvent.org/cathen/05007b.htm. Accessed 29 June 2020

Jesus wore a crown of thorns so that you could wear a crown of life. If Jesus could patiently endure the most brutal death imaginable, and Smyrnaean saints like Justin Martyr, Irenaeus, Origen, and Novatianus could endure their persecutions, you can patiently suffer through your tests. James 1:12 teaches your blessing will be the magnificent crown of life: *"Blessed is the man that endureth temptation: for when he is tried, he shall receive the crown of life, which the Lord hath promised to them that love him."*

Overcomers are not hurt of the second death, which takes place in the lake of fire, based upon Revelation 20:14: *"And death and hell were cast into the lake of fire. This is the second death."* The first death is the end of natural life on earth, one's decease. The body decays and loses its form. So the second death is the end of spiritual life, the life of the soul, and the unbeliever's soul will lose its form and vanish away completely. Sinful souls have an ending point and will come to total annihilation, ceasing to exist. You have likely been told souls are tormented without end, but that is a very shallow belief that God's Word quickly rectifies.

Without devoting substantial time to this point, start with combining truths from 1 John 3:15 and Revelation 21:8 that say murderers do not possess eternal life and will burn in the lake of fire. Without eternal life, which is the Spirit of Jesus Christ, murderers cannot burn or suffer eternally, without end. Wicked ones may burn for millions of years or longer, but at some point they will cease to exist.

Consider how shallow it is to designate eternal life to a location, heaven, instead of a Person, for Christ is the Person of eternal life. Eternal life is not a place you go to; rather, it is a Spirit that comes to live *in* you. Additionally, if a sinner is going to burn eternally, then he already has the same kind of life you have, but you know the error of that thinking. Jesus' life inside you is what makes you eternally different than a sinner. Romans 8:10 declares, *"And if Christ be in you, the body is dead because of sin; but the Spirit is life because of righteousness."*

The Smyrnaean saints received the second life, eternal life, in their lifetimes, which is the same life you receive because you surrendered your earthly life for Jesus' purpose. Being born again, the Holy Ghost in your soul is an earnest, or downpayment in the Greek Lexicon, of eternal life. 2 Corinthians 1:22 declares Jesus' Spirit has *"also sealed us, and given the earnest of the Spirit in our hearts."* The second death cannot hurt you because you already possess a portion of unending life.

Look at Jesus' claim that real believers pass from death to life in John 5:24: *"Verily, verily, I say unto you, He that heareth my word, and believeth on him that sent me, hath everlasting life, and shall not come into condemnation; but is passed from death unto life."* All fear is gone because your soul possesses an earnest of the second life, eternal life.

THE PERGAMEAN CHURCH AGE (312-606) IN REVELATION 2:12-17

Star: Martin of Tours is the angel-star to the Pergamean Age, who was trained in the gospel under Hillary of Poitiers in France. Hillary filled Martin's mind with apostolic teachings straight from Scripture, as he was not under Rome's influence.[1063]

After the Lord led Martin into his individual ministry, he helped his pagan mother and sister convert to Christianity. Martin built both a school and chapel for prayer, and numerous men of God were sent forth from these institutions by the Holy Spirit to do great works in Jesus' name.

God performed many mighty signs and miracles in Martin's ministry as he dedicated himself to study, prayer, and fasting. The laws of nature were defied to vindicate Martin's stand against idolatry, doors supernaturally opened solely by God's power, golden light shone from his body, and the dead were raised to life. Hazeltine writes that Martin's life, from conversion to death, "was one constant miracle."[1064] Full of God's love, Martin traveled over 300 miles to plead with Spanish bishops for the life of his friend.

Martin refused any fellowship with evil men promoting the first church of Rome. He saw how Rome's man-made creeds, which allowed

1063   Hazeltine, p. 241
1064   Hazeltine, pp. 242-246

idolatry, killing, lies, and more, left the Roman church powerless in the Holy Spirit.

After Martin's death, many sick touched his tomb and were healed, just as God honored Elisha's bones in 2 Kings 13:21. Martin was not canonized by Rome, but certainly by God.

Christ's Divinity: Jesus reveals Himself as *"he which hath the sharp sword with two edges."* His third revelation of His deity is His identity as the Word. Scripture verifies Jesus is the Word, the Word is a sword, the Word proceeds out of His mouth like a sword, and His name is the Word of God.[1065] You cannot separate Jesus from the Word, for they are one and the same.

The Word is also truth according to John 17:17, and Jesus calls the Holy Spirit *"the Spirit of truth"* in John 14:17. The world—which includes iniquity-working church members and sinners—cannot receive the Holy Spirit because they disobey God's Word. Yet the disobedient own Bibles, just like the Pharisees owned scrolls, but manifest they are not God's children by blaspheming the true understanding of the Word. John 8:47 says, *"He that is of God heareth God's words: ye therefore hear them not, because ye are not of God."*

The Holy Spirit gives the true interpretation of the Word to every age, and the bride, or true church of Jesus, from each age, hears it and speaks the same truth. Revelation 2:17 says, *"He that hath an ear, let him hear what the Spirit saith unto the churches"*, and Revelation 22:17 says, *"And the Spirit and the bride say, Come. And let him that heareth say, Come. And let him that is athirst come. And whosoever will, let him take the water of life freely."* Christ is the Word, and His bride always believes Him and speaks His truth, like Martin and the Pergamean saints.

Message to the True Vine: Jesus knows the true vine's works, dwelling place, their grip on His name, and stand for His faith even unto martyrdom. He commands some of the true vine to repent for holding two false doctrines—Balaam and Nicolaitanes. Certainly the leading men of this age like Hillary, Martin, and Patrick never agreed with those lies. The

---

1065   John 1:1-3, 1:14, Ephesians 6:17, Hebrews 4:12, 1 John 5:7, Revelation 19:13-15

Balaam and Nicolaitane doctrines and the false vine who propagated them will be covered in the next section.

Genuine Christian flocks labored on in Jesus' name throughout Europe, Asia, and Africa. Despite Rome being overcome with wolves in sheep's clothing working iniquity, the true vine was *"zealous of good works"*, knowing they were *"created in Christ Jesus unto good works."*[1066] They had read *"faith without works is dead"* in James 2:26, and their faith worked by love.

As this would be the age in which the false church united with the Roman state, exponentially growing in wealth, power, and influence, Broadbent notes how the true vine continued to exist by the power and simplicity of the written Word:

> "There remained, however, through all these times one thing capable of bringing about restoration. The presence of the Scriptures in the world supplied the means which the Holy Spirit could use in the hearts of men with a power able to overcome error and bring them back to divine truth, and there never ceased to be congregations, true churches, which adhered to the Scriptures as the guide of faith and doctrine, and the pattern both for individual conduct and for the order of the church. These, though hidden and despised, yet exercised an influence that did not fail to bear fruit."[1067]

In every dwelling place of the true vine, Jesus' presence dwelt there as well. He blessed their works as they held onto His name and received His faith. Human faith is never enough, as Paul says he lived by Jesus' faith, not his, in Galatians 2:20: *"I am crucified with Christ: nevertheless I live; yet not I, but Christ liveth in me: and the life which I now live in the flesh I live by the faith of the Son of God, who loved me, and gave himself for me."* Peter teaches miracles and all works of faith are done through Jesus' name and by Jesus' faith in Acts 3:16: *"And his name through faith in his name hath made this man strong, whom ye see and know: yea, the*

1066 Ephesians 2:10, Titus 2:14
1067 Broadbent, p. 33

faith which is by him hath given him this perfect soundness in the presence of you all."

St. Patrick of Ireland (372-461), whose given name was Sucat, is a saint from the Pergamean Age who held onto Jesus' name and kept His faith. Patrick was robbed of his childhood, and he and his two sisters were kidnapped and sold as slaves, with Patrick being taken to northern Ireland to herd swine. It was there he repented, being converted by God's Spirit. Upon returning home to his mother in France, he enrolled in his uncle's Martin's Bible school. This is the same Martin of Tours who was the star-messenger of this age.[1068] Patrick grew in grace and faith.

Having God's leading to take the gospel to Ireland where he once worked as a slave, he and other ministers did just that and witnessed the Holy Ghost do many miraculous acts. One barbarian chief witnessed so many miracles through Patricks' life that he and his entire household repented and received Christ. Just as Jesus promised in Mark 16:18, Patrick took up serpents and was not hurt. He laid his hands on the sick, and they recovered by Jesus' faith, just as his Uncle Martin did.

Patrick was once approached by an embassy from Rome to visit Rome, but he refused, knowing their wickedness. It is believed the entire island received the pure gospel of the Lord Jesus Christ through Patrick's efforts. Sadly, 100,000 of Patrick's spiritual children were slaughtered through the efforts of Roman Jesuits in 1640. But their genuine faith in Jesus' name undoubtedly provided them a place in glory upon their martyrdoms.

Iniquity of the False Vine: Christ knows Satan's seat of habitation and hates his two devilish doctrines: Balaam and Nicolaitanes.

Satan's earthly seat, or headquarters, had three locations. Genesis 10:10 shows it began in modern Iraq, in the land of Shinar, and became known as the kingdom of Babel. Hislop says Satan's seat moved to Pergamos when the Babylonian Pontiff, Attalus III, was expelled from Iraq by Medo-Persian kings.[1069] Attalus III reigned in Pergamos from

1068 Hazeltine, pp. 247-253
1069 Hislop, pp. 240-241

138-133 B.C. and at his death bequeathed the province to Rome.[1070] Antipas the faithful martyr was slain with other saints in Pergamos, Satan's temporary seat.

Satan's third and final seat became Rome in this church age, as predicted by John identifying Mystery Babylon as the city on seven hills in Revelation 17:5-9. This took place when Constantine I moved Rome's capital to Constantinople in 330, signaling the empire's weakened civil authority and the strengthening of its papal authority. With the empire's civil authority out of Rome, the city's religious authority grew, vested in the first church of Rome. The Ancient Roman Empire fell in the fifth century, but its papal empire began to rise, fulfilling Revelation 13:1-3. Ancient pagan Rome was the beast out of the sea whose one head was wounded, but healed. When pagan Rome fell in fifth century, everyone thought the beast was dead, but it lives to this day in papal Rome, the Roman Catholic Church (See Chapter 9).

This age's first hateful doctrine, the doctrine of Balaam, imitates Balaam's teaching, who infamously caused Israel to stumble into idolatry and fornication at Baal-Peor in Numbers chapters 22-25. Jesus warns that some in the New Testament church would join themselves to idolatry and fornication as "Israel joined himself unto Baal-peor."[1071]

In Numbers 25, a group of Israelis attended a Balaam-designed, Moabite-sponsored feast and stumbled in the sins of fornication and idolatry. Baal-Peor was an immoral union of two groups. Note that Moses, Aaron, Phinehas, and other faithful Jews never attended. God's anger was kindled against the Israeli compromisers, and 24,000 died in the judgment plague.

The New Testament's immoral union was the church uniting with the Roman state during Constantine I's reign. Like Moses despised Baal-Peor and never joined them, the true vine never united with Rome, but many left the true churches to unite with the Roman state.

1070 "Attalus III: Philometor Euergetes ('Loving-his-mother Benefactor')." *Encyclopedia Britannica*, https://www.britannica.com/biography/Attalus-III-Philometor-Euergetes
1071 Numbers 25:3

In 312 A.D, Constantine had a spiritual experience (a dream or vision of Jesus' cross) which led him to a military victory. The next year, his Edict of Milan freed Christians from persecution and began Rome's evolution into a so-called Christian state.

Constantine's early work for Christians included donating lavish buildings and erecting beautiful edifices for worship, courtesy of the state.[1072] Instead of sharing in the poverty of Christ, which included small group gatherings in humble homes and cottage prayer meetings,[1073] the false church inherited royal palaces and gorgeous assembly halls, attracting lukewarm believers instead of Spirit-filled saints.

Sadly, Constantine either never heard the true gospel or rejected it because his life bore many corrupt fruits. One, he never corrected the first church of Rome. It was already a pagan organization, only with the Christian name. Before this time, the first church was already committing the following wickedness among others: statue and Eucharist worship, transubstantiation, bribery, adulteries, infant baptisms, and baptizing the dead. Herein is fulfilled Jesus' rebuke to this Balaam doctrine, as idolatry and sexual sin was permitted. Hazeltine writes the first church of Rome continued to "develop unobserved" by Constantine.[1074] Two, he exalted himself as "the 13th Apostle",[1075] yet his compromise with the first church of Rome and lack of the signs of an apostle make him unfit of this self-imposed title. 2 Corinthians 12:12 reads, *"Truly the signs of an apostle were wrought among you in all patience, in signs, and wonders, and mighty deeds."* Three, he had his eldest son and wife murdered in Constantinople while he was away celebrating his victories in Rome.[1076] These murders occurred over a decade after his supposed conversion. 1 John 3:15 says no murderer, such as Constantine, has eternal life abiding in him.

Just as Baal-Peor had their feast, Constantine had his own 10-month feast in 325 A.D., called the Council of Nicea. His purpose was to unite

1072 "Constantine I"
1073 Hazeltine, p. 316
1074 Hazeltine, p. 221
1075 "Constantine I"
1076 Ibid.

all churches on Jesus' divinity, as Arius' doctrine that Jesus was a created being and not equal with the Father was questioned.[1077] The council rejected Arius' doctrines, which led to the council to plant the seeds of what would later become the Nicene Creed, a Scripture-denying confession of a false "three person" God. Thus the legacy of this compromised council was that preeminence was given to creeds rather than the Word. Here the church stumbled by uniting with creeds instead of the Word. The idolatry, adulteries, and other sins of the first church of Rome were deemed acceptable by their sister churches as the Roman church held to the creeds of the Council of Nicea.

The Nicolaitane doctrine is the second doctrine Jesus hates from this age. Unconverted church leaders continued to be victors over the people by exalting themselves above the laity and instituting false doctrines. The doctrine of transubstantiation worked to exalt the clergy because they claimed to have a miraculous power[1078] to change bread and wine into Jesus' literal body and blood. Additionally, Constantine's church-state union "adopted human rule in place of the guidance of the Spirit," which led clergy to compete for lucrative positions and power just as publicly as political leaders competed.[1079]

With men ruling men instead of the Holy Spirit ruling, the unconverted clergy began using state power to persecute and kill the converted. Through clergy influence, Roman emperor Theodosius' 380 A.D. edict ordered all Christians to be called "Catholic Christians," branding all other names as heretics, with threat of heavy penalties against the disobedient.[1080] Remember, Jesus said the overcomers would hold fast His name in Revelation 2:13—not the Catholic name.

Priscillian,[1081] a Holy Ghost-filled bishop of Spain, and six others, are said to be the first saints executed by the false church in 385 A.D.[1082] While surprising to some, St. Augustine (354-430), usually lauded

---

1077   Broadbent, p. 21
1078   Broadbent, p. 9
1079   Broadbent, p. 23
1080   Hazeltine, p. 287
1081   Hazeltine, pp. 260-265
1082   Broadbent, p. 37

for his theology, is said to have made popes fearless in killing anyone who disagreed with them. When asked of his opinion on the death of a man killed simply for reading Origen's works, Augustine wrote: "It is much better that some should perish by their own fires, than that the whole body should burn in the everlasting flames of Gehenna, through the desert of their impious dissensions."[1083] Broadbent agrees his teachings "incited and justified...methods of persecution by which Papal Rome equalled the cruelties of Pagan Rome."[1084] In 411 A.D., Augustine appealed to his allied Roman bishops and officials to settle his doctrinal dispute with the Donatists, which he won.[1085] Augustine was clearly on Rome's side, as he more than any other writer taught salvation alone through the church and her sacraments.

It is significant that the first pope rises from this age, Damascus (304-384),[1086] and it is possible that the age ended with Pope Boniface III giving himself the title "universal bishop." Like the lawyers in Jesus' day, these popes and others took the key of knowledge from the people by limiting Scripture readings to Latin only. Bible historian Dr. Craig Lampe says the Bible was available in 500 languages in 400 A.D., but was only heard in one—Latin—100 years later.[1087]

Our Lord had warned this age, *"Repent; or else I will come unto thee quickly, and will fight against them with the sword of my mouth"*, but the false vine stiffened their necks. In repayment, God fought against Satan's new Roman seat. Rome was captured by the Goths under Alaric in 410, and the Western Roman Empire ended in 476.[1088] Pagan, Ancient Rome died, but lived again in the papal, Holy Roman Empire.

The Rewards: The Pergamean overcomer is promised to eat of the hidden manna and receive a white stone with a new name written therein.

1083 Hazeltine, pp. 278-282
1084 Broadbent, pp. 26-27
1085 "Saint Augustine." *Encyclopedia Britannica*, https://www.britannica.com/biography/Saint-Augustine
1086 Hazeltine, p. 16
1087 "The Forbidden Book - History of The English Bible." *YouTube*, uploaded by Christian Media Network, 10 October 2019, https://www.youtube.com/watch?v=EjUqTT2I4kA
1088 Broadbent, p. 24

Manna was angel's food given to Israel during their wilderness journey in Exodus 16. In verse 33, God instructs Moses to hide a pot of manna in the Holiest of Holies *"to be kept for your generations."* Only the high priests could ever see this hidden manna, but Jesus came as the Living Bread from heaven to us, which Word we live by.[1089] The Pergamean saints ate spiritual hidden manna as they daily lived in Jesus' presence. They were privileged to partake of this hidden revelation of Jesus Christ, hidden from bishops, popes, and even emperors like Constantine. Every believer also has the future promise to partake of the hidden manna Jesus will give to us in the New Jerusalem. There, He will answer all our questions and feed us the desire of our souls throughout all eternity.

The white stone with a new name represents a lasting revelation of Jesus' righteousness, as revelation is the rock the church is built upon according to Matthew 16:17-18. White is the righteousness of saints, or Jesus' righteousness He shares with us. Recall the false vine of this age rewarded themselves with massive, beautiful structures to hold vain church services while the true vine hid out in caves, dens, homes, woods, and more. The false vine wanted great, natural stones in this life to build churches for their spiritually dead members, but the true vine desired Jesus' future reward of the spiritual white stones. Accompanying this lasting righteousness is your new name, for you held fast the name of the Lord Jesus Christ.

THE THYATIREAN CHURCH AGE (606-1520) IN REVELATION 2:18-29

Star: Columba is the angel-star to this age. He was born of royal blood in northern Ireland, but thankfully his father, Fergus, valued Jesus' cross more than his physical royal blood. Fergus diligently taught Columba the Scripture. Columba became a powerful missionary after hearing Jesus' audible voice call him into missionary work.

Some historians place Columba's supernatural missionary works in second place after Jesus' apostles. Two testimonies stick out in regards to

1089   Matthew 4:4, John 6:51

God's power to save the lost. Visiting one heathen city, Columba prayed outside the gates while magicians inside the city tried to drown out his voice. God increased the volume of his prayers until the Holy Spirit swung open the gates so heathens could hear and receive Christ. A second, similar testimony is told of Columba praying to enter a walled city. Being refused entrance, he turned to leave, but the chief's son became violently ill and the chief called for Columba to pray for his son. After the chief repented, God healed the son and Christ won souls in the city.[1090]

Dr. Craig Lampe credits Columba's work of preserving God's Word in the Dark Ages with making the Reformation possible.[1091] In 563 A.D. Columba started a Bible college in Iona, located in western Scotland. It's believed the barren Ionian ground turned fruitful after Columba planted seeds with one hand and lifted the other in prayer to Jesus. Lampe says Columba's college "would continue through the Dark Ages. The vast majority of evangelism that took place for the next 700 years took place as a result of that Bible college."

Due to its great missionary efforts, the island was nicknamed the "Isle of the Saints."[1092] From it flowed many missionaries into Scotland, Ireland, and England. Building missionary villages was their main method of winning souls. Small groups of saints who were builders, preachers, and teachers would raise walls around their newly formed community and make converts of those who moved into their village. Faithful preachers and teachers were established among the new converts and trained to repeat this method. These Christian villages remained independent from Rome and government aid, keeping the true faith alive in Jesus' little flock during the awful Dark Ages. Few men of God had such lasting and far-reaching influence as Columba.

Christ's Divinity: Jesus reveals to Thyatria that He is *"the Son of God, who hath his eyes like unto a flame of fire, and his feet are like fine brass."* He was most often called the "Son of Man" during His earthly ministry, but here claims His rightful title as Son of God, seated on heaven's throne

1090 Hazeltine, pp. 333-337
1091 "The Forbidden Book - History of The English Bible"
1092 Broadbent, pp. 34-35

at the right hand of the majesty on high. Christ must tell this age He alone is the Son of God to witness against the rise of papal power. Near the end of this age, Thomas Aquinas and Alvarus Pelagius both observed how many saw the pope "not as a man, but a God" with no bounds to his authority.[1093] Rejecting the pope's universal authority, they said, meant being shut out from salvation. This age also saw the rise of Islam, which denies Jesus is God's Son, blaspheming His holy blood as the one and only atonement. But Jesus, full of truth, is God's only begotten Son, as every overcomer believes: *"Who is he that overcometh the world, but he that believeth that Jesus is the Son of God?"*[1094]

Jesus' fiery eyes give warning that He looks upon the evil of this age with vengeance and will bring all wicked deeds into judgment. At Armageddon, Christ returns to destroy all His enemies with *"eyes...as a flame of fire."*[1095] The Son's feet of brass also speak of judgment, as animal sacrifices died in fiery judgment for Israel's sins on the brazen altar. Jesus bore His cross, passing through judgment for us, but at His second coming He will trample down unbelievers in judgment with His holy, nail-scarred feet.

Message to the True Vine: Jesus knew the saints' works, charity, service, faith, and patience. He also knew the last works of the age would outdo the first works. The Lord put no other burden upon the true vine than to hold fast to its love-service until His coming.

Notice Jesus acknowledged the works at the beginning and ending of the age. You've read about the beginning works, which included Columba's foundational missionary method. The Thyatirean saints followed Columba's example for at least the next 700 years, as Jesus also complimented their charity, service, faith, and patience. Since this was the true vine, their ever-increasing and pleasing works were motived by charity. Paul teaches any works without charity are unprofitable in 1 Corinthians 13:1-3. Jesus complimented Columba and countless other saints for their love-inspired works. Their faith worked by love—Jesus' love shed abroad in their hearts by the Holy Ghost.

1093   Broadbent, p. 105
1094   1 John 5:5
1095   Revelation 19:12

The greater works at the end of the Thyatirean Age included those of John Wycliffe, John Huss, Johannes Gutenberg, and Desiderius Erasmus, among many others. Risking their own lives against all evil Roman adversaries, these men spread God's Word in remarkable fashion.

John Wycliffe (1330-1384) systematically attacked Catholicism as the most prominent scholar at Oxford University. His doctrinal lecture notes—which exalted "Scripture alone" as truth—were copied and taken to other countries as ammunition against Rome.[1096] Defying the pope and transubstantiation, Wycliffe fled as a refugee to Lutterworth, England, where he spent the rest of his life working on his greatest achievement—the first complete translation of the Bible into English.[1097] Well after his death, his English Bible was banned by the Archbishop of York in 1408. He was so hated by Rome that in 1428, 44 years after his death, Pope Martin V ordered Wycliffe's bones to be dug up and burned, and his ashes were thrown into the River Swift.[1098]

Czech preacher John Huss (1370-1415) came to follow Wycliffe's teachings through Jerome of Prague, who heard Wycliffe at Oxford.[1099] Huss labored for religious reforms while rebuking the pope. Before being burned at the stake, his last words prophesied of a man to be raised up whose calls for reforms and changes could not be suppressed. Miraculously, 102 years later, God raised up Martin Luther, who would not be suppressed and nailed his 95 Theses to the church door in Wittenberg, Germany. Huss' followers eventually formed the Moravian Brethren, who played a major part in the conversion of the Wesley brothers.[1100]

German craftsman Johannes Gutenberg (1390-1468) dedicated his life to perfecting the printing press with reusable, movable type, allowing

---

1096 Broadbent, pp. 117-121
1097 "John Wycliffe." *Encyclopedia Britannica*, https://www.britannica.com/biography/John-Wycliffe
1098 "The Forbidden Book - History of The English Bible"
1099 Broadbent, p. 123
1100 "John Huss." *Christianity Today*, https://www.christianitytoday.com/history/people/martyrs/john-huss.html

books to be printed more quickly at a lower cost.[1101] Jesus anointed Johannes' painstaking, detail-oriented work, leading to the publication of the Gutenberg Bible in 1455. Through his efforts, both the middle and lower classes could finally access the Bible, fueling spiritual awakenings.

Desiderius Erasmus (1469-1536) was the best known scholar in Europe, his greatest work being the publication of the Greek New Testament, a two part study Bible that included a new Latin edition in 1516.[1102] Previous to this publication, Erasmus had seen first hand the revivals of thousands sparked by John Colet reading the Scripture to people in their own language. The rest of Erasmus' life was devoted to translating Scripture, and his works made possible future Bible translations by Luther and Tyndale.[1103] Lampe echoes Erasmus' famous quote: "I wish that even the weakest woman might read the Gospels and the Epistles of St. Paul…I long for the day when the husbandman shall sing portions of them to himself as he follows the plough."

Jesus assured this age that He accepted their service. Recall His highest compliment is for faithful service in Matthew 25:21: *"Well done, thou good and faithful servant: thou hast been faithful over a few things, I will make thee ruler over many things: enter thou into the joy of thy lord."* It is faithful servants who Jesus rewards.

Thyatira means "odor of affliction" in the Greek, and many saints in this age fulfilled this description by giving their lives as martyrs. Each time a saint died, Christ smelled a sweet-smelling heavenly savor just as the Father smelled a divine aroma when Jesus sacrificed Himself for us. Ephesians 5:1-2 captures this truth: *"Be ye therefore followers of God, as dear children; And walk in love, as Christ also hath loved us, and hath given himself for us an offering and a sacrifice to God for a sweetsmelling savour."*

Christian persecution continued in this age, which undoubtedly was the bloodiest of all ages. Theologian Samuel Schmucker estimated 68 million Christians were martyred from the time Augustine gave his

---

1101   "Johannes Gutenberg." *Encyclopedia Brittanica*, https://www.britannica.com/biography/Johannes-Gutenberg

1102   Broadbent, pp. 114-115

1103   "The Forbidden Book - History of The English Bible"

approval for persecution in the 5th century until Schmucker's lifetime in the 19th century.[1104] The saints in the Thyatirean Age served Christ with godly works until most died at the hands of the first church of Rome, their Crusades, and the Inquisition. Broadbent says the Catholics were absorbed in violent enthusiasm for the Crusades and the "Inquisition finished with the Crusade had left undone."[1105]

Iniquity of the False Vine: Christ chides the false church for suffering Jezebel to teach false doctrines, and seducing His servants into fornication and idolatry. Jezebel was given space to repent, but didn't, causing her to go into the depths of Satan. Righteous Jesus will judge Jezebel, her adulterous lovers, and her children with death.

In this Thyatirean Age, Jezebel is not a literal woman; rather, she is the Roman Catholic Church. In the Old Testament, Ahab married Jezebel for political purposes, and this union led Israel into the depths of Satan. Likewise in the New Testament, Constantine married the state to the Roman church for political reasons in the third age which plunged it into the depths of Satan in the fourth age. Both the original Jezebel and the Catholics in this age were guilty of teaching sexual immorality, idolatry, murder, silencing true preachers, and erecting houses of false worship.

Catholicism stooped to the depths of Satan in this fourth age by first adopting the deeds of the Nicolaitanes in the first age. In the third age, Catholicism made these deeds unbending church doctrines. Satan's depths meant a man, the pope, ruling over men instead of the Holy Ghost. Catholicism was indeed the mother, or first man-made, man-led, demonic system of organization.

Here it is observed that man-made organizations always produce spiritual death. Jesus called this Jezebel-system the depths of Satan. Every denomination is spiritually dead because they have denied further revelation of the Holy Spirit. Every denomination—whether Catholic, Lutheran, Methodist, Baptist, etc.—instantly dies when it writes its tradition-based by-laws and refuses to accept more truth. Jesus said so:

1104 Hazeltine, p. 282
1105 Broadbent, pp. 33, 89

"Thus have ye made the commandment of God of none effect by your tradition."[1106] Denominations limit God to moving solely based upon their interpretation of Scripture. Like Israel, each denomination starts serving God, but ultimately limits God, failing to gain more revelation, fulfilling Psalm 78:40-41: *"How oft did they provoke him in the wilderness, and grieve him in the desert! Yea, they turned back and tempted God, and limited the Holy One of Israel."*

As additional evidence, which denomination has ever had a real, Word-based revival and returned to the teachings of Paul, Peter, and John? None of them have, and they never will, for God's pattern is to call His people out of the Mother-Daughter system of Catholics and Protestants, according to Revelation 18:4: *"Come out of her, my people, that ye be not partakers of her sins, and that ye receive not of her plagues."* Every denomination, without fail, falls further and further from truth, as many now are publicly accepting homosexual clergy and celebrating transgenderism.

In the Thyatirean Age, Satan-filled popes carried out both the Crusades and inquisitions, slaughtering millions. Pope Urban II began the two century-long Crusades in 1095, promising total forgiveness of sins to any of his soldiers who died in battle.[1107] Dr. Lampe says the wars of the popes were carried out to capture the wealth of the world, as some popes fought to steal money to build Rome's extravagant basilicas. Foxe records the papal Inquisition, which later inspired the evil Spanish Inquisition, was instituted by Pope Innocent III (1160-1216) after Peter Waldo (1140-1205) preached boldly against Catholicism, saying, "The pope was antichrist, that mass was an abomination, that the host was an idol, and that purgatory was a fable."[1108]

Another way popes raised finances was by selling indulgences. Pope John XXII (1244-1334) established a list of tariffs for indulgences in which Catholics could kill a man for $1.75, ravish a virgin for $2, or be absolved of all sins for $12.[1109]

1106   Matthew 15:6
1107   "Pope Urban II Orders First Crusade." *History.com*, https://www.history.com/this-day-in-history/pope-urban-ii-orders-first-crusade
1108   Foxe, p. 130
1109   "The Forbidden Book - History of The English Bible"

Papal debauchery ruled this age. Urban VI (1318-1389) in Rome and Clement 7th (1342-1394) in France each claimed to be the true pope, threatening to excommunicate the other. Speaking of popes in general, Foxe says:

> "A worse set of men never corrupted the earth. From the time of Gregory the Great, in the sixth century, to the latest period, the popes have been more or less of abandoned principles. There have been covetous popes, proud popes, profane popes, unchaste popes, dishonest popes, murdering popes, all of whose names and characters may be seen in any impartial history of these pretended representatives upon earth of Him who was 'holy, harmless, and undefiled!'"[1110]

The Lord Jesus ends His rebuke to the false vine by warning He will judge Jezebel, her adulterous lovers, and her children with death. Idol worshippers are often called evil lovers in Scripture, as Malachi 2:11 says Judah was married to the *"daughter of a strange god."* The Jezebel system's lovers in this age were the European governments who bowed to her evils. The Crusades were possible only because European nations obeyed their lover, Jezebel, and her frontman's call to war, Pope Urban II.

Jezebel's children were all the daughter-churches who formed through efforts of the mother's proselytizing. All churches who supported Catholicism and its popes were children of the mother church, and Christ hated their idolatrous works. Having defied Jesus' warning, the false vine will be killed with death, or eternal separation from God, in the second death, the lake of fire. Chapter 9 fully details the mother-daughter relationship between Catholics and Protestants.

The Rewards: Christ's two rewards for the overcomers are power over nations and the morning star.

Power over nations is the perfect reward for all overcomers, but especially the Thyatirean saints. They lived in the darkest age, spiritually speaking, one that was dominated by papal Rome and the devil. It was

1110 Foxe, p. x

almost Satan's millennium, but it was not quite 1,000 years long. Believers like Columba, Peter Waldo, and Wycliffe defied nations for they were of a *"holy nation,"* being born again from above, from the heavenly nation. By forsaking worldly nations, Jesus grants the overcomers power over nations as rulers during the Millennium. Revelation 20:6 says, *"Blessed and holy is he that hath part in the first resurrection: on such the second death hath no power, but they shall be priests of God and of Christ, and shall reign with him a thousand years."* After suffering for Christ during their earthly lives, they are fit to rule and reign over nations.

Jesus appropriately promises to reward overcomers with the morning star, or His light, for He is the Morning Star according to Revelation 22:16: *"I Jesus have sent mine angel to testify unto you these things in the churches. I am the root and the offspring of David, and the bright and morning star."* Christ gives His overcomers the Morning Star because they suffered through the Dark Ages. In this age, popes fervently worked to keep the light of God's Word from the people, forbidding most from hearing and reading Scripture in their own languages. But God anointed men to take the light of His knowledge to every hungry heart and their heavenly reward will be Jesus sharing more of His light throughout all eternity.

In the natural, the morning star is the brightest light in the sky before dawn. Jesus is the true Morning Star, the hope of a new day, for when His day dawns, the Thyatirean saints will reign with Him in the 1,000 year Millennial Reign.

THE SARDISEAN CHURCH AGE (1520-1750) IN REVELATION 3:1-6

Star: Martin Luther is the angel-star to this age. One of the most well known Christians of all time, Luther sparked the Protestant Reformation as "a poor monk" standing against "the whole vast Papal power,"[1111] armed only with the Bible's liberating message of Habakkuk 2:4 and Romans 1:17—the just shall live by faith.

1111 "The Forbidden Book - History of The English Bible"

Luther's legacy is so vast it is hard to measure. Broadbent says Luther "revealed Christ to countless sinners" through "unprecedented power and courage" while writing many teaching tracts for Christian understanding.[1112] Some believe his greatest work was translating both the Old and New Testaments into German, but Luther also added much to the church's music, writing the hymn "A Mighty Fortress Is Our God", and it is believed that Luther operated and possessed all nine gifts of the Holy Spirit.[1113]

Climatic events abounded in Luther' life. Amazingly, he decided to become a monk after surviving a violent thunderstorm. Following numerous years in the ministry, he nailed his 95 Theses to the church door in Wittenberg in 1517 after witnessing a papal worker shamelessly sell indulgences in the streets. Three years later, he publicly burned the pope's letter of excommunication for him. Fully aware he may lose his life at the Diet of Worms, Luther refused to recant. This Sardisean star uttered his most inspired words: "My conscience is my guide. Scripture is my authority, and I can do no other than abide by it's teachings. Here I stand. God help me."

While Luther helped change the whole scope of Christianity, his work was unfulfilled. As he aged, his judgment failed at times. He became dogmatic to a fault, anti-Semitic, negative, and saw many of his followers leave. Luther wrote "not a tenth part" of his converts remained steadfast in the faith and said "we are almost utter heathen with the name of Christian."[1114] In some ways his Lutheran Church was reformed, but not fully. Luther kept the church-state system, the Catholic parish model, infant baptisms, and baptismal regeneration.

Despite these disappointments, Luther's defiance of Rome and Scriptural revelations mightily paved the way for every future preacher and translator.

Christ's Divinity: Revelation 3:1 reveals another aspect of Jesus' divinity, saying, "*These things saith he that hath the seven Spirits of God,*

1112 Broadbent, pp. 142-149
1113 Branham, p. 247
1114 Broadbent, p. 149

and the seven stars." You already know the seven stars are God's human, angel-messengers to the Seven Church Ages, but you need to know what the seven Spirits of God represent.

It is crucial to maintain God is only one Spirit, as taught by Jesus and Paul.[1115] But God manifests Himself in various ways, such as the one Holy Spirit working through nine different gifts of the Spirit in 1 Corinthians 12:4-13.

The seven Spirits appear four times in Revelation: 1:4, 3:1, 4:5, and 5:6. You learn four details about them: they are before God's throne, belong to Christ, appear as lamps of fire, and are sent forth into all the earth. These seven Spirits of God refer to the seven earthly ministries of the seven stars, as proven by the Word. First, God greatly honored their prayers when they came *"boldly unto the throne of grace"*[1116] for mercy and help. Second, they belonged to Christ, as Paul says he was a *"prisoner of Jesus Christ"* in Ephesians 3:1. Third, Proverbs 20:27 teaches the spirit of man is the candle, or lamp in Hebrew, of the Lord. Fourth, Zechariah 4:10 says seven men *"are the eyes of the LORD, which run to and fro through the whole earth."*

As you have seen thus far, these stars, or men—Paul, Irenaeus, Martin, Columba, and Luther—had unique ministries, but the same God supernaturally worked in their lives. Jesus heard their prayers, protected, fueled, and sent them to the world. Two out of the seven stars remain to be described, but you will see the same Lord moving in unique ways to manifest His light to each age. 1 Corinthians 12:5 declares this: *"And there are differences of administrations, but the same Lord."*

Message to the True Vine: Christ knows their works, encourages watchfulness, and instructs them to strengthen the things that remain that are ready to die. The saints were to remember how they received and heard the Word, holding fast to it, and repent because their works were not perfect before God. However, the all-knowing Messiah saw the few who walked worthy and undefiled in white garments.

1115   John 4:24, 1 Corinthians 12:13, Ephesians 2:18, 4:4
1116   Hebrews 4:16

While Jesus acknowledges the works of the true vine, He emphasizes they were not perfect, or unfulfilled. The Reformation is highly acclaimed for its spiritual illumination within the Dark Ages, and rightly so, but it did not fully separate from all Catholic traditions. Thankfully, Luther and other reformers purged the church from papal authority, transubstantiation, idolatry, Maryolatry, indulgences, and much more. But as noted previously, Luther and others leaders of this age retained some errors.

Notice Jesus urging the faithful few to strengthen what remained because the age was ready to die. Remember, Luther said he observed the church as "almost" heathen, showing it was ready to die, or denominate. Historically speaking, the Sardisean believers were to cling to justification by faith—the Reformation's main theme—because the majority of churches were going to die through organizing new daughter denominations. The previous age, Thyatira, saw the saints overcome Jezebel, the Mother Harlot denominational system of the Catholic Church. But Sardis was the age of spiritual Jezebel's daughter, Athaliah. She represented the daughter denominations raising after the mother denomination. The Sardisean Age saw the formation of denominational Lutherans and countless other sects, divisions, and man-made organizations. Denominational zeal was causing many to die spiritually.

Christ implored this age to remember how they first received the reformer's message of justification by faith. Peters emphasizes the power of memory to stir up believers in 2 Peter 3:1: "*Stir up your pure minds by way of remembrance*." This age needed to remember how they repented and became justified under preachers like Luther, Ulrich Zwingli, Heinrich Bullinger, and John Calvin, to name a few. Justification is only the first Work of Grace, with sanctification and the baptism of the Holy Ghost being the second and third work, respectively. God's foreknowledge recognized the majority of Sardisean believers would only accept justification, so He saved the full restoration of the second and third Works of Grace for the last two ages: Philadelphia and Laodicea.

However, a few worthy saints in the Sardisean Age were born again with the third Work of Grace, for that is what white raiment represents.

Putting Jude 1:23, Romans 13:14, Titus 3:5, and Revelation 3:18 together, you understand that Holy Spirit-filled souls are likened to wearing a white robe of Jesus' righteousness while alive on earth. Luther and Zwingli walked worthy in white robes.

Indeed, Luther was born again for he had Holy Ghost power as a witness in Germany and later risked his life defying the Holy Roman Emperor at the Diet of Worms. But his emphasis was preaching justification by faith to a stiff-necked people, who in the generation following him would relax spiritually and denominate, plunging themselves into spiritual death.

Other reformers and saints alike had the genuine, new birth experience, but they were all subject to the conditions of their age and thereby struggled to always magnify truth. Christians living today in the Laodicean Age do well to praise God for the strength of the reformers who triumphed over the utter corruption of the Dark Ages. Surely you can relate to the Sardisean saints' battle against denominationalism for you severely battle today's lazy, lukewarm conditions. Let us rejoice for the faithful few who walked worthy of Christ in white, many of whom gave their lives as martyrs for Jesus' holy name.

William Tyndale (1494-1536) must be remembered from this age. Called "The Prince of Translators" and "The Father of Modern English," Tyndale's translation of the Bible into English serves as one of the greatest contributions to Western civilization.[1117] Despite enduring 11 years of being hunted down for defying the pope and seeking to give the people an English Bible, he diligently translated the New Testament. While dying through strangulation and burning at the stake, Tyndale prayed, "Lord, open the king of England's eyes." Christ Jesus heard his prayer, for the very next year saw King Henry VIII grant permission and license to John Rogers to print the English Bible. The king later printed 20,000 English Bibles composed of 97% of Tyndale's work, called The Great Bible, and sent a copy to every church in England.[1118] The most accurate

---

1117 "Prince of Translators: William Tyndale." *Ligonier Ministries*, https://www.ligonier.org/blog/prince-translators-william-tyndale/
1118 "The Forbidden Book - History of the English Bible"

Bible ever written, the King James Version of 1611, contains 90% of Tyndale's translation work.

Praise the Lord for the few saints, like Luther and Tyndale, who walked worthy of the gospel in the Sardisean Age!

Iniquity of the False Vine: Christ rebukes the false vine for having a name they lived, yet were spiritually dead. This group would not repent of imperfect works, nor watch for Christ so He would come upon them as a thief in an unexpected hour.

Assuredly, the false vine of the Roman Catholic Church associated themselves with the name of Christ, but they lived contrary to His teachings. They arrogantly called themselves Catholics, which means universal. Their claim was to be concerned for the universal, world-wide Christian church, yet Jesus says they were dead. Indeed, they were spiritually dead, for they were more concerned with satisfying their lusts. Sadly, this age was known for vast papal prostitution.

Samuel Schmucker records that in the days of Pope Paul III (1468-1549), the popes were some of the most licentious men in history.[1119] Pope Paul accepted indulgences for sex acts with prostitutes after licensing brothels in Rome. The "holy city" alone had nearly 45,000 prostitutes in their public register. Imagine the total number of prostitutes throughout Rome-influenced Europe!

Foxe says Rome's monasteries and nunneries were "seats of iniquity," with the latter comparable to the worst brothels.[1120] Describing their evils in the days of Henry VIII (1491-1547), Foxe wrote, "When these monasteries were fully explored in England, the abbots, priors, and monks kept as many women each as any lascivious Mohammedan could desire, and their crimes renewed the existence of Sodom and Gomorrah!" In the days of Pope Paul V (1550-1621), the Roman Senate objected against his proposal to suppress licensed brothels because they were worried his priests would instead seduce the senators' wives and daughters.[1121] Yes, the false vine was dead in sins despite their claim to the precious name of Jesus.

1119 Schmucker, Samuel S. *The Glorious Reformation*, 1838
1120 Foxe, p. xi
1121 Foxe, p. 220

This age also saw the false vine promote denominationalism, taking the name of Lutherans and Hussites, but failing to obey their Bible instructions. Like Catholics, they had a denominational name, but were spiritually dead. Luther observed many in his generation were already dead, but the second generation would be worse, as the Lutheran denomination became a replica of the old Catholic system.[1122] The daughter harlot was just like the mother harlot.

Most second generation Lutherans did not live what Luther lived and thus died spiritually. This brings the Pharisees to mind, as they reviled Jesus and His message and claimed to be Moses' disciples in John 9:28. Jesus said they were children of hell. In reality, the Pharisees added and taught their own commandments rather than Moses', which Jesus exposed in Matthew 15:1-9. The Lutherans did the same, for if they had preached and lived what Luther preached, the blessings of justification by faith would have led them away from more false doctrine, organization, and complacency. Obedience to Luther's teachings would have brought strength and led them into sanctification and the baptism of the Holy Ghost. But they denominated, rebelled, and died.

Repentance was available, but refused. The false vine should have watched and waited for Jesus' Spirit to convict their hearts. They should have diligently prepared their lives to meet Jesus in peace, understanding His warning to come like a thief. Instead, they sold out their souls to temporary earthly pleasures and false religion.

The Rewards: Our Lord says the overcomers will be clothed in white raiment. Their names will not be blotted out of the Book of Life, but will be confessed before Jesus' Father and His angels.

The souls of born again Christians are currently adorned in white robes while living on earth, as Paul says we *"put on the Lord Jesus Christ"* and His *"armour of light"* in Romans 13:12-14. In the Greek, "put on" means "to sink into (clothing), put on, clothe one's self." But Jesus promises the future putting on of white robes, referring to the supernatural theophany or celestial bodies that house the Christian's soul after death

---

1122 Broadbent, p. 147

according to 2 Corinthians 5:1-4. All overcomers will have white-as-light raiment like Jesus wore on Mount Transfiguration in Matthew 17:2.

You already learned about the Book of Life in Chapter 6, but the special reward of your name remaining on the Book of Life is what Jesus directs His Sardisean Christians to strive for. This is because the overcomers confessed Jesus' name rather than the pope, Luther, Zwingli, or any other man's name. The few overcomers had Jesus' name and lived by it, walking worthy of the gospel.

Job 14:14-15 captures the truth of Jesus calling and confessing our names after death: *"If a man die, shall he live again? all the days of my appointed time will I wait, till my change come. Thou shalt call, and I will answer thee: thou wilt have a desire to the work of thine hands."* He will call every overcomer to meet Him in the air at the rapture. Then He will call them to sit down and feast at the Marriage Supper of the Lamb. Lastly, He will confess the names of the overcomers as they judge men and fallen angels at the White Throne Judgment, for they will sit with Him on His throne.

THE PHILADELPHIAN CHURCH AGE (1750-1906) IN REVELATION 3:7-13

Star: John Wesley is the angel-star to this age, being the founder of the Methodist movement and champion of the sanctification doctrine. He and his brother, Charles (a gifted song writer), were two of 19 children born to Samuel and Susanna Wesley. Samuel was a busy, traveling clergyman, and Susanna saw her children as talents committed to her by God. Since she had servants to assist her in housework, Susanna devoted much time to prayerful, godly child-training. She frequently gathered her children together to read Scripture and counsel them. Sometimes up to 200 people crowded her home to hear her readings.[1123]

Being trained and obedient to a disciplined Christian life from his youth, John grew in the faith and became an ordained minister. While on a missionary trip to Georgia, the holy lives of the Moravians made

---

1123 Broadbent, pp. 287-288

him realize he was not yet converted. Returning to England, he received inspiring words from Peter Boehler to continue preaching and seeking God. Blessed assurance descended from heaven into his soul on May 24, 1738.[1124]

With his message of a new, greater spiritual experience, John was rejected by the churches he had previously preached for. His old friend George Whitefield introduced him to open-air preaching, and God blessed his efforts with amazing, supernatural results as tens of thousands at a time attended his services.[1125]

The gifts of the Holy Ghost abounded in Wesley's ministry, as believers shook, fell to the ground as dead, wept, and shouted as they were healed and delivered from demons.[1126] The dumb spoke, the insane made sane, and the dead raised to life.[1127]

While Wesley always preached justification by faith, he argued Christians could experience entire sanctification in this life by "loving God and their neighbors, meekness and lowliness of heart, abstaining from all appearance of evil, and doing all for the glory of God."[1128] His organizational genius loosely united believers in faith-societies, or bands, to spread Christianity and yet let each individual church remain independent, proving his stand against denominationalism. Wesley's commitment to sanctification led him to "purge the societies of unworthy members, as he saw fit."[1129] The new life and energy of his movement could not be contained in the dead, established Church of England.

Wesley traveled 4,000 miles per year and preached over 40,000 sermons in his lifetime. Even at 88 years old he said he felt no infirmities of old age. At his death, he twice cried out, "The best of all is, God is with us!" God certainly was with Wesley and the sanctification-loving Methodists.

1124 "John Wesley: Methodist Pietist." *Christianity Today*, https://www.christianitytoday.com/history/people/denominationalfounders/john-wesley.html
1125 Broadbent, p. 291
1126 Broadbent, p. 292
1127 "John Wesley and the Power of the Spirit." *Jamin Bradley's Blog*, https://newfangled.wordpress.com/2010/05/12/john-wesley-and-the-power-of-the-spirit/
1128 "John Wesley: Methodist Pietist"
1129 Broadbent, p. 294

Christ's Divinity: Jesus tells Philadelphia, *"These things saith he that is holy, he that is true, he that hath the key of David, he that openeth, and no man shutteth; and shutteth, and no man openeth."* Christ alone is all holy and all true. Jesus only is exalted as "The Holy One," witnessed by devils, David, Peter, Paul, and John. His holiness was a result of Him always doing the Father's bidding.

Thankfully, Jesus shares His holiness with man via substitution. On the cross, God exchanged our sins for Jesus' holiness. Christ became sin so that we could become holy: *"For he hath made him to be sin for us, who knew no sin; that we might be made the righteousness of God in him."*[1130] Jesus' holiness is a free gift for every believer, but always remains accredited to His work. No man can boast of his own holiness. After healing a lame man, Peter (who was filled with the Holy Ghost) pleads with those marveling at the miracle to recognize it was not done through his *"own power or holiness."*[1131] Only Jesus' holiness heals. It is the only holiness in all the universe.

Jesus' grace imputes His holiness to us as we partake of His sufferings. Hebrews 12:10 says God chastens us *"for our profit, that we might be partakers of his holiness."* Four verses later, you read, *"Follow peace with all men, and holiness, without which no man shall see the Lord."* When Jesus returns in the rapture, believers gifted with the Holy Ghost will be *"holy still."*[1132] How kind for the Holy One to impute holiness to unholy men through the new birth!

Christ is He that is true, for He is the true light, true bread, true vine, true God, and true witness.[1133] Jesus is truth embodied in a Man, as He is the perfect realization of truth. John 1:14 proclaims He is *"full of grace and truth."* As the source of truth, Christ always spoke the truth. Thus, He corrected every false word, including those spoke by His mother, His disciples, the Pharisees, Pilate, Caiaphas, and Satan. In John 17:17, one of His final prayers before being arrested, Jesus said, *"Sanctify them through*

1130   2 Corinthians 5:21
1131   Acts 3:12
1132   Revelation 22:11
1133   John 1:9, 6:32, 15:1, 1 John 5:20, Revelation 3:14

thy truth: thy word is truth." Our True Messiah says His True Word will
sanctify, or separate, you from all profane things.

The key of David is Jesus' right and ability (for He is the *"Son of
David"*[1134]) to sit upon the throne of David as King of Israel in the
Millennium. Jesus has other keys—the keys of death and hell—which
allow Him to raise up His own to live with Him for the 1,000 year honeymoon. Jesus will open the Millennium to His worthy ones and will
close it in preparation for the White Throne Judgment. Isaiah 22:22
teaches the key of David is placed on Jesus' shoulder. The purpose of the
shoulder is to provide strength and range for the arm and hand. Jesus'
hand represents power, and the *"arm of the Lord"* symbolizes His ability
to redeem, save, and judge.[1135] Christ beautifully and powerfully saves
His elect. Luke 15:5 says He rejoices as He lays all His saved sheep on
His shoulders. Jesus takes full responsibility for you, His lamb, and rests
you upon His shoulder of saving, redeeming power.

Message to the True Vine: Jesus knows the works of the faithful
saints, and He sets before them an open door that no man can shut.
Christ sees their little strength, obedience to His Words, and how they
have not denied His name. Our Lord promises to make their enemies
worship before their feet and know that Jesus loves them. Another promise is that He will keep them from the worldwide time of temptation.
Jesus says He is coming quickly, so they must hold fast what they have,
that no man take their crown.

The open door has two interconnected meanings. First, this was
the age of unprecedented missionary work, and it was Paul who called a
new ministry opportunity in Troas an open door in 2 Corinthians 2:12:
*"Furthermore, when I came to Troas to preach Christ's gospel, and a door
was opened unto me of the Lord."* Broadbent says William Carey helped
to bring about "this sense of responsibility and of love to Christ and
to mankind."[1136] Carey's works included 41 years of ministry in India,
over 700 converts, numerous Bible translations, providing education for

1134   Matthew 1:1
1135   Exodus 6:6, 15:6
1136   Broadbent, p. 295

thousands, and initiating social reforms.[1137] His sacrificial works inspired many other missionaries like Hudson Taylor and David Livingstone to enter the global open door that men could not shut.

A second meaning for the open door is the spiritual revelation of Jesus as the door of the sheep in John 10:7: "*Then said Jesus unto them again, Verily, verily, I say unto you, I am the door of the sheep.*" The Philadelphian saints who entered into Christ, The Door, received His "*little strength*" to obey His Great Commission by making disciples of all nations.

The saints in this age confessed Jesus' name and had more strength than those of the Reformation. The Philadelphian saints acted upon Jesus' name by producing some of the greatest sermons and works of literature in history. With Jesus' strength, gifted men like Charles Spurgeon, Jonathan Edwards, and John Bunyan preached and wrote to magnify the name of Jesus Christ.

Just as the second age had lying enemies who called themselves Jews but were not, these Philadelphian saints battled similar liars. Historically speaking, it is difficult to identify this group, but it seems probable this synagogue of Satan was the Roman Catholic Church because she falsely claimed to be the original church. Either way, Jesus encouraged the true vine to be confident that He would show the false vine His love for true believers by making the false vine fall down at their feet at the White Throne Judgment. Liars may not bow now, but every knee shall bow before Jesus and His saints on Judgment Day. 1 Corinthians 6:2-3 promises, "*Do ye not know that the saints shall judge the world? and if the world shall be judged by you, are ye unworthy to judge the smallest matters? Know ye not that we shall judge angels? how much more things that pertain to this life?*"

The Lord's final words to this age emphasize His soon coming, saying, "*Behold, I come quickly.*" After the Philadelphian Age, there would only be one more age: Laodicea. Jesus' second coming was nearer than ever, and sinful human history was coming to a close. These saints kept

---

1137 "William Carey: Father of Modern Protestant Missions." *Christianity Today*, https://www.christianitytoday.com/history/people/missionaries/william-carey.html

the faith through tumultuous times, such as the American Revolution, the Napoleonic Wars, the French Revolution, and the American Civil War, to name a few.

Since the true vine had kept Jesus' word of patience by keeping His Word and confessing His Name, Jesus would keep them from the world-wide hour of temptation spoken of in Revelation 13:15-17. During the Tribulation, the image of the beast is going to try and force all to take the mark of the beast. This is still in the future, but Jesus gave this age blessed assurance that they would not see this wicked event. Chapter 12 outlines Jesus' promise that the true vine in Laodicea will not see this hour of temptation either. Christ will snatch His bride away in the rapture before the Tribulation sets in. God has not appointed us to wrath, but to obtain salvation.

No doubt we will see the ecumenical move grow and further unite with the world's governments. Since the mark of the beast will come out of the United States, or beast out of the earth,[1138] Americans will see the churches unite with the state to enact laws against true Christianity. Jesus' bride may be forced to stop preaching. She may be threatened with the loss of the privilege of buying and selling, but before the hour comes for the mark to be enforced upon all, Christ comes to rapture His bride away.

The true vine who held fast to Jesus' name and strength were to gain their crown and not allow another to take it. Crowns belong to rulers who reign, and two Bible examples illustrate this thought. King Saul was anointed and crowned, but his impatience and self-will caused his crown to be given to David and his sons. Judas Isacariot was given the highest office in the ministry, that of an apostle, but forfeited it, and his place was given to Matthias. Philadelphian saints persevered and kept the faith, ruling and reigning by wearing the full armor of God and overcoming Satan's synagogue. Their crown awaits them, along with a seat on Jesus' throne.

Iniquity of the False Vine: Christ says very little about the false vine in this age because the true vine had the open door and strength in His name. Conversely, the false vine weakened, as seen through the fading

---

1138   Revelation 13:11-18

power of the Inquisition and the fading influence Rome had over rulers. The rise of European nationalism and revolutions around the globe gave greater power to national leaders, who no longer feared popes.[1139]

Two portions of prophecy were being fulfilled during this time. First, the Roman, antichrist spirit was moving into the United States, to become the beast out of the land from Revelation 13. Second, the iron and clay of the "great image" in Daniel 2:42-43 were forming the final Catholic-Protestant kingdom. This image agreed upon false doctrines, but were not completely unified.

As Jesus said, the false vine were liars and their churches of Satan, for they continued persecuting the true vine. Broadbent tells of the persecution Wesley and his preachers faced: "Most violent opposition assailed the preachers from all sides. Riotous mobs attacked them and those who with them had confessed Christ, doing grievous injury to persons and property but all this was met by a courage and meekness which the adversaries were not able to withstand."[1140] Satan's liars name-called, criticized, broke up services, and threatened to kill the true vine[1141], but none could close Jesus' open door.

Jesus promised He would make the false group know His love for the true ones, and it seems this will be done at the White Throne Judgment. During this age, the false could not see Jesus' love for His saints because of the spirit of deception and iniquity they had accepted. Equipped with reprobate minds and blasphemous words, the false vine continued to think their killing was pleasing to God, Rome, and the pope. Their evil works matched the Pharisees of John 16:2-3: "*Yea, the time cometh, that whosoever killeth you will think that he doeth God service. And these things will they do unto you, because they have not known the Father, nor me.*" Had the Catholics known the Father and His Son's prayer for believers' sanctification through truth in John 17:17, they would have honored Wesley's revival.

1139 "When the Pope was Powerful and Why That Changed." *The Washington Post*, https://www.washingtonpost.com/news/worldviews/wp/2013/02/11/the-rise-and-decline-of-the-popes-once-great-power/?noredirect=on&utm_term=.66b401098e77
1140 Broadbent, p. 292
1141 "John Wesley: Methodist Pietist." *Christianity Today*, https://www.christianitytoday.com/history/people/denominationalfounders/john-wesley.html

The Rewards: Overcomers are made pillars in the temple of God and shall no more go out. Herein lies two truths. First, Christ's bride will be residents of the Millennial temple and never leave His side. Revelation 7:9-17 shows His Gentile people are like pillars in the temple, for they are *"before the throne of God, and serve him day and night in his temple: and he that sitteth on the throne shall dwell among them."* You know there is no temple in the New Jerusalem, for the Lamb *is* the temple throughout eternity. Second, overcomers become part of the spiritual temple of God taught in Ephesians 2:19-22. Bride members are built upon the original apostles and prophets with Jesus Christ being the chief cornerstone of the holy temple.

Another reward is for the overcomer to have three names written spiritually on the fleshly tables of his heart[1142]: God's name, the name of His city, and Jesus' new name. God's name is simply the Lord Jesus Christ, for John 5:43 says Jesus came in His Father's name. Jesus means "Jehovah is our salvation", and His name is the name above all names.[1143] Jesus is the image of Jehovah, the Father, for His proper name in Hebrew is Jehovah, or "Yhovah," the self existing One. God's city is named the New Jerusalem, and this name is etched upon the overcomer's heart for this is his eternal home. Jesus' new name is another divine mystery yet to be unveiled and will be magnificent beyond all description.

THE LAODICEAN CHURCH AGE (1906-PRESENT) IN REVELATION 3:14-22

Star: William Branham is the angel-star to this final Gentile age, meaning his Bible-based message from Jesus Christ is what the true church needs to hear today. This entire book is dedicated to sharing Jesus' Bible message for today, and Chapter 13 covers Branham's life, supernatural gifts, and Bible-foretold ministry. Summarizing his ministry's world-wide, lasting impact, the *Dictionary of Pentecostal and Charismatic Movements* states:

1142   2 Corinthians 3:3
1143   Ephesians 1:20-21, Philippians 2:9-10

"The person universally acknowledged as the revival's 'father' or 'pacesetter' was William Branham. The sudden appearance of his miraculous healing campaigns in 1946 set off a spiritual explosion in the Pentecostal movement which was to move to Main Street, U.S.A., by the 1950s and give birth to the broader charismatic movement in the 1960s, which currently affects almost every denomination in the country."[1144]

As the final angel-messenger to the Gentiles, Jesus sent Branham with an undeniable gift of discernment to know the thoughts and intents of hearts. The Holy Spirit repeatedly and boldly spoke with "Thus saith the Lord" through Brother Branham, as He had through prophets like Moses, Joshua, Ezekiel and Jeremiah. Numerous prophesies spoken by the Spirit through Branham have come to pass, and many more remain to be fulfilled as the second coming of Jesus nears.

Since Jesus had Luther emphasize justification and Wesley emphasize sanctification, the Savior had Branham major on the baptism of the Holy Ghost. This is the age of restoration. We are walking where the apostles trod. All mysteries are revealed. Believers' hearts are turned back to the apostolic fathers. Jesus is returning soon to rapture His bride off the earth before judgment falls.

Christ's Divinity: Our Lord signifies Himself as *"the Amen, the faithful and true witness, the beginning of the creation of God."* As our Amen in the last age, Jesus demonstrates His authority of having the last word. Amen means "so it is, so be it, may it be fulfilled" in the Greek. He opened the door to the Gentiles in Ephesus and will close it Himself, at His own appointed time, in Laodicea. His every promise to every age He will fulfill. As 2 Corinthians 1:20 declares, *"For all the promises of God in him are yea, and in him Amen, unto the glory of God by us."* Messiah is also connecting Himself with His "First and Last" title because the word *"Amen"* in the Greek is also used as the "Verily, verily" when beginning

1144 Burgess, Gary, et al. *Dictionary of Pentecostal and Charismatic Movements.* Grand Rapids: Zondervan, 1998

a statement. Jesus begins and ends His messages with the same, loving, eternal assurance that He will do what He said because He is the same yesterday, today, and forever.

Again, Jesus' deity is speaking. It is an astounding historical fact that only the first and last church ages knew Jesus as one Person and not the "second person" of a man-made trinity dogma. Jesus is the invisible God made flesh. He is the image of the one and only God. You will never see the Father, but He has taken on a flesh body so that He can be touched and handled. Indeed, the term Trinity was coined in the second age, mandated in the third, common place in the fourth, and ignorantly carried on through the sixth age. But now in the Amen Age, the seventh age, His bride knows His full deity, as He desires to be known. Jesus is not a part of the Trinity, for there is no such thing. He is the fulness of the Godhead bodily.

Christ is the Faithful and True Witness. Concerning faithfulness, it is through His power that everything consists—the visible and invisible heavens, thrones, dominions, principalities, and powers.[1145] Jesus' Words alone set the universe and its laws in order and keeps them intact. If He can maintain all this, surely He is faithful to start, maintain, and finish His work in you. Philippians 1:6 promises, *"Being confident of this very thing, that he which hath begun a good work in you will perform it until the day of Jesus Christ."*

In this age of lukewarm and lying witnesses, Christ is the True Witness. 2 Peter 3:3-7 says false witnesses in the last days will be willingly ignorant of Jesus' second coming, the earth's creation, and Noah's flood. They will avoid and deny the truth on purpose, witnessing against it. But Jesus is the True Witness, for He was with and loved of the Father before the foundation of the world.[1146] This means He witnessed the earth's founding! Jesus' Spirit was in Noah's preaching, urging mankind to repent. After His crucifixion, Jesus' Spirit descended to hell to preach and witness against that wicked generation. The True Witness is coming

---

1145   Colossians 1:16-17
1146   John 17:24

again and says to watch and pray always that you may be accounted worthy to escape judgment and stand before the Son of Man.[1147]

Recall Chapter 1 when you learned Jesus is the beginning of the creation of God. Before there was time, space, or matter, the invisible God alone existed. His first words, likely *"Let there be light"*, produced a visible Light in time, space, and matter called the Logos, or the Word. This Light was Jesus, for He is the Word, and was the first creation. The First Creation, or Beginner, speaks assurance He is with us in the last age as Finisher.

Message to the True Vine: Jesus again knows the works of Christians and urges them to be *"hot,"* which is possible through buying gold and white raiment directly from Him. Believers are instructed to anoint their eyes with eyesalve in order to see. In love, Jesus rebukes and chastens His own, who zealously repent. His last words to this age place Him knocking at every heart's door, willing to come and sup with them if they will hear His voice and open their hearts to His Spirit.

Although Jesus' message is extremely harsh to this age, as it should be, there is hope for the true church. The overcomer's works will be *"hot"*, which means "boiling hot; metaphorically, of fervour of mind and zeal" in the Greek. Thinking on the word *"fervent"*—also defined as passionate, intense, and sincere—brings to mind Scriptures like the fervent, bold, and diligent teacher Apollos.[1148] Recall Paul's plea for Christians in Romans 12:11 to be *"Not slothful in business; fervent in spirit; serving the Lord."* Jesus' bride in Laodicea must pray fervently, as Epaphras always labored fervently in prayer.[1149] James 5:16 says, *"The effectual fervent prayer of a righteous man availeth much."* Twice in his first epistle, Peter admonishes us to love each other fervently above all else.[1150]

The true vine began this age *"hot"* on April 9, 1906, when the Holy Ghost fell upon believers on Azusa Street, California, after intense seasons of prayer. In obedience to the order of the Word, the saints spoke

1147 Luke 21:36
1148 Acts 18:25-26
1149 Colossians 4:12
1150 1 Peter 1:22, 4:8

in tongues, and every message was interpreted in English.[1151] Fueled by these vigorous works, believers received the revelation that God is one Person within one decade afterwards. This revelation was in direct opposition to the three-person Trinity. The apostolic revelation of Jesus' Supreme Deity and God's one name as the Lord Jesus Christ was restored at the perfect time—just before Jesus' rapture return.

The next two decades would see the false vine hinder the move of God by deceiving men into organizing denominations based upon tongues as the evidence of the Holy Ghost, and the Oneness of God. No longer would God speak through them or any other organization because He said He would spew lukewarm, creed-minded groups out of His mouth. After the churches denominated, Jesus moved right on into the prophetic ministry of William Branham, who began pastoring in 1933 and transitioned into a world-wide healing ministry in 1946. Here is where God would speak His unadulterated truth to the age.

After winning millions of souls to the Lord Jesus in India, Africa, and throughout the world, Jesus used Brother Branham to correctly interpret church history through a series he preached on the Seven Church Ages in 1960. In March 1963, Christ loosed the revelations of the Seven Seals and had Branham preach them with the prophetic validation of "Thus saith the Lord."

Following Branham's death in 1965, the true bride has been taking Jesus' end-time revelations around the world. Believers have experienced the continuation of God's revival by faithfully acting upon Branham's revelations from the Spirit. The bride's eyes are anointed with Jesus' eyesalve in fulfillment of Ephesians 1:17-18:

> *"That the God of our Lord Jesus Christ, the Father of glory, may give unto you the spirit of wisdom and revelation in the knowledge of him: The eyes of your understanding being enlightened; that ye may know what is the hope of his calling, and what the riches of the glory of his inheritance in the saints."*

1151 "The Azusa Street Revival (Documentary)." *YouTube*, Uploaded by End-Time Youth, https://www.youtube.com/watch?v=HPtGJ35jIwA

In this age, Jesus' true church is buying gold and white raiment from Him through spiritual transactions of faith. Provers 23:23 reads, *"Buy the truth, and sell it not; also wisdom, and instruction, and understanding."* Jesus' spiritual gold is time-tested, unwavering faith according to 1 Peter 1:7. White raiment represents the righteousness of Jesus Christ manifested in a life of spiritual integrity and obedience to the Holy Spirit.[1152]

These eternal transactions are possible through Jesus' rebukes and the zealous repentance of the hearers. Bride members in Laodicea are constantly hearing convicting, challenging sermons, which is proof of Jesus' love. Yet the saints rejoice in the constant correction, recognizing God's unchanging method for dealing with His children:

> *"For whom the Lord loveth he chasteneth, and scourgeth every son whom he receiveth. If ye endure chastening, God dealeth with you as with sons; for what son is he whom the father chasteneth not? But if ye be without chastisement, whereof all are partakers, then are ye bastards, and not sons."*[1153]

As Paul promised, the preaching of the five fold ministry will perfect, or complete, Jesus' bride. Believers will hear Jesus knocking on their heart's door for His fellowship and let Him in for supper. The first course of Christ's meal will be milk for the newborn Christian according to 1 Peter 2:1-3. After growing up in maturity, the second course will be meat, feeding the hungry heart with spiritual discernment to judge every action as either evil or good.[1154]

In an age where riches and mega churches are exalted and falsely connected to spiritual attainment, Jesus' true bride will be rich in faith. Through passionate prayers, loving care for fellow Christians, daily repentance, and fellowship with Jesus, she will overcome the spiritual complacency plaguing this age.

The Laodicean Age climaxes with the true vine being raptured to the sky to meet her Husband, Christ, in the air while the world suffers

1152 Romans 8:4, Titus 3:5, Revelation 3:5, 19:8
1153 Hebrews 12:6-8
1154 Hebrews 5:12-14

through the Tribulation. Revelation 4:1-2 offers a beautiful type of this catching away, as John represents the bride called up to heaven, before the throne of God immediately after the end of the Laodicean message:

> *"After this I looked, and, behold, a door was opened in heaven: and the first voice which I heard was as it were of a trumpet talking with me; which said, Come up hither, and I will shew thee things which must be hereafter. And immediately I was in the spirit: and, behold, a throne was set in heaven, and one sat on the throne."*

Iniquity of the False Vine: No other Bible passage records such a scathing judgment as the false vine receives from Jesus as the Time of the Gentiles come to a close. Christ's first assessment is His sickness over their lukewarm spiritual state. The true vine is hot, but the false is lukewarm, which means "tepid, lukewarm…metaphoric of the condition of the soul wretchedly fluctuating between a torpor and a fervour of love" in the Greek. Their wishy-washy works—sometimes fervent, but mostly lethargic—make Christ vomit, calling to mind Isaiah 28:1-13. Specifically, verse 8 says backslidden Israel's tables *"are full of vomit and filthiness, so that there is no place clean."* Isaiah says Israel's pride, drunkenness, and perverted judgments caused the once holy tables to be covered in vomit.

The same conditions have repeated in the modern Mother-Daughter, Catholic-Protestant church system. The pride, natural and spiritual drunkenness, and lack of sound doctrine and Bible-based judgments makes Jesus sick. He spews these churches out of His mouth, meaning He longer speaks through their pulpits. Truly, Jesus is not speaking in Catholic, Lutheran, Methodist, Baptist, and Pentecostal denominations. You hear the groups compromising with and exalting sin. You do not hear them issuing holy judgments with "Thus saith the Lord" like the true vine who is proclaiming the seventh angel's message to the age.

Certainly their church members are drunk with pride, for Jesus records their despicable self-assessment: *"I am rich, and increased with goods, and have need of nothing."* The false vine is delighted with physical riches and goods and feels no further need for the Holy Ghost, spiritual revivals, or repentance. They refuse any additional revelation of Scripture and only accept changes to their by-laws that will swell their number of members. They will accept female clergy, homosexual clergy, transgender members, and repeated adulterers into their vomit-filled sanctuaries. It sounds harsh, but it is Jesus' judgment upon an age that wants its own rights and rules rather than God's rules. Yes, the false vine does not want to follow God's rule, and has long forgot Paul's command for the saints to *"walk by the same rule"*, minding the same thing in Philippians 3:16.

The name Laodicea means "justice of the people" in the Greek, and every church is making their own rules to meet the demands and rights of sinful adulterers, homosexuals, transgenders, liars, blasphemers, child molesters, and the rest. Since the mark of the beast comes out of the United States, also known as the beast out of land in Revelation 13, notice the drastic submission of the government and churches to the rights of sin-loving workers of iniquity.

While America's founding fathers were far from perfect, many possessed sincere faith in Christ. From the time of the Revolutionary War to the Civil War, there were numerous government-proclaimed days of prayer, humiliation, and fasting.[1155] Both Washington and Lincoln called and participated in these holy days. Historian David Barton reports 29 out of the 56 signers of the Declaration of Independence had seminary degrees,[1156] which is why America's founding documents are rich in Biblical references and principles.

Like Israel, America quickly fell from her humble, God-fearing beginnings. The Roaring 20s saw the rise of rebellious women who cut their hair for the first time, wore makeup, miniskirts, smoked, and danced in defiance to God's holiness. Most men permitted it in weakness, fear, and shame. Hollywood rose during the Great Depression and it has constantly ushered in cultural corruption ever since. Rebellious rock'n roll in the 1950s planted the seeds for the Sexual Revolution of the 1960s. The Mother

---

1155   Prince, Derek. *Shaping History Through Prayer and Fasting*, 1973
1156   "FAQs." *WallBuilders*, https://wallbuilders.com/faqs/

Harlot—Roman Catholic Church—mounted on and began riding her final beast, the American beast out of the land, when John F. Kennedy was elected the first Catholic President in November 1960. Prayer was taken out of schools in 1962, followed by the legalization of murdering babies in 1973. Abortion has now claimed over 50 million innocent lives, whose blood cries to God for vengeance from American soil. Homosexuality was removed from the list of mental disorders in 1973, and on June 26, 2015, the Supreme Court legalized this abomination.

Just as Jesus says, this age is indeed *"wretched, and miserable, and poor, and blind, and naked."* Yet He says they do not know their deplorable condition because they have purposely failed to retain God's knowledge in their minds. Romans 1:28 proves this, saying, *"And even as they did not like to retain God in their knowledge, God gave them over to a reprobate mind, to do those things which are not convenient."* Looking deeper in verse 28, the false vine knew the truth at one time, but has since blasphemed the truth and accepted lies. They will be destroyed because they rejected God's knowledge, just as Hosea 4:6 reads: *"My people are destroyed for lack of knowledge: because thou hast rejected knowledge, I will also reject thee, that thou shalt be no priest to me: seeing thou hast forgotten the law of thy God, I will also forget thy children."*

As I conclude writing this book in June 2021, America and the world are in shambles, more ripe than ever for judgment. Through massive voter fraud, America has her second Catholic President, Joe Biden, signaling afresh the Vatican's grip upon both the nation and the world. Coronavirus, foretold by Jesus as a "pestilence" in Matthew 24:7, has weakened the world economy, increased inflation, stolen rights of public worshippers, and taken over four million lives. But this is just the beginning since Jesus says all pestilences and earthquakes are the *"beginning of sorrows"* for this rebellious, sinful world.

Violent rioting and arson has decimated some American cities with one group in Portland, Oregon, burning Bibles and American flags. Other groups are calling for statues of Jesus to come down. The Black Lives Matter movement is leading the protests, which claims to be a peaceful organization, but some of its members escalate their protests into violent destruction, even murdering innocent children and police officers. Christians believe black lives matter, along with all lives, including the unborn. But the spirit of Sodom is upon the BLM movement, as one of its goals is to "disrupt...the nuclear family" in order to exalt the LGBTQ agenda.[1157] Jesus warned the Sodomite culture would return in Luke 17:29-30, and the same violent, holiness-hating mobs from Sodom have reemerged on American soil.

No one knows how long it will be until "Cancel Culture" targets true Christians, but at some point, the false vine will fully support stopping the true vine from preaching and ministering to the needy. In fulfillment of Revelation 13:15-17, the false vine churches will unite with American politicians to change laws, forcing all churches into a unionized religion with the threat of losing money, property, food, and life itself if not obeyed. But before their ungodly, blood-thirsty laws are enacted, Jesus will rescue His bride into heaven in the rapture. Christ promised this protection to the Philadelphian saints, so we know it carries over to this age: *"Because thou hast kept the word of my patience, I also will keep thee from the hour of temptation, which shall come upon all the world, to try them that dwell upon the earth."*[1158]

The false vine will misconstrue Jesus' prayer for oneness in John 17:11-23 in order to promote its evil one world church. It is a tare harvest, a deadly impersonation. Do not believe it, for you are the genuine wheat. 1 Peter 1:22 says oneness with Christ only comes through obeying the truth through the Holy Spirit, and this unionized church will promote inclusion for adulterers, murderers, homosexuals, liars, pedophiles, and more. World leaders will promise *"peace and safety"*, but *"sudden destruction"* is their worthy judgment.

The Reward: The Holy One promises overcomers a seat with Him on His throne, even as He overcame and is set down with His Father in His throne.

1157 "What We Believe." *Black Lives Matter*, https://blacklivesmatter.com/what-we-believe/
1158 Revelation 3:10

Jesus reminds the overcomers how He overcame Satan's temptations in Matthew 4. Messiah overcame the wicked one by simply quoting the rightly-divided Word and obeying It. We overcome the same way—by obeying God's Word while rebuking Satan with God's Word on our lips. Indeed, the Word is our mighty spiritual weapon we use to rule over Satan, the world, sin, and temptation.

No age needs the sharp-cutting, discerning power of the Word like this age, for deception is at its peak. Rejoice that Jesus has already made you a king and priest unto God and His Father. Just as King David smote and subdued the land with his sword, you can smite and subdue every foul, demon power with God's revealed Word on your lips, and the shield of faith protecting your heart and mind.

Christ's final reward is a seat next to Him on the Millennial throne, for the new age is nearly upon us. Certainly Jesus will rule all nations with a rod of iron, but recall He has promised that overcomers will rule in a similar way: "*And he that overcometh, and keepeth my works unto the end, to him will I give power over the nations: And he shall rule them with a rod of iron; as the vessels of a potter shall they be broken to shivers: even as I received of my Father.*"[1159]

By the Holy Ghost's leading and authority, rule over your bodily passions, and situations with family, work, and church. You are not just a conqueror in one area of your life, you are *more* than a conqueror in every aspect of life "*through him that loved us.*" Jesus' love is calling you to rule over sin now so that you can rule over nations later. You can do it by His grace. He is with you, even in you, to the end of the church age.

SUPERNATURAL VINDICATION OF THE SEVEN CHURCH AGES

After witnessing J.F.K.'s election in November 1960 and recognizing it as the rise of Catholicism in the United States, the Holy Spirit led William Branham to embark on his most in-depth study: the Seven Church Ages. Through much prayer and study, Branham preached

1159 Revelation 2:26-27

13 sermons related to the Church Ages from December 4, 1960, to January 8, 1961.

On the evening of the final sermon, the Holy Spirit descended into Branham Tabernacle and visibly appeared as a Pillar of Fire to the congregation on the back wall of the church. As Figure 20 shows, the Holy Spirit shone in the same seven, circular patterns Branham taught for the Seven Church Ages.[1160] The circles showed how the light, or truth, of each age would decrease until moving in an increasing direction beginning at the Sardisean Age. This supernatural event vindicated Branham was preaching heaven's revelation of the ages and not his own.

Figure 20

Audio from the event is available for you to hear, as awe-struck worshippers tremble, scream, and weep at God's visible Light. In orderly fashion, the Holy Spirit first shows the Church Ages revelation was true and then begins to anoint His prophet, Branham, to minister to the sick through the gift of discernment. Here's the text version of this magnificent incident:

> "Now, look this way, you all. Now, that's just like it is when it comes under Glory here, see. See? See? It comes... It's the Light over here. You're moving here, you see. Now, look, it's just--it's just a reflection, just a reflection, that is, see. It's not the Light. Here's the Light hanging right here, see, right here at this woman. I just happened to catch It and I thought It was over somebody. Now, you're seeing one and I'm seeing two. One of them is the natural, and the other One is the Supernatural. There's a man sitting on the outside here, along this line looking over towards that Light. It struck him.

1160 Branham, William. *An Exposition of the Seven Church Ages.* 1965

He's from Seymour, Indiana, and he's got... had a stroke. If you'll believe, sir, God will heal you of that stroke. Amen! Believe now!"[1161]

THE SEVEN SEALS

Chronologically speaking, you must understand the revelation of the seven stars and seven candlesticks in the first three chapters of Revelation in order to understand the rest of the climatic book. With the true understanding of the Seven Church Ages, you can now receive the revelations of the Seven Seals.

For a complete understanding of the Seven Seals, I strongly advise you to read William Branham's *The Revelation of the Seven Seals*, which is a transcription of the sermon series he preached in March 1963. Audio of the sermon series is also available online at no cost.

First, notice the four heavenly beasts around Jesus' throne are connected to the first four Seals. Revelation 4:7 records their specific order with the *"first beast"* being like a lion, the *"second beast"* like a calf, the *"third beast"* with the face of a man, and the *"fourth beast"* like a flying eagle. The order of the beasts matches the order of the first four Seals. In Revelation 6:1-2, the first beast tells John about the First Seal and its horse rider. Revelation 6:3 says the second beast, the one like a calf, announces the Second Seal and the horse rider. The third beast announces the Third Seal in Revelation 6:5, and the fourth beast announces the Fourth Seal in Revelation 6:7.

Notice the Fifth, Sixth, and Seventh Seals have no beasts announcing their symbols and no horse riders. If you recall Chapter 2, this is because the Times of the Gentiles are over after the Fourth Seal. The Fifth Seal deals with blinded Israel being promised eternal life once the Tribulation ends. The Sixth Seal is a description of the earthly effects of the Tribulation, and the Seventh Seal is the rapture of the Gentile bride, which ushers in Armageddon and the Millennium.

1161 Branham, William. *Revelation Chapter Four, Part 3.* January 8, 1961

BIBLICAL NUMEROLOGY OF NUMBER FOUR

Concerning the four beasts and four horsemen of the first four Seals, you see the importance of the number four. In Biblical numerology, four is a number of godly deliverance and an earthly number. Satan copies and perverts God's numbers, so four in his work represents total corruption. Examples include:

- Delivered Israel made their exodus from Egypt in the fourth generation (Genesis 15:16)
- Ezekiel's dry bones vision listed four steps to Israel's restoration: sinew, flesh, skin, breath (Ezekiel 37:1-14)
- Jesus was the fourth Man in the fire, delivering the three Hebrews from Nebuchadnezzar's furnace (Daniel 3:25-28)
- The fourth day of creation saw the earthly and heavenly material finished: sun, moon, stars (Genesis 1:14-19)
- Job was delivered and restored by God after his fourth visitor—Elihu—finished speaking, following his three miserable comforters: Eliphaz, Bildad, and Zophar
- Jesus raised Lazarus from the dead on the fourth day (John 11:17)
- Four important earthly elements: earth, air, water, fire
- Four regions of the earth: north, south, east, west
- Four divisions of the day and four night watches (Mark 13:35, 14:25)
- Earth's eternal city, the New Jerusalem, is foursquare in measurement (Revelation 21:16)
- Four elements most biologically necessary for earthly life: hydrogen, carbon, nitrogen, oxygen
- Four lunar cycles of the earth's moon: new (no), first quarter (half waxing), full, third quarter (half waning)
- Four stages of the destroying insect: palmerworm, locust, cankerworm, caterpillar (Joel 1:4)

- Delilah's fourth attempt to overcome Samson succeeded in his blindness and slavery (Judges 16:9-21)
- Four steps in spiritual corruption: lust enticed, lust conceived, sin, death (James 1:14-15)

THE FIRST FOUR SEALS

The four beasts' association with the first four Seals represent the characteristics of the spiritual power the true church would need during the Times of the Gentiles, or Seven Church Ages. Simply put, the four beasts represent four anointings of the Holy Ghost Jesus would send to the overcomers on earth. A Christian's spiritual power is always the baptism of the Holy Ghost, but these four beasts express special characteristics the Spirit would provide the saints to combat Satan's four horse riders during the Church Ages.

In Scripture, earthly beasts represent earthly kingdoms, such as the beasts in Daniel 7 representing Babylon, Medes and Persians, Greece, and Rome. But the four heavenly beasts represent the kingdom of God upon the earth, as four is an earthly number. Jesus' earthly ministry introduced the kingdom of God which His apostles received within their souls on the Day of Pentecost, for Messiah taught the kingdom of God is within believers in Luke 17:21.

Identifying the four horse riders as belonging to Satan is validated by looking at their works, the fourth rider's name, and follower. The four horse riders are actually one person—death. Revelation 6:8 says the rider's name is *"Death, and Hell followed with him."* The rider is the cursed antichrist spirit. With his identification known, his four step process of evil works are obvious: conquering, killing, money-capturing, and world-wide soul destruction. Chapter 10 shares how today's mega churches dominate and deceive through this four step process.

During the Times of the Gentiles, Satan is now taking the form of four horse riders. His form has often changed, as he began as Lucifer, the heavenly light bearer, then entered the serpent in Eden, filled murderous Cain and his descendants, and then filled the Pharisees and Judas.

Marvel not, for though Satan transforms from an angel of light to serpent, to violent, jealous worshipper, to blaspheming, religious clergy, he is always discerned and overcome by the Holy Ghost.

Yes, the four horse riders are the same rider in different forms, just as the four insects from Joel 1:4—palmerworm, locust, cankerworm, caterpillar—are the same insect in different stages of life, from embryo to adult. The attributes of each horse rider can be perfectly aligned with the church history presented in this chapter to show the four stages of the antichrist spirit as it heads up into death here in the final age, Laodicea.

God always acts first, and then Satan impersonates it, just as God set up His throne in heaven first, and later Lucifer tried to exalt his throne above the stars of God. Historically, God sent His first anointing, the lion, on the Day of Pentecost to seal His saints and prepare them for the battle to come. In a counter attack, Satan rode out against the lion as a white horse. The process repeats until the true bride is raptured off the earth and God judges the sin-soaked world in the Tribulation.

The First Seal: Revelation 6:1-2 records the Lamb opening the First Seal, and the beast has to be the lion because the second, third, and fourth beasts are mentioned by order in the three succeeding seals. John sees a white horse, and the rider has a bow, but no arrows are mentioned. The rider is then crowned and goes forth conquering.

The lion anointing is the fierce boldness of the Holy Ghost the saints embodied during the Ephesian and Smyrnaean Church Ages, and even into the Pergamos Age. Proverbs 28:1 declares, *"The wicked flee when no man pursueth: but the righteous are bold as a lion."* Saints like Paul, Irenaeus, and Martin boldly stood for Christ, and Christ stood for them, manifesting prophecies, healings, visions, and special miracles. The powerful Lion of the Tribe of Judah was with the true vine to combat and overcome the antichrist spirit.

The white color of the horse represents innocent deception, as white often represents holiness. But since the rider is the antichrist spirit, his white horse represents his sly, false teachings which Jesus called the deeds of the Nicolaitans. A horse is a beast and represents power, as horses are appropriately described so in Job 39:19-25.

The rider has a bow, but no arrows are mentioned. Here you learn two truths: the antichrist spirit shot his lies like arrows from the bow of his tongue, as Jeremiah 9:3 describes: *"And they bend their tongues like their bow for lies."* Your shield of faith quenches all of Satan's fiery darts, or lies, according to Ephesians 6:16. Second, you learn Satan is limited in his power, for he was out of arrows. He is the father of lies, and as long as you withstand his untruths, he cannot hurt you, nor make any Christian disobey God.

A crown is given to the rider, representing the first official pope, Damascus, being crowned in 366 A.D. Rome conquered, or overcame the laity, by mixing sinful deeds in worship and exalting the clergy.

The lion-like Holy Ghost anointing battled the white horse rider for about 350 years, from Pentecost in 30 A.D. to 385 A.D. This was the fight between the bold, living Word and false teaching.

The Second Seal: Revelation 6:3-4 records Jesus opening the Second Seal and the second beast inviting John to come and see. Another horse rides, this time a red one, and he takes peace from the earth with a great sword.

The ox anointing is the sacrificial surrender of the Holy Ghost the saints expressed during the Pergamean Age and part of the Thyatirean Age. Oxen were beasts of sacrifice, and so Christians in these ages gave their lives just as freely as God gave them to them. Recall Priscillian and six of his disciples were said to be the first saints executed by the Roman church in 385 A.D.

The red color of the horse represents the blood the rider shed with his great sword. During the Pergamean Age, church and state united through Constantine, and now the false church had power to kill anyone who opposed her. It was Augustine (354-430) who emboldened popes to kill anyone who disagreed with them. As Rome took the Bible from the people, she also took peace from the earth, for Christ and His Word is the only real peace.

The ox-like Holy Ghost anointing battled the red horse rider for nearly 710 years, from 385 A.D. to about 1095 A.D. This was the fight between sacrificial saints and the Roman Catholic sword.

The Third Seal: Revelation 6:5-6 records Jesus opening the seal and the third beast inviting John to see a black horse rider with a pair of balances in his hand. A voice in the midst of the four beasts determines prices for trade, and also protects oil and wine.

The man anointing is the wisdom of God given to saints during part of the Thyatirean Age and in the entire Sardisean and Philadelphian Ages. While mankind is not the largest, fastest, or strongest living thing, we are wisest due to the spirit and soul God imparts to us. The anointing of man's wisdom was needed to prepare the saints to conquer during the Reformation. Recall how the last works of the Thyatirean saints were greater than their works at the beginning of the age in preparation for Reformation.

The black horse represents the Dark or Middle Ages. It was a spiritual midnight for believers, as their numbers were depleted along with their access to and understanding of the Scripture. The balances in the rider's hand represent Rome capturing the wealth of the world, stripping her subjects of all their wealth. Rome grew rich by controlling religion, economics, and agriculture. She also funded her mammoth buildings by waging the Crusades, beginning in 1095 A.D., and fighting other papal wars. Pope John XXII showed future popes how to increase wealth through his profitable business of selling indulgences around 1320 A.D.

The voice in the midst of the four beasts has to be God's, since the beasts were around the throne worshiping the Lord. Surely this is Jesus' voice announcing, exposing, and limiting the financial aspirations of the black horse rider. Heaven is ultimately in control, limiting Rome's financial reach. Heaven is providing for the saints, even in the Dark Ages. Wheat and barley have both a natural and spiritual meaning, as Jesus sees Rome's efforts to get rich by selling natural food—wheat and barley— and selling false spiritual hope through indulgences.

The Lord Jesus protects the wine and oil, forbidding the antichrist from hurting or injuring these two necessities. Of course, Christ is speaking figuratively. Oil represents the permanent seal of the Holy Ghost baptism in a believer's soul, and wine represents stimulation, or joy, from the Spirit's revelation. Satan would not be able to hurt or hinder the true vine during these times. During even the darkest times of the Dark Ages, Satan could not stop believers from receiving the Holy Ghost baptism and the joyful stimulation that accompanies it. Historically, Jesus protected the saints as Holy Ghost revival fires continued to burn in the Dark Ages through men like Pierre de Brueys (martyred in 1126) and Peter Waldo. Waldo's converts, called Waldenses, powerfully spread the Holy Ghost gospel to ensure monasteries and parishes existed in many countries like France, Italy, Austria, Switzerland, Germany, and Bohemia to name a few.[1162] These saints passed on the wine and oil until the pre-Reformation saints like Wycliffe, Huss, Gutenberg, and Erasmus could receive these blessings.

During the Sardisean and Philadelphian Church Ages, Christ administered wine and oil to Luther, Wesley, and many more laborers. None would dare deny the holy man anointing upon Luther, defying every devil-possessd Roman scholar, whose sword-like wisdom cut and rightly divided the truth about salvation by faith alone, apart from sacraments. All the spiritual warriors from these ages possessed this man anointing, overcoming the black horse rider in their unique callings.

The man anointing combated the black horse rider for nearly 850 years, from 1095 A.D. to 1906 A.D. This was the fight between the wisdom of God's men and the money-hungry Mother Harlot.

The Fourth Seal: Revelation 6:7-8 records Jesus opening the seal and the fourth beast inviting John to come and see the pale horse rider go forth with hell following him. Power will be given them over a fourth part of the earth to kill with sword, hunger, death, and beasts.

The flying eagle anointing is watchfulness saints keep during the Laodicean Age. Flying eagles watch for prey and potential adversaries,

---

1162 Broadbent, pp. 85-97

ruling their territory from high altitudes. Jesus urges believers to sit in heavenly places, and watch and pray for His second coming,[1163] making their hearts and lives ready for their Lord's return. Holy Ghost filled saints are rapture-minded, meaning their thoughts are on the heavenly meeting in the air spoken of in 1 Thessalonians 4:17. Our affections should be set on things above, like the rapture, as Colossians 3:1-2 declares. Like a high flying eagle, we must *"press toward the mark for the prize of the high calling of God in Christ Jesus."*

Jesus uses the eagle to represent end time believers in Matthew 24:25-28, saying in verse 28: *"For wheresoever the carcase is, there will the eagles be gathered together."* Verse 27 tells you Jesus is speaking of His second coming, so you must be one of those blessed eagles, anointed with God's flying eagle power. The Lord likens Himself to an eagle in Exodus 19:4, proving you, as His born again child, are of heavenly eagle lineage. Psalm 103:5 and Isaiah 40:31 declare He renews your strength like the eagle. His strength helps you fly, or live above all earth-bound temptations today, and will lift you into the air to meet Jesus at the rapture.

The pale horse represents the incurable disease of spiritual death striking billions now in the end time. Remember the rider's name is *"Death"* from Revelation 6:8, and so the antichrist spirit is death, leading to eternal separation from Christ. In the Greek, *"pale"* means "green" and reminds us of the *"greenish"* plague of leprosy from Leviticus 13:47-49. If untreated and unhealed, uncleanness from leprosy caused separation from the camp and ultimately death.

This green, pale horse also symbolizes the final earthly ride of the person of the Pope-Antichrist whose final ride in the Tribulation will result in a fourth part of the earth being killed with the sword, hunger, death, and beasts. The incarnate devil-Antichrist will lay down the mark of the beast and any dissenters will be killed according to his four-fold strategy. While he is killing on his last earthly ride, Jesus' bride will be safely overhead in heaven, having already flown like an eagle into the skies to meet Jesus at the rapture.

1163 Mark 13:32-37

Note how the rider also kills with *"death."* This speaks of spiritual death, also known as blasphemy of the Holy Ghost, or a reprobate mind in Scripture. Recall Samuel Schmucker's tally of over 68 million Christians who died from the sword in the 5th to 19th centuries. Those were natural deaths. How many souls were killed with spiritual death, or blasphemy of the Holy Ghost during those times? No doubt, millions upon billons died from spiritual death from Rome's false doctrines of idolatry, fornication, and lasciviousness. But in the end time, Death rides into a fourth part of the earth and kills nearly every remaining soul both naturally and spiritually.

Hell always follows death. Like the evil rich man who despised the beggar Lazarus, he found himself in hell after his death: *"And it came to pass, that the beggar died, and was carried by the angels into Abraham's bosom: the rich man also died, and was buried; And in hell he lift up his eyes, being in torments, and seeth Abraham afar off, and Lazarus in his bosom."*[1164] All beast-worshippers share the same fate for denying the Lamb's path to eternal life.

THE FIFTH, SIXTH, AND SEVENTH SEALS

The final three seals make no mention of horse riders or the four heavenly beasts because God's focus is off the Gentiles and on the Jews, signaling the Times of the Gentiles (defined by Jesus in Luke 21:24) are over. God is again dealing with Israel, graciously offering them the New Covenant for the second time.

The Fifth Seal: Found in Revelation 6:9-11, Chapter 2 details the revelation of the Fifth Seal: despite most of Israel being blinded to Jesus' identity as the Messiah, He saves all faithful Jews who gave or lived their lives for the testimony of the Word of God, the Old Testament Scriptures.

The Sixth Seal: Found in Revelation 6:12-17, Chapter 2 also details the revelation of this seal: the wrathful, indescribable punishments in the Great Tribulation upon beast-worshippers. The Seven Trumpets and Seven Last Plagues mentioned in Revelation chapters 8, 9, 11, 15 and 16

1164 Luke 16:22-23

outline each miserable, destructive event. This is the reality-form of the pale horse's final earthly ride.

Jesus provides matching details about the Tribulation in Matthew 24:29-31. Again, none of the four heavenly beasts—lion, ox, man, or eagle—are mentioned in the Sixth Seal because the anointed saints are off the earth, feasting with Christ at the Marriage Supper of the Lamb.

The Seventh Seal: Found in Revelation 8:1-6, the Seventh Seal is the most mysterious. Verse 1 says heaven is silent when this seal opens, which means the four beasts stop their unceasing, day and night crying of "Holy, holy, holy" before God's throne where Jesus sits. The only reason angels would stop worshipping Jesus would be because Jesus left heaven. The next time Jesus leaves heaven will be to meet His bride in the air at the rapture. You can easily see the Seventh Seal is the unknown "day and hour"[1165] of Jesus' second coming. It is the moment of the Last Trump, the third and final event of the rapture: first the shout, then the voice, and lastly, the trump.[1166] At this moment, believers which are alive and remain on the earth are changed from corruptible to incorruptible, then rise to meet Jesus and the dead in Christ in the sky.

Revelation 8:6 gives proof that the judgments of God have not yet occurred because the Trumpets are prepared to sound, but have not yet sounded. Revelation 8:1 shows the rapture takes place before the Seven Trumpets sound. The Tribulation cannot begin until after the rapture. Revelations 7:1-12 teaches the earth cannot be hurt, by the effects of the Seven Trumpets, until the 144,000 Jews are sealed by the Holy Ghost. Clearly, the faithful Jews are sealed by the Spirit during the Tribulation after the Jew-Gentile bride is raptured and the Times of the Gentiles are completed. The Seventh Seal is Jesus snatching His wife off the earth while heaven is making ready for judgments upon the sinners.

Seven is God's number of completion, so the Seventh Seal speaks of Jesus bringing an end to the Times of the Gentiles, or Seven Church Ages. Jesus' Great Commission is finished; every nation has heard and

1165   Matthew 24:36, Mark 13:32
1166   1 Thessalonians 4:16

the elect have received the Holy Spirit. Mercy is over for the Gentiles, and Israel's blindness will now be taken away. The 144,000 guileless, Israeli saints will be grafted back into God's Holy Tree by the baptism of the Holy Ghost.

THE REVELATION OF THE SEVEN SEALS BROUGHT TO EARTH

It may surprise you to know that the interpretation you just read of the Seven Seals was sent to the earth in March 1963. While I understand the gravity of this statement, I maintain its accuracy because God's prophet, William Branham, spoke the interpretation of the Seven Seals with "Thus saith the Lord". Look now to see how Scripture foretold the revelation of the Seals coming to earth.

Revelation 10 shows the interpretation or revelation of the Seven Seals being brought to the earth by a Mighty Angel, which must be Christ in the form of the Holy Ghost because His description matches John's earlier vision of Jesus in Revelation 1:13-16. The Holy Ghost met Branham daily between March 18-24, 1963, to reveal each seal to him before he went to the pulpit to preach.

Revelation 10:2 says a little open book is in Jesus' hand as He reigns over the sea and earth. This is the same seven-sealed book Jesus took in Revelation 5:1-5 and then loosed, or opened, in Revelation 6 and 8:1. The revelation of the Seven Seals had to be brought to earth by Christ's Spirit, for He was the only one worthy to loose the Seals.

In Revelation 10:3, Christ cries like a lion, for He is the Lion of the Tribe of Judah. Seven thunders utter their voices as Christ cries, but John is not allowed to write what was spoken. Verse 7 says *when* the mystery of God, contained in the voices of the seven thunders, would be finished or performed—in the days of the seventh angel.

This seventh angel of Revelation 10:7 cannot be the heavenly, angelic, trumpet-blowing seventh angel from Revelation 11:15 because their ministries are totally different. When the seventh trumpet blows in Revelation 11:15, the kingdoms of this world end, and Christ reigns on the earth in the Millennium. Simply put, the Times of the Gentiles ends, and there is no more saving souls or missionary work to be done once the seventh trumpet sounds.

But Revelation 10:7 and its following verses 8-11 speak of further soul saving to the Gentiles. Verse 11 says the prophecy contained in the interpretation of the Seven Seals must be prophesied *"again before many peoples, and nations, and tongues, and kings."* The Revelation 10:7 seventh angel has to be same seventh angel to the church in Laodicea from Revelation 3:14 because both have a final, world-wide message to the Gentiles. Jesus said in Matthew 24:14 that the gospel must be preached to all nations, and then the end of human history would come.

In simplest terms, Revelation 10 is Jesus' Spirit coming to earth in March 1963 to give the interpretation of the Seven Seals to William Branham. Now you and I, like John, must spiritually eat the revelations of the Seven Seals and preach them to all nations for a witness, and then the end shall come. Share them until the last soul is saved—*"until the fulness of the Gentiles be come in."*

The seven thunders are the revelations contained in the seven sermons William Branham preached on the Seven Seals. When Branham preached *The First Seal* on Monday, March 18, 1963, he shared Jesus' revelation of the First Seal. Since it was Jesus' revelation, it was His Voice thundering upon the earth. Each succeeding sermon about a seal was another thunder until all seven were complete. Numerous Scriptures teach God's Voice is like a thunder. 2 Samuel 22:14 says, *"The Lord thundered from heaven, and the most High uttered his voice."* The people who heard God's Voice speaking to Christ in John 12:28-29 said *"it thundered."*

Christ's Voice has thundered on the earth. Daniel 12:4 has been fulfilled—the once-sealed book is now loosed, for it is the *"time of the end"* when travel, technology, and knowledge has increased. Chapter 13 explains more about the prophesies we are to *"prophesy again"* to the world.

THE CHURCH AGES FORETOLD IN JUDGES AND JOSHUA

Leaving the Seven Seals and returning the Seven Church Ages, recall from Chapter 4 that the Church Ages were foretold in Judges 14 when Samson held a seven day feast for his prospective, Philistine (Gentile) wife. Samson's riddle is not known until his Gentile bride reveals it on the seventh and final day. This typed that the full revelation of God's Bible would be made known to and through Jesus' Gentile bride in the Seventh Church Age, or Laodicean Age. Revelation 10:7 supports this, as *"the mystery of God"* would *"be finished"* through the seventh angel-messenger, and then taken around the world to every Gentile nation by Jesus' bride.

Additionally, William Branham's God-ordained teaching on the Church Ages was foretold in Joshua chapters 18 and 19. Note the sermons were preached in December-January 1960-1961, and the book version, *An Exposition of the Seven Church Ages*, was published in December 1965. I am thankful the Lord revealed the foretelling of the *Exposition* book in Joshua 18 and 19 to my brother Simon, a faithful Bible teacher and missionary.

Joshua 18:1-10 finds the Promised Land subdued before Israel, and Joshua still needs seven tribes to possess their land inheritance. He sends out men into the land to explore it and bring back its descriptions to Joshua so he can divide the land. The men come back with a book describing the land's cities and dividing them up into seven parts. Joshua casts lots before the LORD and assigns the seven land plots to the seven tribes. This assignment had to take place before the prophet Joshua's death. Two applications are apparent.

The first is Jesus as Joshua, placing His foreknown overcomers in the Church Ages of His choosing. The seven-part book symbolizes Jesus' seven letters to the seven Gentile cities in Revelation chapters 2 and 3. You can rejoice that Jesus placed you in the Seventh Age, Laodicea, as you can zealously repent and execute hot, fervent works for His holy name.

A second application is Brother Branham as Joshua. The seven-part book represents his seven sermons on the Church Ages, preached in

December 1960. Having received the revelation of the seven cities as Seven Church Ages, Branham could place the believers of church history in their matching, respective ages, and write his *Exposition*. Their historical placement had to come while the prophet was yet alive, as his book was published just a few weeks before he went home to be with the Lord.

THE REWARDS FOR RECEIVING THE REVELATION OF THE SEVEN STARS AND SEVEN CANDLESTICKS

You will gain at least three rewards if you receive this chapter's revelations. First, you will understand church history correctly. For example, when historians magnify Constantine and paint him as a righteous Christian, you will know that is not the case because his corrupt fruits (murder, pride, etc.) proved he was a corrupt tree. Also, God's plan to permit the true church to lose some of its revelation as it descended into the Dark Ages becomes clear, just as God let Jesus enter the darkness of death. But God's resurrection power brought Jesus out of darkness and into the light, just as He was going to restore the church through Sardis' Reformation, Philadelphia's Open Door, and Laodicea's Hot Restitution.

Second, you will finally understand the Book of Revelation and thereby overcome the false vine of your age. Its symbols, timing, and themes will at last make sense. The same symbols John uses match those of Ezekiel, Jeremiah, Zechariah, and the rest of the prophets. You will see Jesus' separations between the Times of the Gentiles and His return to the 144,000 Jews. Most importantly, you will see your responsibility as an overcomer and the unsearchable rewards awaiting you in the Millennium and New Jerusalem.

Third, the keystone of the entire Bible—God and His ways are unchanging—unlocks the entire Book of Scripture. You identify the true and false vines from Genesis to Revelation. You see Jesus Christ in every Scripture. God's burning stars—His prophets and preachers—illuminate every age and generation from Adam to today. Jesus of the Seven Church Ages is the God of every age, and His marvelous grace and power extend to each.

THE CONSEQUENCES FOR REJECTING THE REVELATION OF THE SEVEN STARS AND SEVEN CANDLESTICKS

There are at least two consequences for rejecting these revelations. First, rejecting Jesus' stars, or Seven Church Age messengers is refusing Jesus' handpicked light-bearers. John 13:20 says, *"Verily, verily, I say unto you, He that receiveth whomsoever I send receiveth me; and he that receiveth me receiveth him that sent me."* Turning down Jesus' stars is essentially turning down Christ, the Light of the world. Jesus Himself was shining through those seven stars.

No doubt, Paul was not perfect, as he committed sins he hated. Martin Luther made mistakes that caused many people much pain. William Branham's memory was imperfect, but remember all of God's servants needed His grace. Abraham lied numerous times and even laughed in unbelief at God's promise. Moses killed a man and magnified himself rather than God, which kept him out of Canaan. David had Uriah killed after selfishly committing adultery with his wife. Jonah ran from God's presence and was angered that He did not destroy Nineveh. Despite each servant's weakness, they were later made strong by God's power. His divine patience forgave His stars so they could again shine His Light.

Jesus says all that is left for rejecting Him and His stars is judgment according to John 12:47-48: *"And if any man hear my words, and believe not, I judge him not: for I came not to judge the world, but to save the world. He that rejecteth me, and receiveth not my words, hath one that judgeth him: the word that I have spoken, the same shall judge him in the last day."* May God be merciful to those who reject His stars.

The second consequence builds upon the first, for rejecting the bright stars in Jesus' hand makes it easier to reject the oil-light from the candlesticks. If you miss God's messenger in an age, you will miss His plans for that period. For example, rejecting John Wesley's ministry leads one to revile the vast, brotherly love-inspired, Open Door missionary efforts of the 18th and 19th centuries. Currently, rejecting Branham's

Bible-message redirects one out of Jesus' Light for these tumultuous times in which we live. Following Branham's Bible revelations is truly following Jesus, as John 8:12 reads: "*Then spake Jesus again unto them, saying, I am the light of the world: he that followeth me shall not walk in darkness, but shall have the light of life.*"

Rejecting Branham's Bible-message today is refusing to walk in the holy Light of the seven golden candlesticks. Remember, Jesus is standing there in the midst of the candlesticks according to Revelation 1:12-13. Jesus is inviting one and all to come to the truth of this age. He will give mercy to those who walk in the Light, but those outside are liars and filthy. 1 John 1:6-7 declares, "*If we say that we have fellowship with him, and walk in darkness, we lie, and do not the truth: But if we walk in the light, as he is in the light, we have fellowship one with another, and the blood of Jesus Christ his Son cleanseth us from all sin.*"

CONCLUSION

Identifying Jesus' seven stars and the light of each candlestick for each age helps you see God's past, current, and future actions. He is empowering His bride to overcome the darkness of Jezebel and her daughters. Jesus' seven stars shine His truth in the midst of the darkness of iniquity. Christ's lights are witnesses and standards. By His grace, you have seen His lights just in time, as we are at the end of the Times of the Gentiles.

Now, let Jesus' candlestick-light reflect upon your life. Imitate the light of the seven stars. Follow the examples of the saints, from Ephesus to Laodicea. It is time to shine! Fulfill Isaiah 60:1-2: "*Arise, shine; for thy light is come, and the glory of the LORD is risen upon thee. For, behold, the darkness shall cover the earth, and gross darkness the people: but the LORD shall arise upon thee, and his glory shall be seen upon thee.*"

ACTION STEPS

1. Since it is most urgent for you to walk in the Light of your age—Laodicea's call for zealous repentance—contact me or go to www.messagehub.info to access the sermons of Jesus' star for this age, William Branham.

2. Locate a home church that teaches God's revelations given to Brother Branham, as the five fold preaching ministry will bring you, as part of Jesus' bride, to perfection (Ephesians 4:7-16).

3. For an in-depth understanding of church history, purchase and read Branham's book, *An Exposition of the Seven Church Ages*. This will lead you into many more enriching studies in church history.

FOLLOW UP

Free online videos, Bible studies, and William Branham's quotes related to this chapter: www.pastorjessesmith.com/12mysteriesbook

Email: jesse.smith11@sbcglobal.net

Text: 330-929-2037

CHAPTER 8
The Mystery of The Kingdom of Heaven

"He answered and said unto them,
Because it is given unto you to know
the mysteries of the kingdom of heaven,
but to them it is not given."

Matthew 13:11

I N THE FOUR GOSPELS of Matthew, Mark, Luke, and John, Jesus teaches 16 parable-mysteries related to the kingdom of heaven. Knowing the meaning of each parable gives you a complete understanding of God's New Testament kingdom. You are able to see your individual role in God's kingdom, the kingdom's enemies, and also how the kingdom continues until the consummation of human history.

To begin with, the kingdom of heaven is not a physical kingdom on earth, but a spiritual one. At this moment, the *"kingdoms of this world,"*[1167]

1167   Revelation 11:15

like Russia, the United States, and China, are not the kingdoms of our Lord Jesus Christ, but one day they will be.

Jesus tells us the location of the kingdom of heaven in Luke 17:21: *"Behold, the kingdom of God is within you."* God's kingdom, or "dominion or rule" in the Greek Lexicon,[1168] is inside the soul of the believer as the baptism of the Holy Ghost (See Chapter 6). Paul teaches when a person is born again, he is *"translated...into the kingdom of his dear Son."*[1169]

This means the kingdom of heaven first came into believers' souls on the Day of Pentecost. Previous to Pentecost, the kingdom of heaven was *"at hand"*, but not yet in believers' souls, according to Matthew 3:1-2: *"In those days came John the Baptist, preaching in the wilderness of Judaea, And saying, Repent ye: for the kingdom of heaven is at hand."* Jesus preached the same truth in Matthew 4:17: *"Repent: for the kingdom of heaven is at hand."*

Since the Holy Ghost has been pouring out for nearly 2,000 years, Jesus has wisely designed for born again Christians to rule and reign in the spiritual kingdom of heaven *while* living in the earthly kingdoms of men. Satan is our opponent and we are promised victory because *"the God of peace shall bruise Satan under your feet shortly."*[1170] Satan is the main influence behind every earthly kingdom, as Jesus teaches Satan has a kingdom.[1171] Once granted permission by God, Satan has power to give earthly kingdoms to those he chooses.[1172] But God's kingdom is greater in every way.

God has equipped us to defeat Satan's spiritual kingdom and influence. Believers are fully armored soldiers, wrestling *"not against flesh and blood, but against principalities, against powers, against the rulers of the darkness of this world, against spiritual wickedness in high places."*[1173] Christians

---

1168   "The Bible: Hebrew and Greek Lexicons." *Voice of God Recordings*, www.branham.org/en/messagesearch
1169   Colossians 1:13
1170   Romans 16:20
1171   Matthew 12:26
1172   Matthew 4:8-9, Job 1:6-12
1173   Ephesians 6:12

war spiritually against the wicked influences of every earthly kingdom and are victorious—*"more than conquerors through him that loved us."*[1174]

Take heed to your Heavenly Father's invitation to be a part of His eternal kingdom. 1 Thessalonians 2:12 says, *"That ye would walk worthy of God, who hath called you unto his kingdom and glory."*

THE CONFUSION ABOUT THE MYSTERY OF THE KINGDOM OF HEAVEN

To begin with, there is no confusion that Jesus' 16 parable-mysteries are from God, as Jesus said He spoke only what the Father taught Him.[1175] It is also widely understood that the parables are natural witnesses of the spiritual world. For example, knowing how to bake bread or plant a mustard seed does not make a person worthy of eternal life.

The confusion about the kingdom of heaven is about how to interpret the parables. Should they be applied directly to our lives today? If so, how far should they be applied? In our politically-correct society, should the *"children of the kingdom"* and *"children of the wicked one"*[1176] be identified? Can the woman hiding leaven in bread be identified? Should Christians warn people about the *"furnace of fire"* and *"wailing and gnashing of teeth"* that await those who offend God's kingdom and work iniquity?[1177] The answer to all of these questions is yes, and the parables should be applied as far as God intended—to the very soul of every man.

The revelation of the kingdom of heaven is those who understand the kingdom's purpose, extent, and organization and give Christ dominion in their earthly lives will be the ones who rule with Christ in His future dominion.

1174   Romans 8:37
1175   John 8:28, 14:10
1176   Matthew 13:38
1177   Matthew 13:41-42

BIBLICAL EVIDENCE FOR THE REVELATION OF THE MYSTERY OF THE KINGDOM OF HEAVEN

The 16 parable-mysteries completely reveal the mystery of the kingdom of heaven when compared with the rest of Scripture. Here are brief summaries followed by full Biblical explanations:

- 1—The Sower and The Four Grounds: Men display four heart-reactions to hearing preaching about Jesus Christ.
- 2—The Wheat and Tares: Each person is either a child of God or Satan, and churches are full of both.
- 3—The Grain of Mustard Seed: The false church started small but grew until it was large and filled with all demonic powers (Chapter 9 reveals the false church).
- 4—The Leaven Hid in Three Measures of Meal: The false church hid lies in her teachings until her entire doctrine became fully corrupted.
- 5—The Treasure in a Field: A true believer joyfully trades all his possessions at the surprising opportunity to gain Christ.
- 6—The One Pearl of Great Price: A true believer abandons his search for many spiritual truths in order to gain the one, most valuable truth: Christ.
- 7—The Net Cast Into the Sea: At the end of the world, the gospel will attract believers and unbelievers, but God's angels will separate the wicked away from the holy.
- 8—The Unmerciful Servant: A person must forgive others if he expects God to forgive him.
- 9—The Laborers in the Vineyard: Eternal life is the reward God gives to all who labor in His kingdom.
- 10—The Wicked Husbandman: The kingdom was rejected by the Jews and then given to the Gentiles to bring forth fruit unto God (See Chapter 2).
- 11—The King's Son: After most Jews reject it, Gentile believers respond to God's invitation for the rapture and

are clothed in the wedding garment, the baptism of the Holy Ghost.

- 12—The Ten Virgins: Wise believers possess oil, or the baptism of the Holy Ghost, as they await their wedding day, the rapture, with Jesus (See Chapter 12).
- 13—The Talents: Christ commits varying amounts of talents and resources to His servants and rewards those who faithfully invest in them.
- 14—The Pounds: Christ provides an equal opportunity to His servants and rewards those who faithfully act upon it.
- 15—The Seed Cast Into the Ground: God causes spiritual growth by invisible means but men observe it in three stages.
- 16—The Great Supper: After most Jews made excuses to reject it, Gentiles should accept Jesus' compelling invitation to His great supper, the Marriage Supper of the Lamb.

1—THE SOWER AND THE FOUR GROUNDS

Revelation: Men display four heart-reactions to hearing preaching about Jesus Christ.

Found in Matthew 13:3-9 and 18-23, this first revelation begins on the individual level and is interpreted by Christ Himself. Men can have only one of four reactions after hearing preaching about Jesus Christ, as the parable details four types of ground that seed falls upon. Seed symbolizes God's Word.[1178] There will be no excuses on the Day of Judgment. Each type of ground received seed. Each heart received the Word. Each person has to ask the same question Pontius Pilate infamously asked when he stated, *"What shall I do then with Jesus which is called Christ?"*[1179] God is watching what you do with the Word you have heard.

1178   Matthew 13:19, Luke 8:11
1179   Matthew 27:22

The first ground or heart is called the *"way side,"*[1180] representing a heart that hears the Word of God but does not understand it. Fowls, representing Satan, *"the wicked one,"*[1181] snatch away God's Word from the person's heart. These fowls play an important role later in the third parable. This heart immediately rejects God's Word, thus not believing and ultimately not saved.[1182] Jesus says that most people fall into this category, declaring there are *"few"*[1183] that are saved.

The second ground is another sad heart condition called the *"stony places."*[1184] This kind of person rejoices over the Word for a season and he can *"for a while believe,"*[1185] but then rejects the truth due to *"tribulation or persecution."*[1186] The rejection occurs because there is no *"root in himself,"*[1187] meaning no deep, genuine love for Christ, as Paul says Christians are *"rooted and grounded in love."*[1188] Jesus says this experience starts excitedly, lasting longer than the *"way side,"* but then slowly withers away. Psalm 1:3 says the godly have leaves that *"shall not wither."* Real Christian love does not wither away.[1189] Jude describes apostates as *"clouds without water"* and *"trees whose fruit withereth."*[1190] Clearly, the stony places heart is apostate and lost, just as the way side heart.

The third ground can be called "thorny" because it receives the seed but then thorns spring up and choke it, making the plant unfruitful.[1191] This third heart hears the Word but then chooses to care for the world, riches, and pleasures more than Christ. Although this heart lasted much longer than the previous two, it still missed the ultimate goal of Christianity—fruitfulness. What good is an apple tree if it doesn't bring forth its fruit? Jesus wants Christians to bring forth their fruits, to serve

---

1180   Matthew 13:4
1181   Matthew 13:4, 19
1182   Luke 8:12
1183   Matthew 7:14
1184   Matthew 13:5-6
1185   Luke 8:13
1186   Matthew 13:21
1187   Matthew 13:21
1188   Ephesians 3:17
1189   1 Corinthians 13:8
1190   Jude 1:11-12
1191   Matthew 13:7

their God-ordained purposes. The rare and precious fruit of the Spirit is *"love, joy, peace, long suffering, gentleness, goodness, faith, meekness, temperance."*[1192] Jesus said He chose the disciples to *"go and bring forth fruit, and that your fruit should remain."*[1193] Paul warns all Christians that riches can cause believers to fall into temptations, snares, and *"into many foolish and hurtful lusts, which drown men in destruction and perdition."*[1194] His advice to Timothy, a man of God, is to *"flee these things; and follow after righteousness, godliness, faith, love, patience, and meekness."*[1195] Paul, in his second letter to Timothy, prophesies that men in the last days will be *"lovers of pleasures more than lovers of God."*[1196] After reading this, you might think it's impossible for this unfruitful heart to be saved, but I will soon show much Bible evidence that salvation is possible for this heart, although the reward will be little to nothing. Examples include Lot and the repentant thief on the cross. Paul says a man can be saved but suffer loss of reward.[1197]

The fourth and final ground is good ground that brings forth fruit in one of three quantities: thirtyfold, sixtyfold, or a hundredfold.[1198] Jesus interprets this ground as *"an honest and good heart, having heard the Word, keep it, and bring forth fruit with patience."*[1199] If you are an honest-hearted Christian you will produce the nine fruits of the Spirit because you are honest about your spiritual condition. You won't let money, riches, or pleasures choke your love for God's Word. As you love God with all your heart, soul, mind, and strength, you will hate even one sin-stain upon your spiritual life.[1200] James says pure religion is keeping yourself *"unspotted from the world."*[1201] You won't let one evil *"root of bitterness"*[1202] spring up and trouble your heart because you are completely focused on seeing an abundant harvest for the Lord's glory.

1192   Galatians 5:22-23
1193   John 15:16
1194   1 Timothy 6:9
1195   1 Timothy 6:11
1196   2 Timothy 3:4
1197   1 Corinthians 3:13-15
1198   Matthew 13:8
1199   Luke 8:15
1200   Jude 1:23
1201   James 1:27
1202   Hebrews 12:15

Genesis to Revelation teaches this Biblical revelation of four heart reactions or heart conditions (See Figure 21). Genesis gives four kinds of heart conditions to God's revelation in Abraham's day. Abraham's heart was "good ground," for he was the friend of God and father of faith, living a fully devoted and separated life. Abraham and Sarah brought forth Isaac as fruit of their union and spiritual devotion. Lot's heart was "thorny," because although he was just and righteous, he erroneously led his family into residing in Sodom, causing him and his family daily torment. There was no real fruit to Lot's ministry efforts in Sodom, just as the thorny ground was unfruitful. Lot's wife represents the "stony ground" because Jesus identifies her as one whose heart and eyes turned back to Sodom due to her love for it, causing her to lose her life.[1203] The Sodomites represent "way side" hearts, for the mob at Lot's house heard him call their homosexuality wickedness,[1204] but then Satan immediately snatched the Seed-Words from their hearts. The mob felt judged and were planning on physically violating Lot until he was saved by the angels.[1205] These were all destroyed with fire and brimstone shortly after the angels pulled Lot and two of his daughters out of the city.[1206]

Good	Thorny	Stony	Way side
Abraham	Lot	Mrs. Lot	Sodomites
Jesus	Saved thief	Judas	Lost thief
Gold	Silver	Wood	Earth
Holy	Righteous	Filthy	Unjust

Figure 21

Jesus' crucifixion exposes these four hearts. Most people think of only three crosses on Golgotha, but there was a fourth cross or tree not far away—Judas Iscariot's tree. Jesus' heart represents the "good ground,"

1203   Luke 17:28-33
1204   Genesis 19:7
1205   Genesis 19:9-11
1206   Genesis 19:24-25

for He always did that which pleased the Father and there was so much fruit to His life that John supposed *"that even the world itself could not contain the books that should be written"*[1207] about Him. The saved thief who was promised paradise by Christ symbolizes the "thorny ground," for his life was fruitless. In fact, the saved thief was mocking Christ with the others shortly before his change of heart, as Matthew 27:44 says, *"The thieves also, which were crucified with him, cast the same in his teeth."* Judas Iscariot's heart was the "stony ground," for he served Christ for a season, even witnessing countless miracles, before withering away and ending in apostasy, betrayal, and hell. The lost thief's heart was the "way side," for he railed against Jesus until the end, without any fear of God.

Paul described the four hearts as four different kinds of vessels: gold, silver, wood, and earth.[1208] The gold represents the "good ground" and the silver symbolizes the "thorny ground." Wood represents the "stony side" heart and earth symbolizes the "way side" heart. Gold and silver vessels are honorable, and thus can be used by the Master for good works. Obviously, gold is more valuable, useful, or better than silver just as the prophet Samuel told Saul that David was *"better"*[1209] than he. God saw David's life was more useful than Saul's because of David's pure heart. The wood and earth are dishonorable, disposable vessels, showing again that two hearts are saved and two are lost. Paul was an honorable vessel, for Jesus literally called Him a *"chosen vessel"*[1210] to bear His name to the Gentiles, kings, and Israel. The Egyptian ruler, Pharaoh, was a vessel of dishonor, for Paul said God raised Pharaoh up as a vessel of wrath *"fitted for destruction."*[1211] Proverbs 16:4 also says, *"The LORD hath made all things for himself: yea, even the wicked for the day of evil."*

Revelation 22:11 lists the four conditions every person will end up in at Jesus' second coming: holy, righteous, filthy, and unjust. The "holy" condition represents the "good ground" while the "righteous" represents the "thorny ground." The "filthy" condition represents the "stony

---

1207   John 21:25
1208   2 Timothy 2:20
1209   1 Samuel 15:28
1210   Acts 9:15
1211   Romans 9:17-23

ground," and the "unjust" condition is the "way side" ground. The "holy" and "righteous" hearts will be saved while the "filthy" and "unjust" will be lost.

Please take a few moments to meditate upon the revelation of The Sower and The Four Grounds, that it may be applied to your soul. You may want to fall to your knees in sincere prayer to Jesus Christ, your High Priest, and ask Him to show you which heart condition you have cultivated thus far in your life. Which ground does your heart resemble? Is the ground of your heart good, honest, and producing much fruit? Or is it thorny because you have let love of pleasures and riches choke the growth of God's Word in your heart? If so, the remedy is to let Jesus' Holy Spirit, the Master Gardener, weed out the cares of the world and ungodly habits from your heart and life. Is your ground like the stony ground, and you have left Christianity after believing for a season? If so, return to Christ and repent of all your transgressions, that God's Word will have a deep love to be planted in. Lastly, if your heart is the way side ground, and you have never followed Christ, won't you repent of your sins now and be baptized in Jesus Christ's name? Won't you lose your sinful life and gain eternal life?

2—THE WHEAT AND TARES

Revelation: Each person is either a child of God or Satan and the churches are full of both.

Found in Matthew 13:24-30 and 36-43, this second revelation is again interpreted by Christ. Here the *"good seed"* is not the Word Itself, as in the first parable, but is the product of the Word preached—the children of God.

Jesus teaches there will be both wheat (God's children) and tares (Satan's children) in the world until the end of time. God's children originate from Jesus, the Son of Man, the sower who first sowed good seed, or believers, in the world, or field. The devil is the enemy who came in afterwards and sowed tares, or unbelievers. At harvest time, or the end of the world, the angels will come to separate unbelievers for their fire judgment. Afterwards, the righteous wheat will *"shine forth as the sun in the kingdom of their Father."*[1212]

This parable's timeline is from the beginning of Jesus' earthly ministry to the end of the *"times of the Gentiles,"*[1213] or end of the Church Ages, which is yet in the future. Jesus said He, the *"Son of Man,"* sowed the good seed. During Jesus' earthly ministry, He either called Himself or was called *"Son of Man"* 80 times. In Matthew 13:24, the Son of Man went sowing first, which was Jesus' three-and-a-half-year earthly ministry. Jesus' preaching and healing ministry caused many to believe the gospel, such as the many Samaritans in the city that believed Jesus was the *"Christ, the Savior of the world."*[1214] But eventually, all the early believers, such as Peter, James, John, and Paul, died, as Matthew 13:25 says, *"While men slept."*

As the early apostles started sleeping, or dying, Satan began sowing his tares, or children, among the believers, as Scripture details. Around 60 A.D., Paul cried for three straight years, warning the Ephesians that wolves, or false teachers, would enter in to their assembly, *"not sparing the flock."*[1215] About six years later, Jude said evil men would pervert grace by making it *"lasciviousness,"* or a license for immorality.[1216] Around 90 A.D., John wrote that there were already *"many antichrists"* working deception in the churches.[1217]

The tares, or *"children of the wicked one,"* are impersonators of the wheat, or *"children of the kingdom."* Physical tares are darnel weeds, which are nearly identical in appearance to wheat, explaining why Jesus commanded that both wheat and tare grow together until the harvest so that wheat would not be rooted up with the tare. To the human eye, it's nearly impossible to distinguish between the wheat and tare, so Christ assigns the angels to separate them at the end of the world. Spiritual tares are impersonators of Christianity, great in number and sitting in every church, looking and acting nearly identical to spiritual wheat.

1212   Matthew 13:43
1213   Luke 21:24
1214   John 4:39-41
1215   Acts 20:29-31
1216   Jude 1:4
1217   1 John 2:18

Tares appear to be twins of the wheat, but they are not true wheat. The Bible is filled with twins, or wheat and tare examples: Cain and Abel, Balaam and Moses, and Judas and Jesus. The only way to know which of the twins is the true believer is to observe which one obeys the Word, as Cain was instructed to obey, but rejected God's will.[1218] Just as tares resemble wheat, these men all had a parallel spiritual life. Balaam and Moses were both known prophets. Judas and Jesus ministered together and both performed miracles.

One reason tares are extremely deceptive is because they can honor and worship God enough to see the Holy Spirit supernaturally move in their services. Jesus said no man that speaks lightly of Him can do a miracle in His name,[1219] proving that tares will speak honorably of Jesus in order to work under His anointing. But afterwards, the tares will work iniquity, engaging in lustful lifestyles, as Jesus taught in Matthew 7:21-23:

> "Not every one that saith unto me, Lord, Lord, shall enter into the kingdom of heaven; but he that doeth the will of my Father which is in heaven. Many will say to me in that day, Lord, Lord, have we not prophesied in thy name? and in thy name have cast out devils? and in thy name done many wonderful works? And then will I profess unto them, I never knew you: depart from me, ye that work iniquity."

Paul speaks of tares, describing their sinful characteristics in these "last days,"[1220] saying tares are "lovers of their own selves, covetous, boasters, proud, blasphemers, disobedient to parents, unthankful, unholy, without natural affection, trucebreakers, false accusers, incontinent, fierce, despisers of those that are good, traitors, heady, highminded, lovers of pleasures more than lovers of God." The apostle says they have a form, or resemblance of godliness, but all deny the power of God that produces genuine godliness. Tares do some good works, but harbor wicked, selfish hearts, putting on

1218 Genesis 4:6-8
1219 Mark 9:39
1220 2 Timothy 3:1-5

a public, church membership act. True Christians let God's power purify and sanctify them wholly because they want to see Jesus face to face and have a body just like His.[1221]

Just as a physical tare causes sickness, a spiritual tare's unholy life nauseates a true believer. The Greek Lexicon says darnel grains, *"if eaten, produce convulsions, and even death."* Jesus described this spiritual condition in the letter to the Laodiceans, saying a lukewarm tare, with lukewarm works, would be spewed out of His mouth because he claimed to be upright but instead was miserable, wretched, blind, and naked.[1222] Witnessing a compromising, unfaithful, undisciplined spiritual life makes both Jesus and Christians sick to their stomachs!

At harvest time, the end of the world, the tares will be gathered and bound *"first"* before the wheat.[1223] This prophetic detail lets us know that the impersonators of Christianity will unite in an ecumenical council before the rapture, or catching away of the Gentile bride of Christ (See Chapter 12). This gathering is manifestly declared in the Pope's 2016 call for unity and love, falsely claiming that Jews, Christians, Muslims, and Buddhists are "all children of God."[1224] With all due respect, the Pope is wrong. The only way to be a child of God is *"by faith in Christ Jesus,"*[1225] so religions that deny faith in Christ, like Muslims and Buddhists, are not God's wheat-children. The binding time is upon us, as the tare churches, or *"children"* of the Mother Harlot, the Roman Catholic Church, and those who commit spiritual adultery with them, will soon be bound in their money-centered ecumenical council in preparation for their burning as foretold in Revelation 2:22-23 and 13:14-18.

Although Christians cannot always identify individual tares, nor is it our desire to, we can identify the characteristics of the group they will unite with. Tares will have some good, supernatural works by God's Spirit, but the majority of their works will be self-loving, self-serving

---

1221 1 Thessalonians 5:23, 1 John 3:2-3
1222 Revelation 3:14-17
1223 Matthew 13:30
1224 "Pope Francis' Prayer Intentions for January 2016." *YouTube*, uploaded by The Vatican -
       Archive, 6 January 2016
1225 Galatians 3:26

endeavors. Tares will ultimately desire to unite with the Mother Harlot and her daughters rather than with the bride of Jesus Christ and His revealed Word of truth.

3—THE GRAIN OF MUSTARD SEED

Revelation: The false church started small but grew until it was large and filled with all demonic powers.

Found in Matthew 13:31-32, this third parable has dual meanings, but the second meaning is the revelation that is far more prevalent than the first.

The first, less prevalent meaning, is that a tiny mustard seed gain is likened unto faith in God's Word.[1226] Jesus says faith the size of a mustard seed can remove mountains, which in context means casting out evil spirits.[1227] According to Christ, the faith-seed will bring forth miracle-fruit when doubt is kept out of the heart.[1228]

The confusing, mysterious second meaning that most people do not see is the false church, which combats the kingdom of heaven, started by the very smallest of lies, or false doctrines, but eventually flourished into a massive, world-wide habitation of devils.

In the early church's infancy, God protected His children by purging them from sinful people: *"And of the rest durst no man join himself to them: but the people magnified them. And believers were the more added to the Lord, multitudes both of men and women."*[1229] But by 90 A.D. John said there were *"many antichrists"* battling the saints. Fast forward 2,000 years, and the false church is now the greatest, largest group in the world.

Who is this mustard tree? The Holy Spirit helps us identify her as the Roman Catholic Church. First, she unashamedly claims to be the "mother church,"[1230] meaning she is the first false church that rejected the leadership of the Holy Ghost, taking inspiration from the wicked one.

1226 Matthew 17:20
1227 Matthew 17:15-21
1228 Mark 11:22-23
1229 Acts 5:13-14
1230 "Roman Catholicism." *Encyclopedia Britannica*, https://www.britannica.com/topic/Roman-Catholicism. Accessed 10 February 2018

Second, this *"great tree"* is lodging birds, which symbolize unclean spirits according to Genesis 15:10-11, Mark 4:15, and Revelation 18:2. When God confirmed His unconditional covenant with Abraham, the father of faith had to drive away fowls as he offered sacrifices to God, which represented evil spirits being cast out, for Satan wants to destroy true worship by devouring[1231] worshippers and by catching away[1232] the Word from their hearts. Revelation 18:2 is the absolute, clearest picture of birds symbolizing demons, for the Roman church is said to be a *"habitation of devils, and the hold of every foul spirit, and a cage of every unclean and hateful bird."* God could not give us a more brutal, honest, and scathing description of Rome. Think of it—every kind of demon, or bird, lives in the Roman Catholic Church system, and the proof is ever before us.

In August 2018, abuse allegations against Catholic priests in Pennsylvania made world news, as over 300 priests abused more than 1,000 victims over the course of 70 years.[1233] Horrific details of abuse filled the grand jury report, including rapes, whippings, and abortions. In a CBS interview, a mother blamed a priest for her son's accidental death by an overdose on pain killers because the priest repeatedly raped her son, causing him irreparable back damage.[1234] Her son then overdosed and died trying to get relief from the unending, agonizing back pain. When asked how this abuse could happen, one Pennsylvania survivor said, "There's something in the DNA of the church that encourages this." The Bible reveals the Roman church's DNA, for she is the Jezebel-church, the Mother of Harlots and abominations, the cage for every demonic spirit, and ultimately a spiritual child of Satan. Priest abuse is not new, as abuse cases have skyrocketed over the past three decades, revealing thousands

1231 1 Peter 5:8

1232 Matthew 13:19

1233 Goodstein, Laurie and Otterman, Sharon. "Catholic Priests Abused 1,000 Children in Pennsylvania, Report Says." *The New York Times*, www.nytimes.com/2018/08/14/ us/ catholic-church-sex-abuse-pennsylvania.html ?action=click&module=RelatedCoverage &pgtype=Article&region=Footer. Accessed 2 November 2018

1234 "Victims of Sex Abuse by Pennsylvania Priests Share Their Stories." *YouTube*, uploaded by CBS This Morning, 9 August 2018, www.youtube.com/watch?v=oHQJCmsFd9k. Accessed 2 November 2018

upon thousands of victims from Australia (2017), Dominican Republic (2014), Netherlands (2011), Germany (2010), Ireland (2009), Boston (2002), Austria (1999), and Louisiana (1985).[1235] This supreme and utter wickedness was not done in just one state, but viciously infected the global community. Shortly after the Pennsylvania grand jury report, at least 18 victims of sexual abuse at hands of nuns came forward, revealing another secret plague in Catholicism.[1236] Both priests and nuns are guilty of sexual immorality. Paul says child molesters, or *"effeminate"* men, shall not *"inherit the kingdom of God."*[1237] No doubt this would apply to pedophile nuns as well. This relentless child-rape epidemic proves the Roman church is truly the habitation of devils, the hold of every foul spirit, and the cage of every unclean and hateful demon (See Chapter 9).

Returning to the symbolism of fowls, there is one bird, and one only—not a group of birds—that symbolizes God's Spirit, and that is the dove. At Jesus' baptism, the Holy Ghost descended *"like a dove,"*[1238] *"abode upon Him,"*[1239] and remained on Him,[1240] empowering His earthly ministry. Multiple birds rarely represent God's Spirit, proving the mustard tree in this parable is the false church, the Roman Catholic Church, and not the true church.

Data proves the Roman Catholic Church is the largest so-called Christian church in the world, which gives evidence that she is the mustard tree that became the *"greatest among herbs."*[1241] The Pew Research Center found that Catholics make up over 50% of the global Christian population, 36% being Protestants, and 11% as Orthodox.[1242] With over

1235   Park, Madison. "Timeline: A Look at the Catholic Church's Sex Abuse Scandals." *CNN*, https://www.cnn.com/2017/06/29/world/timeline-catholic-church-sexual-abuse-scandals/index.html. Accessed 3 November 2018

1236   "Catholic Nuns Accused of Sexual Misconduct." *YouTube*, uploaded by CBS News, 2 January 2019, https://www.youtube.com/watch?v=-Xp9aEzhN3A. Accessed 2 April 2019.

1237   1 Corinthians 6:9-10

1238   Matthew 3:16

1239   John 1:32

1240   John 1:33

1241   Matthew 13:32

1242   Sagal, Neha. "500 Years After the Reformation, 5 Facts About Protestants Around the World." *The Pew Research Center*, https://www.pewresearch.org/fact-tank/2017/10/27/500-years-after-the-reformation-5-facts-about-protestants-around-the-world/. Accessed 4 November 2018

1.2 billion Catholics[1243] and the ever-growing number of abuse victims, this third parable must represent the Roman Catholic Church and not the true church, the bride of Christ. Both Jesus and Paul prophesied that true Christians would decrease in number in the last days. Jesus said *"few"*[1244] would find the narrow road to eternal life because iniquity, not righteousness, would abound.[1245] Christ also declared fewer and fewer souls would be saved as time passed, saying history would be shortened in order that some souls might be saved![1246] Paul said, *"evil men and seducers shall wax worse and worse, deceiving, and being deceived."*[1247] Our time has a great increase of deception, causing fewer people to be saved.

4—THE LEAVEN HID IN THREE MEASURES OF MEAL
Revelation: The false church hid lies in her teachings until her entire doctrine became fully corrupted.

Found in Matthew 13:33, this fourth parable speaks of a woman, or church, hiding leaven in three measures of meal until the bread is completely leavened. Some confuse this woman with the true church, but the Scriptural revelation is that this woman is the false church hiding lies in her teachings. This fourth parable, along with the second and seventh parables, foretells complete doctrinal corruption and world-wide deception inside false churches at the end of the world rather than a major expansion of the true church. Although this parable is very short, it contains powerful symbols.

To begin with, leaven, the yeast added to dough to make it ferment and rise, always has a negative spiritual connotation in Scripture. Mentioned nearly 40 times, leaven represents sin, as Jesus likened leaven unto the Pharisees' false doctrine, saying,

---

1243 "How Many Roman Catholics Are There in the World?" *BBC News*, www.bbc.com/news/world-21443313. Accessed 4 November 2018
1244 Matthew 7:14
1245 Matthew 24:12
1246 Matthew 24:22
1247 2 Timothy 3:13

> *"How is it that ye do not understand that I spake it not to you concerning bread, that ye should beware of the leaven of the Pharisees and of the Sadducees? Then understood they how that he bade them not beware of the leaven of bread, but of the doctrine of the Pharisees and of the Sadducees."*[1248]

Paul labeled a member of the church of Corinth as leaven amongst the brethren because he was committing fornication.[1249]

Second, meal is flour used to make cakes of bread, which was an everyday staple food for Israelis. Meal represents God's pure Word that we should daily hear and obey. Jesus said, *"I am the bread of life,"*[1250] showing He, the Word of God, is the believer's daily portion of spiritual food. The meal offering in the Old Testament represented Christ's cross, as all the offerings foreshadowed His sacrificial work, mission, and character.[1251] Jesus even likened Himself to a grain of wheat that had to die,[1252] and be crushed or bruised,[1253] before it could live again. Since Christ is pure meal or pure teachings, meal with leaven represents impure or corrupted teachings.

Next, what woman, or church, hid leaven, or lies, in her teachings until the whole doctrine was leavened? She is Mystery Babylon, or the Roman Catholic Church, for Jesus warns us of only one woman who is *"drunken with the blood of the saints,"*[1254] and whose false doctrines He hates[1255] because they are completely abominable, calling her both *"Jezebel"*[1256] and the *"Mother of Harlots and Abominations of the Earth."*[1257] This unfaithful church worked deceptively, for she *"hid"* the mixed-in leaven of polytheism (a three-person god) from the people, as Satan delights in masking sin as righteousness or light.[1258]

1248 Matthew 16:11-12
1249 1 Corinthians 5:1-8
1250 John 6:35
1251 Hebrews 8:4-5
1252 John 12:23-25
1253 Isaiah 53:5
1254 Revelation 17:6
1255 Revelation 2:15
1256 Revelation 2:20
1257 Revelation 17:5
1258 2 Corinthians 11:14

Fourth, the three measures of meal denote God's three-fold manifestation as Father, Son, and Holy Ghost,[1259] for God truly is *the Father, the Word, and the Holy Ghost,*[1260] but these three are one—not three persons. Neither God nor His Bible ever say "I am three persons." So the leaven injected into the three measures is the three-person false doctrine that God is three eternal, separate, distinct, yet coequal persons. A three-person god creates polytheism, tritheism, and ultimately idolatry in all churches that confess the Trinity.

Fifth, notice the leaven was hid in the meal early in the baking process. This detail reveals that the false Godhead teaching began early in church history. The earliest record of believers using the false "titles baptism," rather than the true baptism in the name of the Lord Jesus Christ, comes from the Didache, a second century[1261] catechism. The Didache reads, "Concerning baptism, baptise thus: Having first rehearsed all these things, 'baptise, in the Name of the Father and of the Son and of the Holy Ghost,' in running water."[1262] Yet the inspired, inerrant, infallible Book of Acts declares that early church pillars such as Peter, Philip, and Paul all baptized using the literal name of the Lord Jesus Christ[1263] during the church's infancy, in the first century. How contrary is the Didache compared to Peter's infallible words on the day the church was born, the Day of Pentecost, when he declared, *"Repent, and be baptized everyone of you in the name of Jesus Christ for the remission of sins, and ye shall receive the gift of the Holy Ghost"!*[1264] It was also during the second century (many years after the Bible authors and apostles completed the New Testament canon) that the term "trinity" was introduced by both Theophilus of Antioch[1265] and Tertullian,[1266] further demonstrating that the leaven was added by non-apostles early in church history.

1259 Matthew 28:19, 1 Corinthians 12:7, 1 Timothy 3:16
1260 1 John 5:7
1261 "Didache." *Encyclopedia Britannica*, www.britannica.com/topic/Didache. Accessed 7 November 2018
1262 "The Didache." *St. Gemma.com Web Productions, Inc.*, www.thedidache.com. Accessed 7 November 2018
1263 Acts 2:38, 8:16, 19:5
1264 Acts 2:38
1265 "The Trinity." *Encyclopedia Americana*. Grolier, 1996, pp. 116
1266 "Trinity." *The Interpreter's Dictionary of the Bible*. Abingdon Press, pp. 711

Lastly, like leaven permeating throughout the entire bread until the whole is leavened, the Trinity lie has risen, or expanded, corrupting the entire set of Catholic doctrine, which includes the following heresies: transubstantiation, the communion of saints, mandatory clerical celibacy, the office of the Pope, the Holy Father title of the Pope, and the veneration of statues and images, to name a few. The Trinity lie is so wide spread that most church members do not question its validity. One scholar uses fear to threaten his readers that they will lose their souls if they deny the Trinity, stating, "Try to explain it, and you'll lose your mind. But try to deny it, and you'll lose your soul."[1267] How absurd! It is impossible to lose your soul for not believing a dogmatic lie that is not even found in Holy Writ. In fact, the opposite is true—God will save your soul for believing only God's Words. You must not give in to fear and submit to the man-made Trinity dogma, for God does not give us the spirit of fear, but gives us the Holy Spirit, the Spirit of *"power, and of love, and of a sound mind."*[1268] There is nothing Biblically-sound about three individual persons as one deity. Put all your confidence in the Word of God, knowing God is one person, and that you have not added to the Bible, nor taken away from it. Feast on the unleavened meal, the pure, unadulterated Word of God.

5—THE TREASURE HID IN A FIELD

Revelation: A true believer joyfully trades all his possessions at the surprising opportunity to gain Christ.

Found in Matthew 13:44, this fifth revelation likens the kingdom of heaven unto treasure hid in a field, prompting a surprised and joyful man to sell all he has in order to buy the field and treasure therein. The first symbol, treasure, stands for the baptism of the Holy Ghost, for Paul teaches that the gospel light that has shined in our hearts is *"treasure in earthen vessels,"*[1269] for Christ dwells in our *"hearts by faith."* God's Spirit

---

1267 Erikson, Millard J. *Christian Theology.* Baker Publishing Group, 1986
1268 2 Timothy 1:7
1269 2 Corinthians 4:6-7

is treasure, abiding in the heart, or *"inner man."*[1270] This Holy Ghost-treasure fell into the hearts of believers on the Day of Pentecost, for Peter said *"the promise of the Holy Ghost"* is what God *"shed forth,"*[1271] and Paul received the same experience later, saying *"the love of God is shed abroad in our hearts by the Holy Ghost which is given to us."*[1272] To gain Christ is to be filled with His Spirit (see Chapter 6). Furthermore, Jesus says *"the kingdom of God is within you"*[1273] and Paul echos the same, that *"the hope of glory"* is *"Christ in you."*[1274] After His resurrection, Jesus breathed on His disciples, urging them to receive the Holy Ghost-treasure, saying, *"Receive ye the Holy Ghost."*[1275] Christians will always love and consider God's Spirit a treasure above the things of the world, whereas tares will love worldly pleasures and riches more than God.[1276]

Where is this treasure found? It is hidden in the field of the Bible. Recall Jesus' teaching from the introduction chapter about God's desire to hide Himself from the prideful and reveal Himself to the humble. The treasure of the baptism of the Holy Ghost experience is found hidden only in the field of God's Word, foretold by the prophets. Nearly 800 years before Messiah came, Joel[1277] prophesied of the baptism of the Holy Ghost which was fulfilled in Acts 2:16-21: *"And it shall come to pass afterward, that I will pour out my spirit upon all flesh; and your sons and your daughters shall prophesy, your old men shall dream dreams, your young men shall see visions."* Jeremiah, some 600 years before Christ, prophesied of the Holy Ghost, as vindicated by the Book of Hebrews,[1278] saying, *"But this shall be the covenant that I will make with the house of Israel; After those days, saith the LORD, I will put my law in their inward parts, and write it in their hearts; and will be their God, and they shall be my people."*[1279] Some 580 years before Messiah came, Ezekiel foretold the baptism of the Holy

1270 Ephesians 3:16
1271 Acts 2:33
1272 Romans 5:5
1273 Luke 17:21
1274 Colossians 1:27
1275 John 20:22
1276 2 Timothy 3:4, Revelation 3:17
1277 Joel 2:28-32
1278 Hebrews 10:16-17
1279 Jeremiah 31:33

Ghost, writing, *"A new heart also will I give you, and a new spirit will I put within you: and I will take away the stony heart out of your flesh, and I will give you an heart of flesh. And I will put my spirit within you, and cause you to walk in my statutes, and ye shall keep my judgments, and do them."*[1280] The treasure is in the field, meaning the baptism of the Holy Ghost is foretold in Scripture!

This parable says the man *"found"* the treasure in the field, which speaks from the human perspective rather than God's. Scripture declares the eternal perspective is that no man can come to Jesus except the Father draws him[1281] and Jesus is the One seeking the lost,[1282] and not vice versa. God's gracious heart, though, lets the man experience the joy of finding unexpected treasure from his human perspective. Philip's heart burned with excitement when he experienced the joy of finding Christ, telling Nathanael, *"We have found him, of whom Moses in the law, and the prophets, did write, Jesus of Nazareth, the son of Joseph."*[1283] From God's perspective, it was really Jesus finding Philip and Nathanael. While men are surprised at finding Christ, God is not, but there is rejoicing both on earth and in heaven![1284]

This parable emphasizes how God uses the element of surprise in believers' lives, awakening them from complete ignorance. Just as finding unexpected treasure in a simple, common field would delight a man, God's surprising, instant introduction of Himself into a man's life brings joy unspeakable! In John 4:4-42, the Samaritan woman at Jacob's well went to find water, but instead surprisingly found the Messiah's treasure of Living Waters. She hid the treasure in her heart and excitedly went into the city and told others about it! The Bible says, *"Many of the Samaritans of that city believed on him for the saying of the woman, which testified, He told me all that ever I did."*[1285] Imagine the surprise and excitement the Ethiopian eunuch experienced in Acts 8:26-40 when Philip *"preached*

1280   Ezekiel 36:26-27
1281   John 6:44
1282   Luke 19:10
1283   John 1:45
1284   Luke 15:4-7
1285   John 4:39

unto him Jesus" for the first time from Isaiah chapter 53! The eunuch's spontaneous joy in that predestined moment moved him to obey the gospel command to be baptized immediately: *"And he commanded the chariot to stand still: and they went down both into the water, both Philip and the eunuch; and he baptized him."*

This parable says the man hid the treasure before making the purchase of the field. Hiding God's treasure is likened unto meditating and memorizing Scripture, for Psalm 119:11 says, *"Thy word have I hid in mine heart, that I might not sin against thee."* Meditating upon Scripture ensures the Word is stored in your heart, as David says, *"Let the words of my mouth, and the meditation of my heart, be acceptable in thy sight, O LORD, my strength, and my redeemer."*[1286] Psalm 1:2 declares the blessed man delights in God's Word: *"And in his law doth he meditate day and night."* May God's Word be hidden in your heart like it was in Jeremiah's heart, for he says, *"Thy words were found, and I did eat them; and thy word was unto me the joy and rejoicing of mine heart."*[1287]

Selling and buying has both a natural and spiritual meaning in this parable. In the natural, believers gladly sell out any financial gains that might hinder their relationship with Christ in order to receive Him. Moses chose to suffer affliction with the people of God in order to gain the heavenly riches, selling out the financial and worldly pleasures that would accompany being the son of Pharaoh.[1288] Elisha sold out his farming aspirations in order to follow Elijah, slaying his yoke of oxen and feeding the people so he could follow and minister to Elijah.[1289] Brothers Peter and Andrew and James and John left their fishing nets in order to follow Christ as *"fishers of men."*[1290] Jesus promised Peter and all believers[1291] that the rewards for forsaking the world would be *"an hundred fold now in this time"* and eternal life *"in the world to come."*[1292]

1286 Psalm 19:14
1287 Jeremiah 15:16
1288 Hebrews 11:24-26
1289 1 Kings 19:19-21
1290 Matthew 4:18-22
1291 Matthew 19:27-30
1292 Mark 10:28-31

In the spiritual, selling means forsaking Satan's lies while buying represents repenting from those lies and believing God's Word. Jesus says selling is losing your life that you might find your spiritual life, which includes loving Christ more than family.[1293] Proverbs 23:23 says, *"Buy the truth, and sell it not; also wisdom, and instruction, and understanding."* When you buy the field of Biblical truth, you will experience the treasure of the baptism of the Holy Ghost! Not only can you buy the truth, but Jesus tells the Laodicean Church Age, our age, to buy spiritual gold and white raiment from Him.[1294] Gold is time-tested, unwavering faith[1295] and white raiment represents a righteous, spiritual life of integrity in obedience to the Holy Spirit.[1296]

6—THE ONE PEARL OF GREAT PRICE

Revelation: A true believer abandons his search for many spiritual truths in order to gain the one, most valuable truth—Christ.

Found in Matthew 13:45-46, this sixth revelation contrasts the fifth parable which emphasized the suddenness and total surprise when discovering God's treasure. Here in the sixth parable, Jesus illustrates how God satisfies those who are actively seeking many pearls, by letting them discover the ultimate pearl.

The first symbol shows a merchant man seeking many pearls, meaning someone who is actively searching for religious or spiritual truths. The man is not a careless or wicked man, but one who has been awakened and is sincerely seeking truth. Pearls always represent valuable, beautiful, and rare treasures in Scripture, as proved by the following texts: Matthew 7:6, 1 Timothy 2:9, Revelation 17:4, 18:12, and 21:21. Jesus' words from Matthew 7:6 in particular prove pearls represent His life-changing truths, saying, *"Give not that which is holy unto the dogs, neither cast ye your pearls before swine, lest they trample them under their feet, and turn again and rend you."*

1293 Matthew 10:37-39
1294 Revelation 3:18
1295 1 Peter 1:7
1296 Romans 8:4, Revelation 3:5, 19:8

Men can find valuable moral teachings, or pearls, in nearly any religion, but especially in Judaism. Speaking of Moses' law, Paul says the law is *"holy, and the commandment holy, and just, and good."*[1297] There is tremendous moral wisdom in Moses' Law. Yet there is one religion that is far above all others in value—Christianity—because its Founder offers complete forgiveness by grace, power for living godly on this earth, and eternal life.

The *"pearl of great price"* typifies receiving Jesus Christ's Spirit, or the baptism of the Holy Ghost, for this baptism was the mystery hid *"from ages and generations."*[1298] God loves and will reward diligent searchers[1299] of truth by letting them discover the ultimate pearl, the baptism of the Holy Ghost. When a man finds this great pearl by hearing preaching about Jesus Christ, he will sell everything in order to possess it, as seen in two clear New Testament passages.

Acts 19:1-7 provides the first example. Observe how the 12 Ephesian believers sold out their goodly pearls, or their previous, holy teachings learned from John the Baptist, in order to possess the one pearl of great price, the baptism of the Holy Ghost. Once Paul revealed to them that there was one great pearl available to them, the baptism of the Holy Ghost, the 12 were quickly re-baptized in the name of the Lord Jesus,[1300] and received God's Holy Ghost-treasure, for the *"Holy Ghost came on them; and they spake with tongues, and prophesied."*[1301] The Ephesians sold out John's baptism, or moved on to the fresh revelation of the Spirit for their time period, in order to possess the baptism of the Holy Ghost, the one pearl of great price.

Paul's conversion from Judaism to Christianity is a second, clear example of a man selling out his goodly pearls, or moral teachings, in order to gain the baptism of the Holy Ghost. By his own words, Paul was blameless, a *"Hebrew of Hebrews,"*[1302] a dedicated, devoted, and learned

---

1297 Romans 7:12
1298 Colossians 1:26-27
1299 Hebrews 11:6
1300 Acts 19:5
1301 Acts 19:6
1302 Philippians 3:4-6

man with tremendous zeal for Moses' Law. But after once being in the supernatural presence of Jesus Christ, Paul's desires were transformed and he eagerly forsook his previous self-righteousness, renouncing it as "*dung*" in order that he might win Christ! It wasn't long after Paul's conversation that he received the pearl of great price, the baptism of the Holy Ghost.[1303] Paul described the pearl of great price by saying he wanted to

> "*be found in him [Christ], not having mine own righteousness,
> which is of the law, but that which is through the faith of Christ,
> the righteousness which is of God by faith: That I may know
> him, and the power of his resurrection, and the fellowship of his
> sufferings, being made conformable unto his death.*"[1304]

A final thought comes from Revelation 21:21, which says, "*And the twelve gates were twelve pearls; every several gate was of one pearl: and the street of the city was pure gold, as it were transparent glass.*" Herein is the Christian's future home, "*the holy city, new Jerusalem,*"[1305] "*the tabernacle of God,*"[1306] which comes down from God out of heaven[1307] as the eternal abode after all sin, death, and hell are annihilated and forgotten. This eternal city is indescribably beautiful, as "every facet of her beauty tells a story of amazing grace and Jesus' love."[1308] Notice there are 12 gates, three gates on each of the four sides, each made from a massive pearl. Upon entering the holy city, you must pass through a massive pearl of great price as a reminder of God's saving grace to you. No wonder Christ will wipe all the tears from our eyes[1309] as we enter the city and rejoice in His matchless love story of redemption, for we'll remember our life's story, our deep soul desire and passionate longing to possess the ultimate treasure, God's Spirit, and His amazing grace to let us find It! Our hearts will feel eternally grateful that we sold out the many goodly pearls

1303   Acts 9:17-18
1304   Philippians 3:9-10
1305   Revelation 21:2
1306   Revelation 21:3
1307   Revelation 21:10
1308   Branham
1309   Revelation 21:4

of religious truth in order to possess the Holy Ghost. The best word to describe such a happy group is blessed, for Revelation 22:14-15 says, *"Blessed are they that do his commandments, that they may have right to the tree of life, and may enter in through the gates into the city. For without are dogs, and sorcerers, and whoremongers, and murderers, and idolaters, and whosoever loveth and maketh a lie."*

7—THE NET CAST INTO THE SEA

Revelation: At the end of the world, the gospel will attract believers and unbelievers, but God's angels will separate the wicked away from the holy.

Found in Matthew 13:47-50, this seventh revelation is similar to the wheat and tares, as it depicts two different kinds of people closely associated to one another: the wicked and the just. This seventh parable foretells a world-wide gathering unto Christianity that requires a final separation between the wicked and the just.

The *"net…cast into the sea"* that gathers *"of every kind"* denotes the universal invitation to Christianity commissioned by Christ for His disciples to *"Go ye into all the world, and preach the gospel to every creature. He that believeth and is baptized shall be saved; but he that believeth not shall be damned."*[1310] According to Revelation 17:15, the sea represents peoples, multitudes, nations, and tongues. Our Lord prophesied the end would not come until every nation had heard the gospel invitation,[1311] further vindicating this seventh parable as a true end-time revelation.

Jesus called His first preachers, *"fishers of men,"*[1312] so the invitation to become a Christian is the spiritual net that draws men to Christ. However, just as Judas Isacariot was called of Jesus[1313] and later fell by transgression,[1314] the calling does not guarantee salvation, for Christ says, *"For many be called, but few chosen."*[1315]

1310 Mark 16:15-16
1311 Matthew 24:14
1312 Matthew 4:19
1313 Matthew 10:1-4
1314 Acts 1:25
1315 Matthew 20:16

Jesus, John, and Paul prophesied of this *"net"* scenario for the last days, which foretold large numbers of people, or *"every kind,"* who are attracted to Christianity but are mere professors of the faith, rather than true possessors of its power. Jesus witnessed this same vain worship in His earthly ministry, saying, *"This people draweth nigh unto me with their mouth, and honoureth me with their lips; but their heart is far from me. But in vain they do worship me, teaching for doctrines the commandments of men."*[1316] Jesus said the false church would be so close to the true that only the elect would not be deceived.[1317] John's revelation taught that the false ecumenical move would deceive the *"whole world"*[1318] and eventually seek to control each person's ability to buy and sell.[1319] Paul said deceivers would wax worse and worse,[1320] having a *"form of godliness but denying the power thereof."*[1321]

So the question arises, Why would the masses be attracted to gather around Christianity, yet remain wicked and deceived? The answer comes from Jesus Christ and Paul: wicked people enjoy the blessings of the Holy Spirit but do not want to fully surrender to It! In Matthew 5:45, Christ says, *"For he maketh his sun to rise on the evil and on the good, and sendeth rain on the just and on the unjust."* God is so gracious, He sends natural sunlight and rain upon just and unjust people. All sinners enjoy the blessings of the sun and rain, yet many deny God's existence. Likewise, God's mercy also sends spiritual rain, or His Spirit's anointing, upon both just and unjust people.

Sinners can temporarily experience God's joy, freedom, and love, and yet be lost. Psalms says God's presence brings a fulness of joy, which is the same emotion the "stony hearted" ones experienced temporarily before becoming offended by the Word.[1322] Isaiah 10:27 teaches the Spirit's anointing also breaks demonic yokes, or addictions, granting

1316   Matthew 15:8-9
1317   Matthew 24:24
1318   Revelation 12:9
1319   Revelation 13:15-18
1320   2 Timothy 3:13
1321   2 Timothy 3:5
1322   Psalm 16:20, Matthew 13:20

freedom in people's lives. But all too often, as Jesus teaches, the person set free with a clean house allows seven more devils to return, falling back into sinful addiction, and the last state is worse than the first.[1323] Since "*God is a Spirit*"[1324] and "*God is love,*"[1325] sinners can feel God's merciful love offering them truth, but then reject it because they don't love the truth,[1326] since God's Spirit is the "*Spirit of truth.*"[1327]

Paul, by the Spirit, further expounds on this thought in Hebrews 6:4-8, comparing wicked people who temporarily enjoy the blessings of the Holy Spirit, yet later live openly wicked lives, to plants that bear thorns and briers. The apostle says wicked people, whose end is burning, just like the tares, can be enlightened of the Spirit, can taste of heavenly gifts, be partakers of the Holy Ghost, but still fall away from living a true Christian life. Just as the thorn lives off the rain, so do many sinners live off God's anointing, but they are not the seed, or children of God, and cannot bring forth godly fruit because they are workers of iniquity.

Does this teaching surprise you? It did me! Not long after my surrender to Christ in 2000, I was reading my Bible in my college dorm room and came across Matthew 7:21-23, which says,

> "*Not every one that saith unto me, Lord, Lord, shall enter into the kingdom of heaven; but he that doeth the will of my Father which is in heaven. Many will say to me in that day, Lord, Lord, have we not prophesied in thy name? and in thy name have cast out devils? and in thy name done many wonderful works? And then will I profess unto them, I never knew you: depart from me, ye that work iniquity.*"

I was confounded. How could Jesus command that "*many*" eternally depart from Him who had done wonderful works, like prophesying and casting out devils, in His name? How could Christ condemn people who had been anointed of His Spirit to do good works?

1323   Matthew 12:28-29, 43-45
1324   John 4:24
1325   1 John 4:8
1326   2 Thessalonians 2:10
1327   John 14:17

Two years later, the undeniable revelation came as I listened to William Branham's sermon, *The Anointed Ones At The End Time*.[1328] Branham pointed me to Scriptures showing the true anointing of God's Spirit *temporarily* falls on false teachers. Of course, the anointing is not upon the false teacher while he is teaching lies, but it falls on him either before or after while worshipping, operating spiritual gifts, and praying. Branham emphasized Jesus' words in Matthew 24:24, which speaks of *"false Christs and false prophets."* The genuine anointing of the Holy Spirit temporarily manifests through an unsaved person.

Scripture contains multiple examples of *"false Christs,"* or wicked people who want only God's blessings and mercies but not a holy, fully surrendered life to God's Word. In Genesis, Cain worshipped the true God, heard His voice and spoke back to Him, was given God's direct instruction for obedience, begged Him for mercy and received it, but left the presence of God as a reprobate, a son *"of that wicked one."*[1329] In Numbers, Balaam is perhaps the clearest Bible example of a *"false Christ."* This false prophet spoke directly to God in extended conversations, called Jehovah *"my God,"* experienced supernatural visions and trances when the Holy Spirit fell on him, and prophesied correctly about Israel by the Holy Ghost.[1330] Sadly, Balaam ultimately loved money more than God, leading him to teach Israel to commit fornication, which caused 24,000 deaths. The prophecy of Balaam by God's Spirit was correct, but his teaching was false. Peter said Balaam's destiny was hell.[1331]

Judas Iscariot is a third example, for He was chosen by Jesus, yet ended his life unclean.[1332] He was given power to cast out unclean spirits and heal all manner of sickness and diseases, and must have correctly operated in the supernatural as evidenced at the Last Supper when the other 11 apostles questioned if they were the traitor, not instantly suspecting Judas.[1333] Acts says Judas obtained a part of the apostolic minis-

1328   "The Table." *Voice of God Recordings*, http://table.branham.org/#/en/main
1329   Genesis 4:3-16, 1 John 3:12
1330   Numbers 22:8-20, 23:3-5, 16, 24:1-14, 25:1-15, Revelation 2:14
1331   2 Peter 2:15-17
1332   John 6:70-71, 13:10, 18
1333   Matthew 26:21-22

try, but fell from God as a traitor, was lost, and went to his own place as the *"son of perdition."*[1334] Branham, citing Jesus' warning to remove names of reprobates out of the Book of Life in Revelation 3:15, says of Judas,

> "The part that Judas obtained amongst the twelve and then lost was neither inferior to the ministries of the other eleven, nor was it a devilish foreign ministry interjected amongst the ministries of the others. Judas, a devil, lost a God-given Holy Ghost ministry, and killed himself and went to his own place. His name was even in the Book of Life. But his name was blotted out."[1335]

It is through the right approach to God that sinners like Cain, Balaam, and Judas experience God's anointing. God promises to draw nigh to those who draw nigh to Him.[1336] Sinners, like saints, draw nigh to God through sacrifice, humility, and reverence to receive God's mercy, but saints faithfully serve God thereafter while sinners backslide. Cain drew near to God by bringing Him an offering, but it was the wrong kind.[1337] Balaam drew near to God and heard His specific instructions through private worship, prayer, and sacrifice, offering a bullock and ram upon seven separate altars.[1338] Judas knew the right approach to experiencing God's power was being careful to always respect Jesus and never say an evil word against Him, for Jesus said this was the key to doing miracles in His name.[1339] According to Christ, many unsaved workers of iniquity will plead their case to be saved on Judgment Day based upon their experiences with the anointing, but Jesus' judgments will be based upon who obeyed the will of God with their entire life.

This teaching implies that signs, miracles, and wonders done by the Holy Ghost prove only God's presence manifested among a group, and they do not vindicate that group or individual as being truly saved. A

1334   Matthew 10:1-4, John 17:12, Acts 1:17, 25
1335   Branham
1336   James 4:8
1337   Genesis 4:3-5
1338   Numbers 23:1-5
1339   Mark 9:38-40

move of the Holy Ghost proves the group or individual approached God correctly in a temporary manner. No matter the denomination or movement—Charismatic, Pentecostal, Word of Faith, Apostolic Holiness, etc.—miracles do not prove a person is saved or a church is part of the true kingdom of God. Give the individual, denomination, or movement time to manifest the real seed inside of them so you can judge the fruit of the ministry, since Jesus said a tree is known by its fruit.[1340] Miracles and supernatural works prove only that the Holy Ghost was manifesting—not that He is having the full preeminence[1341] He desires in their daily lives.

Once the gospel net is full at the end of the world, having gathered or attracted every kind of person, God's angels will come and separate the wicked from the just so that the wicked may be burned. This separation will take place at the great white throne judgment, as seen in Revelation 20:11-15 and Matthew 25:31-46. The tares, or wicked workers of iniquity, will see Abraham, Isaac, and Jacob in the kingdom of God, but they will be "*thrust out.*"[1342] The wicked will experience wailing and gnashing of teeth in the lake of fire, which is the same judgment pronounced upon the tares in the second parable. It behooves all who call upon the name of Jesus Christ to examine themselves,[1343] to see if they are in the faith and that Christ's Spirit is in their souls. Christians must diligently make their calling and election sure,[1344] faithfully doing God's works, brining forth fruit pleasing unto God.

8—THE UNMERCIFUL SERVANT

Revelation: A person must forgive others if he expects God to forgive him.

Found in Matthew 18:21-35, this parable stresses the necessity of forgiveness. Jesus tells this parable in response to Peter's question about how often he should forgive his brother. Peter estimates seven times but Jesus says "*seventy times seven,*" or an unlimited number of times.

1340 Matthew 7:15-20
1341 Colossians 1:18
1342 Luke 13:27-29
1343 2 Corinthians 13:5
1344 2 Peter 1:5-11

In the parable, the *"certain king"* represents the Heavenly Father Who compassionately and freely forgives a servant who owes 10,000 talents, or an insurmountable debt. So great is our sin debt to God that none could dream of undoing the sin damage we have committed against God's holiness. Sadly, this forgiven servant leaves the king's presence and finds a fellow servant who owes him 100 talents, or 1 percent of the debt he was forgiven, and demands he repay him. The fellow servant begs for patience, but the first servant refuses and has him cast into prison. When the king hears of this injustice, the first servant is brought before him and in wrath declares him as *"wicked."* The king sentences him to torment until his 10,000 talent debt is paid, representing a sentence to the lake of fire. Jesus states, *"So likewise shall my heavenly Father do also unto you, if ye from your hearts forgive not every one his brother their trespasses."*

Although this parable is found only in Matthew, Jesus is recorded stating this same principle from the Sermon on the Mount in Matthew 6:14-15 and during the final week of His earthly life in Mark 11:25-26. Certainly Christ wants us to understand all sins committed against us by others pale in comparison to the sins we have committed against God Almighty.

Forgiveness is so important that Jesus inserts it in the Lord's Prayer, the model daily prayer in Matthew 6:12: *"And forgive us our debts, as we forgive our debtors."* The gift of forgiveness is daily received and daily given. Christ implores Christians to humbly possess a debtor's mindset so we can forgive those indebted to us. The God-designed debtor's mindset produces gratitude and mercy rather than hopeless guiltiness. Our Lord simply wants us to always remember how much we were forgiven so that we can freely forgive others. Jesus promises in Matthew 5:7, *"Blessed are the merciful: for they shall obtain mercy."*

Kingdom citizens keep their hearts, or grounds, free from every life-sucking *"root of bitterness"* that tries to spring up in their hearts.[1345] Through prayer, Christians daily weed their hearts and cast their cares upon the Lord, putting away all roots of bitterness. Choose to forgive with a tender heart. Paul says, *"Let all bitterness, and wrath, and anger, and*

1345 Hebrews 12:15

clamour, and evil speaking, be put away from you, with all malice: And be ye kind one to another, tenderhearted, forgiving one another, even as God for Christ's sake hath forgiven you.[1346]

On a personal note, I strongly encourage you to view my friend's testimony of forgiveness on YouTube: "Michael J. McCloskey - A Testimony of Forgiveness". Seven years after being targeted and shot by a police officer, in which he became paralyzed from the waist down, Michael powerfully and publicly forgave the officer in court holding high his King James Bible as a banner of victory! His story is one of the greatest examples of Jesus' love and forgiveness I have ever witnessed.

9—THE LABORERS IN THE VINEYARD
Revelation: Eternal life is the reward God gives to all who labor in His kingdom.

Found in Matthew 20:1-16, Jesus' parable of laborers in the vineyard magnifies His equity as He gives each of His servants a just reward for their labor. Isaiah rightly describes God as *"a just God and a Saviour."*[1347] Our God fairly deals with mankind in every age as He seeks laborers for His kingdom. Paul supports Isaiah, asking, *"Is there unrighteousness with God? God forbid."*[1348]

Jesus is the *"householder"* Who hires laborers for His vineyard at the first hour of the day and agrees on their wages. The householder hires more laborers at the third, sixth, and ninth hours before making one last hire at the eleventh hour. At the conclusion of the day, the twelfth hour, the laborers come to Jesus for payment. The last laborers, the eleventh hour workers, are paid first, receiving a penny. When the first hour workers are paid the same amount, some murmur against the householder but are rebuked because the initial payment agreement was kept. The householder declares his lawful dealings and affirms he is *"good."*

The main lesson is that some Christians labor longer than others and in much more difficult circumstances, yet eternal life is the reward

1346 Ephesians 4:31-32
1347 Isaiah 45:21
1348 Romans 9:14

for all faithful laborers. The first hour workers worked for 12 hours and endured the sun's most intense heat for an entire day. The eleventh hour workers logged one hour at the sun's setting and decreasing temperature. Apply this principle to spiritual labor as you compare the ministries of Stephen and John, who served one year and 66 years, respectively.

Stephen is the first recorded Christian martyr[1349] having been stoned by a Jewish council around 31 A.D. at the age of 29 years. During his one year of Holy Ghost empowered ministry, Stephen was *"full of faith and power, did great wonders and miracles among the people."*[1350] A great laborer of the kingdom was Stephen, yet he must receive the same eternal life reward as the apostle John. History says John died around 100 A.D. at the ripe old age of 94 years, meaning he faithfully ministered for over 70 years. Both Stephen and John endured the heat of persecution while laboring for the Householder, and both will receive eternal life, the just and good payment promised to them. John labored decades longer than Stephen but each man's steps were ordered of the Lord. Psalm 37:23 reads, *"The steps of a good man are ordered by the LORD: and he delighteth in his way."*

The householder plainly states he can do his own will with own workers, saying, *"I am good."* God is a good and fair Heavenly Father with a plan for every life. The loving Lord has different assignments for believers and today's spiritual labor conditions vary worldwide. United States Christians experience very little persecution but other Christians, especially Middle Easterners, are facing genocide. Newsweek reports Anti-Christian persecution is increasing and its severity is intensifying, making Christians the most persecuted religious group in the world.[1351]

No matter the circumstances, God desires faithful service in the *"hour"* in which you are called. Conditions are only going to get worse. Prophecy says both love and the number of converts will continue to decrease until the end of time. Matthew 24:12 states, *"And because*

1349 Acts 7:58-60
1350 Acts 6:8
1351 "Persecution of Christians is Approaching Genocide Levels, Report Finds: Christianity 'Is At Risk of Disappearing.'" *Newsweek*, https://www.newsweek.com/persecution-christians-genocide-christianity-disappearing-report-1414038

iniquity shall abound, the love of many shall wax cold." Sin destroys love. God has to shorten the days to ensure some people are saved. Our Lord says in Matthew 24:22, *"And except those days should be shortened, there should no flesh be saved: but for the elect's sake those days shall be shortened."* Despite charismatics prophesying of world-wide revival and a great harvest of souls, Scripture foretells the opposite: world-wide deception. Paul prophesies in 2 Timothy 3:13, *"But evil men and seducers shall wax worse and worse, deceiving, and being deceived."* John says *"all nations"*[1352] will be deceived by and cooperate with the false church, the Mother Harlot (See Chapter 9).

The final Scripture in the parable, Matthew 20:16, says, *"So the last shall be first, and the first last: for many be called, but few chosen."* Christ's parable closes with His assurance that He, not man, will determine the order of rewards and honor. Divine wisdom causes Him to honor the last first, and the first last. God calls many to His service but He has chosen a select few to higher, more honorable works based upon His foreknowledge. Rest assured, God's choosing is always right: *"O the depth of the riches both of the wisdom and knowledge of God! how unsearchable are his judgments, and his ways past finding out! For who hath known the mind of the Lord? or who hath been his counsellor?"*[1353]

10—THE WICKED HUSBANDMAN

Revelation: The kingdom was rejected by the Jews and then given to the Gentiles to bring forth fruit unto God.

Found in Matthew 21:33-46, Jesus interprets the parable of the wicked husbandman for us. Christ declares to the Jews, *"Therefore say I unto you, The kingdom of God shall be taken from you, and given to a nation bringing forth the fruits thereof."*[1354]

The symbols are evident. The Heavenly Father is the householder, or owner of the vineyard, representing the kingdom of God. Israel represents the husbandmen to whom the householder entrusted its fruit to.

1352 Revelations 17:15, 18:3, 23
1353 Romans 11:33-34
1354 Matthew 21:43

When the householder sent servants to receive the fruit, the husband-men beat, killed, and stoned them. Jesus says these servants represent the Old Testament prophets God sent to Israel, whom they rejected. Luke 13:34 reads, "*O Jerusalem, Jerusalem, which killest the prophets, and stonest them that are sent unto thee; how often would I have gathered thy children together, as a hen doth gather her brood under her wings, and ye would not!*" Lastly, the householder sent his son to receive the fruit. This represents the Father sending His Son, Jesus, but the chief priests and Pharisees crucified Him "*out of the vineyard,*" or "*without the gate*"[1355] of Jerusalem.

Containing some common sense, the priests and Pharisees infer Jesus is likening them to the wicked husbandmen. Jesus asks if they have read Psalm 118:22-23, which He quotes aloud in their ears. Multiple New Testament passages refer to Christ as the rejected stone: Acts 4:11, Romans 9:33, Ephesians 2:20, and 1 Peter 2:7. Christ interprets the parable, breathing out the sentence against Israel that the kingdom will be given to the Gentiles. Paul echoes this in Acts 28:28: "*Be it known therefore unto you, that the salvation of God is sent unto the Gentiles, and that they will hear it.*"

11—THE KING'S SON

Revelation: Believers respond to God's invitation for the rapture and are appropriately clothed in the wedding garment, or the baptism of the Holy Ghost.

Found in Matthew 22:1-14, this parable typifies the Heavenly Father as a certain king preparing a wedding for his son, or Jesus Christ. The marriage represents the future marriage supper of the Lamb taught in Revelation 19:9. This supper represents the wedding reception of Christ and His bride, the New Testament church, which takes place immediately after Jesus raptures away His bride before the tribulation.

Those "*bidden*" to the wedding who would not come represent Israel because they rejected their own Messiah's invitation to the kingdom of God. Some Jews "*made light*" of the invitation, preferring farming and

1355 Hebrews 13:12

selling merchandise over following Jesus' ministry. The remaining Jews, or "*remnant*," slew Jesus' servants, or preachers He would send following His ascension to heaven. Christ plainly foretells that the Jews will kill His "*prophets, and wise men, and scribes.*"[1356] The wrath of the king's armies and the burning of the city represent the Roman emperor Titus' destruction of Jerusalem in 70 A.D.

Next, the king sends out one last invitation to the farthest extents of his kingdom, to the "*highways*," gathering both good and bad guests so that his wedding is fully attended. This final invite represents the Holy Ghost gospel being given to the Gentiles, who were "*afar off*"[1357] from the promises of God. Paul and Barnabas declare this to Israel in Acts 13:46: "*Then Paul and Barnabas waxed bold, and said, It was necessary that the word of God should first have been spoken to you: but seeing ye put it from you, and judge yourselves unworthy of everlasting life, lo, we turn to the Gentiles.*" The Jews judged themselves "*unworthy*" of everlasting life, just as the king called them "*not worthy*"[1358] of the wedding.

The parable climaxes as the king comes into the wedding to see his Gentile guests but finds a man without a wedding garment. Angered, the king asks the guest how he came into the wedding without the garment but the guest is speechless. Punishment issues forth from the king, as he sends the guest into outer darkness to endure weeping and gnashing of teeth. Why was the king so angry about the guest rejecting the wedding garment?

Scripture teaches how kings and rulers provided changes of clothes as presents for their honored friends or guests, such as in the case of Joseph providing a change of raiment for his brothers, although Benjamin received five changes.[1359] Turning down a wedding garment for a king's marriage celebration for his son would be the highest form of disrespect, especially from a man who was filthy from the elements of living in the highways. Like Esther knew, a king must only be approached in a respectful, clean, and dignified manner. But this guest refused the

1356 Matthew 23:34
1357 Ephesians 2:17
1358 Matthew 22:8
1359 Genesis 45:22

king's requirement for a wedding garment despite it being readily available and freely offered for all guests, showing his disdain for the king, his son, and the other guests.

Symbolically, the wedding garment represents the baptism of the Holy Ghost because it is a *"gift"* God offers to believers, their children, and *"all that are afar off, even as many as the Lord our God shall call."*[1360] Jesus says the Holy Ghost is the promise of the Father that endues, or clothes, believers in power.[1361] Paul, too, uses the garment imagery for the Holy Ghost, saying, *"But put ye on the Lord Jesus Christ, and make not provision for the flesh, to fulfil the lusts thereof."*[1362] In Revelation 3:4, the Lord Jesus admonishes the Sardis church for their holy lifestyle, saying, *"Thou hast a few names even in Sardis which have not defiled their garments; and they shall walk with me in white: for they are worthy."* The wedding garment is also synonymous to eternal life because the baptism of the Holy Ghost is the Spirit of Christ in your soul. Paul says it is *"Christ in you, the hope of glory."*[1363] John supports this, telling believers they already have eternal life in 1 John 5:13: *"These things have I written unto you that believe on the name of the Son of God; that ye may know that ye have eternal life, and that ye may believe on the name of the Son of God."*

The guest without the wedding garment represents believers (Jew and Gentile) who respond to preaching about the end-times and gather in worship with Holy Ghost filled saints but they themselves fail to receive the gift of the Holy Ghost. This guest is just like Judas Iscariot. Jesus says this guest is cast into outer darkness where there is *"weeping and gnashing of teeth,"* which represents being cast into hell according to four other Scriptures.[1364] Most notably, Jesus says the Christ-rejecting Jews will endure weeping and gnashing of teeth being *"thrust out"* or cast out of the kingdom of God as *"workers of iniquity."*[1365] Jesus teaches workers of iniquity can be temporarily anointed of the Holy Spirit to

1360   Acts 2:38-39
1361   Luke 24:49
1362   Romans 13:14
1363   Colossians 1:27
1364   Matthew 8:12, 24:51, 25:30; Luke 13:28
1365   Luke 13:27-28

perform miracles and yet turn from Christ to do their own will instead of His.[1366] Judas performed and witnessed amazing miracles[1367] but forsook the Spirit's leading and did his own will, selling out Christ for 30 pieces of silver.

Like Judas, garment-rejecting worshippers feel the attraction of true worship and understand Jesus' wedding, or rapture, will soon occur. They like seeing the life-changing power of God on others but never experience it for themselves. Somehow the garment-rejectors convince themselves that their own garments are good enough for God's service, but Isaiah 64:6 says, *"But we are all as an unclean thing, and all our righteousnesses are as filthy rags."* You cannot trust in your own righteousness when Christ says your righteousness must exceed that of the Pharisees in order to enter the kingdom.[1368] Christ is freely offering His righteousness in exchange for admission of our sins. 2 Corinthians 5:21 declares, *"For he hath made him to be sin for us, who knew no sin; that we might be made the righteousness of God in him."*

12—THE TEN VIRGINS

Revelation: Wise believers possess oil, or the baptism of the Holy Ghost, as they await their wedding day, the rapture, with Jesus.

Found in Matthew 25:1-13, this parable further differentiates the two kinds of Christians referenced in Figure 21—those with "good" and "thorny" hearts. Jesus now describes these two kinds of Christians as wise and foolish. Wise Christians will be *"ready"* for the bridegroom's coming, or Jesus' return for His bride at the rapture. Foolish Christians will be caught unprepared and will miss the *"marriage,"* or marriage supper of the Lamb that proceeds the rapture.

Ancient Jewish marriage ceremonies in the east were much different than those of modern western civilization. The customs varied among families, but often the bridegroom would begin a procession to the marriage ceremony at an unknown evening hour. Matthew Henry says,

1366 Matthew 7:21-23
1367 Matthew 10:1-4, Luke 9:1-6
1368 Matthew 5:20

"The bridegroom came, attended with his friends, late in the night, to the house of the bride, where she expected him, attended with her bride-maids; who, upon notice given of the bridegrooms' approach, were to go out with lamps in their hands, to light him into the house with ceremony and formality, in order to the celebrating of the nuptials with great mirth."[1369]

The ten virgin bridesmaids served the bride and possibly acted as witnesses of the wedding nuptials, just as Boaz requested ten witnesses when he purchased Ruth to be his wife.[1370]

Examining the symbols, the ten virgins represent both the bride and her wedding party, as they are her closest friends. In short, the ten virgins represent the New Testament church. The fact that they were virgins, having no sexual intercourse, symbolizes complete spiritual purity. Spiritual virgins today do not have any intercourse with worldliness and idolatry. Christ is their only love interest. In complete devotion to Him, they do not flirt with worldly temptations. Paul tells the Corinthians they should be *"chaste"* virgins *"to Christ,"* keeping their minds uncorrupted and undeceived *"from the simplicity that is in Christ."*[1371]

Oil is the symbol of the baptism of the Holy Ghost because Zechariah 4 says the *"golden oil"* that emptied out of the two olive trees into the seven candlesticks is God's Spirit: *"Not by might, nor by power, but by my spirit, saith the LORD of hosts."*[1372] Note carefully that both groups had oil, but the wise had extra oil, choosing to take additional *"oil in their vessels with their lamps."* The foolish virgins only had oil in their lamps but the wise took extra oil in case the bridegroom delayed his coming, which he did. Wise Christians today have an extra measure of oil, representing the anointing of the Holy Ghost in their souls. Foolish virgins have the Holy Ghost anointing in their human spirits or minds, but not in their souls as displayed in Figure 22.

1369 "Matthew 25." *Bible Study Tools*, https://www.biblestudytools.com/commentaries/matthew-henry-complete/matthew/25.html
1370 Ruth 4:2,9
1371 2 Corinthians 11:2-3
1372 Zechariah 4:6

	Wise Virgin	Foolish Virgin
Body	The sin nature permanently dwells in the flesh, but the anointing can temporarily fall upon the body. The desires of the flesh must be crucified daily.	Same as Wise Virgins.
Spirit (Mind)	Oil, or temporary anointing of the Holy Ghost renews the mind daily (Ephesians 4:23). Also called the anointing of a "sound mind" (2 Timothy 1:7).	Same as Wise Virgins.
Soul	Possesses extra oil, or seal of the baptism of the Holy Ghost (Ephesians 1:13).	Lacks extra oil, or seal of the baptism of the Holy Ghost, due to foolishly wasting time with worldly cares (Matthew 13:22, Ephesians 5:14-17).

Figure 22

The bridegroom tarrying represents Jesus tarrying for the rapture, which He has been doing for nearly 2,000 years. The midnight cry of the bridegroom's approaching procession awakening the virgins is equivalent to the rapture "*shout*"[1373] Paul teaches about and symbolizes the supernatural preaching and healing ministry of the late William Branham that awakened all Christendom in the 1940s, 50s, and 60s (See Chapters 7, 12, and 13). Please contact me if you have not heard the Message, or "*shout*," God gave to His prophet William Branham.

Upon hearing the shout, all the virgins trimmed their lamps, removing the charred portion of the wick ensuring their lamps burned their brightest. Lamp-trimming represents sanctification, or the second work of grace that follows justification. William Branham's "*shout*" ministry emphasized the Three Works of Grace: justification, sanctification, and the baptism of the Holy Ghost (See Chapter 5 and Parable 15).

1373   1 Thessalonians 4:16

The five foolish virgins realize they do not have enough oil and ask the wise for some of their oil. The wise admit they do not have enough oil to share and charge the foolish to go buy their own oil. Spiritually, Holy Ghost filled Christians, or wise virgins, cannot give the baptism of the Spirit to anyone. Only Christ baptizes souls with the Holy Ghost, as John the Baptist says, "*I indeed baptize you with water unto repentance: but he that cometh after me is mightier than I, whose shoes I am not worthy to bear: he shall baptize you with the Holy Ghost, and with fire.*"[1374]

This is sound advice from the wise virgins, as Jesus invites all to come and buy spiritual blessings from Him in Revelation 3:18: "*I counsel thee to buy of me gold tried in the fire, that thou mayest be rich; and white raiment, that thou mayest be clothed, and that the shame of thy nakedness do not appear; and anoint thine eyes with eyesalve, that thou mayest see.*" You again see how foolish virgins are more concerned with cares of the world, physical transactions, rather than spiritual transactions, such as prayer. The foolish virgins didn't repent, pray, and obey enough to receive the oil of the Holy Ghost because God promised to fill anyone with His Holy Spirit who truly hungered and thirsted for it.[1375] Yet the foolish lived free from idolatry, having no intercourse with demons.

While the foolish go to buy oil, the bridegroom comes and the wise virgins go in with him to the marriage festivities and the door is shut. The coming bridegroom is the rapture, proving only wise virgins, or Holy Ghost filled Christians, go up to the meeting in the air.

The shutting of the door reminds you of Noah's ark and God shutting the door in conclusion, that no more souls would be saved. This imagery fits our day perfectly. Jesus compares the conditions at the end of the world to the days of Noah in Luke 17:26-30. In Noah's day, all believers gathered in one physical location—the ark. Today, God's people are gathering in one spiritual location—heavenly places, or the baptism of the Holy Ghost. Like the ark, all those outside of the baptism of the Holy Ghost will suffer either partially or completely during the Great Tribulation.

1374   Matthew 3:11
1375   Matthew 5:6, Luke 11:13, Acts 5:32

Once the last Holy Ghost filled Christian has his lamp trimmed and filled with oil, the Times of the Gentiles will be complete. God will cut off the Gentile branch, or people, and "*graff*" the 144,000 Israelis back into the Holy Tree.[1376]

Jesus concludes the parable by instructing believers to "*watch*," which in the Greek means to "give strict attention to, the cautious, active: to take heed lest through remission and indolence some destructive calamity suddenly overtake one." The kingdom of God, the teaching and preaching of the baptism of the Holy Ghost, requires your full attention. Rapture-ready saints will be fully focused on the Bridegroom and actively working in His kingdom.

13—THE TALENTS

Revelation: Christ commits varying amounts of talents and resources to His servants and rewards those who faithfully invest in them.

Found in Matthew 25:14-30 this parable greatly resembles The Pounds parable but has notable differences I will point out in the 14th parable.

The Talents parable was spoken privately to Jesus' disciples only as He sat with them on the Mount of Olives a few days before His crucifixion.[1377] Jesus was answering their three questions: when will the temple be thrown down, what is the sign of Jesus' second coming, and what is the sign of the end of the world? The Talents parable is Jesus' answer to the question, what is the sign of Jesus' second coming because it immediately follows the parable of the Ten Virgins. Both deal with the second coming of Jesus.

Jesus says the kingdom of heaven is like a rich man traveling to a far country who leaves his goods or money with his servants to invest during his absence. The first servant gets five talents, the second gets two talents, and the third gets one talent. The varying amounts of talents speak to

---

1376 Romans 11:21-26
1377 Matthew 24:3

varying abilities and potential the rich man saw in his servants. The two servants with the most talents diligently make business trades to double their money, but the servant with one talent lazily buries it in the earth. After a long absence, the rich man returns to reckon with his servants. He's well pleased with the first two but angry with the third because he did not apply the very least effort to increase his lord's money.

The rich man's long absence represents Jesus going to heaven after His first coming and being there a long time until His second coming. Christians are awaiting His second coming now. During Jesus' time away seated at the right hand of the majesty on high, His servants are given talents, or spiritual gifts to invest in for the benefit of Jesus' kingdom. Examining natural talents helps you understand the value of spiritual gifts. Chapter 11 defines and details the nine gifts of the Holy Ghost.

A "*talent*" is a "sum of money weighing a talent" in the Greek. English clergyman John Gill (1697-1771) notes a single talent was equivalent to 375 English pounds of silver or 4,500 pounds of gold.[1378] Since Jesus did not indicate if the talents were silver or gold, I will show the value of both. Using Eric Nye's online currency converter to convert 1770 A.D. English pounds to 2019 A.D. U.S. dollars,[1379] Figure 23 shows the values of the talents, both in silver and gold.

Imagine your grandfather gifted you some of his money to start a business for him while he was traveling overseas. With a smile, his last words to you before his decade-long absence are, "Do something. Anything. I can't wait to see what you'll accomplish for me." Whether the amount was at either end of the spectrum—having $71,000 (one silver talent) or $4,300,000 (five gold talents)—you'd be extremely fortunate. With either amount, you are not starting in debt, as this money is simply gifted to you. Again, this is not your money. With the largest sum, you could immediately purchase property and build a home for your business. With the smallest sum, you could begin renting a property

---

1378   Myers, Rich. "John Gill's Exposition of the Bible: Matthew 25:15." *E-Sword X,* Version 6.3 (24)
1379   Nye, Eric. "*Pounds Sterling to Dollars: Historical Conversion of Currency,*" https://www. uwyo.edu/numimage/currency.htm

and purchase machines and other assets. At the very least, you could invest the money in the stock market, money market accounts, real estate, or hand the money over to bankers in fixed annuities if you desire guaranteed returns.

	Silver	Gold
One talent	$71,678.48	$860,141.72
Two talents	$143,356.96	$1,720,283.44
Five talents	$358,392.40	$4,300,708.60

Figure 23

The reality of this illustration is Jesus Christ, God's own Son, has gifted you at least one of the nine spiritual gifts and instructed you to do your part in His kingdom. The Lord says, "Help finish the Great Commission. Display My love and power to others, especially your fellow man." Paul urges you to be fervent in business and redeem the time.[1380]

Spiritual gifts are a serious matter, one in which Jesus deals very strictly. Of course, spiritual gifts are secondary to charity, or the baptism of the Holy Ghost. But in this parable you learn how Jesus is going to deal with His servants upon His return: a time of holy reckoning. Some think Jesus' return will be like a party or whimsical celebration. No, Jesus' return is a reckoning with His servants for their efforts to promote the Father's business with His own money, or talents.

Paul teaches each believer is given different measures of gifts, hence Jesus' unequal distribution of talents. The apostle uses the gift of faith as an example in Romans 12:3, instructing believers to be humble because God *"dealt to every man the measure of faith."* Three verses later, Paul says we have *"gifts differing according to the grace that is given to us."*[1381] You may have noticed Paul was endued with many gifts and longed to impart

---

1380 Romans 12:11, Ephesians 5:16
1381 Romans 12:6

spiritual gifts to the saints he ministered to.[1382] Perhaps Paul was a "five talent" servant of Jesus Christ. Paul spoke in tongues more often than all the Corinthians, exercised the gift of prophecy concerning future events, worked miracles, and had the gifts of the apostle and teacher.[1383] Yet, instead of feeling self sufficient and independent of God's assistance because of his many gifts, Paul constantly practiced self denial, forcing his body to obey God's Word to ensure he would not be a spiritual "*castaway.*"[1384] Paul's example teaches us the more gifts we have, the more responsible we must be. In Luke 12:48, our Lord says, "*For unto whomsoever much is given, of him shall be much required: and to whom men have committed much, of him they will ask the more.*"

In the parable, the first two servants doubled the money they were gifted: the five-talent servant now had ten, and two-talent servant now had four. Applying this spiritually, Jesus wants to you invest in your gifts so you're *twice* as wise, for example, as you were when you started serving Him, if wisdom is one your spiritual gifts. Recall there are nine spiritual gifts. If your gift is healing, you'll strive to be twice as effective in praying for the sick than when you started. Jesus' apostles exemplify growing in their healing gifts because they had to learn from Christ that some sicknesses, like the demon of epilepsy, only come out by prayer and fasting.[1385] Christians see growth in their spiritual lives as evidence of dedication to Christ. 2 Peter 3:18 says, "*But grow in grace, and in the knowledge of our Lord and Saviour Jesus Christ.*" The way to grow is to abide in Christ. Jesus says, "*Abide in me, and I in you. As the branch cannot bear fruit of itself, except it abide in the vine; no more can ye, except ye abide in me. If ye abide in me, and my words abide in you, ye shall ask what ye will, and it shall be done unto you.*"[1386] Numerous Scriptures speak of abounding, or increasing "*in every thing*"—love, hope, giving, utterance, diligence, judgment, faith, virtue, knowledge, and all the character qualities of Christ.[1387]

1382   Romans 1:11
1383   Acts 15:12, 19:11; 1 Corinthians 14:18, 1 Thessalonians 4:15-17, 1 Timothy 2:7
1384   1 Corinthians 9:27
1385   Matthew 17:14-21
1386   John 15:4,7
1387   2 Corinthians 8:7, Philippians 1:9, 1 Thessalonians 3:12, 2 Peter 1:5-8

Burying your talent, or running from your giftedness, is not an option. You learn from the parable's third and final servant that hiding your talent in the earth is a *"wicked and slothful"* act. Christians must defeat laziness, letting nothing distract them from doing the Father's business. Additionally, you can see the disastrous effects of the spirit of fear in this parable. The wicked servant says he *"was afraid,"*[1388] and so he did nothing for Jesus' kingdom, even falsely accusing our Lord. Harboring fear causes spiritual paralysis and is a great sin. Revelation says the fearful will burn in the lake of fire,[1389] meaning they are not worthy of eternal life and will not enter the New Jerusalem. There is nothing to fear if Jesus is your Lord because Christ has promised His Holy Spirit will never leave nor forsake us.[1390] Very plainly, Jesus does not give you the spirit of fear, but gives power, love, and a sound mind.[1391] Remember that God has predestined all events and assigned you works He ordained you to do before the world was founded. The faithful God will work out everything if you will just believe Him and humbly invest in your ministry and spiritual gifts. The wicked servant is cast into outer darkness where weeping and gnashing of teeth is. This is a reference to the lake of fire, as Christ says weeping and gnashing is experienced by the group that is *"thrust out"* of the kingdom of God and sees with their own eyes Abraham, Isaac, and Jacob ruling that kingdom.[1392]

The Lord Jesus says the one talent of the wicked servant is given to the first servant with ten talents. It's doubtful this means Jesus gives one person's spiritual gifts to another. But one certain application is that Christ will have one person finish a ministry that another person has forsaken. Acts 1:23-26 exemplifies this truth, as Matthias is chosen to replace Judas Iscariot as one of the 12 apostles. History says Matthias labored greatly for Christ, preaching in Judea before his missionary work of converting souls to Jesus in Cappadocia. Matthias died

---

1388 Matthew 25:25
1389 Revelation 21:8
1390 Matthew 28:20, John 14:16-17, Hebrews 13:5
1391 2 Timothy 1:7
1392 Luke 13:27-29

a martyr by crucifixion in the region about the Caspian Sea.[1393] Our Lord directs you to recognize your ministry and be responsible for it, or else another may take your crown. Revelation 3:11 says, *"Behold, I come quickly: hold that fast which thou hast, that no man take thy crown."* It appears Matthias took the crown Judas forfeited. You must diligently serve Jesus if you want a full reward. 2 John 1:8 reads, *"Look to yourselves, that we lose not those things which we have wrought, but that we receive a full reward."*

The lesson is that Jesus wants His closest, most intimate servants to know He's given them different amounts of varying gifts but each can faithfully invest in them for Jesus' glory. Recall that Jesus had to tell Peter to not worry about God's plans for John's ministry, but rather to fix his eyes solely upon Christ.[1394] Your eyes must always be focused upon Jesus' will for your own life rather than comparing your life to others.

14—THE POUNDS

Revelation: Christ provides an equal opportunity to His servants and rewards those who faithfully act upon it.

Found in Luke 19:11-27, The Pounds parable closely resembles The Talents, but is different in four notable ways.

The similarities with The Talents parable are obvious. First, a rich man or nobleman leaves on a long term trip, representing Jesus' ascension to heaven to be seating at the right hand of the Father during the Times of the Gentiles. Second, before leaving, the rich man leaves three servants in charge of his money with the expectation they will carry on and grow his business until he returns. Third, two servants are faithful with the entrusted goods while the third servant does nothing. Fourth, the nobleman praises the two faithful servants upon his return and severely chastens the third, unfaithful servant. The fate of the third servant is not recorded in The Pounds parable, but he is called *"wicked"* just as the third servant from The Talents parable.

1393 "Saint Matthias." *Encyclopedia Britannica*, https://www.britannica.com/biography/Saint-Matthias
1394 John 21:21-22

The first difference is the group Jesus is speaking to. Here in The Pounds parable, Christ is addressing a multitude of Jews who are under expectation that Jesus is going to immediately overthrow the Roman Empire and institute the Messianic government, the Jewish kingdom of David, free from tyranny and foreign influence. Luke 19:11 declares this, saying, "*And as they heard these things, he added and spake a parable, because he was nigh to Jerusalem, and because they thought that the kingdom of God should immediately appear.*" Jesus knows the Messianic kingdom, or His 1,000 year millennial reign upon the earth, is over 3,000 years in the future so He speaks this parable to correct the multitude's false hope for an imminent appearing of Christ's sinless kingdom. Jesus directs their thoughts to a life of faithful service.

Second, The Pounds parable shows the spirit of hatred the entire world has for Christ and the truth of Christianity. Jesus says the citizens hate the nobleman and send him a message saying they will not be ruled by him. This represents the hatred the world has always had for Christ. Jesus also warned His disciples they would be hated of all men for His sake in Matthew 10:22. Many religious groups publicly and boldly declare their hatred for Christianity. But a sad reality is that many churches who claim to be Christians hate Jesus' Bible commands. Jesus teaches this in Matthew 6:24: "*No man can serve two masters: for either he will hate the one, and love the other; or else he will hold to the one, and despise the other. Ye cannot serve God and mammon.*" Truly, many church members claim to love Jesus but hate the Bible commands against cussing, drunkenness, fornicating, adultery, lustful thoughts, and dressing immodestly. Paul states the fact that homosexuals hate the knowledge of God.[1395] These false Christians have a form of godliness but hatefully deny the cleansing power thereof.[1396] At the parable's conclusion, all the citizens who refused to let Christ reign over their lives will be slain in front of Him, representing the second death when sinners are tormented with fire and brimstone in the presence of the holy angels and the Lamb.[1397]

1395 Romans 1:26-32
1396 2 Timothy 3:5
1397 Revelation 14:10, 21:8

The citizens hate the nobleman because he wants to reign over them. Jesus is showing that He is King of kings and Lord of lords and wants to exercise the highest influence and control over His beloved, blood-bought creation. But the majority of earth's inhabitants will not let Christ's Spirit reign over them, choosing to let the *"law of sin and death"* rule their lives rather than the *"law of the Spirit and life."*[1398] Each person will be ruled by either death and disobedience, or life and obedience. As you love Jesus and let Him rule your life, you *"reign in"* this life as a spiritual king and priest[1399] over sin, the devil, the world, and the flesh.

The third difference is the amount of money each of Christ's servants are given: a pound. Again using Gill and Nye's work, a Biblical pound is equivalent to 75 English pounds, or $14,335.70 in U.S. dollars. While this sum is more modest compared to The Talents parable, a Jewish multitude listening to Christ could easily relate to this realistic wage. Also, this smaller sum matches Jesus' description as a very little amount. Our Lord congratulated the servants saying, *"Well, thou good servant: because thou hast been faithful in a very little, have thou authority over ten cities."* Jesus wanted this multitude to understand their amount of responsibility compared to His was very small but the reward would be very great. Christians should not feel overwhelmed or stressed about their stewardship. God promises to never give us situations and temptations we cannot handle.

It's essential to notice this parable assigning each servant the same amount of money, which greatly differs from The Talents parable. Here, money is equal, which cannot represent spiritual gifts, for gifts are not given equally. Not all speak in tongues, prophesy, or perform miracles.[1400] So what is equal, or nearly equal, among Christians? The answer is an equal opportunity to love Jesus in your home, on your job, around your family members, with your money, and more. Nearly every Christian has a home, family, friends, job, and money. While some Christians are given more years to live than others, all Christians are given one lifetime, one opportunity to love God and their neighbors.

1398   Romans 8:2
1399   Romans 5:17, Revelation 1:6
1400   1 Corinthians 12:29-30

Jesus offers many examples of equal opportunity works every Christian—not just preachers—can act upon, thereby investing their *"pound"* in His glorious, eternal kingdom including, but not limited to:

- Withstanding persecution yields a great heavenly reward (Matthew 5:11-12).
- Giving alms in secret yields an open reward (Matthew 6:4).
- Praying in secret yields an open reward (Matthew 6:6).
- Fasting in secret yields an open reward (Matthew 6:18).
- Receiving a prophet or righteous man yields a prophet's or righteous man's reward (Matthew 10:41).
- Providing food, drink, shelter, or clothes to a Christian or visiting one when he's sick or in prison yields an entrance into life eternal (Matthew 25:34-40).
- Giving an apostle a cup of water for Christ's sake yields a reward (Mark 9:41).
- Loving your enemies, blessing those who persecute you, praying for those who despitefully use you, and lending with no hope of repayment yields a great reward along with the title of being called the children of the Highest (Luke 6:27-33).
- Hosting a feast for the less fortunate who cannot repay you yields a recompense at the resurrection of the just (Luke 14:12-14).
- Fighting the good fight, finishing the course, and keeping the Christian faith yields a crown of righteousness (2 Timothy 4:7-8).
- Providing a Christian's physical necessities (a member of the household of faith) yields a heavenly reward upon a giver's account (Galatians 6:10, Philippians 15-18).
- Doing anything heartily, as doing it to Christ, yields the reward of the inheritance (Colossians 3:23-24).
- Diligently seeking God yields rewards (Hebrews 11:6).

- Enduring temptation yields the crown of eternal life (James 1:12).
- Visiting the fatherless and widows, and keeping oneself unspotted from the world yields the reward of spiritual purity (James 1:27).
- Overcoming sin during any of the Seven Church Ages yields the reward of inheriting *"all things"*[1401] or all the Church Age rewards: eating the Tree of Life, escaping the second death, eating the hidden manna, a white stone with a new name within, power to rule over nations, the Morning Star, white raiment, having your name remain in the Book of Life, being a pillar in the temple of God, having Jesus' new name, God's new name, and New Jerusalem's new name written upon him, and sitting with Jesus in His throne (Revelation 2:7, 11, 17, 26-28 and 3:5, 12, 21).

Fourthly, this parable gives a detail about one of Christ's special rewards: ruling over cities. Jesus tells the servant who had a ten-fold increase upon his pound: *"Well, thou good servant: because thou hast been faithful in a very little, have thou authority over ten cities."*[1402] Two supporting texts about overcoming saints ruling cities, or even nations, include Revelation 2:26-27 and 20:4-6. In the first, Jesus says He will give overcomers *"power over the nations"* to *"rule them with a rod of iron."* This means His saints will be minor rulers underneath His own rule, for Scripture twice records Jesus will *"rule all nations with a rod of iron."*[1403] In the second, the *"blessed and holy"* saints, who overcame *"the beast,"* or Rome, live and reign with Christ for 1,000 years. Recall *"reign"* means "to exercise kingly power." Additionally, Jesus promises His 12 apostles they will sit upon 12 thrones judging the 12 tribes of

---

1401   Revelation 21:7
1402   Luke 19:17
1403   Revelation 12:5, 19:15

Israel.[1404] What wonderful blessings God has in store for those that love Him now!

15—THE SEED CAST INTO THE GROUND

Revelation: God causes spiritual growth by invisible means but men observe it in three stages.

Located in Mark 4:26-29, this parable emphasizes three stages of growth in connection to the kingdom of heaven. Based upon Jesus' words that the kingdom of God is *"within"*[1405] a believer in the form of the baptism of the Holy Ghost in a man's soul, the three stages of growth refers to the Three Works of Grace taught in Chapter 5: justification, sanctification, and the baptism of the Holy Ghost.

Jesus describes a man casting seeds into the ground. The man goes about his daily routine of sleeping and raising as the seeds mysteriously spring up without him knowing how. The earth, Jesus says, brings forth the fruit of herself, without the man's help. Next, Jesus lists the three stages of the wheat plant: blade, ear, and full corn. Once the matured fruit is produced, the man immediately harvests the grain.

This parable's symbols are familiar, but the sower has a different meaning. Previously, the sower represented Jesus, the Son of Man, but now he represents a blood-bought, redeemed human preacher because he doesn't know how seeds grow and cannot cause seeds to increase. But Jesus knows about the growth of seeds, for it was by Him, the Word of God, that all things—including seeds—were created.[1406] Jesus causes growth because His Spirit is quickening power.[1407] Finite human preachers, Paul says, are limited but are united as one in their efforts to both sow and water seeds. 1 Corinthians 3:7-8 reads, *"So then neither is he that planteth any thing, neither he that watereth; but God that giveth the increase. Now he that planteth and he that watereth are one: and every man shall receive his own reward according to his own labour."*

1404   Matthew 19:28
1405   Luke 17:21
1406   Ephesians 3:9, Colossians 1:16
1407   John 6:63

Observe Jesus' emphasis upon the fact that the man does not know how seeds grow. He says the *"earth bringeth forth fruit of herself."* Man plants and waters but cannot force seeds to grow. God's creative growing process causes growth without the help of man. Paul says the same in 1 Corinthians 3:6: *"I have planted, Apollos watered; but God gave the increase."* Christian ministers labor with their human efforts but only God can give an increase of souls. Acts 2:47 declares, *"And the Lord added to the church daily such as should be saved."*

Another point is to show God's growing power while men sleep. God's Spirit is always working, whether you are awake or asleep, and He can cause you to understand truth through dreams. Job 33:15-16 says, *"In a dream, in a vision of the night, when deep sleep falleth upon men, in slumberings upon the bed; Then he openeth the ears of men, and sealeth their instruction."* God changes situations through His ever-working Spirit as He works on your behalf even while you sleep. Psalm 30:5 reads, *"Weeping may endure for a night, but joy cometh in the morning."*

Just as in The Wheat and Tares, the seeds represent genuine Christians. A man's soul receives the incorruptible Seed-Word of God and experiences the baptism of the Holy Ghost. 1 Peter 1:23 says, *"Being born again, not of corruptible seed, but of incorruptible, by the word of God, which liveth and abideth for ever."* Notice that nothing is said of the tares. No doubt every field would have tares, but this parable is focusing only upon the wheat's three stage growth and the immediacy of harvest time.

The parable's main lesson is that wheat grows in three mysterious stages, representing how believers mysteriously but faithfully grow up in three stages. Just like the wheat growing process is certain, Christian maturity is a guaranteed process when the believer remains planted in Christ's teachings. When you delight in and meditate upon the Word you are *"like a tree planted by the rivers of water, that bringeth forth his fruit in his season; his leaf also shall not wither; and whatsoever he doeth shall prosper."*[1408] Psalm 92:13 echoes this truth saying, *"Those that be planted in the house of the LORD shall flourish in the courts of our God."*

1408 Psalm 1:3

The three stages of Christian growth are just as distinguishable as the wheat's three stages (See Figure 14 in Chapter 5). Look at Paul's life for a clear example of the first stage, justification, or the wheat blade. The blade is the narrow leaf that first springs forth from the soil, just a few inches tall. Before the blade is visible, there is no sign of life. Once the blade grows up, there is visible proof of life. Before Paul met Jesus on the road to Damascus, he showed no signs of life, spiritually speaking. In fact, he was an agent of death, advocating for Stephen's stoning and making havoc of the church by entering Christians' homes and dragging them to prisons.[1409] But after Paul was blinded and humbled by his supernatural encounter with the light of Christ, Ananias prayed for Paul's healing and the scales fell from his eyes. Upon receiving his healing, Paul immediately "*arose, and was baptized.*"[1410] Just like a wheat blade springs upward from the dark soil, Paul's new spiritual life arose upward out of his darkened condition of unbelief. New life arose, visible to all. A new wheat plant named Paul raised up, justified from all his sins. For the first time, this new creature in Christ was in plain view to all men.

Jesus' 12 apostles are prime examples of the second stage of grace, sanctification, which corresponds to the wheat's second stage Jesus calls "*the ear.*" Wheat plants grow quickly in the second stage, sprouting stems that range from two to four feet tall. At the top of the stem is the head or spike of the wheat plant. This is "*the ear*" Jesus refers to. The ear contains 35-50 grains or kernels of wheat but in the second stage they are green and need more time to mature. Jesus' 12 apostles grew quickly in the faith, leaving family and careers to preach two by two with miraculous healing power throughout Judea. The four gospels show they were green in many ways and needed to mature. Peter is a clear example because he had faith to walk on water but not long after erroneously rebuked Jesus for foretelling His death and resurrection.[1411] Chapter 5's section called "Jesus' 12 Apostles and the Stature of a Perfect Man" details the apostles' growth in the second stage of grace. John 17:12-19 records Jesus' tender

---

1409   Acts 8:1-3
1410   Acts 9:17-18
1411   Matthew 14:29, 16:21-23

Last Supper prayer for His apostles in which He specifically prays for their further sanctification. Jesus plainly asks the Father for their sanctification in John 17:17, saying, *"Sanctify them through thy truth: thy word is truth."* After three and a half years of following Christ, the 12 apostles still needed more sanctification, which they received after Jesus' resurrection and ascension when Matthias had taken the place of Judas Iscariot. The *"ear"* stage reached its conclusion during the 10 days of prayer and supplication in the upper room in Jerusalem.[1412] The apostles became fully sanctified during this 10 day season of prayer. Scripture describes the believers as being in *"one accord"*[1413] on the truth of God's promise to send the baptism of the Holy Ghost.

The wheat's third and final stage is referred to as *"the full corn in the ear"* by Jesus and corresponds to the third Work of Grace, the baptism of the Holy Ghost. In this final stage, maturing wheat turns from green to straw brown and the kernels become swollen and hard. Previously, in the second stage, the kernel was soft and if pinched would emit a milky substance. After standing long in the presence of the hot sun, the wheat head nods or bows, signaling harvest time. In the same way, a Holy Ghost filled Christian is both beyond "milk" teaching and bows or submits to every Word of the Son of God. Hebrews 5:12-14 records the author rebuking his Hebrew-Christian readers for remaining immature, milk-drinking believers. The author says the believers had enough time to become mature Bible teachers, but instead need to relearn the simple, milky, basic teachings of Christianity. *"Strong meat,"* the author writes, belongs to *"them that are of full age"* who can discern good from evil. Holy Ghost filled Christians are mature enough to handle deep teaching that discerns good and evil in their daily lives. Jesus' *"meat"* was *"to do the will of him that sent me, and to finish his work."*[1414] Mature Christians also do the perfect will of God, no matter how difficult it may seem. Immature Christians, not yet born again of the Holy Ghost, still need basic, milky teaching, just like the immature

---

1412   Acts 1:13-14
1413   Acts 1:14, 2:1
1414   John 4:34

wheat kernel that oozes milk when pinched. Concerning bowing, Paul writes, like a mature, bowing wheat head, he bows his knees in prayer for the Ephesian saints to be strengthened by the Spirit in their inner man, rooted and grounded in love, to know the love of Christ, and to be filled with all the fulness of God.[1415] Peter says Christians must submit, or bow, to *"every ordinance of man for the Lord's sake"*[1416] unless men forbid Christians to preach and teach in Jesus' name.[1417] Logically, Christians additionally submit to every Word of God, for God is so much greater than man. Jesus lived by obeying every Word of God[1418] and Spirit filled Christians follow His holy example. The Book of Acts church serves as an example of the wheat's third stage after receiving the baptism of the Holy Ghost on the Day of Pentecost. The saints bowed to none but Christ, even suffering martyrdom, like courageous Stephen and James. More mature Christians could not be found. Acts 15:26 says they were *"Men that have hazarded their lives for the name of our Lord Jesus Christ."* Their voices joined with Paul's, who said, *"For to me to live is Christ, and to die is gain."*[1419]

The parable's final emphasis is upon the immediacy of the harvest once the wheat is mature, suggesting the imminent rapture of the bride of Christ, or New Testament, Holy Ghost filled church. Mark 4:29 says, *"But when the fruit is brought forth, immediately he putteth in the sickle, because the harvest is come."* Chapter 12 details the mystery of the rapture.

At this very moment, God is still baptizing souls with the Holy Ghost around the world, fulfilling Jesus' Great Commission. When the last predestined soul is born again, the rapture-harvest will begin. Using symbolism from The Ten Virgins parable, when the last wise virgin had arrived at the midnight wedding procession with her oil-filled, bright, glowing lamp, the bridegroom could immediately continue to his home for the remaining wedding festivities. In The King's Son parable, the

1415   Ephesians 3:14-19
1416   1 Peter 2:13
1417   Acts 5:28-29
1418   Matthew 4:4
1419   Philippians 1:21

son's wedding could commence once the last wedding guest was adorning the wedding garment and all those without a wedding garment were removed from the gathering. Christians still pray for the Lord of the harvest to send forth laborers into His vineyard for harvest because there is still work to be done.[1420]

Although some may become discouraged waiting for the rapture-harvest, Jesus Christ values your patience as harvest time nears. James 5:7 reads, "*Be patient therefore, brethren, unto the coming of the Lord. Behold, the husbandman waiteth for the precious fruit of the earth, and hath long patience for it, until he receive the early and latter rain.*" Each mature wheat plant is precious in His holy sight. The Lord of the harvest will not lose or leave behind a single kernel on a single wheat head. Jesus promises, "*And this is the Father's will which hath sent me, that of all which he hath given me I should lose nothing, but should raise it up again at the last day.*"[1421]

16—THE GREAT SUPPER

Revelation: After most Jews made excuses to reject it, Gentiles should accept Jesus' compelling invitation to His great supper, the Marriage Supper of the Lamb.

Located in Luke 14:15-24, this parable emphasizes a great supper representing the marriage supper of the Lamb that immediately follows the imminent rapture of the New Testament church. This parable closely resembles The King's Son parable, but differs in unique ways.

It's similar because a wealthy man is inviting everyone to a special event. In The King's Son parable it was a wedding but here it's a great supper in a house. Both parables contain three separate invitations from the wealthy man. Both describe various worldly motivations for rejecting the special event, including farming, viewing property, selling merchandise, and being a newlywed. Both parables serve as a warning and rebuke to the established Jewish religious system of Jesus' time while offering hope to Gentiles.

1420 Matthew 9:37-38
1421 John 6:39

The parable's context is Jesus speaking to a man at the house of a chief Pharisee.[1422] This man offers a seemingly pious declaration of the future blessedness of he who would eat bread in the kingdom of God. In reality, he expresses a false hope for the future while neglecting the present invitation into Jesus' spiritual kingdom. Jesus' sobering parable validates the man's insincerity. Christ, Who is the Word, corrects and discerns his empty speech by stating that those who eat in the future kingdom of God are those who forsake all, without excuse, to receive Him now during their lifetimes.

Those first invited to the great supper represent the religious, upper class Jews—Pharisees and Sadducees—because judgment begins at the house of God.[1423] The Lord first invites those who claim to represent Him and His kingdom. This group makes three polite excuses to miss the great supper. The first excuse is a man who purchased land and wants to go see it. The second is a man who purchased oxen and needs to prove them. The third is a man who recently married a wife. These excuses can be categorized as "chokers" of the Word, mentioned in The Sower and the Four Grounds parable. Property, work, and marriage are *"cares and riches and pleasures of this life"*[1424] that choke the effects of God's Word when given greater priority than Christ's gospel.

Feeling rejected, the angered master sends a second invitation into the streets and lanes of the city to bring the poor, maimed, halt, and blind to his great supper. This group represents Jesus' loving ministry to the lower class, despised Jews labeled *"publicans and sinners"*[1425] by the upper class group. In Matthew 9:11-13, Christ says this group honestly assesses their spiritually-sick condition and repents of their sins through God's mercy. Mary Magdalene, the immoral woman previously possessed of seven devils, is an example of this lower class group brought in to the great supper by Christ's choosing. James 2:5 says, *"Hearken, my beloved brethren, Hath not God chosen the poor of this world*

1422 Luke 14:1,7,15
1423 1 Peter 4:17
1424 Luke 8:14
1425 Matthew 9:11

rich in faith, and heirs of the kingdom which he hath promised to them that love him?"

When the master learns there is yet room at his supper, he sends a final invitation to the *"highways and hedges"* and charges his servants to *"compel them to come in, that my house may be filled."* Undoubtedly, this invitation symbolizes God offering the kingdom to the Gentiles, who Paul says *"were far off"* but *"are made nigh by the blood of Christ."*[1426] Truly the Gentiles *"were without Christ, being aliens from the commonwealth of Israel, and strangers from the covenants of promise, having no hope, and without God in the world."*[1427] Jesus' Great Commission and Peter's Day of Pentecost sermon both express the *"highway and hedges"* invitation. Christ says in Mark 16:15, *"Go ye into all the world, and preach the gospel to every creature."* In Acts 2:39, Peter teaches the Holy Ghost promise *"is unto you, and to your children, and to all that are afar off, even as many as the Lord our God shall call."*

Compelling preaching is necessary to call and fill God's house, or the marriage supper of the Lamb event.[1428] Jesus says, *"Compel them to come in, that my house may be filled."* Preachers must constrain, or urge sinners to repentance, water baptism, and the baptism of the Holy Ghost with divine zeal. Ministers are offering eternal life and no greater gift could be preached. God's loving heart longs for all men to be saved, as He does not delight in the death of the wicked. Ezekiel 18:31-32 captures God's heart, saying, *"Cast away from you all your transgressions, whereby ye have transgressed; and make you a new heart and a new spirit: for why will ye die, O house of Israel? For I have no pleasure in the death of him that dieth, saith the Lord GOD: wherefore turn yourselves, and live ye."* God passionately pleads for you to live for Him. Despise death and love life. Paul's *"godly jealousy"*[1429] for the Corinthians to live as spiritual chaste virgins to Christ was just that—God's own jealousy for His children's unwavering love and devotion.

1426 Ephesians 2:13
1427 Ephesians 2:12
1428 Revelation 19:9
1429 2 Corinthians 11:2

The parable closes with Christ pulling off the veil of His story, revealing that He is the *"certain man"* and the great supper is His. The Lord says, *"For I say unto you, That none of those men which were bidden shall taste of my supper."* Jesus declares it is *"my"* supper and no meal could ever taste so satisfying as His. No excuse is sufficient for placing a secondary emphasis on the glorious gospel of the Lord Jesus Christ. Being invited to Jesus' wedding supper is the greatest thing that's ever happened to you. Knowing Jesus, His heart, His desires, His truth, and His love is the one and only worthwhile relationship. In Ephesians 3:8-9, Paul calls this relationship *"the fellowship of the mystery,"* or the intimacy of the mystery, and he was privileged to preach *"among the Gentiles the unsearchable riches of Christ."* Accept Christ's invitation to receive the Word of His kingdom now. If you taste of His *"gracious"*[1430] Word in this life and fully digest the Scroll of Truth,[1431] you'll surely taste of Christ's heavenly supper following the catching away of His bride, the Holy Ghost filled, New Testament church.

THEMES OF THE 16 PARABLES

It's helpful to see God's overarching themes in the 16 parable-mysteries. Jesus' most emphasized theme is salvation, or justification (the first Work of Grace), as five parables focus on His gracious redemption plan and free gift of eternal life. The five parables include:

- The Treasure in the Field
- The Pearl of Great Price
- The Laborers in the Vineyard
- The Unmerciful Servant
- The Seed Cast Into the Ground

Stewardship is the second-most emphasized theme being taught in three parables because God delights in His children being accountable and responsible. Once the free gift of salvation has been received, God

---

1430   1 Peter 2:3
1431   Revelation 10:8-11

wants His children to imitate Him, learning to be faithful, focused, and loving like His own divine character. The three parables include:

- The Four Grounds
- The Talents
- The Pounds

The eight remaining parables are categorized in pairs that share themes. God establishes all His truths in the mouth of two or three witnesses. The theme of being prepared for the rapture with the baptism of the Holy Ghost is seen in the two following parables:

- The King's Son
- The Ten Virgins

The theme of the deceitfulness of sin is taught in the following two parables:

- The Grain of Mustard Seed
- The Leaven Hid in Three Measures

The condition of mankind at the end of the world is described in the following two parables:

- The Wheat and the Tares
- The Net Cast Into the Sea

Finally, the theme of the Jews and Gentiles is taught in the following two parables:

- The Wicked Husbandman
- The Great Supper

THE REWARDS FOR RECEIVING THE KINGDOM REVELATIONS

Those who receive the revelations of the kingdom of heaven during their earthly lives and continue living a faithful Christian life will be the same ones who rule in the future when Christ's kingdom comes down to earth. Jesus' words prove this, for He said the mysteries were given to His disciples in Mark 4:11 and later told them that they would *"sit on thrones judging the twelve tribes of Israel"* because they continued with Him in His temptations.[1432] Not only do Jesus' apostles receive a kingdom to reign over, but so does every true Christian, although the apostles' reign will be much grander.

When you understand the kingdom of God during your life, you are *already* both a king and priest unto God on this earth because Christ loved you and washed you from your sins in His own blood.[1433] Colossians 1:13 says you're *already* translated into the kingdom of His dear Son. Of course, you are also promised to reign in Jesus' future kingdom.[1434]

As a spiritual king now, you *"reign in life"*[1435] by ruling over sin, the world, the flesh, and Satan. Like a king, you're empowered with mighty weapons, but yours are for spiritual warfare to cast down every evil or high thing that exalts itself against God's Word[1436] and mortify every sinful deed of the flesh.[1437] You are anointed to speak the Word, *"for the Word is nigh thee, even in thy mouth,"*[1438] like Jesus combated and defeated Satan by repeatedly declaring *"It is written"*![1439] By Christ's spiritual power, you control the three spiritual channels of temptation—lust of the eyes, lust of the flesh, and pride of life[1440]—not allowing sin to enter your life, in order to keep yourself pure.

As a spiritual priest now, God has called you to offer continual prayer, praise, and offerings to His great name. Fully-armored Christians are called to constant prayer by Paul, who said, *"Praying always with all prayer and supplication in the Spirit, and watching thereunto with all perseverance and supplication for all saints."*[1441] It is through praying in the Spirit—not praying in the flesh— that you build up your spiritual power,

---

1432 Luke 22:28-30
1433 Revelation 1:5-6
1434 Revelation 5:10
1435 Romans 5:17
1436 2 Corinthians 10:4-5
1437 Romans 8:13
1438 Romans 10:8
1439 Matthew 4:4, 7, 10
1440 1 John 2:16
1441 Ephesians 6:18

for Jude 1:20 says, "*But ye, beloved, building up yourselves on your most holy faith, praying in the Holy Ghost.*" Daily prayer in the Holy Ghost is the necessary spiritual workout needed to grow stronger faith, just as a daily physical exercise workout is needed to grow stronger muscles.

As a spiritual priest, you offer continual praise to Jesus from your lips, as Hebrews 13:15 reveals: "*By him therefore let us offer the sacrifice of praise to God continually, that is, the fruit of our lips giving thanks to his name.*" In Ephesians 4:29, Paul says, "*Let no corrupt communication proceed out of your mouth, but that which is good to the use of edifying, that it may minister grace unto the hearers.*"

In your spiritual priest office, you offer both spiritual and natural offerings to God. Your spiritual offering is presenting your entire body and mind as a holy, living sacrifice to God.[1442] This is imagery of the Old Testament burnt offering,[1443] a totally-consumed sacrifice. When you give your entire body and mind to Christ, being totally consumed by God's will, it is a "*sweet savour*"[1444] unto God. Natural offerings include giving secret alms[1445] or donations to the poor. The Roman Centurion, Cornelius, was told by God's angel that the record of his alms were kept in heaven as a "*memorial before God.*" Proverbs 19:17 says God views your donations to the poor as lending directly to Himself, and He promises to repay you.

If you receive the revelations of the kingdom now, and rule over sin in this life, Christ will elevate you to rule in His future kingdom, for John says we, as kings and priests, "*shall reign on the earth.*"[1446] While our future reign has some mystery to it, Christ described how His faithful ones will be granted authority and rulership over many things, including cities, during the 1,000 year Millennium. You read in The Talents parable that your future reign is based upon the current fruitfulness in your earthly labors. If you're faithful in a few of Christ's things, He will make you ruler over many. Jesus told the the servant who made a ten-fold increase he'd

---

1442   Romans 12:1-2
1443   Genesis 8:20-21, Exodus 29:18
1444   2 Corinthians 2:15
1445   Matthew 6:1-4
1446   Revelation 5:10

have authority over ten cities. In Revelation 2:26, Christ says, *"And he that overcometh, and keepeth my works unto the end, to him will I give power over the nations."*

May these Scriptures encourage you to keep investing in your spiritual gifts while investing your money into the kingdom of God. This makes you an overcomer, and Christ has great rewards prepared for you. May you *"abound in every thing"*—faith, utterance, knowledge, diligence, and giving.[1447] Paul's words in 1 Corinthians 15:58 ring true: *"Therefore, my beloved brethren, be ye stedfast, unmoveable, always abounding in the work of the Lord, forasmuch as ye know that your labour is not in vain in the Lord."*

THE CONSEQUENCES FOR REJECTING THE KINGDOM REVELATIONS

Those who reject the revelations of God's kingdom become part of Satan's kingdom of darkness[1448] and will eventually be eternally separated from the King of kings, Jesus Christ. Each parable details the consequences of choosing Satan's kingdom over Christ's kingdom:

- The Sower and The Four Grounds: The consequence for the two types of unbelieving hearts are hearts completely void of God's Word, being seared,[1449] confused, useless, and barren.
- The Wheat and Tares: The consequence for a tare is a powerless and feigned impersonation of Christianity that makes Jesus sick to His stomach. Tares are burned in the lake of fire.
- The Grain of Mustard Seed: The consequence of being part of the false church and her daughter-churches is to be judged as a partaker[1450] in their evil ways, sharing the guilt and judgment of their demon-filled assemblies.

1447 2 Corinthians 8:2, 7
1448 Matthew 12:26, Colossians 1:13
1449 1 Timothy 4:2
1450 Revelation 18:4

- The Leaven Hid in Three Measures of Meal: The consequences of eating the fully leavened bread, or false teachings of the mother church, include malice,[1451] wickedness, and insincerity. Making God three separate persons brings the consequence of being a liar and an idolator.
- The Treasure in a Field: The consequence of a man not trading all his possessions at the surprising opportunity to gain Christ is being unworthy of Jesus and the loss of his life.[1452]
- The One Pearl of Great Price: The consequence of one not abandoning his search for many spiritual truths in order to gain Christ is being ever learning but never able to come to the knowledge of the truth,[1453] leading to the destruction of his soul.
- The Net Cast Into the Sea: The consequence of one being partially attracted to the gospel yet living a wicked, iniquity-filled life will result in his soul's destruction in the lake of fire.
- The Unmerciful Servant: The consequence for one not forgiving others is Jesus denying His forgiveness for a man's sins.
- The Laborers in the Vineyard: The consequence for not working in Jesus' vineyard is a loss of eternal life, which is the equal reward God gives to all His faithful kingdom laborers.
- The Wicked Husbandman: The consequence upon the unbelieving Jews who rejected Christ's kingdom is destruction, but Gentiles are issued the same warning in Romans 11:22.

1451 1 Corinthians 5:8
1452 Matthew 10:38-39
1453 2 Timothy 3:7

- The King's Son: The consequence for rejecting God's wedding garment, or baptism of the Holy Ghost, is enduring the awful tribulation period.
- The Ten Virgins: The consequence for not possessing extra oil, or the baptism of the Holy Ghost, is enduring the tribulation period and missing out on Jesus' wedding, the rapture.
- The Talents: The consequence for neglecting Jesus' talents and resources is being called wicked and slothful, and being cast into the lake of fire with weeping and gnashing of teeth.
- The Pounds: The consequence for not investing Jesus' pound is being called wicked and suffering the same lake of fire destiny as The Talents parable.
- The Seed Cast Into the Ground: The consequence of one rejecting God's three stage growing process, or Three Works of Grace, is becoming both a blind guide and liar, as one will lead others away from the baptism of the Holy Ghost while offering potential converts false hope by telling them they are born again when they are not.
- The Great Supper: The consequence of Gentiles rejecting Jesus' compelling invitation to the marriage supper of the Lamb will be suffering His chastening or wrath in the tribulation period.

CONCLUSION

Christ has uttered a 16-fold revelation to His kingdom, making it possible for you to accept His invitation into the kingdom that you might take your place in it. May you submit to every Word of your King now in this spiritual kingdom so that you are assured to be a part of Christ's future Millennial kingdom. What glorious rewards await us, the kings and priests of Jesus Christ!

ACTION STEPS TO THE KINGDOM OF HEAVEN

1. If not done already, repent in faith and be fully immersed in water in the name of the Lord Jesus Christ. Seek to be born again by the Holy Ghost baptism, which places you into the kingdom of God.

2. With Holy Ghost power from on high, Christ will help you redeem your time and lead you into your position in His kingdom, revealing your talents and ministries.

3. Periodically, examine your position, talents, and ministries to be sure you are growing in stewardship and understanding. You'll rejoice as you fulfill God's purpose for your life.

FOLLOW UP

Free online videos, Bible studies, and William Branham's quotes related to this chapter: www.pastorjessesmith.com/12mysteriesbook

Email: jesse.smith11@sbcglobal.net

Text: 330-929-2037

CHAPTER 9
The Mystery of Babylon The Great

"And upon her forehead was a name written,
MYSTERY, BABYLON THE GREAT, THE MOTHER OF
HARLOTS AND ABOMINATIONS OF THE EARTH."
Revelation 17:5

BY THIS POINT, YOU know the true church's identity and her attributes as Jesus' bride. Additionally, the 16 revelations of the kingdom of heaven further differentiate the true church from the false. With this solid, Scriptural foundation, you'll easily recognize the false church's identity.

THE WISDOM REQUIREMENT

The Book of Revelation teaches one requirement to identify the false church—wisdom. Revelation 17:9 says *"the mind which hath wisdom"* recognizes that Mystery Babylon, the false church, sits on seven mountains, which is one of the 11 clues as to her identity. God made the false church's identity extremely obvious—even identifiable geographically by its seven mountains—so that eternal life with Him would be freely available to any and all who desire His love. A second mention of the wisdom-requirement comes from Revelation 13:18, telling us that wisdom counts the number of the beast—666—in order to avoid taking his mark.

God's compassionate heart allows everyone a chance to be saved, for He makes wisdom easily accessible. James 1:5 explains how easily, saying, "*If any of you lack wisdom, let him ask of God, that giveth to all men liberally, and upbraideth not; and it shall be given him.*" In the Greek "*liberally*" means "simply, openly, frankly, sincerely."[1454] All God requires in exchange for His wisdom (needed to recognize the false church and the beast's number) is an honest, selfless prayer requesting wisdom with the right motive.

Few people ever pray an honest prayer because their intentions when praying are selfish, motivated by lusts. James explains that most prayers are not answered because they are asked with lustful intent.[1455] Jesus said "*few*"[1456] would find salvation, meaning few would have wisdom (freely offered through a sincere prayer) to escape the false church destined for the mark of the beast. Consider the past and current global scale of selfish, lustful prayers. Our Heavenly Father turns down billions of selfish prayers from around the globe because of their evil nature, as the false church has deceived "*all nations.*"[1457]

The importance of godly wisdom can hardly be overemphasized. Solomon says, "*Wisdom is the principal thing; therefore get wisdom: and with all thy getting get understanding.*"[1458] If you do not have the wisdom of God, humbly bow your head in prayer and ask God for His divine wisdom at this moment before going forward in this chapter. Pray for more than a minute. Set your face to heaven, praying *until* you feel God's presence surrounding you, granting you the assurance that His wisdom is on the way.

1454 "The Bible: Hebrew and Greek Lexicons." *Voice of God Recordings*, www.branham.org/en/messagesearch
1455 James 4:3
1456 Matthew 7:14
1457 Revelation 18:23
1458 Proverbs 4:7

THE CONFUSION ABOUT MYSTERY BABYLON

The confusion about Mystery Babylon centers around her identity. Is *she*—for she is called a *"woman"* in Revelation 17:6—a real woman yet to rule in the future, or merely a symbolic figure of all false religions, city, kingdom, government empire, or church?

The revelation of Mystery Babylon is her identity as the false mother church, the Roman Catholic Church, and her daughters are Protestant churches who partake in her iniquities.

Please understand this revelation is not a personal attack on Roman Catholics, but rather a desperate, loving call for God's people inside the corrupt Catholic system to *"come out"*[1459] that they be not partakers of the church's sins. This chapter details 11 proofs that witness beyond a shadow of doubt that the Roman Catholic Church willingly upholds *"doctrines of devils,"* abuses its power, and makes merchandise of the souls of men for self-gain.[1460] No other church, city, kingdom, or woman can even come close to meeting all 11 requirements.

Some think Jerusalem is Mystery Babylon due to Scripture's repeated references to her as a *"harlot,"*[1461] but *"the holy city"*[1462] fails to meet a few Scriptural requirements. First, Jerusalem does not *"sit upon many waters"* as taught in Revelation 17:1. Waters represent many peoples, multitudes, nations, and tongues. Jerusalem's influence upon many nations is small in comparison to Rome. There are only around 11 million Jews and about 82% live in Israel and the United States.[1463] The 11 million Jews pale in comparison to the world's 1.3 billion Catholics.

1459 Revelation 18:4-5
1460 1 Timothy 4:1, Revelation 18:13-14
1461 Isaiah 1:21, Jeremiah 3:8, Ezekiel 16:2, 28, 35; 23:4, 19
1462 Nehemiah 11:1
1463 "Israel and the U.S. are Home to More Than Four-Fifths of the World's Jews." *Pew Research Center*, https://www.pewforum.org/ 2013/03/20/israel-and-the-us-are-home-to-more-than-fourfifths- of-the-worlds-jews/

Second, Jerusalem is never called "Babylon" in Scripture whereas Peter refers to Rome as *"Babylon"* in 1 Peter 5:13. Rome is also the *"legs of iron,"*[1464] or modern Babylon-like kingdom vividly described in Daniel chapter 2. Third, Revelation 18:3 requires Mystery Babylon to have strong relationships to the kings of the earth and ties with *"all nations,"* but Israel is despised by many nations and often suffers from bias and discrimination at the United Nations.[1465] On the other hand, the Vatican has diplomats to nearly every nation. Finally, Mystery Babylon is condemned in Revelation 18:21 with prophecy that she will never be *"found"* or rebuilt after God's wrath destroys her. Mystery Babylon has an expiration date! Rome and the Vatican will be destroyed. Jerusalem is promised a rebuilding, a peaceful habitation, and future kingdom in Isaiah 2:2-4, Jeremiah 3:17, and Isaiah 65:17-22. Jesus will set up His millennial throne in Jerusalem and *"all nations"* will gather there to worship and learn the law of God while the *"wolf and lamb"* peacefully *"feed together"*!

If you accept God's revelation of Rome as Mystery Babylon, you are among a large group of believers who have understood Rome's place in Scripture. Church fathers Lactantius, Tertullian, Irenaeus, and Jerome taught this along with reformers Martin Luther, John Knox, John Calvin, William Tyndale, and John Wycliffe.[1466] God has liberally granted His wisdom to many Protestants that they might escape the false mother church, Rome, and her daughter churches.

This chapter labors on Rome's sins, but I am by no means an expert on her rank rebellion and insatiable iniquity. Recommended reads include *The Two Babylons* by Alexander Hislop (1858), and *50 Years in the Church of Rome* by Charles Chiniquy (1885).

1464   Daniel 2:33, 40
1465   "The UN and Israel: A History of Discrimination." *Jewish Policy Center,* www. jewishpolicycenter.org/2017/04/03/the-un-and-israel-a-history-of-discrimination/
1466   "Bill Salus on Mystery Babylon." *YouTube,* uploaded by Christ In Prophecy, 21 August 2018, https://youtu.be/JCnErkq0gOI

BIBLICAL PROOF FOR THE REVELATION OF MYSTERY BABYLON

Revelation chapters 17 and 18 are the main texts that reveal Mystery Babylon's identity as the Roman Catholic Church, but additional Bible books prove this statement beyond doubt.

PROOF #1: THE CATHOLIC CHURCH IS A WOMAN.

Revelation 17:3 describes Mystery Babylon as a *"woman."* Chapter 4 showed how a woman symbolizes a church in Scripture, and is easily seen through two examples: the people of Israel and the New Testament church, referred to as the *"bride"* or *"wife"* of Christ.[1467]

Israel is called the *"church in the wilderness"* in Acts 7:38, and is likened unto a woman in many cases, such as Ezekiel 16. God calls Israel a *"harlot"* unto Him.[1468] Israel's *"sister,"* Samaria, had also been involved in abominations and whoredoms,[1469] just as Israel had. John describes Israel as a woman with a crown of 12 stars, representing the 12 tribes of Israel.[1470] Christ, made *"of the seed of David,"*[1471] is the *"man child who was to rule all nations with a rod of iron,"* Who was *"caught up unto God, and to his throne."*[1472]

The second example of a woman symbolizing a church is the New Testament church, referred to as the *"bride"*[1473] or *"wife"*[1474] of Christ. Ephesians 5:22-33 shows Paul's teaching that a husband is to represent Christ, and a wife is to represent the New Testament church. In John 3:29, John the Baptist labels Jesus Christ as the *"bridegroom"* and His followers as the *"bride."*

Just as Israel and the bride of Jesus Christ are symbolized as women, so is the Roman Catholic Church symbolized as the abominable *"woman"* of Revelation 17.

1467   John 3:29, Ephesians 5:32, Revelation 19:7
1468   Ezekiel 16:15
1469   Ezekiel 16:22, 46
1470   Revelation 12:1
1471   2 Timothy 2:8
1472   Hebrews 12:2, Revelation 12:5
1473   John 3:29, Revelation 21:9
1474   Revelation 19:7

PROOF #2: THE CATHOLIC CHURCH IS THE MODERN-DAY BABYLON.

Revelation 17:5 says this evil woman has *"Babylon"* written upon her forehead. Babylon is first mentioned in Genesis chapters 10 and 11 where we witness the origins of spiritual confusion at the Tower of Babel. This group wanted to reach heaven by man-made means while establishing a name for themselves. God stopped their building by confounding their language.

The Roman Church is the modern Babel because it promotes a false, man-made path to heaven contrary to Scripture. In response to this failed religious system, God has permitted confusing doctrine to deceive this church. Salvation is made confusing through Catholic dogma, which falsely adds a works-requirement for salvation, which one apologist calls "an arduous process."[1475] Catholicism mandates an unscriptural post-death trip to purgatory.[1476] Just as original Babel sought to exalt its own name, Rome also exalts its own name (the Holy See) and Mary's name (Mother of God) far above the name of Jesus Christ.

Further proof that the Catholic Church is Babylon can be found in Daniel chapter 2. In a dream, Nebuchadnezzar saw a great image and his Babylonian kingdom was the head of gold.[1477] Babylon, the literal kingdom, fell to the Medes and Persians in Daniel 5:28, who represented the great image's silver breast and arms. Historically, the Grecian Empire led by Alexander the Great was the next kingdom,[1478] represented by the belly and thighs of brass. The Ancient Roman Empire followed the Grecian[1479] and therefore was the legs of iron. Because the final earthly kingdom represented in the dream is Rome, Mystery Babylon must represent the Roman power.

1475 "Attaining Salvation in Roman Catholicism." *Christian Apologetics & Research Ministry*, www.carm.org/catholic/catholic-salvation-attain

1476 Catholic Church. *Catechism of the Catholic Church*. New York, Doubleday, 1994. Paragraph 1030, pp. 291

1477 Daniel 2:38

1478 "Persian Literature." *Encyclopedia Britannica*, https://www.britannica.com/art/Persian-literature

1479 "Ancient Rome." *Encyclopedia Britannica*, https://www.britannica.com/place/ancient-Rome

Note carefully that Rome is the final kingdom, proven by the fact that only the second coming of Jesus Christ to earth—symbolized as the stone cut out of the mountain that struck the image's feet—can end Rome's reign. The first coming of Christ did not end the Roman Empire. More support is provided by Daniel's description that the kingdom of Christ will spread around the whole world, or fill *"the whole earth,"*[1480] when He, the Stone, returns to end the Roman reign. Christianity does not fill the whole earth at this moment, for most governments ascribe to no official religion. Which church, or woman, is closely associated with the city of Rome? Only the Roman Catholic Church has this distinction.

You may be wondering how Rome can still be ruling today since the Roman Empire fell in the fifth century.[1481] Revelation 13:11-12 holds the answer, for the beast or evil spirits motivating the Roman Empire—that used to be ruling in Babylon, the Medes and Persians, and Grecians—gained a new lease on life by migrating into the papacy. The evil spirits of Rome now rule through a global, ecclesiastical influence rather than through military power. The Catholic Church becomes the modern Babylon because she is empowered by the same evil spirits, but has a different appearance—a church rather than an empire.

In addition to these Bible witnesses, we have a final, prophetic witness that Roman religion reigns until Christ returns at Armageddon. William Branham (1909-1965), a prophet of God, spoke with "Thus saith the Lord" that Romanism would rule the world until Jesus returns. In March of 1962, Branham said:

> "Listen, it's on tape now. To the world I speak or wherever these tapes may go. And to you people here, no matter whatever happens to me, you believe this. Russia, communism isn't conquering nothing. God's Word can't fail. Romanism is going to conquer the world. Jesus Christ was borned in the Roman kingdom and persecuted, His first time come here by the Roman kingdom. And on His second

---

1480 Daniel 2:35
1481 "Roman Empire." *Encyclopedia Britannica*, www.britannica.com/place/Roman-Empire

advent coming now, His message is persecuted by the Roman denominations, which is the mother of all of them. And when He returns, He will come back to wipe out that Roman kingdom, that the Jews has always looked for Him to come and wipe out the Roman kingdom. The Catholic hierarchy with all the denominations in the world, right now coming together as an organization, the confederation of churches organizing themselves together. It isn't Russia, it's Rome. THUS SAITH THE LORD."[1482]

PROOF #3: THE CATHOLIC CHURCH IS A MOTHER OF HARLOTS LIKE JEZEBEL.

Mystery Babylon is called a *"Mother"* in Revelation 17:5, clearly representing she is the original or first church of her kind. The Roman Catholic Church is the first human-organized, man-led church. God is not leading this Mother of Harlots.

The Roman Church unashamedly claims to be the mother church, "the church from which every church took its start."[1483] Specifically, she is the mother of limiting the Holy One of Israel by her tradition-based worship. Jesus says unscriptural traditions make God's Word of *"none effect,"* ultimately producing vain worship.[1484] Rather than contending for the apostolic gospel, her greatest efforts have been in publicly crucifying[1485] the effects of the Holy Ghost to God's people through idolatrous practices (See Proof #6). The true church of the Living God never denominated or organized, like the Catholic Church did. The Roman Church is not the original Holy Ghost-filled "Book of Acts Church."

The "mother" title of the immoral "mother church" implies that she has daughters, or children. Jesus identifies the "mother and daughter harlots" in Revelation 2:20-24, calling the mother church *"Jezebel"* as He pronounces judgment against both Jezebel and *"her children."*

1482 "The Table." *Voice of God Recordings*, http://table.branham.org/#/en/main
1483 "Roman Catholicism." *Encyclopedia Britannica*, www.britannica.com/topic/Roman-Catholicism
1484 Matthew 15:6, 9
1485 Hebrews 6:6

Jezebel clearly represents a church. First, women symbolize churches. Second, she calls herself a prophetess, claiming authority. Third, she has doctrines plunging her into the depths of Satan.

The mother Jezebel is a fitting comparison for the Roman Church, as both she and Catholicism are linked to sexual immorality, death, and idolatry (See Figure 24). Athaliah, Jezebel's daughter, had a murderous, evil spirit just as her mother.[1486] Ezekiel 16:44 states this proverb plainly: *"As is the mother, so is her daughter."*

	Jezebel	Roman Catholic Church
Sexual immorality	2 Kings 9:22, Revelation 2:20	Clergy/nun sex abuse epidemic
Death	1 Kings chapters 18, 21	Wars and The Inquisition
Idolatry	1 Kings 18:19, Revelation 2:20	Veneration of images and statues

Figure 24

If the Roman church is the *"Mother of Harlots,"* who are the daughter-harlots? The daughters are all denominational and nondenominational churches that mimic the Mother Church. These daughters behave exactly like their Mother—substituting traditional creeds for the true Word while overlooking and legalizing sin. A common thread binding the mother and daughters is the three-person, polytheistic, false teaching of the Trinity. Their unity in false doctrine—tritheism—causes the daughter-churches to justify their Mother's evils, failing to speak out against her past and current crimes against God. Proverbs 17:15 says, *"He that justifieth the wicked, and he that condemneth the just, even they both are abomination to the LORD."* Any church denying Scripture while siding with and supporting the Mother Church is manifesting her daughterhood to the Mother.

Notice also the Roman Catholic Church is the immoral mother church because she received the wrong seed, or teaching. God's Word is likened unto seed in Luke 8:11—*"the seed is the word of God"*—but

---

1486 2 Kings 11:1

this mother church denies God's Word and takes Satan's lies, or seed. Chapter 10 shows how the first mother, Eve, also received the wrong seed by believing Satan's lies.

PROOF #4: THE CATHOLIC CHURCH SITS ON MANY WATERS.

Revelation 17:1 and 15 describe the *"many waters"* on which the whore (Mystery Babylon) sits as *"people, multitudes, nations, and tongues."* Recent data shows how the Catholic Church "sits on" or has influence upon many peoples, multitudes, nations, and tongues:

- Nearly 1.3 billion people are professing Catholics (18% of the world's population)
- Nearly 222,000 parishes world-wide
- Parishes in nearly every country on the earth[1487]
- Nearly every nation has either diplomatic or other political relations with the Holy See[1488]
- The number of Catholics is "greater than that of nearly all other religious traditions. There are more Roman Catholics than all other Christians combined, and more Roman Catholics than all Buddhists or Hindus."[1489]

The world's two largest Protestant churches are the Anglican and Methodist, but their estimated sizes of 80 million members[1490] respectively falls far below Catholicism's 1.3 billion members. Anglicans and Methodists do not claim to be "mother" Christian churches, as the Roman Church does. Only the Catholic Church sits *"upon many waters."*

1487 "Frequently Requested Church Statistics." *Center For Applied Research in the Apostolate*, http://cara.georgetown.edu/frequently-requested-church-statistics/
1488 "Diplomatic Relations of the Holy See." *The Permanent Observer Mission of the Holy See to the United Nations*, https://holyseemission.org/contents/mission/diplomatic-relations-of-the-holy-see.php
1489 "Roman Catholicism." *Encyclopedia Britannica*, https://www.britannica.com/topic/Roman-Catholicism
1490 "Member Churches: Our World Wide Church Family." *World Methodist Council*, https://worldmethodistcouncil.org/about/member-churches/

PROOF #5: THE CATHOLIC CHURCH SITS ON SEVEN MOUNTAINS OR HILLS.

Along with sitting on many waters, Revelation 17:9 says Mystery Babylon also sits upon *"seven mountains,"* as well as sitting on many waters. "Mountains" can also be interpreted as "hills" in the Greek Lexicon. The city of Rome, which is the home of the Vatican, is famous for having seven hills on which the ancient city of Rome was built.[1491] While the Vatican is not built among these seven hills, its a mere five miles from the ancient hills.

Some say that the *"seven mountains"* reference could refer to a different location, such as Istanbul, Turkey. It is true Istanbul has seven hills.[1492] The religious majority in Istanbul are Muslim, the second largest religion in the world. But Istanbul is certainly not the headquarters or "mother" city of Islam, which distinction goes to Mecca. Istanbul is not Mystery Babylon because it does not meet the other 10 requirements needed to be considered Mystery Babylon.

PROOF #6: THE CATHOLIC CHURCH IS A HARLOT OR WHORE TO CHRIST.

Revelation 17:1, 15, and 16 call Mystery Babylon a *"great whore"* or *"whore."* Both terms originate from the same Greek word, porne, and can be defined as "one who yields herself to defilement for the sake of gain."[1493] Another meaning literally says porne is "Babylon i.e. Rome, the chief seat of idolatry." Observe the harlot's two great evils—defilement for gain and idolatry.

The Catholic Church is a defiled whore to Christ the Husband because she claims to be the true church, or wife of Christ, but is not faithful to His Word. Romans 7:4 says the true church that is married to Christ will not add to or take away from her Husband's Word according to Revelation 22:18-19. Believers are clean only through Jesus' Word, as He spoke in John 15:3 saying, *"Now ye are clean through the word which*

1491   "Seven Hills of Rome." *Encyclopedia Brittanica,* https://www.britannica.com/place/Seven-Hills-of-Rome

1492   "Istanbul." *Encyclopedia Britannica,* www.britannica.com/place/Istanbul

1493   "The Bible: Hebrew and Greek Lexicons." *Voice of God Recordings,* www.branham.org/en/messagesearch

I have spoken unto you." Sadly, this defiled, unfaithful Roman Church receives and spreads false teachings against her professed Husband, Christ the Word, for monetary gain.

Like a harlot, Catholicism has received the wrong "seed" or false teachings of Satan, and shared those lies with peoples from nearly every nation. Revelation 17:2 and 18:3 says she commits fornication with the kings and nations of the earth by pleasing governments and people rather than pleasing her professed Husband, Christ. For example, during the Pope's September 2015 visit to the United States, his address to Congress called for unity, cooperation, and peace but never mentioned the nearly 700,000 abortions[1494] or murders committed in clinics nationwide during that calendar year. Nor did he mention the nearly 54 million legal abortions committed since 1973.[1495] Abortion is murder, also called an abomination to God in Deuteronomy 12:31. If God heard innocent Abel's blood cry to him from the ground,[1496] would He not also hear the 54 million voices cry to Him in His heavenly temple? If the pope was a true man of God, he would have rebuked America and cried out against her for these senseless, cold-hearted murders rather than praising her and emphasizing climate change needs above the sanctity of life. Instead, like a wolf in sheep's clothing, he was welcomed by the masses "with a fanfare of trumpets and a chorus of amens"[1497] because he is a tickler of ears, a false prophet, and a lover of pleasure more than a lover of God.

Here is a very brief list of some of the "seed" or false doctrine the Mother Harlot has received from evil spirits and then shared and spread all over the world with kings, nations, multitudes, and peoples:

- Mandatory clerical celibacy—The Roman church forces all priests to be celibate,[1498] which contradicts the Bible

---

1494 "CDCs Abortion Surveillance System FAQs." *CDC*, https://www.cdc.gov/reproductivehealth/data_stats/abortion.htm

1495 "Fact Check: 50 Million Abortions Claim Checks Out." *Des Moines Register*, https://www.desmoinesregister.com/story/news/politics/reality-check/2015/03/06/million-abortions-claim-checks/24530159/

1496 Genesis 4:10

1497 "Pope Francis, in Washington, Addresses Poverty and Climate." *The New York Times*, www.nytimes.com/2015/09/24/us/politics/pope-francis-obama-white-house.html

1498 "Celibacy." *Encyclopedia Britannica*, www.britannica.com/topic/celibacy

truth that even Peter was married, whom they claim to be the first pope. The Bible plainly teaches that Jesus healed Peter's mother in law in Matthew 8:14-15. Paul, the celibate prophet of God, also taught that Peter was married in 1 Corinthians 9:5. The apostle Paul also wrote in 1 Timothy 4:1-3 that *"seducing spirits"* and *"doctrines of devils"* teach that marriage should be forbidden. Undoubtedly the world-wide clergy sex abuse epidemic is one result of this false teaching (See The Grain of Mustard Seed Parable in Chapter 8). If Paul's advice for believers to marry rather than burn with desire in 1 Corinthians 7:9 was obeyed, there'd certainly be less abuse.

- Transubstantiation—This false doctrine teaches that the bread and wine in the Eucharist are changed in substance, but not appearance, into the the literal body and blood of Jesus. Catholics claim "the Eucharist becomes Christ's Real Presence—that is, his body and blood."[1499] This lie establishes idolatry—the harlot's second great evil— exalting common bread and wine into deity. Paul calls the wine a symbolic *"cup of blessing"*[1500]—not a cup of liquid deity. Another proof the bread is not divine is Paul's teaching that one can eat the bread unworthily, reaping guilt and damnation upon himself.[1501] Divine bread eaten would instantly and eternally make the consumer divine but that is clearly not taught in Holy Writ. Paul also says we do not know Jesus *"after the flesh"*[1502] anymore. Instead, we know Him by His Holy Spirit being the *"seal"* of God *"in our hearts,"*[1503] or souls.

1499 "Transubstantiation." *Encyclopedia Britannica,* www.britannica.com/topic/transubstantiation
1500 1 Corinthians 10:16
1501 1 Corinthians 11:27-29
1502 2 Corinthians 5:16
1503 2 Corinthians 1:22, Ephesians 4:30

- The pope office and its Holy Father title—The Bible never created the office of a pope, which means "father" in Latin.[1504] The New Testament preaching offices are apostle, prophet, teacher, pastor, and evangelist.[1505] Paul never ordains a pope office. Jesus Christ taught we should *"call no man"* father in Matthew 23:9. The apostle Paul never requested anyone call him "father" even though he gave charges to believers *"as a father doth his children,"*[1506] said elders should be intreated as fathers,[1507] described his relationship with Timothy was *"as a son with the father,"*[1508] and claimed the Corinthians were *"begotten"* to Christ *"through the gospel"*[1509] which Paul preached. The pope is commonly called Holy Father, which is absolute heresy and man-worship because the only time the title Holy Father is used in the Bible is when Jesus prayed to His Father, God Almighty, and called him *"Holy Father"* in John 17:11. The pope is receiving worship and being called a title that was meant for God Himself alone, breaking the first commandment.
- Kissing a pope's ring or priest's hand and bowing to a pope or priest—It is common to see people kissing the pope's right hand and even bowing to him, as worshippers have been doing for centuries.[1510] The Bible teaches that we are not to bow to any man in worship[1511] or kiss any man's hand.[1512] This man-worship breaks the first commandment.

1504 "Pope." *Dictionary.com*, https://www.dictionary.com/browse/pope
1505 Ephesians 4:11
1506 1 Thessalonians 2:11
1507 1 Timothy 5:1
1508 Philippians 2:22
1509 1 Corinthians 4:15
1510 "Pope Explains 'Motivation' for Viral Anti-Ring-Kissing Moment: Germs." *CBS News*, https://www.cbsnews.com/amp/news/pope-francis-pulled-ring-hand-away-from-kisses-for-fear-spreading-germs-vatican/
1511 Exodus 20:5, Revelation 19:10, 22:8-9
1512 2 Samuel 15:5

- Veneration of statues and images—The Catechism of the Catholic Church states that the 7th ecumenical council at Nicea in 787 justified the veneration of images of Christ, the Mother of God, angels, and all the saints.[1513] While this council may have justified veneration, the Bible never did. Nevertheless, Catholics worldwide bow down to, kiss, rub, and weep on images, further exalting them in a way that God never commanded towards any image or man-made statue. All these acts of veneration break the first commandment about having no other gods and making no graven image unto any likeness that is in heaven, on earth, or in the water.[1514] Idolatry is the whore's second great evil, as she is the chief, global seat of idolatry spread through the worship of statues and images.

- Communion of the saints—Catholicism teaches that there can be "an exchange of spiritual goods" through prayers between the disciples currently on earth and those that are in glory.[1515] Catholics are to "pray for the dead that they may be loosed from their sins,"[1516] but the Bible says Jesus' blood already forgives *you all trespasses.*"[1517] The catechism encourages believers to fly to Mary the Mother of God in prayer and request prayer from her.[1518] No where in Scripture does Jesus teach Christians to pray to and for believers who have already died and left the earth. Praying to anyone other than God is a form of spiritualism and should not be taught nor observed, for if the heavenly saints of God are not being contacted, it would mean that evil spirits are being contacted by those misguided prayers.

1513 Catholic Church. *Catechism of the Catholic Church.* Paragraph 2131, pp. 573
1514 Exodus 20:3-4
1515 Catholic Church. *Catechism of the Catholic Church.* Paragraph 955, pp. 271
1516 Catholic Church. *Catechism of the Catholic Church.* Paragraph 958, pp. 272
1517 Colossians 2:13
1518 Catholic Church. *Catechism of the Catholic Church.* Paragraphs 971, 2677, pp. 275, 706

- Deifying the virgin Mary—The idolatrous practice of worshipping Mary, the mother of Jesus, runs deep in Catholicism, for Mary is called the "all holy one" and was supposedly "preserved free from all stain of original sin."[1519] Hebrews 4:15 and Romans 3:23 plainly teach that Jesus is the only person who never sinned and the rest of humanity has sinned and fallen short of God's glory. Mary was not all-holy, for she was a sinner saved by grace and rejoiced in God her Savior in Luke 1:47. In Revelation 5:1-5, Jesus only—not Mary—was found worthy to open the Book and loose the Seven Seals. Additionally, Catholics exalt Mary above God, ascribing to her a "saving office" and the titles Mother of God, Queen Over All Things, Advocate, Helper, Benefactress, and Mediatrix.[1520] Isaiah 43:11 proclaims God is the only Savior—not Mary. The truth is that God the Eternal Spirit has no mother[1521] and Mary was only mother to Jesus' human, mortal body. Jesus is the only Mediator between God and men, and our only Advocate.[1522]

PROOF #7: THE CATHOLIC CHURCH USES THE SCARLET AND PURPLE APPAREL.

Revelation 17:4 says the Mother Harlot is *"arrayed in purple and scarlet."* It is common to see priests, archbishops, and the pope frequently arrayed in these colors during annual festivals, holy days, and seasons of the church year.[1523] You can do a Google image search with the words "pope scarlet purple" and see hundreds of images of past and present popes, priests, bishops, and archbishops adorning these distinctive colors.

1519 Catholic Church. *Catechism of the Catholic Church.* Paragraphs 966, 2677, pp. 274, 706
1520 Catholic Church. *Catechism of the Catholic Church.* Paragraphs 963, 966, 969, pp. 273-275
1521 Hebrews 7:3
1522 1 Timothy 2:5, 1 John 2:1
1523 "Why Do Catholic Priests Wear Vestments (Colorful Robes)?" *Why Catholics Do That,* http://whycatholicsdothat.com/why-do-catholic-priest-wear-vestments/

PROOF #8: THE CATHOLIC CHURCH IS WEALTHY.

It's also clear from Revelation 17:4 that Mystery Babylon is a wealthy church, as she is *"decked with gold and precious stones and pearls, having a golden cup in her hand full of abominations and filthiness of her fornication."* The Vatican receives free will donations from more than 1 billion Catholics world wide and has over $8 billion in assets.[1524] Vatican City also earns interest on its financial investments and has flocks of tourists and visitors for its museums, galleries, and libraries which hold their priceless collections.[1525] The mass services of the Roman Church showcase golden cups and instruments with precious stones,[1526] just as Revelation 17:4 foretold.

PROOF #9: THE CATHOLIC CHURCH IS DRUNKEN WITH THE BLOOD OF THE SAINTS.

Revelation 17:6 says Mystery Babylon is *"drunken with the blood of the saints, and with the blood of the martyrs of Jesus."* Is it possible that the Catholic Church is responsible for the deaths of millions of true Christians? History demonstrates that there was much corruption in the Roman Church and popery during the Roman Empire and Middle Ages. Protestant historians record medieval Roman Church practices in the "most negative terms" and recall the massive corruption of Catholic Church leaders, including adulteries, bribes, extravagant papal art and architecture projects—and most destructive, "wars of conquest."[1527]

Samuel Schmucker, author of *The Glorious Reformation*, details the horrifying tyranny and persecution by the Catholic Church during the Middle Ages. He estimates the Roman Church was responsible for the deaths of nearly 68 million Christians who dissented from her teachings.[1528] This massive slaughter was possible through the Catholic

---

1524 "Vatican Inc.: 5 Facts About the Business of the Catholic Church" *CNN*, https://money.cnn. com/2015/09/24/news/pope-francis-visit-vatican-catholic-church/index.html

1525 "Vatican City." *Encyclopedia Brittanica*, http://www.britannica.com/place/Vatican-City

1526 *Time*, 28 September 2015

1527 "Protestantism." *Encyclopedia Brittanica*, http://www.britannica.com/topic/Protestantism

1528 Schmucker, Samuel. *The Glorious Reformation*, 1838, pp.105

Inquisition[1529] and Crusades against heretics,[1530] which are undeniable, historical examples of the Roman Church being drunken with the blood of the saints. Revelation 18:24 traces all the slain back to Catholicism: *"And in her was found the blood of prophets, and of saints, and of all that were slain upon the earth."*

PROOF #10: THE CATHOLIC CHURCH'S HEADQUARTERS IS A GREAT CITY.

Revelation 17:18 says Mystery Babylon is *"that great city, which reigneth over the kings of the earth."* The Vatican is certainly a *"great city,"* for this city-state is the epitome of church and state. Located on the west bank of the Tiber River, the Vatican is the world's smallest fully independent nation-state. It operates tax free and has its own "telephone system, post office, gardens, astronomical observatory, radio station, banking system, and pharmacy, as well as a contingent of Swiss Guards responsible for the personal safety of the pope since 1506."[1531]

History validates how the Vatican has reigned *"over the kings of the earth,"* particularly in Europe beginning in the fifth century, reaching its height of power during the Middle Ages, then starting its decline in the nineteenth century. Napoleon Bonaparte famously symbolized the Vatican's decline in power when he snatched the French crown from the pope's hands to crown himself at his coronation rather than bowing to him in 1804.[1532] Previously, the Holy See exercised power over Europe's kings and monarchs. Recent popes have had shrinking political legacies rather than being major players in world politics like popes from the Middle Ages. Still, Vatican influence has flexed its muscle at times, as Pope John Paul II is credited with influencing *"kings"* or rulers of the earth by helping to end the Cold War, according to former Soviet leader Mikhail Gorbachev. Former Polish Senator Andrzj Szczypiorski said Pope John

---

1529 "Inquisition: Roman Catholicism." *Encyclopedia Britannica*, https://www.britannica.com/topic/inquisition

1530 "Roman Catholicism." *Encyclopedia Britannica*, https://www.britannica.com/topic/Roman-Catholicism

1531 "Vatican City." *Encyclopedia Britannica*, http://www.britannica.com/place/Vatican-City

1532 "When the Pope was Powerful and Why That Changed"

Paul's "pontificate was responsible for the downfall of Communist rule worldwide."[1533] No church other than the Catholic Church can claim to to be a *"great city"* and have influence, politically and spiritually, over the earth's leaders like Vatican City.

PROOF #11: THE CATHOLIC CHURCH RIDES THE BEAST, THE SPIRIT OF ANCIENT ROME.

Revelation 17:3 explains Mystery Babylon is to *"sit upon a scarlet coloured beast, full of names of blasphemy, having seven heads and ten horns."* By examining each of these descriptions, you can fully recognize that the Catholic Church sits on or rides upon the spirit of Ancient Rome. Scarlet was covered in Proof #7.

In Bible symbolism, a beast represents a human kingdom as taught in Daniel 7:23: *"the fourth beast shall be the fourth kingdom upon the earth."* Daniel chapter 7 lists only four kingdoms upon the earth until the second coming of Jesus Christ to the earth. This time the kingdoms are symbolized as animals rather than as sections of a man, like in Nebuchadnezzar's dream in Daniel chapter 2. Proof #2 details these kingdoms. Babylon is the lion, the Medes and Persians are the bear, the Grecians are the leopard, and Rome is the *"dreadful and terrible"* beast with *"great iron teeth."*[1534] Though this beast, or Ancient Roman Empire, fell in the fifth century, it had already gained new spiritual authority through emperor Constantine in the fourth century. When Constantine changed the empire's capital "from Rome to Constantinople in 330, Rome's civil authority was weakened, but its spiritual authority was strengthened: the title 'supreme priest' (pontifex maximus), which had been the prerogative of the emperor, now devolved upon the pope."[1535]

Constantine's move was a fulfillment of John's prophecy in Revelation 13:1-3; for this beast was *"wounded to death"* but *"his deadly wound was healed."* The Ancient Roman Empire died, or fell in the fifth century, but the

---

1533 "Teacher's Guide - John Paul II: The Millennial Pope." *Frontline*, https://www.pbs.org/wgbh/pages/frontline/teach/leadership/pope/

1534 Daniel 7:7

1535 "Roman Catholicism." *Encyclopedia Britannica*, https://www.britannica.com/topic/Roman-Catholicism

spirit of Rome and its evil influence lived on through the Roman Catholic Church. Observe that this one beast *"out of the sea"* is a combination of the four beasts mentioned in Daniel 7: *"like a leopard"* (Grecians), *"feet of a bear"* (Medes and Persians), *"mouth of a lion"* (Babylon), and *"ten horns"* (Rome). All the violent, evil demons who inhabited each ancient kingdom never died; they have only changed their dwelling places, living now in the Catholic system. The power the Roman church rides upon comes from evil spirits. Revelation 18:2 validates this truth, for Mystery Babylon is *"the habitation of devils, and the hold of every foul spirit, and a cage of every unclean and hateful bird."* Just as each ancient kingdom sought world dominance, so the Roman Church seeks global influence and religious dominance, riding the demonic, beastly power that divides and conquers all nations, peoples, multitudes, and tongues.

TRIPLE BLASPHEMY

Revelation 13:6 says, *"And he opened his mouth in blasphemy against God, to blaspheme his name, and his tabernacle, and them that dwell in heaven."* The beast, or spirit of Rome, blasphemes God in three ways: His name, tabernacle, and the saints that dwell in heaven.

The spirit of Rome in Catholicism blasphemes God's name, the Lord Jesus Christ, by substituting it with "Holy Trinity" and with the titles "Father, Son, and Holy Ghost." Mass services and Catholic wedding ceremonies issue prayers and blessings in the name of the "Father, Son, and Holy Spirit" rather than using the name of Jesus Christ. In Holy Writ, the "Father, Son, and Holy Spirit" titles were never used in worship or in blessing. Colossians 3:17 commands us to do all things, whether in word or deed, in the name of Lord Jesus Christ. Ephesians 3:15 and Philippians 2:9-11 teach that the name of Jesus Christ is the name above all names and that the entire family of God in heaven and earth is named the Lord Jesus Christ.[1536] The Roman Church does not hallow God's revealed name, the Lord Jesus Christ, as Jesus taught us in His model prayer: *"Hallowed be thy name."*

1536 Ephesians 4:14-15

God's heavenly tabernacle is blasphemed because Rome calls itself the "eternal city"[1537] and decks the Vatican with priceless artwork, gold, and precious valuables of incalculable measure. Rome is not eternal, for "*her plagues come in one day*" and she will be judged in "*one hour*" because "*strong is the Lord God who judgeth her.*"[1538] The New Jerusalem, vividly described in Revelation chapters 21 and 22, is the true and only eternal city that is coming to earth from heaven and God—not man—is its builder and maker.

Rome has blasphemed the saints that dwell in heaven through the practice of "communion of saints," or the teaching that men should pray to the saints rather than to God Himself. 1 Timothy 2:5 says Jesus Christ is the only mediator between God and man, and Christ never taught anyone to pray to Mary, or any other believer. Any true believer, whether alive or dead, would instantly reject any prayers, sacrifice, or worship directed to themselves just as Paul and Barnabas did in Acts 14:1-18. After God healed a cripple through Paul's divinely-given words at Lystra, the natives were preparing to make sacrifices to Paul and Barnabas, but these wise apostles were able to talk them out of their idolatry. Our lesson is that human beings are never honored with sacrifices, prayers, or worship; for these expressions are reserved for God alone.

THE MARK OF THE BEAST

Since the Catholic Church rides the beast, or spirit of Rome, you can now understand the mark of the beast. Revelation 13:16-18 says,

> "*And he causeth all, both small and great, rich and poor, free and bond, to receive a mark in their right hand, or in their foreheads: And that no man might buy or sell, save he that had the mark, or the name of the beast, or the number of his name. Here is wisdom. Let him that hath understanding count the number of the beast: for it is the number of a man; and his number is Six hundred threescore and six.*"

1537   "Rome." *Encyclopedia Britannica*, http://www.britannica.com/place/Rome
1538   Revelation 18:8-10

God's spiritual mark for His children is the baptism of the Holy Ghost upon the Christian's soul. Paul and John call God's spiritual mark a seal.[1539] While most people think Satan's mark will be a computer chip, tattoo, or other physical mark, Scripture teaches the opposite, as the beast's mark is also a spiritual mark an unbeliever receives after rejecting God's mark. While the mark of the beast movement may culminate with the implantation of a computer chip during the Great Tribulation, the mark itself begins as a rebellious, stubborn, and prideful human spirit.

Both marks—God's seal mark and Satan's beast mark—are spiritual marks that can be received today. God's mark, the seal of the baptism of the Holy Ghost, is received spiritually when a Christian fully obeys God's requirements for the new birth. Acts 5:32 says God gives the Holy Ghost to *them that obey him.* Obedience always requires sacrifice. For the new birth, Christians must sacrifice their own will, fully dying out to their selfish desires. Chapter 5 explains how Christians die out or crucify the following sins: unbelief, hypocrisy, reasonings, sensuality, impatience, irreverence, selfishness, and resistance.

Satan's spiritual mark is received when unbelievers reject God's seal by disobeying His path to the baptism of the Holy Ghost. Cain is the first prefigure of someone receiving the mark of the beast. Not only did Cain know God's perfect will—animal sacrifice—from God Himself but He also told him he could rule over his sin nature if he simply obeyed.[1540] Cain, like his father, *"that wicked one,"*[1541] blatantly rejected God's Word and soon murdered his brother. It seems God gave Cain a physical mark so that other men would not kill him as he wasted his life wandering like a fugitive and vagabond.[1542]

Genesis shows the beginning of both marks, as Cain was the first marked and immediately left the presence of God. True believers are marked by constant worship, dwelling in God's presence, as Seth's

---

1539 2 Corinthians 1:22, Ephesians 1:13, 4:30, Revelation 7:1-8, 9:4
1540 Genesis 4:7
1541 1 John 3:12
1542 Genesis 4:12-15

example proves in Genesis 4:26: "*And to Seth, to him also there was born a son; and he called his name Enos: then began men to call upon the name of the Lord.*"

Unbelievers after Cain did not receive a physical mark, but instead took a spiritual mark for rejecting God's path to salvation. These wicked, evil, Cain-like rejectors of God's love are termed as "*reprobate*" in Jeremiah 6:30, Romans 1:28, 2 Timothy 3:8, and Titus 1:16. In the Greek Lexicon, "*reprobate*" means "not standing the test, not approved, unfit for, unproved, spurious." According to Romans 1:28-32, God gives a person over to a reprobate mind who continually refuses His love, refusing to retain His Word in his mind while having pleasure in committing wicked, abominable acts. Because God's love is so great, His eyes "*run to and fro throughout the whole earth*"[1543] seeking each soul and offering salvation. The Father is always seeking true worshippers according to John 4:23. There will be no excuses for the reprobates who reject God's continual offer of love on the Day of Judgment because God has revealed His power and Godhead to every person through His creation and the human body.[1544]

Rejection is the key word for understanding the mark of the beast. God desires all men to be saved[1545] but "*few there be that*" will find it,[1546] meaning most will reject His gracious offer. God foreshadowed the mark of the beast in the Old Testament with another physical mark called an "*aul,*" or permanent earring given to Jewish slaves who purposely rejected freedom and wanted to remain slaves forever. Jewish slaves served six years but in the seventh year they could go free. Exodus 21:6 and Deuteronomy 15:17 detail this mark for slaves who rejected their God-given inheritance, which included all the blessings of the land of their forefathers. Today, unbelievers show their spiritual ears are marked with Satan's mark when they reject the good news of the gospel offering them freedom from sin through the Holy Spirit. They choose to love sin

---

1543 2 Chronicles 16:9
1544 Romans 1:19-20
1545 1 Timothy 2:4
1546 Matthew 7:14

and remain a slave to it rather than ruling over it like Cain should have done. Believers submit to God's Spirit and live righteously and godly in this present world.

THE MARK IN THE RIGHT HAND OR FOREHEAD

According to Revelation 13:17, buying and selling during the Great Tribulation will only be accomplished through one of three ways: *"the mark, or the name of the beast, or the number of his name."*

First, the mark of the beast can be in the right hand or the forehead. The right hand mark symbolizes one who has promised or made an oath of allegiance to do the works of the beast under the guise of *"peace and safety."*[1547] In this case the right hand mark may be called the *"right hand of falsehood"*[1548] and means that all people, including church members, will have to do the will of the one-world church system. Hands can represent works, as God promised to bless obedient Israel *"in all the works of thine hands."*[1549] Simple submission and obedience to the will of the antichrist for the sake of financial gain will cause people to take his mark.

The mark in their forehead means the beast's followers will boldly and unashamedly accept the false doctrines of the world church system, which includes trinitarianism, universalism, and other doctrines not found in Scripture. The forehead protects the area of brain known as the frontal lobe where decisions are made, speech is formed, and reasoning occurs. It is fitting that God represents the forehead—a persuaded, made-up mind—as a hard stone such as flint. God told Ezekiel that He would make his forehead *"strong against their* (the house of Israel) *foreheads."*[1550] Sinners' foreheads have minds unashamed[1551] of committing evil while God promised to mark the foreheads of believers who sighed and cried against all the abominations done in Jerusalem as a sign they would be delivered from destruction.[1552] Both God-followers and

---

1547   1 Thessalonians 5:3
1548   Psalm 144:8-11
1549   Deuteronomy 16:15
1550   Ezekiel 3:1, 8-9
1551   Jeremiah 3:3
1552   Ezekiel 9:1-11

beast-followers have marked foreheads and each person must choose the mark he will receive.

THE MARK OF HIS NAME

The second means of buying and selling that will take place in the Great Tribulation is through *"the name of the beast."* Revelation 14:11 teaches sinners will receive *"the mark of his name."* The name of the beast has two applications because there is one name for the person of the antichrist—the beast's figurehead—while the beast or spirit of Rome is *"full of names of blasphemy."*[1553]

The antichrist's name is the name of one man, as taught by Revelation 13:17-18, which says *"the number of his name…it is the number of a man."* What is the name of the man who will be the antichrist? It is the "Vicar of Christ,"[1554] the blasphemous title given to the pope of Rome, who is said to have "full, supreme, and universal power over the whole Church, a power which he can always exercise unhindered."[1555] Vicar means "substitute," originating from the Latin word "vicarius." Consider the other official titles the pope is given: "Bishop of Rome, Vicar of Jesus Christ, Successor of the Prince of the Apostles, Supreme Pontiff of the Universal Church, Patriarch of the West, Primate of Italy, Metropolitan Archbishop of the Province of Rome, Sovereign of the State of Vatican City, Servant of the Servants of God."[1556] Submitting to the name of the antichrist, the Roman Vicar of Jesus Christ, is equal to receiving the mark of the beast.

The beast, or Roman spirit, is *"full of names of blasphemy"* according to Revelation 17:3. What are the beast's many names of blasphemy? They are the different names of so-called Christian churches all claiming to be true churches, for there are "thousands of religious denominations"[1557] existing within the United States and undoubtedly thousands more world wide. Muse on this for a moment: thousands of different

---

1553   Revelation 17:3
1554   "Vicar." *Encyclopedia Britannica*, https://www.britannica.com/topic/vicar
1555   Catholic Church. *Catechism of the Catholic Church*. Paragraph 882, pp. 254
1556   "Pope." Encyclopedia Britannica, https://www.britannica.com/topic/pope
1557   "People: United States." *Encyclopedia Britannica*, https://www.britannica.com/place/United-States/People#ref742503

names—Catholic, Lutheran, Methodist, Baptist, and Presbyterian to name just a few—all claiming to be genuine churches of Jesus Christ without the power and character of true Christianity.

Most church members cuss (blasphemy), enjoy social drinking (drunkenness), watch sinful TV shows and movies (lusts), commit sexual sins (fornication and adultery), and justify themselves above others (pride). Both Peter and Paul condemn all of these sins and more,[1558] stating that Christians are free from these sins and that they were committed *before* a person's conversion to Christ in *"time past of our life."*[1559]

Just for an example, imagine the blasphemy of a "Church of Christ" member enjoying a routine, pleasure-filled (sin-filled) weekend. On Friday night, he goes to a sports bar with the guys, leaving his wife and children at home, to enjoy a basketball game while getting drunk, gossiping, complaining, and cursing players, coaches, and fans alike. Perhaps he flirts with another man's wife and gets her phone number in anticipation of a future affair. On Saturday, after wasting the morning hours watching his favorite sinful Netflix shows, he takes his wife and children to the mall to purchase immodest, sexually suggestive swimwear for their upcoming vacation. To make the children happy, he purchases the newest violent, provocative, and graphic video games. They finish the night going out to eat before catching a movie that exposes them to murders, blasphemies, sexual immorality, lusts, and lasciviousness. Due to their exhaustion from the sin-filled weekend, the family sleeps in and skips church on Sunday but will spend the rest of the day preparing to host their Super Bowl party. It's plain to see that this "Church of Christ" member and his family spent their entire weekend blaspheming the very name they claim to represent—Jesus Christ. If I call this man a "Catholic" instead, which means a member of the universal church, then he just blasphemed Jesus' true universal church, the wife or bride of Christ.

Please remember that I am not attacking the people inside these churches but the antichrist spirit that is guiding their systems because

---

1558 2 Timothy 3:1-5, 1 Peter 4:1-4
1559 1 Peter 4:3

their church bylaws, creeds, and leaders allow this type of blasphemous behavior. The countless church members who live this way are fulfilling Jesus' denunciation in Revelation 3:1: "*I know thy works, that thou hast a name that thou livest, and art dead.*" Unconverted, sin-loving church members have church names they live or confess—Church of God, Church of Christ, etc.—but are spiritually dead. The beast is full of these blasphemous names, and these church-joiners know nothing of Christ's power to make them new creatures: "*Therefore if any man be in Christ, he is a new creature: old things are passed away; behold, all things are become new.*"[1560]

Clinging to one of these thousands of blasphemous names by church-joining and rejecting the new-creature, born again experience is essentially receiving the mark of the beast.

THUS SAITH THE LORD ON THE MARK OF THE BEAST

It's imperative to share that God sent a prophet named William Branham (See Chapter 13) to provide God's warning and revelation regarding the mark of the beast.

Having rejected God's mark, the baptism of the Holy Ghost, the beast's followers will join Rome's evil, world-wide ecumenical move through accepting the mark in one of the three ways: in the forehead or hand, accepting the name of the beast, or accepting the number of his name.

The three succeeding statements about the mark of the beast are available to read and listen to online at no cost.[1561] The Holy Ghost inspired Branham to share these statements while stamping each with "THUS SAITH THE LORD"—God's authoritative phrase signaling His divine will:

- On May 4, 1954, Branham preached, "Without the seal of God, which is the baptism of the Holy Ghost, confederation of apostasy is the mark of the beast. That's THUS SAITH THE LORD."

1560 2 Corinthians 5:17
1561 "The Table." *Voice of God Recordings*, http://table.branham.org/#/en/main

- On January 19, 1964, Branham announced, "I know it's unpopular to speak against organization, but that's the mark of the beast. That's the thing that's carrying us right into that. It's making an image unto the beast. I don't say that for to be angry. I say that because it's the truth, brethren. The day will come when Phoenix will raise up, and maybe I'm gone on, but you'll know that that was THUS SAITH THE LORD."
- On August 23, 1964, Branham said, "THUS SAITH THE LORD—that same thing [unionization] will take place in religion. You'll belong to a denomination of some sort, or you cannot buy or sell."

THE NUMBER OF THE BEAST'S NAME

The third and final way buying and selling will take place during the Great Tribulation is through the number of the beast. The name of the beast has a number, *"for it is the number of a man"*—666. Many have guessed as to what the number 666 represents but there is one clear answer in Revelation. Since the beast is the spirit of Rome, the single *"man"* who is the head of the Roman spirit seeking to unite all people under his leadership can be none other than the pope of the Roman Catholic Church.

How does the pope's name equal 666? The title "vicarius filii dei" or "vicar of God's" in Latin, has been associated to the pope's office for centuries. When the title "vicarius filii dei" is added up using Roman numerals, the sum is 666, as seen in Figure 25. Note that "U" and "V" were used interchangeably until the Middle Ages.

While some contest the validity of the title "vicarius filii dei," saying its earliest appearance is found in a forgery,[1562] it is incontestable that the Catechism of the Catholic Church exalts the pope's office as "Vicar of Christ"[1563] even to this day. Vicar translates to "vicarius" in Latin.[1564] Add

---

1562 "Donation of Constantine." *Encyclopedia Britannica*, https://www.britannica.com/topic/Donation-of-Constantine

1563 Catholic Church. *Catechism of the Catholic Church*. Paragraph 882, pp. 254

1564 "Vicar." *Encyclopedia Britannica*, https://www.britannica.com/topic/vicar

to this fact the 11 proofs of Rome as Mystery Babylon and it seems very probable that the pope at some point in the past held the title "vicarius filii dei" (Vicar of God's), as it is nearly synonymous to his current title "Vicar of Christ."

V = 5	F = No value	D = 500
I = 1	I = 1	E = No value
C = 100	L = 50	I = 1
A = No value	I = 1	
R = No value	I = 1	
I = 1		
U/V = 5		
S = No value		
112	53	501
112 + 53 + 501 = 666		

Figure 25

THE IMAGE OF THE BEAST

Revelation 13:14-15 unveils the beast's plan for humanity to *"make an image to the beast, which had the wound by a sword, and did live."* Since the beast, or spirit of Rome, is invisible, it seeks an image for itself, which is a world-wide ecumenical council. These organized churches will get together in a union with the Roman Catholic Church.

It seems likely that the World Council of Churches will be the main component of this world-wide image unto the beast, as this organization represents nearly 500 million Christians and literally seeks "visible unity" or an image for Christians.[1565] This council is a false unity, for any union without union upon true doctrine is erroneous. The World Council of Churches has member churches who hold false doctrines that allow homosexuality, adultery, and lasciviousness, just

---

1565 "About Us: What is the World Council of Churches?" *World Council of Churches*, https://www.oikoumene.org/en/about-us

to name a few. These churches do not have unity like Jesus' unity with the Father, for Jesus always did those things that pleased the Father.[1566] World Council's churches allow sins that displease and grieve the Heavenly Father.

While Jesus did pray for Christian unity in John 17:11—"*that they may be one, as we are*"—the Bible teaches true unity only comes through adherence to the "*one faith.*"[1567] John states Christians should have no unity with teachers of false doctrine, saying,

> "*Whosoever transgresseth, and abideth not in the doctrine of Christ, hath not God. He that abideth in the doctrine of Christ, he hath both the Father and the Son. If there come any unto you, and bring not this doctrine, receive him not into your house, neither bid him God speed: For he that biddeth him God speed is partaker of his evil deeds.*"[1568]

All churches who reject true Bible doctrine and join the World Council of Churches in a false unity manifest that they are true daughters of the Mother Harlot, the Roman Catholic Church.

The image of the beast, or World Council of Churches, will play a major role in the future Great Tribulation, helping lay down the mark of the beast. Revelation 13:15 says the beast gives "*life unto the image of the beast, that the image of the beast should both speak, and cause that as many as would not worship the image of the beast should be killed.*" The ecumenical move will become so strong politically that governments will enact laws forcing all churches to come under dominion of the World Council, which is under Rome's dominion. Great pressure to join will be placed upon everyone, for this unionized church and state system controls finances and will have power to kill anyone who dissents.

1566   John 8:29
1567   Ephesians 4:5
1568   2 John 1:9-11

THE FALSE PROPHET OR PERSON OF THE ANTICHRIST

Revelation 19:20 and 20:10 describe the judgment of a *"false prophet"* who is closely connected to the *"beast,"* or spirit of Rome. A prophet is one who speaks for God. Who is this false prophet who claims to speak for God but teaches false doctrine and is closely connected to Rome? He can be none other than the pope of Rome.

The Catholic catechism teaches that the pope has the "authority of Christ"[1569] and has an "infallibility in virtue of his office"[1570] when he teaches "on matters of faith and morals."[1571] Yet, the pope and his church are filled with false doctrine, making his office the false prophet connected to the beast, or Roman spirit.

One of those false doctrines was assigning the title Holy Father to the pope, a title given only to the Heavenly Father by Jesus in John 17:11. Any pope who accepts this title shows his completely blind spiritual condition, for he is robbing God of His sacred, distinguished title.

A modern example showing the pope is a false prophet is the Assumption of Mary dogma from 1950. Pope Pius XII announced, "Mary, the mother of Jesus, was taken (assumed) into heaven, body and soul, following the end of her life on Earth."[1572] There is absolutely no historical or New Testament proof for this claim, as it seeks only to further exalt and deify Mary. Instead, it remains a false doctrine from the false prophet.

Another common name for the *"false prophet"* is the Antichrist, or the person who will rule, deceive, and influence the entire world during the Great Tribulation. 2 Thessalonians 2:3-13 is a detailed description of him and his blasphemous actions:

- He's called the *"man of sin"* (2 Thessalonians 2:2).
- He's called the *"son of perdition"* (2 Thessalonians 2:2).
- He's called *"that wicked"* (2 Thessalonians 2:8).

1569 Catholic Church. *Catechism of the Catholic Church.* Paragraph 2034, pp. 547
1570 Catholic Church. *Catechism of the Catholic Church.* Paragraph 891, pp. 256
1571 Catholic Church. *Catechism of the Catholic Church.* Paragraph 890, pp. 256
1572 "Assumption." *Encyclopedia Britannica*, https://www.britannica.com/topic/Assumption-Christianity

- In Jerusalem's future rebuilt temple he *"opposeth and exalteth himself above all that is called God, or that is worshipped; so that he as God sitteth in the temple of God, shewing himself that he is God"* (2 Thessalonians 2:4).
- His *"coming is after the working of Satan with all power and signs and lying wonders"* (2 Thessalonians 2:9) just as the false prophet is said to work *"miracles"* in Revelation 19:20.
- He deceives with unrighteousness and lies, allowing his followers to live in the pleasures of sin (2 Thessalonians 2:10-12).
- Those who overcome him will be believers and lovers of truth (2 Thessalonians 2:10, 13).

Another prophetic book, Daniel, provides more support and evidence about the false prophet, or antichrist-pope's future plans:

- Daniel 8:23-25 is a compound prophecy, fulfilled first by Antiochus IV from 175-164 BC,[1573] and has a future fulfillment in the false prophet-pope, for *"he shall also stand up against the Prince of princes"*—Jesus Christ. The antichrist-pope will have political *"policy"* to cause financial *"craft to prosper,"* magnifying himself in his heart. All nations will support the false prophet-pope because of his successful political and financial solutions.
- Daniel 9:27 states *"he,"* the antichrist-pope, will make a *"one week"* or seven year covenant with many but will break it after three and a half years (*"in the midst of the week"*), causing orthodox Jews to cease offering their animal sacrifices and oblations in their newly built temple. This three and a half year period in the Great Tribulation is the same time period Israel's two anointed witnesses, or

---

1573 "Antiochus IV Epiphanes." *Encyclopedia Britannica,* https://www.britannica.com/biography/Antiochus-IV-Epiphanes

prophets, are prophesying and manifesting God's power according to Revelation 11:2-3.

- Daniel 11:21-31 is another compound prophecy fulfilled by Antiochus IV but with a future fulfillment in the antichrist-pope. The *"vile person,"* or antichrist-pope, will make a peaceful *"league"* or covenant with Israel through deceit and *"flatteries."* His deceitful heart will be against the *"holy covenant"* and he will pollute the newly-built Israeli sanctuary by taking away the *"daily sacrifice."*
- Daniel 11:36-45 is prophecy solely about the antichrist-pope. See the connection to 2 Thessalonians 2:4, as the pope will speak against God, exalting and magnifying himself above everyone and everything. You learn the antichrist-pope will enter *"into the glorious land,"* Jerusalem, and try to set up his own tabernacle in the *"glorious holy mountain."* God will let him swiftly *"come to his end,"* though, and *"none shall help him."*

CATHOLICISM IN THE UNITED STATES

Have you ever wondered if the United States, a world superpower, is mentioned in the Bible? God's Spirit has foretold the prophetic description of the United States in Revelation chapter 13. But did you notice that there are two beasts in Revelation 13? The first is the *"beast out of the sea"* and the second is the *"beast coming up out of the earth."* The latter is the United States.

You have already learned the *"beast out of the sea"* is the spirit of Ancient Rome empowered by the same demonic forces that exercised world-wide dominion in the kingdoms of the Babylonians, Medes and Persians, and Ancient Grecians. Ancient Rome received a *"deadly wound"*[1574] when the Roman Empire fell, but was healed when it gained spiritual authority through Constantine in the Roman Catholic Church.

1574 Revelation 13:3

The second beast in Revelation 13:11-18 is called the *"beast coming up out of the earth,"* who exercises all the power of the *"first beast,"*[1575] or *"beast out of the sea."* The power of the Roman spirit will be exercised by the second beast, or United States. Compare briefly the similarities between Ancient Rome and the United States' world dominance:

- Largest economies
- Strongest militaries
- Most influential politics
- Most advanced technologies
- Freedom and variety in cultural expressions
- Religious tolerance

Examining the five symbols of the second beast will prove it is indeed the spirit of Rome in the United States. First, this second beast rises out of the *"earth"* and not the *"sea"* like the first beast. Since the *"sea"* or *"waters"* represents multitudes of people,[1576] *"earth"* represents a place with with a smaller human population—North America. Second, this beast has *"two horns,"* which symbolize America's civil and ecclesiastical powers. Horns represent power in Scripture, as Jeremiah 48 details Moab's fall from great military power as the LORD prophesies her *"horn"* would be *"cut off."*[1577] Third, it is *"like a lamb,"* a young country, just as a lamb is a young sheep. But it does not have to be a lamb since Scripture says *"like a lamb."* It is the American buffalo, selected as the national mammal of the United States in 2016.[1578] Fourth, America speaks *"as a dragon,"* meaning it makes phenomenal claims and warnings. In front of the United Nations in September 2018, President Donald Trump boasted America's "military will soon be more powerful than it has ever been before."[1579] For decades, Presidents have often issued warnings to rogue regimes,

---

1575   Revelation 13:12

1576   Revelation 17:15

1577   Jeremiah 48:25

1578   "Bison Selected as the Official Mammal of the United States." *History.com*, http://www.history.com/news/bison-selected-as-the-official-mammal-of-the-united-states

1579   "Remarks by President Trump to the 73rd Session of the United Nations General Assembly: New York, NY." *Whitehouse.gov*, https://www.whitehouse.gov/briefings-statements/remarks-president-trump-73rd-session-united-nations-general-assembly-new-york-ny/

such as the Soviet Union, Iran, Saudi Arabia, and North Korea. Finally, Revelation 13:13 says the United States does *"great wonders, so that he maketh fire come down from heaven on the earth in the sight of men."* This prophecy was fulfilled in August 1945 when America dropped atomic bombs on Hiroshima and Nagasaki in an attempt to spare American lives and end World War II.[1580]

History and Scripture detail the spirit of Rome rising in the United States. Colonial America began as a Protestant movement to pursue religious freedom and a "more abundant life."[1581] Indeed, the Pilgrim Fathers, part of the Separatist movement that rejected the Church of England's Roman Catholic-like governmental institutionalism,[1582] came to North America to escape the Church of England's religious persecution and founded Plymouth, Massachusetts, in 1620.

For early Americans, Catholicism, though tolerated, was their religious enemy and remained so for nearly 300 years. Even during John F. Kennedy's 1960 presidential campaign, he had to overcome a "widespread conviction that no Roman Catholic candidate could be elected president,"[1583] narrowly winning the presidency. Kennedy rose above the "religious taboo against Roman Catholics"[1584] through his style, glamour, and wit, pledging his belief of the separation of church and state to Protestant ministers during a televised speech in Houston, Texas.

The Book of Daniel reveals how Catholicism slowly, but effectively, gained acceptance and prominence in the once Protestant-strong America. Daniel 2:40-43 describes the *"fourth kingdom,"* or Roman spirit which began as the Ancient Roman Empire, but was given a new life and appearance in the Roman Catholic Church. Daniel says the Roman spirit breaks and subdues *"all things"* like iron but its feet and toes are part iron and clay, making the end of the Roman rule *"partly strong, and partly*

1580 "Hiroshima and Nagasaki." *Encyclopedia Britannica*, https://www.britannica.com/event/World-War-II/Hiroshima-and-Nagasaki

1581 "Pilgrim Fathers." *Encyclopedia Britannica*, https://www.britannica.com/topic/Pilgrim-Fathers

1582 "Separatist." *Encyclopedia Britannica*, https://www.britannica.com/topic/Separatists

1583 "John F. Kennedy." *Encyclopedia Britannica*, https://www.britannica.com/biography/John-F-Kennedy

1584 "John F. Kennedy."

broken." If iron is Catholicism, then clay is Protestantism, and Daniel says they never truly mix with one another. But Daniel 2:43 says the mixed iron and clay in the image's feet represents the two substances mingling *"themselves with the seed of men."* The devil's plan has been to control both Catholic and Protestant churches, pitting each against the other in a proselytizing battle. Unconverted Catholics and Protestants have been mingling *"themselves with the seed of men,"* or marrying other unconverted people, spreading their corrupt religion by way of family tradition rather than by true spiritual experience. Today's unconverted Catholics and Protestants are the modern Pharisees; as Jesus says in Matthew 15, they draw nigh to God with their mouths and honor Him with their lips, but their hearts are far from God. Truly, they worship God *"in vain… teaching for doctrine the commandments of men."*[1585]

Catholicism gradually became accepted in the United States through mixed marriages of separate beliefs, in which one spouse was Catholic and the other was not. Generation after generation of Catholics took marriage vows according to the Catholic Code of Canon Law promising to "remove dangers of defecting from the faith" while promising "to do all in his or her power so that all offspring are baptized and brought up in the Catholic Church."[1586] Herein was fulfilled Daniel's vision of the iron kingdom, Rome, mingling with the seed of men and pledging to make all offspring Roman Catholic. Mystery Babylon has slowly conquered the world through mixed marriages and unbelieving children who propagate their tradition-based, dogma-centered, man-inspired, and dead religion to succeeding generations.

Mixing unbelief among believers has always been Satan's most effective tactic. The devil knows he can most easily corrupt people's spiritual lives by polluting their daily actions and habits in their homes. Satan delights in destroying families. In the Garden of Eden, he divided and conquered the first family, Adam and Eve, by beguiling Eve[1587] with his

---

1585   Matthew 15:6
1586   "Chapter VI: Mixed Marriages." *The Holy See*, http://www.vatican.va/archive/ENG1104/__
        P41.HTM
1587   2 Corinthians 11:3

lies and misinterpretation of God's Word. In Genesis 6:1-3, God was grieved when *"the sons of God,"* or godly lineage of Seth, married the worldly *"daughters of men,"* or unbelieving women of Cain's lineage, solely based upon their beauty instead of their religious convictions. Marrying outside the faith caused spiritual degradation in Solomon's reign[1588] and in the lives of disobedient Jews in the days of Ezra and Nehemiah.[1589] The apostle Paul warns Christians to not be *"unequally yoked"*[1590] or have intimate fellowship with unbelievers and details how corrupt teachers aim to infiltrate homes of spiritually-weak people in order to lead them astray.[1591] John agrees, warning Christians to refuse false teachers access to their house or from asking God's blessing upon their works.[1592]

THE REWARDS FOR RECEIVING THE REVELATION OF MYSTERY BABYLON

All those who receive the revelation of Mystery Babylon are first able to recognize the mother of false religion and escape her blasphemies, abominations, idolatries, and spiritualism. By rejecting Mystery Babylon, true Christians gain the reward of recognizing the true church, *"the body of Christ,"* and see themselves as *"members in particular"* of this body.[1593]

Perhaps the greatest reward is understanding who your true mother is—the New Jerusalem! This glorious truth is found in Galatians 4:26, which states that the New Jerusalem, or the *"Jerusalem which is above...is the mother of us all."* In the Greek, *"mother"* means *"motherland."*[1594] So, which is your native country: Rome or heaven? Is Mystery Babylon your mother or the New Jerusalem? As a genuine believer in Jesus Christ, heaven is your home, for Ephesians 1:4 says you were *"chosen...in him before the foundation of the world."* You literally came from heaven because you came from God's mind. Heaven has always been your motherland.

1588   1 Kings 11:1-14
1589   Nehemiah 13:23-27
1590   2 Corinthians 6:14-18
1591   2 Timothy 3:6, Titus 1:11
1592   2 John 1:10-11
1593   1 Corinthians 12:27
1594   "The Bible: Hebrew and Greek Lexicons." *Voice of God Recordings*, www.branham.org/en/messagesearch

In John 14:1-3, Jesus promised you when He left this earth, He was going to prepare a place for you so you could be with Him forever. Jesus is just about finished preparing the New Jerusalem for you and the entire body of Christ. Paul says you are seeking *"those things which are above"* and have *"set your affection on things above"*[1595]—your motherland! When you die or at the body change of the rapture, you will return to your mother, heaven. The New Jerusalem, your future dwelling place with Christ your Husband, is your motherland.

The final rewards are the current spiritual benefits you receive after accepting God's wisdom about the false church, Mystery Babylon. This chapter began with God's truths about wisdom being necessary for recognizing Mystery Babylon, and because you prayed and asked God for wisdom, the benefits are sevenfold. James 3:17-18 declares all seven, saying, *"But the wisdom that is from above is first pure, then peaceable, gentle, and easy to be intreated, full of mercy and good fruits, without partiality, and without hypocrisy. And the fruit of righteousness is sown in peace of them that make peace."* Through God's wisdom, your character is pure, peaceable, gentle, compliant, merciful, fruitful, impartial, and sincere.

THE CONSEQUENCES FOR REJECTING THE REVELATION OF MYSTERY BABYLON

Rejecting the revelation of Mystery Babylon as the Catholic Church justifies the Mother Harlot. Proverbs 17:15 reads, *"He that justifieth the wicked, and he that condemneth the just, even they both are abomination to the Lord."* Catholicism's blasphemies, abominations, idolatries, and spiritualism cannot be forgiven because she will not repent. Heaven will not forget her sins. Revelation 18:5 states, *"For her sins have reached unto heaven, and God hath remembered her iniquities."* The next chapter exposes her iniquity-loving characteristics. By not speaking against and leaving the Mother Harlot and her daughters, rejectors of the revelation will be guilty of partaking in her sins.[1596]

1595 Colossians 3:1-2
1596 Revelation 18:4

While Babylon followers are alive, they will suffer the consequences of remaining in the Mother Harlot, antichrist system. Members may be able to attend their spiritually-dead churches, but they will be unable to escape demonic influences, being tormented by the multitudes of unclean spirits present in their gatherings. Revelation 18:2 declares that Catholicism, the mother-church with daughter-churches, is a *"habitation of devils, and the hold of every foul spirit, and a cage of every unclean and hateful bird."*

The fatal, final, future consequences of rejecting this revelation include taking the mark of the beast in your forehead or right hand, bowing to his name, or accepting the number of his name. All those who take the mark of the beast will be *"cast alive into a lake of fire burning with brimstone"* according to Revelation 19:20. The tragic conclusion of rejecting this revelation will be separation from the one true God, being judged in the lake of fire.

CONCLUSION

Our gracious and loving God freely offers His wisdom to all mankind that they might recognize both the true and false church. The book of Revelation provides a clear view of these two churches—the pure, blood-washed wife of Jesus Christ[1597] versus the vile, seductive whore named *"MYSTERY, BABYLON THE GREAT, THE MOTHER OF HARLOTS AND ABOMINATIONS OF THE EARTH."*[1598] All evidence suggests the Catholic Church is Mystery Babylon: the 11 Scriptural proofs, the mark of the beast, the name and number of the beast, the false prophet-pope, THUS SAITH THE LORD from the prophet William Branham, and the rise of Catholicism in the United States.

Revelation 18:4-5 says the Holy Spirit is issuing a final call to God's people, saying, *"Come out of her* [Mystery Babylon] *my people, that ye be not partakers of her sins, and that ye receive not of her plagues. For her sins*

1597 Revelation 7:14, 19:7-8
1598 Revelation 17:5

have reached unto heaven, and God hath remembered her iniquities." If you're a Catholic and one of God's people, please come out of Catholicism and into the true church of Jesus Christ. If you're trapped in a dead Protestant church, a daughter-church of the Mother Church, come out and let the Holy Ghost lead you to Jesus' church.

The choice is up to you as to which church you want to be a part of, but Jesus' church cannot be joined, for Christ says you must be born into it—"*ye must be born again!*"[1599] Unconverted Catholic and Protestant churches can be joined with membership classes, vows, and first communions, but the true church is "*buried*" by baptism[1600] in the name of the Lord Jesus Christ and "*born again*" of His Holy Ghost!

ACTION STEPS TO COME OUT OF BABYLON

1. If you're a Roman Catholic or member of a denomination or nondenominational church holding Catholic dogma (i.e. the Trinity), respectfully and graciously leave your home church and relocate to a new home church that believes the full gospel of Jesus Christ. Contact me if you need help finding a Bible-believing church.

2. If possible, thank your former priest or pastor for his support when you leave his church. It's likely you would not have reached your current spiritual state without his help. You may want to share with him why you're leaving his church based upon the Bible-based truths in this book. Be gentle and speak "*the truth in love.*"[1601] Contact me for a free copy if you feel led to share this book with him.

1599   John 3:7
1600   Romans 6:4, Colossians 2:12
1601   Ephesians 4:15

3. As a new member in your home church, faithfully and diligently stand at your post of duty, supporting the church with tithes, prayers, attendance, and service. Let Christ's five-fold preaching ministry of Ephesians 4:8-16 bring you to a mature state of godliness or perfection.

FOLLOW UP

Free online videos, Bible studies, and William Branham's quotes related to this chapter: www.pastorjessesmith.com/12mysteriesbook

Email: jesse.smith11@sbcglobal.net

Text: 330-929-2037

CHAPTER 10
The Mystery of Iniquity

"For the mystery of iniquity doth already work:
only he who now letteth will let,
until he be taken out of the way."

2 Thessalonians 2:7

KNOWING **R**OME IS **M**YSTERY Babylon, the false mother church, and most Protestant churches are her daughters leads you to investigate how the mother-daughter team attracts nearly 2 billion members. The Bible says their congregations thrive through the deceitfulness of iniquity.[1602] Thus, the Roman Catholic Church is the mother of and propagator of iniquity.

In the Greek Lexicon, "iniquity" means "contempt and violation of the law, wickedness."[1603] Iniquity, or lawlessness, is purposely sinning despite knowing God's will. It's a well covered subject in Scripture with over 300 mentions. Paul says iniquity was *"already"* working at the time he was writing 2 Thessalonians, around 50 A.D. Iniquity's been living in and controlling the hearts of unrepentant church members for nearly 2,000 years, but it will head up in the False Prophet, the Pope-Antichrist.

1602 2 Thessalonians 2:7, 10, 12
1603 "The Bible: Hebrew and Greek Lexicons." *Voice of God Recordings*, www.branham.org/en/ messagesearch

Multiple examples show a lifestyle of iniquity, or habitual sin, brings God's wrath and judgment upon the guilty. God used the Joshua-led Israeli army to drive out the Amorites when their cup of iniquity was full in God's eyes.[1604] Interestingly, God pronounced the Amorites' doom to Abraham 400 years prior to Joshua, but showed divine patience for their cup of iniquity to fill. Lot and his two daughters narrowly escaped God's fire and brimstone wrath upon Sodom poured out due to the *"iniquity of the city."*[1605] Judas Iscariot's destiny was hell and the 30 pieces of silver he received for betraying Christ was his *"reward of iniquity."*[1606] As the previous chapter showed, Mystery Babylon is destroyed in one hour because her iniquities are remembered in heaven.[1607]

Genuine believers will commit single acts of iniquity despite knowing better, but they will always repent and change their future behaviors. Joseph's brothers committed iniquity by selling him into slavery, but they repented and Revelation shows they are saved, crowned, and seated with the 12 apostles around Jesus' heavenly throne.[1608] David committed iniquity by unlawfully taking Bathsheba and numbering Israel, but repented and never repeated those sins.[1609] The apostle Paul admits to doing evil, sinful acts he hated, but assures believers Jesus' blood forgives all their trespasses.[1610] John assures the same, teaching confession of sins allows the faithful and just Christ to *"forgive us our sins, and to cleanse us from all unrighteousness."*[1611]

The universal iniquity problem was so great God sent His dear, innocent, sinless Son, Jesus, to die for past, present, and future iniquities. Isaiah 53:5, 6, and 11 say Jesus was *"bruised for our iniquities...and the Lord hath laid on him the iniquity of us all"*, and He'd justify many by bearing their iniquities. This precious gift was not given in vain, though, and God now requires everyone to accept His Son's power to purge their iniquities. Acts

---

1604   Genesis 15:16, Joshua 10:12
1605   Genesis 19:15
1606   Acts 1:18, 25
1607   Revelation 18:5
1608   Genesis 44:16, Matthew 19:28, Revelation 4:4
1609   2 Samuel 12:9-10, 24:10, 1 Kings 15:5
1610   Romans 7:14-25, Colossians 2:13
1611   1 John 1:8-10

3:26 says God raised Jesus from the dead to bless us *"in turning away every one of you from his iniquities."* If you truly believe in Jesus, you'll gladly accept His blessing of spiritual power to turn from your iniquities.

To believe in Jesus means you stop committing iniquity. Mark 16:16 proclaims, *"He that believeth and is baptized shall be saved; but he that believeth not shall be damned."* Sounds like everyone one would believe in Jesus and be saved, right? Unfortunately, *"all nations"*[1612] are going to be guilty of rejecting Christ through Mystery Babylon's deceptive, sin-loving religion. Now you'll see how this happens.

THE CONFUSION ABOUT THE MYSTERY OF INIQUITY

The confusion about iniquity centers around which actions lead to habitual iniquity and the appropriate, damnable title of "worker of iniquity", which Scripture alludes to over 30 times. How does someone become a worker of iniquity and therefore worthy of the lake of fire? You've probably heard church members attempt to condone their habitual sins by saying, "We all have our demons." But Holy Ghost filled Christians should not be bound by demons as servants of Satan.

> **The revelation of the mystery of iniquity is the antichrist spirit fills and deceives the hell-bound majority into blaspheming God's truth under the guise of a sin-loving, religious experience.**

Workers of iniquity are led by false preachers, filled with Satan's demons, who appear as religious messengers of light but spread spiritual darkness. 2 Corinthians 11:13-14 describe them, saying, *"For such are false apostles, deceitful workers, transforming themselves into the apostles of Christ. And no marvel; for Satan himself is transformed into an angel of light."* These false ones are destined for and worthy of hell because after knowing the truth, they hate, blaspheme, and fight against it. They are more willing to believe lies than Bible truth.

1612 Revelation 14:8, 18:3, 23

As the specific acts of iniquity are identified in this chapter, you'll conclude which groups contain a majority of workers of iniquity, and God's wisdom will help you flee from them, following after *"righteousness, faith, charity, peace, with them that call on the Lord out of a pure heart."*[1613]

BIBLICAL EVIDENCE FOR THE REVELATION OF THE MYSTERY OF INIQUITY

Evidence abounds in support of iniquity's revelation and there's no better place to begin than with Satan, the father of iniquity. As Jesus is the epitome of godliness, leading believers into it, Satan is the opposite—the epitome of iniquity, leading billions into it. In Satan, the father of lies, you see the same characteristics his children bear today.

SATAN, THE FATHER OF INIQUITY

Satan's given name from God is Lucifer, which means "light bearer" in Hebrew. Paul says Satan often transforms himself *"into an angel of light"*[1614] but his lying messages enslave souls in darkness.

Ezekiel 28:11-19 says Lucifer began as the most bright, beautiful angel and was equipped for music ministry in heaven. He was an anointed cherub set by God to be a covering around His throne. It's likely Michael was the other cherub at God's throne, as Moses' Ark of the Covenant included two cherubs covering the mercy seat where God's presence dwelt.[1615]

Lucifer was perfect in every way until iniquity was found in him as his *"heart was lifted up"* because of his brightness and beauty. God says his iniquity—willful disobedience—corrupted his wisdom. Isaiah 14:13-14 reveals his wicked thoughts to exalt himself to be like God: *"For thou hast said in thine heart, I will ascend into heaven, I will exalt my throne above the stars of God: I will sit also upon the mount of the congregation, in the sides of the north: I will ascend above the heights of the clouds; I will be like the most High."*

1613   2 Timothy 2:22
1614   2 Corinthians 11:4
1615   Exodus 25:18-22

Satan infamously said *"I will"* six times in iniquity, providing a stark contrast to Jesus' *"Thy will"* Gethsemane prayer[1616] in godliness. Jesus directly rebuked Satan for regarding only his will rather than God's in Matthew 16:23: *"Get thee behind me, Satan: thou art an offence unto me: for thou savourest not the things that be of God, but those that be of men."* Satan and his workers are not interested in God's will.

Revelation 12:3-4, 7-11 explain Lucifer's heavenly rebellion, as he led the first church split. Accordingly, he's given the titles great red dragon, old serpent, devil, Satan, and accuser of the brethren in this text. Lucifer, *"a liar, and the father of lies,"*[1617] convinced a third of the angels to join his war against Michael and the holy angels. Michael's mighty army prevailed, casting Lucifer's army out of heaven down to earth, and his next act mentioned is beguiling and deceiving a virgin named Eve.

In summary, Satan's characteristics—passed on to his children— include disregarding and rejecting God's will for his own, a prideful heart, accusing others, violent, and desiring promotion, worship, and position.

SATAN, THE SERPENT, AND EVE

Genesis 3 opens with the subtle, sly serpent questioning Eve on God's command about which trees she can eat from. Satan, a spirit being, had possessed the beast-serpent sometime before this conversation because all beasts were created sin-free and *"good"* on the sixth day of creation.[1618] Once cast to earth, Satan came to Eden and found Adam and Eve, as Ezekiel 28:13 confirms: *"Thou hast been in Eden the garden of God."*

Knowing he cannot be god of heaven, Satan observes Adam's domin- ion and connives to take his authority and rule over the earth. 2 Peter 2:19 reads, *"For of whom a man is overcome, of the same is he brought in bondage."* You know Satan succeeded and overcame Adam, which is why Paul calls him *"the god of this world."*[1619] Satan is so shrewd and Scripture

1616   Matthew 26:42
1617   John 8:44
1618   Genesis 1:31
1619   2 Corinthians 4:4

implores you to be aware of his *"devices"* that *"ye may be able to stand against the wiles of the devil."*[1620]

Back to Genesis 3, Eve correctly quotes God's fruit-command in reply to the serpent, but you find Satan doing the same tactic he used in heaven—lying and accusing. Genesis 3:4-5 record Satan's lie she won't die by touching and eating the forbidden fruit and his accusing God of keeping her from an exalted state of wisdom and existence. Verse 6 says deceived Eve believed the serpent and ate the fruit, deciding it was good to eat, pleasant looking, and able to make her wise.

You're aware Eve then gives the fruit to Adam and he eats, but read 1 Timothy 2:14 to gain an important truth: *"And Adam was not deceived, but the woman being deceived was in the transgression."* Adam, not present at Eve's eating, finds her and knows she's defiled and destined for death. His only choices are to abstain from eating and let her die alone, or eat and die with her in hope of God's forgiveness. Knowing she was part of him, taken from his rib, he loves her and becomes a type of Christ, taking her sin upon him, eating the fruit. Christ purposely chose to take His bride's sin upon Himself and die to redeem her.

Notice Satan stealing, killing, and destroying in Eden like Jesus warns us in John 10:10: *"The thief cometh not, but for to steal, and to kill, and to destroy: I am come that they might have life, and that they might have it more abundantly."* Satan first stole Adam's place in Eve's heart as Genesis 3:16 says Eve's desire or longing will be to Adam after the fall. This means Eve longed for the serpent instead of Adam. Then Satan killed Adam and Eve, as death literally entered their bodies and eventually took their lives. Lastly, the tempter destroyed their holy, sinless state and marital unity.

THE ORIGINAL SIN, THE FORBIDDEN FRUIT, AND THE SEED OF THE SERPENT

You might be wondering, how could one apple cause all sin and trouble in the world? Eve didn't eat an apple because 2 Peter 1:4 says corruption *"is in the world through lust."* The forbidden fruit that caused the original

---

1620 2 Corinthians 2:11, Ephesians 6:11

sin was a lustful, sexual act of adultery between Eve and the serpent according to the following nine evidences, but first, here's a Bible-based summary. As you'll soon see, Eve's sexual immortality reveals the mystery of why Jesus Christ had to be born of a virgin.

Eve's adultery with the serpent is often called the Serpent Seed doctrine based upon God's own words in Genesis 3:15, in which He is speaking directly to the serpent: *"And I will put enmity between thee and the woman, and between thy seed and her seed; it shall bruise thy head, and thou shalt bruise his heel."* Notice your God says the serpent has seed, or "offspring, descendants, children" in the Hebrew Lexicon, and this is immediately after the fall. The fruit Eve partook of and shared with Adam created two seeds, or sets of children.

Both the forbidden fruit and two trees—Tree of Life and Tree of Knowledge of Good and Evil—have symbolic, not literal meanings. The forbidden fruit symbolizes adultery because Proverbs 30:20 and Song of Solomon 4:12-5:1 teach eating can represent sexual relations. Proverbs 30:20 says, *"Such is the way of an adulterous woman; she eateth, and wipeth her mouth, and saith, I have done no wickedness."* This explains exactly what Eve did—she was deceived into committing adultery with the serpent, thinking she had done no wrong when Adam found her defiled.

Some believe Song of Solomon 4:12-5:1 records the wedding night of Solomon and the Shulamite, but it's undeniable eating represents sexual relations in this passage. Solomon calls her a garden and she invites him to *"come into his garden, and eat his pleasant fruits."* He says one of her plants is the pomegranate, comparing it to her beautiful head within her locks of hair and she says she's going to bring him into her mother's house and cause him *"to drink of spiced wine of the juice of my pomegranate."*[1621]

Eve first committed adultery with the serpent, lost her virginity, and conceived the serpent's seed, as Paul alludes to in 2 Corinthians 11:2-3:

> *"For I am jealous over you with godly jealousy: for I have espoused you to one husband, that I may present you as a chaste*

1621 Song of Solomon 4:3, 6:7, 8:2

virgin to Christ. But I fear, lest by any means, as the serpent beguiled Eve through his subtilty, so your minds should be corrupted from the simplicity that is in Christ."

Adam then found her fallen in sin and partook in sexual relations with her, causing her to conceive of his seed. Cain was the seed of the serpent and Abel was Adam's seed. Twins conceived of two separate fathers is called superfecundation according to the *Journal of Forensic Sciences.*[1622]

Nine evidences support the revelation of the Serpent Seed doctrine:

Evidence 1: The Bible supports the Serpent Seed doctrine from Genesis to Revelation. Moses, Jesus, Paul, Peter, and John all support the serpent seed doctrine through their teachings.

Moses is the author of Genesis and recorded Genesis 3:15, in which God Himself begins the Serpent Seed doctrine, saying the serpent has a "seed" or offspring, which proved to be Cain, for he *"was of that wicked one."*[1623]

Our Lord Jesus teaches the Serpent Seed in Matthew 13:24-30, and 36-43. In this parable, Jesus describes the children of God as *"good seed"* while the children of the wicked one, Satan, are the tares, or bad seed. The parable, which has numerous applications, teaches two different men, or sowers, planted two different seeds in one field. In one application, the two men are represented as Jesus (*"the Son of man"*) and Satan (*"the enemy"*), and the field represents the world. In another application, this parable helps reveal the origin from Eden of the two kinds of children—the children of God and the children of the devil. Two males—the serpent and Adam—planted their seeds in one field, or one woman—Eve. The seeds, or offspring, grew and manifested their different natures. Cain, the son of the serpent, slew righteous Abel, for Cain was of the cursed seed.

Paul supports the Serpent Seed in 2 Corinthians 11:2-3 by directly comparing the virginity of the church in Corinth to Eve's virginity when she was presented to Adam. Paul said it was his desire to present the

---

1622 *Journal of Forensic Sciences.* American Academy of Forensic Sciences, July 1994.
1623 1 John 3:12

Corinthians as a chaste virgin or spiritual virgin to Christ. Then Paul says he feared the minds of the Corinthians would be corrupted and they would lose their spiritual virginity, just as the serpent corrupted the mind of Eve, causing her to lose her spiritual virginity before losing her physical virginity.

Peter supports the Serpent Seed in 2 Peter 1:4, stating corruption is *"in the world through lust,"* or a desire for what is forbidden. Genesis 3:6 says Eve thought the tree was pleasant looking and good for food, meaning she was physically attracted to the serpent. Then God declares one consequence for Eve's sin is that her desire will be to her husband from henceforth. This means her desire was not to her husband when she fell in sin to her lustful desire to the serpent, who gave her his seed.

John teaches the Serpent Seed in 1 John 3:6-15. Verse 12 records the Holy Spirit saying Cain was *"of that wicked one"*, and Adam was not the *"wicked one"* for this phrase always refers to Satan. Jesus calls Satan the *"wicked one"* twice in Matthew 13:19 and 38. John mentions the *"wicked one"* three other times in his same letter[1624] and each time it means Satan, not Adam.

Cain even has a separate genealogy from Adam's in Genesis 4:17-24, as Adam's is found in Genesis 5:1-32. Seth was *"a son in his [Adam's] own likeness, after his image"*, but the Bible never says this about Cain. Furthermore, the Bible states that Eve was the *"mother of all living"* in Genesis 3:20 but Scripture never says Adam was the father of all living because he was not. The serpent was the father of Cain, and Eve was his mother.

John in Revelation 12:9 calls Satan *"that old serpent"* because he entered and possessed the beast-serpent in Eden. The title *"old"* refers to Satan as the father of lies and murderer from the beginning according to our Lord Jesus in John 8:44. His wickedness is seen in Genesis and continues to Revelation, but thankfully that old serpent comes to his fiery end through the justice and wrath of Almighty God at the battle of God and Magog.[1625]

1624 1 John 2:13-14, 5:18
1625 Revelation 20:10

Evidence 2: The two trees in the midst of the garden were not literal trees because the Tree of Knowledge of Good and Evil was not good for food. The two trees—Tree of Life and Tree of Knowledge of Good and evil—symbolized Jesus and Satan, or the Holy Spirit and Satan's spirit. These two trees were different from all other trees in Eden. Genesis 2:9 says every tree out of the ground was good for food, proving the Tree of Knowledge of Good and Evil was not a regular tree because when Eve partook of its fruit, sin and death occurred. Two truths about this evil tree are evident: it didn't come from the ground and its fruit was not good for food. Any tree whose fruit will kill you isn't good for food.

Notice Genesis 3:6 says Eve believed the fruit was good for food, so this is symbolic of her eating the fruit of adultery. Any sinful act is a fruit of Satan, just as God's prophet rebuked Israel for eating the *"fruit of lies"* in Hosea 10:13.

Evidence 3: The Tree of Life was Jesus' Spirit because there is only one way to eternal life. If the Tree of Life was a normal tree, like a pear tree, it would mean God had a second, works-based way to inherit eternal life. Eating physical food never has and never could give eternal life since eating cannot pardon sin. But there has always been and always will be one way to eternal life—by faith in God, the Holy Spirit.

Hebrews 11 shows all believers from the beginning are saved by faith, as Abel was righteous because of his faith. Similarly, Hebrews 11:26 says Moses followed Christ, or the Holy Spirit, so salvation by faith was the same in the Old Testament as in the New. Jesus claims He is *"the way," "the life," "the bread of life," "with the words of eternal life."*[1626] He's the only way to eternal life and it's only found in Him according to John 5:40 and 1 John 5:11-12.

Evidence 4: The Serpent Seed explains the purpose of the virgin birth of Jesus. The revelation of Jesus' mysterious virgin birth is found in this doctrine. Since mankind's fall into sin came by sex, God had to redeem man without sex and then give him divine power over the sin-nature.

1626   John 6:35, 6:68, 14:6

The original human race was corrupted through the serpent's seed as the sin-nature was passed down to every person from their parents. Job 14:1 says, *"Man that is born of a woman is of few days, and full of trouble."* The same truth is found in Psalm 51:5: *"Behold, I was shapen in iniquity; and in sin did my mother conceive me."*

God's Lamb, His Son Jesus Christ, had to come to earth through virgin birth to bypass the way sin came into the world (sexual reproduction). Since the sin-nature wasn't passed down to Jesus, He could live a sinless life. Instead of a sin-nature, Jesus had a Word-nature in His body because He was conceived of the Holy Ghost. Jesus was the Word *"made flesh."*[1627]

The purpose of the virgin birth was twofold: prepare a sinless Lamb-sacrifice to pay for all sins and begin a new human race. The first fold is magnified in Revelation 5:1-10 in which no man in heaven or on earth was found worthy to loose the Seven Seals until the virgin born Lamb of God came forward to take the Book. Our Redeemer had to be virgin-born, without the serpent's sin-nature inside Him.

Jesus' virgin birth allowed for a new human race to begin. In Revelation 3:14 Jesus says He is the *"beginning of the creation of God"* and Paul says Jesus is the *"firstborn among many brethren,"*[1628] meaning Jesus was the first among many to experience the new birth. Every born again believer today has mighty Holy Ghost power in their souls, like Jesus had. After Jesus received the indwelling power of the Holy Ghost at His River Jordan baptism, He was led into the wilderness to be tempted of the devil. Jesus' new soul-power was going to be tested. In Jesus' three-fold temptation, He defeated the same spirit who defeated Eve by simply quoting and obeying the Word! God was proving His gift of the Holy Ghost baptism could withstand Satan's strongest attacks. Even though Eve first sinned in a garden, her seed, foretold in Genesis 3:15, through the power of the Holy Ghost baptism would eventually crush the head of the serpent in another garden: Gethsemane.

1627   John 1:14
1628   Romans 8:29

Jesus preached about the new birth and urged His disciples to receive it because it would be their inward power to become a new creature from the inside out. Spirit-filled Christians still battle the sin-nature in their members,[1629] but the Word-nature in their souls is a greater, overcoming power according to 1 John 4:4: "*Ye are of God, little children, and have overcome them: because greater is he that is in you, than he that is in the world.*"

Evidence 5: Adam and Eve covered their loins after eating of the forbidden fruit. Genesis 3:6-7 says Adam and Eve knew they were naked after eating the forbidden fruit and sewed fig leaves to make "*aprons*", or loin coverings, in Hebrew. The loins are the area of the human reproductive parts and they covered their private parts because those were the body parts used in their sinful downfall.

If the forbidden fruit was an apple, they would have covered their mouths with figs or sewed a hood to cover their heads, but it was not a literal fruit. Also, if eating apples caused Adam and Eve to know they were naked, why can't we pass out apples to nearly-naked women on beaches so they'll know their near-nakedness and put on modest clothes? Understand eating a natural apple never has and never will bring awareness of sin and evil.

Just like it did for Adam and Eve, sexual sin always produces feelings of shame in nakedness as Ezekiel 16:35-41 teaches. Verses 35 and 36 say, "*Wherefore, O harlot, hear the word of the LORD: Thus saith the Lord GOD; Because thy filthiness was poured out, and thy nakedness discovered through thy whoredoms with thy lovers*". Nahum 3:5 agrees, "*Behold, I am against thee, saith the LORD of hosts; and I will discover thy skirts upon thy face, and I will shew the nations thy nakedness, and the kingdoms thy shame.*" Jeremiah 13:26 is another witness, saying, "*Therefore will I discover thy skirts upon thy face, that thy shame may appear.*"

Evidence 6: God's punishments for Eve's sin centered on her sexual reproduction and longing for Adam. In Genesis 3:16, God issues a twofold punishment on Eve because she was deceived by the serpent: "*Unto the woman he said, I will greatly multiply thy sorrow and thy*

1629 Romans 7:23

conception; in sorrow thou shalt bring forth children; and thy desire shall be to thy husband, and he shall rule over thee."

The first fold of God's punishment was she would experience multiplied or increased sorrow from the conception of to the delivery of children. The first consequence of Eve's sin focused on her sexual reproduction of seed or offspring. Recognize throughout the Bible, God's punishments or consequences always fit the crimes. For example, Exodus 21:24 says an *"eye for eye, tooth for tooth, hand for hand, foot for foot."* A second example is David's sin of adultery with Bathsheba. Both punishments fit his crime. First, the sword of blood would never depart his house because he had Uriah's innocent blood shed.[1630] Second, David's wives were taken from him and Absalom laid with them publicly because David laid with Bathsheba privately.[1631]

In the Eve's case, God was no different than He was with Israel and David. All women experience the pain and suffering in bringing forth seed, or offspring, as a constant, universal reminder from God to all of Eve's daughters that she willingly received or accepted the wrong seed in the beginning from the serpent. Since Eve broke her marriage covenant and received the wrong seed, she would experience suffering bringing forth any and all seed. Because Eve failed in the area of sexual reproduction, all women have increased suffering in sexual reproduction.

If Eve ate a literal apple, why didn't God punish her mouth and all apple trees? God's punishments focused on human reproduction and the body parts of the *"loins"* used for that process.

The second fold of God's punishment upon Eve was her *"desire,"* or longing and craving, would be to her own husband. As God's punishments fit the crimes, He commands Eve to desire, crave, and long for her own husband, which means that before God's command, Eve desired or longed for someone else other than Adam. You know it was the serpent and the fruit of adultery Eve longed for, as she was guilty of lust. 2 Peter 1:4 declares sin entered the world through lust.

1630 2 Samuel 12:9-10
1631 2 Samuel 12:11-12

Notice Adam in Genesis 3:20 recognizing Eve is pregnant—a mother. He names her Eve because her name means "life" and he knew *"she was the mother of all living."* Adam listened to God's Words in Genesis 3:15 and knew two separate seeds were already living and growing inside of Eve's womb and she would be the mother of all living persons—whether they were good or evil. When Eve received the wrong seed, the serpent's seed, she became a mother. The mother denomination, the Roman Catholic Church, did the same: she became the blind mother church by receiving Satan's lies, his seed of discrepancy. Most readers think Genesis 4:1 is the first mention of sexual reproduction, but Adam's naming Eve as a mother in Genesis 3:20 proves Genesis 3:6 is the first mention of intercourse, spoken figuratively.

Previous to Adam naming her, Eve had no individual name, for God called both Adam and his wife *"Adam"* according to Genesis 5:2: *"Male and female created he them; and blessed them, and called their name Adam, in the day when they were created."* Eve's fall from her united name with Adam shows how false churches make their own names—Catholic, Methodist, Baptist, etc.—but the true bride church is restored back to sharing a name with her Husband, Jesus: *"For this cause I bow my knees unto the Father of our Lord Jesus Christ, Of whom the whole family in heaven and earth is named."*[1632]

Evidence 7: The serpent was human-like before the fall. Careful Bible study about the serpent in Genesis 3 reveals he was very different than snakes today. So different, in fact, he had three human-like attributes.

First, verse 1 says the serpent was more *"subtle"*—meaning shrewd, sly, or crafty—than any other beast of the field that the Lord had made. He was the only beast God made with the ability to talk with intellectual reasoning. Observing those human-like characteristics, Satan selected the serpent to possess so he could deceive Eve, as he was present in Eden.[1633] Satan and his demons often possess animals or beasts as Matthew 8:31-32 teaches.

1632 Ephesians 3:14-15
1633 Ezekiel 28:13

Second, the serpent was an upright creature before the fall because after the fall in verse 14 God curses the serpent to go on his belly the rest of his days. Originally, the serpent was likely in between a chimpanzee and a man, but closer to a man, standing upright and able to carry on an intellectual conversation with the deceived Eve.

Third, the serpent had seed that united with Eve's egg cell, causing her to conceive the serpent's own seed according to God in Genesis 3:15. Because of this, God cursed the serpent. He changed every bone in the serpent's body so that he had to crawl on the ground but left genetic information in the serpent as proof of His punishment. In October 2015, the University of Georgia discovered snakes once had legs! Researches reported snakes have DNA that "controls the development and growth of limbs."[1634] Two years later, my children read about this finding in a National Geographic Kids magazine, which said "Snakes once had legs."[1635] Friend, God's Word and its revelation, even in regards to snakes and the Serpent Seed, is eternally true.

Evidence 8: Cain was the serpent's son and not Adam's. According to the Holy Spirit in 1 John 3:12, Cain was not the son of Adam: *"Not as Cain, who was of that wicked one, and slew his brother. And wherefore slew he him? Because his own works were evil, and his brother's righteous."* As shown earlier, the *"wicked one"* refers to Satan, not Adam, since Adam is called a *"son of God"* in Luke 3:38. Here you find the truth of two separate seed lines: Adam's and the serpent's.

Eve's womb carried two separate seeds, or sons, from separate impregnations. She carried twins, with Cain's conception sometime previous to Abel's. To those who think that this is impossible, you need only study superfecundation, as mentioned in the July 1994 *Journal of Forensic Sciences* article.

These two separate seeds had separate characteristics. Adam's seed was blessed in Genesis 5:2 and Matthew 25:34, while the serpent's seed was cursed in Genesis 4:11 and Matthew 25:41. Concerning curses, God

1634 "Blueprint For Limbs Encoded in the Snake Genome." *University of Georgia*, https://news.uga.edu/blueprints-for-limbs-encoded-in-snake-genome-1015/
1635 *National Geographic Kids*, September 2017

Himself cursed both the serpent and Cain, and all lost humanity who are sent to the lake of fire are called *"the cursed."*[1636] Note God did not curse Adam and Eve because He cannot both curse and bless His children according to Numbers 22:12. Instead, the ground was cursed for Adam's sake in Genesis 3:17.

Cain's seed-life bore the full spiritual characteristics of Satan, for he was a liar and murderer just like his daddy in Genesis 4:8-9 and John 8:44. Due to their opposite characteristics, God gave Cain a separate lineage from Adam's.[1637]

One crucial point of emphasis is the two physical, genetic seed lines of Adam and Cain are no longer separate. In the days of Noah, the literal seed of the serpent passed through the Ark through the marriages of Noah's sons and has now intermingled with the godly seed. All mankind are currently affected by the genetic pollution of the serpent's seed. Since the generations after the flood until today, God's seed is known by their reception of spiritual seed, faith in their souls, and not a natural genetic seed. Abraham and Lot had righteous souls when receiving the seed-Word of God's promise by faith.[1638] In the New Testament, God's blessed seed are recognized by the fact they are born again of the incorruptible seed, the Word of God, the Holy Ghost-seal in their souls.[1639]

Evidence 9: The Seed of the woman was a literal man, Jesus, and so was the seed of the serpent a literal man, Cain. Nearly all believers agree the seed of the woman spoken in Genesis 3:15 was Jesus Christ, a literal Man, Who bruised the serpent's head through His death-and-resurrection-victory over sin and death. If the woman's seed, Jesus, was a man-child born apart from human male instrumentality, the seed of the serpent would have to come in the same pattern. Cain fits this pattern, as he was a literal man who came into the world apart from human male instrumentality; he came through the male serpent's seed.

1636 Genesis 3:14, 4:11, Matthew 25:41
1637 Genesis 4:16-26, 5:1-32
1638 Romans 4:3-9, 2 Peter 2:8
1639 Ephesians 4:30, 1 Peter 1:23

As the seed of the woman, Jesus was God's way to reproduce His Word-nature in the human race. Since Satan does not have creative power like God, Genesis 3 shows how he injected his wicked sin nature into the human race through Cain, the serpent's seed.

GENESIS 4:1 IS THE LITERAL INTERPRETATION OF THE SYMBOLISM IN GENESIS 3:6

Genesis 4:1 is often used to try to disprove the Serpent's Seed, but God's revelation shows how it fits into the truth of original sin. It reads, "*And Adam knew Eve his wife; and she conceived, and bare Cain, and said, I have gotten a man from the LORD.*"

Everyone understands the word "*knew*" means sexual relations, but this verse is only a repeat of Genesis 3:6 wherein Eve shares the fruit with Adam. The previous nine evidences support this, for the fruit of adultery and Eve's sexual relations with Adam produced two seeds.

Genesis 4:1 repeats Genesis 3:6 with a literal interpretation along with further information about the act, including Cain's name and gender. Simply put, Genesis 3:6 is symbolic and Genesis 4:1 is literal. The Bible often switches from symbolic to literal interpretation as easily seen in Revelation chapters 17 and 18. Chapter 17 verses 3 and 4 symbolically describe a seven-headed beast and an evil woman, but their literal interpretations are found in 17:9 and 18:10, as the seven heads mean seven mountains and the woman represents a city.

Additionally, Genesis has multiple events repeated in succeeding chapters with additional information provided, such as chapters 1 and 2. Genesis 1:26-31 records mankind's creation on day six, but Genesis 2:7, 21-22 gives more information about the same event by detailing how God created Adam and Eve's bodies from the dust of the earth and breathed life into them.

Before moving on, believers do not need to accept the Serpent Seed doctrine to be saved since it does not pertain to salvation. Justification by faith is the doctrine needed for salvation.

But the Serpent Seed doctrine shines more light upon the gospel story, taking away the confusion about original sin. Knowing the forbidden fruit was adultery, not an apple, helps you understand why God sent Jesus Christ via virgin birth. Sin came into the world through sex, so our Deliverer from sin's curse had to be virgin born and free from the sin-nature in order to take all our iniquities upon Him and pay our sin debt.

INIQUITY'S ATTRIBUTES IN SATAN AND CAIN

Having found iniquity's starting place in Lucifer's heart and his injection of his nature into the human race in Cain, you witness iniquity's six attributes, although there could be more. Armed with this knowledge, you must discern and withstand the wicked one, his demons, and his human children while diligently doing opposite works.

First, the lawless go through vain, beautiful religious acts and create their own traditions. It's uncertain how long Lucifer helped lead heaven's worship while having iniquity in his heart, but it's certain he went through some acts in vain. His words from Isaiah 14:14 prove he wanted the religious worship to continue but with him as the object and recipient.

Cain, in a religious act, brought a beautiful, colorful offering of fruits fully aware it was not what God required. To onlookers, his fruit may have looked more classy, pious, and beautiful than Abel's bloody lamb offering, but God rejected it. Satan always hides behind worldly beauty while God hides in simplicity. Jesus had *"no beauty that we should desire him."*[1640]

Genesis 4:6-7 show the Lord questioning Cain about his anger regarding his rejected offering, saying He'd accept him if he only offered the correct sacrifice. Cain went through his religious act willingly and stubbornly disobedient.

Religious acts are often masks the wicked hide behind. The serpent hid his agenda behind a religious promise for Eve to become like God. Recall Jesus saying false doctrine is hidden among truth like yeast is

---

1640 Isaiah 53:2

mixed in dough in His parable on The Leaven Hid in Three Measures of Meal. More will be taught on the religion-mask later in this chapter.

Paul teaches workers of iniquity have a *"form of godliness"*, or outward resemblance of godliness in 2 Timothy 3:1-7. Outwardly, they look holy, but are void of inward holiness, never coming to believe all the truth. The apostle says they slowly corrupt themselves and others, like leaven's slow spreading, by creeping into houses and leading families into lustful indulgences.

Iniquity-filled worshippers, like Cain, create their own traditions to teach and live by, rather than adhering to God's. Matthew 15 captures Jesus Christ rebuking the scribes and Pharisees for transgressing God's commands by their traditions. He says their worship is vain because they teach man-made commands instead of Scripture.[1641] Jewish leaders in Jesus' day were using the Oral Law, later organized and called the Mishna in 3rd century A.D., to interpret the written Law of Moses.[1642] Nearly all modern churches create their own Mishnas, called by-laws and creeds, being equally guilty of transgressing God's Word by their sinful traditions. Thus, you can say all Bible-denying, man-made religions and denominations started in Genesis through Cain's example.

No matter how religious a person seems, discern his heart to see if he believes the truth, which leads to the next attribute.

Secondly, iniquity workers do not abide in the truth and therefore despise it. Jesus describes Satan accordingly, saying he *"abode not in the truth."*[1643] Lucifer left his original heavenly position and Cain left his family. After murdering Abel, Cain was marked by God and *"went out from the presence of the Lord."*[1644] 1 John 2:18-19 says antichrists, iniquity workers, leave groups of true worshippers, saying, *"They went out from us, but they were not of us; for if they had been of us, they would no doubt have continued with us: but they went out, that they might be made manifest that they were not all of us."*

1641 Matthew 15:1-9
1642 "Mishna." *Encyclopedia Britannica*, https://www.britannica.com/topic/Mishna
1643 John 8:44
1644 Genesis 4:16

Concerning Cain's mark, you already learned the mark of the beast is received when a person rejects God's mark, the baptism of the Holy Ghost, for the final time. Paul calls this a reprobate mind in three instances.[1645]

Cain despised the truth about offerings, being wroth because God required blood rather than his fruit offering. Paul says the perishing, unrighteous ones despise the truth that could save them in 2 Thessalonians 2:10: *"And with all deceivableness of unrighteousness in them that perish; because they received not the love of the truth, that they might be saved."* You must love the truth and abide in it.

Third, the lawless deny the full power of the Holy Spirit. God's Spirit urged Cain to repent while reminding him the Spirit could empower him to rule over his brother if he only obeyed, but Cain denied the Spirit's work. Jesus explains in Matthew 7:21-27 that workers of iniquity accept temporary power to perform miracles in His name, but reject God's power to help them do His will in their daily habits. Acts 7:51 shows Stephen rebuking the Israeli high priest and Jewish council because they always resisted the Holy Ghost, despite their religious acts.

Paul says they're guilty of *"denying the power"*[1646] of godliness despite having its outward resemblance. Christianity's power is faith in Jesus' blood, as Hebrews 13:20-21 says *"the blood of the everlasting covenant"* makes *"you perfect in every good work to do his will, working in you that which is wellpleasing in his sight, through Jesus Christ."* The Holy Spirit is the life of Jesus' blood, so when you obey the Spirit in faith, you're accepting the power of the blood.

Fourth, Satan's children lie. Jesus says Satan is a liar and the father of lies in John 8:44. Cain lied to our holy God in Genesis 4:9, claiming he didn't know where Abel was after murdering him in a field. 2 Peter 2:19 declares false preachers promise hearers blessings they themselves never attain. Revelation 21:8 teaches unrepentant liars are cast alive into the lake of fire.

1645   Romans 1:28, 2 Timothy 3:8, Titus 1:16
1646   2 Timothy 3:5

Fifth, the wicked persecute and kill the righteous. Lucifer verbally accused heaven's leadership before waging his losing campaign to persecute angels and overthrow heaven. His accusations against believers continue without ceasing, day and night, according to Revelation 12:10.

Cain committed the first murder, rising up against his brother Abel and slaying in him a field. In Matthew 23:34-35, Jesus distinguishes the act of murder as a key trait when recognizing the serpent's seed, saying, *"That upon you may come all the righteous blood shed upon the earth, from the blood of righteous Abel unto the blood of Zacharias son of Barachias, whom ye slew between the temple and the altar."* Christ says the Pharisees are guilty of all the blood shed from Abel to Zacharias—that's compounded guilt from 4,000 years worth of martyrs!

While unrepentant murderers will surely perish, Jesus says many are in *"danger of hell fire"*[1647] for harboring unjust anger against others even if they never hurt anyone. This shows a sinner can murder someone in their heart even without committing the violent act.

WORLDY SORROW VERSUS GODLY SORROW, OR TRUE REPENTANCE

Sixth, Satan's seed sorrows over their sins but never repents. Paul calls this worldly sorrow and it needs its own section. Workers of iniquity feel bad after sinning, but never repent and change their behavior.

There's no record of wicked Cain expressing godly sorrow for murdering Abel, but he does express worldly sorrow after God curses him *"from the earth"*, sentencing him to become a fugitive and vagabond.[1648] The pitiful, lying, wretched Cain is only sorry for himself, complaining about his punishment for murder, having no remorse for his dead brother. Serpent seed only care for themselves.

In his second letter to the Corinthians Paul rejoices that his first letter made them sorrowful unto repentance. The apostle distinguishes between two kinds of sorrow—worldly and godly:

1647 Matthew 5:21-22
1648 Genesis 4:9-15

"Now I rejoice, not that ye were made sorry, but that ye sorrowed to repentance: for ye were made sorry after a godly manner, that ye might receive damage by us in nothing. For godly sorrow worketh repentance to salvation not to be repented of: but the sorrow of the world worketh death."[1649]

Sorrow is emotional pain or grief both sinners and saints experience after sinning. God builds this painful conviction into every human's spirit (called conscience) along with a soul-thirst to know God, so there are no excuses on Judgment Day. Souls who choose hell are worthy of its torment because they refused to respond correctly to their sorrow. Rather than forsaking their sin and accepting our loving God's forgiveness, they choose to hate holiness, fight against it, and blaspheme it. God strives with man, sometimes for decades, but if a man won't repent, the Lord gives him over to believe the lies he loves. Paul writes, *"And for this cause God shall send them strong delusion, that they should believe a lie: That they all might be damned who believed not the truth, but had pleasure in unrighteousness."*[1650]

Repentance is the goal of painful, emotional sorrow. True repentance is threefold: a change of mind and behavior, making amends for sin, and hating sin. The first son in Jesus' parable of two sons asked to work in their father's vineyard displays a change of mind and behavior.[1651] Initially, the first son refused his father's command to work, but repented and did the work. Zacchaeus models making amends for sins, as he pledges to restore fourfold the amount he'd gained by false accusation.[1652] Paul, saved and born again, admits hating his sins he sometimes committed.[1653] Jude 1:23 says to hate any sin-defilement in our lives: *"Hating even the garment spotted by the flesh."*

Worldly sorrow is deceiving because a sinner exudes emotion, feeling awful for his sins. But the threefold requirement for repentance, or

---

1649   2 Corinthians 7:9-10
1650   2 Thessalonians 2:11-12
1651   Matthew 21:28-31
1652   Luke 19:8-9
1653   Romans 7:14-15

the *"fruits meet for repentance,"*[1654] is never visible in his life. Sadly, I've witnessed worldly sorrow first hand, twice praying at an altar with an emotional man for a combined three hours, only to see him immediately return to his wickedness. Bible examples of worldly sorrow include:

- Pharaoh, called a vessel unto destruction, admitted his sin against the Lord on multiple occasions, even asking Moses to bless him, but continually hardened his heart after each admission of guilt (Exodus 8:15, 9:27, 10:16, 12:32, Romans 9:14-27).

- Balaam admitted his sin in going to Balak when he talked with the angel of the Lord, yet was permitted to go on account of his love for money and was later slain by Israel (Numbers 22:34, 31:8, 2 Peter 2:12-22).

- Achan acknowledged his sin against the Lord, but in His fierce anger was stoned and burnt by Israel (Joshua 7:16-26).

- King Saul admitted his sins of rebellion and stubbornness against God to the prophet Samuel, yet spent years hunting David's life until his repentance shortly before his death and salvation (1 Samuel 15:10-31, 26:21, 28:19). Ahab, upon hearing God's assessment of his abominable, idolatrous, and wicked life, temporarily humbled himself with fasting and rent clothes, but soon returned to his hatred for holiness and died in shame (1 Kings 21:25-29, 22:8, 29-38).

- Judas Iscariot repented and returned the 30 pieces of silver he earned for betraying Jesus, but went and hung himself, sealing his doom (Matthew 27:3-10, Acts 1:25).

1654   Matthew 3:8

HOW INIQUITY ORIGINATES IN AND FILLS HUMAN MINDS

As Lucifer's example teaches, iniquity originates in the heart, or mind. Your mind is your conscious state wherein thinking occurs and decisions are made, while your soul is your conscious nature.

Every soul begins with a God-given holy thirst[1655] to know God and long for His fellowship so men are without excuse on Judgment Day. Like a man ignoring his need to get help from a doctor, iniquity begins when a mind ignores its soul's need to know God. Iniquity workers fill their minds with evil instead of good, purposely starving their soul's hunger and thirst for holiness. When an iniquity-filled sinner makes a final determination he will never submit to his thirst for God's fellowship, God gives him over to a reprobate mind, also known as the mark of the beast.

Luke 12:16-21 records a rich man's decision to silence his soul's thirst for God. His crop harvest was so great he had to decide to store up treasure for himself or God. Sadly, he chose personal treasures. His mind said to his soul, "*Soul, thou hast much goods laid up for many years; take thine ease, eat, drink, and be merry.*" Jesus calls him a fool because he should have given his extra food to others, which would have resulted in heavenly treasure,[1656] rather than selfishly saving it for himself.

All acts of disobedience are done by evil spirits influencing human minds. Eve is the first human example of disobeying God's Word after letting her mind be influenced by the serpent's lie. Paul supports this in Ephesians 2:2, saying sinners walk according to Satan's fallen angels, or spirits "*that now work in the children of disobedience.*" Evil spirits cause humans to do evil works. As a believer, your spirit works by love and faith according to Galatians 5:6.

Ephesians 2:3 says we were all guilty, at one point, of "*fulfilling the desires of the flesh and of the mind; and were by nature the children of wrath, even as others.*" Your body, mind, and soul all have desires. You know the body and mind only have evil desires, so God's children crucify the

---

1655   Psalm 42:1-2, 63:1, 143:6, Romans 1:19-20
1656   Luke 12:33

desires of the body and mind and bring them into subjection[1657] to the holy desires of their souls. Galatians 5:24 reads, *"And they that are Christ's have crucified the flesh with the affections and lusts."*

People commit sins after yielding their minds to harbor and accept evil thoughts. Devils anoint and live in their minds. Indeed, their minds become a home for devils, which Paul warns us of in Ephesians 4:27 saying, *"Neither give place to the devil."* Then Paul calls demon-controlled minds *"strongholds"* in 2 Corinthians 10:4: *"For the weapons of our warfare are not carnal, but mighty through God to the pulling down of strong holds."* The wicked have spiritual castles or fortresses set up by demons in their minds. Sinners willingly let fallen angels live in and control their minds. They are guilty of thinking the Bible has errors, God doesn't heal anymore, sexual sins have no consequences, or God doesn't exist. The mighty weapon of God's Word is the only power that can bring down these fortresses.

After a person sins once, it's easier to commit the same sin the next time. Sinning becomes a habit. Evil habits are from evil spirits, just as the opposite is true—godly habits are from the Holy Spirit.

Matthew 12:25-30 illustrates godly habits being spoiled or ruined by devils entering once-strong minds. The Lord likens a believer to a man dwelling in his house stocked with goods. Demons then enter the house and steal the goods. Christ is saying a *"strong"* believer can possess goods or habits of His kingdom, but have those habits stolen by opening the door of his mind to lies and deceitful thoughts. Paul urges us not to give heed, or open the door, to *"seducing spirits, and doctrines of devils."*[1658] Don't allow yourself to think evil thoughts.

Jesus teaches the strong man, or faith, is bound by a devil and then the house is plundered. A devil who constantly robs believers today is the evil spirit of fear. 2 Timothy 1:7 teaches us fear causes weakness, hatred, and mind trouble because God's Spirit gives the opposite: *"power...love, and ...a sound mind."* The fear demon paralyzes faith,

---

1657   1 Corinthians 9:27
1658   1 Timothy 4:1

robbing your confidence in God, like Israel's fear of the giants while at Kadesh-Barnea. Numbers 14 shows the evil report of the 10 spies caused fear to spread like wild fire among the Israelis, despite Caleb and Joshua's valiant attempt to raise faith. It was too late—fear demons had already spoiled Israel's spiritual goods. Friend, don't allow Satan to steal your confidence, joy, strength, song, victory, or faith.

Imagine every evil thought Satan brings you as a box of poisonous snakes a delivery man wants you to sign for. In the natural, it's your American right to deny any package sent to your door. Just because someone sent you death doesn't mean you have to accept it. If the box is left at your door, don't bring it inside. Take it to the burn pile and ignite it in Jesus' name, just as Paul shook the serpent off himself and cast it into the fire. Satan is sending lies to billions today and when he sends you death, turn him down by quoting God's Word. Resist the devil and he will flee.[1659]

Keep your mind free from corruption, or defilement, as Paul says in 2 Corinthians 11:3. Give your mind over completely to Jesus and His Words. Speak the truth in love and season your words with grace rather than bitterness. He says *"men of corrupt minds"* are *"destitute of truth,"* specifically resist truth, and hold perverted disputes.[1660] Renewing your mind is the way to keep corrupt thoughts from ruling your mind.[1661]

You can't help from thinking evil thoughts but you can cast them away. Like a farmer, you can't keep birds from nesting in your barn, but you can drive them out once you're aware of their presence. 2 Corinthians 10:5-6 teaches your God-given control over thoughts will lead to obedience: *"Casting down imaginations, and every high thing that exalteth itself against the knowledge of God, and bringing into captivity every thought to the obedience of Christ; And having in a readiness to revenge all disobedience, when your obedience is fulfilled."*

Revelation 12:10-11 teaches you overcome Satan by two things: Jesus' blood and your verbal testimony. Jesus' blood provides redemption

1659　James 4:7
1660　1 Timothy 6:5, 2 Timothy 3:8
1661　Romans 12:2, Ephesians 4:23

and total forgiveness when you confess your sins.[1662] Your verbal testimony is speaking or swinging God's Word-sword against Satan and his demons. Like Jesus cutting down Satan's temptations in Matthew 4 by repeatedly saying, *"It is written"*, you cut down Satan's traps by obeying the Word and rebuking Satan. Eve failed in this, the battlefield of the mind, but you can overcome. The only way you know you're an overcomer is by overcoming, so daily confess your sins and defeat Satan by speaking God's Word and casting down his deceitful lies. It doesn't matter what you have to overcome as long as you know how to overcome because God's Word is the greatest power in the universe.

Stockpiles of Scriptures say the evil are full of darkness, meaning their minds are totally full of evil thoughts. Peter condemns these beastly-minded sinners, saying they have *"eyes full of adultery, and that cannot cease from sin; beguiling unstable souls: an heart they have exercised with covetous practices; cursed children."*[1663] They fill their minds with debauchery and habitually sin. If you're filled with a love for God's Word, you'll serve Him, but if you hate truth, you'll be full of darkness and serve the world according to Jesus:

> *"But if thine eye be evil, thy whole body shall be full of darkness. If therefore the light that is in thee be darkness, how great is that darkness! No man can serve two masters: for either he will hate the one, and love the other; or else he will hold to the one, and despise the other. Ye cannot serve God and mammon."*[1664]

Paul describes the minds of homosexuals in a similar manner, saying their minds knew God's Word but refused to retain it. Therefore, God gave them over to a rejected, or reprobate mind, being filled with all unrighteousness:

> *"For this cause God gave them up unto vile affections: for even their women did change the natural use into that which*

1662 Ephesians 1:7, Colossians 1:14, 2:13, 1 John 1:9
1663 2 Peter 2:12-14
1664 Matthew 6:23-24

is against nature: And likewise also the men, leaving the natural use of the woman, burned in their lust one toward another; men with men working that which is unseemly, and receiving in themselves that recompence of their error which was meet. And even as they did not like to retain God in their knowledge, God gave them over to a reprobate mind, to do those things which are not convenient; Being filled with all unrighteousness, fornication, wickedness, covetousness, maliciousness; full of envy, murder, debate, deceit, malignity; whisperers, Backbiters, haters of God, despiteful, proud, boasters, inventors of evil things, disobedient to parents, Without understanding, covenantbreakers, without natural affection, implacable, unmerciful: Who knowing the judgment of God, that they which commit such things are worthy of death, not only do the same, but have pleasure in them that do them."[1665]

THE INIQUITY-FILLED SCRIBES, PHARISEES, AND SADDUCEES

Lucifer and Cain were religious but their acts were eventually meaningless. Their iniquity-filled hearts hid behind religious masks until their true colors were manifest. Fast forward to Jesus' earthly ministry and the scribes, Pharisees, and Sadducees repeat the same religious vanity.

Two portions of Scripture highlight the depths of iniquity in these groups: Jesus' Sermon on the Mount, and His eight-woes-discourse against them in the week leading up to His crucifixion.

Matthew chapters 5-7 contain the most details on Jesus' Sermon on the Mount, partially taught in private to His disciples, but also to a great audience.[1666] In chapter 5, Jesus' beatitudes emphasize blessings upon spiritual purity. His disciples were to keep and teach His commands in sincerity and their righteousness was to exceed that of the Pharisees, the legalist, popular religious party of the day. Our Lord magnifies Moses' Law, giving insight on anger, mental lust, adultery, swearing, resisting not evil, giving, and loving enemies.

1665   Romans 1:26-32
1666   Matthew 5:1-2, Luke 6:17-20, 7:1

Matthew chapter 6 records Jesus' three attacks on religious hypocrites residing in Jewish synagogues, which would include the aforementioned Pharisees. Messiah blasts hypocritical alms giving, praying, and fasting, urging believers to do more secret service in God's sight instead of public service in man's sight. Public worship performed for man's praise yields no heavenly reward. Jesus shows the religious hypocrites really serve "*mammon*", or riches, and not God. True worshippers seek first Jesus' kingdom rather than basic human needs.

In Matthew chapter 7, Jesus' fourth hypocritical charge is on those who judge others despite being guilty of the same sins. Our Lord promises to hear our prayers and proclaims the Golden Rule fulfills "*the law and the prophets.*"

Chapter 7 ends with a sobering, concise contrast between true and false religion. Jesus says there are two gates, two ways, two kinds of prophets, two trees with separate fruits, and two kinds of builders using two different foundations. The two builders—workers of iniquity and wise workers—express the difference between sayers versus doers. Iniquity-filled builders give God lip service, saying "*Lord, Lord*", but fail to do God's will. Wise workers perform God's will, as Chapter 11 of this book pursues in depth.

The few wise workers seek, find, and enter the strait, or narrow gate, leading to eternal life. Most people choose the easy-to-find broad way as workers of iniquity, whose end is destruction in the lake of fire. Both types of prophets look like sheep, but the workers of iniquity are greedy wolves inwardly. They're also likened to corrupt trees known by their corrupt fruits, or sinful deeds.

Verses 21-23 reveal the shocking truth that wolf-preachers temporarily have God's genuine anointing for legitimate miracles and signs, but spend most of their lives in disobedience and habitual sin. Jesus specifically denounces their works, as they did not keep God's laws. Proof of knowing Jesus is obeying Him and working righteousness.

In verses 24-27, Jesus says you build your life upon a solid rock by hearing and doing His commands. Chapter 5 of this book identifies this rock as genuine, divine faith. Wisely listening to Jesus helps you add virtue to your faith, then knowledge, temperance, patience, godliness, brotherly kindness, and charity. Spiritual rains and floods cannot destroy this kind of life. In contrast, a life built on loose, sinful, sandy living comes to desolation in the storms of life. Great is the fall of the lying testimonies of religious wolves, matching the great falling away predicted in the end days when the Antichrist is revealed.[1667]

Moving on to Matthew 23, you read Jesus' scathing discourse of eight woes against the scribes and Pharisees, one chapter after He silenced their foolish questions. Observe Jesus in verse 28 saying they are full of hypocrisy and iniquity. That said, Messiah calls them children of hell, serpents, and a generation of vipers.[1668] They are the demon-possessed, spiritual seed of the serpent.

A woe is an exclamation of grief in the Greek, and Jesus' eight woes for their hypocrisy include:

- Woe for not entering Jesus' kingdom and keeping others out (23:13)
- Woe for devouring widows' money and offering long, pretend prayers (23:14)
- Woe for worldwide travel to make doubly-wicked, hell-bound converts (23:15)
- Woe for swearing or making invalid oaths while exalting religious gifts for selfish gain (23:16-22)
- Woe for straining over or overemphasizing details of commands while omitting the *"weightier matters of the law, judgment, mercy, and faith"* (23:23-24)
- Woe for dressing clean and holy while being inwardly dirty, full of robbery and incontinence (23:25)
- Woe for being like cleaned, whited grave stones, yet being full of death, uncleanness, hypocrisy and iniquity (23:27-28)

1667   2 Thessalonians 2:3
1668   Matthew 23:15, 33

- Woe for honoring dead prophets yet disobeying them and being children of their murderers (23:29-33)

Jesus ends this discourse by promising to send His true servants—prophets, wise men, and scribes—to these hypocrites, some of whom they will kill. As always, the guilt of bloodshed would be upon the workers of iniquity. Our Lord laments for the entire city of Jerusalem, whom God tried to bring close to Him, but they would not love Him back.

"THERE THEY CRUCIFIED HIM" AND CRUCIFYING JESUS AFRESH

Four words in Luke 23:33—*"there they crucified him"*—hold depths of meaning to the mystery of iniquity. In context, the words reveal the extreme wickedness workers of iniquity stoop to:

- *"there"*: in Jerusalem, the city of God, the most holy place on earth
- *"they"*: the world's most powerful government, Rome, in agreement with Israelis, the most holy people on earth
- *"crucified"*: the world's most gruesome, torturous, painful death
- *"him"*: the world's most holy, innocent, perfect Person—Jesus

You read it right—the most religious people commit the most wicked crimes against the most holy Person they claim to love. Israel, God's own people, came to this truth-hating condition by sin's slow-spreading and all encompassing effects. Pride, covetousness, and complete spiritual corruption overcame Israel's leaders and people.

Shockingly, the Hebrews author teaches Christ is constantly crucified *"afresh"* by individuals who publicly disgrace Jesus. Did you know Jesus is crucified daily? Not physically, but spiritually, because workers of iniquity disobey truth and teach others to do the same.

Hebrews 6:1-8 explains Christ is presently crucified by ones who temporarily experience God's blessings only to publicly disobey Jesus' teachings at a later time. Verse 6 says apostates *"crucify to themselves the Son of God afresh, and put him to an open shame."* In God's eyes, these rebellious ones are like thorn bushes who rejoice in receiving rain, but produce sharp, prickly thorns. Likewise, the religious lawless enjoy the blessings and feelings of God's Spirit, but commit sharp, despicable iniquities. They are like Judas, publicly kissing Jesus in betrayal for selfish benefit.

Hebrews 10:29 describes their crucifixion of truth as smashing it under their feet: *"Of how much sorer punishment, suppose ye, shall he be thought worthy, who hath trodden under foot the Son of God, and hath counted the blood of the covenant, wherewith he was sanctified, an unholy thing, and hath done despite unto the Spirit of grace?"* Sore punishments await those who deny the Spirit's work of continuous sanctification. God's gracious Holy Spirit leads us to a sanctified life; not a sinful, disobedient life.

This proves one can temporarily receive God's grace but then fail to let it continue its cleansing work. Grace never fails believers, but workers of iniquity can fail grace by rejecting it: *"Follow peace with all men, and holiness, without which no man shall see the Lord: Looking diligently lest any man fail of the grace of God; lest any root of bitterness springing up trouble you, and thereby many be defiled."*[1669]

Multitudes of preachers currently crucify the effects of the Holy Spirit by denying the true interpretation of God's Word. Yes, the ones who mention the cross are often the enemies of the cross, for their god is their belly and wallet.[1670] They deny the power needed to live a holy life, giving license for immorality while presently an outwardly clean and wealthy appearance. Jude 1:4 foretold the wicked would turn grace into lawlessness. Paul says, *"from such turn away."*[1671]

1669   Hebrews 12:14-15
1670   Philippians 3:18-19
1671   2 Timothy 3:5

Real Christians do experience daily crucifixion, dying daily like Paul,[1672] to their selfish desires. Jesus urgently requires daily cross-carrying in Luke 9:23. Paul says proof of you belonging to Christ is that you crucify and mortify the deeds and lusts of the flesh, and the world.[1673] You'll either crucify God's Word or crucify your selfish lusts with God's Word. Christians kill their own sinful wills so they can perform God's will.

THE MYSTERY OF INIQUITY CONTINUED WORKING IN PAUL'S DAY THROUGH MANY ANTICHRISTS

Jesus' iniquity-filled religious opponents succeeded in killing Him, but He resurrected and filled His followers with the Holy Ghost and power. Christ's followers have battled the workers of iniquity ever since.

Paul says the mystery of iniquity—a sin-loving, religious guise—was already working at the time he wrote 2 Thessalonians, around 51 A.D. He said it would continue until heading up in that wicked person, the Antichrist, as 2 Thessalonians 2:7-8 proclaims: *"For the mystery of iniquity doth already work: only he who now letteth will let, until he be taken out of the way. And then shall that Wicked be revealed, whom the Lord shall consume with the spirit of his mouth, and shall destroy with the brightness of his coming."*

A few antichrist doctrines Paul rebuked include a legalistic requirement for circumcision,[1674] declaring the rapture already occurred,[1675] requiring abstinence from marriage, and meat eating.[1676] Paul goes as far as saying the iniquity-filled church goers hate sound doctrine, heaping to themselves false teachers who tickle their ears and turn them from truth to believe fables.[1677]

Nearly 50 years later in 100 A.D., the apostle John gave the workers of iniquity a new label—antichrists. 1 John 2:18 declares, *"Little children, it is the last time: and as ye have heard that antichrist shall come, even now*

1672 1 Corinthians 15:31
1673 Romans 8:12, Galatians 5:24, 6:13-15, Colossians 3:5
1674 Galatians 2:1-5
1675 2 Timothy 2:16-18
1676 1 Timothy 4:1-5
1677 2 Timothy 4:3-4

are there many antichrists; whereby we know that it is the last time." In the Greek Lexicon, antichrists means adversaries of the Messiah.

John continues describing antichrists, saying they eventually leave true churches, deny Jesus is the Christ, deny the Father and Son, and fail to confess Jesus Christ is come in the flesh.[1678] The world's 1.5 billion Muslims,[1679] 1 billion Hindus,[1680] and millions of Buddhists, atheists, agnostics all deny Jesus is the Christ, proving they are antichrists. But more Scripture needs examined to see how many of the 2 billion[1681] professing Christians are antichrists as well.

RECOGNIZING ANTICHRISTS BY THEIR HELL-DESERVING AND NON-KINGDOM WORKS

Antichrists abound today, as Paul foretold their drastic increase—waxing worse and worse—but promised the *"holy scriptures"* would make us *"wise unto salvation"* in 2 Timothy 3:13-15.

In addition to Jesus' previously mentioned descriptions of the lawless, you recognize modern antichrists by their hell-deserving and non-kingdom works. Revelation 21:7-8, 2 Peter 2:9-22, and Jude 1:1-25 list specific sins of hell-bound souls. You'll see some overlap in the lists and I'm leaving repeats for emphasis. Of course, all these sins can be repented of so souls can be saved, but Jesus says few will choose the narrow way leading to eternal life.

In Revelation 21, John says *"the fearful, and unbelieving, and the abominable, and murderers, and whoremongers, and sorcerers, and idolaters, and all liars, shall have their part in the lake which burneth with fire and brimstone."*

Peter's second epistle lists the following hell-deserving acts: walking in fleshly lusts, despising government, being self-willed, speaking evil of good, adultery, sin addiction, coveting, loving money, forsaking the right way, serving corruption, unbridled lusts, and other pollutions of the world.

1678   1 John 2:19, 22, 4:3, 2 John 1:7
1679   "Islam." *Encyclopedia Britannica*, https://www.britannica.com/topic/Islam
1680   "Hinduism." *Encyclopedia Britannica*, https://www.britannica.com/topic/Hinduism
1681   "Christianity." *Encyclopedia Britannica*, https://www.britannica.com/topic/Christianity

Jude's powerful chapter tallies the following damning acts: turning grace into lawlessness, fornication, sinfully defiling one's flesh, despising dominion, speaking evil of dignities, corrupting one's self, greed, not fearing God, shameful violence, wandering, ungodly deeds, hard speeches, murmuring, complaining, walking after one's own lusts, and mocking.

Antichrists act in opposition to the kingdom of God, and Paul provides three texts to identify their non-kingdom works to eliminate any confusion about who is in Jesus' kingdom and who isn't: 1 Corinthians 6:9-11, Galatians 5:19-26, and Ephesians 5:1-8. Greek definitions in parentheses follow unfamiliar words to provide understanding.

In the Corinthians text, Paul says *"be not deceived"*—the following unrighteous works of iniquity will not inherit the kingdom of God: fornicators (sex before marriage), idolaters, adulterers (sex with someone other than your first and living spouse), effeminate (child molesters), abusers of themselves with mankind (homosexuals), thieves, covetous, drunkards, revilers (complainers), and extortioners (robbers). Verse 11 rejoices believers' hearts, though, as it magnifies Jesus' cleansing power from the guilt of these sins: *"And such were some of you: but ye are washed, but ye are sanctified, but ye are justified in the name of the Lord Jesus, and by the Spirit of our God."*

In Galatians 5, Paul says people who commit the following sins, without repentance, *"shall not inherit the kingdom of God"*: adultery, fornication, uncleanness (lustful, luxurious living), lasciviousness (unbridled lust), idolatry, witchcraft (which includes drug use), hatred, variance (contention), emulations (rivalry, jealousy), wrath, strife (electioneering for office), seditions (divisions), heresies (man-made tenets), envyings, murders, drunkenness, revellings (late night parties), and such like.

Paul's Ephesians letter warns the following acts give one no *"inheritance in the kingdom of Christ and of God"*: fornication, uncleanness (lustful, luxurious living), covetousness (greedy desire to have more), filthiness (immoralities), foolish talking, jesting (evil humor), whoremongering (all unlawful sex), unclean persons (evil thoughts and acts), idolaters, and speakers of vain words (devoid of truth).

The reality is most church members are antichrist, following anti-christ preachers who legalize and commit the preceding list of sins. Many antichrist preachers flaunt their greed, adulteries, and sins publicly, putting Christ to an *"open shame."*[1682] Flee from any preacher and church that condones any of the sins you just read. Just as Jesus attacked every aspect of worship of the Pharisees and scribes, the Holy Spirit rebukes every worship aspect of modern workers of iniquity because they are demon-influenced. Only evil works flow from their evil hearts. Corrupt trees produce only corrupt fruit.

Antichrist preachers build their own self-serving kingdoms and ultimately destroy men's souls. Recall Chapter 7's teaching about the four horse riders in the first four seals of Revelation 6:1-8. The horse riders are the selfsame person: the antichrist spirit. His four step process for kingdom building and dominion is conquering through deception, killing, money-capturing, and world-wide soul destruction. Demon-filled preachers build their kingdoms through the same steps. First, they deceive with false doctrine, allowing listeners to indulge in their sinful lusts. Second, they kill the reputations of true preachers and Christians. Third, they elicit millions of dollars in financial support from their blind followers. Megachurches and mega bank accounts soon come afterwards. Fourth, they lead their worshippers into the unredeemable condition of having reprobate minds. All blind preach-ers will lead their blind followers into union with the Mother Harlot, the Roman Catholic Church.

Remember, God has saved preachers and church members in every organization, but they are few and far between. Of the saved, most are foolish, denying the full revelation in Scripture, as Chapter 4 details 15 of Paul's simple, sound doctrines most churches deny in the section "Judging Christian Groups and Denominations By Their Fruits." Look how religious Catholics are and how beautiful their churches stand in architectural majesty, yet many of their teachings are abominable. The same can be applied to many Lutherans, Methodists, Baptists,

---

1682 Hebrews 6:6

Pentecostals, and independents. Only a small, wise group, will believe and live all Jesus' New Testament commands.

ABOUNDING INIQUITY IN THE END TIMES

In the years leading up to Jesus' return in the rapture, iniquity will abound to its greatest measure in the antichrist groups, causing genuine love for God to be extremely rare. Jesus announces this in Matthew 24:11-13: *"And many false prophets shall rise, and shall deceive many. And because iniquity shall abound, the love of many shall wax cold. But he that shall endure unto the end, the same shall be saved."* Paul gives the same warning in 2 Timothy 3:13: *"But evil men and seducers shall wax worse and worse, deceiving, and being deceived."* America's churches work the worst iniquity, as Revelation 13:11-18 shows their future union with the government in issuing the official mark of the beast, which will unleash massive death upon the whole world.

Ezekiel 16:49 and Revelation 3:14-19 show Israel and modern Christians falling into iniquity by the same means: pride, abundance of goods, and idleness. Laodiceans are lukewarm and prideful, saying they have no more need of God due to their riches and increased goods. Let us be hungry and thirsty for more divine righteousness while busily working for the kingdom of God.

Chapter 12's section called "The Conditions or 'Times and Seasons' of the Rapture" provides further description of the times we are living in so you can know how to escape antichrists.

THE TRAIL OF THE SERPENT AND SPIRITUAL TWINS

You can trace "The Trail of the Serpent"—a phrase used by Larkin—from Eden in Genesis all the way to Gog and Magog in Revelation. Satan's spirit, the antichrist spirit, closely observes, then insincerely imitates the true believer's behavior in order to deceive the masses. Spiritual twins emerge off the pages of the Bible—one is God's child, the other is Satan's.

The Lord Jesus Christ provides two proofs of this "battle of the twins" beginning in Matthew 13:24-30 and 36-43 with His Wheat and

Tares parable. Tares, poisonous to eat, closely resemble wheat and are only distinguished by their failure to bow at harvest time. This signifies their defiance against and failure to obey God's Word. Tares live among the wheat, just like the wicked can worship right alongside the righteous.

Jesus' second mention of spiritual twins is Matthew 24:24: *"For there shall arise false Christs, and false prophets, and shall shew great signs and wonders; insomuch that, if it were possible, they shall deceive the very elect."* False Christs are temporarily anointed by the genuine Holy Spirit but their heretical teachings and sin-loving lives reveal their true seed of discrepancy. Paul says the reason God allows evil men to spread heresies is to reveal the two distinct groups of the twins in 1 Corinthians 11:19: *"For there must be also heresies among you, that they which are approved may be made manifest among you."* Only the elect children of God will not be deceived by the antichrist because they are born again of the Spirit of Truth, the Holy Ghost.

The evil twins always exhibit the six iniquity attributes—vain religion, rejecting and despising the truth, denying the full power of the Spirit, lying, persecuting and killing the righteous, and worldly sorrow. Jesus uses the evil twins' fifth attribute, murderous, to trace the serpent's trail from Cain's murder of Abel to the Pharisees of His lifetime:

> *"Wherefore, behold, I send unto you prophets, and wise men,*
> *and scribes: and some of them ye shall kill and crucify; and*
> *some of them shall ye scourge in your synagogues, and persecute*
> *them from city to city: That upon you may come all the righteous*
> *blood shed upon the earth, from the blood of righteous Abel unto*
> *the blood of Zacharias son of Barachias, whom ye slew between*
> *the temple and the altar."*[1683]

Notice Christ assuring us the serpent's seed would keep murdering even after His ascension to heaven. Thus, throughout mankind's 6,000 year history, the Trail of the Serpent is forever stained with the blood of Jewish and Christian martyrs.

1683   Matthew 23:34-35

Watch the serpent silently slither through history, beginning in heaven and then moving to earth. The first set of twins were Lucifer and Michael. Both were exalted, holy angels until iniquity caused Lucifer to battle against his twin in a losing effort. On earth, the first set of twins was the Tree of Life, Jesus' Spirit, and the Tree of Knowledge of Good and Evil, Satan. The serpent and Adam were the next twins, but Eve's sin in longing for the serpent rather than her own husband began mankind's sin-slavery. Next came Cain and Abel, both offering worship to God, but in jealousy Cain killed his twin.

Cain's tare-children multiply with such abundance that God destroys nearly all living things with a flood. Shem and Ham, Noah's sons, are the next set of spiritual twins, as Ham was cursed by his father, but Shem's descendant was Abraham, the father of the faith. Abraham was separated out of the remnant of tares from the Tower of Babel movement, and you see twins rise again in his grandchildren: Esau and Jacob.

Esau, like Cain, profanes God by forsaking his firstborn rights to spiritual leadership while Jacob eagerly snatches the birthright, blessing, and connection to the Messiah. God's true prophet Moses, next battled multiple tares, including Jannes, Jambres, Balaam, Korah, and Dathan. Balaam, despite accurately prophesying through his knowledge on how contacting God, proved he was a tare when he lured thousands of Israelis into sexual immorality at Baalpeor. Achan, Joshua's twin, showed his tare-nature by lustfully harboring forbidden treasures while dwelling with Israel's victorious army.

The serpent's trail leads to the days of Israel's kings. Micaiah, God's true prophet, stood upon truth against 400 tare-prophets anointed with a lying spirit. The same lying spirit anointed the false prophet Hananiah in the days of Israel's final king, Zedekiah, whom the wheat-prophet Jeremiah withstood.[1684]

The New Testament opens with the serpent slithering into its pages, as John the Baptist identifies and rebukes the generation of vipers (Pharisees and Sadducees) who attended his services, but refused his

---

1684 Jeremiah 28:1-15

baptism unto repentance.[1685] In like manner, Jesus chides the same religious, impersonating-tares, saying *"ye serpents, ye generation of vipers"* in Matthew 23:33.

As a prefigure to the future, final person of the Pope-Antichrist, Judas Isacariot is Jesus' twin, temporarily serving with Christ in the power of the Spirit for over three years until his Satan-filled heart of iniquity betrays Christ for 30 pieces of silver. Observe Satan silently slithering into Jesus' inner circle. Jesus was incarnate God and Judas became incarnate Satan.

Both Peter and Paul contended with evil spiritual twins. God's Spirit helped Peter discern Ananias' Satan-filled heart that sprang up shortly after the outpouring of the Holy Ghost baptism in Acts 5:3. Paul, like Christ and Judas, was betrayed and forsaken by Demas, who loved this present world as proof God's love was not in his heart.[1686] The apostle John was falsely accused and rejected by prideful Diotrephes,[1687] who loved *"to have the preeminence among them."*

Finally, you reach the prophesied end of the serpent in the Book of Revelation. Chapter 7 in this book shows how the serpent morphed into an antichrist horse rider, violently riding through the Times of the Gentiles, or Seven Church Ages. Revelation chapters 19 and 20 show Satan's final two attempts at conquering Jesus' kingdom in the battles of Armageddon and Gog and Magog, respectively.

Revelation 19 finds Satan possessing the pope's body and reigning as the world-flattering and world-ruling Antichrist during the Tribulation. He gathers nations, kings, and captains for the Battle of Armageddon as a sort of rematch between Satan's army and Michael's, but this time Christ leads heaven's invasion of earth. Jesus' army of white horse riders breaks through the skies and the Sword-Word from Jesus' mouth destroys the Pope-Antichrist's armies. Birds eat until full with the flesh of these reprobates. The beast (spirit of Rome) and false prophet (Antichrist-Pope) are both cast alive into the lake of fire.

1685 Matthew 3:7, Luke 7:30
1686 2 Timothy 4:10, 1 John 2:15
1687 3 John 1:9-10

Revelation 20 shows Satan's final, climatic attempt at defeating heaven's king, King Jesus. After 1,000 years of confinement, the old serpent is loosed from the bottomless pit, deceiving and gathering all nations, whose number is *"as the sand of the sea."* Christ's Jerusalem-dwelling bride finds herself completely surrounded and outnumbered, but her help comes from above. Heavenly fire descends and burns the wicked. Psalm 57:3 rings true: *"He shall send from heaven, and save me from the reproach of him that would swallow me up. Selah. God shall send forth his mercy and his truth."* Satan is tossed into the lake of fire to be continually tormented day and night. With Satan tormented in the lake of fire, the mystery of iniquity is defeated and brought to an end. All accounts will be settled—with the impossibility to lie or deny truth in an act of iniquity—at the White Throne Judgment.

THE REWARDS FOR RECEIVING THE REVELATION OF INIQUITY

Those who receive the revelation of the mystery of iniquity enjoy three closely related rewards. The first is the blessing of your iniquities being forgiven through confession of sins with faith in Christ's cleansing blood. God graciously revealed to you the dangers of iniquity and you've repented. Romans 4:7 excites believers, saying, *"Blessed are they whose iniquities are forgiven, and whose sins are covered."* David knew this blessedness, expressing it in Psalm 32:5: *"I acknowledged my sin unto thee, and mine iniquity have I not hid. I said, I will confess my transgressions unto the LORD; and thou forgavest the iniquity of my sin. Selah."*

Christians know how to genuinely repent from sins, admitting their sins while confessing them to Father God, Who guarantees pardon: *"If we confess our sins, he is faithful and just to forgive us our sins, and to cleanse us from all unrighteousness."*[1688] For certain, Jesus was sent to bless you in turning you away from your iniquities according to Acts 3:26: *"Unto you first God, having raised up his Son Jesus, sent him to bless you, in turning away every one of you from his iniquities."*

1688 1 John 1:9

Secondly, you have the reward of a purified soul after obeying God's commands. Iniquity makes one forever disobey, but you obey God and feel clean down in your soul as 1 Peter 1:22 expresses: *"Seeing ye have purified your souls in obeying the truth through the Spirit unto unfeigned love of the brethren, see that ye love one another with a pure heart fervently."*

A final reward is having the testimony of forever departing from iniquity as an overcomer. Paul says departing from iniquity is God's foundational seal for His children in 2 Timothy 2:19: *"Nevertheless the foundation of God standeth sure, having this seal, The Lord knoweth them that are his. And, Let every one that nameth the name of Christ depart from iniquity."* Everyone has two choices: either depart from iniquity or depart from Jesus. Christians choose to depart from all iniquity—not some. Jesus *"gave himself for us, that he might redeem us from all iniquity, and purify unto himself a peculiar people, zealous of good works."*[1689]

The key to the revelation of the mystery of iniquity is Christians are constantly conformed to a holier life, being guided into all truth by the inward dwelling of the Holy Ghost. This is the law of the Holy Spirit—making you progressively live more holy, like Christ lived. Workers of iniquity are lawless, becoming progressively more wicked as Romans 6:19 teaches: *"I speak after the manner of men because of the infirmity of your flesh: for as ye have yielded your members servants to uncleanness and to iniquity unto iniquity; even so now yield your members servants to righteousness unto holiness."*

THE CONSEQUENCES FOR REJECTING THE REVELATION OF INIQUITY

There are at least four consequences for rejecting the revelation of the mystery of iniquity. A first consequence for condoning iniquity is suffering loss of spiritual positions and blessings during life on earth. 1 Samuel chapters 2 and 3 record God judging Eli's house for his iniquity. Eli was a the priest, a descendant of Ithamar, one of Aaron's two remaining sons, along with Eleazar. Rather than removing his disobedient and lustful

1689 Titus 2:14

sons from priestly work, Eli let them continue ministering, honoring his sons above God. The priestly duties eventually moved solely to Eleazar's descendants rather that Eli's. Just look around you to see scores of men and women who've fallen from spiritual leadership positions due to unconfessed iniquities.

Israel's unconfessed iniquity caused her slow, violent, and painful removal from the Promised Land. Lamentations details this, as chapter 4:6-10 shows iniquity caused the removal of God's blessings. Iniquity brought death by sword, starvation, and more. Verse 6 reads, *"For the punishment of the iniquity of the daughter of my people is greater than the punishment of the sin of Sodom, that was overthrown as in a moment, and no hands stayed on her."*

Just as the saved thief on the cross in Jesus' day, there are many today who commit iniquity, but can repent and be saved moments before death. They'll have no reward other than being granted eternal life at the White Throne. God's long-suffering kept these saved from never accepting a reprobate mind, thereby keeping them from blaspheming the Holy Ghost. Like the saved thief, they admit their sins and confess the purity of God's Word in their dying moments, and will join the surprised, saved sheep on Jesus' right hand spoken of in Matthew 25:31-46.

Second, rejecting this revelation leads a reprobate mind to speak blasphemy against the Holy Ghost. In the Greek, blaspheme means "to speak reproachfully, rail at, revile." Jesus says blasphemy, or criticism of the Holy Ghost is an unforgivable sin:

> *"Wherefore I say unto you, All manner of sin and blasphemy shall be forgiven unto men: but the blasphemy against the Holy Ghost shall not be forgiven unto men. And whosoever speaketh a word against the Son of man, it shall be forgiven him: but whosoever speaketh against the Holy Ghost, it shall not be forgiven him, neither in this world, neither in the world to come."*[1690]

1690 Matthew 12:31-32

Paul witnessed envy and hate-filled Jews in Antioch blaspheme his preaching in Acts 13:44-48. The apostle said the Jews' blasphemous words judged themselves unworthy of everlasting life, causing him to focus on preaching to Gentiles only.

Angry, vile criticizers of full-gospel, Holy Ghost preaching likewise blaspheme God's Spirit today, sealing their eternal judgments while living on earth. No doubt they'll continue to live in lustful, luxurious pleasures, but their souls remain dead while alive. 1 Timothy 5:6 describes this consequence of being alive naturally, but dead to the Holy Spirit: *"But she that liveth in pleasure is dead while she liveth."*

A third consequence is torment in the Tribulation for workers of iniquity who live past the day and hour of the rapture. Once the Tribulation period begins, they'll suffer God's wrath for rejecting and crucifying the spiritual effects of Jesus' blood. Disobeying the gospel yields the flaming fire of God's vengeance. 2 Thessalonians 1:8 says, *"In flaming fire taking vengeance on them that know not God, and that obey not the gospel of our Lord Jesus Christ."*

Finally, a fourth consequence is the most dreadful of all—the ultimate damnation in the lake of fire. Before the indescribable damnation, though, is the shock workers of iniquity will experience at the Day of Judgment, the White Throne. Matthew 7:21-23 and 25:41-46 detail this shock, as the first text says many will plead with Jesus for salvation by reminding Him of the miracles they worked in His name during their life. But Jesus will say, *"I never knew you: depart from me, ye that work iniquity."* You learn Jesus sees through their hypocrisy of knowing enough about God to perform miracles, but failing to simply repent from sins and lovingly obey Jesus.

The second text reveals how workers of iniquity focused on satisfying their own sinful lusts rather than serving the needy through six acts: feeding the hungry, giving drink to the thirsty, housing strangers, clothing the naked, visiting the sick, and visiting prisoners. The simplest acts of service would have been enough to gain eternal bliss, but the self-centered lawless despised the needy and exalted self.

The Lord Jesus Christ warns the religious leaders who worked iniquity will receive the greatest damnation in Matthew 23:14: *"Woe unto you, scribes and Pharisees, hypocrites! for ye devour widows' houses, and for a pretence make long prayer: therefore ye shall receive the greater damnation."* The lake of fire's worst punishments are reserved for religious deceivers who failed to enter into salvation, kept others out, and failed to warn others as Ezekiel 33:6-9 and James 3:1 echo.

The congregations and other hearers who heard but rejected righteousness will also suffer worse than others. In Matthew 10:13-15, Jesus says those cities who rejected His disciples' preaching will suffer worse than the violent, homosexual gangbangers from Sodom and Gomorrha.

It's a saddening, sobering thought to picture billions upon billions of souls tormented in the lake of fire and brimstone day and night, *"for ever and ever,"* in the presence of the holy angels and the Lamb[1691] all because of their unconfessed iniquity. How easily torment could have been avoided by simple, humble repentance!

Take this opportunity to bow in prayer, confessing any and all iniquities. Jesus only asks you to acknowledge your sins and depart from them. Be like Jesus—love righteousness and hate iniquity. Then His anointing and power will come upon you and you'll finally feel alive. Hebrews 1:9 reads, *"Thou hast loved righteousness, and hated iniquity; therefore God, even thy God, hath anointed thee with the oil of gladness above thy fellows."*

CONCLUSION

The mystery of iniquity begins and ends with Satan, the father of iniquity, but obedience begins and ends with Jesus, the Son of Righteousness, and the Mystery of Godliness. Christ is the Author and Finisher of our faith. Indeed, Satan is a worthy adversary, tempter, and accuser who comes to steal, kill, and destroy, but Jesus is the Way, Truth, and Life.

Though all nations and churches work iniquity under the guise of religion, your love for the Holy Spirit, the Spirit of truth, helps you

---

1691 Revelation 14:10, 20:10

discern imposters and keeps your spirit sincere, pure, and unmasked without guile in service to Jesus. Psalm 32:2 records this blessed state, saying, *"Blessed is the man unto whom the Lord imputeth not iniquity, and in whose spirit there is no guile."* Lost souls rejoice in iniquity—stubborn rebellion against God—but you love, obey, and rejoice in truth because the love of God is shed in your heart by the Holy Ghost.[1692]

ACTION STEPS

1. Purge your heart from all iniquity through confession and faith in Jesus' blood, and ask Him for strength to obey all His commands.

2. Discern and forsake all association with workers of iniquity, following faith, charity, and peace with them that call on the Lord out of a pure heart.

3. Continually examine your spiritual state to ensure sincere growth in grace and knowledge of the Lord by letting the Spirit guide you into all Bible truth.

FOLLOW UP

**Free online videos, Bible studies, and William Branham's quotes related to this chapter:
www.pastorjessesmith.com/12mysteriesbook**

Email: jesse.smith11@sbcglobal.net

Text: 330-929-2037

1692   Romans 5:5, 1 Corinthians 13:6

CHAPTER 11
The Mystery of God's Will

"Having made known unto us the mystery of his will, according to his good pleasure which he hath purposed in himself."

Ephesians 1:9

MULTITUDES OF RELIGIOUS PEOPLE say they want to know God's will for their lives. For certain this is an admirable confession, but how many would accept it if they knew God was calling them to holiness? In the Greek Lexicon, "holiness" means "sacred, physically pure, morally blameless."[1693]

Paul emphatically states God's call upon every Christian's life is a holy calling in 2 Timothy 1:9: *"Who hath saved us, and called us with an holy calling, not according to our works, but according to his own purpose and grace, which was given us in Christ Jesus before the world began."* First, note that God loves you so much that His purpose for you started before the world began. The Bible tells you where you came from (God's mind) and where you're going (back to God's presence).

1693 "The Bible: Hebrew and Greek Lexicons." *Voice of God Recordings*, www.branham.org/en/messagesearch

Ephesians 1:4 agrees, saying we should be holy based upon our love for God: "*According as he hath chosen us in him before the foundation of the world, that we should be holy and without blame before him in love.*" You will learn where you are now in relation to God's will and how to remain in His perfect will.

God calls us to holiness, away from the world. You cannot live immorally and claim to be obedient to God's will. You're not called to enjoy sin. In 1 Thessalonians 4:7-8, Paul claims we are not called to uncleanness, but to holiness. Men despise us for this calling, but our leading to be holy is through the Holy Spirit within us. Jesus' holy Voice daily calls you to live holy.

In fact, holiness is a requirement to see Jesus in His mercy. Hebrews 12:14-15 read, "*Follow peace with all men, and holiness, without which no man shall see the Lord. Looking diligently lest any man fail of the grace of God.*"

You read that correctly—religious people can fail, or "fall short… be destitute, lack" God's grace and miss heaven. Many fail or reject grace by disobeying Jesus' commands. God's warning for this is recorded in Hebrews 10:29: "*Of how much sorer punishment, suppose ye, shall he be thought worthy, who hath trodden under foot the Son of God, and hath counted the blood of the covenant, wherewith he was sanctified, an unholy thing, and hath done despite unto the Spirit of grace?*"

Doing the will of God is at the core of the Christian experience and is a requirement to enter heaven. In the Greek, "*will*" means choice, desire, or pleasure. Since God is eternal, infinite, omniscient, and omnipotent His will or choices for us are our joy and comfort. Humans constantly make disastrous choices, so God's will saves us from our helpless, fallen, sinful, selfish, and failing condition.

Jesus' prayer in Gethsemane, in the moment of His greatest anguish marked by bloody sweat drops, is likely the most memorable and famous quote regarding God's will. Luke 22:42 records this prayer, "*Saying, Father, if thou be willing, remove this cup from me: nevertheless not my will, but thine, be done.*" The Father's will superseded the will of Jesus' flesh and mind, which did not want to suffer, let alone die the brutal death of the cross. Yet Jesus chose God's will and Christ is exalted, glorified, and worshipped because of His momentous surrender of His own will.

Jesus' ability to always do the Father's will is what made Him a worthy substitutionary sacrifice for mankind. He said in John 8:29, "*For I do always those things that please him.*" Your ability to surrender to and obey God's will is what makes you worthy of heaven, according to our Lord in Matthew 7:21: "*Not every one that saith unto me, Lord, Lord, shall enter into the kingdom of heaven; but he that doeth the will of my Father which is in heaven.*"

THE CONFUSION ABOUT THE MYSTERY OF GOD'S WILL

The confusion about God's will centers on whether or not it can be known, and if so, how can it be known? Is His will known by just reading the Bible or does God speak in other ways? Additionally, many wonder if it's their responsibility to seek God for His will or if God is obligated to initiate His will by supernaturally revealing Himself and His will to them.

The revelation of the mystery of God's will is that God initiates and reveals His will to every person, making them responsible for responding to Him and seeking His future desires.

BIBLICAL EVIDENCE FOR THE REVELATION ABOUT GOD'S WILL

Scripture teaches God initiates a relationship with every human, undeniably revealing Himself and His eternal power. Romans 1:19-20 proclaims:

> "*Because that which may be known of God is manifest in them; for God hath shewed it unto them. For the invisible things of him from the creation of the world are clearly seen, being understood by the things that are made, even his eternal power and Godhead; so that they are without excuse.*"

God makes everyone know His existence by giving them proof in close proximity to them—in their body, mind, and all creation in the universe around them. As preacher Ray Comfort correctly reasons, "Atheists believe the scientific impossibility that nothing created everything… Every building is proof of a builder. Every painting is proof of a painter. Creation is proof of a creator. It's impossible for it to make itself."[1694] There will be no excuses on Judgment Day for denying God's existence, grace, and mercy. His love is proven in the air you just breathed, the grass you walk on, and the 35 million times your heart beat in the past year without needing your help or permission.

Through God's mercy, we *"live, and move, and have our being."*[1695] Life is such a beautiful opportunity to experience God's love and share it with others. Solomon states the glory of life's opportunities but perfectly balances it with God's requirement for accountability in Ecclesiastes 11:9: *"Rejoice, O young man, in thy youth; and let thy heart cheer thee in the days of thy youth, and walk in the ways of thine heart, and in the sight of thine eyes: but know thou, that for all these things God will bring thee into judgment."*

Armed with this inward, spiritual knowledge and outward, scientific evidence, all men are responsible for responding to God by searching after, knowing, and doing His will. Every soul has a thirst for God and truth. Psalm 42:2 reads, *"My soul thirsteth for God, for the living God."*

God mercifully grants each person the gift of life, an awareness of his Creator's existence, and free moral agency. But God is going to demand back, or require each soul to give account of his choices. Luke 12:20 says of the lost soul, *"Thou fool, this night thy soul shall be required of thee."* The wise soul will seek after God and find Him through the cross of Jesus. The sinful, foolish soul will deny his Creator and spurn His mercy.

Validated by John 3:16 and 19, the sad truth is God loves the humanity He created but most men greatly love darkness. Those who love God will be with Him eternally. Those who hated and despised Him will be

---

1694 "An Atheist Gets His Evidence." *Living Waters,* https://www.livingwaters.com/an-atheist-gets-his-evidence/
1695 Acts 17:28

separated from Him eternally. Our Lord is too gracious and loving to force anyone to be in His presence eternally.

GOD'S SOVEREIGN WILL

There are three aspects to God's will:

- God's sovereign, immutable, eternal, unconditional will
- God's known will for man
- God's progressive, unknown, or future will for man

Ultimately, God's will is sovereign, immutable, and eternal. Before the foundation of the world, the eternal God preplanned all human history based upon His foreknowledge of every human decision. Beginning with believers, 1 Peter 1:2 says we are elect, or chosen, based upon God's foreknowledge: *"Elect according to the foreknowledge of God the Father, through sanctification of the Spirit, unto obedience and sprinkling of the blood of Jesus Christ."*

God never had to, neither had need to, ask anyone about how to plan human existence. He needs no counselor, as Isaiah 40:13-14 proclaims: *"Who hath directed the Spirit of the Lord, or being his counsellor hath taught him? With whom took he counsel, and who instructed him, and taught him in the path of judgment, and taught him knowledge, and shewed to him the way of understanding?"* The obvious answer is no one.

God declares the beginning from the end and does exactly what He wants. Isaiah 46:9-10 reads, *"Remember the former things of old: for I am God, and there is none else; I am God, and there is none like me, Declaring the end from the beginning, and from ancient times the things that are not yet done, saying, My counsel shall stand, and I will do all my pleasure."* What pleases God, He does.

It pleased God to plan the flood in Noah's day. Nearly 2,000 years afterwards, He planned Jesus' substitutionary death beforehand,[1696] along with His resurrection. His future plans for the rapture, Tribulation, Battle of Armageddon, Millennium, White Throne Judgment, and New

---

1696 Acts 2:23, 4:28-29

Jerusalem-future home are all steadfast, sure, and unchangeable. We can't stop His will, nor delay it or alter it. But we can embrace it and prepare for it. If you haven't yet done it, make your plans to repent of you sins and live with Jesus in His future home.

Every nation under heaven is subject to God's will. Worldly rulers cannot alter God's eternal purposes. Our Lord allows them freedom in decision making, but He alone ultimately decides what will happen based upon His eternal plan. Psalm 33:10-11 declares, *"The Lord bringeth the counsel of the heathen to nought: he maketh the devices of the people of none effect. The counsel of the Lord standeth for ever, the thoughts of his heart to all generations."*

Daniel 2:21 says God alone changes the times and seasons of earthly leaders, removing and setting them up. After being humbled by God for seven years, one of the world's most powerful leaders of all time, Nebuchadnezzar, described God's sovereign will over the earth thusly:

> *"I blessed the most High, and I praised and honoured him that liveth for ever, whose dominion is an everlasting dominion, and his kingdom is from generation to generation: And all the inhabitants of the earth are reputed as nothing: and he doeth according to his will in the army of heaven, and among the inhabitants of the earth: and none can stay his hand, or say unto him, What doest thou?"*[1697]

Job's life teaches that everything the devil does must first be allowed by God, giving us great trust in our Heavenly Father as we go through trials and tests. Chapters 1 and 2 show Satan having to ask permission to tempt Job[1698] and God allowed it because He knew in His foreknowledge Job would eventually overcome the temptation and not fall to it. 1 Corinthians 10:13 says all temptations upon man are similar and shared, and God will only allow a test in your life that He has already equipped you to overcome.

1697   Daniel 4:34-35
1698   Job 1:6-12, 2:1-6

Yes, God works everything according to His own counsel, and pre-plans every event for the spiritual benefit of His children, believers. Ephesians 1:11 says we are *"predestinated according to the purpose of him who worketh all things after the counsel of his own will."* Romans 8:28, Deuteronomy 6:24, 8:16, and 10:13 all agree that God works every event for our good, always. You never have to wonder why good or evil happens to you. Your heart rests in heaven's assurance that every event that occurs in your life will make you love God more. The best way to prove your love to God is by believing in His sovereign will and choosing thankfulness and joy while you go through trials of faith that His infinite wisdom allowed to come to pass.

Jesus promises you peace that passes all understanding and a life free from anxiety as you prayerfully thank God for everything in your life while making your personal requests known to Him.[1699]

GOD'S KNOWN WILL FOR MAN

Moving to man's perspective of God's will, there is a will of God He makes known to men and then a progressive, future will men must seek Him for.

Starting with God's known will, He first gives every soul an awareness and thirst for fellowship with Him. The individual's inward conscious and knowledge of his Maker's desire to save his soul makes him thirst to respond to God and seek Him. He either quenches his soul-thirst by seeking and finding Christ, or hushes and silences it with sinful pleasures.

God's will is further known through the Holy Bible, which contains all His holy commands. Simply put, God's will is His Word. Notice Ephesians 1:9 says the mystery of God's will is purposed in Himself, and He is the Word.

There are two crucial aspects of God's known will: His desire for every human to be saved, and then be born-again, or filled with His Spirit.

First, the eternal God wants all men to be saved from hell, but in His love, will not force anyone to love Him in return. He will patiently wait

---

1699 Philippians 4:6-7

until every person who longs to be saved, is saved. 2 Peter 3:9 states, *"The Lord is not slack concerning his promise, as some men count slackness; but is longsuffering to us-ward, not willing that any should perish, but that all should come to repentance."* Paul agrees to this in 1 Timothy 2:4: *"Who will have all men to be saved, and to come unto the knowledge of the truth."* Do not allow the devil to tell you God doesn't love you and doesn't want you saved. Here's Biblical proof He wants you saved. Trust God and His Word, for Satan is the father of lies and Jesus is *"the faithful and true witness."*[1700] Jesus promises *"It is not the will of your Father which is in heaven, that one of these little ones should perish."*[1701]

Jesus wants you and every believer in heaven with Him, for He said in John 6:40, *"This is the will of him that sent me, that every one which seeth the Son, and believeth on him, may have everlasting life: and I will raise him up at the last day."* Galatians 1:4 says it is God's will to *"deliver us from this present evil world."*

Our God does not delight in the death of the wicked, for He wants and pleads for the souls to love Him and live. Ezekiel 33:11 declares, *"Say unto them, As I live, saith the Lord God, I have no pleasure in the death of the wicked; but that the wicked turn from his way and live: turn ye, turn ye from your evil ways; for why will ye die, O house of Israel?"*

When a soul hears the good news of Jesus Christ preached and explained, he knows the revelation of the mystery of God's known will. Paul says the revelation of God's will is that all things in heaven and earth will be gathered in Christ, and believers will have an unending inheritance as they praise Jesus' glory eternally:

> *"Having made known unto us the mystery of his will, according to his good pleasure which he hath purposed in himself: That in the dispensation of the fulness of times he might gather together in one all things in Christ, both which are in heaven, and which are on earth; even in him: In whom also we have obtained an inheritance, being predestinated according to the purpose of him who worketh all things after the counsel of his own will: That we*

1700   John 8:44, Revelation 3:14
1701   Matthew 18:14

should be to the praise of his glory, who first trusted in Christ."[1702]

The second truth about God's known will is His desire for Christians, and all men, to be born-again. God loves when believers hear the good news, accept it and get saved because part of the known will of God is obeyed, giving God great pleasure. However, full redemption is a three step process: justification, sanctification, and the filling of the Holy Ghost (See Chapter 5). This was typed by Israel coming out of Egyptian bondage. Deuteronomy 6:23 says God brought them out to bring them in: *"And he brought us out from thence, that he might bring us in, to give us the land which he sware unto our fathers."* Jesus brought you out of sin, justifying you, but He doesn't want you to stop there. He wants you to come through the spiritual wilderness of sanctification and into the Promised Land of the Holy Ghost baptism in your soul. 2 Corinthians 5:17 says you're a new creature when you are *"in Christ."*

Jesus first commands all to be born again in John 3:7: *"Ye must be born again."* Remember Israel leaving Egypt—she must reach Canaan or else she would fall short of God's will. Then, Christ invites all to be born again in John 7:37-39, crying, *"If any thirst, let him come unto me, and drink...this spake he of the Spirit, which they that believe on him should receive: for the Holy Ghost was not yet given."* The universal invitation to the new birth is also resounded by the Holy Spirt and the bride-church in Revelation 22:17: *"And the Spirit and the bride say, Come. And let him that heareth say, Come. And let him that is athirst come. And whosoever will, let him take the water of life freely."* Again, cast down any doubt Satan puts in your mind about God not wanting to fill you with the Holy Ghost. Deny the seducing serpent and accept the loving Lamb.

If you want to obey both aspects to God's known will—being saved and Spirit filled—you need only genuine love. All Jesus' precepts are summarized and fulfilled in one word: love. In Matthew 22:37-40 Jesus says loving God with all your heart and loving your neighbor fulfills every command. Three times Paul echoes Jesus' summary, saying

1702 Ephesians 1:9-12

love is the fulfilling of the law.[1703] If you can truly love God, you will do His will.

In 1 John 5:1-4, the apostle John writes that being born again is the source of this divine love, empowering Christians to keep all Jesus' commands:

> "Whosoever believeth that Jesus is the Christ is born of God: and every one that loveth him that begat loveth him also that is begotten of him. By this we know that we love the children of God, when we love God, and keep his commandments. For this is the love of God, that we keep his commandments: and his commandments are not grievous. For whatsoever is born of God overcometh the world: and this is the victory that overcometh the world, even our faith."

Friend, if you are seeking salvation through Jesus Christ and the filling of His Holy Spirit in your soul, you can undoubtedly know you're doing the will of God.

GOD'S KNOWN WILL THROUGH THE HOLY BIBLE IS YOUR SPIRITUAL FOOD

After a believer is saved, he comes in contact with earth's greatest book—the Holy Bible. Man begins to satisfy his soul's thirst to know God through daily reading of Scripture. While meditating upon his readings, he finds more of the known will of God.

Some of the following doctrines have been mentioned previously in this book but bear repeating to emphasize their place in your spiritual diet—the known will of God. Let these commands, as God's will, be your meat, or spiritual food. Jesus says, "My meat is to do the will of him that sent me, and to finish his work."[1704] Jesus Christ desires, or wills, all Christians to

- Experience sanctification, or purification of thoughts and actions (also called the Second Work of Grace), before

---

1703   Romans 13:8, 10, Galatians 5:14
1704   John 4:34

a Christian is born again as Jesus' Seed Cast Into the Ground parable teaches (Mark 4:26-28, John 3:7, 17:17, 1 Thessalonians 4:3, 1 Peter 1:23)

- Abstain from sexual immorality, meaning no sexual activity before marriage (fornication), no homosexuality, and marrying only one person (Matthew 19:1-9, Romans 1:26-32, 1 Corinthians 6:9-11, 1 Thessalonians 4:3-4)
- Find a home church, listen to male preachers only, and gather increasingly more as the rapture approaches (1 Corinthians 14:34-36, 1 Timothy 2:11-15, Hebrews 10:24-25)
- Give tithes (ten percent of income) and offerings (any free will amount) to the home church (1 Corinthians 9:9-14)
- Abstain from all substance abuse, including tobacco, alcohol, marijuana, etc.(Romans 14:21, 1 Corinthians 3:17, 6:19-20, 8:13)
- Abstain from wicked and lustful movies and television shows (Psalm 101:3, 1 Thessalonians 5:22)
- Wear modest clothing (Proverbs 7:10, 1 Timothy 2:9)
- Allow the correct hair length for gender—uncut hair for women and short hair for men (1 Corinthians 11:1-16)
- Keep three physical ordinances: water baptism, feet washing, and communion (Mark 16:16, John 13:14, 1 Corinthians 11:23-26)
- Pray continually, express thanksgiving, fast, and give alms to the poor (Matthew 6:1-21, 1 Thessalonians 5:17-18)
- Financially support oneself if single or their families by working hard to supply their needs (1 Timothy 5:8, 1 Thessalonians 4:11-12)
- Obey government laws unless they contradict God's commands (Acts 5:29, 1 Peter 2:13-15)
- Worship God in the Spirit and in truth (John 4:23-24)

Plainly stated, if you're guilty of breaking any of these commands, you're disobeying God's will. Committing sexual sin, skipping church gatherings, abstaining from charitable giving, smoking, drinking, dressing immodestly, and breaking the law put you out of God's will for your life.

It's possible you're learning about these commands for the first time. If so, know that it's God fulfilling prophecy from Matthew 17:11, Acts 3:21, and Malachi 4:5-6. The Lord promised to restore all Biblical truths in the last days. He loves you and wants you to know truth. God orchestrated His mysteries to be finished in your lifetime so He could lead you to the revealed Word for your day (See Chapter 13). He's getting His bride ready for her rapture-wedding day. God has made a way for you to know His plan to restore all things and be *"established in the present truth."*[1705]

Be like your Messiah, Who focused on and sought after God's will, saying, *"I seek not mine own will, but the will of the Father which hath sent me."*[1706] John 6:38 teaches Christ's purpose for coming down from heaven was *"not to do mine own will, but the will of him that sent me."* That's your purpose as well, and Peter says you lived for your own will before being saved but now that you're a Christian, you live for God's will: *"That he no longer should live the rest of his time in the flesh to the lusts of men, but to the will of God."*[1707]

Have a humble, hungry heart like David, who said, *"Teach me to do thy will"* in Psalm 143:10. Ask God for wisdom to understand His will and He'll bountifully give it to you. Ephesians 5:17 states, *"Wherefore be ye not unwise, but understanding what the will of the Lord is."* James 1:5 promises, *"If any of you lack wisdom, let him ask of God, that giveth to all men liberally, and upbraideth not: and it shall be given him."*

Patience is the key attribute you need as you follow God's will. God's order for answering prayers is ask in prayer, do God's will, wait, and then receive the promise. Hebrews 10:35-38 declares this truth:

1705 2 Peter 1:12
1706 John 5:30
1707 1 Peter 4:2

"Cast not away therefore your confidence, which hath great recompence of reward. For ye have need of patience, that, after ye have done the will of God, ye might receive the promise. For yet a little while, and he that shall come will come, and will not tarry. Now the just shall live by faith: but if any man draw back, my soul shall have no pleasure in him."

THE STATURE OF A PERFECT MAN IN CONNECTION TO THE KNOWN WILL OF GOD

Through Peter's Stature of a Perfect Man teaching, you can know your spiritual location in the known will of God. Hebrews chapter 4 types Israel's journey from Egypt to Canaan as the Christian's growth from sinner to Holy Ghost-filled saint. Hebrews 4:11 tells us to *"labour...to enter into that rest"* as Israel labored to reach Canaan. Jesus says He gives us rest for our souls in Matthew 11:29, which must be the Holy Ghost-baptism He repeatedly urged His disciples to receive,[1708] breathing *"Receive ye the Holy Ghost."*[1709] Just as Moses, Joshua, and Caleb could know exactly where they were on their journey—whether the baptism at the Red Sea, the wilderness of sanctification, at the border of Canaan, or crossing Jordan—so you can know where you stand with God.

Chapter 5 explained God's eight-step plan for bringing Christians from salvation to the new birth, called the Stature of a Perfect Man. Faith, the First Work of Grace, comes at the moment you get saved and water baptized in the name of the Lord Jesus Christ. Then you being the Second Work of Grace called sanctification. Herein God imparts or adds more character attributes of His own life to yours: virtue, knowledge, temperance, patience, godliness, and brotherly kindness. The Third Work of Grace is the baptism of the Holy Ghost, or God's charity, His love, coming to dwell in your soul.

Remember Paul said God has *already* made known to us the mystery of His will. You know it's God's will for you to be saved (faith),

1708 Matthew 20:23, Luke 24:49, John 7:37-39, Acts 1:4-8
1709 John 20:22

sanctified (virtue through brotherly kindness) and Spirit-filled (born again with charity).

TWO PRINCIPLES GOVERNING GOD'S PROGRESSIVE WILL FOR MAN

After following God's known will—being saved, Spirit-filled, and obeying the Bible doctrines—you naturally begin to wonder what else God has in store for the rest of your life.

God's future plans for your life can be called the progressive will of God. The plans are eternally known to God, but unknown to you. He reveals His future desires to you as you seek His guidance traveling on your earthly pilgrimage.

Abraham is your example for seeking God's progressive, future will. God called him to leave his country and family, and he didn't know where he was going. Hebrews 11:8 says Abraham was called out and obeyed, *"not knowing whither he went."* Abraham obeyed the known will of God, but God didn't tell him all the details about his travels, nor his final destination. Abraham was content seeking God's progressive will daily, and as a spiritual faith-child of Abraham, you'll do the same. Be faithful to God's most recent revelation of His will until the next revelation comes. As Abraham lived by faith, moving from city to city, you live *"from faith to faith,"*[1710] from revelation to revelation, *"from glory to glory."*[1711]

Two principles govern God's progressive will: it'll align perfectly with His known will revealed in the Holy Bible, and will happen in His ordained time and season.

God's future will always harmonizes with His known will expressed in Holy Scripture and also through the prophets. Satan's threefold temptation of Christ in Matthew 4 exemplifies this truth about obeying the known Word. One particular temptation was for Christ to immediately rule over the nations, rather than wait. Jesus knew He'd rule the nations

1710   Romans 1:17
1711   2 Corinthians 3:18

at some point in the future, but was it now? How did Jesus know God's progressive will in the exact moment of temptation? Jesus triumphed over the wicked one not by miracles, but by obeying the known will of God, which said to never worship anyone but God.

In 2 Samuel 6, David attempted to bring the Ark of the Covenant into Jerusalem, but his first attempt failed, causing Uzzah's death, for one reason—he disobeyed the known will of God that said the Ark must be carried on the shoulders of the Levites.[1712] David first put the Ark on a new cart but when the oxen shook it and Uzzah touched the Ark to steady it, God smote him. Three months after the tragedy, David fully obeyed the known will of God, pleasing God this time. He again worshipped God with all his might in the same manner he previously did, and brought the Ark to Jerusalem with joy.

In Daniel 9:1-2, Daniel was seeking God to know His progressive will for his people, Israel. How did Daniel know God was going to soon move on Israel's behalf and let them return to Jerusalem? Verse 2 says he knew the 70 year exile period was about up due to reading Jeremiah's books. God's progressive will for Israel was known by one prophet, Daniel, through its harmony with another prophet, Jeremiah.

Jeremiah's victory over the false prophet Hananiah in Jeremiah 28 is an example of God's progressive will aligning with his own previous prophesies. How did Jeremiah know Hananiah was wrong by saying God would break Nebuchadnezzar's yoke upon Israel within 2 years? He knew because God had already spoken the yoke would last 70 years through Jeremiah's own lips,[1713] showing a true prophet's prophecies will always agree with his previous predictions spoken in the Lord's name.

Applying this to your life means no matter how strongly you may feel about a potential decision, first see if it obeys God's known will. For example, if you're a woman and someone pleads with you to cut your long, uncut hair for any reason, even to help make wigs for cancer patients, you

---

1712 Exodus 25:14, 1 Chronicles 15:15
1713 Jeremiah 25:11-12

know not to because of God's known will. Rather than cutting your hair, God's Word says to lay your hands on the sick in prayer and ask for healing. Or, if you're a married man and you're tempted to commit adultery with another man's wife or divorce your wife and remarry another, you know it's not God's progressive will. God's known will commands you to remain married to one wife until death.

Never trust a sign or wonder if it contains instructions that disagree with God's known will. Deuteronomy 13:1-5 expresses this lesson as Moses tells Israel not to follow a prophet who urges you to worship false gods even if he shows a sign or wonder that comes. Moses says it's a test of your love for God. If you love God, you'll always keep the known will of God as you're trying to discern His progressive will. Signs and wonders and the messages that follow must all harmonize with God's known will. As Exodus 4:8-9 demonstrate, God's signs have a voice or instructions that follow them, and they will always point you to holiness and obedience.

Perhaps you have a beautiful dream you think comes from God and it's allowing you to break His Word. Jesus Himself might appear in the dream, but if the command is against Scripture, you know its Satan disguised as an angel of light.[1714] Don't trust any dream, nor angel, or preacher if they contradict Jesus' holy Words in the Holy Bible.

God works in specific times and seasons, and His progressive will always aligns with His predetermined timing. Believers must obey God's known will and patiently wait until it's God time to fulfill His promise. You don't want to try and enforce God's will too early, nor miss God's moment in which He wants to move.

One reason God rejected King Saul was because he couldn't wait upon God's timing. In 1 Samuel 13:8-14, Saul was told to wait seven days for the prophet Samuel to come and offer sacrifices before battling the Philistines. Towards the end of the time period, Saul took it upon himself to offer sacrifices, encroaching into the prophet's office. As soon as the sacrifices were offered, Samuel arrived and pronounced God's

---

1714   2 Corinthians 11:14

displeasure with Saul forcing himself into an office not assigned to him. Saul, by missing God's progressive will by a few hours, lost out on generations of blessings.

David's adulterous sin with Bathsheba happened when he was out of position in the season of battle. 2 Samuel 11:1 tells that the kings went out to battle at a particular time of the year but instead of being in position in battle, David neglected his position, leading to his adultery with Bathsheba and murder of Uriah. This serves as a lesson for Christians to be in position, or obeying all the known will of God, in every season. 2 Timothy 4:2 says, *"Preach the word; be instant in season, out of season; reprove, rebuke, exhort with all longsuffering and doctrine."*

There is also great sin in refusing to act in God's season, missing His leading, as Jesus rebukes a multitude for not discerning His supernatural ministry. Jesus chides the multitude in Luke 12:56 saying, *"Ye hypocrites, ye can discern the face of the sky and of the earth; but how is it that ye do not discern this time?"*

In my short time as a Christian, I've seen many erroneously attempt to predict the season of the rapture. In 2011, the late Harold Camping rented billboards across America declaring the rapture would occur on May 21, 2011. It miserably failed. The next year, 2012, many believed the Mayan calendar predicted the world's end but it came and went without a fulfillment. Blood moons in 2015 were next in line to predict the rapture, but this phenomenon came and went without ending history. Thankfully, Spirit-filled Christians are promised to know the time and season of the rapture based upon 1 Thessalonians 5:1 and don't spend their time trying to force the rapture-season to occur.

SERVICE, SUBMISSION, AND SUFFERING IN GOD'S PROGRESSIVE WILL

New Christians, and sometimes seasoned ones, often ask themselves about God's will for their relationships, vocations, locations, ministries, and gifts. They say, "Who should I marry?" or "What job should I have?" Many ask, "Where should I live and what gifts has God given me?" These are legitimate, worthy questions God knows you're considering and He has answers for all of them.

You'll have to ask God about some of these subjects and remember to honor the two principles for God's progressive will: He'll never ask you to break commands in Scripture and everything must be done in His season—not yours.

Before diving into knowing God's will for relationships and more, understand service, submission, and suffering are at the heart of God's will for every life. You are called to serve and submit to others. David's life exemplifies service and New Testament authors expound on Christian submission and suffering.

Serving others is at the core of your calling for each of these areas. For example, Acts 13:36 states, *"For David, after he had served his own generation by the will of God, fell on sleep, and was laid unto his fathers, and saw corruption."* David's vocation and location are easy to identify, as God chose him to be king over all Israel in Jerusalem because he was a man after God's heart.[1715] Acts 13:22 declares the very reason God chose David was because He knew David would do all of His will: *"I have found David the son of Jesse, a man after mine own heart, which shall fulfil all my will."* David served God's will, feeding, protecting, and judging Israel, for 40 years.

David's marriage relationship with Bathsheba began in sinful disgrace but God still used this couple to serve His purpose in shaping Israel's future. Their second son, Solomon, was loved of the Lord and later became the wisest and richest king of his time period.[1716] At the end of David's life, it was Bethsheba's service to God, her influence and efforts, that stopped Adonijah from stealing the throne from Solomon, who eventually ascended to his kingly, God-given authority.[1717]

David served God's purpose for both the music and military ministries. In 1 Chronicles 15 and 16, David established Levitical worship using various instruments to continually and skillfully thank and praise

1715   1 Samuel 13:14, Acts 13:22
1716   2 Samuel 12:24-25, 1 Kings 10:23
1717   1 Kings 1:11-21

God. With his military, David served God's purpose of expanding Israel's borders to boundaries they were promised under Joshua but never achieved until David's lifetime.[1718] These victories were possible because David always enquired of the Lord before battles, and each time Scripture records him seeking God before battle, he was undefeated.[1719] As you learn to humble yourself and pray before decision-making, you'll see constant victories as well.

History affirms David's gifts to write songs and prophecy served God's purpose for His life. David contributed more than 70 of the 150 songs in the Book of Psalm, many of which are sung to this day in Christian churches worldwide. Described as a prophet in Acts 2:30, David served God's will to foretell many details of Jesus' crucifixion and resurrection nearly 1,000 years beforehand.[1720]

It is also God's will that you submit to others, beginning with God. James 4:7 commands, *"Submit yourselves therefore to God. Resist the devil, and he will flee from you."* Then, learn to sacrifice your selfish desires and submit to others. Ephesians 5:21 says, *"Submitting yourselves one to another in the fear of God."* Every Christian should submit to godly leadership in their local church: *"Obey them that have the rule over you, and submit yourselves: for they watch for your souls, as they that must give account, that they may do it with joy, and not with grief: for that is unprofitable for you."*[1721]

Peter tells us submission to government is the will of God and silences those who criticize Christianity in 1 Peter 2:13-15:

> *"Submit yourselves to every ordinance of man for the Lord's sake: whether it be to the king, as supreme; Or unto governors, as unto them that are sent by him for the punishment of evildoers, and for the praise of them that do well. For so is the will of God, that with well doing ye may put to silence the ignorance of foolish men."*

1718   Joshua 1:4, 2 Samuel 8:3
1719   1 Samuel 23:2-4, 30:8, 2 Samuel 2:1, 5:19, 23
1720   Psalm 16:10, 22:7-16, 27:12
1721   Hebrews 13:17

Suffering is a necessary, but often unwanted, part of doing God's will. As humans, we need a renewed vision of suffering's purpose. The Lord has chosen suffering as your teacher and his lesson is obedience. Even God's spotless, holy Son, Jesus, learned obedience through suffering. Hebrews 5:8 declares, "*Though he were a Son, yet learned he obedience by the things which he suffered.*" You know of Jesus' suffering during His Gethsemane prayers, but this Scriptures tells us much of His life was spent suffering for the gospel.

Expect suffering in your earthly journey, as "*all that will live godly in Christ Jesus shall suffer persecution.*"[1722] There is no escaping suffering for Christians as it's required for future responsibility. If you hope to reign with and for Christ in the Millennium, embrace your sufferings. 2 Timothy 2:11-12 says, "*It is a faithful saying: For if we be dead with him, we shall also live with him: If we suffer, we shall also reign with him: if we deny him, he also will deny us.*"

Peter's first epistle constantly deals with your required suffering. Chapter 2, verse 20 claims God accepts you when you endure suffering with patience. In chapter 3, verses 13-17, the apostle tells you to be happy if you suffer for righteousness' sake. Next, 1 Peter 4:19 says to commit the keeping of your soul to God in constant well doing when you're suffering according to God's will. In the times God desires you to suffer, remember the vast, eternal benefits. One benefit is your perfection, or completion. You'll never be what God intended for you to be without a little suffering. Chapter 5:10 reads, "*But the God of all grace, who hath called us unto his eternal glory by Christ Jesus, after that ye have suffered a while, make you perfect, stablish, strengthen, settle you.*" Paul says all suffering is only momentary "*light affliction*" that produces "*a far more exceeding and eternal weight of glory.*"[1723]

Your suffering allows God's power to manifest through your life. Paul explains the following order for powerful instances of God's Spirit: suffering, weakness, then strength. 2 Corinthians 12:1-10 provides insight

---

1722   2 Timothy 3:12
1723   1 Corinthians 4:17

on Paul's physical sufferings from a satanic messenger to keep him humble. After three prayers requests for it to be removed, Jesus tells Paul His strength is perfect in Paul's weakness. Paul then glories in his weakness because Christ's power rested on him. You also see how God's power is not always seen in healing the sick or raising the dead. Sometimes it's power to give thanks in the midst of suffering and weakness: *"In every thing gives thanks: for this is the will of God in Christ Jesus."*[1724]

It's through suffering that you develop intimacy with Christ. Most Christians want to know Jesus' power but few His sufferings. Paul knew both were mandatory. Philippians 3:10 tells you, *"That I may know him, and the power of his resurrection, and the fellowship of his sufferings, being made conformable unto his death."* How well do you want to know Jesus? Enough to suffer for Him? If so, you'll not only suffer for Him, but fellowship with Him, as He'll never leave you nor forsake you.

HOW TO FIND THE PERFECT WILL OF GOD FOR YOUR LIFE

Romans 12:1-2 provides two simple steps to finding the perfect will of God for your life:

> *"I beseech you therefore, brethren, by the mercies of God, that ye present your bodies a living sacrifice, holy, acceptable unto God, which is your reasonable service. And be not conformed to this world: but be ye transformed by the renewing of your mind, that ye may prove what is that good, and acceptable, and perfect, will of God."*

Observe in verse 2 that there is a perfect will and permissive will of God for your life. The perfect will of God is full obedience to the Word of God while the permissive will is a path of disobedience and compromise. David says the Word of God is the lamp unto our feet and light unto our path.[1725] Disobeying God's Word and struggling through life

---

1724   1 Thessalonians 5:18
1725   Psalm 119:105

in God's permissive will is like losing your light source in the dark and fearfully stumbling about.

Jesus is the only Person to ever walk in God's perfect will for His entire life. But many saints recorded in Scripture spent much of their lives in the perfect will of God, such as Abraham, Joseph, David, Daniel, and Paul. These men's lives are marked by constant obedience to God's commands. Their mistakes God allowed recorded in the Bible show brief missteps into the permissive will of God with appropriate consequences, but God's grace always guides them back into the perfect will.

All who willingly disobeyed God's Word in Bible records are examples of walking in the permissive will of God. Four examples include Cain, Balaam, Saul, and Hezekiah. The first two men were lost;[1726] the last two were saved. Satan inspires people into the permissive will, for they choose their own will over God's. Lucifer said, "*I will*" five times in Isaiah 14:12-15. Be like Christ and say, "I will do God's will; not my will."

Cain disdained God's perfect will requiring animal sacrifice before murdering his brother, Abel.[1727] The son of the wicked one, Cain even turned down God's plea for his repentance in a personal supernatural encounter with the Holy One. Balaam heard God's first command, His perfect will, to avoid visiting Balak but prayed again to see if God would allow it. The Lord gave him permission to take the permissive will and go see Balak, but Balaam was ultimately slain in disgrace for his sins.[1728] King Saul started his kingship in great victory and obedience but ultimately rebelled against God's direct commands, causing him to lose out on God establishing his kingdom forever.[1729] King Hezekiah lived in the perfect will of God for much of his life but staggered into the permissive will when he asked for more years for his life. Once granted 15 more years, Hezekiah catered to the Babylonian ambassadors, showing them all the treasures in the Lord's house.[1730]

1726   2 Peter 2:17, 1 John 3:12
1727   Genesis 4:1-16
1728   Numbers chs. 22-25, 31:8, Rev. 2:14
1729   1 Samuel 13:13-14
1730   2 Kings 20:1-6, 2 Chronicles 32:24-31

The first step in finding God's perfect will is to present your body as a living sacrifice unto God. Paul says to consider God's mercy and then willingly offer your body to God for His service, sacrificing opportunities to make your body feel good. God won't force you to offer yourself; but His mercy will plead with you to do so. This means forcing your body to serve God when your body's sin nature doesn't want to. Usually this equates to eating less food, and eating the healthy kinds when you do, and voluntarily starving your body at times, called "fasting" by Jesus in Matthew 6:18. Benefits of fasting are many, including power for healing and deliverance, focus to feed the poor, and getting answers from God.[1731]

Since you're a living sacrifice, your altar is also your own, personal cross. In Luke 9:23 Christ says, "*If any man will come after me, let him deny himself, and take up his cross daily, and follow me.*" Your cross is the loss of your desires, for the next verse says, "*For whosoever will save his life shall lose it: but whosoever will lose his life for my sake, the same shall save it.*" You must learn to let God lead your life every single day. He will lead you only into holy separation, not lusts of the flesh.

Also, keep your body out of harm's way. Avoid all appearances of evil, not walking in "*lasciviousness, lusts, excess of wine, reveling, banquetings, and abominable idolatries.*"[1732] Keep your body out of bars, sporting events, concerts, movie theaters, and all sinful gatherings. Control your work hours as well. Satan has enslaved many a well-meaning Christian into the idolatry of money-making and position-seeking.

Indeed, if you're to be a sacrifice and reasonably serve God's purpose for your life, something has to die. Your will must daily die, as Paul says, "*I die daily.*"[1733] Remember you're a living sacrifice, which requires the daily crucifixion of your lusts and selfish will.

Secondly, your mind needs renewed daily: "*Though our outward man perish, yet the inward man is renewed day by day.*"[1734] Jesus says to seek the

---

1731   Isaiah 58:1-14, Daniel 9:3, Matthew 17:21
1732   1 Thessalonians 5:22, 1 Peter 4:3
1733   1 Corinthians 15:31
1734   2 Corinthians 4:16

kingdom of God first, so pray and read your Bible first every morning. Reading your Bible once a week isn't enough. Daily reading is essential to renew your mind. This daily renewing of your thinking causes your spiritual transformation.

Recall your mind has five channels: conscience, memory, reason, affection, and imagination. 2 Corinthians 10:4-5 says any evil thought pattern or mental complex that exalts itself against God's Word must be pulled down, cast down, and forgotten through the mighty weapon of God's Word. When Satan floats a hurtful memory near your mind, cast it down. If you're building a complex by imagining someone's hatred for you and planning how to counter a possible attack, pull down that sinful strong hold. If you're affectionally admiring and coveting earthly riches, cast down those thoughts and set your affections on things above.[1735]

Yes, the key to mind renewal is simply putting off old, sinful thoughts, or the "old man," and putting on the "new man," or new, holy thought, according to Ephesians 4:22-24: *"That ye put off concerning the former conversation the old man, which is corrupt according to the deceitful lusts; And be renewed in the spirit of your mind; And that ye put on the new man, which after God is created in righteousness and true holiness."* Give your mind wholly to the Word. Think upon all eight of Paul's subjects: whatsoever is true, honest, just, pure, lovely, of good report, virtuous, and praise worthy.[1736] Meditate all day and *"pray without ceasing."*[1737]

You now see doing God's perfect will requires complete consecration of your body (presented as a living sacrifice) and mind (daily renewed). You know your being has three parts: body, mind (spirit), and soul.[1738] But did you notice how Paul never mentioned the soul of man in Romans 12:1-2? The reason is because Paul knew the Christian's soul was already housing God's nature, sealed by His Holy Spirit, which directs all actions. A Christian's soul is already perfect before God. It cannot sin, for it possesses God's own seed, His life.[1739] Paul's showing you

1735 Colossians 3:1-2
1736 Philippians 4:7-8
1737 1 Thessalonians 5:17
1738 1 Thessalonians 5:23
1739 1 Peter 1:23, 1 John 3:9

how to bring your two outward parts into subjection to your inner core, your soul.

Prayer is one indispensable tool to know God's will. In Jesus' model prayer, He says to daily pray for God's kingdom to come and His will to "*be done in earth, as it is in heaven.*"[1740] In fact, Jesus says this kind of consistent prayer will be hard to find on the earth at His second coming,[1741] so be one of those faithful prayer warriors.

Praying Jesus' way through His Spirit raises your faith, and faith does the works God desires for your life. Jude 1:20 states, "*But ye, beloved, building up yourselves on your most holy faith, praying in the Holy Ghost.*" Paul writes in Ephesians 2:10 God created you to do His will, or good works: "*For we are his workmanship, created in Christ Jesus unto good works, which God hath before ordained that we should walk in them.*"

Through your prayers, you can support other believers in doing God's will. Paul's helper Epaphras had this special burden as a prayer warrior in Colossians 4:12: "*Epaphras, who is one of you, a servant of Christ, saluteth you, always labouring fervently for you in prayers, that ye may stand perfect and complete in all the will of God.*" Paul prayed similarly for the Colossians:

"*For this cause we also, since the day we heard it, do not cease to pray for you, and to desire that ye might be filled with the knowledge of his will in all wisdom and spiritual understanding.*"[1742] If you can't do anything else to help others, you can pray for them to do all the will of God.

PROVING GOD'S PERFECT WILL IN YOUR RELATIONSHIPS, VOCATIONS, LOCATIONS, MINISTRIES, AND GIFTS

Daily renewing of your mind leads to transformed living. Equipped with a transformed being—a fully consecrated body and mind—you can now prove God's perfect will for your life as He progressively reveals it to you. You won't have to guess about it; you'll know and do Jesus' perfect will.

1740   Matthew 6:10
1741   Luke 18:1-8
1742   Colossians 1:9

Always diligently obey all the known will of God before deciding upon relationships, vocations, locations, ministries, and gifts.

RELATIONSHIPS

Paul's first letter to the Corinthians helps establish God's will for relationships. Chapter seven addresses virgins, the unmarried, married, and the widowed. Read the whole chapter for a complete understanding.

Single believers should pray and seek God to know whether they have the gift to be single or whether they should seek marriage.[1743] Marriage is the second most important decision you'll make in life outside of salvation, so pray, fast, and seek God before agreeing to marry. Quote James 1:5 aloud in prayer and God will freely give you the wisdom to know whom to marry and when.

It's crucial to know that your vow to marry a person cannot be broken. Too often, engagements become official and then are broken off. This is sin because a promise or vow is what marries two people in God's sight. Matthew 1:18-20 shows the power of the vow, as the angel of the Lord appearing to Joseph in his dream called Mary his wife and they were only espoused, or engaged. Numbers 30 offers added insight on vows.

If you're single and committing fornication with your partner, you know you are out of God's will.[1744] It's not wise to jump into marriage with the partner just so you can have sexual relations without seeing if God is leading you to marry this person. Stop fornicating, begin living in sanctification, and wait upon the Lord for His will.

If you are already in a marriage relationship and you wonderfully come to Christ as a new convert, Paul says to stay married, even if your spouse is not a Christian.[1745] He encourages you that your sanctified life may help win your spouse and children to Christ.

Notice Paul emphasizes how marriage is about pleasing and serving your spouse through love.[1746] When marriage infatuation ends, let God's

---

1743   1 Corinthians 7:7, Matthew 19:10-12
1744   1 Thessalonians 4:3
1745   1 Corinthians 7:12-16
1746   1 Corinthians 7:13, 34, Ephesians 5:25, 33, Colossians 3:19, Titus 2:4

love motivate you to serve and please your mate. Malachi 2:16 says God hates divorce and anyone who divorces and remarries another becomes adulterers, and if left unconfessed, keeps them from the kingdom of God.

Jesus teaches the only occasion a person can remarry after divorce is a man who puts away his wife due to unconfessed fornication committed before marriage. Read Matthew 5:31-32 and 19:1-9 for more on this. This one and only divorce-and-remarry clause exists because the woman made a false vow, claiming to be pure when she wasn't. Joseph and Mary best teach this truth, as he was going to put her away for fornication but God supernaturally intervened to validate Mary's virginity. Adultery is not a cause for remarriage—only unconfessed fornication according to Jesus Christ. All marriage vows last until death.

God's will for parents is to diligently love, teach, discipline, and provide for their children. Read Proverbs 19:18, 20:11, 22:6, 22:15, 23:13, 29:15-17, 29:21, and Colossians 3:21 for these truths. Psalm 127:1-5 proclaim children are God's heritage (possession), rewards from His creative hand, and are arrows you must sharpen (increasing their godly character) to defeat future enemies.

For all non-family relationships, endeavor to live at peace with all men as much as possible.[1747] Have answers ready for those who ask about your faith and season them with grace.[1748] Jesus says bless and love enemies rather than cursing them, overcoming evil with good.[1749]

VOCATIONS

God's will for your job can be an urgent question for some. Know first that parenting is the most important vocation if you have children. Never abandon your child: *"The rod and reproof give wisdom: but a child left to himself bringeth his mother to shame."*[1750] If the choice is between more money through a job or staying at home to parent your children and have less, choose less in the natural and more in the spiritual. You can

---

1747 Romans 12:18, Hebrews 12:14
1748 Colossians 4:6, 1 Peter 3:15
1749 Matthew 5:44, Romans 12:19-21
1750 Proverbs 29:15

work the rest of your life after your children grow up. Love and invest in your children's souls while there is hope. Proverbs 19:18 admonishes, *"Chasten thy son while there is hope, and let not thy soul spare for his crying."*

As with relationships, ask God for wisdom when deciding upon a vocation. If you love God, He'll use your choices for His glory and all will work together for your good. Be open to God doing something different from your first plans. You might follow in your parent's footsteps, like Jesus working as a carpenter. Paul made and sold tents, Luke was a physician, Matthew was a tax collector, Peter was a fisherman, and Lydia was a seller of purple. God will provide a vocation for you, too.

No matter the vocation, God's will is for you to work diligently, as if you're working for Him. Ecclesiastes 9:10 says, *"Whatsoever thy hand findeth to do, do it with thy might; for there is no work, nor device, nor knowledge, nor wisdom, in the grave, whither thou goest."* Paul expresses the same urgency in Romans 12:11: *"Not slothful in business; fervent in spirit; serving the Lord."* Ephesians 6:6 records Paul's instructions for servants to serve from their hearts: *"Not with eyeservice, as menpleasers; but as the servants of Christ, doing the will of God from the heart."*

Always remember your vocation is not given you to become rich. It's not a sin to be wealthy, nor to be poor, but God's goal for you is contentment. 1 Timothy 6:6 teaches, *"But godliness with contentment is great gain."* Money is a means to an end—the end is loving God and your fellowman. God loves a cheerful giver.

LOCATIONS

Where should you live? This answer is most often determined by your vocation, but know God determined your physical location so you would learn to seek Him. Acts 17:26-27 declares,

> *"And hath made of one blood all nations of men for to dwell on all the face of the earth, and hath determined the times before appointed, and the bounds of their habitation; That they should seek the Lord, if haply they might feel after him, and find him, though he be not far from every one of us."*

God determined your starting location, so trust Him to guide all the places you'll inhabit. You might never leave the region of your birth. Or, there may be surprises about your future dwellings.

Abraham, by God's will, moved at least 15 times,[1751] from Ur, to Egypt, to Damascus, to Hebron. Despite the constant activity from his many movings, he was a friend to God and father of faith.

It wasn't easy for Joseph when God allowed him to be sold into slavery at age 17. He was completely surprised and his life was turned upside down. Joseph was moved from Canaan across the Sinai Peninsula to Egypt. God's purpose for Joseph's life, as savior of many lives, caused his move. All God-directed moves glorify God and position man for His service.

Lot, nephew of Abraham, demonstrates the importance of your physical location. In Genesis 13, Lot and Abraham agreed they could not live together due to spacing limits, so Lot chose the well-watered plains of Jordan and pitched his tent toward Sodom. This turned out to be a disastrous choice, as eventually he lost wife (turned into a pillar of salt) and other family members in fire and brimstone. Lot's location choice seemed to be made upon financial prospects only. He may have prospered financially, but suffered great loss spiritually. He was daily vexed by things he saw and heard—especially the violent, homosexual lifestyle of Sodom's men. Choose to put your family among godly people and influences even if it means less money and benefits.

Let your place of worship, your home church, be a major factor in your location. Frequent, increasing gathering with Christians while hearing live preaching from the fivefold ministry is God's will for your life, so choose a location that allows you to fulfill this command. Satan wants to scatter the sheep (congregation) from their shepherd (pastor), so his wolves can devour the flock.[1752] Your location should allow you to have a pastor and church family you regularly serve and worship with.

1751 "Map: Abraham's Journeys." *Reading the Bible Chronologically in 365 Days*, https://hisstillsmallvoice.wordpress.com/2013/02/07/400/

1752 Acts 20:28-29

MINISTRIES

Important Christian ministries, outside local church ministry, include missionary work, prayers, and providing relief for the poor and needy. Ask God which ministry you are to support. Fulfill Jesus' command to seek first the kingdom of God.

God's will must be sought for each move in missionary work. For instance, some have said all missionary efforts are the will of God. Acts 16:6 proves otherwise, as Paul is *"forbidden of the Holy Ghost to preach the word in Asia."* While on his second missionary trip, God's will for Paul cut him off from doing missionary work in Asia Minor at that time. Acts 13:1-3 shows Paul fasting, denying his body food, before deciding where to go and who to take with him on his trips. You must constantly seek God's progressive will in every ministry effort.

For missionary efforts, you'll find Paul frequently leaning on God's will and timing for his visits. He knew everything had to be done in God's time and season, not his. Christians must recognize and accept the same. Paul tells the Romans he's hoping for a *"prosperous journey by the will of God to come unto"* them *"with joy by the will of God"* so they all could be refreshed.[1753] He wanted to visit his Christian family, but everything depended upon God's will—his actual ability to visit, provisions, joy, and refreshment. Your every missionary or evangelistic trip should follow this pattern.

Prayer is a crucial ministry for saints, as Paul prayed and fasted before trips. But all saints can join in praying to heaven for successful missionary efforts and general Christian needs. Acts 12 records the unceasing prayers of the church during Peter's imprisonment and in response God sent an angel to rescue him out of prison.

Providing relief to the poor and needy is a God-called ministry referred to as *"helps"* in 1 Corinthians 12:28. In the Greek, *"helps"* means "aid; relief." Jesus calls this almsgiving, and saints like Joanna, Tabitha, Phebe, and the Macedonian Christians are examples of relief ministries. Joanna, *"wife of Chuza Herod's steward"* teamed up with *"Susanna, and*

1753   Romans 1:10, 15:32

many others" to provide food and other needs for Jesus as He preached in cities and villages.[1754] Tabitha was *"full of good works and almsdeeds"* making *"coats and garments"* for the needy. [1755] Paul urged the Romans to assist Phebe in her business of succoring, or aiding the needy, for she had previously helped meet Paul's needs.[1756] Paul rejoices in the efforts of the deeply-poor Macedonians who sent Paul and his ministry provisions. Scripture says the Macedonians first gave themselves to the Lord and then unto Paul *"by the will of God."*[1757] This harmonizes with this entire chapter, as you find God's will after you yield yourself completely to Him.

This pattern of saints (non-preachers) helping and supporting preachers is foundational as seen in Jesus' ministry (Luke 8) and in Acts. New converts saw such holiness in the preachers and cared so much for other believers that they laid financial offerings at the apostles' feet, assured the money would be used wisely for God's kingdom.[1758] The 12 apostles in the early church soon ordained deacons, through prayer and reports of honest men, to provide relief to hungry Christinas in Acts 6:1-8.

Take Paul's advice and find within your home church a family who diligently serves the needy, and then offer to help them. 1 Corinthians 16:15-16 says, *"I beseech you, brethren, (ye know the house of Stephanas, that it is the firstfruits of Achaia, and that they have addicted themselves to the ministry of the saints,) That ye submit yourselves unto such, and to every one that helpeth with us, and laboureth."* Stephanas' addiction to serving believers was a testimony that refreshed Paul's spirit. Would to God adults and teenagers would be addicted to serving others by the will of God rather than suffering addiction to drugs and alcohol! Be like David, serving your generation by the will of God.

GIFTS OF THE HOLY GHOST

Paul lists the nine gifts of the Holy Ghost in 1 Corinthians 12:8-10. Gifts are extraordinary powers God bestows upon all to help all. Paul teaches

1754   Luke 8:1-3
1755   Acts 9:36-39
1756   Romans 16:1-2
1757   2 Corinthians 8:1-5
1758   Acts 4:34-37

gifts are given to every man to profit others.[1759] Romans 11:29 says God gives gifts and callings regardless of whether a person repents or not. Your gifts are in you before birth.

Two people have told me they knew I was a preacher before I stepped into the pulpit to minister. A high school friend said she saw a leadership gift in my life even when I was a sinner, seven years before I began preaching. Years later, a pastor's wife told me she knew I'd be a preacher the very first time we met, well before I even considered preaching. Jeremiah 1:5 is true—God knew us before our birth and ordained us for His purpose.

Since your gift is not for yourself, you only operate it in love. Seek not to use your gift for your benefit but use your gift that sinners might testify to God's manifest presence.[1760]

God gives you a gift or gifts because there is a need for your service. You'll never have to force your gift into a situation or church ministry because Provers 18:16 declares, *"A man's gift maketh room for him, and bringeth him before great men."* Your gift has a God-ordained place for it to fit into.

Gifts edify, or build, the church, and keep it clean. Paul says prophecy is greater than one person's ability to speak in tongues because it helps more believers: *"I would that ye all spake with tongues, but rather that ye prophesied: for greater is he that prophesieth than he that speaketh with tongues, except he interpret, that the church may receive edifying."*[1761] Peter's gift of discernment cleaned the spirt of deception out of the early church when Ananias and Sapphira tried to lie to him. Afterwards *"great fear came upon all the church, and upon as many as heard these things."*[1762]

Many seek gifts, like unknown tongues, rather than the Giver of the Gifts, Jesus Christ. Seek first to be born again and afterwards follow charity, desiring spiritual gifts. Get born from above and God will naturally lead you to using your gifts. 1 Corinthians 14:1 proves this: *"Follow after charity, and desire spiritual gifts, but rather that ye may prophesy."* You

---

1759   1 Corinthians 12:7
1760   1 Corinthians 14:23-25
1761   1 Corinthians 14:5
1762   Acts 5:1-11

should not be ignorant of gifts and it's godly to desire the best gifts so that more saints are helped.[1763]

While everyone has a gift, the apostle also stresses realistically assessing your portion of faith, or whichever gift you possess. Our gifts have different measures of power. Your faith might move mountains while mine moves only hills. Romans 12:6 says to operate your gift *"according to the proportion of your faith."* Another's gift of healing might cure a cancer case while another might relieve a headache. In His wisdom, Jesus gave differing amounts of talents to each person and we must happily invest in our portion.

DEFINITIONS AND EXAMPLES OF THE 9 GIFTS

All nine gifts will now be defined, accompanied by both Bible and real life examples.

The Word of Wisdom: Listed first by Paul, wisdom is the chief gift because it manages all others. Solomon says it is *"the principal thing."*[1764] God honored Solomon because he asked for wisdom and wrote Proverbs, a treasure-trove of practical wisdom. However, he had only the gift of wisdom, and in his later years he failed to apply it to his life when his many wives turned his heart from the Lord.[1765] Jesus Christ is the fulness and essence of wisdom.

This ability, sometimes referred to as sound advice, manifests skill and discretion in timely decision-making. Jesus says wisdom is validated by the results it bears, saying, *"wisdom is justified of her children."*[1766] The Bible says, *"Wisdom hath builded her house"* and a wise man builds his house upon a rock.[1767] Like a project manager building a house, wisdom tells you what to do and when to do it. Here are some examples:

- Jesus' answer about paying taxes to Caesar and also giving money to God (Matthew 22:15-22).

1763   1 Corinthians 12:1, 31
1764   Proverbs 4:7
1765   1 Kings 11:1-8
1766   Matthew 11:19
1767   Proverbs 9:1, Matthew 7:24

- The wise virgins preparing extra oil for light in case the bridegroom tarried while the foolish neglected to prepare (Matthew 25:1-13).
- Paul's perception to share his belief in the resurrection before a divided, angry Jewish council, thereby saving his life (Acts 23:6-11).
- A minister said I gave him a word of wisdom about how to decide upon and manage extracurricular activities for his children after he was wrongly accused of being an unfit father.
- Another minister said I gave him a word of wisdom to continue in his ministry when he had almost decided to give up.

The Word of Knowledge: If wisdom tells you how to build a house, knowledge is your raw building materials. You need both to build a house, so you'll find knowledge and wisdom associated together over 30 times in Scripture.[1768] Knowledge is information from God—usually a Scripture from the Bible.

Another divine illustration is Jesus calling knowledge a key allowing you to enter into the door of God's will in Luke 11:52. Knowledge is an understanding of God's Word needed to possess His promises and escape Satan's devices. Peter says we escape *"the pollutions of the world through the knowledge of the Lord and Saviour Jesus Christ."*[1769] Here are some examples:

- Peter and Philip both gave Scriptural knowledge, citing Joel 2:28-32 and Isaiah 53:7-8 respectively, allowing 3,000 souls and the Ethiopian eunuch to enter the door of salvation through repentance and water baptism (Acts 2:1-47, 8:26-40).

1768   Exodus 31:3, Proverbs 2:6, 10-11
1769   2 Peter 2:20

- Acts 19:1-6 shows Paul opening the door of the baptism of the Holy Ghost to 12 believers in Ephesus who previously had no knowledge of the new birth.
- After receiving the knowledge of 1 Corinthians 6:12, God opened the door to my deliverance from tobacco addiction.
- My wife gave me a word of knowledge I shared with a brother struggling to know whether or not he could be both a preacher and deacon, setting him free from doubt and allowing God to use him repeatedly in supernatural ways in our assembly.

Faith: This gift is an assurance and inner substance[1770] of God's desire and power to move obstacles, problems, sicknesses, or adversaries, figuratively described as mountains,[1771] by speaking God's Word. Jesus teaches that faith, a revelation of God's will about a specific work, makes anything possible.[1772] Here are some examples:

- Jesus commends the Roman centurion's great faith for requesting Jesus to speak the Word only for his servant's healing, which happened the same hour (Matthew 8:1-13).
- Paul and a crippled man in Lystra both had faith for healing, causing Paul to loudly command the man to walk for the first time (Acts 14:7-10).
- A friend's gift of faith pronounced a barren couple would have a baby after we prayed for them and about a year later their baby boy was born on my birthday.
- Similarly, one morning in prayer I felt led to command another couple's mountain of barrenness to leave, and less than a year later they embraced their God-sent baby girl.

1770 Hebrews 11:1
1771 1 Corinthians 13:2
1772 Matthew 17:20

- After months of battling a critical spirit on a couple in our assembly, I felt led to stand by their seats while praying alone in church, commanding the evil spirit to leave and 11 days later the husband, an officer in our church, abruptly resigned and left, restoring peace.
- A pastor friend of mine felt led to tell his friend to speak his faith in God's Word regarding his hunting trip the day beforehand. The hunter spoke an eight point buck in faith and harvested it the next day.

The Gifts of Healing: Healing is the deliverance from the oppression of the devil from both body and mind,[1773] as mental torment often causes physical ailments. There are numerous gifts of healing, such as laying on hands, speaking the Word, and natural remedies. Divine healing isn't spontaneous, which differentiates it from miracles. Here are some examples:

- Saul's mental torment from an evil spirit troubled his body, but David's skillful harp playing cast the demon from him (1 Samuel 16:13-23).
- Ezekiel 47:12 declares leaves and plants can be used as medicine, and figs were used to heal boils (2 Kings 20:7, Isaiah 38:21).
- Jesus Christ promises to heal the sick when we lay hands on them (Mark 16:16-17).
- Paul prayed and laid his hands on Publius' father, and he was healed of fever and bloody flux, an intestinal infection (Acts 28:8).
- Women on two separate occasions, one in Pennsylvania and another in our Ohio church, were healed of arm weakness or paralysis using Jesus' keys to the kingdom in prayer.
- After battling a throat sickness for over a week which hindered me from singing, a visiting minister from India

1773   Acts 10:38

prayed for me and I left the church building with full
ability to sing and praise God loudly.

- As I preached on divine healing in a service, my wife felt
God reveal her healing from migraines and through faith
and a healthier lifestyle, has not suffered from them since.

The Working of Miracles: These are instant, spontaneous manifestations of healings or other phenomenon performed by faith. Galatians 3:5 says, "*He therefore that ministereth to you the Spirit, and worketh miracles among you, doeth he it by the works of the law, or by the hearing of faith?*"

Jesus' innumerable healing miracles included stopping a woman's bleeding and delivering souls from life-threatening fevers. Other miraculous phenomenon included raising the dead, turning water to wine, and multiplying fish and bread.[1774] More Biblical and modern examples include:

- Casting out certain types of demons (Mark 9:38-39).
- Jesus causing a lame man to walk and leap by the hand of
Peter and John (Acts 3:1-11, 4:16).
- Using handkerchiefs Paul had touched to drive out
demons from the sick (Acts 19:11-12).
- God's healing my mother from liver cancer as my father
laid his hand upon her and prayed in Jesus' name in 1988.
- While praying for the sick in Guyana, I witnessed God
instantly heal a young mother from a kidney stone, as well
as an elderly man suffering from arthritis.

Prophecy: This ability foretells the future, giving believers "*edification, exhortation, and comfort.*"[1775] Prophesies can be spontaneously pronounced aloud with "*Thus saith the Holy Ghost*" like Agabus in Acts 21:11, or God can send a prophetic dream as He did with Nebuchadnezzar in Daniel chapter 2.

1774 Mark 5:25-34, 6:52, John 2:11, 4:49-54, 6:1-14, 12:17-18
1775 1 Corinthians 14:3

When prophesies are pronounced in a public gathering, they are to be judged by two or three witnesses according to 1 Corinthians 14:29 and 1 Thessalonians 5:19-21. Here are some examples:

- Jesus foretold Peter's three denials (Matthew 26:34,75).
- Agabus prophesied a famine (Acts 11:27-28).
- Philip had four virgin daughters who prophesied (Acts 21:9).
- In 2013, a pastor friend of mine foretold the passing away of numerous preachers during that year.
- My wife and I have had prophetic dreams come to pass warning individuals of Satan's snares.

Discerning of Spirits: This gift judges or distinguishes between the source or motivation behind actions, prophesies, or words. All actions come from either the Holy Spirit or one of the many unholy spirits—fallen angels—and discernment identifies if it's from God or a demon, whether a spirit of divination, lying spirit, or other.

Discernment is the gift that judges publicly announced prophesies and interpretations of unknown tongues: *"Let the prophets speak two or three, and let the other judge."*[1776]

Hebrews 4:12 likens discernment to a sword that divides a man's soul and spirit, and discerns the *"thoughts and intents of the heart."* God's Word ministers to the unique, individual needs of the body, human spirit, and soul (See Chapter 5). Discernment allows secrets of hearts to be made manifest. Below are some Biblical and modern examples:

- Solomon used discernment to reveal the good intentions of the real mother of a baby when another woman falsely claimed to be its mother (1 Kings 3:16-28).
- Jesus discerned both Nathanael's guileless spirit and the woman at the well's sexual immorality with six men (John 1:47-51, 4:4-29).

1776   1 Corinthians 14:29

- Peter exercised discernment by revealing Ananias' secret lie and Simon the sorcerer's wicked heart condition (Acts 5:1-5, 8:18-24).
- Paul says sinners will recognize God's Spirit is in a local church when their secrets are revealed through gifts of prophecy, interpretation, and discernment (1 Corinthians 14:24-25).
- Through dreams, God gave a couple in our church discernment about the source of contention in a matter, likening the evil spirit as a wolf (Acts 20:29-30).
- God helped me discern and deny a lying spirit on a former church member when he requested permission to share his false teachings in front of the church to draw away members after his group.

Divers Kinds of Tongues: This gift allows believers to speak in unknown or known human languages, or even tongues of angels.[1777] Jesus promised believers would speak in new tongues in Mark 16:17. Tongues may be given in public worship, but only if they are interpreted and judged.[1778] Paul says publicly-spoken tongues without interpretations create a barbaric, insane atmosphere.[1779] With no interpreter, tongues are strictly for private prayer and individual edification.

1 Corinthians 12:30 says not all Christians speak with tongues. Paul strongly supported prophetic, interpreted tongues because they edified the entire church rather than just one believer.[1780]

On the Day of Pentecost, the 120 Spirit-filled believers were speaking in unknown tongues so the hearers from 17 different regions could hear them in their own native languages. All tongues were known and understood. You can speak in an unknown tongue at the moment you're born again, but it should be understood by a hearer close by. Modern

1777 1 Corinthians 13:1
1778 1 Corinthians 14:28-29
1779 1 Corinthians 14:11, 23
1780 1 Corinthians 14:1-5

churches err greatly when they allow instant, constant, and uninterpreted tongues in public services, leading to confusion and chaos, which God does not author.[1781] Below is a list of examples where tongues were used appropriately:

- While Peter preached at Cornelius' house, the Holy Ghost fell upon the hearers, who spoke in tongues and magnified God (Acts 10:44-48).
- Paul laying hands on 12 Ephesians, who being filled with the Holy Ghost, spoke in tongues and prophesied (Acts 19:1-6).
- In 2010, a visiting minister to our church spoke in an unknown tongue and interpreted it, with three people testifying the message was a warning to them about their spiritual backsliding.
- Three other times our church has had unknown tongues spoken; and we've prayed for interpretations as Paul commanded in 1 Corinthians 14:13, but none came, and we are always open to more.

Interpretation of Tongues: This gift directly connects to Divers Kinds of Tongues. The examples above also apply to it.

Begin seeking God first to be born again and afterwards seek to know His gift or gifts in your life. Paul says, *"Follow after charity, and desire spiritual gifts."*[1782] You might have more than one gift, as Paul had multiple gifts, including speaking in tongues, miracles, and divine healing. Remember, with love as your motivation, you're commanded to desire and covet gifts. 1 Corinthians 12:31 reads, *"But covet earnestly the best gifts: and yet shew I unto you a more excellent way."* May you covet God's supernatural power and ministry in both your daily life and church services.

Study God's way to use your gifts and prayerfully ask God to help you operate them. After you double the impact of your spiritual gifts,

1781   1 Corinthians 14:33
1782   1 Corinthians 14:1

Jesus will say, *"Well done, thou good and faithful servant: thou hast been faithful over a few things, I will make thee ruler over many things: enter thou into the joy of thy lord."*[1783]

MY TESTIMONY ABOUT FINDING GOD'S WILL FOR MY LIFE

Reading my testimony about finding God's will may help you find His will for yours. Currently, I'm 40 years old, happily married with eight children. My two vocations are teaching in public school and pastoring a small church. Humbly, I truly believe with all my heart I'm living in God's perfect will for my life. How did I get here?

Relationship: My wife and I joke we met in a sandbox because we were both long jumpers in track and began dating in 1998 at 17 and 15 years old, respectively. We weren't saved at this point, but we knew we shared a special bond. After I left for college, we both repented and gave our hearts to Jesus Christ on the same night, completely unaware of it—she in Toledo and me in Columbus. We had obeyed God's known will for salvation, but was it God's will for us to be married?

Before our engagement, we had been dating for over four years and we had seriously prayed, asking God to show us His will for our relationship. We were both open to God separating us as well, since we wanted only His will. After multiple conversations I had with pastors and married couples, God's peace settled into my heart that I did not want to live without her. I admired everything about her and knew her strengths would compliment my weaknesses. Our wedding in June of 2003 still stands as the second happiest day of my life—right after the day we were saved from our sins through faith in Jesus Christ.

Vocations: While on college visits, I realized I didn't want to become a doctor, as I had previously hoped, completely naive to the workload. After my first college semester in Akron, Jesus wonderfully saved my soul, but I was still undecided on my major. Trying course after course, I joined a friend in a child development class and instantly fell in love

1783 Matthew 25:21

with the classroom. It became a joy to go to class and learn about teaching and learning.

In 2004, God supernaturally opened up a teaching position for me right out of college when jobs were scarce and despite hundreds of applicants seeking it. Multiple parents have told me having their child in my classroom was the answer to their prayers. Additionally, the Lord has inspired me help lead two Bible Clubs—one before school at the middle school and one after school club at an elementary building. Hundreds of children and teens have heard the gospel of Jesus.

My second job is pastoring, as my friends and I started our own church in 2006, and I've served as the only pastor. The reason I knew God had called me to preach was because I began to feel a strong burden to minister. After receiving an invitation to preach, I prayed and fasted, asking God to clearly show me if He was calling me. The Lord answered in full assurance. Seconds before I began preaching, Jesus anointed a sister in the audience to give a loud word of discernment, making known the very subject I was going to preach. At the sermon's conclusion, the altar was full of saints repenting, seeking deliverance, and more. I've known it's God's will for me to preach ever since.

Locations: I've lived in only two Ohio locations my entire life— Toledo and Akron. You know God brought me to college in Akron before mercifully saving me, but you might be surprised to know He used a full-ride football scholarship to do it. Being that my parents were divorced, our family was poor and it was impossible for me attend college without it being paid for. I now see God's hand in the scholarship to move me away from all I ever knew and loved. This separation showed me my need for Jesus' love and guidance, and He was also providing a pastor for His small Akron church.

After my 2004 college graduation and subsequent hiring at a local school district, we started the church two years later. I've never felt God's leading to leave this city, but I am open to God moving my family according to His pleasure.

Ministries: My family's main ministry is providing three weekly church services to our Akron church members. A few of my older children have began to serve in music ministry, in which I also perform a small role. I believe God gave me my eight children "*for song in the house of the Lord*" and "*for service of the house of God*" like Heman, father of 17 children, from the days of David.[1784]

It's my joy to do most of the preaching and all the church's deacon and financial work. Our church supports missionaries, helps the poor and needy, and provides Bible studies for new converts.

Over the past eight years, I've felt led to work in video-making and book writing ministries. I waited on these ministries for almost 10 years, but since investing heavily into these works, God has given us wonderful testimonies of His Spirit helping believers around the world.

Gifts: You've read some of the testimonies God has done through the gifts in my life, whether in preaching, or in faith, healing, or miracles. Jesus' words in John 15:5 are my testimony to any good happening through my life: "*I am the vine, ye are the branches: He that abideth in me, and I in him, the same bringeth forth much fruit: for without me ye can do nothing.*" I am nothing without Jesus. Absolutely nothing.

I can honestly say I feel unworthy during the times God has gently and mercifully used me to help others. In the moment of any supernatural work, Jesus has captured my entire thought process, and I'm just doing what seems right or natural. As Romans 12:1-2 declares, being used of God happens as I lay myself on His altar, laying aside my thoughts, time, plans, and preferences. My dearest prayer is that I can always be His living sacrifice that He may be exalted more.

THE REWARDS FOR RECEIVING THE REVELATION OF GOD'S WILL

Eternal life is the first and greatest reward for doing the will of God. 1 John 2:17 expresses, "*And the world passeth away, and the lust thereof: but he that doeth the will of God abideth for ever.*" Living God's will in this

1784   1 Chronicles 25:1-6

short, fleeting life entitles you to an unimaginably amazing eternal life to come.

A second reward is joining (by the new birth) and fellowshipping with God's eternal family. Jesus teaches your spiritual family is in fact your real family. While preaching, Jesus was interrupted and told that his mother, Mary, and siblings were seeking Him. Jesus' answer about who is His true family astounds the hearers. Mark 3:33-35 says, "*And he answered them, saying, Who is my mother, or my brethren? And he looked round about on them which sat about him, and said, Behold my mother and my brethren! For whosoever shall do the will of God, the same is my brother, and my sister, and mother.*" Doing God's will makes you a part of His forever-family.

Natural family relationships are important, but pale in comparison to being in God's spiritual family. You must love Jesus, your Savior, more than anyone else. Jesus' knew His preaching would divide family relationships within houses:

> "*But whosoever shall deny me before men, him will I also deny before my Father which is in heaven. Think not that I am come to send peace on earth: I came not to send peace, but a sword. For I am come to set a man at variance against his father, and the daughter against her mother, and the daughter in law against her mother in law. And a man's foes shall be they of his own household. He that loveth father or mother more than me is not worthy of me: and he that loveth son or daughter more than me is not worthy of me. And he that taketh not his cross, and followeth after me, is not worthy of me.*"[1785]

In this life you'll benefit from being in God's family. When Peter tells Jesus he's left everything for Him, implying about his losses, Jesus informs him of his gains in Mark 10:29-30:

> "*And Jesus answered and said, Verily I say unto you, There is no man that hath left house, or brethren, or sisters, or father,*

[1785] Matthew 10:33-38

or mother, or wife, or children, or lands, for my sake, and the gospel's, But he shall receive an hundredfold now in this time, houses, and brethren, and sisters, and mothers, and children, and lands, with persecutions; and in the world to come eternal life."

Holy Ghost-filled Christians have great heavenly inheritances waiting them, but all inherit a loving family in this earthly journey.

More rewards for doing God's will include being blessed by God, abiding in His love, and assurance that Jesus hears our prayers.[1786] Our Lord promises those who do His will and teach others to do the same *"shall be called great in the kingdom of heaven."*[1787]

As you confidently wait upon God's will for a little while, you gain three more great rewards. First, you eventually receive the promise—whether it's a bodily healing, knowledge of whom to marry, or financial supply. Hebrews 10:35-38 notes,

"Cast not away therefore your confidence, which hath great recompence of reward. For ye have need of patience, that, after ye have done the will of God, ye might receive the promise. For yet a little while, and he that shall come will come, and will not tarry. Now the just shall live by faith: but if any man draw back, my soul shall have no pleasure in him."

While patiently waiting for God to make His progressive will known and manifest, you're promised the second reward of renewed strength. Isaiah 40:31 says, *"But they that wait upon the Lord shall renew their strength; they shall mount up with wings as eagles; they shall run, and not be weary; and they shall walk, and not faint."* Hasty believers who try to force their will instead of waiting on God's will grow weaker in faith—not stronger. Jesus strengthens your faith as you wait upon His time and season.

The third reward is understanding God's progressive will, as Paul describes in Ephesians 5:14-21. With Christ' light of understanding, you

---

1786   John 15:10, James 1:25, 1 John 3:22-23
1787   Matthew 5:19

walk precisely in God's will, redeeming the time. Notice Paul separates wise from foolish by their use of time—just like Jesus separates the wise and foolish virgins. Wise virgins use their time to do exactly God's will for their lives.

You can understand your purpose doing God's will. Moses says the same as Paul, telling Israel that God's commands are *"your wisdom and your understanding in the sight of the nations."*[1788] Your life makes sense as you read the Bible for God's known will for your life and pray for His progressive will. In John 7:16-17, Jesus says you gain a witness inside your being when you do God's will. You'll feel, know, and understand true doctrine through the Spirit's presence in your soul.

THE CONSEQUENCES FOR REJECTING THE REVELATION OF GOD'S WILL

The most serious consequence of rejecting God's known will is being lost to hell and eternally separated from God via the lake of fire. Jesus' teaching about true and false prophets in Matthew 7:13-29 explains the severe punishment for false prophets who have enough faith in God to operate their spiritual gifts correctly, yet afterwards devote their lives to iniquity. Verses 21-23 read:

> *"Not every one that saith unto me, Lord, Lord, shall enter into the kingdom of heaven; but he that doeth the will of my Father which is in heaven. Many will say to me in that day, Lord, Lord, have we not prophesied in thy name? and in thy name have cast out devils? and in thy name done many wonderful works? And then will I profess unto them, I never knew you: depart from me, ye that work iniquity."*

It's not enough to do miracles and operate spiritual gifts. God wants simple, humble obedience to His will—both known and progressive. The evils of these false prophets are the worst because they knew God's will and blatantly refused to obey, loving sin more than righteousness.

1788 Deuteronomy 4:6

A second consequence is unfulfilled potential, which applies to the saved, or foolish virgins, who are truly Christians but live with some disobedience to God's will. They could have potentially attended the wedding supper but failed to prepare enough oil, or live close enough to God's will to receive the baptism of the Holy Ghost. Jesus also says they miss out on producing fruit, likening them to having thorny hearts which care for the world, riches, and pleasures more than Christ.

King Saul is a prime example of falling short of his potential, yet being saved. Samuel promised Saul he would be saved and with him in paradise after his death in battle[1789] but Saul lost out on untold blessings, wasting years embroiled with jealousy and murderous hatred for his son-in-law, David. God would have established Saul's kingdom forever if only he had done His will.[1790]

A third consequence is inward confusion, sadness, sorrow, and grief. Mark 10:17-25 records Jesus offering the highest calling in church—apostle—to the rich young ruler. Parallel passages prove Jesus loved this man,[1791] as he had kept nearly all the commandments. But to gain God's will for his life and the eternal life he lacked, Jesus asked him to forfeit his trust in riches, which the man refused. Verse 22 says, *"And he was sad at that saying, and went away grieved: for he had great possessions."* Although he may have grown to possess even greater riches, he would always possess an even greater sorrow for turning down eternal life. He may have even kept the commands on giving his money in tithes and offerings to the temple, which would have been a sacrifice, but he always lived with the grief of loving money more than Jesus. Obedience to God's will is greater than sacrifice. You can live in the joy, assurance, and confidence of obedience.

1789 1 Samuel 28:19
1790 1 Samuel 13:13-14
1791 Mark 10:21

CONCLUSION

God's power is limitless, and He's predestined and ordained everything in human history and your life, perfectly weaving His sovereign will with man's free moral agency. He chose the location of your nativity that you'd respond to His loving invitation to be saved and know Him intimately. You might go from the shepherd's field to the throne like David, or from Pharisee-fame to the prison like Paul. But you can trust Jesus' plan, purposes, timing, and commands.

You easily identify God's known will by simply reading the Bible. But His progressive will is a mystery you must seek out for yourself. It's not a maddening, arduous task; rather, it's a joy, comparable to a gold prospector who is guaranteed to strike it rich. Proverbs 2:4-5 illustrates, "*If thou seekest her as silver, and searchest for her as for hid treasures; Then shalt thou understand the fear of the Lord, and find the knowledge of God.*" It's like the Queen of Sheba enduring travel pains but eventually experiencing the indescribable joy of having all her questions answered by Solomon in God's holy presence.

You're guaranteed to know God's will if you'll search for it. As you seek Him, He promises to be found. The infallible Christ says, "*Every one that asketh receiveth; and he that seeketh findeth; and to him that knocketh it shall be opened.*"[1792]

Serve your family, church, community, and generation by God's will. Live in the perfect will of God and pray like Epaphras for others to obey all of God's will. Lastly, my prayer for you is everyday service to God's will, like Zachariah prayed in Luke 1:71-75. May we serve Him "*without fear, In holiness and righteousness before him, all the days of our life.*"

1792 Matthew 7:8

ACTION STEPS

1. Do the known will of God first, obeying every Bible command. Repent and be baptized in the name of the Lord Jesus Christ if you haven't been saved. Then go through sanctification, the Second Work of Grace, so you can be born again by the Holy Ghost in the Third Work of Grace.

2. After the new birth, develop the daily habits of Romans 12:1-2, being a living sacrifice, taking up your cross, and allowing your renewed mind to transform your life.

3. Before any decision—relationship, vocation, ministry, etc.—patiently wait on God's timing while keeping every commandment. Ask, seek, and knock, and Jesus will let you receive, find your desire, and open every door He wants you to walk through.

FOLLOW UP

Free online videos, Bible studies, and William Branham's quotes related to this chapter: www.pastorjessesmith.com/12mysteriesbook

Email: jesse.smith11@sbcglobal.net

Text: 330-929-2037

CHAPTER 12

The Mystery of the Rapture

"Behold, I shew you a mystery;
We shall not all sleep, but we shall all be changed,
In a moment, in the twinkling of an eye,
at the last trump: for the trumpet shall sound,
and the dead shall be raised incorruptible,
and we shall be changed."

1 Corinthians 15:51-52

T IS ONLY FITTING that the final mystery is the rapture of Jesus Christ's bride, the New Testament church, because the rapture will be final event of the Times of the Gentiles. Immediately after the rapture of the Gentile bride, God will graft Israel back in to the *"holy tree"* and send her the two prophets mentioned in Revelation 11:3-13.

The rapture is the unknown day and hour Jesus Christ secretly and physically comes back to earth. Christ will stop in the air, not touching the sin-soaked earth, to eagerly receive His bride for their wedding day before returning to heaven with her for their wedding reception, the Marriage Supper of the Lamb.

As recorded in the epigraph, Paul specifically calls this event *"a mystery."* Thankfully, the Bible promised that all the mysteries of God, including the rapture mystery, would be revealed in the end times. Revelation 10:7 says that the *"mystery of God"* would be finished or revealed, and then the revelation would be taken and prophesied *"before many peoples, and nations, and tongues, and kings."*[1793] God is currently fulfilling this prophecy by anointing and sending apostles and evangelists to prophesy again all the revelations of the New Testament mysteries.

The word "rapture" is not in the King James Bible, but many Christians use it because it gives us a common term referring to this momentous future event. However, the Bible also gives others names for the rapture: the *"caught up"* meeting or the *"first resurrection."*[1794]

Some may argue that Christians should not use the word "rapture" because, like the "Trinity," it is not found in the Bible. The difference is that the definition of the rapture is fully Scriptural while the definition of the Trinity, "God in three persons" is completely absent from God's Word. It's completely acceptable to use the term "rapture."

The Holy Spirit will perform six raptures, with four already occurring and two upcoming:

- Enoch (Gen. 5:24).
- Elijah (2 Kings 2:11).
- Jesus ascending to the Father alone (John 20:17).
- Jesus ascending with the Old Testament saints, leading *"captivity captive"* to heaven (Mark 16:19, Ephesians 4:8).
- Gentile bride rapture (1 Thessalonians 4:15-17).
- Two witnesses (Revelation 11:11-12).

THE CONFUSION ABOUT THE RAPTURE

The confusion about the rapture centers around *when* it will occur. Bible students believe the rapture will take place in one of three different future times centering around the major event of the Great Tribulation. Will the rapture take place before, during, or after the Tribulation?

1793   Revelation 10:11
1794   1 Thessalonians 4:17, Revelation 20:5

The revelation of the rapture mystery is Jesus uses a shout, voice, and trump to secretly and suddenly snatch away His Holy Spirit-filled bride off the earth as the last climatic, culminating event of the Times of the Gentiles before the wrathful Tribulation.

A fourth and smaller group believes the rapture has already taken place. Thankfully, we can know assuredly that the rapture has *not* yet happened and is a future event. Paul's last letter before his martyrdom condemned those who said the rapture or *"resurrection"* was past already, saying their false doctrine was overthrowing the faith of some.[1795] The apostle also wrote to Titus, saying that Christians should deny worldly lusts in this present world, *"Looking for that blessed hope, and the glorious appearing of the great God and our Saviour Jesus Christ."*[1796] The rapture is the future event all Christians are still looking for 2,000 years later—the appearing of our Lord Jesus Christ in the air.

There is also confusion about who will be in the rapture. Is it for everyone on earth, all those who call themselves Christians, or just a small, faithful, Spirit-filled remnant of Christians?

BIBLICAL PROOF FOR THE REVELATION ABOUT THE RAPTURE

To begin with, the Bible defines the rapture mystery as the *"caught up"* experience Paul teaches about in 1 Corinthians 15:51-54 and 1 Thessalonians 4:15-18, respectively:

> *"Behold, I shew you a mystery; We shall not all sleep, but we shall all be changed, In a moment, in the twinkling of an eye, at the last trump: for the trumpet shall sound, and the dead shall be raised incorruptible, and we shall be changed. For this corruptible must put on incorruption, and this mortal must*

1795   2 Timothy 2:17-18
1796   Titus 2:12-13

put on immortality. So when this corruptible shall have put on incorruption, and this mortal shall have put on immortality, then shall be brought to pass the saying that is written, Death is swallowed up in victory."

"For this we say unto you by the word of the Lord, that we which are alive and remain unto the coming of the Lord shall not prevent them which are asleep. For the Lord himself shall descend from heaven with a shout, with the voice of the archangel, and with the trump of God: and the dead in Christ shall rise first: Then we which are alive and remain shall be caught up together with them in the clouds, to meet the Lord in the air: and so shall we ever be with the Lord. Wherefore comfort one another with these words."

The question as to *who* will be in the rapture can now be answered. These texts teach two groups of Christians will have their bodies changed at the moment of the rapture so they can be caught up to meet Jesus Christ in the the air: the *"dead in Christ"* and the living Christians. The dead in Christ are the Holy Ghost-filled Christians who have died over the past 2,000 years. This group will be resurrected in immortal bodies first, as Paul says *"the dead shall be raised incorruptible"* and *"shall rise first."* John correctly describes the rapture as the *"first resurrection"* because the *"dead in Christ"* are being resurrected.

The living Christians, the second group, will be changed from mortal bodies to immortal, and will be like Enoch and Elijah, who never had to taste death. Paul says their mortal bodies will be *"swallowed up in victory."* This group of Christians *"which are alive and remain unto the coming of the Lord"* received the "oil" of the baptism of the Holy Ghost, or eternal life, during their lives, being called "wise virgins" by Jesus Christ in Matthew 25:1-13.

The rest of the entire world population who denied Christ as unbelievers, along with those "foolish virgin" Christians who did not receive the "oil" or baptism of the Holy Ghost, will have to die during the Tribulation Period or the Battle of Armageddon, and will miss the 1,000 year millennial reign with Christ. The foolish virgins miss the millennium because they foolishly choose to live lives void of the Holy Ghost-baptism on earth, being unfit to rule and reign with Christ. Revelation 20:5 explains, *"the rest of the dead lived not again until the thousand years were finished."* The bodies of the rest of the world population and "foolish virgin" Christians will remain *"in the graves"* according to Jesus[1797] and will be resurrected for their day of judgment at the Great White Throne, which is called the second resurrection, detailed in Matthew 25:31-46 and Revelation 20:11-15. The souls of the "foolish virgin" likely go to a heavenly dimension to peacefully wait for the second resurrection, just like the faithful, yet blinded-to-Christ Jews who had a heavenly waiting place under the altar of God in heaven according to the Fifth Seal of Revelation 6:9-11. The souls of unbelievers will undoubtedly go down to *"the heart of the earth,"* hell's prison house, to await judgment.[1798]

It's crucial to understand how the Greek word for *"caught up"* in 1 Thessalonians 4:17 supports a pre-Tribulation rapture. In the Greek Lexicon, *"caught up"* is harpazo, meaning "to seize, carry off by force, to seize on, claim for one's self eagerly, to snatch out or away."[1799] The rapture is Jesus eagerly seizing or snatching away His bride, His wife, so that He may take these Christians to heaven, or the *"Father's kingdom"*[1800] with Him for a wedding in the sky followed by a *"marriage supper."*[1801] Simultaneously, the inhabitants of the earth are being judged and tormented for their sins in the Tribulation for rejecting the gospel.

SIX REASONS THE RAPTURE IS PRE-TRIBULATION

Six reasons prove that the rapture is before the Great Tribulation—not during, nor afterwards.

Reason 1: The Great Tribulation is described as *"trouble"* for Israel, the "foolish virgins," and sinners, but not for the Holy

1797 John 5:28
1798 Matthew 12:40, 1 Peter 3:19, Hebrews 9:27
1799 "The Bible: Hebrew and Greek Lexicons." *Voice of God Recordings*, www.branham.org/en/messagesearch
1800 Matthew 26:29
1801 Revelation 19:9

Ghost-filled Christians. The Spirit-sealed Christians are already washed in the blood of Jesus Christ and are not in need of purifying, purging, or trouble during the Great Tribulation.

Daniel 12:1 and Jeremiah 30:7 refer to this season of unparalleled trouble by similar names—*"time of trouble"* and *"Jacob's trouble."* Both clearly reference Israel.

The foolish virgins, or Christians without the baptism of the Holy Ghost, will experience some degree of trouble in the Tribulation because two of Jesus' parables describe it. First, Jesus describes these foolish Christians as being locked out (obvious *"trouble"*) of the *"marriage"* in Matthew 25:10-12. This corresponds to missing the *"marriage supper"* in heaven mentioned in Revelation 19:7, despite living *"virgin"* or pure lives because they had no *"oil,"* or the Holy Ghost baptism. Another parable from Christ in Matthew 22:10-13 describes those without the wedding garment, which represents the Holy Ghost baptism, cast into outer darkness, with weeping and gnashing of teeth. Notice God's repeating pattern that despite making great human effort to be a part of the supper, or rapture, only those who are born again of the Holy Ghost will qualify for this holy gathering.

Sinners will face the worst trouble during the Great Tribulation, for God is going to *"Execute judgment upon all, and to convince all that are ungodly among them of all their ungodly deeds which they have ungodly committed, and of all their hard speeches which ungodly sinners have spoken against"* Jesus Christ and His bride.[1802]

Reason 2: There is no mention of Christ's bride or church in the Tribulation texts in the Book of Revelation. The word *"church"* appears 19 times in Revelation but is absent from 3:22 to 22:16. The reason Christ's bride, or *"wife"*, is not mentioned during the Great Tribulation taking place on earth is because she will be with Jesus at the heavenly Marriage Supper of the Lamb.[1803] Christ will rapture his bride at the end of the Laodicean Church Age[1804] (See Chapter 7), and the next time she

---

1802   Jude 1:15
1803   Revelation 19:1-10
1804   Revelation 3:14-22

is seen near earth is when she returns to the earth from heaven with Jesus Christ for the battle of Armageddon in Revelation 19:5-21, which takes place at the very end of the Tribulation.

The true church is not mentioned in Revelation chapter 8 during the first four trumpets, nor in Revelation chapter 9 in the fifth and sixth trumpets and when the first woe passes. Revelation chapter 10 deals with the completion of the Gentile bride's Great Commission, so it's not a Tribulation text. When the second woe passes in Revelation 11, the bride is still not mentioned. Israel is the theme of Revelation 12 and doesn't deal with Jesus' Gentile bride. In Revelation 13, you see the beast's transition to Papal Rome, her influence in the United States, and her war with the Jewish saints in the Tribulation, but there's no mention of Jesus' church. During the final harvest of the 144,000 Israeli believers in Revelation 14, there is again no mention of the bride of Christ. Jesus' wife is not mentioned in Revelation 15 and 16 when the seven last plagues and seven vials are poured out upon the earth. Revelation chapters 17 and 18 reveal Mystery Babylon's union with earth's kings, as well as her day of destruction in the Tribulation.

Some wrongly point to Revelation 14:6-10 and 16:15 to prove Jesus' bride goes through the Tribulation. These Scriptures are simply warnings for Jesus' church to be rapture-ready as she reads through the Book of Revelation during the 2,000 year time period of the Times of the Gentiles before the Tribulation. Revelation 18:4 is another plea for Bible readers to come out of Babylon before it's too late.

Reason 3: The bride or true church is specifically promised a pardon from God's divine wrath. The following seven Scriptures speak of God's gracious promise, beginning with Paul's two records of pardon in context directly after the *"caught up"* description from 1 Thessalonians:

- *"But ye, brethren, are not in darkness, that that day should overtake you as a thief."* (1 Thessalonians 5:4)
- *"For God hath not appointed us to wrath, but to obtain salvation by our Lord Jesus Christ."* (1 Thessalonians 5:9)

- *"And to wait for his Son from heaven, whom he raised from the dead, even Jesus, which delivered us from the wrath to come."* (1 Thessalonians 1:10)
- *"Much more then, being now justified by his blood, we shall be saved from wrath through him."* (Romans 5:9)
- *"Because thou hast kept the word of my patience, I also will keep thee from the hour of temptation, which shall come upon all the world, to try them that dwell upon the earth."* (Revelation 3:10)
- *"Watch ye therefore, and pray always, that ye may be accounted worthy to escape all these things that shall come to pass, and to stand before the Son of man."* (Luke 21:36)
- *"For in the time of trouble he shall hide me in his pavilion: in the secret of his tabernacle shall he hide me; he shall set me up upon a rock."* (Psalm 27:5)

In the seventh Scripture, take notice that David mentions being hidden from *"trouble,"* so this prophecy can only pertain to the bride of Christ, for the three other groups, specifically Israel in Daniel 12:1, endure trouble during the Great Tribulation.

The word *"wrath"* is used 13 times in Revelation and refers to God's wrath upon the religious system of Mystery Babylon and those who aligned themselves with her during the Tribulation. The final mention of *"wrath"* in Revelation 19:15 is Jesus treading out God's wrath against Satan and the ungodly at Armageddon.

Consider Christ's affection for His wife, the New Testament bride, and compare it with a natural husband preparing to marry his wife. Would a loving husband purposely allow his espoused wife to endure his wrath before their wedding? No, a godly husband would have no wrath towards his future wife because she has already found favor in his sight. On the contrary, he would do everything in his power to keep his wife from wrath and suffering. How much more will Jesus Christ keep His espoused wife from His wrath? Listen to Scripture's testimony about Jesus' wife: she's a *"glorious church, not having spot, or wrinkle, or any such thing."*[1805] Bride members are *"blameless and harmless...without rebuke."*[1806] Jesus' blood has forgiven all her trespasses.[1807] Christ's wife has *"no condemnation,"* and no man *"shall lay any thing to the charge of God's elect,"* for *"It is God that justifieth."*[1808] Undoubtedly, Jesus Christ will not allow His wife to endure His wrath because she is the wife of His choosing, already justified in His eyes.

Revelation 3:10 and 13:16-17 seem to suggest that the true church will experience a great trial just before the rapture, but surely this will be a *"light affliction"*[1809] compared to the divine wrath reserved for the wicked. Jesus promised Christians would be kept from living through the world-wide mark of the beast temptation, called the *"hour of temptation"* in Revelation 3:10. It seems inevitable that true believers will feel some of the mounting political, ecclesiastical, and financial pressure moments before Revelation 13:16-17 is fulfilled: *"And he causeth all, both small and great, rich and poor, free and bond, to receive a mark in their right hand, or in their foreheads: And that no man might buy or sell, save he that had the mark, or the name of the beast, or the number of his name."* But just as one in the *"form...like the Son of God"*[1810] speedily stepped into the fiery furnace milliseconds before the three Hebrew children were burned, so will the true Son of God snatch away us, His bride, the church, moments before the Tribulation is unleashed.

Reason 4: The bride or true church is foreshadowed to receive a pardon from God's divine wrath. Three historical Old Testament events and two of Jesus' parables foreshadow the bride's pardon from divine wrath.

Enoch, whose name means "dedicated" in Hebrew, foreshadowed the true church because he was raptured, not tasting death: *"And Enoch walked*

1805   Ephesians 5:27
1806   Philippians 2:15
1807   Colossians 2:13
1808   Romans 8:1, 33
1809   1 Corinthians 4:17
1810   Daniel 3:24

with God: and he was not; for God took him.[1811] Being the seventh generation from Adam,[1812] Enoch typed the current, seventh Gentile Church Age, the Laodicean Age, which will escape the wrath of the Tribulation.

Noah, the tenth generation from Adam,[1813] was spared from the wrath of God because he found grace in God's sight.[1814] 2 Peter 2:5 says Noah was a preacher of righteousness, and was spared from the worldwide destruction of the flood. Jesus validated that the end-times would resemble Noah's day in Matthew 24:37-39 and Luke 17:26-27. Thus, Noah types the "foolish virgin" group of Christians who miss the Enoch-like rapture before judgment and thereby experience the great temptation to take the mark of the beast. Revelation 13:15-17 seems to point to all foolish virgins being martyred due to their rejection of the mark of the beast. Their deaths would mean being spared from the wrath of the seven trumpets, seven vials, and three woes.

Righteous Lot, nephew of Abraham, was spared from God's wrath poured out on Sodom and Gomorrah in Genesis 19:1-29. Abraham's merciful intercession for Lot and all righteous people in the wicked cities was remembered by God[1815] and proved He would not destroy the *"righteous with the wicked."*[1816] Lot, like Noah, types the "foolish virgin" group of Christians who will not be raptured but will escape the indescribable wrath of the trumpets, vials, and woes. Herein we see God's faithful principle He will not destroy the righteous with the wicked. The two kinds of believers—holy and righteous—always escape God's wrath upon the wicked, as Jesus' Sower and the Four Grounds parable denotes.

Continuing on Lot's story, Jesus said His second coming would occur when world conditions resembled the days of Lot in Luke 17:28-30. We are living in a modern Sodom, as the growing global acceptance of homosexuality and the LGBT movement shows the fulfillment of Jesus' prophetic words.

1811   Genesis 5:24
1812   Jude 1:14
1813   Genesis 5:21-29
1814   Genesis 6:8
1815   Genesis 18:23-33, 19:29
1816   Genesis 18:25

Jesus' The King's Son parable in Matthew 22:1-14 foreshadows true Christians escaping God's wrath. Christ tells of a king making a marriage for his son, typing God the Father preparing the true church for their marriage to His Son, Jesus Christ at the *"caught up"* rapture. When the king came in to see the guests gathered for the wedding, he found a man that did not have the wedding garment. He was bound and cast into outer darkness, where there was weeping and gnashing of teeth. *"Outer darkness"* symbolizes the Great Tribulation since the wedding represents the rapture. Wedding garments represent the spiritual power or clothing *"from on high"*[1817] of the baptism of the Holy Ghost, because *"endued"* means "clothed with." Any person who is not born again of God's Spirit will not partake of Jesus Christ's wedding, and will have to give his life by denying the mark of the beast in the Tribulation.

Jesus tells a second parable about a wedding, or the future rapture in Matthew 25:1-13. Two groups of virgins hear the cry to attend the wedding but only one group has the *"oil,"* or baptism of the Holy Ghost, as described in Zechariah 4:1-6. "Wise" virgins have oil, meaning they are born again. "Foolish" virgins have no oil and are therefore shut out of the marriage-rapture. Those shut out of the rapture will endure the Tribulation, being forced to give up their lives rather than take the mark of the beast.

Reason 5: Jesus and Paul taught the rapture was imminent at an unknown day as an approaching thief while other views can number or count to the day. Jesus taught this truth on four occasions and Paul twice.

First, Jesus says, *"But of that day and hour knoweth no man, no, not the angels of heaven, but my Father only."*[1818] Later in the same chapter, Christ says *"But know this, that if the goodman of the house had known in what watch the thief would come, he would have watched, and would not have suffered his house to be broken up. Therefore be ye also ready: for in such an hour as ye think not the Son of man cometh."*[1819] The third reference is in

1817 Luke 24:49
1818 Matthew 24:36
1819 Matthew 24:43-44

the succeeding chapter when our Lord says, *"Watch therefore, for ye know neither the day nor the hour wherein the Son of man cometh."*[1820] Revelation 3:3 is the fourth witness, as Jesus says, *"Remember therefore how thou hast received and heard, and hold fast, and repent. If therefore thou shalt not watch, I will come on thee as a thief, and thou shalt not know what hour I will come upon thee."*

In 1 Thessalonians 5:2-4, Paul twice describes Christ's coming as a thief, saying Christians will escape the Great Tribulation's sudden, secret destruction time:

> *"For yourselves know perfectly that the day of the Lord so cometh as a thief in the night. For when they shall say, Peace and safety; then sudden destruction cometh upon them, as travail upon a woman with child; and they shall not escape. But ye, brethren, are not in darkness, that that day should overtake you as a thief."*

The two other, erroneous views and timelines of the rapture—mid-tribulation and post-tribulation—could potentially calculate the day of Christ's coming. Mid-tribulation supporters could count 3.5 years or 1,260 days after Israel's two prophets appear and calculate the day they believe Jesus will return. Likewise, post-tribulation supporters could count 7 years or 2,520 days after the two prophets appear and pinpoint the day of Christ's return. The pre-tribulation rapture is the only teaching that allows Christ to return at an unknown day and hour before the world-wide Great Tribulation.

The rapture must remain a secret for two reasons. First, Satan could do great damage if he knew the timing of Jesus' second coming, the rapture. Satan and a third of his angels[1821] did awful damage at Jesus' first coming when they anointed Herod and his soldiers to slay *"all the children that were in Bethlehem, and in all the coasts thereof, from two years old and under."*[1822] What type of killing spree would Satan inspire if he knew Jesus was going to come and take away His people this year or the next?

1820   Matthew 25:13
1821   Revelation 12:4
1822   Matthew 2:16

Second, a secret rapture reveals both good and evil hearts, according to Jesus Christ's parable in Matthew 24:45-51. A good hearted, faithful, and wise servant will be ready for the rapture while serving spiritual *"meat in due season"* to his fellow servants. The *"evil servant"* will behave as though the rapture is delayed, smiting his fellow servants in his drunken state. Peter explains that love motivates true Christians to endure trials of faith in anticipation of Jesus' appearance.[1823]

Reason 6: The rapture is the removal of the grace of God for Gentiles in preparation for the Antichrist's public revelation and God's return to the Jewish people.

Gentiles are now receiving *"salvation"*[1824] by the grace of God and will retain this privilege *"until the fulness of the Gentiles be come in."*[1825] God has blinded Israel from recognizing Christ as their Messiah that we, the Gentiles, might know Christ and be saved. Jesus defines this current time period as the *"times of the Gentiles"* in Luke 21:24.

Once the last Gentile Christian has *"come in"*—been saved and sealed by the Holy Ghost into the kingdom of God—the rest of the unbelieving Gentiles will be *"cut off"* from the mercy of God, and Israel will be grafted back into fellowship with God, *"their own olive tree."*[1826]

In 2 Thessalonians 2:2-13, Paul labels the person of the antichrist as the *"man of sin"* and *"son of perdition"* who has not yet been revealed, but will be revealed after a great *"falling away"* or apostasy occurs by churches. As apostasy increases, verses 7 and 8 further declare the antichrist will be revealed after God takes His Holy Spirit *"out of the way."* The rapture is God taking Holy Spirit-filled Christians out of the antichrist's way to Jerusalem, where he will sit in the Jewish *"temple of God, shewing himself that he is God."* Christians need not fear the apostasy movement, nor the antichrist. Paul identifies their characteristics, declaring they will exalt themselves above God's Word, not love the truth of God's Word, have pleasure in doing unrighteous acts, and believe lies. If you believe God's

1823 1 Peter 1:6-8
1824 Romans 11:11
1825 Romans 11:25
1826 Romans 11:22-24

Word is truth, love the truth, and do righteousness, God's grace will remove you from the earth in the rapture before the antichrist is revealed. God's perfect love casts out all fear about the antichrist's appearance.

THE CONDITIONS OR 'TIMES AND SEASONS' OF THE RAPTURE

Having proved the rapture is pre-tribulation, God's grace has also revealed even more about the world's conditions at the time of the rapture.

Jesus clearly taught the rapture takes place at an unknown day and hour. But many people fail to recognize Paul's bold claim that Christians will know the *"times and seasons"* of Jesus' coming! Immediately after teaching on the *"caught up"* event in 1 Thessalonians chapter 4, Paul follows up in the proceeding chapter by assuring Christians they'll be ready for Jesus Christ's return:

> *"But of the times and the seasons, brethren, ye have no need that I write unto you. For yourselves know perfectly that the day of the Lord so cometh as a thief in the night. For when they shall say, Peace and safety; then sudden destruction cometh upon them, as travail upon a woman with child; and they shall not escape. But ye, brethren, are not in darkness, that that day should overtake you as a thief. Ye are all the children of light, and the children of the day: we are not of the night, nor of darkness. Therefore let us not sleep, as do others; but let us watch and be sober. For they that sleep sleep in the night; and they that be drunken are drunken in the night. But let us, who are of the day, be sober, putting on the breastplate of faith and love; and for an helmet, the hope of salvation. For God hath not appointed us to wrath, but to obtain salvation by our Lord Jesus Christ, Who died for us, that, whether we wake or sleep, we should live together with him."*[1827]

The apostle describes the *"times and seasons"* of the rapture with two descriptors. First, sinners will be unaware of the rapture just as drunken, sleeping robbery victims are caught off guard by a night-time

---

1827   1 Thessalonians 5:1-10

thief. Jesus teaches this same idea when He likens the day of the Lord as the days of Noah, in which the lost kept eating, drinking, and marrying right up *"until the flood came and took them all away."*[1828] Paul compares the sinners to sleeping drunks. Second, Paul proclaims the world's mantra will be *"Peace and safety"* at the time of Christ's sudden rapture event. It's striking to imagine how contrary the thoughts and plans of sinners will be compared to those of God. As God is planning for war (Armageddon) and destruction (with earth's sinless, holy restoration in mind), the world is planning, albeit in vain, world peace and safety. Are Christians living in a world that matches these descriptions? Partially, no doubt, and each day we're closer to seeing the full rapture conditions.

Building upon these two descriptions, the Bible provides further proofs that we are near the time and season of Jesus' return:

- Scoffers will be mocking Jesus' second coming (2 Peter 3:3-4).
- The conditions of Noah's time will be repeated: violence, lust-based marriages, continually evil thoughts (Luke 17:26-30, Genesis 6:1-13).
- The sodomite conditions of Lot's time will be repeated (Luke 17:28-30).
- Evil men and deceivers will grow more evil with greater deceptions (2 Timothy 3:13).
- Many churches will commit a great falling away from God's truth (2 Thessalonians 2:3).
- Few will have genuine faith expressed through regular prayer (Luke 18:1-8).
- Pestilences (swine flu, coronavirus, etc.) and earthquakes will increase as sorrows before the Tribulation (Matthew 24:7-8).
- Men will love themselves more than God and be covetous, boasters, proud, blasphemers, disobedient to

---

1828 Matthew 24:38-39

parents, unthankful, unholy, without natural affection, trucebreakers, false accusers, incontinent, fierce, despisers of those that are good, traitors, heady, high-minded, and having a form of godliness but denying the power thereof (2 Timothy 3:1-7).

- The New Testament gospel will have been preached to all the world (Matthew 24:14).
- Through united efforts of false churches and politicians, new laws will stop true churches from preaching and pressure them to join the evil ecumenical move but Jesus anoints believers with the latter rain and rescues them in the rapture (Psalm 27:5, Revelation 3:10, 13:16).
- Israelis will be physically returning to live in the Holy Land and seeking to rebuild a new temple (Deuteronomy 30:1-10, Luke 21:24, Revelation 11:1-2).
- Nominal churches will be in a Laodicean, lukewarm condition, concerned with riches and goods, having no need of more truth, and unwilling to repent (Revelation 3:15-19).

FULLY ARMORED IN THE RAPTURE SEASON

Paul says a Christian's only hope for being spiritually awake and soberly watching for Christ's return is by putting on the full armor of God. In 1 Thessalonians chapter 5, Paul describes two of the six pieces of armor fully detailed in Ephesians 6:10-18. It behooves Christians to understand and put on each piece of armor that we *"may be able to withstand in the evil day, and having done all, to stand."* Here's a brief summary of your spiritual armor:

- **Breastplate of faith, love, and righteousness** (1 Thessalonians 5:8, Ephesians 6:14). A physical breastplate protects the heart and other vital organs from the chest down to the waist, just as a righteous, obedient Christian life of integrity protects our heart from Satan's attacks on our character. Christians trust in Christ's righteousness imputed to us and not our own.[1829]

- **Helmet of salvation** (1 Thessalonians 5:8, Ephesians 6:17). A physical helmet protects the head, the command center and most complex organ in the human body, just as the *"hope of salvation,"* the assurance that we are saved and forgiven by Jesus' sacrifice, protects us from Satan's attempts to make us doubt our salvation. Jesus' helmet makes us victorious in the battlefield of the mind, the greatest battle ever fought, as we cast down every imagination that exalts itself against the Word of God.[1830]

- **Loins girt about with truth** (Ephesians 6:14). Girded loins meant a man could tuck his long, flowing robe into his belt, enabling him to travel, run, or work. In the same way, a Christian's mind is girt up in Bible-truth,[1831] calmly prepared to be victorious in spiritual mind battles and successful in his ministry's work.

- **Feet shod with the preparation of the gospel of peace** (Ephesians 6:15). Solider's' feet and lower legs were protected by sandals and *"greaves"*[1832] to ensure their protection in traveling or war. In the same way, the Christian's daily travels and decisions are made only after prayerful preparation produces God's peace in his heart.

- **Shield of faith** (Ephesians 6:16). Just as the soldier's shield protected all the aforementioned pieces of armor from fiery arrows, faith in Christ completely protects a Christian's armor by extinguishing or stifling every falsehood Satan shoots from the bow of his lying tongue.[1833]

- **Sword of the Spirit** (Ephesians 6:17). Just as a solider's sword was his main offensive and lethal weapon, the Word

---

1829 Philippians 3:9
1830 2 Corinthians 10:5
1831 1 Peter 1:13
1832 1 Samuel 17:6
1833 Jeremiah 9:13, John 8:44

of God spoken through a Christian's mouth will resist,[1834] wound, even "*bruise*"[1835] the devil, eventually putting to flight his evil forces. Jesus used the spoken Word-sword three times during Satan's temptation in the wilderness, causing the devil to flee Him "*for a season.*"[1836] At Christ's physical return to the earth after the Great Tribulation,[1837] a sword of judgment comes from His mouth, smiting all His enemies.

It is no wonder Paul admonishes us to be alert soldiers of the daytime if we want to go to heaven in the rapture. If you want to be ready for the rapture, you must be willing to fight for this privilege! God's most successful Solider, Jesus Christ, says the the kingdom of God is experienced when spiritual soldiers "*take it by force.*"[1838] Amazingly, the Greek word for "force" is the same word Paul used for "*caught up,*" meaning Christians must actively snatch away their spiritual victories from Satan as Jesus is going to snatch away His bride from Satan's Great Tribulation!

Satan, the god of this world-system,[1839] has laid many traps and snares[1840] around us. The devil's angels have been and will continually be sent to war against our cause[1841] but we are fully equipped and more than conquerors[1842] fighting the good fight of faith with our divine armor.

WHERE WILL THE RAPTURE TAKE PLACE?

The rapture will be a universal event, meaning it will take place on a global scale, and believers will *not* have to be in one physical location in order to be a part of the rapture. In Matthew 24:23-28 Jesus plainly teaches us not to be deceived by men who claim to be Christ and call us

1834   James 4:7
1835   Romans 16:20
1836   Luke 4:1-13
1837   Revelation 19:15-21
1838   Matthew 11:12
1839   2 Corinthians 4:4
1840   1 Timothy 3:7
1841   Matthew 12:43-44
1842   Romans 8:37

out to the desert or secret chambers. Christ's coming will be as fast as lightning, "*in a moment, in the twinkling of an eye,*"[1843] so there is no need to gather physically for the exact moment of the rapture.

At the precise moment of the rapture, "wise virgin" Christians might be working or sleeping in their beds on the other side of the world, according to Christ's teachings in Luke 17:34-36 and Matthew 24:40-42. Jesus says, "*I tell you, in that night there shall be two men in one bed; the one shall be taken, and the other shall be left. Two women shall be grinding together; the one shall be taken, and the other left. Two men shall be in the field; the one shall be taken, and the other left.*" You are admonished to be ready, watching for Christ's return whether you are sleeping or working. Let us pray sincerely before bed and before the work day begins each morning, for our Savior is coming back as quick as lightning!

It will not matter where a true believer is physically located at the moment of the rapture as long he possesses the "*oil*" or the "*wedding garment*" of the baptism of the Holy Ghost. Wise virgins will be ready for the rapture, and Jesus will call them to the air to meet the rest of the saints in the sky.

Don't miss this—there *is* one spiritual location (not physical) a Christian must be concerned about for the rapture, for a true Christian must be located "*in Christ*" according to Romans 8:1: "*There is therefore now no condemnation to them which are in Christ Jesus, who walk not after the flesh, but after the Spirit.*" Believers are spiritually "*in Christ*" when Christ is in them by the baptism of the Holy Ghost according to Colossians 1:27: "*To whom God would make known what is the riches of the glory of this mystery among the Gentiles; which is Christ in you, the hope of glory.*" Galatians 3:27 says Christians "*have been baptized into Christ,*" meeting Christ's direct command to "*be baptized with the Holy Ghost.*"[1844] Paul announces that if the Holy Spirit "*that raised up Jesus from the dead dwell in you, he that raised up Christ from the dead shall also quicken your mortal bodies by his Spirit that dwelleth in you.*"[1845]

1843 1 Corinthians 15:52
1844 Acts 1:5
1845 Romans 8:11

Jesus foretold His disciples about His desire to dwell in them by His Spirit in John 14:17, saying, *"Even the Spirit of truth; whom the world cannot receive, because it seeth him not, neither knoweth him: but ye know him; for he dwelleth with you, and shall be in you."* A few verses later in John 14:20, Messiah revealed a most glorious truth about those He would dwell in—He revealed that those believers were already in Him, in His mind and plan, before the foundation of the world: *"At that day ye shall know that I am in my Father, and ye in me, and I in you."* Paul elaborates on this fact, teaching, *"According as he hath chosen us in him before the foundation of the world, that we should be holy and without blame before him in love."*[1846] Praise God for the revelation of where Christians need to be for the rapture—we must be *"in Christ,"* meaning that Christ's Spirit is dwelling in our souls by the baptism of the Holy Ghost!

Jesus does, though, give us a clue about where Christians will be frequently gathering physically as the rapture draws closer. Matthew 24:28 says Holy Ghost-filled Christians will be gathered together like eagles feasting on a carcass, representing constant, increasing church attendance[1847] in which believers feast on the preaching of God's Word. Paul validates that five preaching gifts will perfect, edify, and bring total unity to the body of Christ.[1848] God likens Himself to an eagle[1849] and so we as His children must be eaglets. Just as eagles are carnivores, Christians feast on the *"meat"*[1850] or deeply spiritual insights that help us to discern good and evil in our daily lives. Believers cannot remain on a *"milk"*[1851] diet and expect to go in the rapture, just as eagles cannot expect to soar in the heavens without a steady meat diet.

WHY WILL THE RAPTURE OCCUR?

The *"caught up"* rapture occurs because Christ is snatching away His wife from the earth, rescuing her from the awful wrath of God meant

1846 Ephesians 1:4
1847 Hebrews 10:25
1848 Ephesians 4:11-15
1849 Exodus 19:4
1850 Hebrews 5:14
1851 Hebrews 5:12-13, 6:1

to purge the earth before the millennium. Our Lord says, *"Because thou hast kept the word of my patience, I also will keep thee from the hour of temptation, which shall come upon all the world, to try them that dwell upon the earth."*[1852] What amazing grace Christ offers us, *"being now justified by his blood, we shall be saved from wrath through him"*![1853]

According to John 14:1-3, Christ desires to be married with His eternal companion—the holy, separated, many-membered bride-church. Christ wants to receive His people, His bride, unto himself and take her to the place He has prepared for her to live eternally. As pilgrims and strangers on this earth, the Holy Ghost-filled bride shares the same desire as her Husband and wants to leave this world to be with Christ, just as Paul desired *"to depart, and to be with Christ."*[1854]

The rapture is the moment we shall *"ever be with the Lord"*[1855] because we *"were ready"* to go *"in with Him to the marriage."*[1856] Truly, the Lamb's wife is blessed to be able to make herself ready for her marriage to Christ![1857]

God's rich, marvelous, and longsuffering grace gives every man and woman opportunity to repent before the rapture. The perfectly just and fair Savior offers *"space to repent"* to every generation, even as Christ announced to the Gentile city of Thyatira in Revelation 2:21: *"And I gave her space to repent of her fornication; and she repented not."* Nearly 4,000 years ago, God's grace was equally offered to the Amorites, possessors of Canaan, in Abraham's lifetime. The Lord told Abraham He would give the Amorites a space of 400 years to repent until their iniquity would be *"full."*[1858] Of course, the omniscient God knew the Amorites would not repent and thus ordained for Joshua to lead Israel into Canaan as a possession for Abraham's seed.

Today, God's grace is extending to Mystery Babylon, the Roman Catholic Church, and her daughters, the denominational and

---

1852   Revelation 3:10
1853   Romans 5:9
1854   Philippians 1:23
1855   1 Thessalonians 4:17
1856   Matthew 25:10
1857   Revelation 19:7-9
1858   Genesis 15:13-21

nondenominational churches, who practice iniquity, harboring every unclean and hateful evil spirit. But there will come a day when their iniquity will be full, and like the Amorites, they will be destroyed for their unbelief and hard, unrepentant hearts. God's Word says, "*Come out of her, my people, that ye be not partakers of her sins, and that ye receive not of her plagues. For her sins have reached unto heaven, and God hath remembered her iniquities. Reward her even as she rewarded you, and double unto her double according to her works: in the cup which she hath filled fill to her double.*"[1859] If you are Christ's bride, you will come out of sin-loving churches and into Christ by the baptism of the Holy Ghost.

HOW WILL THE RAPTURE OCCUR?

The rapture will occur by the power and authority of Jesus Christ's Spirit through a shout, voice, and trump: "*For the Lord himself shall descend from heaven with a shout, with the voice of the archangel, and with the trump of God: and the dead in Christ shall rise first.*"[1860]

First, the word "*shout*" in the Greek means the "order, command, stimulating cry" from Jesus Christ to get His people ready for the wedding, or rapture. This "*shout*" or "*cry*" must be the same "*midnight*" cry described in Matthew 25:6 because both texts deal with Jesus' wedding to His bride, which is the rapture. The cry that awoke the ten virgins (both wise and foolish) caused them to trim their lamps (sanctification) but only the wise filled their lamps with oil (baptism of the Holy Ghost) in order to go meet the Bridegroom.

History witnesses that God's ministry through the late William Branham was the "*shout*" or "*cry*" that awakened the Christian church worldwide. The supernatural preaching and healing ministry of Branham was introduced in Chapter 7 and is fully developed in Chapter 13, but for now you can rejoice that the first of three steps in the rapture plan is in progress! God's Bible-message preached through Branham is still being preached by ministers, being taken around the world, awakening

1859 Revelation 18:4-6
1860 1 Thessalonians 4:16

both wise and foolish Christians. As you've read this book, you've been made aware of this worldwide "shout," and now it's your responsibility to obey it.

Second, the *"voice of the archangel"* is a future event that will be the voice of resurrection for the *"dead in Christ"* group mentioned in 1 Thessalonians 4:16. The *"voice of the archangel"* is the same Voice that resurrected Lazarus in John 11:43 and will one day resurrect all the *"dead in Christ"* who faithfully served the Lord Jesus Christ during the past 2,000 years. The literal bodies of the *"dead in Christ"* will rise first, being united with glorified bodies, and then sometime afterwards at the *"last trump,"* we which are *"alive and remain"* on the earth will receive our body change.

It's possible that wise virgin Christians who are *"alive and remain"* may see the glorified bodies of the resurrected *"dead in Christ"* saints for a short time period before the rapture. Immediately following Jesus' resurrection, the Bible says, *"And the graves were opened; and many bodies of the saints which slept arose, And came out of the graves after his resurrection, and went into the holy city, and appeared unto many."*[1861] If the future rapture-resurrection is patterned the same as Jesus' resurrection from the grave in Matthew 27, then we may see Paul, Peter, James, and John in their glorified bodies for a short time before our bodies are changed. What a faith-building experience it would be to see with our own eyes the saints we've read about in the Holy Bible all our lives! Oh, how exciting it is to be a Holy Ghost-filled Christian and imagine the wonderful things God has in store for His Son's bride!

Third, the *"trump of God"* or *"last trump"* will sound to finish the three-step rapture plan, which will change the bodies of the living saints and call for the gathering of the dead and living in Christ to the sky to meet Jesus in the air at the wedding ceremony. Paul writes, *"Then we which are alive and remain shall be caught up together with them in the clouds, to meet the Lord in the air: and so shall we ever be with the Lord."*[1862]

1861 Matthew 27:52-53
1862 1 Thessalonians 4:17

The apostle continues,

> *"Behold, I shew you a mystery; We shall not all sleep, but we shall all be changed, In a moment, in the twinkling of an eye, at the last trump: for the trumpet shall sound, and the dead shall be raised incorruptible, and we shall be changed. For this corruptible must put on incorruption, and this mortal must put on immortality."*[1863]

Just as the bride's processional music signals for the bride to come forward to meet her waiting bridegroom during an earthly wedding, so the *"last trump"* signals for the union in the sky of Jesus Christ and His bride.

The last trump is also known as the Seventh Seal. Recall Chapter 7's teaching that the Book of Revelation's Seven Seals are seven revelations the New Testament church needs to understand the Bible. The last and Seventh Seal was the unknown day and hour of the rapture, known only to the Father according to Mark 13:32, making the last trump and Seventh Seal identical.

The shout, voice, and trump are all performed by the Holy Ghost, which is the same Spirit that quickened Jesus' own body at His resurrection from the dead: *"But if the Spirit of him that raised up Jesus from the dead dwell in you, he that raised up Christ from the dead shall also quicken your mortal bodies by his Spirit that dwelleth in you."*[1864]

THE LAST SIGN BEFORE THE RAPTURE

Genesis 18:9-15 powerfully foreshadows God's "last sign" before the rapture. Before referencing the last sign, observe the context of this story. In Genesis 18:1-8, God and two angels visit Abraham and Sarah, appearing in flesh bodies and eating butter, milk, and veal. Verses 9-15 detail God confirming to Abraham that he will have a son through Sarah. Standing behind them, Sarah overhears this and laughs within herself. Instantly,

---

1863   1 Corinthians 15:51-53
1864   Romans 8:11

God discerns her doubt and questions Abraham about Sarah's laughter, asking, *"Is any thing too hard for the LORD?"* Sarah hears God and proceeds to lie to Him, saying she did not laugh but God says, *"Nay, but thou didst laugh."* Genesis 19 describes Lot's escape as Sodom and Gomorrah is destroyed. Genesis 20 shows Abraham's second lapse in lying about Sarah being his wife to Abimelech and also God's graceful restoration of Sarah to Abraham. God keeps His Word and visits Sarah in Genesis 21, allowing Isaac to be born to 100-year old Abraham and 90-year old Sarah.

Foreshadowing is seen in the arrival of the promised son, Isaac, who represents Jesus, the promised Son, arriving for the rapture. Before Isaac arrived, though, Abraham and Sarah's bodies needed changed because his ability to reproduce was *"dead"* and *"the deadness of Sara's womb"*[1865] wouldn't permit a pregnancy. Their body-change, from infertility to fertility, foreshadows the body-change at the rapture, for *"we shall all be changed, In a moment, in the twinkling of an eye, at the last trump: for the trumpet shall sound, and the dead shall be raised incorruptible, and we shall be changed."*[1866]

What was God's last sign to Abraham and Sarah before each experienced a body-change? Genesis 18:9-15 reveals God's "last sign" to Abraham and Sarah before the promised son arrived was a Man (God) discerning Sarah's doubting heart through a supernatural gift of discernment. Since God is the Word (John 1:1), He was *"a discerner of the thoughts and intents"*[1867] of Sarah's heart despite the fact that she was standing behind Him and made no noise with her voice.

Notice this Biblical pattern—God in a flesh body discerning the thoughts and intents of the heart. This same pattern repeated in the "Son of Man" ministry of Jesus Christ during His earthly ministry. A "son of man" is simply a prophet, as Ezekiel was given this title over 90 times, and the Lord Jesus, the only God-prophet, bore this title over 80 times. As "Son of Man," Jesus twice used His discernment to reveal the thoughts and intents of believers' hearts. In John 1, Christ discerned Nathanael's

---

1865   Romans 4:19
1866   1 Corinthians 15:51-52
1867   Hebrews 4:12

thoughts, telling him that He saw him under a fig tree when Philip called him. Aware that only Christ could have known his previous whereabouts and conversation with Philip, Nathanael instantly identified Jesus as "*the Son of God...the King of Israel.*"[1868] Jesus' supernatural discernment proved He was God's prophet.

Later in John 4, Christ discerned the thoughts and intents of the Samaritan woman at Jacob's well. She told Jesus she had no husband, to which Christ agreed but then told her she had had five husbands and the current man she was living with was not her husband. Convinced of the supernatural gift of discernment, she uttered, "*Sir, I perceive that thou art a prophet.*"[1869]

Notice Jesus used His gift of discernment among the Jewish people in John 1 and then among the Samaritans in John 4. The gospels often differentiate three races: Jews, Samaritans (half Jew and half Gentile), and Gentiles. Jesus, then, used His discernment gift with two races—Jew and Samaritan—but never with the Gentiles. Wouldn't the ethical and just God be obligated to manifest Jesus' discernment gift to the Gentiles?

In Luke 17:30, the Lord promised that the "*Son of man*" would be revealed "*in the day*" when societal conditions mirrored the days of Noah and Lot.[1870] These were two of the 14 conditions for the rapture previously listed in this chapter. This "Son of man" ministry must be intended for the Gentiles because God is currently dealing with the Gentiles, having blinded the Jews to their Messiah. Thankfully, tape recorders from the 1940s through 1960s have preserved evidence that the Gentiles have *already* received this final, Gentile "Son of man" discernment ministry. Yes, you read that correctly—the Gentiles have already received the "Son of man" ministry, as it came and went in God's ordained time and season.

The prophetic, supernatural ministry of the late William Branham (1909-1965) fulfilled Jesus' promise (Luke 17:30) to send a "son of man" to the Gentiles. Branham's ministry is fully explained in Chapter 13, but

1868 John 1:49
1869 John 4:19
1870 Luke 17:26-29

know that the Holy Spirit vindicated his ministry with the same gift of discernment Jesus used in John chapters 1 and 4. In a 1954 prayer line, Branham told a female patient 15 secrets by God's discernment power, including her name, address, and many details about her sicknesses.[1871] Discernments like these were commonplace in Branham's ministry, as tape recordings of his sermons contain hundreds of these same amazing occurrences. Branham's discernment ministry *"was not done in a corner,"* just as Paul testified before *"most noble Festus"* of his obedience to the heavenly vision.[1872] Hundreds, even thousands, were beneficiaries of Branham's obedience to his heavenly commission.

Furthermore, on six occasions the Spirit of God prompted Branham to publicly declare that his discernment gift was the "last sign" the Gentile church would receive before the rapture. All six declarations can be read or listened to online.[1873] Not only was the "last sign" declared, but it was stamped with "THUS SAITH THE LORD"—the authoritative phrase signaling God's literal self-revelation:

- On April 11, 1961, in Bloomington, Illinois, Branham said, "Remember, let me tell you, THUS SAITH THE SPIRIT OF GOD that's on me, this is the last sign to the Gentile church before the rapture."
- Three days later in Bloomington, Branham added, "Remember, THUS SAITH THE HOLY SPIRIT, this is your last sign. Write it in your Bible. And if something rises besides this, and greater than this, call me a false prophet."
- On May 19, 1961, in Dawson Creek, British Columbia, Branham announced, "Just remember, THUS SAITH THE LORD, you will never in any—no more Gentile church age ever see any sign to succeed this, go greater. This is the last sign to the Church."

1871 "3 Prophesies of William Branham." *YouTube*, uploaded by Pastor Jesse Smith, 4 October 2014, https://youtu.be/7PiEO2OK5e0
1872 Acts 26:19-26
1873 "The Table." *Voice of God Recordings*, http://table.branham.org/#/en/main

- On July 7, 1962, in Grass Valley, California, Branham declared, "You'll never receive another sign. This is It. THUS SAITH THE LORD. Would a prophet of God make a statement like that if it wasn't true? You're receiving your greatest sign, and your last sign, before the appearing of Christ."
- On April 11, 1964, in Birmingham, Alabama, Branham charged the believers: "This is the last sign. Remember, THUS SAITH THE LORD! Did you ever hear me say that but what it was true? You are seeing your last sign. That's Scriptural. You've seen your last sign, Pentecost."
- On April 26, 1965, in Los Angeles, California, Branham prophesied: "And, remember, Abraham and his group never received one more sign from God, until the promised son arrived. How many knows that's true? That sign of discernment! And the royal Seed of Abraham, let me hear you…Let me tell you, THUS SAITH THE LORD, you're receiving your last sign. That's according to the Scriptures and the revelation of God that's in my heart, that speaks that this is the Truth."

A few years back, I had the pleasure of meeting two people—unfortunately both are now deceased—who experienced Branham's discernment gift in very personal ways. My first meeting was with Tom Brown, a Lima, Ohio, resident who attended Branham's home church in Jeffersonville, Indiana, for nearly five years (1960-1965). Brown described multiple instances in which Branham would discern his questions and provide answers *before* Tom even asked the questions.[1874] A second witness I've met of Branham's "son of man" ministry was Florence Humes, healed of tuberculosis after Branham prayed for her on August 6, 1955. This supernatural interaction is recorded on tape and available to

---

1874 "Tom Brown - Times With a Prophet William Branham." *YouTube*, uploaded by Biblijski krskani, 4 October 2013, https://youtu.be/bAb8pCMkxOM

read or listen to online.[1875] God's Spirit led Branham to foretell Florence's healing, saying that she would gain weight on two consecutive Mondays as a sign of her healing. Florence's healing took place exactly as foretold by God's prophet. Florence, who already had three daughters before the tuberculosis, lived to birth another daughter and four sons, leading to 25 grandchildren and over 40 great grandchildren.

Brahman's discernment gift appeared at the correct time chronologically, just as God in flesh appeared to Abraham and Sarah at the right time. God in flesh appeared before both the destruction of Sodom and Gomorrah and Isaac's birth. The son of man ministry of Branham appeared before both the rapture and Great Tribulation.

Even though you, like me, probably missed experiencing the Gentile "son of man" ministry first-hand, it is no cause for discouragement. Most prophetic gifts are rejected by the ones God intends should receive them. For instance, Jesus taught that both His ministry and that of John the Baptist were sent to the Jews but rejected by the majority.[1876] Be encouraged that you now have the chance to receive God's last sign to the Gentiles just before the rapture. You can listen to Branham's sermons and discernments online, and then see God do similar things through the living bride-church today. Blessed are your eyes if they can see God's last sign to Abraham's seed and receive the Bible instructions preached by God's prophet!

REWARDS FOR RECEIVING THE REVELATION OF THE RAPTURE

The eternal rewards for receiving the revelation of the rapture are perfectly beautiful. You'll need an active imagination in your attempt to fathom the immensity of Christ's rewards for His bride.

Previously in this chapter, you read a few rewards worth recalling, such as escaping the wrath of God during the Great Tribulation period and knowing the nearness, or the *"times and seasons"* the rapture occurs

---

1875 "The Table." *Voice of God Recordings*, http://table.branham.org/#/en/main
1876 Matthew 17:12-13, John 1:10

in. Accepting God's truth right now ensures you'll be prayerfully prepared for Jesus' return and miss the global destruction and torment of the seven trumpets, seven vials, and three woes.

There are at least four more rewards for receiving this revelation. First, you'll have much assurance in knowing you are part of Christ's bride, or true church. Scripture refers to this assurance as a *"seal,"* which in the Greek means "security from Satan" and "a mark upon by the impress of a seal or a stamp." The *"seal"* is the baptism of the Holy Ghost, so it's even more apparent that our gospel comes *"not in word only, but also in power, and in the Holy Ghost, and in much assurance."*[1877]

Another way Scripture describes this seal of assurance is a *"token."* Old Testament examples of tokens include the rainbow, circumcision, the Passover lamb's blood upon the door posts, Aaron's rod, and the scarlet cord given to Rahab. In particular, it behooves you and me to meditate on two tokens: the blood of the Passover lamb and Rahab's scarlet cord. The public display of the Passover lamb's blood was required for Israel's exodus out of Egypt. In fact, without the blood publicly displayed, the death angel destroyed the firstborn of every family. Similarly, the blood, or life of Jesus Christ, must be publicly displayed in the lives of Christians in order for them to make an exodus from this world to the rapture in the air and escape the oncoming Great Tribulation.

Rahab's scarlet cord was publicly displayed so she and her house would be spared from Jericho's destruction. Through her observable token, she and her family made an exodus from God's wrath. Again, the red cord represents a public testimony of the red blood of Jesus Christ. Since the Bible teaches the life is in the blood,[1878] these Old Testament symbols represent the life of Jesus Christ, which is the Holy Spirit baptism, must be publicly displayed by Christians because *"the Spirit is life."*[1879] Just as your boarding pass is the assurance you'll have a seat on a flight, the baptism of the Holy Ghost is your seal, token, or assurance you have a ticket for the rapture!

1877   1 Thessalonians 1:5
1878   Leviticus 17:11
1879   Romans 8:10

A second reward is escaping death, for those who are *"alive and remain"* will not die but will instead have their vile, mortal bodies changed into immortal ones. Though countless funerals have been observed for thousands of years, there will be a small group of Christians that will not need funeral services! The rapture is a one time, world-wide, escape death pass. This miraculous event will be the first and only time a large group of saints will escape death. This has never, ever happened in world history. Up to the current time, only two individuals have had the high calling of missing death—only Elijah and Enoch! All other saints have had to die. Think of it—*we* may be that fortunate, blessed, and privileged generation to join Elijah and Enoch as raptured saints! If not us, it will certainly be a generation in the near future because the signs of the rapture are evident.

A third reward is experiencing two glorious events in heavenly places while the earth is being plagued during the Great Tribulation: the meeting in the air and wedding supper of the Lamb. Imagine meeting Paul, Peter, Mary the mother of Jesus, Tabitha, and the rest of the saints in the sky at the rapture! Picture in your mind shaking hands with and instantly recognizing Martin Luther and John Wesley. How will you feel seeing your loved ones who have died but now you're reunited with them in young, youthful new bodies? This event includes the greatest reward—finally seeing Jesus Christ, God's only begotten Son, the Risen Lord of Glory, face to face! Oh, how my heart races and tears begin forming in my eyes when I think of this moment when I shall not *"see through a glass darkly"* but shall see Christ *"face to face."*[1880] Not only we will see Him, but He *"shall change our vile body, that it may be fashioned like unto His glorious body."*[1881] Our eyes shall behold the Desire of Nations, the Bright and Morning Star, the Fairest of Ten Thousand, the Root and Offspring of David, the Holy One of Israel, and the Faithful Bridegroom. Your faith will become sight at the rapture. No longer will we be able to say Peter's words, *"Having not seen, ye love,"*[1882] for we will say "I have seen my Jesus, the One I have loved!"

1880 1 Corinthians 13:12
1881 Philippians 3:21
1882 1 Peter 1:8

The wedding supper takes place in heaven after the meeting in the air. While Scripture does not offer many details about this wedding reception, it for sure entails both a bride-presentation and communion service.

Paul reveals the bride-presentation in 2 Corinthians 11:2: *"For I am jealous over you with godly jealousy: for I have espoused you to one husband, that I may present you as a chaste virgin to Christ."* The Corinthian church was supernaturally birthed under Paul's ministry in Acts 18:1-17 by Christ's divine direction. The apostle writes about his duty to present the Corinthian believers as chaste virgins to Christ and the only logical time this could occur would be at the wedding supper of the Lamb. No doubt the believers died one by one after Paul left their city, leaving Paul no chance to present them to Christ. But every faithful Corinthian who received Paul's preaching about the baptism of the Holy Ghost will be resurrected for the rapture and will be gathered in heaven at the wedding supper. This is when Paul can present the bride members from Corinth to their Husband, Jesus Christ. It seems possible that all seven stars or human messengers to the seven churches will present the bride of his church age to Jesus Christ.

Following the bride's presentation, raptured saints will partake in a heavenly communion service. Just as Jesus desired *"with desire"*[1883] to have communion with His disciples before His crucifixion and ascension to heaven, the Bishop of our souls will desire sweet communion with His bride after the Gentile Church Ages have finished. Christ held communion with His disciples to signal the end of their intimate, earthly communion but promised the next communion service would signal renewed, intimate eternal fellowship. Melchisedec's communion with Abram foreshadowed this communion in Genesis 14:14-20. How entirely appropriate for Christ to conduct communion after the trials of life are finished! Abram, having defeated four kings with his trained army and restoring his nephew Lot, was met with bread, wine, and blessings by Melchisedec. Communion at the wedding supper will also express

---

1883   Luke 22:15

that blessings and fellowship follow victorious battle. Christ, the great Promise Keeper, will fulfill the promise He gave to His disciples: *"But I say unto you, I will not drink henceforth of this fruit of the vine, until that day when I drink it new with you in my Father's kingdom."*[1884]

Experiencing Christ's 1,000 year millennial reign as kings and priests is the fourth reward. This millennial period represents the honeymoon period for Christ and His bride, naturally following the wedding ceremony (rapture) and reception (marriage supper of the Lamb). Only a select group of people will enjoy this blessed, sinless 1,000 year "day," for *"one day is with the Lord as a thousand years, and a thousand years as one day."*[1885] Revelation 20:4-6 states exactly who will reign on the earth for 1,000 peaceful years:

> *"And I saw thrones, and they sat upon them, and judgment was given unto them: and I saw the souls of them that were beheaded for the witness of Jesus, and for the word of God, and which had not worshipped the beast, neither his image, neither had received his mark upon their foreheads, or in their hands; and they lived and reigned with Christ a thousand years. But the rest of the dead lived not again until the thousand years were finished. This is the first resurrection. Blessed and holy is he that hath part in the first resurrection: on such the second death hath no power, but they shall be priests of God and of Christ, and shall reign with him a thousand years."*

Catch the fact that the *"rest of the dead"* do not live during the millennium—only faithful Christians who worshipped Jesus in Spirit and truth will live and reign with Christ. The foolish virgin will miss the millennium because she foolishly neglected the *"oil,"* the baptism of the Holy Ghost. Christians are warned and admonished to not *"neglect"*[1886] the powerful, Holy Ghost gospel. Additionally, untold billions of unbelievers will not experience the glory and beauty of a 1,000 year period without sin.

1884   Matthew 26:29
1885   2 Peter 3:8
1886   Hebrews 2:3-4

Imagine a millennium without the devil, temptation, lust, greed, murder, destruction, and politics. For 365,000 straight days you'll enjoy only pure peace, grace, victory, beauty, and joy! Some Christians will even reign over nations[1887] while others over small regions of the earth, for Jesus promised good, faithful servants would have "*authority over ten cities.*"[1888] Submitting only to Christ's Spirit in this life as a cross-carrying follower of Jesus entitles you to lead cities, perhaps even nations in the next life. Christ's words remain true: "*He that is faithful in that which is least is faithful also in much.*"[1889] A Christian "*faithful over a few things*" will be made "*ruler over many things.*"[1890] Branham writes, "And now He [Jesus] says, that he who keeps doing His works faithfully until the end will be given power over nations, and will be a strong, capable, unbending ruler who can cope so powerfully with any situation, that even the most desperate enemy will be broken if need be. His demonstration of rule by power will be like unto the very Son's. This is very amazing."[1891]

CONSEQUENCES FOR REJECTING THE REVELATION OF THE RAPTURE

The main consequence for rejecting the revelation of the rapture is unpreparedness for Christ's return. Learn from Jesus' teaching on stewardship to be prepared for the rapture by honoring those in your care, being sober, and doing Christ's will.[1892]

God's "*shout*" has sounded and is now sounding in your ears. Neglecting the divine "*shout,*" or Bible-based message God sent through William Branham, produces a spiritual state of slumber. Paul says most people will be "*overtaken*"[1893] when Jesus returns. Likewise, the apostle admonishes Christians to not let this opportunity to be baptized with the Holy Ghost and exit earth in the rapture "*slip*"[1894] away from our minds.

1887 Revelation 2:26
1888 Luke 19:17
1889 Luke 16:10
1890 Matthew 25:21
1891 Branham, p. 240
1892 Luke 12:45-48
1893 1 Thessalonians 5:4
1894 Hebrews 2:1

God's mercy has placed an end-time exodus right in our laps. Foolish is the only word suitable for describing those who reject this Christ-indwelling experience that was *"hid from ages and from generations, but now is made manifest to his saints."*[1895]

Believers who reject the rapture revelation but die before the rapture will not have to experience the awful Great Tribulation period. Their consequences for rejection include being absent from the rapture, the Marriage Supper of the Lamb, and Millennium.

Believers who reject the rapture revelation but live long enough to physically miss the rapture will have to die in the Tribulation. Being righteous, yet not filled with the Holy Ghost, God will not let them suffer the worst torments with the wicked. Before death, Jesus teaches that the foolish virgins will ask for an opening into the rapture after it has happened, but Christ's Voice will answer back in their hearts, saying *"Verily I say unto you, I know you not."*[1896] The way to know Jesus is to possess *"oil,"* the baptism of the Holy Ghost.

Indescribable torments of hail, fire, brimstone, and inescapable demonic oppression contained in the seven trumpets and seven vials await unbelievers, the Bible-rejecting group. Sudden destruction and travail is determined upon them, *"a time of trouble, such as never was since there was a nation even to that same time."*[1897]

CONCLUSION

Clearly defined by Paul as a mystery, the rapture or *"caught up"* experience is now revealed as a secret, sudden going away of Christ's bride with her beloved Bridegroom to their marriage supper just before the Great Tribulation sets in upon the rest of humanity. Knowing the six reasons that prove the rapture occurs before the Tribulation is a great blessing and should inspire Christians to be awake and alert, daily wearing and utilizing the full armor of God. By God's amazing grace, we'll accept His

1895 Colossians 1:26
1896 Matthew 25:11-13
1897 1 Thessalonians 5:3, Daniel 12:1

invitation and be prepared for this once-in-history event—the privilege of skipping death with a small group of Christians as Jesus' Spirit changes our bodies for the meeting in the air.

Now that all 12 mysteries are revealed, Chapter 13 shows how they were foretold to be revealed, or finished, nearly 2,000 years ago in Revelation 10:7: *"But in the days of the voice of the seventh angel, when he shall begin to sound, the mystery of God should be finished, as he hath declared to his servants the prophets."* Just as Jesus identified the fulfillment of Scripture at His first coming in Luke 4:21, we too can echo His declaration of another Scripture being fulfilled: This day, this Scripture—Revelation 10:7—is fulfilled!

ACTION STEPS TO BE IN THE RAPTURE

1. Be sure you are baptized in the name of the Lord Jesus Christ and filled with the Holy Ghost baptism.

2. Find, grow in, and remain in your position in your family, local church, and ministries.

3. Daily watch and pray for the imminent return of Jesus Christ and you'll be prepared because all that love Him will see His appearing (2 Timothy 4:8).

FOLLOW UP

Free online videos, Bible studies, and William Branham's quotes related to this chapter: www.pastorjessesmith.com/12mysteriesbook

Email: jesse.smith11@sbcglobal.net

Text: 330-929-2037

CHAPTER 13
Elijah Shall Restore All Things

"And Jesus answered and said unto them,
Elias truly shall first come, and restore all things."

Matthew 17:11

THE SUBJECT OF ELIJAH and his shared-anointing (Elisha and John
the Baptist had the Spirit of Elijah[1898]) has both baffled and astounded
believers for centuries, but Daniel 12:4 and Revelation 10:7 assure
us the mystery of God will be finished in the end time. God is obligated
to reveal this mystery in our day because the world-wide rapture conditions are evident (See Chapter 12). The mystery of Elijah's anointing is
actually part of the seventh mystery, the Seven Stars, because the final
star-angel to the Laodicean Age was to be an Elijah-anointed prophet.

ELJIAH SHALL RESTORE ALL THINGS BEFORE THE GENTILE RAPTURE

Six passages of Scripture—Acts 3:20-21, Matthew 17:11-12, Malachi
4:5-6, Revelation 10:7-11, Amos 3:7, and Luke 17:30—declare an
authoritative, Biblical truth about Elijah's Spirit in the end time:

1898   2 Kings 2:15, Luke 1:17

Jesus will remain in heaven and not physically return to the earth until all things—including Bible doctrines and the hearts of believers—are restored to their original, apostolic conditions by the preaching of a prophet anointed with the Spirit of Elijah.

Acts 3:20-21: Beginning here, Peter teaches Jesus will remain in heaven *"until the times of restitution of all things."* In the Greek, *"restitution"* means "restoration." All things pertaining to Christianity need restored, or put back into their original condition. Look at modern churches and ask yourself, "Do churches today resemble the churches in the Book of Acts?" Of course not, as they are lacking power, holiness, diligence, truth, sincerity, and more. Joel 2:25 agrees with God's promise to restore the true church back to its original glory: *"I will restore"*!

Matthew 17:11-12: Restoration is also Jesus' theme in Matthew 17:11: *"Elias* [Elijah] *truly shall first come, and restore all things."* Three points need emphasized. First, all things must be restored, which agrees with Joel and Peter's restoration prophesies. Second, Jesus says Elijah alone—not Elijah and Moses—is going to come and restore everything before Jesus' Millennial reign occurs. Third, Jesus affirms in Matthew 17:12 that John the Baptist had Elijah's Spirit upon him: *"But I say unto you, That Elias is come already, and they knew him not, but have done unto him whatsoever they listed."* Both Matthew 17:12 and Luke 1:17 agree John the Baptist had Elijah's Spirit upon him.

Putting these findings together, Elijah's anointing comes upon four other men besides Elijah himself, tallying five total appearances of Elijah's Spirit:

- Elijah (1 Kings 17:1)
- Elisha (2 Kings 2:9-15)
- The "preparation" Elijah: John the Baptist (Malachi 4:5-6 with Luke 1:17, Isaiah 40:3 with Matthew 3:1-3, Malachi 3:1 with Matthew 11:10, Matthew 17:12-13)

- The "restoration" Elijah: William Branham (Malachi 4:5-6, Matthew 17:11, Luke 17:30, Revelation 10:7 with Amos 3:7)
- Elijah in the Tribulation, accompanied by Moses (Revelation 11:3-13)

Malachi 4:5-6: This text mentions the Spirit of Elijah working in two separate ministries before judgment strikes the world—*"before the coming of the great and dreadful day of the LORD."* These two ministries belong to John the Baptist and William Branham. John prepared the way for the Messiah's first coming and Branham restored the way for Jesus' second coming.

Malachi 4:6 reads, *"And he shall turn the heart of the fathers to the children, and the heart of the children to their fathers, lest I come and smite the earth with a curse."* The two ministries Elijah's Spirit fulfills are:
- turning *"the heart of the fathers to the children"*
- turning *"the heart of the children to their fathers"*

According to Luke 1:17, John the Baptist fulfilled the first ministry of turning the hearts of the fathers to the children: *"And he shall go before him in the spirit and power of Elias, to turn the hearts of the fathers to the children, and the disobedient to the wisdom of the just; to make ready a people prepared for the Lord."* John, by Elijah's Spirit, prepared the people for the Messiah, Jesus, by preaching repentance. Mark 1:4 proclaims, *"John did baptize in the wilderness, and preach the baptism of repentance for the remission of sins."* Repenting and obeying God is the definition of a turned heart. Romans 6:17 agrees, saying, *"But God be thanked, that ye were the servants of sin, but ye have obeyed from the heart that form of doctrine which was delivered you."* Acts 7:39 shows a disobedient heart is turned back into worldliness: *"To whom our fathers would not obey, but thrust him from them, and in their hearts turned back again into Egypt."*

The *"fathers"* John preached to were the first generation of believers who accepted the Messiah. The first generation included early "father" apostles like Paul and Peter. These original apostles were deeply burdened for the *"children"*, or last generation of Christians, who would see Jesus' return to the earth, and wrote about it.[1899]

John the Baptist had the preparation ministry for the Messiah, preparing believers' hearts through repentance to receive Jesus. Malachi 3:1 foretold this, saying, *"Behold, I will send my messenger, and he shall prepare the way before me."* Jesus affirmed this spoke of John in Matthew 11:10: *"For this is he, of whom it is written, Behold, I send my messenger before thy face, which shall prepare thy way before thee."* Isaiah 40:3 and Matthew 3:1-3 teach the same, saying John's voice would cry, *"Prepare ye the way of the LORD."*

But there had to come a restoration ministry. Another preacher anointed with Elijah's Spirit had to come to turn the hearts of the children, or last generation of Christians, back to their fathers, the first generation believers. This book is one of many witnesses that William Branham's ministry is turning hearts back to Bible-based repentance and obedience, so that end time Christians can love, serve, and understand God just like the early apostolic believers. Branham's Bible-revelations are currently restoring the Book of Acts church, world-wide.

Branham's restoration ministry is the *"former rain"* ministry from Joel 2:23, as *"former"* can mean "teacher" in Hebrew. After two decades of studying Branham's teachings, I can testify to the depths of sound instruction God has restored to His bride in every single area of doctrine: the 12 mysteries, true repentance, salvation by grace, prayer and fasting, marriage and divorce, modest appearance, abominations still in effect, two kinds of Christians, Melchizedek, the Serpent's Seed, predestination, Daniel's 70 Weeks, the Feasts and Holy Days of Israel, tithes and offerings, torment in the lake of fire is not eternal, divine healing, the nine gifts of the Spirit, male-only preachers, male-only angels, and so much more. While rejoicing and growing through the former rain's teaching, we eagerly await the *"latter rain"*—the final anointing of rapturing faith.

1899 1 Thessalonians 4-5, 2 Peter 3

Some want to delete the fourth Elijah-ministry to the Gentiles and make the fifth Elijah-ministry of the Tribulation a restoration, but that would be a gross error for two reasons. First, John the Baptist came *alone* to turn the hearts of the apostolic fathers to the children in Malachi 4:6, so the turning of the hearts of the children back to their apostolic fathers must be done by one Elijah-anointed man—not two. William Branham came alone to turn the hearts of the children to the fathers. The fifth Elijah-ministry of Revelation 11:3 consists of two men—Elijah and Moses. Second, the fifth Elijah-ministry during the Tribulation is a ministry of judgment, or torment, according to Revelation 11:10. This of course differs greatly from the fourth Elijah-ministry which brought restoration before the rapture. Additionally, the 144,000 Jews are restored only after Jesus physically returns to them following the rapture of the two prophets. Zechariah 13:6 seems to support this because they are ignorant of the nail prints in Jesus' hands and His death on the cross: "What are these wounds in thine hands?" Reconciliation and restoration occur only through the knowledge of the blood of Jesus' cross, according to Colossians 1:14, 20, and 22.

Revelation 10:7-11: These Scriptures reveal Jesus giving the open Book, formerly sealed with Seven Seals, to an earthly seventh angel. The open Book's revelations are then taken around the world.

Notice first the open Book can only come to the earth at the end time, agreeing with Daniel 12:4: *"But thou, O Daniel, shut up the words, and seal the book, even to the time of the end: many shall run to and fro, and knowledge shall be increased."*

Revelation 10:11 places this end time revelation at the end of the Times of the Gentiles, because the open Book is eaten and taken around the world to Gentiles: *"Thou must prophesy again before many peoples, and nations, and tongues, and kings."* The open Book is not sent to Israel only, but to every nation under heaven. Revelation 10:11 reveals God is going to finish Jesus' Great Commission—preached in Matthew 28:19-20— by the loosing of the Seven Seals.

The seventh angel of Revelation 10:7 must be the same fourth Elijah-ministry because they both happen at the end time, before the Times of the Gentiles finishes. Thus, the seventh angel preaches during the Seven Church Ages, or Times of the Gentiles. Labeled as *"the seventh angel"* in Revelation 10:7, he must be *"the angel of the church of the Laodiceans"* in Revelation 3:14 because Laodicea was the seventh and final Gentile church Jesus addressed.

Amos 3:7: The seventh angel of Revelation 10:7 must also be a prophet because Amos 3:7 assures God only reveals His mysteries to prophets: *"Surely the Lord GOD will do nothing, but he revealeth his secret unto his servants the prophets."* Branham revealed the secrets of these 12 Bible-defined mysteries, and also correctly foretold the future by the Holy Spirit. Sick believers were foretold of their healings by Branham, and they were well shortly thereafter. Brother Branham correctly prophesied the immoral condition of the churches in the United States, how no greater ministry would rise to the Gentiles than what God gave to him, and no Christian denomination would return to an apostolic ministry. Additionally, Christ revealed the Seven Seals to Branham, the United States' identity, position, and destiny in Revelation 13, and spoke with "Thus saith the Lord" regarding numerous Bible doctrines.

Luke 17:30: The last of the six verses about God's end time restoration was detailed in Chapter 12 under the section "The Last Sign Before the Rapture." The Son of Man ministry had to be revealed to the Gentiles before the rapture, and Jesus anointed Brother Branham to fulfill this prophecy. It's notable there are three "R's" emphasized in this day: revelation, restoration, and rapture. Branham's ministry was the revelation of the Son of Man; his ministry brought restoration of Bible teachings, turning hearts back to the apostolic fathers. With the baptism of the Holy Ghost, believers are ready for the rapture.

I trust you can now see the clear Bible evidence for Brother Branham's ministry. It was foretold by Jesus, Malachi, Peter, and John and witnessed by millions world-wide.

HISTORICAL EVIDENCE OF BRANHAM'S RESTORATION MINISTRY

Historical evidence abounds for substantiating William Branham's restoration ministry. First hand witnesses of his gifts of healing and discernment testify to God's anointing upon his life. Amazingly, the Pillar of Fire was photographed in his meetings. Speaking with "Thus saith the Lord," Branham spoke God's opinion on sound doctrine and foretold the future. Researching Branham's life, you see the characteristics of Elijah's Spirit upon the Kentucky-born prophet.

HEALINGS AND DISCERNMENT

Branham's healing ministry is legendary, as God used it initiate the post-World War II healing revival.[1900] Although his healing campaigns began in 1946, Branham had been pastoring a local church in Jeffersonville, Indiana, since 1933.

Met by an angel and commissioned to pray for the sick in May 1946, healings multiplied throughout his state, the nation, and then the world. Observe Branham's ministry began first, well before other evangelists because God Himself ordained it. Oral Roberts began his own healing campaigns in 1947 and Billy Graham rose to national acclaim in 1949.[1901] After only four years of supernatural ministry, over 1,000 ministers gathered at a *Voice of Healing* convention in 1950 to recognize Branham's influence on the healing revival. They praised God and paid tribute to Branham for inspiring them to start praying for the sick.

As Moses was given two signs to prove he was God's deliverer,[1902] God commissioned Branham with two signs: a sign in his hand to identify sicknesses and discernment to know the secrets of hearts. Divinely equipped, "The power of a Branham service...remains a legend unparalleled in the history of the charismatic movement."[1903] The largest stadi-

---

1900   Burgess, Stanley, et al. *Dictionary of Pentecostal and Charismatic Movements.* Grand Rapids: Zondervan, 1988,

1901   "Billy Graham." *Billy Graham Evangelical Association,* https://billygraham.org/about/biographies/billy-graham/

1902   Exodus 4:9

1903   Burgess, p. 95

ums and auditoriums in the world were filled with worshippers and Jesus Christ mightily healed and saved His people.

Branham's sign in his hand detected diseases when a sick person put their right hand into his left hand. Meda Branham, William's wife, was detected as having a tumor on her left ovary around 1948, well before it caused Meda pain. Over the next 15 years, the tumor grew until it bulged out of Meda's side, causing her to hobble as she walked. But in November 1963, the Angel of the Lord met Branham and told him to speak to the tumor. He prayed, "Before the doctor's hand shall touch her, the hand of God shall take the tumor away, and it won't even be found."[1904] So it was—the tumor literally vanished as she sat in the doctor's office, seconds before her doctor asked to touch it.

Authentic healings were commonplace in Branham's ministry. Guided by a vision, Branham traveled to Milltown, Indiana, to pray for 28 year old Georgia Carter. Tuberculous had caused her to wither away to 50 pounds and had kept her bedridden for nearly nine years. Branham grabbed her hand and called upon the name of the Lord Jesus, and she was instantly healed. She spent the rest of her days as the pianist at the local Baptist church. Another saint named Florence Humes was healed of tuberculous in 1955. Almost all hope was lost, as Florence, mother of three girls, was rapidly losing weight. In a prayer line in Campbellsville, Kentucky, Branham first discerned her disease, then condemned Satan in prayer and turned Florence loose in the name of Jesus Christ. Florence miraculously recovered, having five more children, 25 grandchildren, and over 40 great grandchildren. You can listen to the audio of this miraculous event online. I had the pleasure of meeting Florence before she passed in 2015.

The healing of Congressman William Upshaw in 1951 remains one of the most powerful healing testimonies from Branham's meetings. After being a paraplegic for over 50 years, bound to a wheelchair and crutches, Upshaw attend Branham's meeting and rose from his wheelchair walking in complete healing. He preached Christ the rest of his

1904   Branham, William. *Look Away to Jesus.* December 29, 1963

days. Testifying of Christ's mighty power, Upshaw claimed to have sent his written testimony to President Truman, every senator and congressman, King George VI, Winston Churchill, and even Joseph Stalin.[1905] Again, you can listen to Upshaw's own voice give this testimony online.

Healing magazines like the *Voice of Healing* catalog Jesus' power in Branham's ministry. At Branham's memorial service in January 1966, the late evangelist Tommy Osborne well said:

> "The man we know as William Branham was sent to demonstrate God again in the flesh...Branham came our way as the prophet of God and showed us in the twentieth century precisely the same things that were shown us in the Gospels. Where we read of a few incidents in the Gospels, we have seen hundreds in our generation no less great nor wonderful, but far more numerous. We have seen them in our day."

Unfortunately, most historians reject Branham's teachings, but gladly accept and praise God for the supernatural healings via his two signs. The same was true of Jesus' earthly ministry; multitudes rejoiced over His miracles, but many of His own disciples left His ministry because of His doctrine.[1906] Faithful saints accept the Bible-based words of life Jesus revealed to Branham, just as Peter stayed with Jesus when the majority left, saying, *"Lord, to whom shall we go? thou hast the words of eternal life."*[1907]

THE RETURN OF THE PILLAR OF FIRE

It's historically proven that the Pillar of Fire returned to vindicate Brother Branham's ministry. You first learn of the Pillar of Fire, or the LORD in a visible manifestation, leading Moses and the children of Israel as they journeyed from Egypt. The Pillar of Fire has to be Jesus' Spirit, or the Holy Spirit, for Hebrews 11:26 plainly says Moses esteemed *"the reproach of Christ."* The LORD, as the Pillar of Fire, met Moses to give him the Ten Commandments, and also inspired him to write the Pentateuch, or

1905 Branham, William. *Testimony*, May 9, 1951
1906 John 6:66
1907 John 6:68

the first five Old Testament books. Since the Pillar of Fire was visible at the onset of the Old Testament, It had to come at the founding of the New. Acts 9:3-6 and Galatians 1:17 point to Jesus being the Pillar of Fire Who met Paul and later inspired him to write the majority of the New Testament's foundational epistles.

Since restoration was foretold—the mystery of God was to be finished—and desperately needed at the close of the New Testament, it was necessary for the Pillar of Fire to return. Overall, the church was in a lukewarm state and couldn't understand the Old or New Testament, but God promised to restore. Daniel 12:4 says the Book would be sealed until the end time, when Jesus brings the open Book to earth after loosing its Seven Seals as told in Revelation 10.

In March of 1963, the LORD met Branham in the desert near Tucson, Arizona, and commissioned him to preach the Seven Seals with "Thus saith the Lord." These revelations rightly divided the Word of truth, making the Bible understandable and God's presence real. Once again God had visited His prophet in a desert to bring the Word of the Lord. God previously met Moses in the wilderness to inspire the writing of the Old Testament, and Jesus led Paul to the Arabian desert to inspire his writing of the New. Now God was fulfilling Revelation 10:1-7 by meeting with His prophet, Branham, in the desert to finish His divine mystery.

Two evidences support the Spirit's visible return in Brother Branham's ministry. On January 24, 1950, a picture was taken of Branham at a debate on divine healing in Houston, Texas (See Figure 26). Above his head is the Pillar of Fire, and this photo remains the most well known picture of the post-World War II healing era. George J. Lacey, an official examiner of questioned documents, verified the photo was not retouched, but light struck the negative.

A second evidence of the visible Pillar of Fire was on January 8, 1961, when the Spirit became visible to the entire Branham Tabernacle congregation at the conclusion of Branham's sermon about the Book of Revelation (See Chapter 7). Audio exists from this supernatural occurrence.

Figure 26

THE RETURN OF 'THUS SAITH THE LORD'

Accompanying the Pillar of Fire's return was the necessary return of a prophet speaking for God with the full authority of "Thus saith the Lord". Moses spoke this authoritative phrase to both Pharaoh and Israel.[1908] Paul prophesied the rapture *"by the word of the Lord"*,[1909] and challenged the Corinthians to recognize his prophetic authority to speak for God: *"What? came the word of God out from you? or came it unto you only? If any man think himself to be a prophet, or spiritual, let him acknowledge that the things that I write unto you are the commandments of the Lord."*[1910] Branham's picture with the Pillar of Fire validates God choosing him to speak on behalf of heaven.

1908 Exodus 9:13, 32:27
1909 1 Thessalonians 4:15
1910 1 Corinthians 14:36-37

With all due respect, note that preachers like Oral Roberts and Billy Graham never spoke with "Thus saith the Lord," for they were not commissioned by God to do so. Both men had their gifts and positions, but not as prophet of the Lord. Modern preachers like T.D. Jakes and Joel Osteen never prophesy with "Thus saith the Lord" like Brother Branham did. Truly, no man in recent history has spoken like Branham—"in the name of the Lord"—and exercised such an awesome, unparalleled gift of discernment. Remember, it's "Thus saith the Lord" we'll never see a greater gift to the Gentiles before the rapture than Branham's discernment gift.

Open your Bible and heart to receive the following 30 statements Brother Branham spoke with the same "Thus saith the Lord" authority as Moses and Paul.

'THUS SAITH THE LORD' REGARDING DOCTRINE

The divine presence of the Pillar of Fire in Branham's meetings led him to preach doctrine with the authoritative phrase "Thus saith the Lord." Doctrine is instruction, a direct order, or command. This means God was speaking direct orders, originally found in Scripture, through His prophet to Christians of this final age. While most left Branham because of his doctrine, the true bride of Christ were and still are drawn like a magnet to his Bible-based teachings.

The main reason believers follow Branham's doctrines is because they are found in the Word of God. In my personal life, I went to many churches and always left feeling disappointed and unfulfilled before Jesus gave me my heart's desire with Branham's Bible-centered doctrines. His Bible references answered my questions about every aspect of my life. I could physically point to the Scripture in the Bible providing me specific instructions on how to live. I finally knew I was doing God's perfect will.

Concerning the doctrinal mysteries in this book, six of the 12 were delivered with "Thus saith the Lord" from God through Branham:

- Chapter 1, regarding the doctrine of the Godhead as one Person and not an unholy Trinity of three persons—"Trinitarianism is of the Devil! I say that THUS SAITH THE LORD! Look where it come from. It come from the Nicene Council when the Catholic church become in rulership. The word 'trinity' is not even mentioned in the entire Book of the Bible. And as far as three Gods, that's from hell. There's one God."[1911]

- Chapter 2, regarding the doctrine of Israel's blindness to their own Messiah, originally taught in the Fifth Seal—"If you've never heard, if you ever believed I ever said anything in a sermon, inspired, you take them tapes of the Seven Seals...And if you ever heard anything that's really, as I can say it's THUS SAITH THE LORD, get those."[1912]

- Chapter 6, regarding the doctrine of the baptism of the Holy Ghost—"I want to make myself very clear on what the Baptism with the Holy Ghost is according to the Word. It is not according to me, and it is not according to you. It has to be according to 'Thus saith the Lord,' or we are falsely led. Amen."[1913]

- Chapter 7, regarding the revelations of the Seven Church Ages—"Now, the vision, plus the Word, plus the history, plus the church ages; and all blend together. So I could truly say that to the best of my understanding and according to the Word of God and the vision and the revelation, the interpretation thereof is THUS SAITH THE LORD."[1914]

- Chapter 9, regarding the Roman Catholic Church as the Mother Harlot of Revelation 17—"And then, finally, she [the Roman Catholic Church] was 'The Mother of Harlots.' She gave birth unto churches, after her, 'cause they couldn't have been boys; they had to be girls. And

1911 Branham, William. *Revelation Chapter Four, Part 3.* January 8, 1961
1912 Branham, William. *Perseverant.* August 2, 1963
1913 Branham, p. 144
1914 Branham, William. *The Seventh Seal.* March 24, 1963

we find out that the Protestant church is a product of the Catholic church, by searching the Scriptures and looking at your history book. We see that the Protestant church is the product. And the Protestant can't holler at the Catholic, because the both, says they are 'harlots' and 'whores' That's flat, but that's THUS SAITH THE LORD."[1915]

- Chapter 10, regarding the mystery of iniquity working by the antichrist spirit—"Now, but you see, antichrist come in, as we've pictured it and showed it. What a revelation, my, my. And to think all these years we've seen it moving up, and here it--it's absolutely directly THUS SAITH THE LORD."[1916]

Additionally, Branham highlighted eight individual doctrines as "Thus saith the Lord" with their validating Scriptures:

- Recognizing Jesus' enigma in Matthew 28:19, water baptism is to be performed in the literal name of Jesus Christ (Acts 2:38, 8:16, 10:48, 19:5, 22:16) rather than the titles of Father, Son, and Holy Ghost—"THUS SAITH THE LORD, the baptism using the title of Father, Son, Holy Ghost is false. THUS SAITH THE LORD, I command every one of you on here or on tape that hasn't been baptized in the Name of Jesus Christ, be baptized again in the Name of Jesus Christ."[1917]
- Marriage and divorce (Matthew 5:32, 19:3-13) and the Serpent Seed doctrine (Genesis 3:15, Proverbs 30:20)—"And here they are, the true mystery of marriage and divorce, and the serpent's seed, and all of these things that's been fussed about. It's THUS SAITH THE LORD. What is it? The quickening power coming to the Church,

1915 Branham, William. *The Seal of God.* May 14, 1954
1916 Branham, William. *The Seventh Seal.* March 24, 1963
1917 Branham, William. *A True Sign That's Overlooked.* November 12, 1961

making Her ready, this hour that we're approaching.
Quickening power!"[1918]

- Ancient Rome morphed into Papal Rome and rules
the world at the end time as the fourth kingdom from
Daniel's interpretation of Nebuchadnezzar's dream
(Daniel 2:40-43)—"Russia, communism, isn't conquering
nothing. God's Word can't fail. Romanism is going to
conquer the world. Let's take Daniel's vision. That's
the Word of God. 'Thou, O Daniel…' 'Thou, O King
Nebuchadnezzar, is this head of gold,' Babylon. 'Another
kingdom will succeed thee, which is silver,' see, which was
Medes-o-Persia. Another one was Greece, Alexander the
Great. Next, come in, Rome. And there wasn't nothing
said about a communism. Rome conquered the world…
The Catholic hierarchy with all the denominations in
the world, right now coming together as an organization,
the confederation of churches organizing themselves
together. It isn't Russia. It's Rome. THUS SAITH THE
LORD. Yeah. Show me a Scripture where communism, or
anything else besides Rome, will rule."[1919]

- Women who purposely dress in sexy, provocative clothes
will answer for committing adultery because they caused
men to lust after them (Proverbs 7:10, 27, Matthew
5:28)—"They don't know what decency means. Out here
with little, old tight dresses on, and things like that, and
men lusting after them, and think that they're decent. You
might not have done nothing wrong, sister, but let me
tell you something, you're a tool of the Devil. And at the
Judgment Bar, THUS SAITH THE LORD, you'll answer
for committing adultery, and your soul will be gone. You
know better."[1920]

1918 Branham, William. *The Easter Seal*. April 10, 1965
1919 Branham, William. *The Greatest Battle Ever Fought*. March 11, 1962
1920 Branham, William. *The Way of a True Prophet*. May 16, 1962

- A woman who cuts her hair shames both her husband and Christ, and is spiritually dead, having rejected the quickening or life-giving power of the Holy Ghost baptism (1 Corinthians 11:1-16, Ephesians 2:1-3)—"The woman that's a child of God, lets her hair grow, to show that's she's consecrated to every Word of God. If she cuts it off, I don't care how much she dances, sings, is in the choir, speaks in tongues, runs up-and-down, or has all kind of aid societies, she is dead. That's THUS SAITH THE LORD, the Word of God."[1921]

- Branham's Bible-based teachings are restoring God's people back to the fulness of Pentecost (Joel 2:23-26)— "The people of God are being made ready by the Word of Truth from the messenger to this age. In her will be the fulness of Pentecost for the Spirit will bring the people right back to where they were at the beginning. That is 'Thus saith the Lord.' It is 'Thus saith the Lord' for that is what Joel 2:23-26 says."[1922]

- The Elijah-messenger to the Gentiles (Malachi 4:5-6), the fourth ministry of Elijah, appeared in the United States in the 1960s—"God has promised Malachi 4 for this last day. And Malachi 4 has not yet been fulfilled, but it must be fulfilled, for it is a germitized Word of God spoken through Malachi the prophet. Jesus referred to it. It is to be just before the Coming of Christ, the second time...All Scripture that has not been fulfilled, must be, before that time. The Bible is to be finished, to--to be finished. The Gentile dispensation is to be finished, with the church age, when this anointed messenger arrives. Of course, he will plant the Seed of the entire Bible, plumb from the serpent to the messenger in the former rain. Then he will be

---

1921 Branham, William. *The God of This Evil Age.* August 1, 1965
1922 Branham, p. 379

rejected by the denominational people, as his forefather, John and Elijah, as was spoken by our Lord...So it's at this time, in this country, that that person will appear, for it's in the Scripture and it's THUS SAITH THE LORD."[1923]

FULFILLED PROPHESIES AND THREE IN THE PROCESS OF COMING TO PASS

One qualification for being a genuine prophet is to foretell something in the Lord's name and then see it come to pass. William Branham was a true prophet, for he correctly prophesied the passing of Florence Shekarian in 1965 and the healing of Florence Humes in 1955.

In Shekarian's situation, she was diagnosed with inoperable cancer and after seeing a vision of her passing, Branham said, "Thus saith the Lord, their daughter [Florence] is going to die."[1924] While it's not difficult to prophesy death for a cancer patient, the context shows it's supernatural origin. Florence's brother, Demas was a famous minister, and several friends in their Pentecostal ranks had prophesied in the name of the Lord that Florence would be healed. But with Florence's passing, Branham's word from the Lord was proven to be true. Even when death is certain, God sometimes uses prophets to warn the sick of their deaths, just as Elijah foretold king Ahaziah of his certain death in 2 Kings 1:1-17.

Humes' situation, described earlier, was just as desperate as she was noticeably thin, dying with tuberculosis. But God's prophet condemned Satan "in Jesus Christ's name" and foretold her healing, saying, "God bless you, sister. Tell you what to do to know whether I told you truth. You go Monday and weigh, then next Monday weigh again, see what I've told you. Amen."[1925] Indeed, in the name of the Lord, Humes saw the prophecy come to pass. She was turned loose, being made well, living 60 more years!

Three prophesies are in the process of coming to pass, with the first being his 1961 prophecy of no greater gift arising to the Gentiles than

1923 Branham, William. *The Spoken Word is the Original Seed, Pt. 2*. March 18, 1962
1924 Branham, William. *A Man Running From the Presence of the Lord*. February 17, 1965
1925 Branham, William. *Jesus Christ The Same Yesterday, Today, and Forever*. August 6, 1955

the gift of discernment God gave him. Chapter 12 details Branham's discernment gift in the section "The Last Sign Before The Rapture." For 60 years this prophecy has stood firm. Preachers have come and gone, some even performing miracles, but none have come close to the discerning ability to know the thoughts and intents of the hearts like Jesus repeatedly performed in Branham. Video exists from Branham's 1954 meetings in Washington, D.C., in which he told a cancer patient 15 secrets, including her name, address, and ailments, before pronouncing her healing in Jesus' mighty name. Instances of infallible discernments like this were common place in Branham's prayer lines.

A second prophecy coming to pass is the immoral condition of American churches. In April 1965, Branham shared a symbolic vision with "Thus saith the Lord" in which a group of women represented American churches. The women had bobbed hair, painted faces, were dancing to rock and roll, smoking cigarettes, and hardly wearing any clothes in an attempt to sexually seduce. History shows most churches—especially Pentecostals—in 1965 condemned all these evil practices. Recently, we've seen the acceptance of these sins in nearly every church, specifically the celebration of rock and roll. When I shared Branham's vision with my mother, now 70 years old, she admitted her Pentecostal denomination once forbid rock and roll until a decade ago. Her heart broke at a recent youth convention as she watched young people dance to rock, rap, and more, something she thought would never have been accepted in her denomination. Undoubtedly, this sinful trend will only increase, since it was a warning in the name of the Lord.

The third prophecy, from July 1965, foretold the impossibility of Christian denominations returning to the apostolic gospel and the certainty of their acceptance of the future Pope-Antichrist. God's prophet pronounced:

> "It's predicted that they're going to do it. And they're going to do it, for it's THUS SAITH THE LORD they're going to do it. You think them nominations will ever break up, their denomination come back to the Word? It's THUS SAITH

THE LORD, they won't! Will they go into the antichrist? Exactly. It's THUS SAITH THE LORD, they will!"[1926]

Friend, there is no hope for denominational systems. In 56 years since this prophecy thundered out, true apostolic revival has not come to a single denomination and never will come to their dead systems. While the warning is stern, God's grace to call out His people from organization is amazing. Revelation 18:4 pleads with millions yet today: *"Come out of her, my people, that ye be not partakers of her sins, and that ye receive not of her plagues."*

FUTURE PROPHESIES WITH 'THUS SAITH THE LORD'

In divine mercy, God has given us 11 future prophesies to help us prepare for Jesus' rapture return. The first is driverless cars, prophesied in 1933, but not recorded on tape until 1958. Branham said, "Now, I said, 'It'll come to pass that those cars will not be run by a steering wheel; it'll be something another run.' It's them cars they're bringing out right now, remote control, for safety…Now, you remember; that's THUS SAITH THE LORD."[1927] It's likely Waymo, a sister company of Google, along with Tesla, General Motors, and other companies will help bring this prophecy to pass.

Backslidden United States has seven judgment-prophesies against her:

- "We are coming into a religious persecution with the same things that they did in pagan Rome many years ago, for it's THUS SAITH THE LORD."[1928]
- "And I say THUS SAITH THE LORD: the God, that America claims to serve, will destroy her."[1929]
- "This America has become condemned. And what did she do, according to the vision? She elected the wrong person. I don't know how long it'll take it to run out, but it will be

1926 Branham, William. *The Anointed Ones at the End Time*. July 25, 1965
1927 Branham, William. *Why We Are Not a Denomination*. September 27, 1958
1928 Ibid.
1929 Branham, William. *Influences*. February 15, 1964

someday. THUS SAITH THE LORD. It will. She's on her downward move right now. She'll never come back again. She's gone. That's right. She's been gone since 1956 when she condemned and turned away God from the great revival hours."[1930]

- "And remember, THUS SAITH THE LORD there will be a woman rule before the end time. She'll either be President, Vice President, or it'll be the Catholic church as a woman. I've seen her: A great woman, the nation bowed to her. It'll be one before the end time. THUS SAITH THE LORD. Write it down and find out, you young people. See if it happens. If it isn't, I'm a false prophet."[1931]

- "I remember, just my last Message in California, where I thought I'd never go back again, when I predicted, 'Los Angeles will go beneath the ocean, THUS SAITH THE LORD.' It will. She is done. She is washed. She is finished. What hour? I don't know when, but it will be sunk."[1932]

- "Someday, THUS SAITH THE HOLY SPIRIT out of the Word of God, that, 'America, there had been whole turning God down, and will receive the mark of the beast according to Revelations the 13th chapter.' And we're moving into it."[1933]

- "The last and seventh vision was wherein I heard a most terrible explosion. As I turned to look I saw nothing but debris, craters, and smoke all over the land of America."[1934]

Along with Branham's earlier prophecy that every denomination would take the mark of the beast, he also described it as a form of unionized religion:

1930 Branham, William. *Condemnation By Representation*. November 13, 1960
1931 Branham, William. *From That Time*. July 16, 1960
1932 Branham, William. *The Rapture*. December 4, 1965
1933 Branham, William. *Jubilee Year*. October 3, 1954
1934 Branham, p. 322

"Pertaining to labor union: I know you work... You men have labor unions and things that you... If you want to work, you have to belong to it. That's exactly right. You have to do that. But watch it (See?), because it's going to come from labor to religion one of these days. See? Now, you just remember; it's a forerunner of everything becoming unionized. You can't work; they won't let you on the job; you're--you're a 'scab,' unless you--unless you belong to this union. Now remember, you young people, remember what Brother Branham's saying. And may my words be graved with a iron pen in a--a--a mountain of steel. THUS SAITH THE LORD, that same thing will happen in religion. You'll belong to a denomination of some sort, or you cannot buy or sell. So be real careful, brother. Let it go just to labor alone. Watch it; it's a warning."[1935]

God's Spirit warns Christians to spiritually battle against the effects of Catholicism. In punishment for failing to repent of untold iniquities, a harsh prophecy is spoken against the Vatican:

- "Don't you never try to fight communism. Fight Romanism. For, that's THUS SAITH THE LORD. The Lord said Romanism is going to rule, not communism. It's just a puppet."[1936]
- "And remember, I say this as God's prophet: The Russian empire will drop an atomic bomb of some sort on the Vatican City and destroy it in one hour. THUS SAITH THE LORD."[1937]

Armed with these "Thus saith the Lord" doctrines and fulfilled and future prophesies, Jesus' earthly bride is now fulfilling Revelation 10:11 by sharing these prophesies, essentially prophesying again: *"And he said unto me, Thou must prophesy again before many peoples, and nations, and tongues, and kings."* Possessing "Thus saith the Lord"—the word of the King— makes you ready for the final showdown before the rapture. This

1935 Branham, William. *Questions and Answers, Part 1.* August 23, 1964
1936 Branham, William. *The Restoration of the Bride Tree.* April 22, 1962
1937 Branham, William. *The Mark of the Beast.* May 13, 1954

last showdown is between the true bride-church of Jesus Christ and the false, united denominational churches. Recall Haman's wicked plot to kill Esther and her people through evil laws. That's a type of the Catholic-beast system's plot to lay down its worldwide mark in deadly religious persecution against Jesus' bride through government legislation. Esther's intercession for the king's favor at the second wine banquet in the presence of her enemy, Haman, secured deliverance. The bride of Christ's favor with King Jesus will grant her deliverance from Satan's false church at the latter wine banquet, or the time when rapturing faith is poured out.

BRANHAM'S ELIJAH CHARACTERISTICS

Since William Branham fulfilled the fourth coming of Elijah's Spirit, he fittingly displayed numerous characteristics of Elijah and John the Baptist.

First, all three men spoke the Word of the Lord. Elijah spoke with "Thus saith the Lord" when he prophesied of Ahaziah's demise in 2 Kings 1:1-18. The Word came to John in the wilderness whereby he foretold Jesus would take away the sins of the world and baptize with the Holy Ghost.[1938] As this chapter chronicles, Brother Branham correctly spoke in the name of the Lord more than 30 times.

Second, all three were set apart from and opposed the popular religious organizations of their day. Elijah rebuked Ahab, Jezebel, and their false 450 Baal prophets in 1 Kings 18:17-22 and 21:20-25. John called the Pharisees and Sadducees a generation of vipers in Matthew 3:6-8. As God revealed the incurable iniquities of denominations, Branham condemned preachers who rejected Bible revelations:

> "And, today, I indict this bunch of ordained ministers; in their creeds and denominations, they are crucifying, to the people, the very God that they claim that they love and serve. I indict these ministers, in the Name of the Lord Jesus, upon their doctrine, that claim that 'the days of miracles is past,' and that 'the water baptism in the Name of Jesus Christ is not sufficient and not right.' Upon any of

---

1938 Luke 3:2, John 1:29, 33

these Words, that they have substituted creeds for, I indict them, as guilty, and the Blood of Jesus Christ upon their hands, for crucifying afresh the Lord Jesus, the second time. They are crucifying Christ, to the public, taking from them the thing that they're supposed to be giving to them. And they substituted something else in Its place; a church creed, for popularity."[1939]

Third, these men condemned prominent, immoral women. Elijah condemned Jezebel's murder of innocent Naboth in 1 Kings 21:17-29. John the Baptist rebuked Herod for his unlawful marriage to Herodias, prompting her to take off his head.[1940] Branham condemned the evil influences of Marilyn Monroe and Jackie Kennedy. About Monroe, he warned, "I don't want you be influenced by Marilyn Monroe. I want you to be influenced by Jesus Christ, see, and by His Word. He is the Word. If the Word don't influence you, then Christ can't, because He is the Word."[1941] Branham rebuked Kennedy for encouraging women to cut their hair, breaking 1 Corinthians 11:1-16. He preached, "I said a hard thing about Mrs. Kennedy, a couple times, about her setting fashions for the world, with these water-head haircuts, and, 'How our sisters and them cut their hair, and dress like Mrs. Kennedy,' I said, 'like a Jezebel of old.' That's true."[1942]

Fourth, all three were men of the wilderness. Elijah was from Gilead, a mountainous region near the River Jordan. He spent time at the Brook Cherith, being fed by ravens. Later, he rested under a juniper tree and dwelt alone in a cave, hearing God's voice.[1943] John dwelt in the wilderness, receiving God's Word and baptizing there. John is well known for wearing camel's hair, and eating locusts and honey.[1944] Brother Branham spent much of his free time in the woods and wilderness in order to refresh his mind and body. His gift of discernment sapped much of his physical strength, just as Daniel experienced in Daniel 8:26-27. Nature

1939 Branham, William. *The Indictment.* July 7, 1963
1940 Matthew 14:3-10, Luke 3:19-20
1941 Branham, William. *Influence.* January 12, 1963
1942 Branham, William. *The World is Again Falling Apart.* November 27, 1963
1943 1 Kings 17:1-7, 19:4-9
1944 Mark 1:4-6, Luke 1:80, 3:2

was also his refuge; a place to meet with God. Branham shared, "And my nature has always been to the woods. I was born in the woods, and I just seemed like was raised up there. And even my conversion never took it out of me. Not so much to get the game; but just to be in the woods. I think God is there; to see Him, how He moves."[1945]

Lastly, all three men battled the sin nature when not under the Holy Spirit's anointing. Fearing Jezebel's death threat, Elijah fled in 1 Kings 19:1-8, despite having so recently called fire down from heaven to consume his sacrifice. While in prison, John doubted whether Jesus was the Messiah, despite having baptized Jesus and having seen the Spirit descend upon Him like a dove.[1946] Under God's powerful anointing, Brother Branham repeatedly and publicly declared he was God's prophet. When correctly discerning a woman's infirmity, he proclaimed, "And that you might know that I be God's prophet, and His Spirit is here on me now, you also have a condition of the colon and bowel."[1947] But when Jesus' mighty anointing left, Brother Branham doubted he was a prophet, hesitating to label himself so: "The people, many times, regard me as being a prophet. I do not regard myself that. No, sir. I do not. I have... I don't say that to be humble. I say that to be truthful. I do not regard myself to be a prophet of the Lord. I--I haven't that honor."[1948]

FALSE CLAIMS TO BE ELIJAH

Although many men and women have falsely claimed to have Elijah's anointing, two stand out in particular: John Alexander Dowie and Tony Palmer.

Dowie (1847-1907) was a pastor from Australia who moved to America and gained many followers in the Chicago area. Dowie did indeed possess a legitimate healing ministry, having won nearly 100 suits against doctors and clergy who denied his healing testimonies.[1949] Sadly,

---

1945   Branham, William. *He Was To Pass This Way*. March 21, 1964
1946   Matthew 11:1-6
1947   Branham, William. *Witnesses*. October 4, 1964
1948   Branham, William. *Taking Sides With Jesus*. June 1, 1962
1949   "John Alexander Dowie." *Encyclopedia Britannica*, https://www.britannica.com/biography/John-Alexander-Dowie

he declared himself "Elijah the Restorer" in 1901 and was later removed from leading the city of Zion for fiscal irresponsibility.

What's significant about Dowie is the timing in which he falsely claimed to possess the Elijah anointing, as 1901 was only 8 years before the true Elijah was born—William Branham. A Biblical precedent exists for men recognizing God's season for prophecy to be fulfilled, but prematurely injecting themselves into it. In Acts 5:34-39, the Jewish teacher Gamaliel names Theudas and Judas of Galilee as men who boasted themselves as great ones and gained many followers, to their shame and destruction. These evil men sensed it was time for a great one to come, and He did—Jesus Christ—but they selfishly exalted themselves as great rather than waiting for God's Chosen One. Gamaliel wisely advised the Jewish council to abstain from persecuting Peter and the Christians, for if the move was of men, it would cease.

Moving on to our day, Jesus Himself taught many would rise and claim to be Him right before His second coming in Matthew 24:24. Spiritual men recognize this is the season of Jesus' second coming, and some allow Satan to deceive them into pretending to be Messiah, but they lie. Do not fear, for Jesus says you'll know all the false prophets by their evil fruits. You'll know the true church, Jesus' bride, for she'll have the correct interpretation of the Bible and the power of the Spirit accompanying her.

Bishop Tony Palmer (1966-2014) is best known for unifying the charismatic Word of Faith movement with the Vatican. In February 2014, Palmer visited Kenneth Copeland's leadership conference "in the Spirt of Elijah" to reunite Protestants and Catholics.[1950] It was a lie, for the Spirit of Elijah had already spoken "THUS SAITH THE LORD" through Branham to fight against, not unite with, Romanism! The bishop claimed the protest against Rome was over, and all Christians were Catholics. However, Revelation 18:5 says heaven will not forget Rome's sins. Palmer was right about one thing; he knew

1950 "Pope Francis Sends Video Message to Kenneth Copeland - Let's Unite." *YouTube*, uploaded by Prove All Things, 21 February 2014, https://www.youtube.com/watch?v=uA4EPOfic5A

Elijah had to return before Jesus' second coming, but must have overlooked Branham's unequaled ministry. The bishop erred by teaching the anointing unites us, not the doctrine. 2 John 1:9 teaches otherwise: "*Whosoever transgresseth, and abideth not in the doctrine of Christ, hath not God. He that abideth in the doctrine of Christ, he hath both the Father and the Son.*" True Christian unity requires *both* the anointing and true doctrine. Many false prophets and false Christs have the anointing but are void of truth.

Copeland's group swallowed up Palmer's false unity plea, blessing Pope Francis with all their hearts and souls, an idolatrous statement, and visited the Vatican a few months later to officially unite in brotherhood. Yes, the iron, Catholics, and clay, Protestants, of Daniel 2:43 are mixed, but not cleaving one to another. True, God-fearing Protestants remain staunchly opposed to Rome, for the blood of millions of martyrs is on her hands, and she is guilty of continual idolatry, Maryolatry, pedophilia, and every other unclean spirit.

Tragically, Palmer died in a head-on motorcycle accident in July 2014, and we mourn for his wife, children, and family. But the question remains: if Elijah's Spirit upon Branham had already come with "THUS SAITH THE LORD" to condemn Catholicism's iniquity, how could God send another man with Elijah's Spirit, Palmer, to condone Rome's wickedness and urge complete unity with the Mother Harlot? Scriptural and prophetic authority validates Branham as God's true and only Elijah-messenger to this age.

WILLIAM BRANHAM WAS NOT JESUS

In recent years, two extreme, erroneous groups have risen up around Branham's movement. One exalts Branham as infallible, essentially equal with Jesus, and the other labels him a charlatan.

William Branham was not Jesus—far from it, according to his own words. He admitted he was a sinner saved by grace, making thousands of sins per year and repenting frequently: "I make thousands of mistakes in each month, in each year. Sure. I do. But when I see I'm wrong, I say,

'God, I didn't mean to do it, You know my heart. I didn't mean to do that. I was trapped into that. I didn't mean to do it. You forgive me, Lord.'"[1951] Branham plainly said, "I'm not infallible" in 1963 after telling his congregation it was awful and tommyrot to say he was such in October of 1962. Branham never wanted nor accepted Jesus' honor.

The ever growing Branham-worship group says every word Branham said was "Thus saith the Lord". This is blatant heresy in light of Romans 3:4: *"Yea, let God be true, but every man a liar."* The rest of Romans 3 says there is none righteous and every tongue has used deceit. Jesus alone is the only infallible Man. If Branham was a true prophet, he, like every prophet, would be infallible when he spoke "in the name of the Lord" and with "Thus saith the Lord". It's my conviction Branham was a true prophet, but not every word he uttered was inspired, as he often admitted.

During his lifetime, Brother Branham battled and rebuked men who worshiped him. Two years before his death, Branham wondered if God would take him off the earth because men were giving him more attention than they were to Christ's Bible message: "I'm nothing. I'm your brother. Don't you pay any attention to a messenger. You watch the message. Don't watch the messenger. God will take it away from you. He will share His Glory with nobody. That's right. Don't you watch the messenger. Watch the message."[1952] The man-worshipping, antichrist spirit never left after Branham's death, as many worship Branham secretly by claiming his every word was infallible.

Branham's supernatural gifts caused some to exalt him, just as some confused John the Baptist for Jesus in John 1:19-20: *"And this is the record of John, when the Jews sent priests and Levites from Jerusalem to ask him, Who art thou? And he confessed, and denied not; but confessed, I am not the Christ."* Anyone worshipping a man is deceived of Satan. However, servants of God always battle this Satanic scheme, like Paul and Barnabas desperately condemned worship directed to them in Acts 14.

1951   Branham, William. *Hebrews Chapter Seven, Part 2.* September 22, 1957
1952   Branham, William. *An Absolute.* January 27, 1963

Like John the Baptist, Branham only pointed believers to Jesus. John said *"Behold the Lamb of God"* and Branham directed believers away from his mortality, pointing to the Immortal Christ, praying:

> "May they look away from this mortal clay of a servant. May they look to Him Who is the Omnipotent, Who is. And we know, Lord, that we are finite. No matter who we are, we're still mortal. But, not the messenger, but the Message. Grant it, Lord. That's where we point, to Jesus Christ the Son of God. Grant that He will be so real to every one here today, even to the little children, that He will become the absolute of the entire congregation. We ask in Jesus' Name. Amen."[1953]

Any student of Branham's teachings knows he grew in revelation. Some of his doctrinal understandings greatly changed over the course of his ministry. For example, Branham grew in his understanding of the Godhead and the Seven Seals. In 1952, he thanked God for the "great, third person of the Trinity" who burned in his heart[1954], but nine years later he boldly preached Trinitarianism was of the devil. Branham originally believed the white horse rider of Revelation 6:2 "was the Holy Spirit"[1955], but three years later declared he was the antichrist spirit with "Thus saith the Lord". In both doctrines, his later interpretations contradicted his first teachings, proving not every word he said was divine since God doesn't contradict Himself. Branham's growth in understanding is a sign of his humble, teachable, Christ-like spirit.

WILLIAM BRANHAM WAS NOT A CHARLATAN

The anti-Branham group claims he was a charlatan, but their assumptions are evidence of their ignorance.

One claim against Branham was that he purposely lied and exaggerated stories in order to gain influence. It's true details in Branham's stories change at times, but nothing suggests he was lying. Humans

---

1953 Branham, William. *Absolute*. December 30, 1962
1954 Branham, William. *Early Spiritual Experiences*. July 13, 1952
1955 Branham, William. *The 10 Virgins and the 144,000 Jews*. December 11, 1960

sometimes forget details, which I can relate to as a minister of the gospel. Also, unlike nearly every other human, Brother Branham spent much time daily seeing visions in a heavenly dimension. Many associated with him witnessed him constantly breaking in and out of visions. As Daniel suffered physically and mentally from visions, Branham did too. A weary mind is prone to forgetfulness, but God's amazing grace kept Branham sharp with "Thus saith the Lord".

Branham wasn't afraid of being challenged, as he openly invited listeners to test his teachings by the Word, quoting *"prove all things"* repeatedly. He knew the Bible was always right and accepted correction from it: "Now, we must prove all things by the Scripture. Not what…If It's contrary to my faith, and yet the Scripture says so, the Scripture's right and I'm wrong. See? The Scripture's always right. And only way you can do anything, is come back to the Scripture."[1956]

A second, more serious attack is saying Branham's prophesies failed. But Branham has evidence of accurately foretelling events in the name of the Lord, as you've already read five prophesies that have either come to pass or are in the process of being fulfilled.

The anti-Branham group makes three mistakes regarding Branham's prophesies. First, they claim prophecies have failed because they haven't come to pass, but ignore the fact that Brother Branham never put a date on their fulfillment.

Next, they fail to recognize some prophetic visions are conditional while others are unconditional. Conditional promises come to pass through human obedience, and thus can remain unfulfilled due to disobedience. Joshua 1:1-4 shows God's conditional promise to Israel through Joshua—equivalent to "Thus saith the Lord"—regarding their potential boundaries or coasts. But Judges 1 and 2 show Israeli tribes failed to drive out all the inhabitants of Canaan, thus not fully claiming their coasts. Did God's own "Thus saith the Lord" fail? No, that generation of Israelis failed God's conditional "Thus saith the Lord" promise due to disobedience, and missed their opportunity to expand their borders.

1956 Branham, William. *Israel and the Church, Part 1.* March 25, 1953

On the other hand, Jesus' earthly life and mission is an example of an unconditional promise. Despite Herod's efforts to kill all Israeli male babies, two years old and under, God protected baby Jesus by sending Him and his parents to Egypt. Isaiah's "Thus saith the Lord" prophesies about Jesus' life, death, and resurrection in Isaiah 53 were going to be fulfilled no matter what.

A final mistake is denying the fact that God can use other men to fulfill Brother Branham's prophesies if they have not yet come to pass. In 1 Kings 19:15-17, the Lord commanded Elijah to anoint Hazael, Jehu, and Elisha. Elijah could have said, "Thus saith the Lord, I'm going to anoint three men," but Elisha was the only one he anointed. Hazael seems to be anointed by Elisha in 2 Kings 8:13-15, and Jehu is anointed by a son of a prophet in 2 Kings 9:1-13. Scripture doesn't offer a reason why God didn't allow Elijah to anoint the other two men, but you learn we cannot interpret prophesies by human reasoning. God is the only true interpreter of His Word.

I must insert a friendly challenge to readers to contact me if you think a Branham prophecy has failed. After two decades of studying and preaching revelations God revealed to Branham, I'm convinced Branham was a genuine prophet of God who was accurate with "Thus saith the Lord".

Brother Branham was as genuine as Christians come, with impeccable character. Financially, Branham lived a very modest life, shunning luxurious living, unlike today's many prosperity preachers. He lived true to first wife, Hope, and after her death, did the same with his second wife, Meda. Branham kept his ministry small when other ministers of his time, like Oral Roberts, spent millions to expand theirs, all while compromising on Bible truths. Branham's purpose in staying small was to be able to preach to any size congregation, and to abstain from begging for money:

> "But I've kept my meetings small; I've never tried to get big, or some great big program, where I have to beg people for money. When it gets like that, I'll fold the Bible and go back to my Tabernacle. See? I never have to do that; may God help

me to never do it. I've never had big programs, so I can go to a church that holds ten and hold a revival. Or if the Lord wants me to preach to a hundred thousand, He sends somebody along to pay for it, so I go on and preach to a hundred thousand. So that's the way we live. So just don't have to have money. Just very small."[1957]

No, these are not the words of a charlatan; rather, they reveal Branham was a humble, honest Christian who was loved and vindicated by God, but despised and rejected by the majority of Christendom.

WILLIAM BRANHAM AND THE 12 MYSTERIES

Two Bible passages foretold Brother Branham's ministry of restoring the 12 Mysteries: the 12 pieces of shewbread and Elijah repairing the altar with 12 stones.

On December 30, 1962, William Branham preached two sermons, and the latter, evening message was different than any other sermon he had ever preached. The sermon, titled *Is This The Sign of the End, Sir?*, contained a cluster of interrelated dreams and visions he couldn't interpret. Yet he spoke "in the name of the Lord"[1958] that something important was going to happen soon. Branham wondered if the dreams and visions meant his death or Jesus' coming, but three months later the Lord showed him they signaled a furthering of his ministry into its third and final phase.

The last phase of Branham's ministry was to finish the mystery of God in fulfillment of Revelation 10:7. He spent the second half of the *Is This The Sign of the End, Sir?* sermon preaching all the Bible mysteries that needed to be explained before the end time, many of which he had already preached. Branham began the teaching by quoting C.I. Scofield's comments on Matthew 13:11, which define 11 New Testament mysteries, and then added more Bible revelations God's people needed (See Appendix B). It became clear to me that Scofield and Branham were on to something divine, and I began studying these mysteries.

1957 Branham, William. *The Queen of the South.* June 20, 1958
1958 Branham, William. *Is This The Sign of The End, Sir?* December 30, 1962

To begin my search, I used my electronic Bible concordance to search the King James Version for every Scripture that used the word "mystery" and found 27. After reading them all, I concluded there were 12 mystery-doctrines—not 11. Scofield left one out, the Mystery of God's Will, found in Ephesians 1:9. 12 mysteries connects to 12 loaves of shewbread in the Old Testament Holy Place, just as the Seven Church Ages were represented by the seven golden candlesticks. The types have to match the antitypes. There were not 11 loaves of bread, but 12.

Next, the Spirit of God brought to my remembrance how Branham taught the waters of separation and Moses' Tabernacle typed our New Testament worship experience. Old Testament worshippers first had to be sprinkled with the waters of separation before they could even enter Moses' Tabernacle,[1959] so the red heifer typed Jesus' death on the cross, and the sprinkling of the water typed a believer's first act of repentance. 1 Peter 1:2 shows New Testament sprinkling is God's anointing to repent and obey: "*Elect according to the foreknowledge of God the Father, through sanctification of the Spirit, unto obedience and sprinkling of the blood of Jesus Christ.*"

Once sprinkled, the cleansed and forgiven believer could enter the outer court, and offer sacrifices, which typed justification, the first New Testament Work of Grace. Branham taught this, and said Old Testament worshippers in the outer court still lacked fellowship with Almighty God, for there were two courts they could not enter: Holy Place and the Holiest of Holies. In the New, many believers repent and worship God, but fail to advance in worship, with the Holy Place representing sanctification, and the Holiest of Holies typing the baptism of the Holy Ghost, or true fellowship with God. Branham taught:

> "Now, my Baptist brother, I want to ask you something, if justification is all God requires, I'd like to ask you this: When the man was separated by the waters of separation, sprinkled, then he could not yet enter into the—the worship of the glory of the Lord. He could not do it,

1959 Numbers 19:1-22

because he was only sprinkled from his sins. It separated him from his sins, but did not put him in fellowship. That's right. It only separated him from his sins. Now, Ephesians said, 'We are washed by the water of the Word.' Now, hearing the Word and being just as religious as you want to be, and your—your pastor a scholar, and your Doctor of Divinity, a scholar, still that don't put us in fellowship. No, sir, it will not do it, because they were only separated from their sins. Now, that's a... Justification was Martin Luther's doctrine. We know that. Being justified by faith and still it didn't bring a fellowship."[1960]

The antitype of the Holy Place is the second Work of Grace, called sanctification. Sanctified Christians today must worship with all three furniture pieces: the seven golden candlesticks, the 12 loaves of shewbread, and the altar of incense. The seven candlesticks speak of Branham's "Thus saith the Lord" interpretation of the Seven Church Ages (See Chapter 7). Believers must recognize their Church Age, Laodicea, and maintain a brightly burning testimony for Christ as every other age accomplished. Then, believers feast on the fresh spiritual shewbread, the "bread of His face," or the 12 New Testament mystery-doctrines, tasting the goodness of the Lord. Before entering the Holiest, Christians become prayer warriors, offering fiery, sincere prayers, including sighing and crying for the abominations done in the world.

A crucial point about the 12 loaves of shewbread as the 12 New Testament mysteries is that Paul said you can understand all mysteries, yet not have love in 1 Corinthians 13:2: *"And though I have the gift of prophecy, and understand all mysteries, and all knowledge; and though I have all faith, so that I could remove mountains, and have not charity, I am nothing."* Just as priests could devour the shewbread yet still not enter the Holiest, believers today can devour the 12 mysteries and still not be born again. Yes, you can understand all the mysteries—the 12 previous chapters of this book—and still not be filled with the Holy Ghost-baptism experience. A dedicated, sincere prayer life is needed to be born again, as

1960 Branham, William. *The Basis of Fellowship.* February 14, 1961

evidenced by the altar of incense being the final piece of furniture before entering the Holiest.

The Third Work of Grace, the baptism of the Holy Ghost, is typed by the Holiest of Holies. God meets with and speaks to Christians in their souls, as Exodus 25:22 says it was the place of meeting and communion, or speaking. The Ark of the Covenant contained two tables of stone, the pot of manna, and Aaron's rod. The stone tables speak of the New Testament Word-covenant written on the *"fleshly tables"* of our hearts, according to 2 Corinthians 3:3. The pot of manna represents God sharing His original, supernatural Word with believers in every generation. God's Word is incorruptible, and satisfies the hungry soul: *"For he satisfieth the longing soul, and filleth the hungry soul with goodness."*[1961] Aaron's rod represents a resurrected, quickened soul according to Ephesians 2:5: *"Even when we were dead in sins, hath quickened us together with Christ, (by grace ye are saved;)."*

I believe there's a second Scriptural precedent for Branham restoring the 12 Mysteries. 1 Kings 18:30-31 shows Elijah repairing the altar of the Lord with 12 stones at the Mount Carmel showdown. Once the altar of worship was restored, Elijah prayed, and the fire fell, vindicating him as God's true prophet. Elijah's showdown typed the final showdown coming before the rapture, which Branham calls the Mount Zion-latter rain showdown: "Then in the latter rain will come a Mount Carmel showdown…He will be indicated (pointed out in the Word, Revelation 10:7) and God will vindicate his ministry. He will preach the truth as did Elijah and be ready for the Mount Zion showdown."[1962]

In our day, Branham had the Spirit of Elijah, and restored true worship by placing 12 stones, or the 12 Mysteries, in their proper place. Matthew 16:17-18 teaches a stone, or rock, is a revelation. One day soon the Holy Ghost-fire will fall, vindicating Branham as God's true prophet, as evidenced by his followers being raptured into the sky to meet Jesus in the air.

1961   Psalm 107:9
1962   Branham, p. 174, 176

BRANHAM'S EMPHASIS ON THE BIBLE
AND CONCORDANCE

Amazed by the revelations of Moses' Tabernacle typing New Testament worship, I wondered how to teach the 12 New Testament mysteries. The Holy Spirit reminded me how He taught Branham to interpret the Seven Seals, and I followed his example. Each day before preaching one of the Seals, God showed Branham a vision interpreting its meaning. Then Branham would spend the rest of the day finding Bible support for each vision's meanings, using his concordance to locate Scriptural evidence for God's revelations. Here Branham explains it well:

> "And then I thought, 'Well, what is it, Lord?' And I walked up and down the floor awhile. I'd kneel down and pray, go back and pick up the Bible, set down, and read, walk back and forth. And then all of a sudden when I got quiet, here it [vision] just unfolded like that. Then I'd grab a pen right quick, and go to writing it down like that, whatever I was seeing and doing, watching it like that till I got it wrote down. Then I'd take the rest of the day and go down and chase this out and see if it tied all the way down through the Scriptures. Then it... 'Prove all things.' See?"[1963]

Further, Brother Branham likens this method to raising a building stone by stone, which connects to his Elijah-like ministry of restoring the altar of worship using 12 stones, or 12 mystery-truths:

> "So help me, I never knew it before; none of these things [revelations of the Seals] have I ever knowed before. That's right. And I just don't--just go up there and take the Bible and set down and set there until... When it [vision] goes to breaking forth like that, I just pick up my pen and start writing (See?), and just stay there, maybe for hours, till It gets--a--It gets finished. Then I go back, and I find out as I see where He said this... I thought, 'Well, looks like I've seen that somewhere.' I get my concordance, go look back (Is there something like that?) and here it is right here. And

1963 Branham, William. *The Seventh Seal*. March 24, 1963

then here it is over here again; here it is back here and down here and over here. Then I just tie it right in. I know that's God as long as it's comparing Scripture with Scripture. That's the way it has to do. Just like putting a building together, the stones have to fit stone by stone."[1964]

In my case with the 12 Mysteries, I'm not a prophet, so I never saw visions, but I started with the unfailing "Thus saith the Lord" teachings from Branham as my foundation. With each mystery, such as Chapter 5's Mystery of Godliness, I used a concordance to look up each occurrence of "godliness" in the King James Version (there are 15). Then I looked up each of the eight character traits—such as virtue and temperance—in the concordance, and every Bible occurrence had to be taken into prayerful consideration in understanding the trait. It's indisputable that the Bible interprets itself, so the revelation of virtue, temperance, and every other trait must already lay in Scripture. This book's aim has been to clearly prove the revelations of the 12 Mysteries are already in the Bible.

Branham's experience in the spiritual realms, supporting heavenly visions using his Bible and concordance, caused him to distinguish his teachings on the Seven Seals as his greatest meetings. He says the Spirit's revealing of truth is greater than divine healing:

> "Of all the times that I've been behind the pulpit at the Tabernacle, I have never, never in any time of my ministry ever worked into the realms of God and the spiritual realms as it's been this time. Yeah, it's beyond anything I ever did in any time of my ministry, in any meeting at anywhere like this. Mostly, it's on healing; this is revealing of Truth by the same Spirit. See? Same Spirit."[1965]

BRANHAM ON MYSTERIES AS BREAD

While no quote exists of Brother Branham saying "12 Mysteries," numerous quotes associate mysteries and bread.

1964 Branham, William. *The Fourth Seal.* March 21, 1963
1965 Branham, William. *Questions and Answers on the Seals.* March 24, 1963

In Moses' Tabernacle, the shewbread was hidden from the public inside the Holy Place. Priests alone could eat of it, once a week. The pot of manna was even more exclusive, accessible only once a year to Israel's high priest. Interestingly, there's no Biblical record of any priest eating from the pot of manna.

Spiritually speaking, the 12 Bible Mysteries are hidden from most Christians, accessible only to spiritual priests who are living sanctified lives. Born again Christians, who enter into the Holiest by the baptism of the Holy Ghost, behold the pot of manna, or original, eternal Word delivered on the Day of Pentecost.

Branham's first quote connecting mysteries and bread is fittingly from December 1960, immediately after he preached the revelation of the Mystery of Seven Stars and Seven Golden Candlesticks—the Seven Church Ages. According to a dream or vision from the Lord, he says his preaching was a mountain of bread the saints were feasting on:

> "Help me, God, because I seek sincerely to know Your will, that I might do it to bring (as You showed me many years ago when I left this church) the Bread of Life to the peoples of the world. When I saw that great mountain of Bread, and white-robed Saints coming from all over the earth to eat this Bread of Life. O God, let me--O God, let me never, never fail to feed the people on the Bread of Life. Bless these hungry souls in here that raised their hands just now."[1966]

In June 1964, Brother Branham likens Christians to spiritual kings and priests who enter into the Holy Place and Holiest of Holies, eating shewbread, or Bibles with brand new revelations:

> "It may be, but, you see, inside, behind that badger skin, behind that human skin, in there is the Shekinah Glory, in there is the power, in there is the Word, in there is the shewbread. And the Shekinah Glory, which is the Light, that makes Light that ripens grain. You Kansas people know

1966 Branham, William. *Revelation Chapter 4, Part 1.* December 31, 1960

that, by your wheat crops. Without that sun, it won't light. And until you come in behind that badger skin, until you get out of your old skin, your old thoughts, your old creeds, and come into the Presence of God; then the Word becomes a living reality to you, then you're awakened to the Shekinah Glory, then the Bible becomes a new Book, then Jesus Christ is the same yesterday, today, and forever. You're living in His Presence, eating the shewbread that's only provided that day for believers, priests only. 'And we are priests, royal priesthood, a holy nation, peculiar people, giving spiritual sacrifices to God.' But you must come in, to behind the veil, to see the unveiled God. And God is unveiled, that's His Word made manifest."[1967]

Next, in what may be the most important quote associating mysteries and bread, Brother Branham uses Malachi 4:5-6 and Revelation 10:7 to say God is turning our hearts back to eating all the revealed mysteries, calling them the Shewbread of this Laodicean Church Age:

"...the Shekinah Glory...it ripens the Shewbread that we feast on, and drive across the country for, hundreds of miles, see. It's the believers' Food. It's only for a believer. Remember, the Shewbread was only for the believer only, see, Shewbread Seed. Notice. What does it do? That Shekinah Glory, over the Shewbread, kept It from spoiling...What's this Shekinah Glory today? To break beyond the veil, to see Who God is standing before you, see Who God is standing here before us, the--the Pillar of Fire. He is veiled in human flesh. But what does the Shek'nah, what did it do? The Shewbread Seed, the Word that we're to live on in this day, by these promises, the Shekinah Glory ripens that Shewbread, brings it to pass, makes it Bread to the believer; that laid in the pages of the Bible, year after year, the Word for this age. To the denominations, It's a stumbling block. To the denominations, they stumble at It. Down through the years, Luther, Wesley, Martin Luther, and all, Sankey, Finney, John Smith, Knox, all stumbled at It. But what's it to be done in the last days? What is 'to reveal'? 'Bring forth!' What's Malachi 4 to do? To turn

1967 Branham, William. *The Identified Christ of All Ages.* June 17, 1964 back the people from that stumbling block, to break down the traditions, and to reveal the Bread with the Shekinah Glory. Watch It ripen and produce just exactly what It said It would do, oh, my, the Shewbread for this age. To the denomination, a stumbling block, 'a bunch of fanatics.' But, we who believe! But now as Revelations 10 has promised, 'All the mysteries of God, that's been hid in the pages down through them years, would be ripened, brought forth in the age of the seventh angel's Message.'"[1968]

RESTORED TRUTHS

Another observation from *Is This The Sign of the End, Sir?* is Branham listing more mysteries after he read Scofield's list of 11, such as the Serpent Seed, the true understanding of grace, non-eternal hell, water baptism in Jesus Christ's literal name, and the return of the Pillar of Fire. But notice these doctrines are not specifically labeled as "mysteries" in Scripture, like the 12 Mysteries of each previous chapter. Since God's Word omits the "mystery" label, I choose to do the same.

The conclusion is twofold. First, some of these doctrines are part of the 12 Mysteries, showing they are mysterious. They include the Serpent Seed as part of the Mystery of Iniquity, grace accepted and grace failed in the Mystery of Godliness, and water baptism as part of the Mystery of the Godhead.

Second, the doctrines not labeled as mysteries in the KJV, such as non-eternal hell and the return of the Pillar of Fire, can be categorized as "restored truths" Christians lost during the Church Ages. Recall the end time is the age of restoration according to Joel 2:23-26, Matthew 17:11, and Acts 3:20-21.

REVELATIONS ARE HIDDEN WISDOM GIVEN TO THE WISE

The 12 Bible-defined mysteries and Branham's God-given revelations are so simple and plain you would think multitudes of church

---

1968 Branham, William. *The Unveiling of God.* June 14, 1964

members would rejoice in them. Sadly, most fulfill the denunciation given to the Laodicean Church Age, thinking they have everything spiritually, and desire nothing more from God. In most of my conversations sharing about the mysteries, church members disregard them, showing no interest in the deep things of God. If they had the Spirit, they would desire the deep things, for *"the Spirit searcheth all things, yea, the deep things of God."*[1969] Lukewarm is God's description of this revelation-rejecting group.

Another reason church members reject the mysteries is because they're hidden from them. 1 Corinthians 2:7 supports this saying, *"But we speak the wisdom of God in a mystery, even the hidden wisdom, which God ordained before the world unto our glory."* Why is it hidden? Because they have rejected God's previous attempts to show them truth. Billions will be left behind after the rapture and suffer God's wrath in the Tribulation because they refused God's counsel. Proverbs 1:24-26 reads, *"Because I have called, and ye refused; I have stretched out my hand, and no man regarded; But ye have set at nought all my counsel, and would none of my reproof: I also will laugh at your calamity; I will mock when your fear cometh."* The Tribulation is the reaping of their sinful planting. David speaks of God's just dealings with mankind that apply to today in 2 Samuel 22:26-28:

> *"With the merciful thou wilt shew thyself merciful, and with the upright man thou wilt shew thyself upright. With the pure thou wilt shew thyself pure; and with the froward thou wilt shew thyself unsavoury. And the afflicted people thou wilt save: but thine eyes are upon the haughty, that thou mayest bring them down."*

Jesus endured the same truth-rejecting, demon-filled religious groups we battle. The Pharisees flat out denied and ignored all the Scriptures about Jesus like groups today do to followers of Brother Branham's ministry. John 7:52 exposes one major error the Pharisees

---

1969   1 Corinthians 2:10

made—they never asked Jesus where He was born. They assumed He was born in Galilee, but Bethlehem was his birthplace. How many today hear Brother Branham's doctrines, like the One-Person Godhead, the Serpent Seed, women having uncut hair, and never search the Scriptures to see if they are true? Shame and folly is all that is left for such world-loving church members. Proverbs 18:13 confirms this: *"He that answereth a matter before he heareth it, it is folly and shame unto him."*

Holy Ghost-filled Christians want to know God's mysteries. We delight in the deep things, for they reveal God's heart. We want to please God. He is seeking true worshippers now, for His eyes go to and fro throughout the earth to reveal Himself to truth-hungry souls.

JESUS' HEART TRUSTS HIS WIFE

Paul says in 1 Corinthians 4:9: *"We are made a spectacle unto the world, and to angels, and to men."* The word *"spectacle"* means "theatre or public show," giving us the imagery of a Broadway show. Human history is a great drama being played out before the world, angels, and men. Thankfully, the Author and Finisher of the script loves and protects those that love Him, and will not suffer them to be tempted above their capacity.

The final act in this climatic Times of the Gentiles scene is for Heaven's Hero, our Husband, Jesus Christ, to return to rapture His bride off the earth. Revelation 19:7 says our charge, as Jesus' future wife, is to make ourselves ready. The Bible is our Husband's love letter, giving us both clear and secret instructions to prepare for the rapture. The secrets, or mysteries, are only revealed to Jesus' bride because she truly hungers to obey Him. Deuteronomy 29:29 proclaims this, saying, *"The secret things belong unto the Lord our God: but those things which are revealed belong unto us and to our children for ever, that we may do all the words of this law."*

The distinctive characteristic of true Christians is their desire to lovingly obey Jesus as a wife obeys her husband. Thus, the purpose of God revealing His mysteries is so you can do the will of God. James 1:22 says, *"But be ye doers of the word, and not hearers only, deceiving your own selves."* Jesus' bride is a doer, not a hearer only.

Since you've received Jesus' Spirit in the depths of your being, your soul, He has confidence that you'll do His good pleasure in everything. Recall how God confidently allowed Job to be tested by Satan himself. God wasn't worried about Job falling, neither is He worried about you falling because you have already received His own Life in your soul, the Holy Ghost. Like Job and the Proverbs 31 Woman, Jesus' heart is confident in your obedience. Proverbs 31:10-11 proclaims, "*Who can find a virtuous woman? for her price is far above rubies. The heart of her husband doth safely trust in her, so that he shall have no need of spoil.*"

Truly, God doesn't think—He *knows*—you're going to overcome Satan and keep His Word, for you are the spiritual seed of Abraham. Genesis 18 is repeating now, as God is preparing to destroy the sin-loving Sodomites of this world. But God is graciously revealing all His plans to you, like He did Abraham, because you're keeping His Bible commands:

> "*And the LORD said, Shall I hide from Abraham that thing which I do; Seeing that Abraham shall surely become a great and mighty nation, and all the nations of the earth shall be blessed in him? For I know him, that he will command his children and his household after him, and they shall keep the way of the LORD, to do justice and judgment; that the LORD may bring upon Abraham that which he hath spoken of him.*"[1970]

Since you love Jesus Christ with all your heart, you're in the Abraham-group, to whom Jesus revealed His 12 mystery-doctrines. Recall the four heart reactions to Jesus from Figure 21 in Chapter 8. Jesus hid these revelations from the other three groups: the Lot-group (foolish virgins), Mrs. Lot group (make believers like Judas Iscariot), and Sodomites (unbelievers).

Whether the rapture comes in this generation or a future generation, Jesus' blessing will rest upon you and your children because you're Abraham's spiritual seed. You've obeyed His Voice and kept His

---

1970   Genesis 18:17-19

commands. Isaac, the seed of Abraham, received this same promise in Genesis 26:4-5: "*And I will make thy seed to multiply as the stars of heaven, and will give unto thy seed all these countries; and in thy seed shall all the nations of the earth be blessed; Because that Abraham obeyed my voice, and kept my charge, my commandments, my statutes, and my laws.*"

Your ministry is making yourself ready, finishing Jesus' Great Commission, and waiting for your Heavenly Husband to appear not on stage, but above the stage, in the air! Our promise remains: "*Then we which are alive and remain shall be caught up together with them in the clouds, to meet the Lord in the air: and so shall we ever be with the Lord.*"[1971] You don't know the day and hour of His return. Neither do the angels, or the Husband Himself, but He knows your heart, and He's trusting you'll be ready.

CONCLUSION WITH A COMMA

Scripture is clear that God promised to send a prophet anointed with the Spirit of Elijah to restore all things before Jesus returns to the earth. Amos 3:7 agrees, saying God always sends a prophet to reveal His secrets. Our Lord was obligated by His promises to send a prophet before the Times of the Gentiles were finished, and he has come and gone, speaking in Jesus' name with "THUS SAITH THE LORD."

The apostolic ministry of Bible days has returned, though small in number. Jesus' bride patterns herself after Paul's divine pattern, pointed to Paul's Scriptures by Branham. As a member of Jesus' bride, never let your hunger for God wane. Feed your soul daily upon God's fresh bread, His Word.

God doesn't condemn people for being born in sin, but for loving darkness rather than light. If your soul is full of Holy Ghost love, you'll never denominate upon your own opinions. Instead, you'll constantly seek more revelation from God. Branham had to stand against every denominational system because they grew lukewarm and thought they

---

1971   1 Thessalonians 4:17

had no more need of God's power, like Revelation 3:17 expresses. God's prophet said:

> "That way, when I speak against some denomination, or the denominational system, it isn't the people in there. It's the system that I'm against, you see, that holds them apart, holds us from receiving. See? They draw up their declarations, say, 'We believe this, period!' If they would end it with a comma, 'We believe this, plus as much as the Lord can show us out of His Word,' it would be all right. But they do not do it that way. You know that. It couldn't be a denomination and do that, see. It would just be the move of God, moving on all the time, you see."[1972]

I'm a witness that God is active and moving in my life and our local church, by His grace. We're thrilled to be a part of God's restoration of the Book of Acts Church. The best part is, the move of God is only going to increase in bride churches, according to prophecy in Joel 2:23-26. Imagine a church full of fresh bread, fresh preaching. Imagine a church overflowing with wine (joy and gladness) and oil (saints being born again). Imagine being satisfied leaving church every single time. Imagine long stretches of joyous praise to Jesus. Imagine being unashamed of the gospel in every area of your life. Some saints are already experiencing these blessings, but the bride worldwide is coming into them in order to fulfill God's promises.

My final prayer is for God to help us boldly utter the revelations He has made known to us, as Paul prayed in Ephesians 6:18-20. We are called to boldly share God's secrets, not hide them from others. Dear Jesus, open doors of utterance to the lost, and embolden our spirits to make known the mystery of the gospel in their ears!

At the beginning of this book, Jesus' secrets were at your fingertips, but now they are written in your heart by the Holy Ghost. God's secrets are both with you and in you. Proverbs 3:32 affirms, "*His secret is with the righteous.*" 2 Corinthians 4:7 says God's treasure is inside you: "*But we*

[1972] Branham, William. *Once More*. November 17, 1963

have this treasure in earthen vessels, that the excellency of the power may be of God, and not of us."

I'm ending this book with a symbolic comma as a tribute to Branham's dedication to constant revival through receiving further revelation from the Holy Spirit. Branham never denominated, thinking he knew everything. Bride members today will keep the same humble attitude as their star-messenger, Branham. May you believe God sent William Branham to finish the mystery of God and obey the Bible truths he pointed to. With all my heart, I believe Brother Branham's Bible-based revelations, plus as much additional revelation the Lord Jesus Christ will reveal to me out of His Word,

APPENDIX A

Bible Study Reference List For The Mystery of the Godhead

Q UICK REFERENCE BIBLE STUDIES for the 12 Mysteries are essential for two purposes: defending the gospel against skeptics, and teaching Christians reasons they should hope in the Word of God. This book's length naturally begs for a quick reference guide for Biblical proof "*the mystery of God*"[1973] has been finished, or revealed.

Below you'll find Bible study references for Chapter 1 only. References for remaining chapters are available for free at www.pastorjessesmith.com/12mysteriesbook. You can also reach me via email, jesse.smith11@sbcglobal.net, or text 330-929-2037.

As Christians, we must verbally defend our faith. Twice Paul says he was set for the defense of the gospel in Philippians 1:7 and 17. In Greek, "defence" means "verbal defence, speech in defence, a reasoned statement or argument." The same Greek word for "defence" is also

---

1973 Revelation 10:7

translated as "answer" in Peter's first epistle: *"But sanctify the Lord God in your hearts: and be ready always to give an answer to every man that asketh you a reason of the hope that is in you with meekness and fear."*[1974] You can be ready to share the truth with any inquirer.

Ministers especially must faithfully test all beliefs. Paul commands us to *"Prove all things"* in 1 Thessalonians 5:21. Prove means "to test, examine, prove, scrutinize (to see whether a thing is genuine or not), as metals" in the Greek. Since the Bible is our Absolute, all revelations are proven true by the pure words of Scripture alone.

Paul's message to Timothy in 2 Timothy 2:15 is: *"Study to shew thyself approved unto God, a workman that needeth not to be ashamed, rightly dividing the word of truth."* Acts 17:11 labels the Bereans as a noble group because they searched the Scriptures daily to verify Paul's preaching.

Special thanks to Pastor Craig Booher for his inspiration in compiling quick reference Bible studies.

1ST MYSTERY: THE GODHEAD

Revelation: God is one invisible Person—three persons is essentially tritheism—Who created the body of His Son, Jesus, to be His one eternal image and tabernacle.

Paul calls the Godhead a mystery:
- Col. 2:2-3 *mystery of God, and of the Father, and of Christ*

The Heavenly Father alone reveals the mystery of Jesus' deity through revelation—not a creed:
- Mat. 16:16-17 *for flesh and blood hath not revealed it…but my Father which is in heaven*
- Mat. 11:25 *I thank thee, O Father…thou hast hid these things from the wise and prudent, and hast revealed them unto babes*

1974   1 Peter 3:15

Godhead-related creeds that add to the pure words of the Bible are false and dangerous:

- Prov. 30:5-6 *Every word of God is pure... Add thou not unto his words, lest he reprove thee, and thou be found a liar*
- Rev. 22:18-19 *If any man shall add unto these things, God shall add unto him the plagues*

Scripture debunks contradictions in the Athanasian Creed:

- John 4:24 [We] *worship Him... in spirit and in truth;* Creed: "we worship one God in Trinity"
- Rev. 3:14 [Jesus is] the beginning of the creation of God; Creed: "the Son uncreated"
- Mark 13:32 Jesus doesn't know day and hour of His return; Creed: "the Son unlimited"
- Matt. 1:20 Jesus' body *conceived... of the Holy Ghost;* Creed: "the Son is of the Father alone"
- John 14:28 *The Father is greater than I* [Jesus]; Creed: none is greater, or less than another
- Heb. 1:3 Jesus is the *"express image"* of the one *"person"* of God; Creed: God is "three persons"

Shield of the Trinity falsely claims "the Holy Spirit is NOT the Father":

- Eph. 4:4 *One Spirit;* [There is One Spirit; not two]
- John 17:11 *Holy Father* [The Father is holy]
- Eph. 4:30 *grieve not the holy Spirit of God* [The Spirit is holy]

If the Shield of the Trinity is true, Jesus had two separate persons living inside Him:

- John 1:32 *the Spirit... abode upon him* [The Holy Spirit dwelt in Jesus]
- John 14:10 *the Father that dwelleth in me, he doeth the works* [The Father dwelt in Jesus]

Jesus and His apostles taught and affirmed pure Hebrew monotheism—not trinitarianism:

- John 4:19-26 *We know what we worship: for salvation is of the Jews*
- Mark 12:28-34 *Jesus answered...The first of all the commandments is, Hear, O Israel; The Lord our God is one Lord*
- Deut. 6:4 *Hear, O Israel; The Lord our God is one Lord*

God the Father *is* the Holy Spirit—God is a Spirit, one Spirit, only Savior, and is holy:

- Jhn. 4:24 *God is a spirit*
- Jhn. 17:11 *Holy Father, keep through thine own name those whom thou hast given me*
- Deut. 6:4, Mark 12:29, Gal. 3:20 *God is one*
- Isa. 43:11 *even I, am the LORD; and beside me there is no saviour*

God is invisible, Jesus is His bodily image, and the fulness of God's Spirit dwells in Jesus' body:

- Col. 1:15-19 *Who is the image of the invisible God...it pleased the Father that in him should all fulness dwell*
- 2 Cor. 5:19 *God was in Christ, reconciling the world unto himself*

God the invisible Father will never been seen; He's only visible through Jesus' body:

- John 1:18 *No man hath seen God at any time; the only begotten Son...he hath declared him*
- 1 Tim. 1:17 *Now unto the King eternal, immortal, invisible, the only wise God*
- 1 Tim. 6:16 *whom no man hath seen, nor can see*

God Manifests Himself in Three Ways—Father, Son, Holy Ghost:

- Mal. 2:10 *Have we not all one father? hath not one God created us?*
- 1 Tim. 3:16 *God was manifest in the flesh*
- 1 Cor. 12:7 *But the manifestation of the Spirit is given to every man to profit withal*

Jesus, the Word, is God—not a "second person"—manifest in the flesh:

- 1 Tim. 3:16 *God was manifest in the flesh*
- John 1:14 *And the Word was made flesh, and dwelt among us*
- John 8:58 *Verily, verily, I say unto you, Before Abraham was, I am*
- John 10:30 *I and my Father are one*
- John 14:8-10 *he that hath seen me hath seen the Father*
- Rev. 1:4-8 *I am Alpha and Omega, the beginning and the ending, saith the Lord, which is, and which was, and which is to come, the Almighty.*

The word "manifest" to describe Jesus:

- John 1:31, 14:21, 17:6, 1 Cor. 12:7, 1 Tim. 3:16, 2 Tim. 1:10, 1 Pet. 1:20, 1 John 1:2, 3:5, 3:8, 4:9

Jesus' bodily image reveals the Father:

- Mat. 11:27 *neither knoweth any man the Father, save the Son, and he to whomsoever the Son will reveal him.*

See "The Oneness Wheel" showing Jesus' unity with the Father:

- https://gracenews.wordpress.com/2007/11/20/wheel-of-prophecy-who-is-god/

The One Person Godhead uses plural nouns because Jesus' human body was not divine, unlike the Father, yet had a Word-nature:

- John 14:23, 17:21 *we will come* and *make our abode* and *may be one in us*
- John 14:28 *for my Father is greater than I* [The Father was greater than Jesus' humanity]
- Luk. 22:42, Heb. 4:15, Jam. 1:13 Jesus was tempted but God can never be tempted
- Heb. 1:3 Jesus is *express image*, or exact expression, of God's holy nature

Understanding Genesis 1:26 does not refer to three persons:

- Mal. 2:10 *one Father…one God created us*—one Creator; not two creators
- Isa. 44:24 *the LORD…maketh all things…stretcheth forth the heavens alone; that spreadeth abroad the earth by myself*—God alone created; not two persons
- Gen. 11:7 *let us* refers to angels—doesn't mean three divine persons
- Isa. 6:8 *who will go for us?* refers to God and seraphims; no mention of three heavenly persons
- Eph. 3:9 *God…created all things by Jesus Christ*—"Let us" might mean God created through Jesus, Who is the Word, just like Jesus used plural nouns in John 14:23, 17:21

Understanding Matthew 28:19 and water baptism:

- Mat. 28:19 *baptizing them in the name of the Father, and of the Son, and of the Holy Ghost*
- Acts 2:38 10 days after Mat. 28:19, Peter commands baptism *in the name of Jesus Christ*
- Acts 8:16 Samaritans were *baptized in the name of the Lord Jesus*

- Acts 10:48 Peter baptized Cornelius' house *in the name of the Lord*
- Acts 19:1-6 Paul baptized the Ephesians *in the name of the Lord Jesus*; rebaptism is permitted
- Acts 22:16 Paul was baptized *calling on the name of the Lord*
- Mat. 13:34-35, Ps. 78:2-3 Father, Son, and Holy Ghost was a foretold *dark saying*, or enigma

God has many titles but one Name above every Name:

- Mat. 28:19 *the name...Father...Son...Holy Ghost* are titles referencing one name: Lord Jesus Christ
- Phil. 2:9-11 *name which is above every name*—the Lord Jesus Christ is the highest name
- Rev. 12:9 Satan's four titles, yet one person: *great dragon... old serpent...Devil...Satan*
- Isa. 9:6, Jere. 23:5, Hag.2:7, Zec. 9:9, Dan. 9:25, Job 19:25, Ps. 118:22, Mal. 4:2 some of Jesus' Old Testament titles: Wonderful, Counselor, the Mighty God, the Everlasting Father, the Prince of Peace, the Righteous Branch, the Desire of All Nations, King, Messiah the Prince, Redeemer, the Head Stone of the Corner, and Sun of Righteousness
- 1 Cor. 10:4, Rev. 22:16, John 11:25, John 15:1, John 1:9, Rev. 19:13, 22:13 some of Jesus' New Testament titles: Rock, Root and Offspring of David, Bright and Morning Star, Resurrection and the Life, True Vine, True Light, the Word of God, Alpha and Omega, the Beginning and the End, the First and Last, Lord God Almighty
- Luke 10:17, Acts 16:18 demons cast out using the literal name of Jesus Christ
- Acts 2:38, 8:16, 19:5 believers baptized only in the literal name of Jesus Christ

- Acts 3:6 miracles performed only in literal name of Jesus Christ

Power in the Name of Jesus Christ:
- Acts 3:16 *And his name through faith in his name hath made this man strong*
- 1 Sam.17:45 David defeated Goliath *in the name of the Lord of hosts*
- John 1:12 those that receive Christ receive His power because they *believe on His name*
- Acts 4:7 a name is synonymous with power: *By what power, or by what name, have ye done this?*
- 2 Tim. 3:1-5 last days imposters will be *denying the power* or name of Jesus Christ
- Rev. 13:5-6 Satan blasphemes God's *name…tabernacle* and the saints *in heaven*

Understanding 1 John 5:7:
- 1 John 5:7 *Father…the Word…Holy Ghost*—never says "three persons"; all three bear record or witness in heaven
- Mat. 28:19 *Father…Son…Holy Ghost*—Son and the Word are interchangeable titles
- John 1:1,14 *In the beginning was the Word, and the Word was with God, and the Word was God. And the Word was made flesh, and dwelt among us*
- Rev. 19:13 *his name is called The Word of God*
- Deut. 30:19 The Father bears heavenly witness (1 John 5:7) of His covenant with Israel
- Mal. 2:13-14 Jehovah (the Father) witnessed Israeli men *dealt treacherously* against their wives
- John 5:36-37 Jesus' works and the Father bore witness of Him

- John 12:48 Jesus' preaching will be a heavenly witness in judgment: *The word that I have spoken, the same shall judge him in the last day*
- Acts 5:31-32 Holy Ghost baptism gives witness to Jesus' death, resurrection, and exaltation
- Heb. 2:1-4 miraculous, Holy Ghost empowered ministry is God's witness to all generations

Jesus' baptism shows the invisible God anointing His visible human image, or tabernacle:

- Mat. 3:13-17 Jesus baptized, Spirit like a dove, voice from heaven (three manifestations)
- Ex. 3:1-6 Moses see God manifest Himself in two ways (voice and fire) yet He's one Person
- Acts 2:3-4 120 licks of fire does not equate to the Spirit being 120 separate, distinct persons
- 1 Tim. 6:16 God dwells *in the light*—120 licks were 120 manifestations of the one God
- Acts 10:38 Jesus was *anointed…with the Holy Ghost*—if Jesus was already coequal in his own separate personhood, why did He need anointed?
- John 5:19 *The Son can do nothing of himself, but what he seeth the Father do*—Jesus' body was powerless with the anointing
- John 14:10 *The Father that dwelleth in me, he doeth the works*—Jesus gives credit to the Father for performing miracles
- Isa. 42:1, John 14:10 The Father said He'd put His own Spirit in Jesus, but when did He do this if the third person (Holy Ghost) came upon Jesus at His baptism?
- Luke 4:1, John 14:10 since both the Holy Ghost and Father dwell in Jesus, does Jesus have two separate, distinct, coequal persons living inside Him?

- Rev. 4:2 *one sat* on heaven's throne: Jesus; no mention of three persons, or a heavenly dove
- Mat. 3:15, John 1:32-22, 3:34, Col. 2:9 Jesus fulfilled all righteousness at His baptism and received the Holy Spirit *without measure,* as the *fulness of the Godhead* dwelt in His body
- Matt. 20:22 Jesus verified He received the baptism of the Holy Spirit: *Are ye able to drink of the cup that I shall drink of, and to be baptized with the baptism that I am baptized with?*
- Ex. 40:30-35 Moses, Aaron, and his sons washed in water before *the glory of the LORD filled the tabernacle* as a type of Jesus being washed, or baptized, before being filled with the Holy Ghost
- Lev. 1:1-9, Eph. 5:2 Jesus' baptism was the antitype of the washing of the burnt offering, as both were sweet savors unto the Lord

Jesus' prayers in Gethsemane:
- Luke 22:39-46 Jesus prays for help with a separate will than the Father, proving He is not a second coequal, coeternal person
- 1 Cor. 2:16 *we have the mind of Christ;* we imitate Jesus' mindset of subordination to the Father, rather than coequal status

Other threefold references to Father, Son, and Holy Ghost:
- 2 Cor. 13:14 *The grace of the Lord Jesus Christ, and the love of God, and the communion of the Holy Ghost* doesn't declare "three persons" but proves God's three manifestations
- Rom. 1:7, 1 Cor. 1:3, 1 John 1:3, 2 John 1:3 God and Jesus mentioned; no mention of the Holy Ghost because it's implied the Father *is* the Holy Ghost

- John 1:14 Jesus was *full of grace and truth*—matches the grace of...*Jesus Christ* (2 Cor. 13:14)
- John 3:16, Rom. 8:38-39 God's love emphasized—matches *the love of God* (2 Cor. 13:14)
- John 14:26 Holy Ghost teaches and brings all things to remembrance—matches *the communion of the Holy Ghost* (2 Cor. 13:14)

Jesus is not the "Eternal Son":
- Gal. 4:4 Jesus' human body was *made of a woman*, proving it did not exist eternally in heaven
- Isa. 6:1, Ezek. 1:26-28, Rev. 4:2 the prophets Isaiah, Ezekiel, and John the revelator had fellowship with only one person—not three coeternal persons—in their heavenly visions
- Isa. 40:25, 46:5 The Holy One has no equal—no such thing as three coequal persons
- Isa. 44:24 God created everything alone, all by Himself—not with two other coequal persons
- Rev. 3:14 Jesus says He's *the beginning of the creation of God*
- John 1:1 *In the beginning* Jesus was the first visible image of God, called *the Word*, or Logos
- John 17:5, 24 before the foundation of the world, God shared His glory with the Logos
- Prov. 8:12, 22-31 the Word, or Logos, personified as wisdom before the foundation of the world
- 1 John 5:11-12 eternal life is in the Son of God, who is God's eternal, visible image

APPENDIX B
Quotations From William Branham

HOLY GHOST FILLED CHRISTIANS recognize William Branham was a genuine prophet of God and therefore seek his interpretations of Scripture. Amos 3:7 says God first reveals His secrets to His prophets, and He did this by showing Branham the secrets of the Church Ages, the Seven Seals, marriage and divorce, and much more.

Believers who study Branham's teachings will be delighted to read Branham's quotes that inspired me to write this book. I have a quote from Brother Branham to support nearly every teaching in this book. Appendix B only includes quotes for Chapter 1 on the Godhead. Please contact me or go online for the quotes for the remaining chapters—330-929-2037 or www.pastorjessesmith.com/12mysteriesbook.

In Chapter 13 I mentioned Branham's quotes listing the specific mysteries the Seventh Angel was to reveal, but did not share the quotes. Below, Brother Branham cites Scofield's list of mysteries. Note there are 11, but if we are in the spiritual Holy Place with the candlestick representing the Seven Church Ages, then there must be 12 shewbread-mysteries:

> 241 The seventh angel of Revelations 10:7 is the seventh church-age messenger. See? Now watch. "And in the days..." Now watch here.

But in the days of the voice of the seventh angel, when he shall begin to sound, the mystery of God should be finished,...

242 Now, sounding forth, this messenger, the seventh angel here is sounding forth his Message to the Laodicean church. Notice his type of Message. Now, it wasn't to the first angel, wasn't given That; second angel, third, fourth, fifth, sixth. **But it is the seventh angel that had this type of Message. What was it? Notice his type of Message, "Finishing all the mysteries of God, that are written in the Book." The seventh angel is winding up all the mysteries that's laying loose-ended, all out through these organizations and denominations. The seventh angel gathers them up, and finishes the entire mystery.** That's what the Bible said, "Finishes the mystery of the written Book."

243 Now let's note a few of these mysteries, and if you want to write them down. First, I'll take what Scofield says here, in Matthew 13. If you'd like to type some of them down, if you haven't got a Scofield Bible. You might read what he thinks some of the mysteries are. Now, in the 11th verse.

And he answered and said unto them, Because it's given to you (his disciples), because it is given to you to know the mysteries of the kingdom of heaven, but not to them, but to them it is not given.

244 The mysteries, here is "the mystery." A mystery is Scripture, is a previously hidden Truth now Divinely revealed, but (which is) a supernatural element still remains despite the revelation. The greater mysteries and the great mysteries are:

245 Number one, the mystery of the Kingdom of Heaven. That's the one we're talking on now. 13, Matthew 13:3 to 50.

246 Now, second mystery is the mystery of Israel's blindness during this age. Romans 11:25, with the context.

247 Third, third mystery is the mystery of the translation of the living saints at the end time of this age. First Corinthians 15, and also Thessalonians 4:14 to 17.

248 The fourth, mystery of the New Testament Church as one Body composed of both, Jews and Gentiles. Ephesians 3:1 to 11, Romans 16:25, and also Ephesians 6:19, Colossians 4:3.

249 The fifth mystery is of the Church as the Bride of Christ. Ephesians 5:28 to 32.

250 Sixth mystery is of the living Christ, same yesterday, today, and forever. Galatians 2:20, and Hebrews 13:8, and many places like that.

251 The seventh mystery is of God, even Christ as the incarnate fulness of the Godhead embodied, in Whom all Divine wisdom.

And godliness is restored to man.

252 Ninth mystery is the mystery of iniquity, found in Second Thessalonians, and so forth.

253 The tenth mystery is of the seven stars of Revelations 1:20. We just been through that, "The seven stars of the seven churches, the seven messengers," and so forth.

254 And the eleventh mystery is Mystery Babylon, the prostitute. Revelations 17:5 to 7.

255 That's some of the mysteries that this angel is supposed to wind up, all "the mystery," all the mysteries of God.

— 62-1230E - Is This The Sign of the End Sir?

See Chapter 13 for Brother Branham's quotes about how the Holy Ghost taught him to use his Bible and concordance to defend every revelation, as well as his quotes about bread's symbolism for revealed mysteries.

MORE BIBLE INFORMATION ABOUT THE SAME REVELATION

In the Church Age Book, Brother Branham says we can receive more Bible information about the same revelation. God doesn't give a second revelation, but He does give more information about his first revelation. For example, God gave the Hebrew prophets more information about Jesus' birth. Brother Branham writes:

> "Thou hast tried them that say they are apostles, and are not, and hast found them liars."

> My, that is a blunt statement. "Thou hast tried them who call themselves apostles." Isn't that presumptuous? What right has a people to try those who call themselves apostles? And how do they try them? Oh, I love this.

> Here it is in Galatians 1:8,

> "But though we, or an angel from heaven, preach any other gospel unto you than that which we have (already) preached unto you, let him be accursed."

> It was the apostles who brought the original Word to the people. That original Word could not change, not even a dot or dash of it. Paul knew it was God Who had spoken to him so he said, "Even if I come and try to give a second revelation, try to make one little change in what I gave originally, let me be accursed." You see, Paul knew that first revelation was correct. God can't give a first revelation, then a second revelation. If He did, He would be changing His mind. **He can give a revelation and then add to it,** as He did in the Garden of Eden when He promised the Seed to the woman, and then later

designated that Seed had to come through Abraham, and then later said it would come by the same blood lines in David. **But it was the same revelation. It only gave the people more information to help them receive and understand it.**

But God's Word can't change. The Seed came exactly as revealed. Hallelujah. And see what those false apostles were doing. They came with their own word. Those Ephesians knew that Word as Paul had taught it. They were full of the Holy Ghost by the laying on of Paul's hands. They looked those false apostles in the eye and said, "You are not saying what Paul said. You are, therefore, false." Oh, that sets my heart on fire. Get back to the Word! It is not you that really tries the apostle, and prophet and teacher, IT IS THE WORD THAT TRIES THEM.

One of these days there is going to come a prophet to the Laodicean Church Age and you will know if he is the real one sent from God or not. **Yes you will, for if he is of God HE WILL BE IN THAT WORD EXACTLY AS GOD GAVE IT TO PAUL. HE WON'T DEVIATE FROM THAT WORD FOR A MOMENT, NOT BY ONE IOTA.** In that last age, when there will be many false prophets appearing, watch and see how they keep telling you that if you don't believe them and what they say, you will be lost; but when that LAST DAY PROPHET comes on the scene, if he is truly that prophet, he will be crying out, "Get back to the Word or you are lost." He won't build on a private revelation or interpretation, but on the Word. Amen, and Amen!

— Church Age Book - Chapter 3 - The Ephesian Church Age

Applying this concept to our day, I believe the revelations in this book are more information about the same revelations Brother Branham already received from the Holy Ghost. Again, Chapter 13 shows 6 of these mystery-doctrines are backed up with "Thus saith the Lord", and all 12 mysteries align with every other "Thus saith the Lord" statement Brother Branham made.

With all due respect, I have not added my own interpretations to Brother Branham's quotes, like the false movements of the Seven Thunders, Two Souls, or Parousia. I'm not asking anyone to follow me; rather, I'm pleading with believers to be born again, show complete dedication to their home church, feast on Jesus' fresh bread-mysteries, and invest in their God-given talents. Truly, in my 17 years of preaching ministry and 8 years on YouTube, I have never asked for anyone to follow me, nor donate one cent to my ministry.

THE IMPORTANCE OF PREACHERS RIGHTLY DIVIDING THE WORD

Brother Branham said the most important thing is a gifted man who can rightly divide the Word. This agrees with Paul's emphasis on the five fold ministry in Ephesians 4 and Jesus' promise to guide us into all things:

> Now, to bring up this faith in Christ, there's ministers. **That's the most important thing of the day, is a good God-sent preacher.** I admire them. **And their gift is far beyond anything could be done in anything else, is a preacher, a man who knows how to rightly divide the Word of God.** It's the most wonderful gift in the world, is to be a minister.

— 53-0614E - I Perceive That Thou Art a Prophet

Additionally, anything the Bride says, with the Holy Spirit's leading, must already be in the Bible:

> The corn of wheat (the Bride Wheat) that fell into the ground at Nicaea has come back to original Word Grain again. Praise God forever. Yes, listen to the authenticated

prophet of God who appears in this last age. What he says from God, the bride will say. The Spirit and the prophet and the bride will be saying the same thing. **And what they will say will have already been said in the Word**.

**— An Exposition Of The Seven Church Ages -
9 - The Laodicean Church Age**

The next two quotes show Brother Branham's role as the Seventh Angel was to gather up the loose ends of the mysteries, already found in Scripture, and reveal the secrets. The legitimacy of this ministry was "Thus saith the Lord" out of Revelation 10:1-7:

But it is the seventh angel that had this type of Message. What was it? Notice his type of Message, **"Finishing all the mysteries of God, that are written in the Book."** The seventh angel is winding up all the mysteries that's laying loose-ended, all out through these organizations and denominations. The seventh angel gathers them up, and finishes the entire mystery. That's what the Bible said, "Finishes the mystery of the written Book."

— 62-1230E - Is This The Sign Of The End, Sir?

And now, we know that this Book of Redemption will not be thoroughly understood: it's probed at through six church ages, but at the end, when the seventh angel begins to sound his mystery, he winds up all of the loose ends that these fellows probed at, and the mysteries comes down from God as the Word of God and reveals the entire revelation of God. Then the Godhead and everything else is settled. All the mysteries: serpent's seed and whatevermore is to be revealed.

Now, you see, I'm just not making that up. That's what... It's THUS SAITH THE LORD. I'll read it to you out of the Book: the sounding of the seventh angel's message, the mystery of God should be finished that's been declared by His holy prophets. That's the prophets who has wrote the Word. At the sounding of the seventh church age, the last church age, all the loose ends that through these church ages have been probed at, will be wound up together. And when the Seals are broke and the mystery is revealed, down comes the Angel, the Messenger, Christ, setting His foot upon the land and upon the sea with a rainbow over His head. Now remember, this seventh angel is on earth at the time of this coming.

— 63-0317E - The Breach Between the Seven Church Ages and the Seven Seals

The prophet also hoped men would be able to make his Bible-restored Message come to life after he left:

Now, Her messenger is promised, in Malachi the 4th chapter. He's promised to do it. **And the Message is to bring back the Word**, bring the people back to the Word. Birth is to be. She's to be delivered, of a new Birth, from according to Malachi 4…**These men, if they pick up This and goes out with It, they can make more sense to It, see, to bring It to a place you would. I just want to lay this Seed, then hope they make It come to Life.**

— 65-0124 - Birth Pains

THE IMPORTANCE OF DOCTRINE

Due to the rise of many false teachers in the Message, some have dismissed the need for doctrine, to their detriment. The Bible is clear true doctrine saves both the preacher and hearer (1 Timothy 4:16). In fact, 2

John 1:9 says Holy Ghost filled Message believers will abide in Christ's doctrine: *"Whosoever transgresseth, and abideth not in the doctrine of Christ, hath not God. He that abideth in the doctrine of Christ, he hath both the Father and the Son."* In this quote, Brother Branham says the Bride will have true doctrine:

> **The antichrist refuses the true Bride Doctrine,** and therefore he takes his own bride now and builds her up, under a creed of his own. Takes his own bride and makes her a denomination! She gives birth to other denominations, as quoted in this Holy Scriptures; gives birth to daughters. And she don't...She becomes just like her mother, natural, worldly, denominational; opposing the spiritual Bride, the Word.
>
> **— 63-0321 - The Fourth Seal**

In 1 Timothy 5:17 Paul says laborers in doctrine are worthy of double honor: *"Let the elders that rule well be counted worthy of double honour, especially they who labour in the word and doctrine."* If there's a deep call for true doctrine, there has to be a deep to respond. You know the true Bride will have both the Spirit, supernatural works of the Holy Ghost, and the truth, true doctrine.

Some forget Brother Branham's quote that Jesus' first doctrine was on the new birth, or the baptism of the Holy Ghost. This proves true doctrine leads you to the new birth, and once born again, the Spirit keeps guiding you into more true doctrine. Brother Branham said:

> Now, God bless His Word. And I want to take the subject this morning of Jesus' first doctrine. **The first doctrine of Jesus was, "You Must Be Born Again."** That was His first doctrine.
>
> **— 61-1231M - You Must Be Born Again**

It's wrong for preachers to say they aren't trying to preach doctrine because every single sermon includes doctrine, since it means instruction. Preachers are either giving instruction for miracles, divine healing, salvation, etc. Brother Branham says every preacher has doctrine, whether he knows it or not, as he cannot have a ministry without doctrine:

> Now, and to my friends all over the different parts of the world that will be hearing this by the magnetic tape, in here I might say that I have to express doctrines and so forth to make this. **And any man that has not a doctrine has not a ministry.** So if you don't think that your congregation should hear the tape, then keep it from them. But I'm just expressing my own opinion and my own feelings, my own revelation of the Word of God.

— 61-0618 - Revelation, Chapter Five #2

Brother Branham loved teaching the Bible and wished he had charts to reference when teaching his people God's revelations, saying it would be a "little heaven". This is why PowerPoints or visuals can be helpful to believers to grow their understanding. Brother Branham said:

> How you all enjoying the Revelation? All right? I believe a whole lot like my little girl, Sarah, back there, it's become "revolutions" to me, it's just--it's just revolutions going over and over. You know, I wish we just had now until about March or April, just to put a great big canvas across the back here and just come down in daytime and draw out those pictures and the whole chart, and just raise them up and down like window shades, you know, like I've always dreamed sometime of having a great big tabernacle somewhere where I could reach down and pull this chart down, come all the way across the platform; and revelations and the interpretations the Lord has given me, and take a pointer and start through there and bring these ages down. Then when we get through with that, raise that one up, pull

the other one down like this and start on that, and teach it through. **Oh, that would just be like a little heaven, wouldn't it?** Just sit the complete winter through, just sit it out with the Lord.

— 61-0101 Revelation Chapter Four #2

THE WATERS OF SEPARATION

As taught in Chapter 13, I feel compelled to add one more quote about Brother Branham's teaching on the waters of separation. Christians worship Christ in the three court spiritual tabernacle as the antitype of Moses' three court natural tabernacle. Here in February 1965 Brother Branham said repenting and being baptized, the first Work of Grace, or justification, does't yet bring the believer into complete worship. This is because he has to be sanctified and then filled with the Holy Ghost to be a true worshipper:

Now, the thing of it is, if we find where the place is…The worship place is nowhere accepted, only in Christ. **You can repent, you can do that, but you're not worshipping yet. You're asking for pardon.** Peter said…

On the Day of Pentecost, when they seen them all speaking with tongues, and great signs and wonders taking place, they begin to laugh, the church did, and said, "These men are full of new wine. They act like drunk people. The…" Mary the virgin, all of them, was together, hundred and twenty of them. And they were staggering like drunk men, and speaking in tongues, and carrying on. They said, "These men are full of new wine."

But Peter, standing up, said, "Men and brethren, these men are not full of new wine, for this is just the third hour of the day. But this is that which was spoke of by the prophet Joel, 'And it shall come to pass in the last days, saith God, I'll pour out My Spirit upon all flesh; your sons and daughters shall prophesy; upon My handmaids and maidservant will I pour out of My Spirit. I'll show signs in the heavens above, and on earth; fire, pillars of fire, vapors of smoke. It shall come to pass, before the great and terrible Day of the Lord shall come, that whosoever shall call upon the Name of the Lord shall be saved.'"

When they heard this, they were pricked in their heart, and said, "Men and brethren, what can we do?"

Peter said, "Repent, every one of you, and be baptized in the Name of Jesus Christ for the remission of your sins, and you shall receive the gift of the Holy Ghost. For the promise is that all future generations." Now we find that.

Now we want to find how we get into Him. How do we get into this place of worship? First Corinthians 12 settles it, for, "By one Spirit!" Not by one church, not by one creed, not by one pastor, not by one bishop, not by one priest. But, "By one Holy Spirit we are all baptized into one Body," which is the Body of Jesus Christ, and subject to every gift that lays in that Body. Yes, sir! No joining, no reciting of creeds, no pumping up, letting down, handshaking, or nothing else. But, by Birth we are baptized into the Body of Jesus Christ! Amen. **"By one Holy Spirit we are all baptized into one Body."**

— 65-0220 - God's Chosen Place Of Worship

Here are quotes from Brother Branham that support the Godhead mystery:

1ST MYSTERY: GODHEAD

It's my opinion that few Message preachers would reject my Bible teachings on the Godhead. Please contact me if that's not the case.

But it's critical to see Brother Branham didn't make a big issue out of the idea of three persons in the Godhead until December 1960. Here's a quote from November 1960 in which Brother Branham tells Shreveport believers the third person is working in their flesh:

Jesus Christ, the resurrected One, **the One you call the third Person, is the same Person, that's in our midst now working in our flesh**, as He--as God worked in the flesh of His own Son, Jesus Christ, is working in the flesh of adopted children through Jesus Christ as He promised.

— 60-1126 - Why

Then, the next month, Brother Branham told his home church that three persons was wrong:

First Timothy 3:16, "Without contradiction, great is the mystery of godliness: for God was manifested in flesh, seen of Angels, believed on in the world, received up into Glory." God! Not a third person or a prophet, but God Himself, made manifest in human form. Now, this is the revelation, remember.

— 60-1204M - The Revelation of Jesus Christ

It's interesting to see how Brother Branham progressively grew in revelation, as he expressed his love for the third person of the trinity and his indwelling presence in 1952:

We love Him, that great, third Person of the trinity Who burns through our hearts. And we love Him. O Holy Spirit, I thank You for Your Divine leading, and how You led me here to Hammond.

— 52-0713A Early Spiritual Experiences

These quotes are important to remember when reading Brother Branham's Godhead quotes because he clearly grew leaps and bounds on the Godhead revelation after preaching the Seven Church Ages. This monumental study led him to pronounce God's authoritative Word in relation to the Godhead in January 1961:

> Now, my precious brother, I know this is a tape also. Now, don't get excited. Let me say this with godly love, the hour has approached where I can't hold still on these things no more, too close to the Coming. See? **"Trinitarianism is of the Devil!"** I say that THUS SAITH THE LORD! Look where it come from. It come from the Nicene Council when the Catholic church become in rulership. The word "trinity" is not even mentioned in the entire Book of the Bible. And as far as three Gods, that's from hell. There's one God. That's exactly right.

— 61-0108 - Revelation Chapter 4, Part 3

ACKNOWLEDGMENTS

First, I give eternal thanks and all glory to the Lord Jesus Christ for forgiving my sins, sanctifying my mind, and filling my soul with His Holy Spirit. Without You, Lord Jesus, I can do nothing (John 15:5). I will keep watching and praying for your rapture return and compel others to do the same.

To my wife, Kristen, thank you for being my constant companion and faithful friend. Without your support I couldn't accomplishment much in this life. As our children know, you're an amazing mother, teacher, wife, counselor, and more. Your love and wisdom has helped me tremendously through our 18 years of marriage. And as Brother Branham said of his own wife, thanks for being "my correction" (*Questions and Answers on the Holy Ghost*, December 19, 1959).

Third, I am very grateful to Pastor Cameron Smith and the trustees at Living Waters Tabernacle—David LeWallen, Dustin Salmi, and Simon Smith—for their generous help with this outreach project. Brothers, I love you all dearly, and you serve as a rare, special, and godly example of unity in a home church. May the Lord Jesus Christ continue to strengthen and guide you into His blessings, power, and truth.

Fourth, many thanks to Paul Smith, my natural and spiritual brother. Your generous support for this book has amazed, blessed, and humbled me. Your friendship is a true treasure to my heart. God richly bless you, your talents, and family for His glory.

Fifth, thank you to my editors, Joyce Greeley and Lydia Smith. Joyce, your insights, ideas, and corrections on the majority of the chapters blessed my heart. You're a true godsend and I'm very thankful to the Lord for allowing you to help me again. Lydia, it's a joy to see God using your talents to help me with editing. You never cease to be a huge help, sensitive encourager, and delightful oldest daughter.

Lastly, a huge thanks to my home church, Bride of Christ Fellowship. This book is possible only through your prayers, support, patience, and devotion. Your love for God's End Time Message thrills my soul and it's a true joy for me to weekly preach Jesus' unsearchable riches to all of you. Your godly lives preach to the world that Jesus Christ is soon to come, and He's the same yesterday, today, and forever.

WORKS CITED

"3 Prophesies of William Branham." *YouTube*, uploaded by Pastor Jesse Smith, 4 October 2014, https://youtu.be/7PiEO2OK5e0.

"About The UPCI." *United Pentecostal Church International*, https://www.upci.org/about/about-the-upci. Accessed 2 February 2019.

"About Us: What is the World Council of Churches?" *World Council of Churches*, https://www.oikoumene.org/en/about-us. Accessed 15 April 2019.

"An Atheist Gets His Evidence." *Living Waters*, https://www.livingwaters.com/an-atheist-gets-his-evidence/. Accessed 10 May 2020.

"Ancient Rome." *Encyclopedia Britannica*, https://www.britannica.com/place/ancient-Rome. Accessed 6 April 2019.

"Anu." *Encyclopedia Britannica*. www.britannica.com/topic/Anu. Accessed 31 January 2019.

Apple. "Hypocrisy." *Dictionary*, Version 2.3.0. Accessed 22 May 2019.

Apple. "Modalism." *Dictionary*, Version 2.3.0. Accessed 19 January 2019.

"Apple Fruit and Tree." *Encyclopedia Britannica,* https://www. britannica.com/plant/apple-fruit-and-tree. Accessed 12 May 2019.

"Assumption." *Encyclopedia Britannica,* https://www.britannica.com/ topic/Assumption-Christianity. Accessed 17 April 2019.

"Athanasian Creed." *Christ Reformed Church,* https://www.crcna.org/ welcome/beliefs/creeds/athanasian-creed. Accessed 30 November 2018.

"Attaining Salvation in Roman Catholicism." *Christian Apologetics & Research Ministry,* www.carm.org/catholic/catholic-salvation-attain. Accessed 21 March 2019.

"Attalus III: Philometor Euergetes ('Loving-his-mother Benefactor')." *Encyclopedia Britannica,* https://www.britannica.com/biography/ Attalus-III-Philometor-Euergetes. Accessed 2 July 2020.

"Baptism." *Encyclopedia of Early Christianity.* 1997, pp. 161.

"Baptism." *New Standard Encyclopedia.* Chicago, Standard Educational Corporation.

"Baptism." *The Interpreter's Dictionary of the Bible.* Abingdon Press. 1962, pp. 351.

"Bill Salus on Mystery Babylon." *YouTube,* uploaded by Christ In Prophecy, 21 August 2018, https://youtu.be/JCnErkq0gOI.

"Billy Graham." *Billy Graham Evangelical Association,* https:// billygraham.org/about/biographies/billy-graham/. Accessed 21 August 2020.

"Bison Selected as the Official Mammal of the United States." *History. com,* http://www.history.com/news/bison-selected-as-the-official- mammal-of-the-united-states. Accessed 20 April 2019.

"Blueprint For Limbs Encoded in the Snake Genome." *University of Georgia,* https://news.uga.edu/blueprints-for-limbs-encoded-in-snake-genome-1015/. Accessed 26 May 2020.

Branham, William. *An Exposition of the Seven Church Ages.* 1965.

Broadbent, E.H. *The Pilgrim Church.* 1935.

Burgess, Stanley, et al. *Dictionary of Pentecostal and Charismatic Movements.* Grand Rapids: Zondervan, 1988, pp. 372.

"Can Birth Control Pills Kill Unborn Babies?" *ChristianAnswers.Net,* https://christiananswers.net/q-eden/edn-bcpill.html. Accessed 7 May 2020.

Catholic Church. *Catechism of the Catholic Church.* New York, Doubleday, 1994.

"Catholic Nuns Accused of Sexual Misconduct." *YouTube,* uploaded by CBS News, 2 January 2019, https://www.youtube.com/watch?v=-Xp9aEzhN3A. Accessed 2 April 2019.

"CDCs Abortion Surveillance System FAQs." *CDC,* https://www.cdc.gov/reproductivehealth/data_stats/abortion.htm. Accessed 27 March 2019.

"Celibacy." *Encyclopedia Britannica,* www.britannica.com/topic/celibacy. Accessed 30 March 2019.

"Chapter VI: Mixed Marriages." The Holy See, http://www.vatican.va/archive/ENG1104/__P41.HTM. Accessed 23 April 2019.

"Christianity." *Encyclopedia Britannica,* https://www.britannica.com/topic/Christianity. Accessed 4 June 2020.

"Christianity in China." *Council on Foreign Relations,* https://www.cfr.org/backgrounder/christianity-china. Accessed 28 April 2020.

"Clarence Larkin: The Book of Daniel." *Earnestly Contending For The Faith*, https://www.earnestlycontendingforthefaith.com/Books/ Clarence%20Larkin/Daniel ClarenceLarkinTheBookOfDaniel11.html. Accessed 24 March 2020.

"Clarence Larkin: Chapter 26 - The Covenants." *Blue Letter Bible*, https://www.blueletterbible.org/study/larkin/dt/26.cfm. Accessed 19 February 2020.

Connor, Kevin J. *The Feasts of Israel.* City Bible Publishing, 1980.

"Constantine I." *Encyclopedia Britannica*, https://www.britannica.com/ biography/Constantine-I-Roman-emperor. Accessed 18 June 2020.

Coxe, A. Cleveland. *Ante-Nicene Fathers: Volume 1: The Apostolic Fathers, Justin Martyr, Irenaeus.* 1885.

Coxe, A. Cleveland. *Ante-Nicene Fathers: Volume 4: Tertullian, Part Fourth; Minucius Felix; Commodian; Origen, Part First and Second.* 1885.

Coxe, A. Cleveland. *Ante-Nicene Fathers: Volume 8: The Twelve Patriarchs, Excerpts and Epistles, The Clementina, Apocrypha, Decretals, Memoirs of Edessa and Syriac Documents, Remains of the First Ages.* 1886.

"Didache." *Encyclopedia Britannica*, www.britannica.com/topic/ Didache. Accessed 7 November 2018.

"Diocletian." *Encyclopedia Britannica*, https://www.britannica.com/ biography/Diocletian/Domestic-reforms#ref1832. Accessed 18 June 2020.

"Diocletian." *New Advent: The Catholic Encyclopedia*, https://www. newadvent.org/cathen/05007b.htm. Accessed 29 June 2020.

"Diplomatic Relations of the Holy See." *The Permanent Observer Mission of the Holy See to the United Nations*, https://holyseemission.org/ contents/mission/diplomatic-relations-of-the-holy-see.php. Accessed 21 March 2019.

"Donation of Constantine." *Encyclopedia Britannica*, https://www.britannica.com/topic/Donation-of-Constantine. Accessed 14 April 2019.

"Edict of Milan." *Encyclopedia Britannica*, https://www.britannica.com/topic/Edict-of-Milan. Accessed 18 June 2020.

Encyclopedia Britannica: A Dictionary of Arts, Sciences, Literature and General Information. University Press, 1910.

Erikson, Millard J. *Christian Theology.* Baker Publishing Group, 1986.

"Fact Check: 50 Million Abortions Claim Checks Out." *Des Moines Register*, https://www.desmoinesregister.com/story/news/politics/reality-check/2015/03/06/million-abortions-claim-checks/24530159/. Accessed 30 March 2019.

Foxe, John. *Foxe's Book of Martyrs.* 1563.

"Frequently Requested Church Statistics." *Center For Applied Research in the Apostolate*, https://cara.georgetown.edu/frequently-requested-church-statistics/. Accessed 20 March 2019.

"George Whitefield." *Christianity Today*, https://www.christianitytoday.com/history/people/evangelistsandapologists/george-whitefield.html. Accessed 20 June 2020.

"Global Christianity-A Report on the Size and Distribution of the World's Christian Population." *Pew Research Center*, https://www.pewforum.org/2011/12/19/global-christianity-exec/. Accessed 2 May 2020.

Goodstein, Laurie and Otterman, Sharon. "Catholic Priests Abused 1,000 Children in Pennsylvania, Report Says." *The New York Times*, www.nytimes.com/2018/08/14/us/catholic-church-sex-abuse-pennsylvania.html?action=click&module=Related Coverage&pgtype=Article&region=Footer. Accessed 2 November 2018.

Hackett, Conrad and McClendon, David. "Christians Remain World's Largest Religion Group, But They are Declining in Europe." *Pew Research Center*, https://www.pewresearch.org/fact-tank/2017/04/05/christians-remain-worlds-largest-religious-group-but-they-are-declining-in-europe/. Accessed 24 November 2018.

Hazeltine, Rachel. *How Did It Happen?* 1958.

"Hinduism." *Encyclopedia Britannica*, https://www.britannica.com/topic/Hinduism. Accessed 4 June 2020.

"Hiroshima and Nagasaki." *Encyclopedia Britannica*, https://www.britannica.com/event/World-War-II/Hiroshima-and-Nagasaki. Accessed 21 April 2019.

Hislop, Alexander. *The Two Babylons*. 1853.

"How Long Did It Take Noah To Build The Ark?" *Answers In Genesis*, https://answersingenesis.org/bible-timeline/how-long-did-it-take-for-noah-to-build-the-ark/. Accessed 12 June 2019.

"Inquisition: Roman Catholicism." *Encyclopedia Britannica*, https://www.britannica.com/topic/inquisition. Accessed 3 April 2019.

International Gem Society, *https://www.gemsociety.org*. Accessed 23 May 2018.

"Introduction to the Holocaust." United States Holocaust Memorial Museum, https://encyclopedia.ushmm.org/content/en/article/introduction-to-the-holocaust. Accessed 20 January 2020.

"Islam." *Encyclopedia Britannica*, https://www.britannica.com/topic/Islam. Accessed 4 June 2020.

"Israel and the U.S. are Home to More Than Four-Fifths of the World's Jews." *Pew Research Center*, https://www.pewforum.org/2013/03/20/israel-and-the-us-are-home-to-more-than-fourfifths-of-the-worlds-jews/. Accessed 25 March 2019.

"Israel's Innovation Story is Extraordinary." *I Am Media,* https://www.iam-media.com/law-policy/israels-innovation-story-extraordinary-just-assuming-it-will-continue-would-be-big. Accessed 6 March 2020.

"Istanbul." *Encyclopedia Britannica,* www.britannica.com/place/Istanbul. Accessed 23 March 2019.

"Johannes Gutenberg." *Encyclopedia Brittanica,* https://www.britannica.com/biography/Johannes-Gutenberg. Accessed 9 July 2020.

"John 7:37." *Bible Study Tools,* https://www.biblestudytools.com/commentaries/gills-exposition-of-the-bible/john-7-37.html. Accessed 7 December 2019.

"John Alexander Dowie." *Encyclopedia Britannica,* https://www.britannica.com/biography/John-Alexander-Dowie. Accessed 5 September 2020.

"John F. Kennedy." *Encyclopedia Britannica,* https://www.britannica.com/biography/John-F-Kennedy. Accessed 22 April 2019.

"John Huss." *Christianity Today,* https://www.christianitytoday.com/history/people/martyrs/john-huss.html. Accessed 9 July 2020.

"John Wesley and the Power of the Spirit." *Jamin Bradley's Blog,* https://newfangled.wordpress.com/2010/05/12/john-wesley-and-the-power-of-the-spirit/. Accessed 25 July 2020.

"John Wesley: Methodist Pietist." *Christianity Today,* https://www.christianitytoday.com/history/people/denominationalfounders/john-wesley.html. Accessed 25 July 2020.

Jones, Floyd Nolen. *Which Version is the Bible?* KingsWord Press, 2006.

Journal of Forensic Sciences. American Academy of Forensic Sciences, July 1994.

Larkin, Clarence. *Dispensational Truths or God's Plan and Purpose in the Ages.* 1918.

"Legalism." *Oxford English Dictionary,* https://en.oxforddictionaries.com/definition/legalism. Accessed 27 April 2019.

"Leviticus 23." *Bible Study Tools,* https://www.biblestudytools.com/commentaries/scofield-reference-notes/leviticus/leviticus-23.html. Accessed 21 April 2020.

"Luther's Jewish Problem." *The Gospel Coalition,* https://www.thegospelcoalition.org/article/luthers-jewish-problem/. Accessed 3 April 2020.

"Map: Abraham's Journeys." *Reading the Bible Chronologically in 365 Days,* https://hisstillsmallvoice.wordpress.com/2013/02/07/400/. Accessed 15 May 2020.

"Matthew 25." *Bible Study Tools,* https://www.biblestudytools.com/commentaries/matthew-henry-complete/matthew/25.html. Accessed 1 August 2019.

"Member Churches: Our World Wide Church Family." *World Methodist Council,* https://worldmethodistcouncil.org/about/member-churches/. Accessed 23 March 2019.

"Mishna." *Encyclopedia Britannica,* https://www.britannica.com/topic/Mishna. Accessed 10 June 2020.

"Modern History Sourcebook: Martin Luther (1483:1546): Address to the Nobility of the German Nation, 1520." *Fordham University,* https://sourcebooks.fordham.edu/mod/luther-nobility.asp. Accessed 20 June 2020.

"Monarchianism." *Encyclopedia Britannica,* www.britannica.com/topic/Monarchianism. Accessed 20 January 2019.

"Monotheism." *Encyclopedia Britannica*, www.britannica.com/topic/monotheism. Accessed 31 January 2019.

Myers, Rich. "John Gill's Exposition of the Bible. Matthew 25:15." *E-Sword X*, Version 6.3 (24). Accessed 7 August 2019.

National Geographic Kids, September 2017.

Nye, Eric. "*Pounds Sterling to Dollars: Historical Conversion of Currency,*" https://www.uwyo.edu/numimage/currency.htm. Accessed 7 August 2019.

Park, Madison. "Timeline: A Look at the Catholic Church's Sex Abuse Scandals." *CNN*, https://www.cnn.com/2017/06/29/world/timeline-catholic-church-sexual-abuse-scandals/index.html. Accessed 3 November 2018.

"People: United States." *Encyclopedia Britannica*, https://www.britannica.com/place/United-States/People#ref742503. Accessed 12 April 2019.

"Persecution of Christians is Approaching Genocide Levels, Report Finds: Christianity 'Is At Risk of Disappearing.'" *Newsweek*, https://www.newsweek.com/persecution-christians-genocide-christianity-disappearing-report-1414038. Accessed 26 July 2019.

"Persian Literature." *Encyclopedia Britannica*, https://www.britannica.com/art/Persian-literature.Accessed 6 April 2019.

"Pilgrim Fathers." *Encyclopedia Britannica*, https://www.britannica.com/topic/Pilgrim-Fathers.Accessed 22 April 2019.

"Pope Francis Sends Video Message to Kenneth Copeland - Let's Unite." *YouTube*, uploaded by Prove All Things, 21 February 2014, https://www.youtube.com/watch?v=uA4EPOfic5A.

"Pope Urban II Orders First Crusade." *History.com*, https://www.history.com/this-day-in-history/pope-urban-ii-orders-first-crusade. Accessed 10 July 2020.

"Prince of Translators: William Tyndale." *Ligonier Ministries*, https://www.ligonier.org/blog/prince-translators-william-tyndale/. Accessed 22 July 2020.

"Proselyte." *Bible Study Tools*, https://www.biblestudytools.com/dictionaries/eastons-bible-dictionary/proselyte.html. Accessed 6 April 2020.

"Protestantism." *Encyclopedia Brittanica*, http://www.britannica.com/topic/Protestantism. Accessed 3 April 2019.

"Proverbs 31 As An Acrostic Poem." *Bible Odyssey*, https://www.bibleodyssey.org/en/passages/related-articles/proverbs-31-as-an-acrostic-poem. Accessed 9 May 2020.

"Pope." *Dictionary.com*, https://www.dictionary.com/browse/pope. Accessed 1 April 2019.

"Pope." *Encyclopedia Britannica*, https://www.britannica.com/topic/pope. Accessed 12 April 2019.

"Pope Explains 'Motivation' for Viral Anti-Ring-Kissing Moment: Germs." *CBS News*, https://www.cbsnews.com/amp/news/pope-francis-pulled-ring-hand-away-from-kisses-for-fear-spreading-germs-vatican/. Accessed 1 April 2019.

"Pope Francis, in Washington, Addresses Poverty and Climate." *The New York Times*, www.nytimes.com/2015/09/24/us/politics/pope-francis-obama-white-house.html. Accessed 30 March 2019.

"Pope Francis' Prayer Intentions for January 2016." *YouTube*, uploaded by The Vatican - Archive, 6 January 2016, www.youtube.com/watch?v=-6FfTxwTX34.

"Roman Catholicism." *Encyclopedia Britannica*, https://www.britannica.com/topic/Roman-Catholicism. Accessed 10 February 2018.

"Roman Empire." *Encyclopedia Britannica*, www.britannica.com/place/Roman-Empire.Accessed 19 March 2019.

"Rome." *Encyclopedia Britannica*, http://www.britannica.com/place/Rome. Accessed 8 April 2019.

Sagal, Neha. "500 Years After the Reformation, 5 Facts About Protestants Around the World." *The Pew Research Center*, https://www.pewresearch.org/fact-tank/2017/10/27/500-years-after-the-reformation-5-facts-about-protestants-around-the-world/. Accessed 4 November 2018.

"Saint Augustine." *Encyclopedia Britannica*, https://www.britannica.com/biography/Saint-Augustine. Accessed 4 July 2020.

"Saint Matthias." *Encyclopedia Britannica*, https://www.britannica.com/biography/Saint-Matthias. Accessed 9 August 2019.

Schmucker, Samuel S. *The Glorious Reformation*, 1838.

"Separatist." *Encyclopedia Britannica*, https://www.britannica.com/topic/Separatists. Accessed 22 April 2019.

"Seven Hills of Rome." *Encyclopedia Brittanica*, https://www.britannica.com/place/Seven-Hills-of-Rome. Accessed 23 March 2019.

"Shew-bread." *Bible Study Tools*, https://www.biblestudytools.com/dictionaries/smiths-bible-dictionary/shew-bread.html. Accessed 30 March 2019.

"Shield of the Trinity." *Wikipedia, The Free Encyclopedia*, https://en.wikipedia.org/w/index.php?%20title=Shield_of_the_Trinity&oldid=878878640. Accessed 26 January 2019.

"Shulamite, The." *Bible Study Tools*, https://www.biblestudytools.com/dictionaries/smiths-bible-dictionary/shulamite-the.html. Accessed 18 October 2020.

"St. Peter the Apostle." *Encyclopedia Britannica*, https://www.britannica.com/biography/Saint-Peter-the-Apostle. Accessed 1 January 2020.

"Synod of Laodicea (4th Century)." *New Advent*, https://www.newadvent.org/fathers/3806.htm. Accessed 15 June 2020.

"Teacher's Guide - John Paul II: The Millennial Pope." *Frontline*, https://www.pbs.org/wgbh/pages/frontline/teach/leadership/pope/. Accessed 5 April 2019.

"The Azusa Street Revival (Documentary)." *YouTube*, Uploaded by End-Time Youth, 13 January 2015, https://www.youtube.com/watch?v=HPtGJ35jIwA

"The Bible: Hebrew and Greek Lexicons," *Voice of God Recordings*, www.branham.org/en/messagesearch. Accessed 10 February 2018.

"The Didache." *St. Gemma.com Web Productions, Inc.*, www.thedidache.com. Accessed 7 November 2018.

"The Forbidden Book - History of The English Bible." *YouTube*, uploaded by Christian Media Network, 10 October 2019, https://www.youtube.com/watch?v=EjUqTT2I4kA.

"The Gods." *Encyclopedia Britannica*, https://www.britannica.com/topic/ancient-Egyptian-religion/The-Gods. Accessed 31 January 2019.

"The Gutenberg Press." *The Museum of the Bible*, https://museumofthebible.org/book/minutes/440. Accessed 22 June 2020.

The Holy Bible. King James Version, Holman Bible Publishers, 2012.

The Interpreter's Bible. Abingdon-Cokesbury Press. 1954, pp. 49.

"The Table." *Voice of God Recordings,* http://table.branham.org/#/en/main. Accessed 18 November 2018.

"The UN and Israel: A History of Discrimination." *Jewish Policy Center,* www.jewishpolicycenter.org/2017/04/03/the-un-and-israel-a-history-of-discrimination/. Accessed 25 March 2019.

"Thousands of Muslims Reportedly Turning to Christ in Middle East." *Fox News,* https://www.foxnews.com/world/thousands-of-muslims-reportedly-turning-to-christ-in-middle-east. Accessed 28 April 2020.

Time, 5 December 1955, pp. 5.

Time, 28 September 2015.

"Transubstantiation." *Encyclopedia Britannica,* www.britannica.com/topic/transubstantiation. Accessed 30 March 2019.

"Trinity, The." *Encyclopedia Americana.* Grolier, 1996, pp. 116.

"Trinity, The Blessed." *The Catholic Encyclopedia, Vol. 2.* New York: The Encyclopedia Press.

"Trinity." *The Encyclopedia of Religion, Vol. 15.* New York: Macmillan Publishing Company, 1993, pp. 54.

"Trinity." *The Interpreter's Dictionary of the Bible.* Abingdon Press, pp. 711.

"Trinity." *World Book.* 2003, pp. 447.

"Vatican City." *Encyclopedia Brittanica,* http://www.britannica.com/place/Vatican-City. Accessed 3 April 2019.

"Vatican Inc.: 5 Facts About the Business of the Catholic Church" *CNN,* https://money.cnn.com/2015/09/24/news/pope-francis-visit-vatican-catholic-church/index.html. Accessed 21 September 2019.

"Vicar." *Encyclopedia Britannica,* https://www.britannica.com/topic/vicar. Accessed 12 April 2019.

"Victims of Sex Abuse by Pennsylvania Priests Share Their Stories." *YouTube,* uploaded by CBS This Morning, 9 August 2018, www.youtube.com/watch?v=oHQJCmsFd9k.

Warren, Rick. *Purpose Driven Life.* Zondervan, 2012.

"What We Believe." *Black Lives Matter,* https://blacklivesmatter.com/what-we-believe/. Accessed 6 August 2020.

"When the Pope was Powerful and Why That Changed." *The Washington Post,* https://www.washingtonpost.com/news/worldviews/wp/2013/02/11/the-rise-and-decline-of-the-popes-once-great-power/?noredirect=on&utm_term=.66b401098e77. Accessed 5 April 2019.

"Why Do Catholic Priests Wear Vestments (Colorful Robes)?" *Why Catholics Do That,* http://whycatholicsdothat.com/why-do-catholic-priest-wear-vestments/. Accessed 2 April 2019.

"William Carey: Father of Modern Protestant Missions." *Christianity Today,* https://www.christianitytoday.com/history/people/missionaries/william-carey.html. Accessed 27 July 2020.

INDEX

CPSIA information can be obtained
at www.ICGtesting.com
Printed in the USA
BVHW070715020821
612755BV00002B/5